Swear to Tell the Tr[uth]

> Certain people, events, organizations, and storylines in wrestling history have gotten a bum rap. Some writers have presented overtly critical comments and outright lies as fact, and others have followed suit. Well no more! "In Defense of..." has one reason: to bring the truth to the wrestling fan!

This was part of the opening lines to every issue of the classic anthology series **In Defense Of...**, a 64-part exposé that fought to dispel the myths surrounding the Internet Wrestling Community's (IWC) most hated targets. Now, all 29 cases have been brought together under one title, edited into in a streamlined format, and buoyed with rare and never before seen bonus material!

Join author, consultant, entrepreneur, and all-around defender of truth J.P. Prag as he sheds lights on much maligned professional wrestling targets such as Eric Bischoff, Bill Goldberg, Lex Luger, the Ultimate Warrior, Jeff Jarrett, Hulk Hogan, and more. Further, the Finger Poke of Doom, Earl Hebner screwing Bret Hart, Vince McMahon not buying out WCW's contracts, the McMahon-Helmsley Era, and other key events in wrestling history are explored and exonerated.

Remember: the trial is not over until the defense rests!

TABLE OF CONTENTS

SWEAR TO TELL THE TRUTH 1
TABLE OF CONTENTS 2
DEPOSITION 14
    SUBMITTED EVIDENCE 14
    REMEMBERING LARRY CSONKA 15
    PRE-TRIAL FACT GATHERING 17
ERIC BISCHOFF 21
    INTRO 21
        Some dame walked into my office and said 21
        Why this? 21
    ERIC BISCHOFF ONLY CREATED ONE THOUSAND STARS 21
    CRUISERWEIGHTS EQUAL WORKRATE 23
    BILLIONAIRE TED'S MONEY 23
    GIVE A MAN AN INCH 24
    ERIC BISCHOFF CREATED THE IWC! 25
    THE COLD, CALCULATING, EVIL BUSINESSMAN 26
    AND SPEAKING OF BUSINESS 27
    THE REWARDS 28
    FOR EVERY HATER, THERE'S A LOVER 28
    THE WWE 29
    NUMBERS DON'T LIE 30
    MORE REASONS WHY ERIC BISCHOFF IS A BETTER HUMAN BEING THAN YOU 31
    SURVEY SAYS… 32
    AFTER THE TRIAL 32
        Hung Jury 32
        Response 33
        Additional Evidence 36
THE ELIMINATION CHAMBER 39
    INTRO 39
        Some dame walked into my office and said 39
        Why this? 39
    ONCE A MAN HAD A DREAM 40
        The ostrich effect… in reverse 40
        The Art of Professional Wrestling 41
        But nothing speaks louder than my credit card 42
    IT'S A LAST MINUTE THROWN TOGETHER MATCH… WITH SIX MONTHS OF PLANNING 44
        Establishing the Brand 44
        Another heading about planning? Aiya! 49
    THE AFTERSHOCK! 49
    RUNNING JOKES 50
        The Evolution of Evolution 50
        The Regulars 50
        Where's my championship? 51

  Christian can't get inside 51
 THE PINFALL VICTORY 52
 AFTER THE TRIAL 52
  Hung Jury 52
  Response 52

KEVIN NASH 55

 INTRO 55
  Some dame walked into my office and said... 55
  Why this? 55
 THE WORST DRAWING CHAMPION OF ALL TIME – PART 1 55
 THE WORST DRAWING CHAMPION OF ALL TIME – PART 2 57
 WRAPPING UP THE NUMBERS 58
 LET ME TELL YOU ABOUT A LITTLE CITY... 59
 THE "BIG MAN" PUSH.. 60
 ARISTOTLE'S RULES OF FRIENDSHIPS... 61
 WATCH OUT FOR THE BOOKER MAN 62
 SUPER FRIENDS, UNITE!... 64
 SIX MOVES OF DOOM 65
 HERE COMES THE MONEY OR NASH THE HUMANITARIAN 67
 UNBEATEN RECORDS.. 69
 THE JACKKNIFE POWERBOMB 69
 AFTER THE TRIAL 70
  Hung Jury 70
  Response 70

THE FINGER POKE OF DOOM 74

 INTRO 74
  Some dame walked into my office and said... 74
  Why this? 74
 BACKGROUND.. 74
 THE LOGIC OF WRESTLING 75
 THE RASH DECISION.. 76
 YOU REMEMBER MY GOOD FRIENDS, THE NUMBERS? 77
 THE DEATH OF WCW 79
 ONE MORE TO THE PIN 79
 AFTER THE TRIAL 80
  Hung Jury 80
  Response 80

DUSTY RHODES: HEAD BOOKER.. 85

 INTRO 85
  Some dame walked into my office and said... 85
  Why this? 85
 ALL HAIL THE AMERICAN DREAM 86
 THOSE FATEFUL SIX YEARS 86
 FUN WITH NUMBERS... ERRR... WORDS 87
 REVENGE OF THE STARDUST 88
 ON THE SIDELINES?... 90
 CH-CH-CH-CHANGES!.. 91

AN OLD ENEMY COMES A-KNOCKIN' AND SOME NEW FRIENDS	93
THE DUSTY FINISH	95
GOIN' TO THE PAY WINDOW!	96
AFTER THE TRIAL	97
Hung Jury	*97*
Response	*97*

EARL HEBNER SCREWING BRET HART 100

INTRO	100
Some dame walked into my office and said...	*100*
Why this?	*101*
YOU SCREWED BRET	101
TRY THINKING FOR YOURSELVES BEFORE YOU PELT AN INNOCENT MAN WITH CIGARETTES!	102
THE SEEDS WERE PLANTED 10 YEARS BEFOREHAND	106
A CASE WITHOUT TALKING ABOUT BUYRATES?	107
THE OLD 1-2-3	107
AFTER THE TRIAL	108
Hung Jury	*108*
Response	*109*

VINCE MCMAHON NOT BUYING OUT WCW'S CONTRACTS 111

INTRO	111
Some dame walked into my office and said...	*111*
Why this?	*111*
WHERE HAVE ALL THE GOOD PEOPLE GONE?	112
ECONOMIC VS. NORMAL PROFIT	115
THE MILLIONAIRES YOU ALREADY KNOW	117
THE "X" FOOTBALL LEAGUE	117
YOU OWN WHAT?!	119
LET'S TAKE IT TO A HIGHER POWER!	122
THE INTENTIONS OF THE MAN	123
SIGN ON THE DOTTED LINE	126
AFTER THE TRIAL	127
Hung Jury	*127*
Response	*127*

GOLDBERG 130

INTRO	130
Some dame walked into my office and said...	*130*
Why this?	*131*
STONE COLD RIP OFF	132
THREE HUNDRED SIXTY-FOUR JOBBERS?	134
DEVELOPING INTO A WRESTLER	136
QUID PRO QUO	140
PEANUTS FOR SALE!	141
PROTECTING THE CHARACTER OR WHEN TO FALL DOWN AND GO BOOM	142
TURN THIS!	145
WHY WON'T YOU FIGHT ME, GREENBERG?	148
DANGER WILL ROBINSON	150
BROCKBERG?	152

WE'VE GONE ALL THIS TIME AND WE HAVEN'T TALKED ABOUT THE NUMBERS?	153
HUMANITARIAN AND HERITAGE	155
SPEAR, JACKHAMMER, PIN, GO HOME	157
AFTER THE TRIAL	158
Hung Jury	*158*
Response	*158*
More Good Things	*163*

THE BRAND EXTENSION 166

INTRO	166
Some dame walked into my office and said...	*166*
Why this?	*166*
WHAT IS A BRAND?	167
BUT WHY OH WHY OH WHY WOULD THEY EVER DO THIS?	169
THE BEGINNINGS OF THE EXTENSION TO TODAY	170
WHERE'S MY BRAND?	174
THE BIG GUNS	175
THE DREAM MATCH. OR IS THAT THE DREAM EHARMONY?	177
NEW RULES, NEW GAMES	178
THE DEATH OF SO-AND-SO	180
BEWARE THE LOOMING SHARK	181
THE NUMBERS THAT DON'T AGREE	182
REUNION SAYS WHAT?	185
WHERE THE FUTURE LIES	187
TIME TO SPLIT	187
AFTER THE TRIAL	188
Hung Jury	*188*
Response	*188*

WCW THUNDER 191

INTRO	191
Some dame walked into my office and said...	*191*
Why this?	*191*
WHERE THE HECK DID THIS SHOW COME FROM?	191
WHERE ARE MY MAIN EVENTERS?	192
UNIQUE SITUATIONS	193
MORE BIG SURPRISES AND THAT OLD NITRO FEELING	194
FEEL THE THUNDER	194
AFTER THE TRIAL	195
Hung Jury	*195*
Response	*195*

LEX LUGER 197

INTRO	197
Some dame walked into my office and said...	*197*
Why this?	*198*
HE LOVES ME, HE LOVES ME NOT	198
WHO NEEDS MAT SKILLS WHEN YOU'VE GOT PECKS LIKE THESE?	201
I CAN'T REMEMBER ANYTHING IMPORTANT	202
BOY THIS ARENA SURE IS EMPTY	203

DAMN THAT BOY IS JACKED!	203
A COUPLE OF MORE CRIMES	206
GIVING THE BOY A SHOT	208
LISTEN TO THE FANS	209
THE NARCISSISTIC FINAL COMMENT	211
AFTER THE TRIAL	212
Hung Jury	212
Response	212
Mini-Case: Lex Luger (Follow-Up)	216

THE UNDERTAKER — 219

INTRO	219
Some dame walked into my office and said...	219
Why this?	220
A LITTLE HISTORY, AND SOME EARLY COUNTER-ARGUMENTS	220
BALL... ERRR... BELT HOG!	222
YET THEY STILL WANT HIM	224
HOW COME HE ALWAYS GETS UP?	224
WHO ARE THESE PEOPLE?	225
STEALING THE SPOTLIGHT	227
ENOUGH FOES, HOW ABOUT SOME FRIENDS?	227
BUT HE JUST WRESTLES WHEN HE WANTS!	228
FILLER FUN FACTS!	228
BUT CAN THEY ~~DANCE~~ WRESTLE?	229
USUALLY WHEN I TALK ABOUT SELLING, WE'RE IN THE NUMBERS SECTION	231
SO IF THIS WERE AN EVOLUTION SCHEMATIC, WOULD HE BE ON PHASE 943,304,424-C?	232
NOW, LET'S TALK BLING BLING	234
WHERE DO YOU GO FROM HERE?	236
BURIED ALIVE!	237
AFTER THE TRIAL	237
Hung Jury	237
Response	238

SID VICIOUS — 240

INTRO	240
Some dame walked into my office and said...	240
Why this?	241
A LITTLE HISTORY, AND SOME EARLY COUNTER-ARGUMENTS... WAIT, DIDN'T I DO THIS BEFORE?	241
TOP THREE MOST INFAMOUS MOMENTS	245
No respect for the Hulkster, brother	245
What are you gonna do, clean my windows?	246
TWENTY PUNCTURE WOUNDS?!?!?	246
THE SECRET OF LIFE: SOFTBALL STYLE	249
WHAT IS THIS WORK ETHIC YOU SPEAK OF?	250
I'LL TRADE YOU THESE THREE BEANS FOR ONE SID VICIOUS	251
WHY'D YOU SAY THAT? WHY'D YOU HAVE TO TELL ME?	253
MARK OUT MOMENTS	256
POWERBOMB... SMASH!	257
AFTER THE TRIAL	257
Hung Jury	257

    Response 258

MIKE AWESOME LEAVING ECW **259**

  INTRO 259
    Some dame walked into my office and said... 259
    Why this? 259
  WHAT'S THE STORY HERE? 260
  WHO REALLY TRASHED THE TITLE? 260
  WHAT ABOUT THE CONTRACT? 262
  DOING THE RIGHT THING 264
  BUT THE BOYS STILL HATE HIM 265
  WHAT ABOUT PAUL E.? 266
  THAT'S AWESOME! 268
  AFTER THE TRIAL 269
    Hung Jury 269
    Response 269

THE MCMAHON-HELMSLEY ERA **274**

  INTRO 274
    Some dame walked into my office and said... 274
    Why this? 274
  HOW DID THIS ALL BEGIN? 275
  WHY TRIPLE H? 277
  WHY STEPHANIE? 279
  AND THEN WHAT HAPPENED? 280
  THE SHORT-TERM GAINERS 282
  THE LONG-TERM GAINERS 284
  WHAT WE SAW FOR THE FIRST (THOUGH NOT LAST) TIME 286
  THE THINGS THAT DID NOT HAPPEN 288
  NUMBERS GALORE! 289
  AND WHAT BECAME OF OUR WARDS? 290
  THE SLAP HEARD ROUND THE WORLD 291
  AFTER THE TRIAL 291
    Hung Jury 291
    Response 292

NEW JACK **294**

  INTRO 294
    Some dame walked into my office and said... 294
    Why this? 294
  HOW'D I COME TO BE? 295
  THE ORIGIN, PART 2 296
  YOU HAVE THE RIGHT TO REMAIN SILENT... 297
    The Mass Transit Incident 298
    Scaffold Fall 300
    Killing ECW on TNN 302
    Stabby Stabby! 302
    More incidents 304
  A WRESTLER? DOING HIS BEST? GIVING BACK? WHAT?! 305
  BALCONY PLUNGE 308

AFTER THE TRIAL 309
    Hung Jury *309*
    Response *309*

SCOTT HALL **312**

INTRO 312
    Some dame walked into my office and said.... ....*312*
    Why this? *313*
THE HISTORY OF THE EDGE (NOT THAT KIND)..313
CURSE OF THE BIG MAN 316
ONLY HIMSELF? 318
GOT AWARDS? WHY NOT! 319
WAIT, THAT WAS HIS IDEA? 319
ALCOHOLISM 321
    What are you asking of me? *324*
    Where does it all come back to? *326*
THE TOOTHPICK FLICK 326
AFTER THE TRIAL 327
    Hung Jury *327*
    Response *327*

LARRY ZBYSZKO **330**

INTRO 330
    Some dame walked into my office and said.... ....*330*
    Why this? *330*
THIRTY YEARS IN THE INDUSTRY..331
IS HE TRIPLE H? 342
THE LINE IN THE SAND 344
IT'S SUING TIME! 345
AND WHAT HAS HE DONE WITH THAT TRADEMARK? 350
THE LEGENDARY WRAP-UP 351
AFTER THE TRIAL 351
    Hung Jury *351*
    Response *352*

VINCE MCMAHON IN THE DEATH OF OWEN HART **354**

INTRO 354
    Some dame walked into my office and said.... ....*354*
    Why this? *355*
VINCE KILLED OWEN 355
THE SETTLEMENT 362
THE SHOW MUST GO ON...365
MARTHA HART: ULTIMATE MARTYR...366
ONE LAST WALK DOWN THE TUNNEL 368
AFTER THE TRIAL 368
    Hung Jury *368*
    Response *369*

THE ULTIMATE WARRIOR **374**

INTRO 374

Some dame walked into my office and said...	374
Why this?	375
HISTORY PART 1 – WHO IS JIM HELLWIG?	376
HISTORY PART 2 – AND THEN THERE WAS...	378
IT WAS ABOUT PAYING DUES.	382
HISTORY PART 3 – THE ULTIMATE JOURNEY BEGINS	383
WHAT REALLY HAPPENED?	387
Unprofessional	387
Contract Problems	388
Crazy Angles	392
F•R•I•E•N•D•S	393
TO HAVE WRESTLING ABILITY, OR NOT TO HAVE, THAT IS THE QUESTION	395
LOVE OF THE BUSINESS	397
ONE LAST TIME OUT TO BAT	399
WHAT'D HE SAY?	401
SHOOT 'EM IF YOU GOT 'EM	403
THE FIRST RULE OF CONSERVATION	409
THE ONCE AND FUTURE	413
AND SO ENDS THE ULTIMATE CHALLENGE	416
AFTER THE TRIAL	417
Hung Jury	417
Response	418

SCOTT STEINER ... 421

INTRO	421
Some dame walked into my office and said...	421
Why this?	421
SCOTT STEINER PART 1 – SCOTT STEINER	422
SCOTT STEINER PART 2 – THE BIG BAD BOOTY DADDY	427
WHEN AND WHEN NOT TO GO	429
HAVE YOU SEEN MY LOST PUPPY?	432
MISUNDERSTAND THIS!	433
NOW THAT'S DEDICATION	435
THE AWARDS	435
MMMMM... DRUGS	437
TO ALL MY FREAKS OUT THERE	439
AFTER THE TRIAL	439
Hung Jury	439
Response	440

THE WORLD HEAVYWEIGHT CHAMPIONSHIP ... 443

INTRO	443
Some dame walked into my office and said...	443
Why this?	444
SUPPOSED HISTORY	445
TRUE ORIGINS	445
THE CASE FOR TRIPLE H	448
OVER YOUR SHOULDER OR AROUND YOUR WAIST	450
AFTER THE TRIAL	451
Hung Jury	451

    Response 452

HULK HOGAN 458

  INTRO 458
    Some dame walked into my office and said... 458
    Why this? 460
  CALIFORNIA... GEORGIA... WHAT'S THE DIFFERENCE? 461
  RASSLIN' DOWN SOUTH 463
  WRESTLING UP NORTH 465
  WRASSLIN' IN MIDWEST AND PURO IN THE LAND OF THE RISING SUN 467
  AND SO THE TRUE AMERICAN ICON IS BORN 470
  TIME TO REALLY START RUNNING WILD 472
  HOW TO BUILD A WRESTLEMANIA 475
  HOLLYWOOD! LA LA LA LA LA LA... HOLLYWOOD! 476
  THE SHOT (TO THE VEIN) HEARD ROUND THE WORLD 477
  THERE'S A NEW HOGAN IN TOWN 480
  THIS IS THE NEW WORLD ORDER OF WRESTLING, BROTHER! 481
  HOW MANY TIMES MUST I EXPLAIN HOW WCW DIED? 483
  AND THEN THERE WAS QUIET 485
  THE POISON IS INTRODUCED 485
  BUT CAN HE STILL DRAW? 486
  SHOOT 'EM IF YOU GOT 'EM! 487
  HERE COMES THE PROSECUTION! 494
  DO YOU HAVE A HART? 500
  CAN HOGAN WRESTLE? 503
  NOW WHAT? 506
  HE IS THE IMMORTAL ONE 506
  AFTER THE TRIAL 507
    Hung Jury 507
    Response 507

DDP 510

  INTRO 510
    Some dame walked into my office and said... 510
    Why this? 511
  THE JERSEY TRILOGY PREQUEL 512
  STILL NOT QUITE FEELING THE BANG 516
  AND THEN THERE WAS ANOTHER "W" 517
  I'M A 'RASSLER! 519
  SO THAT'S WHY THEY CONSIDER HIM A TRAINER! 520
  WCW GROWS AND GROWS AND PAGE... GETS RELEASED?!? 523
  SNAP INTO HIM! OOOOOOOOOH YEEEEAAAAAHHHH!!! 525
  THE END OF WCW 527
  INVASION 528
  TIME TO MAKE AN IMPACT! 530
  AND AFTER THAT? 533
  FUN FACTS 533
  THE CHING-CHING 533
  DIAMOND CUTTER 535
  AFTER THE TRIAL 536

 Hung Jury *536*
 Response *536*

JEFF HARDY **538**

 Intro 538
  Some dame walked into my office and said... .... *538*
  Why this? *539*
 On a little tobacco farm... 540
 A career begins, like a willow in the wisp 544
 I'm single, baby! 547
 Why don't you care anymore? 549
 Back to the small venue 552
 Total Nonstop Jeff 554
 Oh these little pills 556
 You are out of here! 558
 Bumper 560
 You know what I'm thinking? 562
 Wipe that brush off 563
 Whisper that into the wind 564
 After the Trial 565
  Hung Jury *565*
  Response *565*

THE EUROPEAN CHAMPIONSHIP **567**

 Intro 567
  Some dame walked into my office and said... .... *567*
  Why this? *568*
 Where? When? WHY?!?! 569
 The best we could do 570
 Is it a steppingstone? 571
 What did the wrestlers think? 572
 Today... what are they doing? 574
 Strap it on 575
 After the Trial 575
  Hung Jury *575*
  Response *575*

THE NWO SPLIT **577**

 Intro 577
  Some dame walked into my office and said... .... *577*
  Why this? *577*
 What's the story here? 578
 Face? nWo? What? 580
 The B-team 583
 Opportunity 583
 Topic 1: The End 584
 Billionaire Ted says... 585
 What did it all do in the end? 587
 Take out the spray paint one more time 588
 After the Trial 589

 Hung Jury *589*
 Response *589*

JEFF JARRETT **591**

 INTRO 591
  Some dame walked into my office and said......*591*
  Why this? *593*
 WHERE DID WE GET THIS COUNTRY BUMPKIN?..593
 WIN A TITLE, LOSE A TITLE, WIN A TITLE, LOSE A TITLE... 596
 J-E-DOUBLE F J-A-DOUBLE R-E-DOUBLE T. DOUBLE J, JEFF JARRETT 599
 TOP OF THE TOP... NAH, I'VE HAD ENOUGH 600
 WHERE THE BIG BOYS PLAY 602
 WWF... ERRR... NWA... NO, I WAS RIGHT THE FIRST TIME 604
 GOODBYE AGAIN, OWEN 608
 ONE LAST TIME 610
 NOW IT'S TIME TO BE CHOSEN 613
 CHOP IT DOWN WITH THE SIDE OF MY HAND 617
 IT'S A BIG WORLD 619
 HAVE YOU EVER TRIED TO PROTECT A MOUNTAIN? 621
 SWING THAT GUITAR 623
 AFTER THE TRIAL...624
  Hung Jury *624*
  Response *624*

CHYNA WINNING THE INTERCONTINENTAL CHAMPIONSHIP **626**

 INTRO 626
  Some dame walked into my office and said......*626*
  Why this? *626*
 DYNASTIES IN CHYNA 627
 WHERE IS INTERCONTINENTAL? 629
 THE EMPEROR'S NEW GROOVE 631
 FUTURE IMPERFECT 633
 THAT WONDERFUL LISP 634
 AFTER THE TRIAL...635
  Hung Jury *635*
  Response *635*

MINI-CASES **638**

 OVERVIEW..638
 TONY SCHIAVONE "THAT'LL PUT BUTTS IN SEATS..638
 BROCK LESNER LEAVING THE WWE FOR FOOTBALL 639
 THE WWE BANNING HIGH-RISK NECK MOVES...640

APPENDIX: SUSPENDED SENTENCE **645**

 NEWS FROM PRAG'S PLACE 645
  Some dame walked into my office and said......*645*
 IN DEFENSE OF... IN DEFENSE OF... 647
  Where's the prosecution? *647*
  This should be a debate *649*
  More counter-evidence *650*

Manipulating the last word	652
The "rules" are unfair	654
You don't follow the "rules"	654
The vote is skewed	657
Preaching to the choir	658
Why do I put up with it?	660
Real world impact	661
My secret reason for doing this	662

AFTERWARDS **663**

    ABOUT THE AUTHOR 663
    OTHER WORKS 664
    DEDICATIONS AND NOTES 666
    VERSION HISTORY 667
    COPYRIGHTS AND DISCLAIMERS 668

Deposition

Submitted Evidence

On May 1, 2005, my first anthology series **In Defense Of...** premiered on pop-culture website 411mania.com. I had been hired by **Wrestling Zone** editor Larry Csonka and site owner Ashish Pabari after submitting my sample case of **In Defense Of... Eric Bischoff** the prior month. Before being employed by 411mania, I had no professional writing experience whatsoever, so they were certainly taking a chance on me. But all worked out well as I stayed with 411mania until November 2010, launching two other major anthology series (**Hidden Highlights** and **The Hamilton Ave Journal**) before officially leaving the writing world behind for nearly a decade.

During that time, I wrote nearly 500 articles—of which 64 were for **In Defense Of...**, spanning 29 unique cases. Additionally, I penned a set of "mini-cases" as add-on content inside **Hidden Highlights** before I was comfortable that the premise could work fully on its own (it would take nearly half a year until I felt that). While I was scribing for 411mania, I was also working full-time-plus as an on-the-road consultant, and the two priorities were often in massive conflict for my attention. Since each issue of **In Defense Of...** usually required in the neighborhood of 20 hours of work, something eventually had to give, and it was this article. While Larry, Ashish, and the fans would have been happy for me to continue, I simply could not make the commitment.

Due to the passage of time, the errors of technology, and other factors, much of my work had disappeared from the public internet. While laboring to compile my entire writing history for my website jpprag.com, I discovered what was still available live, what was at least captured once on archive.org's **Wayback Machine**, and what I had to rebuild from my original files. To be clear, all of the cases in this book are available for free in their original format (or as close as possible) on my website at https://www.jpprag.com/blog/categories/in-defense-of. If you want to experience how each of these cases was originally presented, it is accessible to you now without even buying this book.

But while going through that aggregation effort, I also saw an opportunity, which has resulted in this collection. Because **In Defense Of...** was written as a weekly article in a myriad of other articles, it is full of content locked to a time and place that has nothing to do with the subject at hand. And both because of space limitations on posts and due to general marketing, cases were split up into two or three parts. All of that resulted in large swaths of space dedicated to recapping (colloquially known as "stenography"), plugging other articles, creating hype, doing general intros, and talking about unrelated content that was relevant to the news of the day. All of that was because the important thing at that time was getting "hits", and those were the tools we had.

As such, that is the superior value of reading the cases in this book instead of on the website. That excess material has been stripped out and the cases have been put together into a single streamlined format as they were meant to be read. Each have been cleaned up with better editing than we had available in the wild west of the internet and formatting that was near impossible that makes everything a much easier read. Further, I used this opportunity to post some of the feedback that has only ever existed in my inbox—including one infamous message from someone involved in the death of Owen Hart.

As a word of caution: all of this was originally written between 2005 and 2006. As such, certain references will not just seem dated, but will be downright perplexing in light of later events. For instance, there are several praises of Chris Benoit and use of him as a character witness. For those unaware, Chris Benoit murdered his wife and son before killing himself in June 2007. After his death, it was discovered that Benoit appeared to have severe brain damage from years in the ring, being described as similar to an 85-year-old Alzheimer's patient. But this was unknown a year or two prior, in a timeframe where he was beloved by many fans.

Additionally, many of the people discussed have gone on to more actions (or have subsequently passed away). Our first defendant Eric Bischoff has a long history post May 2005 that includes executive and creative stints with iMPACT Wrestling and WWE, all of which could provide expanded issues for the case to address. However, I have elected to leave the cases mostly intact and as their point-in-time references—although I have added some additional material if it added to an argument already being made. For instance, when discussing Chyna's life circumstances, she was very much alive at the time of the writing. Adding in details about her death by overdose helped wrap up the picture I was painting. Or in another example, at the time of the original writing Nick Patrick had never discussed his count during the Sting/Hogan match at Starrcade 1997. But in 2017 that all changed when he finally came forward with his perspective and others responded to his revelations. As such, it was worthwhile adding a bit of content there as it reinforced the point already being made.

That said, most of the material is still as first presented—just polished, made clearer, and reorganized for a better read. The overall thesis and arguments remain the same whether additional material was added or not, so it was better to just leave the cases as they were originally designed.

With all of this in mind, please enjoy the redux of **In Defense Of...**!

J.P. Prag
October 30, 2019, updated July 22, 2020

REMEMBERING LARRY CSONKA

On May 18, 2020, the immeasurable force in the wrestling journalism industry known as Larry Csonka passed away. Larry's impact was felt far and wide as writers, fans, wrestlers, and management all paid tribute to his influence and massive work ethic. I also wrote a brief remembrance:

> For those who don't remember me, I wrote In Defense Of..., Hidden Highlights, The Hamilton Ave Journal, and other odds and ends here at 411mania/411wrestling from 2005 to 2010. I can say without a doubt that not only would I not be the fan I am today, not only would I not be writer I am today, and not only would I not be the professional I am today—but I would not be the person I am today without Larry Csonka. The man has had an outstripped influence on my life, and everyone above has done a wonderful job capturing what it was like to work with and know Larry.
>
> Larry not only gave me and many others an opportunity, he helped us thrive and pushed us to be better, but never once controlled what we did. He let me experiment and find my own way while shining a light on what he did so well. There was so much behind the scenes that no one here is privy to. I remember calling Larry when my mother died, and just read a conversation we had about his health about a year later. Going through the archives, I wanted to find the perfect encapsulation of what it was like working with Larry. I think I found it in this:
>
> The Hidden Highlights 12.25.05: Issue #17
>
> Scroll down to **Hidden Highlights for WWE SmackDown! presents Armageddon: Sunday, December 18, 2005 by Larry Csonka**
>
> The first line captures it all:
>
> *Larry Csonka: HAHAHA! FORMAT? I laugh at thy format! Hello there kids, it's the Big LTC here, bailing out JT and JP on my VACATION! MY VACATION! Fuckers.*
>
> Ah, that's the Larry Csonka we all knew and loved!

Everything in this book would not exist without Larry Csonka. As such, it is all dedicated to his memory.

J.P. Prag
July 6, 2020

PRE-TRIAL FACT GATHERING

Every issue of In Defense Of... began with an introduction discussing the prior week or the case just completed. Once that was out of the way, it moved on and introduced any new readers to the concept. This was presented as "a pretty simple premise":

> Certain people, events, organizations, and storylines in wrestling history have gotten a bum rap. Some writers have presented overtly critical comments and outright lies as fact, and others have followed suit. Well no more! "In Defense of..." has one reason: to bring the truth to the wrestling fan!

Similarly, at the end of every case (save the first one), readers were given the ability to vote GUILTY or NOT GUILTY for each client. The voting took place entirely over e-mail by people clicking a link that created an e-mail message with the topic and verdict in the subject line. This also gave an opportunity for the voters to get in their thoughts (more on that later) and for me to minimize any stuffing of the ballot box that you would see in generic online polls. At the time, online polling technology was not readily available, but even once it was I stuck with the same method for reasons that will be discussed in the appendix.

At the end of a case, a very specific array of accusations were presented. Over time, a set of "rules" were developed to assist in how people voted to keep everyone on track. Those were presented as:

> And please take into consideration the rules (well, they're more what you might call guidelines than rules) of a fair court system:
>
> (1) All parties, events, circumstances, etc... are innocent until proven guilty. In this court, the defendants have already been found guilty without trial, and so therefore this is an appeals court. Finding a defendant guilty means you disagree with the evidence presented.
>
> (2) The jury must find the defendant guilty beyond reasonable doubt. That means that if there is doubt in your mind that the defendant is guilty, then you cannot find the appellant guilty. Reasonable doubt means that the average person, looking at the facts presented, could

> not find the defendant guilty on all counts despite personal feelings.
>
> (3) This is a court of fact, not fiction. Fantasies of what could have been or should have been do not fly here; especially fantasies of the impossible (such as a wrestler not getting injured at an untimely moment). All we have is what did actually occur and the intentions of those being accused.
>
> (4) A defendant cannot be judged by events outside the case at hand. For example, if we were trying a particular contract signing by a wrestling promoter, you cannot use that ten years later that wrestler died from a heart attack relating to the drug use that the wrestler started when he signed with the promoter. One has nothing to do with the other in terms of the case at hand.
>
> (5) You do not have to like the accused before or after the case at hand, and a vote of not guilty does not change your personal preferences. You can make it clear that you feel the accused is the worst thing you have ever seen, but if the facts compel you to see that the accused cannot be found guilty beyond reasonable doubt, then voting guilty would be unconscionable.

All of the cases below are presented in the order in which they were written with the exception of the mini-cases and the wrap-up in the appendix. Further, because they are shown in order my style will change drastically as the cases move on. Reading them now, they have a high level of energy and bit of "yelling at you" that does not reflect how I would present the topics today. With that in mind, you may find shifts in tone as I move between original content and new.

Additionally, there are some terms that it would be helpful for you to be familiar with. These include:

- **IWC:** This stands for "Internet Wrestling Community" and refers to the fans of wresters who populated the message boards and news-sites of the early internet. This is generally considered a negative term as people in the IWC could be considered close to the "trolls" of 2020.

- **Mark:** Since wrestling came out of the old carnival traditions, they share many terms. A "mark" is a person who treats the product as real or at the very least just takes the product at face value and does not look for anything beyond what is presented. This can be a negative term making fun of someone for being naïve, but it can be a positive term for someone who does not let the backstage antics impact their feelings for the product.

- **Smark:** This stands for "Smart Mark", which is what people in the IWC considered themselves. You see, they were "smart" to the backstage antics and knew how the product was put together. Again, this term could be negative because it could be seen as a person who is jaded and caustic about the product or positive because of their knowledge.

- **Kayfabe:** Another carnival term, this one means interacting with the world of wrestling as if it were real. For instance, if two wrestlers are feuding and someone spots them out in public, they will then go into their act in order to not break the illusion. Anything presented as "in universe" would be kayfabe.

- **Shoot:** When something is real, not pre-determined.

- **Sell:** When a wrestler makes a move look believable, especially when they are on the receiving end of the offence. "No Selling" may indicate that the wrestler is intentionally not making their opponent look good.

- **Green:** New and inexperienced, often hinting at lack of ability to make moves believable and sell, and also potentially making noticeable mistakes.

- **Dirt Sheet:** This is what the news-sites were called, taking their name from the old physical papers that were created to follow wrestling news. These were usually cheap copy machine created "newsletters" that people subscribed to through a mailing list. The name followed the reporters to the internet.

- **'rasslin:** A diminutive form of "wrestling" that infers a particular mat-based style known in more southern-based promotions. A way to think about it is the WWE presents more of "show" that is about characters and not the in-ring product, while an organization like WCW was presented more around the substance of the in-ring product to the detriment of characters and storylines.

- **Workrate:** Similar to the last term, this is about a wrestler's skill in the ring to present a crisp product that looks impressive and wows the audience. A lack of workrate would be considered a negative as someone might just lumber around the ring and not really do anything great.

- **Sports Entertainment:** A term invented by the WWE to describe wrestling. Since wrestling is "pre-determined", it is not really a competitive sport. However, it is still an athletic exhibition mixed with stories, acting, and the like. Hence, the term "Sports Entertainment" was created in order to avoid being regulated by actual sports agencies in each State.

- **House Show:** A non-televised event, often with a lot more freedom than when on television but also used for wrestlers to practice those matches for big events.

- **Face and Heel:** Faces are the good guys and heels are the bad guys. When they change from one to the other it is called a "turn".

- **Jobber:** A wrestling character that is a perpetual looser, rarely if ever winning a match. These people are usually known as "enhancement talent" because their job is to make the other person(s) look better.

- **Go Over:** The person who is decided to win a match.

- **Booker:** The person in charge of planning the matches and storylines. Not to be confused with Booker T, who was a wrestler.

- ***:** Any reference to a * is a "star rating" or a "snowflake", a subjective measurement that those in the wrestling review community give to the quality of matches.

- **Squash:** When a win in the wrestling ring is decisive and there is no offense from the other side. Usually these matches are short; under a minute.

- **Pop/Popping and Heat:** These are crowd reactions, or as known in another way how "over" a person is with the crowd. Faces will pop a crowd if they are getting a large reaction while heels will generate heat. There is also a term "X-Pac Heat" which refers to a crowd acting negatively towards someone not because they are reacting to the character, but are reacting to the performer and don't want to see them. The idea for heels is that the crowd should love to boo them, not hate them for real.

- **Lower/Mid/Upper Carder and Main Eventer:** Positions in the pecking order or perceived rank of the wrestlers. The higher they are, the more they are considered "legitimate" contenders and the more their characters and merchandise may be desired.

Now that that is all squared away, let us bang the gavel and get to court!

Eric Bischoff

Intro

Some dame walked into my office and said...

Normally, this section would be filled with the original e-mail or the like that I received asking for a particular case. Being the premier issue, Eric Bischoff was my first choice. Although a near life-long wrestling fan, I grew up watching NWA and WCW, not the WWE. After the WWE bought all relevant assets of WCW in 2001, most of the fans like me disappeared from the real world and the nascent internet as they chose to move on rather than watch WWE programming (televisions ratings prove this later on). As the years moved on, I became more disillusioned with professional wrestling because I did not like how the WWE presented their product and upstart organizations like TNA failed to maintain a consistent unique value proposition.

Because of my feelings, I took to writing to rediscover my love of professional wrestling, and that quickly morphed into the case you are about to read here. I actually wrote the original draft poolside while on vacation in Arizona visiting my brother. Without 411mania hiring me to present this case to the world, I most likely would have given up on wrestling completely within a few months. This case is so important to me because it reinvigorated me as a fan and fueled my next 6 years as both an audience member and a reporter.

Why this?

My all-time favorite promoter, on-air character, philosopher, and dealmaker in wrestling is Eric Bischoff. That's it. I think he's absolutely fantastic at what he does, at least way better than you or I would be, and many others have tried to be. Don't believe me? Think that Uncle Eric is nothing compared to Vinny Mac or [throw in miscellaneous independent promoter that no one cares about here]? Well here's setting the facts straight...

Eric Bischoff only created one thousand stars

The utmost biggest lie I read every week about Eric Bischoff is that he only created one star: Goldberg. Are you insane? Did you even watch wrestling in the mid-90's? Well let me tell you, I was a total mark, and here is a short list names I never knew before WCW that I saw rise under Bischoff's tutelage: Chris Benoit, Chris Jericho, Rey Mysterio, Giant, DDP, Torrie Wilson, Stacy

Keibler, Ernest "Cat" Miller, Eddie Guerrero, Chavo Guerrero, Dean Malenko, Kanyon/Mortis, Raven, Konan, Lance Storm, and Shane Helms.

Do you see that? I could go on forever! Bischoff created stars on all levels of the card, but he wasn't just good at creating, he was excellent at re-inventing.

I'm an entrepreneur, and for the layman that might mean starting your own business. Entrepreneurship, though, should not be so pigeon-holed; it can be about re-creating and re-energizing, about taking something old and making it new and great again. Personally, I deeply believe in corporate entrepreneurship, that a company that is old and tired and full of bureaucracy can become lean, mean, and young again. Don't believe a company can become young again? Here's a list of companies that completely changed from their old ways to grow to new heights: HP, Apple, PepsiCo, Virgin, Sunkist, Viacom, Miramax Studios, and, oh wait, the then WWF! Do you remember the Attitude Era? Vince Russo, Ed Farrarah, and Vince McMahon completely changed how the company was run, perceived, and did business. You should be thankful.

So what does this have to do with Eric Bischoff? Well, I contend that re-creating a star's valor is just as big, if not a bigger accomplishment, than creating a new star. Here's a list of stars whose careers were dead or dying that Bischoff gave new life to (sometimes multiple times): Hulk Hogan, Kevin Nash, Scott Hall, Syxx, Ted DiBiasse, Rick Rude, Curt Henning, Sting, Booker T, Stevie Ray, Rick and Scott Steiner, Lex Luger, Kevin Sullivan, Meng, Barbarian, Larry Zybsyco, and Dusty Rhodes (even if the last two were only as announcers. I'm goin' to the pay window!).

And as for "stealing" Vince's talent and characters, that is complete bull. Bischoff never violated a copyright law or made a WWF character show up on WCW television. He just signed INDEPENDENT CONTRACTORS to an exclusive contract with his company. Since people like Scott Hall and Kevin Nash are independent contractors—and those are their true names—their public persona cannot be copyrighted. So sure, Kevin Nash could not run around pretending to be a truck driver in WCW, but Kevin Nash the persona cannot be copyrighted, and therefore he can act however he wants anywhere.

Thus you can see by all of this that Eric Bischoff is an incredibly creative man, whether it is with his own creations or remaking an older model. It takes talent and skill to build the roster and program he made, not luck, stealing, and money (wait a little bit and we'll get back to this last point).

By now you may be saying, "Boy, that's great, but did he really add to the legacy of wrestling?"

Glad you asked...

CRUISERWEIGHTS EQUAL WORKRATE

What is the one thing from WCW that still exists in the WWE today? That's right: it's the Cruiserweight Championship of the World! Being the only title that never combined with any WWE title (unless you count when Ultimo Dragon had nine belts in WCW), and the only one that maintained its original sheen months after the end of the InVasion, the Cruiserweight Championship is the last true piece of WCW iconography available.

And would we even have had a Cruiserweight division if not for Eric Bischoff? Would people like Rey Mysterio, Juventud Guerrera, Psycosis, Villano IV y V, La Parka, Ultimo Dragon, Silver King, Lizmark Jr, Eddie Guerrero, Chavo Guerrero, or Chris Jericho ever have gotten the chance to wow and amaze us? Would we have gotten the opportunity—no privilege!—to see these amazing stars in action? Did we even know what workrate really was before we saw these guys bust their behinds for us day in and day out?

Eric Bischoff reminded us what it meant to be a wrestler, and not just a gimmicky clown or a group of skin heads or [insert race here] supremacy group with very little to offer for entertainment and excitement.

Eric Bischoff brought 'rasslin back to wrestling.

BILLIONAIRE TED'S MONEY

You might say to yourself, "Sure, Bischoff could have done those things, but he'd be nothing without Ted Turner's money. Billionaire Ted just bought whatever Bischoff wanted and damned the consequences. All he cared about was having a 'rasslin show on his SuperStation."

And I might tell you that you need to get your facts checked.

Bischoff only went to Ted Turner ONCE for money, and that was to acquire Hulk Hogan. After that, Bischoff was really on his own. He had a set budget determined by TBS, and he had to stick with it. And on top of all that, Ted Turner was not even in charge of Time-Warner from 1994 on! Everyone always acts like Ted Turner was the CEO of Time-Warner and took care of everything. Well, guess again, corporate conspiracy sleuth. Yes, Ted Turner was on the Board of Directors, but he gave up running the company or any of its sub-divisions in any meaningful way by 1994. Yes, he had a lot of influence and owned a lot of stock, but he had no real control anymore. He was just a figurehead to point a finger at. As time went on, it became more and more apparent that Turner had little to do with the company, especially when the AOL merger was announced and his later resignation from the board. Ted Turner can be found nowadays growing his mid-sized family eatery chain "Ted's Montana Grill" in a Midwest state near you.

But I digress. Since Turner had so little control over the everyday life of his company, Bischoff was on his own; but he had great ideas!

The last thing Bischoff asked Turner for was Nitro. Turner came to him near the end of his reign and asked what Bischoff needed to compete against the WWF. Bischoff didn't ask for money or celebrities or stealing contracts; he asked for a Monday night primetime slot to take the competition right to Vince, and it was granted. The rest is history. This would be one of the last truly great things that WCW's parent company did for WCW and Bischoff. After that, things went haywire.

You would think in a huge media giant like the then (and once again) Time-Warner, they would want to have synergy across the brands. Eric Bischoff thought so. According to his shoot interview, Bischoff wanted to create a more "adult" version of his programming on HBO, but that was shut down. He wanted to use music from Warner Records, but they would not allow him to do so. Now Warner Records has been sold off due to slumping sales (and yes, I am suggesting there is a connection between their lack of inter-brand promoting and the sale of the division). When Bischoff could not use Warner Records, he asked permission to negotiate outside the company for mainstream music, and he was refused. At every turn, Bischoff was thwarted from those above him from taking WCW to new heights, and Ted Turner could do nothing to help him.

GIVE A MAN AN INCH...

Despite all standing in his way, Eric Bischoff did everything possible to be creative and expand the brand and the audience. Outside of his famous storylines (nWo, Sting, Television Title fun), what Eric Bischoff was exceptionally good at was making deals and creating cross promotion with partners. For instance, WCW and Disney had an excellent working relationship, and Nitro ran at Disney for weeks at a time, despite the fact that they were part of competing parent companies. Remember when Rey Mysterio was launched like a dart? That was at Disney! What a fun ride!

Not enough? How about the highly successful NASCAR tie-in which saw the WCW racer get into the top rankings, and even the nWo car making a splash. We in the IWC like to pretend we are so sophisticated, but there is a significant portion of the audience that loves NASCAR and wrestling and is loyal to both brands.

Want more? Look no further then Dennis Rodman and Jay Leno. Say what you will about their ability and the time they stole away from real workers, WCW got a ton of attention, ratings points, and buyrates from these guys. And Jay Leno donated all the money he made from his appearances to charity, so there!

But that was not all: Eric Bischoff also had excellent working relationships with companies in Japan and Mexico, allowing us to see great stars from all over the world. He had independent organizations working as an early version of a farm system, and went to Sturgis every year to have the second coolest audience in wrestling history: MOTORCYCLES (top kudos goes to Smackdown! in Iraq 2003, that was simply an amazing sight).

OK, so Sturgis may not have been your or the workers' thing, but it still was new, interesting, and did create cross promotion and make certain sponsors very happy.

And speaking of sponsors, Bischoff was an early pioneer of product placement, which we now have in every television show and movie. From Surge bottles on the announce table (savesurge.org) to Little Creaser on the turnbuckle, WCW was all about making money for everyone involved.

Oh, and by the way, WCW/JCP's only profitable time was under Eric Bischoff. And he used the profit to run the company and grow it bigger, not Ted Turner and his so-called wallet. Eric Bischoff is one of the best businessmen of all time.

But he should be more than that to you...

ERIC BISCHOFF CREATED THE IWC!

You read the title, and I mean it! You should be on your hands and knees now thanking the Bisch for giving you a place to gripe about the pointlessness that is our obsession with wrestling. Still don't believe me after everything we've been through? Let's take a trip back in time.

Waaaaaay back when, there was this Internet Service called Prodigy. Prodigy was the pioneer of at home internet access for the everyday man. They were just a few years too early, and the technology was not ready for what they wanted to do (think Apple Newton:Palm, as Prodigy:AOL). Still, they launched one of the very first global bulletin boards (and you do not want to know what the BBS was like before Prodigy, henceforth called P*), and a couple of years later had interactive chat rooms!!!!!!! OK, so that isn't a big deal to you 14-year-olds out there, but it was an amazing advancement in my day and age.

And who was one of the first people to have interactive chats on P*? That's right: Eric Bischoff. His chats were so popular that they had to create a MODERATOR system! And then people wanted transcripts of the chats, and they wanted to talk about what they had just read about. Suddenly, newsgroups (ask your older brother) were storming with wrestling news and ideas and thoughts and opinions and clubs! It was a golden age of the internet, before smarks and statutory rapists. It was a good time.

But that was not enough for Bischoff. WCWWrestling.com became one of the first websites about wrestling, and from there launched WCW Live!, the first interactive, online show. Oh, and they started broadcasting events over the internet, and had special cyber-events that only us hardcore fans on the website knew about (by this point I was less a mark and more a smark). They also created kayfabe sub-sites (nWowrestling.com) and continued to maintain an open-door policy of talking to the internet "reporters". WCW never put a ban on talking to the internet, nor did they stop their wrestlers from going anywhere and saying whatever they wanted (with appropriate consequences, of course).

The IWC really grew out of what Bischoff did on the old P* chat rooms, and how he continued to act as time went on. He never saw us as the enemy, only dollar signs waiting to be plowed. And frankly, I see nothing wrong with that.

THE COLD, CALCULATING, EVIL BUSINESSMAN

In case you haven't guessed by now, I'm a businessman have a lot of respect and admiration for other businesspersons. Too often I think we label every corporation as "evil" and every businessperson as "dirty" simply because we do not understand their actions (As much as I love George Carlin, sometimes he is just full of it). Take this from me: I was one of those punk kids who thought a socialist system would be cool. But as I learned from SLC Punk (go watch it, but don't get Suburbia), we are all posers, and you can only do what's right for you.

Bischoff gets chastised a lot for the way he conducts business sometimes. The oft repeated offence is when he fired Steve Austin by FedEx. Well, we have recently learned more about Steve Austin and how he is an alleged liar, manipulator, wife-beater, and general psychopath, so how much of his story can we believe? Well, here's a compilation of what really happened from Bischoff's perspective, taken from the Monday Night Wars DVD, interviews, books, and my own deductive reasoning:

Imagine it is Christmas time at Macy's and your first shift cashier doesn't show up a bunch of times. You call his house and his wife answers saying he is not there. Pretend that you do not even hear him in the background screaming about what a terrible manager you are. Just knowing he is out somewhere else when he is supposed to be at work is enough. What do you do? He won't come into the store, so you can't fire him there; and he won't answer the phone so you can't fire him there. All you can do is send him a letter with his final check and wash your hands of it. You are a busy guy, too, and you now need to find a new first shift cashier during one of your busiest times of the year.

This is what Steve Austin did. As a solid mid-carder at the time, he was responsible for helping to progress the show and keep it interesting. He could be out first to get the crowd excited or be out in the middle to keep the flow and tempo right. But one day—for his own selfish reasoning—he decided not to show up. Bischoff was patient and understanding, and tried to talk to Steve, but Austin would have none of it. Bischoff tried every way to get in contact with him, but Austin still refused, up until the point when Bischoff heard Austin in the background while talking to his wife. That was the final straw for him, and he had to be let go.

So you see, there are two sides to every story, and when you think a businessperson is being mean and callous, maybe you need to take a step out of your own shoes for a minute and realize why they act the way they do.

AND SPEAKING OF BUSINESS

What saddens me is when WWE writers re-write history and make it look like Eric Bischoff killed WCW. What is worse is when Eric isn't allowed to respond back with the truth. Well fear not, Uncle Eric, I am coming to your aid!

First off, AOL-Time-Warner killed WCW. They were the ones who decided to cancel the highest rated series on their networks, and also one consistently in the Top 15 of all of cable. Eric Bischoff believed so much in WCW that he was willing to put his and a bunch of his friends' money into buying the company away from A-T-W and bringing it back to its former glory.

Mind you, Bischoff was not in charge of WCW at the end. By that point, he was a consultant who wasn't being paid attention to, so he went home. And while at home, he came up with many millions of dollars and a long-term plan for WCW. But no, he was thwarted again by politics and bad business moves. Listen, if someone is willing to pay you nearly ten times what the next highest bidder is offering, and all they want in return is 4 hours of time a week, then the decision should be easy. Somehow, it was very, very stupid.

This was not the only time Time-Warner messed with Eric Bischoff's long term and daily planning. For starters, Bischoff never wanted to launch Thunder or make Nitro three hours. He knew that it would create over-exposure (especially because they still had Saturday Night, Main Event, and Worldwide at the time) and lower ratings in the end. But the execs at the top of Turner would hear none of it. They saw huge ratings and big advertising dollars and wanted more. They made the decisions, then poorly supported them (such as refusing to run spots during other shows promoting WCW and its programming), leaving Bischoff to pick up the mess. And frankly, he did as a good of a job as one human being could do. You try to book 9 hours of original programming a week while also running the business end of a company and tell me how you do.

How long until you burn out and need a vacation? How many vacations have you already taken?

If you are Eric Bischoff, the answer is zero... over six years. Six years!! This man worked seven days a week, running both the creative and financial end of a company, while also playing an on air character for six years without taking a significant vacation and barely a day off. That takes dedication, pride, commitment, and a love of one's job beyond what most mortal men are capable of. How much sacrifice of his friends and family do you think Bischoff made for our entertainment? I cannot even imagine the true toll of what this man has paid to make us forget our troubles for a couple of hours a week.

THE REWARDS

Of course, just entertaining us was not Bischoff's only motivation; he wanted to make money. And he did a damn fine job of it, having an incredibly high paid roster and support staff. Plus, rolling his profits into Turner Sports and TBS (without ever crediting him or WCW) made those divisions look like a fantastic growth opportunity. This allowed Turner Sports and TBS/TNT to secure more funding and begin original programming, gaining respect among all networks. But they would never thank Eric Bischoff, only scowl at the mention of wrestling.

There was one fairly significant acknowledgement of Bischoff, though. For years, Bischoff was the Vice President of WCW reporting to the President of TBS or Turner Sports, depending on when in history we are talking. But in 1997, Turner (the company) was so impressed by Bischoff that they CREATED the position of President of WCW just so they could give him a promotion and a raise and a nicer office (OK, I'm only guessing at the latter). They wanted to promote this man so badly and give him incentive to stay, but they had nowhere else for him to go without taking him away from WCW. Thus, they had to create an entire position and level in the company just for him. How many people do you know have whole jobs created just for them, nonetheless the highest in a company?

FOR EVERY HATER, THERE'S A LOVER...

I have gone over some amazing facts about the history of Eric Bischoff and WCW, and what a remarkable place and man he must have been to work for. Yet, we hear all the time from some former employees about how they hated it there, and their life felt meaningless, yadda yadda. But here is a common fact of life, kids: People are more vocal when they want to complain than when they have something nice to say. When you go to the supermarket and everything goes smoothly, do you write a letter to the manager telling him how much you enjoyed the experience? Of course not! But that one time when they shortchanged you by $1.13, you get all up in arms and demand refunds and coupons and everything else! I bet you still talk about it today.

There's nothing wrong with that. It's in our nature to accept that things should be good, and that we don't need to acknowledge when things are going right. The same can be said about the news. You won't hear about the 6 billion people that went about their day and nothing significant happened; you'll hear about the one that got murdered, raped, robbed, or won the lottery. No one cares to hear about when things are just fine.

So when Ric Flair and Bobby Henan are out screaming about how much they hated WCW and how it ruined their lives and how they were completely wasted there, why do we take that as gospel? They are just a couple of the hundreds of employees WCW had through the 90's, and two of the most vocal people anywhere in the world.

There are many who have gone on record with how much they enjoyed WCW, including Larry Zybsyco, Dusty Rhodes, DDP, Ernest Miller, Mike Tenay (with the exception of Tony Schiavone), every luchador under the sun, any guy who came up from the Power Plant (Goldberg didn't say anything bad about WCW until Vince Russo took over), and countless others who have just chosen to remain quiet because it does not matter if they liked working there or not.

There are many great companies to work at in the world, but you will always find a few people who did not like it there. It is just a culture thing. Every company has a culture that has developed over time, and not everyone can fit into it, no matter how smart, talented, nice, or accommodating they may be. So WCW was not the right place for a few people, big deal. Spanky, Vince Russo, Nathan Jones, Brian Adams, Dave Sahadi, Bill Goldberg, Brock Lesner, Molly Holly, and many others have said the WWE is not the right place for them and have moved on. That does not mean the WWE is a bad place to work, that just means it is a bad place to work for some people.

THE WWE

But can you believe that the WWE is the right place to work for Eric Bischoff?! You cannot tell me you have not enjoyed his performances and his ability to try to make sense of a nonsense storyline. And he works house shows sometimes and even got to make out with the CEO of the company (that's Linda, Vince is the Chairman [oh La Parka, I need you for this storyline]).

What is more amazing is despite everything Bischoff did to Vince and the then WWF, Vince still forgave him and gave him a job (not that Bischoff needed the job, he was doing quite fine on his own). That may be because he thinks it is better to keep Bischoff under his wing so he can't go off and start/help another wrestling promotion, but he has proven his worth and staying power, even more than the daughter of the Chairman. While Smackdown! has seen Stephanie McMahon, Paul Heyman, Kurt Angel, and Theodore R. Long be GM, Bischoff has continued unabated on Raw. And despite trying to team him with Stone Cold and Mick Foley as co-GM (or Sheriff or whatever), Bischoff still has a job in the WWE while the latter two are off in their own la-la lands (OK, so Steve is sort-of back, but only to make movies).

Can you imagine that? The man who tried to put the WWF/E out of business has more staying power in the company than two of the top draws of all time, and two of the most loyal people to Vince. Simply amazing.

Numbers Don't Lie

Like I said, though, Vince has every reason to fear what Bischoff could do for another wrestling company. I received some (semi-negative) feedback from 411's own Mike Campbell. But one line really stuck out for me that sounded like it could be a legitimate fact, but I wasn't so quick to believe it:

> As for their buyrates. The only WCW PPVs that were really a monumental success were Bash at the Beach 1994 and Starrcade 1997.

Makes sense, the entrance of Hogan into WCW and the culmination of a year and half storyline of Sting VS. the nWo. But that doesn't feel right. Something seems... off.

Well, OK, let's do the math!

Bash at the Beach 1994 drew a 1.02 buyrate and Starrcade 1997 drew a 1.90 buyrate. Now, let's say that a "successful" PPV is one that is 15% below Bash at the Beach (0.87) to anywhere above. Well, in the period from February 1993 (when Bischoff became head booker) to September 1999 (when President Bischoff was fired), WCW had 14 "successful" PPVs. At their peak, over a 12-month period they had 7 of those "successful" PPVs.

Here's what's more. Over that period of 80 months, the WCW and WWF had 52 "head-to-head" PPVs (had a PPV in the same month). Of those, WCW had higher buyrates in 20 of them (or 38%). So we take a look deeper. Overall for the entire length of time, WCW's one-month winning average (how many months they had a higher buyrate then WWF compared to the total head-to-head months up until that point in time) was above 50% 11 times, or 21%. But wait! If we look over 12-month periods, WCW's one-month winning average was above 50% 23 times, or 44% of the time! So using the relativity of time to take away long-term advantages, WCW's buyrates were beating WWF's on a month-to-month basis anywhere from 21-44% of the time, all the while having an overall success rate of 25% (far above the 3% Mr. Campbell suggested) and a peak 58% success rate over a 12 month period.

Wait again! There's more! For 19 months, from March 1997 to September 1998, WCW overtook the WWF in 12-month buyrate average and 12-month "success" rate average!

True, overall the WWF never lost the Buyrate average or "Success" rate average for these 80 months. But Bischoff had to start at the bottom (with SuperBrawl '93 drawing a 0.50 buyrate and WrestleMania IX a month later drawing a 2.00 buyrate), and crawl and scrape and make his product great so that Starrcade '97 could draw a 1.90. And Vince had to fall, so that in the same month IYH: Degeneration X would only draw a 0.44 rating. Bischoff's averages were dragged down from earlier performances he had to pull up from, while Vince had the advantage of a well-drawing product at the beginning of Bischoff's reign, and he had to lose almost all of it.

But that's not the point of this piece. We're here to prove how great Bischoff is, not whether he beat the WWF on all fronts. But what this proves is that he could and did beat the WWF, and had "success" by many, many different measures, much more than your average smark will give him credit for.

MORE REASONS WHY ERIC BISCHOFF IS A BETTER HUMAN BEING THAN YOU

As if everything Bischoff has done and continues to do is not astounding enough, here are a few more tidbits:

- Bischoff is a legitimate blackbelt, which takes immense training and athletic and metal ability

- He nearly qualified for the 1976 US Olympic team as a steeple chaser

- The Birmingham Vulcans (World Football League) drafted him

- He has a pilot's license

- <Kayfabe> He has defeated Ric Flair, Kane, JR, Shane McMahon, and Vince McMahon (Yes, I'm counting THAT one) </Kayfabe>

- Jean-Claude Van Damme came to him and asked Bischoff to produce a martial arts fitness infomercial

What's more, Bischoff is really great to the fans. Through everything we have seen about him, we know Bischoff has been on top of the world and has every reason to be pompous, but amazingly he still remembers what this is all about: entertaining us. I now call John Dee of the Dee Spot sub-column in Evolution Schematic (and Matthew Sforcina deserves major props for taking on a challenging and hate-mail-generating topic like Jeff Jarret) to the stand.

John, please tell us your (disclaimer: edited for grammar, spelling, and space) account of meeting Eric Bischoff.

> It was just before the event they did here in Newcastle (about 3 hours before). Me and several others were standing outside the back gates at the venue it was at... I told Bischoff that I thought he

> *was a genius and I loved what he did with WCW, to which he responded "Yeah, it was fun." Then a kid asked him if Stone Cold was here, [and] Bischoff replied with "No he's at home drinking beer." Someone pointed out to him that we have beer here and Bischoff had to admit this was true. I asked him if he liked our Aussie beer and he said yeah, it was OK. Just in general he was being really nice to the fans.*

And there you have it. Eric Bischoff being nice to us—the fans and 411mania columnists—the world over.

Survey Says...

You see, there is a whole world of Eric Bischoff that we have refused to acknowledge just because some terrible IWC writer decided that his opinion was fact and others followed suit. This man deserves better than the outright lies we have been reading about him for years. He deserves the truth... he deserves a defense.

Next time you read some throwaway line out there presented as fact, challenge it. The truth matters, and you have a right to know.

The defense rests.

After the Trial

Hung Jury

Being the first case, I did not have the voting system set up yet, so did not have an "official" count of Guilty versus Not Guilty verdicts. However, I always said that I won this case by default! For those looking to go deep behind the scenes, the voting system actually came from this man:

> *Hey, JP. I love the column, great concept. I just wanted to run an idea past you. How about after the defense of a certain wrestler or on-air character, you could have the jury deliberate and put up a poll or something. You know, see if your case has actually had an effect on the public*

> *perception (at least perception of your readers) of that person. I mean, these people are being judged in the court of public opinion, right? I don't know. Just a thought.*
>
> *Sincerely,*
> ***Julian Smith***
> ***Atlanta, GA***

RESPONSE

The e-mail responses started immediately, as did the debates. I always felt it was best to have a case fully laid out in all of its parts before getting full feedback, but the intermediate responses were sometimes helpful. More often than not they were points that I was going to get to anyway in later parts, but they could provide interesting insights and perspectives, such as this one:

> *JP,*
>
> *Great column, but just a little problem with the facts, saying Eric Bischoff created the IWC is a little bit of a stretch. Vince McMahon himself had something to do with this as well, as around the same time Bisch was ranting on Prodigy, Vince and Co. signed an exclusive deal with AOL. If you remember, there was a special Keyword: WWF launched in early 1996, newsboards, downloads and the famed chat rooms where interviews with the stars and in my opinion, where it kind of all started with their play-by-play during PPVs where we could talk to each other. The cool part was I remember Vince Russo actually hosted most of these chats.*
>
> *Again, this may sound like a pro-WWE mark, but I do give Bisch credit where credit is due, and I wanted to share my experience where MY Internet Wrestling Community experience started.*
>
> *-Anthony*

To which I replied:

> *I do agree with you. Other people became instrumental in forming the IWC as time went on, and WWF's presence on AOL was one of them (which I always thought it was amusing that AOL bought Time Warner while still being home to the WWF's online product). And yes, newsgroups and wrestling clubs existed long before the P* chats. But I feel it was those chats that really brought shape to the IWC in its formative years (1995/6), and also had a grand effect on the internet in general.*

Anthony was not the only person to point out some internet history and it is amazing to think after living through it that it is actual history and these comments are some of the only captures of what happened online in the 1990's in certain smaller communities.

While some people were easy to have discussions with like that, others were not so much. Starting in Part 1 I had a reader who was... verbose... in his... interesting view of history and his use of language. I will spare you all of the original back-and-forth and most of the final messages, wanted to show a tiny bit (multiple what is here by 100) of the extreme opposition:

> *Dear Sir:*
>
> *I promised to read your part 3 of attempting to defend Eric Bischoff and to give you feedback on it, so here it is... Your assumption that Vince McMahon and a group of unnamed Internet writers (2 factions that never agree on anything) have come together to rewrite history to make all us sheep believe that Bischoff is less than a god is ridiculous because fans and people in the wrestling industry know what they have witnessed and have no reason to make up things about a washed up television show producer (which is all Bischoff is).*
>
> *... I love how you give me a hard time about speaking in absolutes then write a crock like "every luchador under the sun" loves Bischoff, which is completely untrue because Rey Mysterio, Konnan, the Guerreros, and Juventud Guerra to name a few have been outspoken about their abuse under Bischoff...*
>
> *...*

> *Until you have read the "Death Of WCW," which details all the WCW buy rates including the lack of numbers following the Hogan debut and after the debacle of the blown finish at Starrcade 1997 you should hold off on talking about buy rates. ... You ignore the horrible buy rates of pay per views Bischoff personally came up with like Souled Out (Bischoff making out with fat broads), Uncensored (so bad they should have been censored), and Hog (until Harley Davidson threatened to sue) / Road Wild (no live gate or buy rate, but at least Bischoff got a paid vacation to Sturgis)....*
>
> *The rest of the crap about Bischoff being a better person because of what he did 30 years ago or in his spare time is all utter nonsense....*
>
> *Bischoff deserves credit for being able to buy a... trophy wife...*
>
> *...*
>
> *Sincerely,*
>
> **Matthew Alan Roberts**
> **Lakewood, Ohio**

OK, time to cut it off there. There were some other words between "buy a" and "trophy wife", but I am very uncomfortable printing them. This was an early lesson that I should not always engage with certain people, but I was a naïve novice so thought that logic could work its way through:

> *Sigh. Well, I tried. And you did live up to your end of the bargain, so I thank you for giving me a fair chance.*
>
> *We could probably go on with this argument for years, so if you don't mind I'll skip over most of your refutations and only touch on points I'm truly confused about.*
>
> *First, I don't recall ever saying nor insinuating that there is a conspiracy between Vince McMahon and some IWC writers to bury Bischoff. That sounds absurd even reading it. I do have two mutually*

> exclusive arguments; one being that the WWE rewrites history to the detriment of Eric Bischoff, WCW, and its fans. The other argument is that certain negative writers in the IWC say overtly negative opinions and outright lies of Bischoff to suit themselves and others have taken those opinions and lies as fact and have spread them. Those are two separate arguments, and I would never intentionally try to suggest they are in any way connected.
>
> Every Luchadore under the sun was a joke, but you are right, I should not have said everyone in the Power Plant, especially Hard Body Harris. The Power Plant line was just to keep tempo in the article.
>
> ...
>
> Also, I don't need to read a book about someone's opinions on the death of WCW to know how to analyze numbers.... I have years of training on how to analyze what numbers mean. And to counteract what you said, the first Uncensored drew a 0.95 rating, well within the "success" range we defined in the column. You are right, the first Souled Out did not draw well, with 0.47 rating, but Uncensored that year drew a 0.89, again in our "success" range. Then again, in the following year Souled out drew a 1.02 (Bischoff learned from his mistake and got better) and Uncensored drew a 1.10. And just for kicks, Road Wild drew a 0.91 that year, too. Numbers don't lie, Bischoff's personal PPVs did just fine. But like I said in my article, it wasn't about always winning, just that he could and did and had a 19-month streak of being on the top....
>
> ...
>
> What is it you have against Bischoff's wife? ... This is just me, but I could never say such harsh things about someone I've never met.

ADDITIONAL EVIDENCE

Ten months after wrapping up my case on Eric Bischoff, I received an e-mail from Anthony Maurizio of WCWLive.com (which was an excellent site that was just starting up and being filled with lots of old school WCW stuff and current news on former WCW talent. Anthony mentioned that he had recently read my article on Eric Bischoff and would be passing it along to friends who worked for WCW.

Because of that, I re-read my article, too, and really got to thinking about something I said in the latter part. I talked about how despite the fact that there are plenty of people who hate Bischoff and talk smack about him (Ric Flair and Bobby Hennan come to mind), that there were lots of people who liked, appreciated, and looked up to Bischoff and have gone on record to say so or have just remained silent.

And much to my delight, I found this on the newsboard. From Mike Johnson's recap of Sting's press conference on January 11, 2006:

> *When asked about Eric Bischoff, he said he has nothing but good things to say. He said that everyone likes to remember him as the one who sunk the WCW ship but it was a "group of us" overall who undermined each other and had a lot of secret agendas. He said that Bischoff was the first one who would talk to wrestling fans and get feedback and he surrounded himself with people he could trust. He said that they had a good working relationship. He said the night they launched Nitro, the rest was history.*

Plus earlier in the recap:

> *He said that he remembered when Hulk Hogan came to WCW in 1994, he was often asked if he was upset he was pushed aside. He said he wasn't because it took the pressure off of him personally and that it would help the overall company. He's hoping that he can do the same for TNA.*

This just puts to rest so many rumors that have lasted a decade. As Sting said, everyone thought he hated Bischoff for bringing in Hogan, pushing him aside, and (as some think, not me) messing up his year and half long storyline to Starrcade '97 in the main event match. Well, Sting has put it all to rest! He not only had no problem with any of it, he preferred it!

Sting then highlighted several of my own points. One being that Bischoff was not the one who sunk WCW. Another being the Eric Bischoff was excellent with the fans and really took time out to interact with them. Also, as noted, he was a lot more open to suggestion and new ideas then others would have you believe.

On top of that, Sting was very complimentary to Eric Bischoff. What did he have to gain from being nice to Bischoff? Absolutely nothing! Eric Bischoff has no stroke anymore and is (currently) employed by the WWE. He had no reason to say anything nice unless he meant it.

In the end, I just wanted to add Sting's testimony as evidence that Eric Bischoff was a much better person, promoter, and performer than many in the IWC have given him credit for, and to thank Eric Bischoff for all of the years of WCW I enjoyed under his tutelage.

The Elimination Chamber

Intro

Some dame walked into my office and said...

In the future chapters, I'll use this space to paste the (probably heavily edited) letter of the person asking for my services. But this time, I go to bat again for myself. Unlike last time, our suspect does not have a long history to follow. This one only has about two and a half years of history and three incidents to examine. I am talking about the second-latest gimmick match in pro-wrestling, THE ELIMINATION CHAMBER!

Why this?

As has been habit recently in the IWC, writers have crapped on a gimmick or wrestler or storyline before they have seen it executed. Sometimes they are right in their skepticism (see Katie Vick), but more often they have jumped the gun (see WGTT debut and push, Eugene, Jericho/Christian/Trish Love Triangle, John Cena, etc...). The Elimination Chamber was another such event in wrestling history where the IWC had horrible things to say about it, even though NO ONE (and I mean NO ONE) saw what it looked like until the PPV (that's Survivor Series 2002 for the record). How can you judge something before you have seen it?

And worse yet? The post judgmental comments by those who STILL had not seen it. Let me tell you, I watched that PPV, and I thoroughly enjoyed the match, the concept, and generally the result.

We will examine the build-ups, the fallout, and the actual matches themselves. The Elimination Chamber will prove itself, and haters will prove that they just know how to hate. Let's get rolling.

ONCE A MAN HAD A DREAM...

On October 21, 2002 Eric Bischoff came out on Raw and said that there would be the first ever Elimination Chamber match at Survivor Series. By the next week, we knew two things: who was in the match and that that match itself was a combination of War Games, Royal Rumble, and Classic Survivor Series. Let the intrigue begin!

The following week, some vignettes began running that only whet our appetite even more. And again, on the following week we finally learned the rules! But we had not even seen the chamber for what it really was. How were we supposed to react?

You would think with a little awe or at the very least optimistic intrigue. But I'm afraid that wasn't quite true.

THE OSTRICH EFFECT... IN REVERSE

First, let's take a look at people's reaction to Bischoff's announcement, right on 411mania's own message boards:

After the first Elimination Chamber video...

> - What the hell was that all about? On the video it showed a circular cell surrounding one ring...ONE ring!! I want two rings!! And what's with the circular cell? That's a stupid idea. There better be more to it than this.
>
> - JUNGLE GYM OF DOOM!
>
> - WHOA WHOA WHOA! Cylinder? Dome? Alright Bischoff, be honest, is the Elimination Chamber just a giant steel penis?

After rumors leaked of the possible rules...

> • Okay I'm not looking forward to this at all now. A lot of people are saying the same thing and it [is] starting to make sense. If you look at the official Survivor series website, look at the drawing closely, you can see 4 semi-circular cages inside the sides on the chamber. Very Unhappy and Angry!

Very unhappy and angry? That's a stupid idea? What are these posters so against? What did we know about the Elimination Chamber at this point? Heck, when we did not even know the rules people were saying that it was the worst gimmick match going.

And this is the negativity that spread without any provocation. The Elimination Chamber had been found guilty without a trial, or even so much as a chance to say "Hello!" How was it supposed to ever recover from that start?

THE ART OF PROFESSIONAL WRESTLING

But we weren't the only ones who hadn't seen the Elimination Chamber. There were a few other people who knew only a little bit more than we did. Their names were Chris Jericho, Booker T, Triple H, Kane, Shawn Michaels, and Rob Van Dam.

The six participants in the Elimination Chamber had no clue what they were getting into!

You see, the complaint we hear from many wrestlers in the WWE (especially those who have left) and old school guys who watch the product is that the WWE plots out entire matches backstage. Not only that, but they use house shows as practice ground for guys to get the matches down before their big PPV showdown. So in the end, wrestling becomes a tedious series of moves planned out in an exact way, and it shows.

That's not to say that that is always bad. Sometimes guys do need to get a feel for each other, and the best way is to practice.

But that is a method, not an art.

I am of the belief that art is not limited to painting, writing, sculpting, and acting, but that art can be wherever you are creative. Moreover, I believe business is an art form, that the ability to create or grow a company and manage the flow of people and resources is an art that is practiced and perfected, not a method that can just be learned. That's why most MBAs don't go on to become millionaires, they want to learn a method to move up, not really risk it all for an art.

(And please, I'm not advocating not going to school. I think school is very important for helping you develop your art, whether it is business or wrestling. The most important thing is to listen to the lessons of those who came before you and integrate it into your own experience.)

So a lot of people, especially in the 70's and 80's, got into wrestling to make money and that was it. They had no love of the business as an art. The vast majority of them failed, but a few managed to stick around for a while. But eventually while someone like Terry Funk cannot stop wrestling because he loves it so much, people like Brock Lesner are perfectly content to have nothing to do with the business that made them. Some people are artists, some people are workers.

The Elimination Chamber was a moment of pure art. Six artists came together for the first time in a brand-new environment. They put on a spectacle of a show with nothing but their proverbial feather pens. There was no practice, there was no understanding of what you could or could not do in the Elimination Chamber. They risked themselves, not just physically, but spiritually. If they could not deliver, it would be because they had failed as artists, as people who could not work on the fly.

But they did deliver. It was a phenomenal match. People held on to the edges of their seats. People went home happy.

Still, people going home happy means nothing to this stockholder.

BUT NOTHING SPEAKS LOUDER THAN MY CREDIT CARD

As you may not realize, the Elimination Chamber cost $500,000 to build! That's quite a bit of money there kids, even if you do make $90 million in revenue a year. So not only does the Elimination Chamber have to be initially profitable, it needs to have longevity.

Well, the WWE was so impressed with the match and the artisans involved that Linda McMahon took a considerable amount of time talking about it during a conference call with investors shortly after the event. In that interview she promised that the Elimination Chamber would return... and sure enough it did... TWICE!

In 2002, the WWE was still sailing on old recognition. The brand extension was in its infancy, and the WWE wanted to recreate the competition of the past without any of the backhanded slaps. At the same time, they wanted to create an opportunity for new talent to rise, something we are just starting to see the results of in 2005. In the short term, ratings were dropping and so were buyrates. They needed something to keep interest while the rest of their needs caught up.

The Elimination Chamber provided that. At Survivor Series 2002 it delivered a 0.86 buyrate. Not too shabby. Granted, Survivor Series had done better in the past, but the WWE was trying a few new things and fighting a falling business. It certainly was better than the previous month's No Mercy 0.77 buyrate.

But the real proof doesn't come until SummerSlam 2003. The WWE was falling on harder times; Judgment Day drew a 0.58, Bad Blood 0.75, and Vengeance 0.49. That was the buildup to SummerSlam. And then SummerSlam got the Elimination Chamber II, and took in a 0.94. Yes, a lot of that had to do with just the SummerSlam name. But to prove names don't draw, and it is still the main event that matters, Survivor Series 2003 without an Elimination Chamber drew 0.71, less than the previous year's No Mercy. People had seen what the Elimination Chamber was and were excited for its return.

And finally, there was Elimination Chamber III at a brand new PPV called New Year's Revolution. It's so new that we haven't even seen a second one yet! It was just 4 weeks after SmackDown!'s Armageddon, which drew a 0.59 buyrate. More importantly, it was 3 weeks before the Royal Rumble! OK, so we have everything going against it: a no name PPV, two weeks where Raw wasn't watched much because of Christmas and New Years, coming off a lackluster SmackDown PPV, but going into the second biggest PPV of the year—New Year's Revolution seemed doomed. Oh, and they somehow needed to get the ten tons of steel to Puerto Rico. Despite all of that, New Year's Revolution and the Elimination Chamber brought in a respectable 0.68 buyrate.

Not the best ever, and very much outside the success rate we defined in our last case, but pretty good considering everything it was going up against. How much money do you have after the holidays and New Years? Which PPV are you going to buy with your limited cash supply: New Years Revolution or the Royal Rumble? A PPV that you have no idea about except the main event or the event that is going to set up the next three months of angles and WrestleMania? Yeah, that's what I thought.

Has the Elimination Chamber paid for itself? Oh yeah! Has it made a profit? You bet! But there is more!

And if you read the Movie/TV Zone, you know that something else. Most movies make about 40% of their sales in the theatres, and the rest come from DVD/Video sales and rentals. Well, when dealing with children's movies and Star Wars, the real money comes from the merchandise. We know, too, that the WWE is nothing but one of the best merchandisers going. Why don't you scroll up to the top of this case for a second?

Ah, welcome back down here. That picture: the Elimination Chamber toy. See, there's always more money to be made elsewhere, and you can bet that the WWE will exploit the Elimination Chamber for all its worth!

IT'S A LAST MINUTE THROWN TOGETHER MATCH... WITH SIX MONTHS OF PLANNING

The outright worst lie I have heard about the Elimination Chamber is that it is just a thrown together match to pop buyrates with no long term planning or booking. It has been said that the Elimination Chamber just serves to get as many guys in the main event as possible.

Yes, the Elimination is good for business, and yes, it does get a lot of people in the main event.

But thrown together it is not!

To prove this we will examine all of the events that led up to the first Elimination Chamber. I would do this for the second and third, but as you can see, this is pretty huge by itself. Here we go!

ESTABLISHING THE BRAND

As you know, our story began on October 21, 2002, when Eric Bischoff first announced the Elimination Chamber match.

Except that's not where our story began.

Jump back in time with me to August 25, 2002. The event was SummerSlam, and a lot was going on. Eric Bischoff had recently been brought in as GM of Raw, and the brand split was taking a new direction. The GM's (Bischoff and Stephanie McMahon at the time) were starting to put more control on their talent, keeping them locked onto one show. This became a problem when Chris Benoit decided to jump to SmackDown! with the IC title around his waist (boy, that guy sure switches brands a lot). Luckily, RVD still had a title shot and managed to bring the belt back home to Raw, so Bischoff was very much in RVD's debt. Meanwhile, former co-owner Ric Flair was feuding with the evil Chris Jericho, and even managed to get Jericho to submit on that hot summer's night. Later in the evening, Shawn Michaels would get the pinfall victory over Triple H in an "Unsanctioned Match". Triple H, though, would get the last laugh by hitting Shawn in the back with a sledgehammer and taking him out of commission for a while. But the most important thing that happened was the recently jumped Brock Lesner became the Undisputed WWE champion be defeating the Rock.

The next night on Raw, things seemed business as usual. Kane made his triumphant return to stop the UnAmericans from burning a US Flag with the help of Booker T and Goldust, who had also been feuding with the UnAmericans over the World Tag Team Championships. In the main event, Triple H defeated the Undertaker to become the #1 Contender to the Undisputed WWE Championship. But, a short time later, Stephanie McMahon showed up backstage at Raw to let Bischoff know that Brock Lesner was exclusive to SmackDown!, and so was the WWE Championship.

Things were looking grim, especially when the Undertaker jumped to SmackDown! that week and defeated Chris Benoit and Kurt Angle in a triple threat match (how poetic) to become the new #1 contender.

What was Eric Bischoff to do? Well, all though the weekend, there was much backstage wheeling and dealing, but McMahon would not budge. He had one choice. On Raw on September 2, 2002, Eric Bischoff said the Undisputed Championship was now in dispute. Since Brock Lesner refused to meet the #1 contender for the title, the rightful #1 contender Triple H would be awarded what made up one half of the Undisputed Championship: the venerable World Heavyweight Championship.

Debate all you want about the lineage of that belt (and we will in a later chapter), there is plenty of precedent for stripping the champion of the belt and awarding it to the challenger if the champion refuses to meet him. In 1929, the National Boxing Association withdrew its recognition of Gus Sonnenberg as World Heavyweight Champion when he refused to meet credible challengers. The NBA (and later the National Wrestling Association) then had a tournament to crown the rightful World Heavyweight Champion, which was won by Dick Shikat when he defeated Jim Londos. This branch of the title would remain disputed until 1948 and through 1952, when Lou Thesz started gathering all the World Heavyweight Championships to become a true Undisputed World Heavyweight Champion. Thus we can see from this example that Bischoff has plenty of history to look back on when it comes to withdrawing recognition of a champion and awarding it to someone who he thinks is the rightful and worthy title holder.

Still, a few more things happened that night. For starters, Ric Flair came out and let Triple H know he needed to earn that title, so Bischoff made the match between the two. The 16-to-42-time world champion lost, and Jericho came out for some revenge by locking Flair in the Walls of Jericho. IC Champ RVD then came out for the save, having found out earlier in the night that he was going to defend that title against Jericho at a later date. But because of his interference, Triple H demanded a match with RVD. As such, Bischoff made the match of Y2J and Triple H vs. RVD and Flair for later that night. And RVD pinned the newly crowned World Heavyweight Champion.

Now mind you, being the IC champ makes you the de facto #1 contender if there are no other #1 contenders around. On top of that, pinning the champ in a non-title affair does bump you up quite a few notches in and of itself. Not to mention that Shawn Michaels had also pinned the champion just a week beforehand, and Chris Jericho was #1 contender to the IC title. But the week before, he lost to Flair, so who had what standing?

It was a bit too much for Bischoff, so he set up a Four Way Elimination match for the #1 Contender spot on the September 9, 2002 edition of RAW. The participants were RVD (the seeming #1 contender), Chris Jericho (the seeming

#2 contender), the Big Show (he's big), and Jeff Hardy (he's painted). In the match itself, Jericho got the Big Show eliminated by DQ when he feigned getting hit by a chair, and then pinned Jeff Hardy. Despite running down Triple H earlier in the night, Triple H decided to try to help Jericho by distracting RVD, but to no avail. RVD hit the five-star frog splash to become the absolute-definite-no-doubt-about-it #1 contender.

That brings us to RAW on September 16, 2002, where Bischoff was in a good mood after invading SmackDown! and pulling off a huge scam at Billy and Chuck's wedding. He gave Rico a match versus Ric Flair, which Rico actually won! Backstage, Triple H let Flair know how pathetic he had become, and Flair let Triple H know that he didn't know how to be a champion. Meanwhile, Bischoff also decided that both champion and #1 contender needed to defend their titles that night. So Triple H defeated Jeff Hardy for fun, but RVD lost the IC title to Chris Jericho after interference from Triple H (which also led to a Jericho vs. Flair rematch for the IC title at the next PPV). Now this is important: Jericho had defeated the #1 contender to the World Heavyweight Championship just a week before his championship match. Remember that.

Then it was September 22, and it was Unforgiven. You see, back then all PPVs were co-branded. But on the RAW side, two important things happened: (1) Chris Jericho defeated Ric Flair via submission (thus getting back his loss the month before, defeating someone who challenged for the title just a few weeks before, and holding the IC title he won from the #1 contender high) and (2) Triple H defeated RVD. Now, this is important, because RVD had Triple H pinned twice while the ref was knocked out, and then it was Ric Flair coming in and hitting RVD with a sledgehammer that helped Triple H win the match.

The next night on RAW, a whole bunch of things happen that set up some seemingly random matches. Just know that Jericho ended up pinning Booker T's tag team partner Goldust, and RVD put Triple H through a table. Flair also explained that Triple H made him realize how low he had sunk and was the only one honest with him, and that he was going to rise up again and teach Triple H how to live the life of a WOOOOOOO Champion.

Oh, and Eric Bischoff introduced some kid named Randy Orton as the newest RAW superstar. How peculiar.

Now, on the following RAW on September 30, 2002, Bischoff let us know that IC and World titles were going to unify at No Mercy, so again the IC champ was the #1 contender. At this point in history, that man was Chris Jericho, who was having some arguments with that Booker T character. But that would have to be put on hold because Jericho had to face Kane later in the night for said title. And Kane managed to take the title away from Jericho, despite interference from Triple H. Meanwhile, backstage Bischoff asked Flair about some former SmackDown! talent he was bringing over, but the intrigue would have to wait, for the following week was RAW ROULETTE!!!

OK, let's summarize here. Shawn Michaels and RVD both held pinfall victories over Triple H. RVD got his shot, but only lost due to mass cheating from Flair.

While RVD was #1 Contender, though, Jericho pinned him and never got a title match. Jericho then became #1 Contender for about two hours until Kane pinned him. So Shawn Michaels held the last full pinfall over Triple H, RVD needed revenge from mass cheating, Jericho never got his shot, and Kane was the #1 Contender. Got it? Good!

That brought us into the fall and the RAW ROULETTE on October 7, 2002. As much as I loved this episode of RAW, only a few relevant things happened. First, Booker T defeated the Big Show in a Steal Cage and then Jericho beat him up afterwards, saying that Booker T's taunting the previous week caused him to lose the match to Kane... SUCKAAAAA! But Kane was not to be made fun of, as he went through a whole mess of people in a TLC match to claim the World Tag Team Championships with the Hurricane (who was laid out in the back).

The next week was October 14, 2002, Jericho and Christian won the tag team titles, so again Jericho defeated the #1 contender a week before his championship match. And due to much stuff happening, it would be Jericho and Christian vs. Booker T and Goldust at No Mercy for the titles. RVD vs. Ric Flair was also made, but first there would be a Canadian Lumberjack match on RAW between RVD and Triple H. And then... OK, this gets to be a bit much, here it is in my original notes form:

> *Meanwhile, HHH has been teasing he knows something about Kane, and that he is a murderer of some kind. Shortly thereafter we learn about Katie Vick. Oh my. Big Show d. Booker T in a falls count anywhere match when Jericho hits Booker with a steal chair in the women's shower. HHH meanwhile backs a forklift into a door, stopping most of the lumberjacks from making it to his match. RVD had HHH pinned, but Jericho pulled him out. The faces led by Booker T make their way out, a schmoz happens, and then Flair comes in, hits RVD with the title belt, and then HHH gets the pin. Kane comes in to destroy everyone.*

Finally, it was October 20, 2002, and there was NO MERCY. Jericho and Christian defeated Booker T and Goldust; RVD defeated Flair; and last, but not least, Triple H defeated Kane with lots of interference from Flair and sledgehammers to unify the World and IC championships.

That brings us back to our first sentence: October 21, 2002, RAW. Of course the Elimination Chamber itself was announced, but other things were going on as usual. We're going to ignore the start of the Katie Vic storyline except to say it made Kane upset. Kane and RVD also defeated Triple H and Flair when RVD pinned Flair.

On the October 28, 2002 program of RAW, there was a non-title casket match between Kane and Triple H, which Kane won when Shawn Michaels popped out of the casket to get Triple H. Earlier in the evening, Bischoff had offered a spot in the Elimination Chamber to Shawn Michaels, but he had one week to get back to him. Oh, and the Big Show got traded to SmackDown!

All right, time for another summary. Shawn Michaels had a legitimate pin over Triple H just before he "won" the Championship. RVD had a pinfall victory over Triple H and still needed revenge after Flair cost him the match. Since then, he had beaten Flair a number of times. He had also beaten Triple H in tag team contests (without pinning him, though). Jericho pinned RVD when RVD was #1 Contender, but never got his shot. Kane defeated Jericho when Jericho was IC champ and #1 Contender to take the spot from him. He lost to Triple H but then defeated him again in a casket match. Meanwhile, Booker T had defeated the Big Show, but Jericho had been harassing him and cost him a match against the Big Show. So Booker T was looking for revenge on Jericho and had some high profile wins. Jericho wanted revenge on Booker T and Kane, but also wanted his #1 contender's spot. Kane wanted revenge on Triple H for the Katie Vick stuff and his #1 contender's spot after beating Triple H in a casket match. RVD still needed revenge for his two losses to Triple H from insane outside interference and needed a closed in environment. Shawn Michaels wanted revenge on Triple H for the sledgehammer and had a right to the #1 contender spot as the man who pinned Triple H just before Triple H was granted the championship. Big Show might have had a spot since he pinned Booker T, but since he was moved to SmackDown! all of that was null and void.

And a few weeks later, we had the first Elimination Chamber.

Did you read all of that? Now that, my friend, is "buildup". There was legitimately three months of buildup to the Elimination Chamber, including an incredibly complex interweaving of storylines to make the environment possible. And I left out a LOT of details and many of the subplots also going on (The UnAmericans, Buh Buh Ray Dudley, the Hurricane, Bischoff and Stephanie, etc...).

I started to do the same thing for the second chamber, and traced the storylines that led to it all the way back to April 7, 2003. Don't forget that the Elimination Chamber II did not take place until SummerSlam! And I'm sure I could do the same with Elimination Chamber III, but we have simply run out of room and time.

Oh, and anyone who says that this was still thrown together, you need to realize how far back the Elimination Chamber was planned. That monstrosity took six weeks to build. Now, first it needed to be designed and conceptualized, then it had to be bided out to contractors, and finally made and transported. That's not something you can do on a whim. The Elimination Chamber was planned for a long time, and these storylines were the culmination of that long-term concerted effort.

Still, the buildup was not the end of the impact of the Elimination Chamber.

There's always an aftermath. But first...

ANOTHER HEADING ABOUT PLANNING? AIYA!

There is something important that happened with the RAW main event scene after the first Elimination Chamber:

There was one.

You have to remember, before Eric Bischoff became GM of RAW, SmackDown! was the show with the main eventers and heavily controlled the Undisputed Championship. After shaking up the rosters with the new GMs and splitting the championship, RAW had a lot to prove. Who was in the main event? What were the programs between these people? Could they draw?

The Elimination Chamber did a pretty concise job of answering these questions. We quickly saw that the top of RAW's card had Triple H, Shawn Michaels, Chris Jericho, Kane, RVD, and Booker T. And directly with and after this we set up feuds and storylines that led to Jericho-Michaels, Vitamin C-BookDust, RVD/Kane tag team (and the eventual fallout), and the Triple H-Booker T WrestleMania program. Also, new (old?) blood was injected with Scott Steiner (no pun intended) and Kevin Nash, so at the end of the day, RAW became a credible place to dwell. And as we saw with the buyrates, RAW also made money.

THE AFTERSHOCK!

By the time the second and third Elimination Chambers rolled around, there were so many main eventers that you could not fit them all in the Chamber. While the second Elimination Chamber match was going on, Kane and RVD were fighting each other and by the third Elimination Chamber RVD and Booker T were over on SmackDown! and Kane was fighting Snitsky. Despite the fact that Nash, Goldberg, and Steiner were all gone, and HBK was a ref, there were still six people in the chamber to remind us just how good the RAW main event scene was, and to set up the angles for the coming months.

And that is something the Elimination Chamber has always excelled at. The second chamber led right into Triple H vs. Goldberg and Goldberg's title reign which led to Goldberg vs. Brock Lesner at WrestleMania. Edge's getting screwed by HBK in the third chamber led to continuing that feud and Edge's heel turn and decent into insanity. The Elimination Chamber set the pace for months before with the storylines leading to it, and months after with its repercussions.

Still, there was always a little something going on in the middle.

Running Jokes

In each Elimination Chamber match, there have been a number of consistent stories. Now, I can't say if that is because of creative writing, a person on the booking committee that has a good sense of continuity and sense of humor, or if it is all just happenstance. Either way, though, there are some running stories you can find across the Elimination Chamber:

The Evolution of Evolution

Every Elimination Chamber has been a major point in the development of Evolution. In the first Elimination Chamber, Ric Flair had just recently given his allegiance to Triple H, and Randy Orton had just re-debuted on RAW. Meanwhile, Ric Flair was touting that he had acquired a huge former SmackDown! wrestler, who we later would learn was Batista. The Elimination Chamber had all the blocks of Evolution forming, and also gave the major impetus when Triple H lost. Triple H saw that he needed a full group for backup because of all the challengers and dangers for him on RAW, and his loss in the chamber solidified that need. The Elimination Chamber really signaled the beginning of Evolution.

The second Elimination Chamber had the growth of Evolution. Randy Orton began his climb to the main event by being in the chamber and set up his long-term feud with Shawn Michaels. Also, the events of the chamber led to the Triple H-Goldberg match at Judgment Day (which Goldberg won), which led directly to the return of Batista to RAW and Evolution to try to take Goldberg out. The Elimination Chamber really signaled the beginning of the height of Evolution and the rise of Randy Orton.

When the third Elimination Chamber came around, Randy Orton had long since been gone from Evolution, but was still in the match looking for his title and revenge on Triple H. The match actually ended with Triple H, Orton, and Batista. Batista basically eliminated everyone else, until Orton RKO'd him while Triple H watched on in the corner. And then Triple H went on to pin Randy Orton. These events all led to the Royal Rumble a few weeks later that Batista won and then finally Batista's big win at WrestleMania. The Elimination Chamber really signaled the beginning of the end of Evolution, and the final steps to the rise of Batista.

The Regulars

Besides just Evolution, three men have been inside every single Elimination

Chamber: Triple H, Chris Jericho, and Shawn Michaels. Yes, Shawn Michaels was just a ref in the third chamber, but he was still inside. Triple H was always in there solely for defending/regaining the title; Shawn Michaels was always in there for a little revenge and super kicked someone that led directly to Chris Jericho pinning that person (One: Kane pinned by Jericho, Two: Nash pinned by Jericho, Three: Edge pinned by Jericho); and Jericho was always in there because he's Chris Jericho.

WHERE'S MY CHAMPIONSHIP?

Aside from the regular cast, two people in the chamber always had never been a world champion in the WWE. In the first Elimination Chamber it was Booker T and Rob Van Dam. In Elimination Chamber II, those roles were played by Goldberg and Randy Orton. And finally, in Elimination Chamber III, Batista and Edge were the men. This always added a "darkhorse" level on intrigue to the chamber, as people would wonder if it was time for these guys to step up to the top of the ladder. And three out of six of those men have gone on to win a world championship in the WWE, and a fourth should be happening sometime this year.

CHRISTIAN CAN'T GET INSIDE

Finally, there is always a story about Christian trying to get into the Elimination Chamber and just can't seem to get in.

In the first Elimination Chamber, Christian initially challenged RVD for his spot in the chamber, but just could not pull off the victory. The next week, Christian's tag team partner (and co-champion) Chris Jericho started taking everyone out, and Christian told him that Bischoff said he can take anyone's place who doesn't want to be in the chamber. Fearing for his spot, Y2J hit Christian in the back of the head with a steel chair.

For the second Elimination Chamber, Christian was the IC champ and was not even booked for the show. He sure let everyone know that he was upset that he didn't have a match, and that he should have been in the chamber, too.

By Elimination Chamber III, Christian was back in the full swing of things. First, he lost a match to Chris Jericho on Raw during "Beat the Clock" night. At New Year's Revolution itself, Edge offered Christian his spot because he knew the HBK was going to screw him (which he did!), except Bischoff would not allow the substitution.

Christian was always trying to get into the Chamber, as again it was part of his character's long term story of always getting screwed out of title shots, except in a funnier version than Edge's character.

The Pinfall Victory

You may not always agree with the short-term outcome (Triple H winning twice), but there is no denying the long term impact of the Elimination Chamber. It has shown itself to be a creative success, a monetary success, and a continual growth success. Each Elimination Chamber has been new and fresh, and they have spaced them far enough apart that there is no burnout yet. And look what can happen in the coming year: After the draft, who will be on RAW? What about guys who have been moving up the card like Shelton Benjamin and Christian? What about new possible players like Eddie Guerrero or Kurt Angle?

What happens over the next few weeks and months will certainly be interesting, and you can sure bet that someone is thinking of Elimination Chamber IV. Watch RAW closely, and you might just see the little things that are building up to this next momentous event.

Until then, the defense rests.

After the Trial

Hung Jury

IN THE CASE OF THE IWC VERSUS THE ELIMINATION CHAMBER, THE ELIMINATION CHAMBER HAS BEEN ACCUSED OF BEING A CHEAP PLOY, NO BUILD, BAD MATCHUP.

With 94% of the vote, the Elimination Chamber was found:

NOT GUILTY!

Response

While in the last case we looked at some of the pushback (some helpful, others quite painful), this case provided the opportunity to start to see how my writing was making an impact:

> *You are like a light shining in the vast darkness that is the IWC. I truely blame most of wrestling's problems on an IWC that cannot see past their own nose. Sometimes, yes, bad decisions are made, but time tells the full truth. Thank you for defending wrestling and showing that it should be enjoyed and not torn apart.*
>
> **- Rachel Hagan**

> *I never realized how the booking in summer/fall 2002 really did lead up to the Elimination Chamber. I guess that's the problem - it was never explained like that on TV. It was presented as just another "let's stack the odds against Triple H" angle, and seemed to me at least like a great way to get the title of him while managing to make him look like MORE of a superman since it took so many guys (and a friggin' crushed larynx, but I guess that was an accident - "true artists", eh?) to beat him. Bischoff never outlined the complexities of the angles previous, but instead built the cage up as his own evil little creation to make Raw better than Smackdown. I would have much preferred your way.*
>
> **- Steve Furmaniuk**

Another interesting component of the article started here as well when I began to receive backstage information related to our cases:

> *My biggest problem with the Elimination Chamber has always been that wrestlers are constantly preventing one another from pinning anyone else.*
>
> *This would make sense in the context of a first-fall-wins scenario, but when we're talking elimination, it makes absolutely no sense for anyone else to be preventing anyone else's pinfall attempt.*
>
> *Eric Bischoff has also described the chamber's glass as bulletproof... yet we've seen wrestlers put one another's heads through it like it was papier mâché.*

Two facts I politely pointed out to Stephanie McMahon's assistant Jennifer a couple of years ago when they were interviewing me for a position on the creative team. It was my very first criticism of the product, and also my last; Jennifer stopped speaking to me after that, so don't expect things to improve with regards to the Chamber anytime soon.

- Dusty the Fat Bitter Cat

Kevin Nash

Intro

Some dame walked into my office and said...

Andrew Strom, hailing from Hotmail, VA (apparently somewhere in nWo 4-Life county), had this to say:

> [C]ould you defend Kevin Nash for me sometime? He gets an awful lot of Hell on the net for stuff he did, and he and Scott Hall are my favorites of all time. I believe that his "bad booking" and "lack of work rate" has completely overshadowed the fact that he was a marvelous on-air character from 1996-2000. When he got back to the WWE Vince McMahon wouldn't let him be himself and he flopped because of it.

Andrew, your time is now.

Why this?

Kevin Nash has been called a lot of names over the years. And I'm not talking about "Diesel", "Big Sexy", or "the Giant Killer". I'm talking about "the Lumbering Disaster", "the Promotion Killer", and "the Worst Drawing Champion of All Time". People attack his title reigns, his reasons for being on top, his ability as a booker, and his drive for being a professional wrestler. Instead of enjoying everything Kevin Nash has done for the wrestling business, history seems ready to write him off as a walking path of destruction and 1/1000 * matches. Well, it's time to defend the honor of the big man, and let's start right at the biggest lie of all:

The Worst Drawing Champion of All Time – Part 1

During my research, that term came up so many times, but there was never any proof. All I usually read was something along the lines of "Was Kevin Nash the worst drawing champion of all time? Yes he was, and the buyrates and rating prove it." Except, that would be it. Where are the buyrates? Where are the ratings?

You know where they are: right here. Now let's get some truth going.

Ratings before the launch of Nitro in September 1995 are hard to come by, but I managed to find some. Before we delve into that, though, we need a little history lesson. Monday Night Raw launched in 1993 as an hour-long show with one purpose: to sell tickets. Back then, the WWF's business model was to use the TV time to highlight their big names beating jobbers and then use the time during the show to advertise local house shows and the major PPVs. Money came from seat sales and merchandise. When Monday Nitro launched, WCW proved not only could you put quality matches on ad-supported TV, but that there was lots of money to be made from increasing ratings and charging higher advertising rates. The Monday Night Wars changed the way the wrestling business was run and made money. Now we see that house shows are about practice while the PPVs and programming fees are where the WWE makes all of their real money. Ticket sales are really secondary.

That said, before September 1995, rating for Monday Night Raw were generally in the high 1's and low 2's range. Do you know what they were during Kevin Nash's reign as WWF Champion (as Diesel)? In the low to high 2 range. Ratings never got above 3 during his reign, but then again, they did not get above 3 until February 19, 1996. But as soon as that 3 threshold was broken, it was lost again with most weeks in the low to upper 2's (with one 4.7 in the middle). Then, from May 20, 1996 to April 28, 1997 ratings dove again into the low 2's, and then some 1's. This also included the lowest rating ever with a 1.5 on December 23, 1996. It would not be until January 1998 and forward that RAW started to put on ratings higher than 3.0 on a regular basis.

So yes, ratings of RAW during Diesel's reign were hardly the best compared to the top of the WWF/E's run, but they were a far cry from the worst. And when he was champ (at least the first six months of his reign), ratings were not even a consideration or a factor of success.

But even if they were, Diesel could hardly be blamed for the low ratings on Monday night. During his entire reign, Diesel fought 6 times on Raw. Six! Well, seven if you count the show where he fought Razor Ramon twice. And the rest of the time, he wasn't always on the show or even commenting. The man was not a factor in what was going on during WWF TV. On a weekly basis, you were more likely to see Bret Hart, Owen Hart, Yokozuna, Mabel, 1-2-3 Kid, Shawn Michaels, Davey Boy Smith, Razor Ramon, Bam Bam Bigelow, the Undertaker, or a slew of jobbers. Yet, those men who were actually performing on RAW do not get blamed for the low ratings, while the man who made six match appearances takes all of the blame onto himself. How unfair.

THE WORST DRAWING CHAMPION OF ALL TIME – PART 2

But if ratings were not how you would judge a champion, then what would you?

House Shows are one way to look at it. We said they were important to the WWF at the time. Unfortunately, finding house show attendance figures from 10 years ago is a bit of a challenge. I will say this, though: the WWE has cancelled a number of shows in the past month alone. That is how far down they have fallen. RAW, SmackDown!, and PPVs are not selling out arenas. WCW faced a similar problem after the end of the nWo era. And before 1995, the WWF was not selling out arenas, and after 1996 they were not selling out arenas. Nash's attendance figures were no worse and no better than those before him since the heyday of Hulkamania, and were no better than those who came after him until the nWo and later Attitude Era. And since the end of Attitude, attendance figures have fallen to similar levels.

Still, we need some hard numbers. Let's take a look over to the other side of the coin: PPV buys.

After Diesel won the title, he went on to a nearly one-year reign. During that time, Royal Rumble drew a 1.0 buyrate, WrestleMania drew a 1.3, and SummerSlam had a 0.9. Those three PPVs were well within the "success" range we defined in the Eric Bischoff case. Want to know more? The first four In Your Houses EVER were during Diesel's reign. You have to realize, the idea of a PPV outside the Big 5 had never been attempted before, but the WWF needed to respond to the monthly PPV model that WCW had launched. So the idea of the minor PPV was born with In Your House 1, as Diesel defeated Sid Vicious by DQ for a 0.83 buyrate. Not a bad way to start at all.

So yes, the other In Your House PPVs did not fare as well, eventually settling at a 0.4 for In Your House 4. But look at these cards:

Royal Rumble
Diesel and Bret Hart battled to a draw, Shawn Michaels won the Royal Rumble

WrestleMania
Diesel defeated Shawn Michaels, Lawrence Taylor defeated Bam Bam Bigelow in the main event

In Your House 1
Diesel defeated Sid Vicious by DQ

King of the Ring
Mabel wins KoTR, Diesel and Bam Bam Bigelow defeated Sid Vicious and Tatanka

In Your House 2
Lumberjack match: Diesel defeated Sid Vicious

SummerSlam
Diesel defeated Mabel

In Your House 3
Diesel and Shawn Michaels defeated Yokozuna & The British Bulldog for the World Tag Team Championships

In Your House 4
British Bulldog d. Diesel by DQ

Survivor Series
Bret Hart defeated Diesel for the championship

Three non-endings, two tag team matches, one PPV headlined by a football player, and one match with Mabel. That's enough to anger any wrestling fan into not wanting to watch WWF, go to their shows, or order their PPVs.

And who's fault is that? Did Kevin Nash go to Vince McMahon and say, "Vince, I want to fight in a bunch of matches that don't have endings. And while you are at it, could you make Mabel the King of the Ring?"? Of course not! The WWF bookers and Vince McMahon are responsible for the content and results, not the man with the belt on his waist.

But let's pretend it was all Nash. Let's say Nash is 100% responsible for the PPV buyrates. During Diesel's 12-month title reign, the average PPV buyrate was a 0.78. Yes, that is below our minimum overall success range, but it is not the worst of all time. From May 1996 to April 1997 (or July 1996-June 1997, depending on how you round), the 12-month average PPV buyrate was a 0.59 for the WWF. So there you have it. Diesel was not the worst drawing WWF champion on PPV buys either.

WRAPPING UP THE NUMBERS

Was Diesel the best drawing champion of all time? No. Were his ratings on Raw, house show attendances, and PPV buyrates somewhere from mediocre to mildly successful? Yes. Were they the worst ever? Absolutely not.

Kevin Nash may not have been the best champion ever, but he was a far cry from the worst. He went out, did his job, had two 4+* matches with Bret Hart, and did what he loved to do: wrestle. And we'll prove his love of wrestling soon enough, don't you worry.

His real success came later when he left the WWF and returned (that's RETURNED) to WCW to join with Scott Hall and Hulk Hogan as the nWo. And there is no denying the impact he had in the nWo and the money that was made from it (and don't tell me I have to go out and show how much money the nWo made, please). The nWo would not have been anything like it was without the attitude, personality, and storylines involving Nash. There's very little to look at as far as championship reigns, since reign #1 lasted a week, #2 two months, #3 two hours, #4 a week, and #5 a month, so that is not where to look at Nash's drawing ability. The man generated money away from the title. He was an important player when he was at the top and made money with all those around him.

Just as another example, I was selling wrestling shirts (FULLY LICENSED!) around 1997 or so at a flea market, and the Wolfpac shirts were the top of the top, even better than Austin at times. Nash makes money, maybe not Hulk Hogan or Rock money, but money nonetheless.

Say what you want about the politicking and booking and whatnot, the numbers prove it. Whether ratings, PPV buys, house show attendance, or merchandise sales, Kevin Nash is far from the worst. As it stands, he's a draw—and a money generating one at that.

LET ME TELL YOU ABOUT A LITTLE CITY...

Born on July 9, 1959 outside Detroit, Michigan, Kevin Nash had no idea that he was going to grow up and be a pro-wrestler. Some would have you believe he has no love of the sport and is only in it for the money. Well, you should know that growing up he went to the arena to see The Sheik, Bobo Brazil, and Pampero Firpo. That's right, Kevin Nash was a fan of wrestling, and had to work to be a fan as any old school kid will tell you.

But he was just a fan, and really did not have the inclination to train to be a wrestler. As a matter of fact, he was following the path of many other 6' 11" men: he was going to be a pro-basketball player. Laugh all you want, but Nash was the second-most recruited man out of Michigan in his senior year of high school, right after the legendary Magic Johnson. He went on to play for the Tennessee Volunteers from 1979-1980, but did not rise to the top of the team. He soon found himself in Europe playing basketball there (which we see a lot more in reverse now-a-days) until he had a serious knee injury that took him out of the game forever.

Now, many other sports stars that have had serious injuries and have ended up in wrestling—from Hacksaw Jim Duggan to Bill Goldberg. But that is not where Kevin Nash went next. He joined the United States Army and was stationed in Germany for two years. That's right, the man took orders and learned discipline for two years. Actually, Nash is quoted as saying "The army taught me discipline, and the value of hard work." Nash believes in hard work, it would seem, though others may tell you he only believes in laziness.

Not being lazy, Nash ended up in Atlanta working as a bouncer. While there, Dusty Rhodes chanced upon him and was impressed with his size, look, and attitude. He suggested that Nash go to WTBS headquarters and have a tryout.

And that is exactly what Kevin Nash did. Are you going to turn down an open invitation from Dusty Rhodes? The executives at Turner liked what they saw and told Nash he should enroll in the Power Plant. And so, risking everything he had, Nash did that and worked his way through the Power Plant until he was ready to join the big show.

Except getting to the dance isn't exactly the same as being a success.

THE "BIG MAN" PUSH

Kevin Nash was getting a second chance. His first dream of being a pro-basketball player had failed, but now he could live out a childhood love of pro-wrestling.

After his training period, Nash was ready to debut for Jim Crockett Promotions as none other than...

STEEL! ONE HALF OF THE MASTER BLASTERS!!!!

You see, people are under the impression that Nash—just because he was a big man—got all the breaks in the business. That could not be further from the truth. Yes, he got lucky in breaking into the business, but he still had to work from the bottom up. And how low can you go starting with Steel?

Well, shortly thereafter he dropped the orange Mohawk and became OZ, managed by the ever-impressive Merlin the Wizard! Does this sound like an instant push to you?

Well how about this: After finishing as Oz, Nash moved on to become a member of the Vegas Connection as Vinnie Vegas, working for none other than Diamond Dallas Page. But this was well before DDP was WCW Championship material. Hell, this was well before DDP was WCW TV Title material. Nash was backup for a nobody, making him less than a nobody. He did get one major thing out of this, though: Snake Eyes! Why do you think when he drops someone face first on the top turnbuckle it is called Snake Eyes? That was his finishing maneuver as Vinnie Vegas, king of the craps!

Having not accomplished much, he left WCW in late 1993 and signed with the WWF. Shortly thereafter he debuted as "Big Daddy Cool" Diesel, playing backup to Shawn Michaels. No, Nash was not pushed right to the top. But the fans started to get behind him, and they loved when he finally turned on Shawn Michaels. After four or five years, he had done it; Nash had worked his way to the top of the game. But he was used to following orders, he was used to doing what he was told, and he let the program be decided by those above him. He was not ready to become the booker yet, but what he saw during his own reign made him worry about the future. He had realized his worth and wanted to make those changes when his time came again.

ARISTOTLE'S RULES OF FRIENDSHIPS

During his time in WCW and WWF, Nash had made friends with a short list of people. These men included Scott Hall, Shawn Michaels, the man who would later become Triple H, and Sean Waltman. Nash has been accused of using these friendships, and his later friendships with Hulk Hogan and Eric Bischoff, in order to keep himself at the top. Well to that, I say, so what?

If you've read Aristotle, you know that he proposes there are three types of friendships:

(1) Friendships of utility, where the people do favors for one another
(2) Friendships of activity, where the people enjoy doing the same things
(3) True friendships, where the people just enjoy each other

Now, there is nothing wrong with having a friend who is just about favors and business. This is how the world works; someone has something that the other wants and a trade happens. Also, a friendship of activity can also be a friendship of utility and a true friendship can contain elements of both. So who are we to even judge what type of friendships Nash had with these people. If Shawn Michaels was his true friend, could not his true friend do him a favor?

Chris Rock once noted that 80% of the people in his audience got their job because a friend recommended them. We already talked about how Dusty Rhodes gave Nash a recommendation, and that helped him get his foot in the door. But getting your foot in the door does not equate to success. You have to prove yourself or you will be gone.

Thus if Shawn Michaels recommended Nash for a push for the title, so what? If Eric Bischoff was so charmed by Nash that he wanted him at the top of the game, so what? This type of personal interaction is what gave him the opportunity, but he was the one who took the opportunity and did something with it.

My company just hired eight new people. Do you know what the major criteria was for their hire? It was how well they would fit into the company, how we judged that they would be able to work with our current crew. But that got them in the door. They still have to prove they can do the work and move up the ladder. It will take time, and they will need to learn and grow. If they don't, then their future is limited.

Nash got into a good position because of his personality, because he can fit into an organization, and because he makes people believe he has the potential. You can guarantee, though, that if he did not live up to his potential that McMahon and Bischoff would never have put up with him. Now go back to earlier and note how he drew as a champion, pay close attention to the numbers he drew. The bottom line is: the fans like him. And when the fans like you, you sell, and you work your way to the top of the game, and then you are a success.

No friend can bring you to the top, only you can. A friend can give you the opportunity, and you have to exploit it to its fullest. Kevin learned that lesson well, and also learned that when the opportunity presents itself, you have to protect yourself.

WATCH OUT FOR THE BOOKER MAN

Nash had already seen what disastrous booking could do to a reign, even one as long as his. After the culmination of a year and half of storylines, Sting had finally defeated Hulk Hogan and the nWo. But the question remained: what now?

That question plagued WCW for the next year as they began to lose focus and the WWF caught up in the ratings, having finally found their "attitude". Things began to shift internally, and Kevin Nash was given a chance he never knew he could have.

Kevin Nash joined the booking committee in late 1998 and began to use his influence. Remember, though, that Bischoff was still around, as were others, so final decisions were not his. As such, when Starrcade 1998 rolled around and Kevin Nash had a match against Goldberg for the World Heavyweight Championship, do not think for a minute that he booked himself to win. He wanted to win, I'm sure. Who wouldn't? Who would pass up the chance to be champion?

But let's go back for a second. Like we said, since Starrcade 1997 WCW was lacking in direction. The nWo had split into the Wolfpac and Hollywood, and Hogan had gone into semi-retirement. The WWF had finally caught up to the WCW in ratings and had overtaken them. But that was not horrible. For instance, on the January 4, 1999 edition of the Monday Night Wars, WWF had a 5.7 rating and WCW had a 5.0 rating. That is a combined 10.7 for wrestling! What did Raw score on a week in 2005? A 3.8?

That was also the night of the Nash vs. Goldberg rematch from Starrcade, which turned into the Nash vs. Hogan-coming-back-from-retirement match when Goldberg got arrested for sexually harassing Miss Elizabeth, which in turn turned into the infamous FINGER POKE OF DOOM (stay tuned)!

If Nash had so much power, why would he allow himself to just lose to Hogan? Because at the end of the day, Nash knew what was good for business and that there were other decisions to make. He had proved that he could draw money without the title and saw the reformation of the nWo as a way to make more money for himself, his friends, and WCW.

And did Nitro die right after that? Absolutely not! The next week drew a 5.0 rating again, and a 4.4, 5.0, 4.7, and a 5.7 in the weeks thereafter. Nitro would remain mostly in the 4's until the end of April. Back then, it was said that this was terrible, and these were horrible ratings, and that the bookers were destroying everything. Looking back on it now, the WWE would love to have ratings today as good as during that particular "death of WCW". But we let the stigma of these being "terrible ratings" persist through time, even though they are excellent ratings, even compared to Rugrats.

Now, let's return to Starrcade 1998, which pulled in a 1.15 buyrate, well above our "success" range. As a matter of fact, I was in a store in the mall when I overheard another man in the store talking about the upcoming match. Now, I cannot remember the last time I ever heard someone talk about being excited for a match and event, hearing a mark just going on about it in the middle of a store. I was actually much more jaded due to reading too many internet reports, but this man's simple love of the suspension of belief, him wanting to just see two big guys beat the crap out of each other, reminded me of why I was a fan. Suddenly, Starrcade looked a whole lot better.

Nash won with the help of a taser. That hardly seems like the mark of a man trying to put himself above everything. Don't forget that Nash was a face at this time, too, so we are not talking about a heel just dominating the show. No, that turn would have to come a couple of weeks later.

Still, Nash was not in charge, and time moved on. But people were interested in him. Heck, that Nitro above was in the Georgia Dome and drew 40,000 people! 40,000 for a regular Nitro? How many people showed up for SmackDown! during a particular week in 2005, 8,000?

But despite Nitro doing well, there was little fanfare going into Souled Out and SuperBrawl, and their buyrates proved it.

Immediately following SuperBrawl, Nash was given the book. He wanted to change the program and stop the hemorrhaging from the last year. To begin with, there were more backstage vignettes and skits to add more solid entertainment to the show. Next, matches began to have more concrete endings, less run-in and garbage collections. Nash realized that the run-ins of the past were just that: the past. Times had changed and he wanted to change with them. Finally, he decided that no one was above losing, especially himself. So to set things right and let everyone know the tone, he lost to Rey Mysterio cleanly on Nitro.

The effects were seen right away. Uncensored drew a 0.73 buyrate. Nash was doing his job.

Still, things would turn against Nash. Just as we noted in the Bischoff case, Time Warner Corporate was not in the position of supporting WCW. Standards and Practices interfered, they would not let them make many changes, and soon Bischoff was fired and the whole company was about to go through an astounding transformation.

But even with his limited control, people still say Kevin Nash only looked to make things better for himself and his friends. Well, we'll have to take a closer look at that.

Super Friends, unite!

While Kevin Nash was head booker, people say he only pushed his friends on the shows. Oh really? Well, we have already talked about how he lost cleanly to Rey Mysterio on Nitro, but many people will just say that Rey Rey was an extended member of the WCW Klique. Well how about on the same Nitro that Nash lost to Rey Mysterio (the night Nash became head booker), another Booker was victorious. Booker T defeated Bret Hart in a 20-minute awesome match-up.

Now, Nash and Hart had had some four-star matchups back in the WWF, but Nash was not a big fan of Hart. Even still, Nash understood that business was business, and got Hart back into the title hunt and major storylines. So on one hand he had Hart making Booker T, and on the other he had Hart reaching for the top of WCW. Mind you, Nash wasn't even in the title hunt after "losing" to Hulk Hogan, so others were getting his spot, and not necessarily people he liked.

Speaking of titles, Booker T and Scott Steiner began a feud over the Television Title that within a few months was over the US Title. And as we know, that feud would later headline WCW in its final years. Booker T and Scott Steiner were really coming into their own under the watchful eye of Kevin Nash's booking.

Also another title returned to prominence. For a while, the cruiserweight title almost disappeared from WCW. But when Nash took the reins, Kidman returned with the Cruiserweight belt and had excellent matches with Psychosis, Chavo Guerrero, Chris Jericho, and Mikey Whipwreck, before finally losing in an all-out match with Rey Mysterio. Later yet, Kidman maintained prominence and went on to heavyweight tag team gold with said Mysterio.

Oh, that's right, tag team gold! Suddenly, teams were formed again with the aforementioned Mysterio/Kidman, Saturn/Raven, Windham/Henning, and a nice little team of Benoit/Malenko. The latter were treated as credible threats over everyone. Not bad for a couple of the "vanilla midgets" that one would say Nash is not high on. Wait, I almost forgot. They then went on to join the new and last Four Horsemen, cementing them as the best of the best.

But back to the World Heavyweight Championship, fellow Horseman and insane President Ric Flair went on to defeat Hollywood Hogan and take the title. And who would he defend that title against? As an interesting twist, Rey Mysterio got a shot after defeating the likes of Bam Bam Bigelow, Scott Norton, and Buff Bagwell. Still, Hogan was the definitive friend of Nash and Bischoff, yet it was

Flair who got to carry the strap and take most of the focus of the show while Nash was in charge, even though Flair had a rough history with Nash, especially after the Horsemen-Spot incident.

Meanwhile, there were a few things going on that Nash doesn't get credit for. When Raven, Hak, and Bigelow were putting on vicious brawls and showing real hardcore in WCW, Nash was supporting that. When Jerry Flynn was getting the Barry Windham push, Nash was there. When the Disco Inferno got a real finishing move and storyline with Konnan, Nash was there.

But it was not just people that were feeling the benefit of a Nash booking reign. Thunder was given a lot of focus and time, and often saw Hogan, Flair, and others in the main event scene. For a while, Thunder was being treated like a recap show, but under Nash it became must-see-TV again, and continuity spread among all of WCW television.

Still, there is one man missing in all of this that you would think would take prominence. Where was Scott Hall? Even with all his personal problems, don't you think that if Nash were really only looking out for his friends that Scott Hall would be there? But he wasn't. Nash knew what was right for business, and put the business before his friends, no matter how much it hurt himself.

Again, though, we have gone too far ahead. Before and after Nash was a booker, he was a wrestler. But how good of a wrestler was he?

SIX MOVES OF DOOM

People often say that Kevin Nash only has six moves, that he is an extremely limited worker, if the word worker can even be applied to him.

To prove this point wrong, I decided to review a match between two people that are considered non-workers by the vast majority and took Kevin Nash vs. Goldberg I from Starrcade 1998 and also a look at Kevin Nash vs. Goldberg II from Spring Stampede 1999.

OK, during the first match, Kevin Nash did the following moves (not including punching, which is illegal): collar-and-elbow tie up, headlock, knee wrench, forearm shot (legal, and a move!), hip check, elbow, boot choke (illegal, but I'll allow it), reversal of a leg lock, reversal of a jackhammer, side slam, reverse leg lariat, jackknife powerbomb.

All right, let's count. That's 12 moves at least! And he didn't even use snake eyes! Want to add a little more into the mix? In Kevin Nash vs. Goldberg II, Nash pulled off a leapfrog over Goldberg!!! Why aren't you amazed? This is a 6' 11" man leaping at least 5 feet in the air to get over a man running towards him. I can barely jump a foot and have about a third of the mass of Kevin Nash. And don't we always hear about how Kevin Nash isn't athletic and can't pull off big moves?

Well maybe it is because he doesn't have to. Remember during Tough Enough IV when the Bashams whipped out some excellent amateur moves on the contestants and we suddenly saw more than their brawling style, that they really are actually excellently trained wrestlers? Well, Nash is a trained wrestler. Maybe he is not as expertly tuned as Chris Benoit, but he still knows a lot more than he puts into his matches.

And why is that? Why would Nash hold back on his abilities and not wow people with his in-ring aptitude? Well, why doesn't the Big Show pull off the Giant-sault that we know he perfected in WCW? Why doesn't Booker T use the Harlem Hangover to end every match?

Because they don't have to.

And it's not laziness. It's smart and knowing what works in the business.

I take you back to my example earlier of the mark in the jewelry store who was all excited about this match. Well, it did not end with him. Watching that match, the crowd was on the edge of their seats. They were screaming and cheering before the bell rang. The first part of the match was both men making faces at each other and the crowd. That was it! And the crowd loved every second of it.

I love to watch a Chris Benoit match any day of the week, but I think back to Royal Rumble 2003 when he fought Kurt Angle. I was there live in the then Fleet Center, and it was an incredible match. But for the first 10 minutes, the crowd could not care. This is a man who does have to lay it all out in the ring because that is the only way to get the fans to really care about him. That match is one of the best I have ever seen live in my entire life, but it pales in comparison to a match of lumbering giants.

Hulk Hogan vs. Andre the Giant at WrestleMania III, or even the more recent Hulk Hogan vs. the Rock at WrestleMania... these are matches that were made by the crowd. The crowd did not care about move-for-move, excellent mat Wrestling. They did not need to see breathtaking moves with flying around blood and guts. And I do love to see these things, too, but what the crowd comes for is intensity. Their emotional involvement in the match is all that matters. And the crowd cares about Kevin Nash, whether to see him rise to the top or to see their favorite hero take him down.

Kevin Nash is a much better mat technician than he has ever gotten credit for. Then again, he had never needed to prove it in the ring. He had all the tools he needed: the crowd in the palm of his hand.

HERE COMES THE MONEY OR NASH THE HUMANITARIAN

Despite everything that Nash has given in the ring and to the business, people say he only wanted one thing: money.

Sure, money was a major factor in Kevin Nash's career, but it was not his only goal. As we have seen in the booking section, he cared about trying to make the product better across the board, not just himself. And yes, he did not always make the best decisions, but who has? He made mistakes, but did not let them hold him down from going ahead with plans to make things even better.

In an interview with the Associated Press, Nash had this to say about his career:

> "God made me almost 7-feet tall, and now I'm 300 pounds. I don't think I was made an accountant or a bookkeeper," Nash said. "I was put on this earth for something. I guess this is what it was."

Nash has an understanding of what his role is, not only in business but in life.

More so, here is an excerpt from an article in the Ottawa Sun just before TNA's Turning Point:

> "When I first broke in, I'd already had seven knee operations (from basketball). I was limited physically by a bad knee. But those are the cards that were dealt to me.
>
> "I'm 45 years old now, but I look in the mirror and I see the body of a 35-year-old guy. I'm fortunate. I can sit back and work when I want to work and not work when I don't want to work.

> "I'm a dad and a husband. It's a 90-minute drive each way (to TNA's studio in Orlando), so I'm home in the morning and home at night. It's the best possible situation."
>
> He's more limited in what he can do in the ring, but that's not such a big deal.
>
> "I don't think doing flips off the top rope has ever drawn money," he said. "I've been in a lot of bar fights and it's pretty much punching and kicking. I don't remember flying off the top rope."
>
> Nash says some of today's wrestlers don't understand the tried and true formula that is wrestling.
>
> "When I broke in, all the guys would say that less is more. A lot of these guys think more is more.
>
> "Years ago, my four-year-old punches me in the nose. You sell it. You go, 'Ow!'
>
> "Sometimes, these guys don't sell. They're so consumed with getting everything possible into an eight-minute match."

Nash has a deep understanding of the business and how to work a crowd, and he went to TNA to try to teach the guys there that. Was he making more than most on the card per appearance? You bet! But how long has this man been working? How much of a draw is he? He deserves his money, which is not much compared to what he was making in WCW. You read what he said, he could get back to his family in a day; it was great for him. He could give back a little while he was there. Now he is off making movies, but do not believe that he will not make an appearance now and again.

And it is not like this is the first time that Nash has tried to give back to the young generation in the business. Towards the end of WCW, Nash found himself in the role of "coach" for the Natural Born Thrillers. This onstage role quickly turned into a backstage one, as he became a mentor in all of the Thrillers' developments. Above Average Mike Sanders, Shawn O'Haire, Chuck Polumbo, and Mark Jindrak have all gone on record to say how influential Nash was in their careers and thanked him for all his help and guidance.

Nash was a man trying to give back to a business that gave him so many opportunities. More important, he wanted others to see that opportunity was not the end all, be all. You have to take that ball and run with it, or break your knees trying.

UNBEATEN RECORDS

Just to keep these little tidbits up, here's a few other records that Nash holds:

- Holds the fastest time to winning the championship by defeating Bob Backland in nine seconds

- The only wrestler in history to acquire the Tag Team, Intercontinental, and WWF Championships in one calendar year

- The longest reining WWF/E Champion since Hulk Hogan, and longest rein until JBL

- One of four men to retain his title at WrestleMania (Hogan, Triple H, and Eddie Guerrero are the others)

- Got the role as Super Shredder in Teenage Mutant Ninja Turtles 2 because he was the only person big and strong enough to fit the costume

OK, that last one was just too sweet not to put in there.

THE JACKKNIFE POWERBOMB

Kevin Nash is a man who the IWC turned against because he does not appear to be a workrate king. But the man has shown a deep understanding of the business and done everything in his power to give back to it. He wasn't the best, the top of tops, or the greatest at anything, per se. But he was damn good. Nash worked hard and tried to make every time he came out a special one, kept the crowd involved, and took the opportunities he was given to create a better environment for himself, the fans, and those who would come after him.

Kevin Nash is a man who should not have been given the harsh treatment he has seen over the years. He is a man who deserves to be given credit for everything he has done.

Kevin Nash deserves this.

The defense rests.

After the Trial

Hung Jury

IN THE CASE OF THE IWC VERSUS KEVIN NASH, NASH HAS BEEN ACCUSED OF BEING A NO-TALENT, SELF-SERVING, FRIEND-PUSHING, POLITICKING, MONEY-GRUBBING WRESTLER WHO WAS ALSO THE WORST DRAWING CHAMPION OF ALL TIME.

With 89.7% of the vote, Kevin Nash was found:

NOT GUILTY!

Response

Wrestlers like Kevin Nash were often the favorite of many people who felt they were alone in the world. Seeing a singular defense outside of their own community meant a lot to these people and was a common theme throughout the entire run of the article.

> *Nash has always had my respect. He's a class act all the way, and he has a deep respect for his fans (I do a lot of artwork for his webmaster for his Official Fanclub). I've met and spoken with him several times now and he's a good guy who cares a great deal about the business. Your defense of him and his contributions to the wrestling biz was A-1. I applaud your courtroom prowess.*
>
> *Not Guilty!*
>
> **Valentina**

> *[Let's] just say that the Kevin Nash you see in the ring and on TV is the exact opposite of the real man.*
>
> *I was privileged to be able to attend his first fan club dinner last Dec in Orlando. We were promised a few hours with him, dinner, one picture and one autograph..... the man spent over 6hrs talking to*

> us and sharing stories. He posed for any and all pictures we wanted..... signed anything he [was] asked.... including one member's lower back.... and was genuinely sorry to leave us. He gave each of us a hug and thanked us personally for "coming all this way just to see me". Kevin and his wife even went out and purchased a new camera/printer combo so we could all have immediate photos of him with us... and group shots.... a nicer and sweeter man [cannot] be found.
>
> Thanks for FINALLY defending him!
>
> **Bobbi**

These were hardly the only people who had spent time with Nash in person, as I told Bobbi in my response:

> You are very welcome Bobbi. I've heard from a few other people who attended the same dinner, and all said equally great thing about the man. I really enjoyed defending Nash, and have been glad to hear other people's wonderful real world stories with him.

Of course, although the numbers were fantastic for this case, there were people who voted guilty:

> [Y]ou've conveniently skewed some of the facts in favor of making Kevin Nash appear like the misunderstood saint of wrestling.
>
> **Prince Zardos**

But it was those earlier fans who had met Nash in person who provided the fodder for my reply:

> Strangely enough, a number of people who have met Nash have written in, and the words "humble", "selfless" and "really cares about the fans" came up a lot. I don't think my facts were skewed to make Nash look like a saint, but they

> were definitely designed to highlight the good that he has done. Generally, I believe the facts (or more so opinions/lies) are skewed to make Nash look like a terrible person. Like I said in my article, he's certainly not the best, but deserves better than we give him!

More responses were closer to this, which is exactly what the intent of this article was:

> I think you put up a good case for the Big Man. I had read a lot of what other people have had to say about Kevin Nash over the years and even though I try to keep an open mind about things, I guess I just assumed that most of what was said was true. Great job.
>
> **Quique74**

This was my perspective as well, as I told Quique74:

> Thanks for reading Q, and I'm glad I could change your mind. Honestly, I was surprised by a lot of what I found out about Nash as I was doing my research. I did the same thing you did, and there was no reason to believe otherwise. Everything I've read about Nash sounded like it could be true! But I'm glad to help the Big Man get a fair shake, and hopefully we'll see more of these Kevin Nash facts popping up than the lies we've read for years!

And while changing others minds always made me happy, I was most delighted to hear perspectives like this one:

> I have to say, you're one of two IWC columnists I actually enjoy reading on a regular basis.
>
> You don't have the preachy, self-righteousness of [others], and you actually have a point to make, unlike oh-so-many others.

> *Even if I were to disagree with your defense of Kevin Nash, I could still actually read your column enjoyably, and not feel as if I were being preached to, or called stupid for disagreeing with you....*
>
> **-Sincerely,**
> **Chuck Stahlheber**

I blanked out the name of the columnist that Chuck mentioned, but nothing tickled me more than being the antithesis to this person who I was basically writing the article to.

THE FINGER POKE OF DOOM

INTRO

SOME DAME WALKED INTO MY OFFICE AND SAID...

This actually comes from a friend of mine. He loves the Finger Poke of Doom, and puts it over like the deadliest move of all time. If anyone ever says it was stupid, he'll go through all of the ways the finger poke hit certain pressure points and shuts down the nervous system. Try arguing with him about why this isn't a legitimate devastating move, I dare you!

WHY THIS?

Well, insane kayfabe aside, the Finger Poke of Doom is oft lamented as the prime example of what was wrong with WCW. My friend and I disagree. The Finger Poke of Doom actually made perfect sense from all perspectives, progressed storylines for a year, and—most of all—was good for business. Ready to find out why? I know I am!

BACKGROUND

On January 4, 1999, newly crowned President of WCW Ric Flair announced a rematch from Starrcade: New World Heavyweight Champion Kevin Nash vs. the man he defeated for the title: Goldberg. Seemingly unknowing, Nash won the match after Scott Hall hit Goldberg with a taser to finally end the undefeated streak. Not wanting to lose his Wolfpac love with the fans, Nash accepted the match, and everything was in place.

That same night, Hollywood Hogan was set to make a special guest appearance after being in semi-retirement for months and toying with the idea of running for President of the United States (just to stick it in Jesse Ventura's face). Meanwhile, without his presence, the nWo Black and White had fallen into a disarray of B-stars and the Wolfpac was nothing more than a coddling piece of WCW, not the great machine the nWo used to be.

What had happened to the nWo of the past? They were a separate organization set to take over WCW, but those days were behind. They had become the establishment—as could be seen with co-branding—and were soon to lose everything, even then their own PPV Souled Out. The nWo was lost... or was it?

Behind the scenes, the best of the best got together. Hulk Hogan, Kevin Nash, Scott Hall, Lex Lugar, Scott Steiner, and Buff Bagwell came up with a plan to get rid of Goldberg (who had truly driven Hogan away), turn the nWo back into a dominating force, and keep the rabble in the nWo busy so they would not hinder the real work being done.

The plan was set into motion before Starrcade, but this would be their shining moment.

Miss Elizabeth went to the Atlanta police and got Goldberg arrested for sexual misconduct towards her, as she feared for her safety. Everywhere she went, Goldberg was there! Of course, Goldberg countered that that's because they travel around the country together. But Elizabeth said that even when she went to the gym at home Goldberg was there waiting for her. Goldberg said that was because he owned the gym. Oh well!

But this kept Goldberg busy enough. While away, Kevin Nash said Goldberg got screwed at Starrcade, and was getting screwed by Hogan now. He asked President Flair for a match against Hogan that night, and Flair gave the go ahead. Later, Hogan came out for a special interview to announce his VP candidate, but said the situation with Goldberg made him sick. What also made him sick was Kevin Nash thinking he was scared of him. Thus he decided to have "one last match" that he owed to his fans.

And everything was set.

The main event came. Steiner came out with Hogan. Nash came out alone, and then pointed to the back and Scott Hall followed. 40,000 fans in the Atlanta Dome were on their feet screaming. The tension could be cut with a knife. They stared each other down. Nash shoved Hogan. Hogan came back with a punch. He pulled it. And then he hit the most devastating move in wrestling:

THE FINGER POKE OF DOOM!!!

Hogan covered for the One-Two-Three and the championship!

And the plan was set in motion.

THE LOGIC OF WRESTLING

People say, what was the logic of Nash dropping the title to Hogan after just winning it? Why would he do that?

Well, look at it from his character's perspective. Through the nWo to the present, the Kevin Nash character has cared about one thing: making a lot of money. Remember when the nWo had a match for the entire gate of a live event? Or how they always pushed their t-shirts?

And that's what Kevin Nash was noticing. Wolfpac sold decently but was reaching its saturation point. It was nothing like the nWo of the past. He didn't have the clout anymore that he used to and was now really a part of WCW accepting their terms instead of dictating his own.

He needed to refocus and get back into a power position. He knew one man who could do that for him: Hulk Hogan.

But what could Hogan to gain from this? He was already rich beyond most and had nothing to prove in the sport. Wasn't he going to run for President?

Well, Hogan had decided that he needed more time before that happened and realized that he only had so much time left in the business. He wanted one last shot at the top, but feared one thing: Goldberg. How could he get the title off of Goldberg yet never have to face him? That's where this plan turns genius.

You see, when a champion loses his title, he generally has an automatic rematch clause in his contact against the person that beat him. Well, that meant that when Nash beat Goldberg, Goldberg had the right to ask for the rematch on Nitro. But since he was unable to make it, Hogan got the match. When Hogan won and became the new champion, Nash became the defacto number one contender. Now he was the former champion who could exercise a rematch clause whenever he wanted! Except, being in a team, he never would! So now Hall and Nash could keep Goldberg busy for months to come, while Hogan was off celebrating with the gold.

Meanwhile, the nWo got to reform into a powerhouse unit, but things were just getting underway.

THE RASH DECISION

Despite the starkness of the devious plan, members of the IWC still believe that this was an on-the-fly booking decision; that all of the events leading up to the Finger Poke and afterwards were just out of the booking committee's backside that day. Look, though, at the long-term focus WCW was trying to put in:

Refocus the forces
WCW had split into a ridiculous number of factions, all filled with people no one cared about. The first step was to set up the elite nWo, then start to dismantle the rabble in the black and white. At the same time, they had President Flair get rid of the lWo so that there would be certainties about who was on what team and how the storylines were going. Keeping everything fractured into groups that people could not get behind was not helping anyone, and this was the start of the new direction of WCW.

Drawing out the point
At this point in time, WCW began to set the pace for where things were going

for months. For instance, the antics of Hall, Nash, Hogan, and the rest of nWo led to Flair's eventual insanity and the heel turn for the Horsemen. Looking back, the seeds were built for everything, and the storylines all began to intertwine again into something special.

Continuity
As time went on, WCW did not try to bury the Finger Poke or pretend it never happened. It came up again, especially when Kevin Nash and Hulk Hogan started feuding. A lot of it began with Hogan implying the Finger Poke was real, and he had totally devastated Nash. Torrie Wilson, of all people, was speeding along the process and using the Finger Poke to ebb Nash into turning on Hogan. WCW did not just try to make things happen for no reason at this point; they wanted the long story to continue.

GOLD! And Newbies!
And let us not forget about the gold. The World Heavyweight Championship obviously took a lot of emphasis and good stories evolved surrounding the title leading up to Hogan's loss to Flair at SuperBrawl. At the same time, there was an excellent Tag Team tournament, with Hall and Nash trying to remind everyone how good they were. The Television title got a lot of shine from Steiner now being in the top of the nWo. Also, just coincidently, the cruiserweights were getting a lot of air-time and were often getting beat up by nWo members. This actually led to the nWo being used to elevate new stars, most notably Rey Mysterio and Konnan. Both were treated as legitimate threats to the nWo and were given the proper ball to run with. Of course, let us not forget that within the nWo that said Steiner was on the rise, and was soon to take a Booker T with him.

The Finger Poke of Doom did not lead directly to all of this, but it was the forefather for things to come. It was the necessary step to set WCW's direction in the coming months, and those months were planned to some detail. There was no rashness to this choice; it was all played out exactly as it was meant to.

YOU REMEMBER MY GOOD FRIENDS, THE NUMBERS?

How did this new direction and focus affect WCW? Well, since this is a corporation we are talking about, let's look at things in quarters (3 months/12 weeks). Let's start out with the Nitro ratings:

Date	Rating	Note
January 4, 1999	5.0	*Finger Poke of Doom*
January 11, 1999	5.0	*Post Finger Poke people are still back in full force*
January 18, 1999	4.4	*A slight dip that was the harbinger of doom then, now higher than RAW's ratings.*
January 25, 1999	5.0	*Back to where it was. Whew!*
February 1, 1999	4.7	*On no! Another drop!*
February 8, 1999	5.7	*Wow, largest rating in the longest!*
February 15, 1999	3.9	*Oh my, WCW is going out of business next week!*
February 22, 1999	4.8	*Ummm... nevermind. Let's wait out the rest of the quarter*
February 29, 1999	4.3	
March 8, 1999	4.4	
March 15, 1999	4.3	
March 22, 1999	4.0	

Well OK then. For the entire quarter, WCW averaged a 4.6 rating. And look at the ratings right around the Finger Poke of Doom. People were not turned off by it as the IWC would have you believe. All of these old stereotypes for what is a good and bad rating from the past have stopped us from seeing what is plain in numbers: people were entertained and tuned back in. They wanted to see what would happen next.

Over the next several months, the WWF picked up a lot more steam and WCW started to stall again. But that does not mean the Finger Poke of Doom drove away the fans. Quite the contrary, looking at the immediate numbers the following week, we can see they were acutely interested in what was going on.

Taking an interesting turn, we can also check the Thunder ratings. And wouldn't you know it: The January 7, 1999 edition of Thunder immediately following the Finger Poke of Doom was the highest rated Thunder EVER with a 4.3. This followed up with a 3.9 and two weeks at 4.2's. So for a month within the Finger Poke of Doom, the average WCW rating for its two main shows was a 4.5. I would say that that meant people were not turned off at all, and that the Finger Poke of Doom did not just increase interest in Nitro, but in WCW overall.

THE DEATH OF WCW

Yet we hear all the time how the Finger Poke killed WCW. During my research, I often found people who said the Finger Poke of Doom brought WCW to its end, and several people wrote in with the same comments every time I brought it up. It seems that to these people, the finger poke happened, everyone ran to WWF the next week, and WCW was immediately out of business.

Let's clear the air. WCW died on March 26, 2001, a full two years and nearly three months after the Finger Poke of Doom. As a matter of fact, by that point in time, neither Kevin Nash, Hulk Hogan, nor Eric Bischoff was really involved with WCW anymore (although Bischoff was trying to purchase it before AOL-TW pulled the plug on an actual show!). There seems to be this magical gap in memory that life went on for a long, long time, and WCW was profitable for quite a while after this event, too.

But as we just saw with the ratings, the Finger Poke did not only NOT drive away the fans, it led to some of the highest rated Nitros and Thunders on record. Those involved saw that what they had done was good for business, was good for WCW, and that meant it was the right thing to do all along.

ONE MORE TO THE PIN

With a simple push to the chest, wrestling history was changed in one night. The Finger Poke of Doom was the culmination of a plan to change the direction of WCW and accomplished so much in one little touch. Some would have you believe that this was a horrible mistake that immediately caused the end of WCW, but the numbers show the opposite as fan interest rose across the board in WCW with the Finger Poke of Doom. It was talked about, it was watched, and it made money in the long run.

The Finger Poke of Doom rarely has had anyone talk about all of the positives it has done. Instead, simple idle lines about it have tarnished reasonable thought for too long. Step back and look: The Finger Poke of Doom was amazing. It wasn't the horror that the IWC has claimed for so long, but was an enjoyable and shocking moment in wrestling history; a moment that will be remembered for a long time to come. So instead of wallowing in some supposed tragedy that never happened, let us remember how to enjoy the moment as it was.

The defense rests.

After the Trial

Hung Jury

IN THE CASE OF THE IWC VERSUS THE FINGER POKE OF DOOM, THE FINGER POKE HAS BEEN ACCUSED OF CAUSING THE DEATH OF WCW, DESTROYING ENJOYMENT IN WRESTLING, AND BEING ONE OF THE WORST SWERVES IN WRESTLING HISTORY THAT SENT THE FANS AWAY IN DROVES.

With 64% of the Finger Poke of Doom was found:

NOT GUILTY!

Whew, that was a close one! Every vote counted up until the last minute! Most people who voted guilty had legitimate reasons and expressed them to me, and I appreciate that. Some people, though—well, you know how message boards are. At least if you are going to accuse me of anything or lambaste my choice of topics, have some evidence to back it up!

Response

Although I dominated in the prior case, I knew this one was going to be an uphill battle:

> *I've read all your columns and certainly they're interesting, though I think you're sometimes too 'fanatic' about things. But you did convince me that Kevin Nash isn't an overpushed immobile heap of muscles, which IWC seems to imply quite often.*
>
> *However, I do not agree with the defense of Fingerpoke of Doom. You've got some valid points and some less valid (I don't think that ratings have too much to do with FoD. People might have watched WCW because they always watched it and even horrible things couldn't steer them away from TV. And, as Diva Search II proves, horrible things can draw ratings, but they're still horrible), but there is more to this.*
>
> *It was [the] WCW World Title. The straightest descendant of the first ever World Heavyweight Title. The Belt held by legends like Flair, Thesz,*

> Lewis. You don't give up the *fucking* most prized title in wrestling business. You don't fucking do this. This is where WCW failed. They presented the political power of [the] nWo as more important than anything else. Not even the big belt. Evil prevailed. People don't want to see things like that. Vince understood this. Despite all his on-screen power, he couldn't take the WWF belt from Austin - Austin could fight. And even when Vince was this close to winning, often his own troops fought among themselves to claim the belt, allowing Austin to sneak away in [the] chaos. Screwjobs are fine, political games are not. The most important championship belt shouldn't be subject to politics, or else it's worthless...man, I got carried away.
>
> To sum up, Fingerpoke is GUILTY!!
>
> Cheers,
> zv

So here we have outside evidence working its way in, especially emotional evidence to a piece of hardware that meant so much to so many. However, this was hardly the only reasoning:

> You made some good points with the Finger Point of Doom angle/storyline, but not enough to [convince] me. The angle still seems to me that a lot off bullshit by the same tired characters (Nash, Hogan, Hall and NWO in general) just to get the "oh my god" reaction that lasts for a few seconds, while the WWF was at the same time actually pulled off dramatic good matches and pushed new stars (Mankind, Rock) The latter stars went on to be some of the most successful stars in history while the former weren't even around for Nitro's final show.
>
> ...
>
> Nitro had some very good ratings after, but as your chart shows they went down fast and never went back up. It's the [epitome] of a hot shot angle (people watch to see if anything happens in the aftermath of a shocking angle, find out nothing of note happens and tune out)...

> *[Your] best points were the character motivations. You [obviously] are a much more sophisticated [viewer] than the average IWC and especially mark out there... The WCW needed to tell viewers (outright) that Nash was a greedy, money hungry guy, even reminding them about the t-shirt days and his old role in the NWO. Sometimes not being subtle is a way to drive angle home.*
>
> **Nicholas Wellbaum**

While I may not have been able to argue too much with someone's personal attachment to this history of an object, at least this one I could respond reasonably to:

> *I believe, though, you missed your own connection. The reasons the ratings went down a few months later were for the reasons you listed: the rising stars of the WWF. The WWF was getting hot, and WCW stopped long-term planning. It was not the Finger Poke of Doom that led to those lower ratings, but the storylines in WCW not being attractive enough and the storylines and wrestling in the WWF being more interesting. It would still be another half-year after that before ratings really began to hurt for WCW, not the direct result of the poke.*

These were the reasonable types. Others became increasingly agitable:

> *[G]reat booking strategy. [T]ake the title off of a popular champion to give it back to the desperate old man trying to cling to his spot. You must also understand that at that point wrestling was so huge even the [A.W.A.] could have drawn big business ([I] mean the A.W.A. with such stars as [M]aster [B]laster and [R]ocky [M]ountain [T]hunder.) [Y]our evidence is flimsy to say the least.*
>
> **Melanie Phillips**

> You make up ratings numbers, and your only defense is "the IWC is lying, the FOD did huge business" without any non-fabricated evidence to back it up.
>
> Your case was a joke, at best.
>
> **LiutenantSalt**

I did give the respondent my original source and told him to tell the source that their data was wrong and to keep me in the loop. Strangely, I never received a follow-up.

On the other end were those who absolutely loved it and would have voted "Not Guilty" no matter what:

> Thank you! I have been defending that match to my friends for years now. I think it was a brilliant swerve that worked for the characters and the storyline. I think the internet people were just upset because they got suckered in by a heel turn like they were normal marks.
>
> **Christopher Carroll**

> NOT GUILTY! If only we had more worked shoot incidents like this today, wrestling would be much edgier. I wasn't even alive when Lou Thesz was wrestling. Why am I supposed to uphold his legacy as the best???
>
> **Theo1923**

To which I responded:

> Well, I still love the history stuff, but I honestly do not believe this tarnished the World Title at all. And Lou Thesz had PLENTY of controversial finishes and screwjobs in his matches. People seem to have selective memories when it comes to information like that.

The real win, though, was on those I was able to turn:

> *Your points are well taken, I was one of those people that thought that The Finger Poke of Doom caused the demise of WCW, but you have made [me] see the error of my ways.*
> *Thanks!!!!!!!!!!!!*
>
> **Jose Torres**

> *Wow...just wow.*
>
> *I went into the article, expecting to disagree with you, and vote guilty. I still hate the angle, and feel it could have been executed in a way less infuriating manner, while still accomplishing the goals of reuniting the NWO. But hindsight is 20/20, and the IWC is full of armchair bookers who are sure that they could have done a much better job. (Thankfully, I have Adam Ryland's Total Extreme Warfare game to soothe my ego and show that I'm a great booker, hence why I don't have a column somewhere on the internet, ranting about the WWE roster cuts, etc.)*
>
> *Anyway, back on topic-I wanted to vote guilty, but quite frankly, facts are facts. You truly proved, via hard statistics that the fingerpoke didn't kill WCW, and may have helped ratings in the short term.*
>
> *I have no valid argument to any of the points you brought up, beyond my whole opinion of the angle, and it would serve no purpose to place an opinion against facts.*
>
> *Not guilty, and by a large margin. This wasn't even something I had to think about.*
>
> *Best Wishes,*
> **Chuck**

DUSTY RHODES: HEAD BOOKER

INTRO

SOME DAME WALKED INTO MY OFFICE AND SAID...

Steve Cook of Cook's Corner sent this thought along to me:

> *I have an idea for your column though... how about Dusty Rhodes as a booker? I'm not the biggest fan of his, which is kinda why I'd like to see you take him on.*

See people, this is what I'm talking about. Steve isn't a big fan of Dusty's but he's willing to have an open mind about him! That's the enlightened attitude I'm looking to create!

Or he's daring me with something he thinks I'll miserably fail at and the 411mania staff can laugh at me for the rest of my tenure.

Either way, I'll take the case!

WHY THIS?

As I said to Steve:

> *Dusty Rhodes as a booker is a great idea! I always read comments about what a terrible booker he is and the infamous "Dusty Finish", yet he was head booker for years in many different promotions, including running his own. If he was so terrible, why do promotions keep giving him a shot? This should be an interesting case!*

And that's the question that starts this all: Why was Dusty given the book in the first place?

ALL HAIL THE AMERICAN DREAM

Who is the "American Dream" Dusty Rhodes? For those born into the Rock and Wrestling era (like myself) or the New Generation or the nWo/Attitude era, all you may know about Dusty Rhodes is that he is a fat man with some funny sayings. You might ask yourself, why oh why would this man ever be allowed to be in the business, nonetheless allowed to run the show?

In 1966, the man born Virgil Runnels Jr. began training for wrestling under Joe Blanchard (who was also the father of future horseman great Tully Blanchard). Dusty had overcome childhood ailments that attacked his hip, learned to walk again, and went on to successfully play football for West Texas State. Being a man of determination, he wanted to take a chance at the wrestling business, and so began his two years of training.

Finally in 1968, Dusty made his debut in Pat O'Connor's Central States territory of the NWA. He found much success there and went on to defeat Tommy Martin for the NWA Central States Championship in the last month of the year. But real success would find him when he teamed up with "Dirty" Dick Murdock in the last year of the Age of Aquarius and the early Disco days to form the uber-hated Texas Outlaws. The Outlaws went on to cheat their way to a vast number of tag team championships, winning notoriety across the entire industry.

After the Texas Outlaws went their separate ways, Dusty moved on to the AWA, and then to Eddie Graham's NWA Florida. There, despite his cheating and heelish ways, the crowd began to cheer Dusty and force his face turn, a la the Rock in the late 1990's. It was there that Dusty became the "man of the people" and earned his nickname "The American Dream". He went on to capture a vast number of titles while battling all of the top heels of the time until finally defeating Harley Race in 1979 for his first of three NWA World Heavyweight Championships. He would quickly lose the title and not win it back until 1981. That reign only lasted a couple of months when he lost the title to Ric Flair, a win he would not get back until 1986 for his last NWA World Heavyweight Championship.

And what does this all prove? Dusty Rhodes had paid his dues and knew the wrestling industry. He did not become a head booker until 1983, seventeen years after he began training. There was a man who had traveled the world and done it all. He knew this industry from the inside out, so why not get a shot at running it?

THOSE FATEFUL SIX YEARS

From 1983 until 1989, Dusty Rhodes was head booker for the NWA, managing all of the top angles and storylines of the time. But it was not as if he was just thrust into power in 1983; there was long process to get there.

In 1974, Florida promoter Eddie Graham saw the potential in Dusty to not only be a star, but to be a leading man in the industry. His understanding of the audience and ability to draw and make money led Graham to show Dusty the other side of the business. He taught him what it takes to run a show, how to plot out matches, how to maintain and organize talent, and how to find new prospects for future growth. Dusty was an eager student and used all of these lessons in his personal career and in helping others.

In 1983, the wrestling landscape was changing as Ted Turner had already launched his SuperStation WTBS with Georgia Championship Wrestling as a keystone program. That year, with the larger audience outside Georgia, GWC television became World Championship Wrestling. The timeslot would go to Vince McMahon's WWF for less than a year in 1984 (WWF's World Championship Wrestling?), and quickly returned to the NWA with Jim Crocket Promotions. All this time, though, Dusty Rhodes had been given the book.

And with that book, did Dusty Rhodes put himself at the top of promotion? Contrary, he let Ric Flair run with the ball and the title, only once defeating him in 1986. But that win was a quick one, losing the title back to Flair less than two weeks later. Now wouldn't a man who was only interested in putting himself over give himself the title for years at a time? Instead, he completely separated himself from the title, making that one moment when he won that much more special.

The booking strategy was counter to what the WWF was presenting at the time. The WWF became all about cartoon characters and the Rock and Wrestling connection. Hulk Hogan was the perpetual champion, the babyface who could not be overcome. The NWA knew they needed to be a different product if they wanted to compete so they became all about the wrestling. Matches were the focus above characters (though there were still their fair share). More so, having the faces chase the heel made the fans clamor to see the evil Flair dethroned. Flair himself was an interesting performer for the fans and had the skills that the NWA wrestling audience loved to watch. Similar to Kurt Angle of 2005, Ric Flair was a man the fans loved to hate.

Dusty recognized all of this and made sure that this was the storyline of the 1980's for the NWA. Jim Crocket didn't always agree with the direction of NWA, and his decisions were often reflected on WCW television. But the committee was behind Dusty, and Dusty continued to change the concept of professional wrestling.

FUN WITH NUMBERS... ERRR... WORDS

With the landscape of professional wrestling shifting, Dusty knew he needed to take the NWA into other media markets. The first playground was with PPV by creating Starrcade and the Great American Bash. And I mean _creating_ them. He came up with the concepts, the name, and the cards. And how successful were these events? Well, 1987 Starrcade got a 3.3 buyrate, in 1988 1.8, and in 1989 a 1.3. And then the Great American Bash scored a 2.2 in 1988 and a 1.5 in 1989. Seeing the success of his initial PPVs, Dusty wanted to branch out even more and had the one and only Bunkhouse Stampede on January 24, 1988. And how did that no-name, never repeated PPV do? Oh, it scored a 3.5 PPV buyrate. Well, Dusty seemed to have some idea what he was doing, despite most people saying that the PPVs of the NWA were financial disasters. Check back in our Eric Bischoff case to see why we consider these to be "successful" PPVs.

By the way, a PPV buyrate translates into roughly 400,000 buys, in case you don't know. Do the math and multiple by about $20 a pop at the time. Now multiply times 3% to the N where N is equal to the number of years since the event and 3% is the average rate of inflation. That is how much money that PPV would have made today on buyrates alone! What? I left my calculator at work.

During this time, Dusty also came up with and booked one of the most beloved gimmick matches in all of wrestling, IWC and mark alike. War Games was a creation of Dusty Rhodes, a match won by the Road Warriors over JJ Dillon—hardly putting himself above the card again. Dusty even used his greatest creations to put others over huge instead of himself and keep his opponents strong (notably Ric Flair) in the long chase.

Still, despite everything he had done for the NWA, World Championship Wrestling television, and the business in general, Dusty Rhodes had to go.

REVENGE OF THE STARDUST

In 1989, JCP would fall on hard financial times. Despite the success of Dusty's PPVs and booking strategy, Crockett had made a number of bad financial decisions. He had been out acquiring rival promotions and signing wrestlers to guaranteed contracts in an effort to grow faster than Vince McMahon. This concentration on trying to beat McMahon without the business fundamentals first put JCP into bankruptcy.

Not wanting to see his highest rated television show just disappear, Turner acquired the assets of JCP and officially renamed it World Championship Wrestling, the same name as his television show. Concurrently, Ric Flair and Dusty Rhodes were in a bitter backstage feud on the future of Flair as champion. Dusty saw that it was now time to use Flair to make new stars, while Flair thought that he should continue to ride high and long with the title. Turner would not buy JCP without Flair (being a huge mark for the man), so the NWA sent Dusty packing and Turner put Jim Herd in charge. In turn, Herd made Ric Flair the head booker, and the early 90's went to Flair country in WCW.

Dusty took this opportunity to go the WWF where Vince tried to humiliate

Dusty for all of his years of booking against the WWF. Despite the polka dots, the plumbers, and everything else, Dusty remembered his lessons from Graham and his natural charisma and ability and was being cheered in the WWF at levels near Hulk Hogan. Once again, Dusty proved he knew the business.

Meanwhile, back in WCW, the wrestlers were revolting against Ric Flair constantly putting himself over, so he resigned from the booking committee and was replaced with Jim Barnett who also brought Jim Crockett back into the committee. This group reversed a lot of the booking decisions Flair had made and confused the fans to no end. Thus Barnett's reign quickly ended and Ole Anderson was given the book. Ole pushed older stars and was jobbing out the younger crew and driving them away in droves. This quickly led to him being fired at the end of 1990.

In January 1991, WCW decided only one man could book their show, only one man could help the fledgling WCW grow. And that man was none other than the "American Dream" Dusty Rhodes.

Dusty was through with wrestling on a regular basis, so this time around there was less worry over him wanting to put himself over (though he did not do that much, as we have previously seen). This time around, too, Dusty tried to help the younger wrestlers develop personalities and gimmicks. Sure, some of them were as bad as Oz, but others were as good as "Stunning" Steve Austin. The most important aspect is that he was out there trying to find new talent and give them a shot.

As I said in the Kevin Nash case, it is one thing to be given the opportunity, it is another thing entirely to run with it. Dusty Rhodes had gotten over with a polka dot gimmick. The gimmick does not matter, the performer does. Carlito probably has one of the silliest gimmicks going in 2005 on RAW, but the performer behind it makes it all believable and enjoyable.

Also during this time, the main event was shuffled up as more wrestlers were given an opportunity to show what they were made of. Scott Steiner received a shot against Ric Flair at Clash of the Champions in his first ever main event. Bobby Eaton also got a main event title shot in his first and only time headlining a show. Dusty was never trying to hold these guys back, only give them legs to run on. If they could not run that was hardly his fault. Sometimes people need time to develop (Kevin Nash needed another three years of seasoning before he was ready), and sometimes they are ready to go (Vader became a monster in WCW under Rhodes).

Rhodes also worked to get back the prospects and talents that Ole had chased away, including IWC favorite Cactus Jack. And understanding the direction of the industry towards athletic competition and again going against the cartoons of the WWF, Dusty created the short-lived Light Heavyweight Championship that was won by Brian Pillman. Perhaps he was a bit ahead of his time with this concept, but Dusty knew what the fans wanted to see: action.

In that vein, he went on to Starrcade 1991 with the Lethal Lottery Tag Team Tournament, pairing odd teams together in an action-packed evening.

Still, business was not turning around fast enough for Herd, and Herd also failed in his negotiations with Ric Flair, losing the World Heavyweight Champion to the WWF. So at SuperBrawl 1992, Dusty was given his last night with the book by the desperate Herd. Going out with a bang, Dusty had the 17-minute Pillman-Liger classic for the Light Heavyweight Championship and Sting over Luger for the World Heavyweight Championship in Luger's last match before going on to the World Bodybuilders Federation. And despite drawing a 0.96 buyrate (well above our success range), Dusty was pushed down to the announce booth and Cowboy Bill Watts took over the committee.

ON THE SIDELINES?

When Jim Herd removed Dusty Rhodes from his position as head booker, did you think it would be the end of Dusty Rhodes in a creative capacity? Of course not!

Herd may have been too impatient to turn business around, but at the very least he realized he was not the man to do it and men like Dusty Rhodes would have to be the answer. Besides, WCW was still on hard times and the last thing he would have wanted was for Dusty to go back to Vince. So Dusty remained on as an announcer and occasional wrestler, but lent a hand behind the scenes, pitching ideas and pushing for the next generation.

Time marched on. Eric Bischoff came in and took over. But Dusty was not pushed to the side. Bischoff took him in as a confident, let him continue to pitch ideas and be a part of the creative process. Dusty got to see his protégées Scott Hall and Kevin Nash rise to prominence in the nWo, all while helping Bischoff recognize that wrestling was the key to WCW's continued success. The Cruiserweight Championship took prominence much like the Light Heavyweight Championship of the past. The wrestlers controlled the in-ring action, not the writers. Dusty's fingerprints could be seen on every episode of Nitro and Saturday Night during WCW's only profitable time.

But much like looking for the superstars of tomorrow, Rhodes also looked for the future bookers—the people who could lead the program long after he was gone—much like Eddie Graham did for him. And he found such a man in Kevin Nash.

Rhodes had this to say in an interview conducted in June 2001:

> *"Creatively, Kevin is very good and we worked well together.*

> "He was just coming into his own [on the Booking Committee] when the company made changes. Kevin is very modern, but still sees things old-school. He's so in-tune with the atmosphere of the country, and that helps. I often was more of the old-fashioned cowboy, but he was into other things ... but could combine our thinking.
>
> "I think he's a real force as far as a creative person."

See, Dusty was not just about trying to give himself power or put his friends over. Much like a parent with his children, Dusty wanted his successors to be better than him. And humbly he admitted that Nash was the better man for the job during that phase of WCW, not himself.

Dusty went on to talk about some of their booking decisions:

> "With the Lenny & Lodi characters, we were way ahead of our time, obviously.
>
> "Corporate people came in one day and said, 'Shut that down.' We objected, but they didn't listen. The funny thing is, the ending to that whole [story line] was that they were just brothers.
>
> "Everyone always wanted us to say they were gay, but they weren't, [which would have come to light had the storyline been fully developed.]"

There it is again. There was no off the cuff booking going on. Dusty always had a plan, but others were too quick to judge. Given the chance, Dusty could have the best long-term storylines going on any level of the card. But with so many political influences going on, Dusty would soon be out again.

CH-CH-CH-CHANGES!

With the dawn of the Vince Russo era and the change of direction of WCW corporate, Dusty soon found himself removed from WCW in general. He took a trip down to ECW to help get Steve Corino over, but that was only a part-time gig.

During this period, Dusty also started Turnbuckle Championship Wrestling.

In an interview with the Wrestling Digest, Dusty had this to say about TCW:

> "After I got fired from WCW... I walked out the door there and said, `I'm gonna take it one step farther. It's my vocation, and I love it, I've done well at it, I've had my ups and downs, so I said I want to start something that's really meaningful and in the next three or four years will really mean something."

And so Dusty started to train eight young competitors in the business before launching TCW. But TCW was not about just lining Rhodes pockets, as some would have you believe:

> "The between 40 and 60 guys we turned down, financially would've made me pretty wealthy, but they had no place to go, no place to do anything but be smartened up and, my god, enough people in this country have been smartened up to my business, so I'm gonna turn the tide back around."

Rhodes used his booking aptitude to gain a following for TCW, expanding from Georgia into Florida, North Carolina, Alabama, and Tennessee. His goal consistently remained to become the #2 company to the WWE, and to later overtake it.

When WCW folded, TCW became the haven for exiled WCW stars without guaranteed contracts that Vince was not interested in, such as Daffney, Scotty Riggs, Lodi, and Larry Zybzsko (see the later chapter). Rhodes wanted to use those with talent who would not fit in with the WWE get a shot and to help build his promotion.

Still, Rhodes did not just want to use names to sell his cards. He understood what we in the IWC have realized for a while:

> "You're gonna see television become not as important for promoting your talent as the Web, and the Web sites and computers and all that knowledge will be in the next five years. You're gonna see that come into play more than how many syndications or how many syndicated cities your show goes on."

Rhodes as a booker embraced today's technology instead of trying to fight it. The future seemed like it could be bright for the creative Rhodes and TCW.

An Old Enemy Comes A-Knockin' and Some New Friends

Someone beside the fans of TCW noticed the efforts that Dusty put in as head booker. In July 2002, Vince McMahon arranged a meeting with Dusty Rhodes to recruit him to a booking position in the WWE. Much like the Vince Russo's tryout, the WWE environment was not one for Dusty Rhodes. His decisions would butt heads too much with Vince McMahon, and Vince could have none of that.

In another interview with IGN Sports, Dusty was asked his opinion of what a booker means:

> **IGN Sports:** One of your roles traditionally has been not only as a wrestler, but as a booker. What exactly is the role of a booker backstage?
>
> **Dusty Rhodes:** It's a head coach, it's an executive producer of television, it's all of those things wrapped into one. Now, though, it's done more by committee where they have all of these writers writing the pay-per-views like Survivor Series, and that works, but I'm from that school where it's my ball and if we're going to play with my ball, I'll pick the music, I'll tell them when to play it, I'll pick what interviews to do, I'll write the show, I'll be the executive producer, and I'll be the star of that son of a bitch. That's the way it was. That was the role of a booker. There are no more bookers any more. That term is gone. I was probably the last of what you'd call bookers. It's the head coach, the head guy. The whole deal.

Dusty could not be part of a committee, and he did not see a future as a booker, so he returned to TCW to continue to train the next generation.

Meanwhile, a couple of other exiles had formed another promotion known as Total Nonstop Action. TNA already had a PPV distribution deal and had financing well beyond TCW. Dusty realized that he had already lost the battle to be #2, so he had one choice: when you can't beat them, join them.

Dusty started making appearances for TNA and later closed shop on TCW in 2003. But it was not until 2004 when TNA handed the book over to Dusty.

Do you see this continued pattern? People keep coming back to Dusty Rhodes as a booker! Does that sound like the resume of a failure? Why would people who have made millions off of this business continually return to Dusty Rhodes if he were as bad as many claim.

It's because he is not. He is a competent, long-term, old-school thinker. He is a man who wants to push young talent and recognize the legends of the past. He also understands when others are better than he is.

The Wrestling Observer recapped their interview with Dusty Rhodes by saying:

> *Dusty says that as well as Jeff Jarrett has done, he knew that AJ Styles and Abyss were the two men to bring it home at Lockdown.*
>
> *Dusty really wants to see TNA work. He thinks the 6 sided ring has worked out well. He is very high on Shocker. He hopes to tap into the Latino audience. Bryan asks about coaching on interviews. Dusty has been working with AJ Styles a lot. He is trying to bring his natural great personality out of him. That's the one thing missing with him right now. Dusty jumps back to Crockett. He says when Magnum TA went down, that was another big loss. He saw him as the next Hogan. He says that era was no different to now. The interviews are as important as the in-ring product. Dusty doesn't like long backstage interviews, but gave Raven extra time this week because it was such a great interview.*

A lot covered in that short paragraph, but here's the story:

(1) Dusty does not suck up to the bosses and does what is best for the product and the fans

(2) Dusty wants to make an environment that is in unique, wrestling-intensive, and counter-WWE

(3) Dusty recognized overall trends in society and wants to tap into them (IE, Latinos are far outpacing the Gringo growth-rate in the economy)

(4) Dusty works hard to help the younger stars be better than themselves and move into the roles of tomorrow

(5) Dusty did not want to hold Magnum TA down to make himself look better, but wanted Magnum to surpass him in the business

(6) Dusty does not want to waste time in back, but likes to have action in the ring

Dusty has an obvious understanding of the product, and even more so of himself:

> *"Bruce (Springsteen), 'The Boss,' is still singing at his age, and I'm still singing, but I by no means think that I'm gonna draw a tremendous amount of people anymore. We use Dusty Rhodes... as an anchor to get other people over."*

And what more could one ask for from their booker than that?

Still, this was not enough for TNA in the short term. Much like the Lenny/Lodi storyline, TNA did not fully understand where Dusty was going with such issues as the Monty Brown heel turn and Outlaw/BG James situation. And since they removed him before those storylines could finish, they were booked into the corner. Who knows what great twists Dusty might have had for us in the end?

But this will not be the last shot for Dusty. Every era has found a reason to return to Dusty Rhodes: Head Booker, and the book will call Dusty back again.

> *Dusty, in fact, did reach further acclaim—most especially after returning to the WWE several months after this was originally written. At various points he held a "creative consultant" role and eventually ended up being head writer and creative director for NXT. Later, he stepped back into a more sporadic performer role before finally passing at the age of 69 on June 11, 2015*

THE DUSTY FINISH

Dusty Rhodes has done a lot for this business with his time at the top, but one thing is named after him: the Dusty Finish.

The Dusty Finish takes many forms. In the most popular form, a ref is knocked out and a second ref comes down. The second ref counts the win for the face, but the first ref revives and reverses the decision. In another variation, the ref misses something, like the heel having his feet on the ropes, and reverses the decision later. Or in yet another version, the two aforementioned refs are in the ring at the same time, and each counts the other opponents shoulders down.

Basically, somehow a match decision gets reversed.

Now let's get a few things straight:

These types of finishes existed long before Dusty Rhodes was born. They were used all around the world as champions took on the local challengers. Dusty Rhodes also used these on the local NWA circuits, but used them on television as much as the WWE does today. But dirt sheets of the day compared local arena results and saw a pattern, and thus started to blame Dusty.

These old school dirt sheet writers were the first people on the internet, and their description of this type of ending as a "Dusty Finish" persisted through time. So even though we are in a whole generation and half of readers later, the term Dusty Finish has taken a negative connotation.

When used correctly, though, the Dusty Finish is just what it takes to keep a good storyline going. I was at a WCW house show when Hollywood Hogan had just turned face and was feuding with the heel President Flair. Hogan won the match, but Flair reversed the decision and remained champion. The fans got to see an exciting match and see their hero win, but nothing changed for TV and the real ending could be done on PPV. The fans went home happy, and things kept on going.

Did Dusty Rhodes use this finish a lot? Sure he did. Did he use it effectively in local markets making it so only a small segment of the market realized this was happening on a larger scale? Absolutely. I will never claim that a small minority cannot have a major impact (see: the PTC or World Wildlife Fund vs. WWF/E), but I will never claim that a minority of viewers reflect the opinions of the majority of the audience.

While the internet audience today is much larger than the WWE has given it credit for until recent weeks, the dirt sheets never came near the levels of some of the lowest hit wrestling websites. The vast majority of the audience was not as outraged as these people were, yet it is their opinion that has persisted. My father was privy to these events, but he was a casual fan, not a reader of the sheets. He enjoyed what he saw, and never once uttered the term "Dusty Finish".

GOIN' TO THE PAY WINDOW!

Dusty Rhodes as Head Booker has been misunderstood for several reasons. First, dirt sheet writers of the past laid the path for the internet, and their early biases affected the development of the budding IWC. As time went on, these prejudices continued to be displayed in so many people's writings, and thus were instilled in a generation and half of readers.

But as we have seen, Dusty took a successful career in the ring and parleyed it into a successful booking career on top of the NWA. And despite being shown the door, he's been brought back time and time again because he gets the job done. He brings in the money, he brings in the talent, and he brings in the ratings. Dusty grows new talent, honors the past, and recognizes his own flaws.

Some would have you believe that Dusty is all about himself. His decisions and notes, though, show that he is concerned more with the young talents and the future of the business, even if that means hurting himself. Dusty is gone from the books for now, but he'll be back, because he is that good.

Dusty Rhodes has worked hard as head booker, and he deserves his chance to shine.

The defense rests.

After the Trial

Hung Jury

IN THE CASE OF THE IWC VERSUS DUSTY RHODES: HEAD BOOKER, RHODES HAS BEEN ACCUSED OF BEING A TERRIBLE BOOKER WHO DID NOT DESERVED HIS POSITION, ONLY PUT HIMSELF OVER WITH THAT POWER, NEVER TRIED TO BUILD A BRAND MORE THAN HIS OWN SELFISH GOALS, AND USING REPETITIVE BOOKING THAT DROVE FANS AWAY IN DROVES.

With 81.5% of the vote, Dusty Rhodes: Head Booker was found:

NOT GUILTY!

Less votes than the Finger Poke of Doom, that's for sure, but still a good showing for a true legend. Sadly, the man I set out to do the case for, Steve Cook, voted guilty! Way to turn your back on the guy, Steve. Thankfully, Dusty had me and 81.5% of the audience on his side instead of you. And then I plug you anyway?! What's the matter with me?

Response

What was especially fun about a case like this is how much it was history lesson for the readers and me. For those who lived through it, though, it gave them the chance for nostalgia and to teach the next generation:

Never was a Dusty fan but give him his due as a great booker. He also booked Championship Wrestling from Florida for several years in the early 80s. They were ahead of their time with:

1) *Occult storylines: Kevin Sullivan and his merry band of [Satanists]*
2) *[Impromptu] TV matches: Gave the show an unpredictable feel kinda like Raw shoots for*
3) *multipart angles: Example: JJ Dillon digging into Dusty's skeletons in the closet in several weekly segments. (think Dibiase's investigation of Bossman)*
4) *characters: Dusty knew he had to have a "hook" to get people interested.*

CWF was ahead of its time and had the most unpredictability and action out of all the wrestling I watched during that time period. Not that [it's] an exhaustive sample but does include World Class, WWF and Jim Crockett's Mid Atlantic territory.

Chris Pineo

I grew up watching [M]id-[A]tlantic [C]hampionship [W]restling and right after the first Starcade... you could definitely see a difference in the product. During these times[,] there was a live house show every other weekend at the Richmond coliseum... the main event was always the same..."Ric Flair vs Dusty... Ric Flair vs Dusty"[.] Then He alternated with Terry "Magnum TA" Allen. After Allen's car accident Then he alternated the card with Nikita Koloff.

Unfortunately after Starcade Crockett lost of major stars (Steamboat, Piper, Valentine) not saying Rhoads had anything to do with these guys leaving, but just reading interviews with these guys (Steamboat in particular said When Rhoads came in... He said he was going to be the number one babyface)...

But anyway... [that's] my take on the matter.... [your] article made a lot of good points... Dusty wasn't the worst booker in NWA/JCP/CWF history... But it was very irritating to watch the decline of Mid-Atlantic Championship wrestling during those years.

Christopher Grosvenor

I lived and [breathed] WTBS wrestling from 79 until its end. Those Dusty years were some of the best for JCP, the NWA and the fans. The gimmicks [weren't] too over the top (don't say Lasertron because he was cool in an uncool costume) and the action topped just about everything going on in the WWF.

Chad Eiler

I first got into wrestling because of JCP circa 1985-86, and it was booked by Dusty. A lot of people on the internet praise JCP, yet at the same time seem to give no credit to the man who ran the show. If you watch old tapes from those days, you'll notice that the fans go nuts (and I mean nuts!) for the faces and boo loudly for the heels. Everyone and I mean even Sam Houston was over like crazy! ...

Dusty created new stars and booked them to seem like they were the best in the business (and usually they were. Tully Blanchard, Arn Anderson, Magnum T.A. Rock'n' Roll Express, Ron Garvin, Nikita Koloff, Midnight Express, Barry Windham, and arguably the Road Warriors and Ric Flair had their greatest fame during that time frame. Lex Luger and Sting had their first pushes to superstardom under Dusty. Did Dusty book himself as the top face? Sure, [because] he was a huge draw and already a legend, but by late 1986, he was NOT in the main events with Flair. He let the new guys take over (Lex, Koloff, et al.) If you notice, the old Mid-Atlantic guys who were at the top in 1984 were phased out and the new, younger, hipper stars were phased in in 1985 - which ended up drawing lots of money. Look at the line up for Starcade 1984 and then for Starcade 1985 to see the difference[.]

Nick

EARL HEBNER SCREWING BRET HART

INTRO

SOME DAME WALKED INTO MY OFFICE AND SAID...

It all started when I got an e-mail from the promo-man himself, <u>Tim Hamilton</u>:

> *Some ideas I have thought of that would work well for your column include... the Montreal Screwjob and how Vince did what he had to do (obvious choice).*

That was soon followed up when my number one detractor **MATTHEW ROBERTS** suggested a number of topics he felt were better than some upcoming cases I shared with him:

> *Defending McMahon, Michaels, Hebner, and Triple H against the Montreal [Screwjob.] Yes, Bret screwed [Bret]. [Bret] should have done business the right way instead of being a mark for himself. It actually helped [Bret]'s failing career. [Bret] should stop being bitter.*

And even very recently I heard from **Gino** who had this to say:

> *I don't know if you have done it yet, but can you defend Vince for screwing Bret? If nothing else, it's a challenge.*

And the answer to all of them is this:

No.

Why this?

Well, actually, to MATTHEW Roberts it is "kind of".

You see, I will not defend Vince for screwing Bret. Don't get me wrong, it has nothing to do with what happened in the ring.

When Vince and Bret were backstage, Vince lied straight to Bret's face and said Bret could have it his way, and that was the end of it. Right there, Vince lost any ground he would have had. I do not defend lies on this scale, despite intentions. He had the option to refuse Bret, to say he'd think about it, or to not give him any answer. Instead, he said Bret was right, and that it was fine and dandy. For that reason, Vince McMahon will not be defended here.

But don't read into this too much; I am not anti-Vince. As you will see at the end of this case, he is defendable in many other circumstances, and I'll be glad to defend him then.

Now, this case is NOT about whether or not the Montreal Screwjob should have happened. Vince should not have lied to Bret to his face, this is true. Bret should not have tried to leave with the title. Leaving with the title hurts a promotion (see Ric Flair: Real World Champion or Medusa and a trash can). Both of these parties were in the wrong for their wants and actions. But one man was stuck in the middle... literally. And one man still gets blamed for it all across the great white north.

You Screwed Bret

Until a few days before this was originally published, Earl Heber was employed by World Wrestling Entertainment as a referee on RAW. As part of the WWE circuit, the RAW crew found themselves in Canada three or four times a year. And every time they went there, Earl would hear this chant:

"You screwed Bret! You Screwed Bret!"

On November 9, 1997 at Survivor Series, Shawn Michaels had Bret Hart locked in his own finishing move—the Sharp Shooter—and Hebner called for the bell. Shawn Michaels was declared the winner and new WWF Champion, and Heber was raced out of the ring.

He ran through the locker room and straight into a waiting car running in the parking lot that was set to drive him to the hotel to grab his things and then straight to the airport. Hebner would have the next two days of RAW tapings off. Unfortunately, Hebner was not quick enough at the hotel and some wrestlers made it back there while he was still collecting his possessions. A good friend of Bret Hart's confronted Hebner and asked him how he could screw over his friend like that. Fearing for his safety, Hebner said he was so mad about it he would quit the company. This, of course, would not happen. But this was not some backstage dealings we are talking about, but the man's safety. Hebner needed to get out the country, and he did.

Yes, Hebner was definitely in on the plot to screw Bret Hart, someone Hart considered one of his closest friends in the industry. Why would Hebner screw over his friend like that? Why would Hebner put himself at great personal physical risk for this? Why would he take the chance that he'd be ostracized from every other worker in the company?

> **TRY THINKING FOR YOURSELVES BEFORE YOU PELT AN INNOCENT MAN WITH CIGARETTES!**

Because Earl Hebner was doing his job.

And this is where people get confused. I think the best example comes from the film Clerks:

> **LISTENER 1:** It's not that easy to quit [smoking].
>
> **ACTIVIST:** Of course it's not; not when you have people like this mindless cretin so happy and willing to sell you nails for your coffin!
>
> **DANTE:** Hey, now wait a sec...
>
> **ACTIVIST:** Now he's going to launch into his rap about how he's just doing his job; following orders. Friends, let me tell you about another bunch of hate mongers that were just following orders: they were called Nazis, and they practically wiped a nation of people from the Earth... just like cigarettes are doing now! Cigarette smoking is the new Holocaust, and those that partake in the practice of smoking or sell the wares that promote it are the Nazis of the nineties! He doesn't care how many people die from it! He smiles as you pay for your cancer sticks and says, "Have a nice day."
>
> **DANTE:** I think you'd better leave now.
>
> **ACTIVIST:** You want me to leave? Why? Because somebody is telling it like it is? Somebody's giving these fine people a wake-up call?!
>
> **DANTE:** You're loitering in here, and causing a disturbance.

> **ACTIVIST:** You're the disturbance, pal! And here... (slaps a dollar on the counter) I'm buying some... what's this? ... Chewlie's Gum. There. I'm no longer loitering. I'm a customer, a customer engaged in a discussion with other customers.
>
> **LISTENER 2:** (to DANTE) Yeah, now shut up so he can speak!
>
> **ACTIVIST:** Oh, he's scared now! He sees the threat we present! He smells the changes coming, and the loss of sales when the nonsmokers finally demand satisfaction. We demand the right to breathe cleaner air!
>
> **LISTENER 3:** Yeah!
>
> **ACTIVIST:** We'd rather chew our gum than embrace slow death! Let's abolish this heinous practice of sucking poison, and if it means ruffling the feathers of a convenience store idiot, then so be it!
>
> **DANTE:** That's it, everybody out.
>
> **ACTIVIST:** We're not moving! We have a right, a constitutional right, to assemble and be heard!
>
> **DANTE:** Yeah, but not in here.
>
> **ACTIVIST:** What better place than this? To stamp it out, you gotta start at the source!
>
> **DANTE:** Like I'm responsible for all the smokers!
>
> **ACTIVIST:** The ones in this town, yes! You encourage their growth, their habit. You're the source in this area, and we're going to shut you down for good! For good, cancer-merchant!
>
> (The small crowd begins to chant and jeer in DANTE's face.)
>
> **CROWD:** Cancer merchant! Cancer merchant! Cancer merchant!

In the grand scheme of things, the fact that Hebner was in on the screwjob and part of it does not make him one of the worst people on Earth. Yes, always following orders is not the smart or ethical thing to do, and you should stand up for your beliefs. I was not backstage, but I am sure Hebner expressed his disappointment in what he was going to be a part of. Still, when you weigh your options, and you look at your choices, just because you choose the path of the bad guy it does not mean you are always bad.

Standing by and doing nothing is an atrocity, but no one's lives were on the line. No nations were going to be overrun, no people oppressed and killed, and no years of war were going to follow. There was going to be backlash and regret, but at no point was Hebner putting anyone but himself at physical risk.

Dante was just selling cigarettes; it was people's choice whether or not to buy them. He personally did not agree with them but was not about to force his opinions down their throat. He'd be out of a job with nothing to show for it. No one would stop smoking from listening to him. Even the Chewlie's Gum representative couldn't do it, as one of the pelting parties bought a package of cigarettes immediately following this scene.

If Earl Hebner had made a moral stand, what would have happened? He would have been fired. I turn you to Week Forty-Two of Fact or Fiction:

> *6. Earl Hebner should not have been fired by WWE after the loyalty he showed in the Montreal Screwjob.*
>
> *Stephen Randle:* **FICTION.** *Hell, the Montreal Screwjob actually sets the precedent. Nobody (except Vince's family, and I wouldn't hold him to it) is untouchable. Loyalty, friendship, they don't mean anything if you do things like [publicly embarrass] the company, get in the way of company plans, or, in this case, apparently steal from the company. Steal a car, go to jail. Steal from Vince (or any boss, really), go to the unemployment line and be thankful you aren't in the spoon position with Jimmy Hoffa.*

Randle has it right. Hebner would have been fired on the spot for not doing his job. And two things would have happened. One, the screwjob would still happen because some other ref would be in there who would listen to Vince. Two, Hebner would have nowhere to go. WCW was full of referees at the time. Being fired means he would not have been part of the angle, so there would be no interest from that perspective to bring him in. Referees are not like wrestling personalities, and although they play an important role in the pace and layout of a match, they do not add enough that a company would just hire more. Even though WCW was making money hand over fist at the time, they still would not just hire anyone. Maybe Bret could have pulled some strings, but that was not a guarantee, and he might have been upset with Hebner for not telling him in the first place. There was simply too much risk.

On the same note, Earl could not go back to the independents. He had worked for years on the independent scene to get to the WWF, but there was no guarantee of work there either. There were plenty of young refs out there already who worked cheap enough part time that Earl would never find any work. Also backstage, his brother Dave worked in a management capacity. Dave, too, would feel the backlash effect of Earl's actions, just like he has now with the merchandizing scandal.

But why should we listen to another outsider? Let's ask Referee Scott Dickinson his thoughts:

> **Question 11:** Earl Hebner: Loyal company employee, or backstabbing two-faced phony?
>
> **Scott Dickinson:** Earl did what he had to do under very tough circumstances.
>
> **Question 31:** If you were in Earl Hebner's position and had a family to support and your career on the line, would you have gone through with the double-cross, knowing you'd lose your best friend?
>
> **Scott Dickinson:** Since I was never full time [it's] hard to answer but I would [probably] be a company guy.

Just because you are doing a job, it does not make you responsible for everything. Earl Hebner was told to do something, and it was going to happen with or without him. He weighed his options and saw what he was doing was not the worst thing in the world. Even the man he was hurting, Bret Hart, was going to be fine. Bret already had a $3 million a year guaranteed contract at WCW waiting for him. There really was not that much to worry about aside from his own personal health.

In an interview with Alan Wojcik, Dennis "Mideon" Knight had this to say about the Montreal Screwjob:

> The only bad thing that no one talks about is Earl Hebner who refereed that match, he almost quit the business. He took tons of heat but he did what the boss told him to do. How did Bret get screwed when he left and went... to the highest contract in wrestling history?

THE SEEDS WERE PLANTED 10 YEARS BEFOREHAND

What is even more amazing, though, is that this type of action is not out of the nature of Earl Hebner the character. I refer you to Saturday Sentinel with Professor Newton Gimmick (which was lifted from 1wrestling which in turn lifted it from Wikipedia):

> Hebner debuted as a referee during a WWF World Heavyweight Championship match pitting champion Hulk Hogan against challenger André the Giant, which aired live on February 5, 1988, on NBC's The Main Event. Hebner's twin brother, Dave, was the assigned official, but unbeknownst to Hogan, André's manager, Ted DiBiase, had bribed Earl to take his brother's place. Earl then counted André's pin against Hogan, even though Hogan's shoulders were clearly off the mat. As André and DiBiase were celebrating (with André quickly "selling" his title to an overjoyed DiBiase), Dave Hebner - whom DiBiase had locked in a closet prior to the match - ran to the ring and confronted Earl. Hogan turned around just in time to see the two brothers arguing and Earl knock down his brother.

And I had almost forgotten this! Earl Hebner the character debuted in a screwjob, that is his MO. Not only that, Earl was such a successful con artist that over time he convinced us that he was the good referee and that Dave was actually the evil one that DiBiase had paid off. We had been fooled for almost ten years into believing that Earl was actually a good man looking out for the best interests of the faces. But he often chose interesting methods to get there.

Let us not forget that he later intentionally screwed over Triple H in favor of the Rock. Or that he was often seen "toasting" in the ring with Steve Austin. Hebner the character definitely had personal biases and never hid them. He would kick a heel's hand off the rope who was using it for leverage instead of making them break the hold. That goes far beyond refereeing, and straight into full blown personal interference.

The character of Earl Hebner was definitely the type to do the screwjob. He had done it before, and would do it again.

A CASE WITHOUT TALKING ABOUT BUYRATES?

Meanwhile, back in the real world, Hebner the person was rewarded for his actions and for protecting the company. As we have recently learned, Earl was making upwards of $500,000 a year, even more than Johnny Ace, head of talent relations. Earl could not have known this was going to happen, as he just wanted to protect his initial paycheck and his family. But the rewards were there for him proving that he at least did the right thing for his own personal life.

Yes, he did lose a good friend in the process, but even Bret Hart has forgiven Hebner for his role in the Montreal Screwjob. In an interview with Steve Gerweck, the Hitman had this to say:

> **SG:** Are you still friends with referee Earl Hebner?
>
> **BH:** No, I'm not friends with any of them. At the same time, I don't carry around a lot of anger. Earl Hebner is really just a victim.

If Bret Hart isn't bothered that Hebner screwed him, then why are any of us?

THE OLD 1-2-3

Earl Hebner was a man with one of the best jobs in the world: a referee for the WWE. He did not want to jeopardize his career or his family in 1997, and knew nothing was going to stop the oncoming storm. So he weighed his options, saw that everyone was going to be safe and monetarily secure in the end, took a big personal physical risk, and then screwed Bret Hart.

But in the end, Hart forgave Earl, and knew Earl had to do what he had to do. The character of Earl Hebner also knew that this is what he had always done and would do again. Everything made sense on the camera, and the world was safe backstage.

Earl Hebner screwed Bret Hart. No one is denying that. But for Earl Hebner the person and character, it was the correct choice to make, and he was justified in his decision.

Hebner may have lost his way over time with his large paycheck, but that does not change history. What happened in 1997 occurred just as it was supposed to: with Earl Hebner as the ref that screwed Bret.

The defense rests.

After the Trial

Hung Jury

IN THE CASE OF THE IWC VERSUS EARL HEBNER SCREWING BRET HART, HEBNER HAS BEEN ACCUSED OF BEING JUST LIKE A NAZI FOR FOLLOWING ORDERS TO END THE MATCH IN MONTREAL AND NOT DOING THE RIGHT THING FOR BRET HART AND THE WRESTLING WORLD.

And with some decidedly split decisions, having just 59.8% of the vote, Earl Hebner Screwing Bret Hart was found:

NOT GUILTY!

I feel like I could have converted about 10% more of the people if I had addressed one issue: According to Dave Meltzer, Bret Hart said that Earl Hebner said, "I swear on my kids lives that I'd quit my job before double-crossing you." And many of you called me out on this and asked how I could defend Earl Hebner for lying to Bret Hart but not Vince? Well, here's my answer:

I knew about this statement well beforehand but chose not to include it because I do not believe it is corroborated evidence. Look at what I wrote: Dave Meltzer said that Bret Hart said that Earl Hebner said. That's third hand evidence, what I would call hearsay at best. We do not know enough about what was really said, if those even were Earl's words, or just the words Bret wanted to hear (i.e., as time went on, Bret believed what he thought he heard in his head until he was positive it was exactly what he heard). We also do not know if Earl knew about the plan at this point or if he did not find out until the next morning. I personally believe Earl said something to the effect of "I'll make sure nothing bad happens to you" meaning that he'd make sure Bret was not physically hurt. And that's exactly what Earl Hebner did; he kept Bret Hart physically safe and sent him on his way.

Since this isn't a speculation piece, though, I did not want to address it. I do not believe it is firm evidence of anything Earl may have said, and I do not have any evidence to attack it, only opinion. Therefore, those of you who voted guilty, I'd ask you to rethink your position since you are basing it off of a most likely false statement.

RESPONSE

Of course, my response was not the end of the controversy. Among the many responses was:

> *Hey[,] I just wanted to comment on what you said about Dave Meltzer saying Bret said Earl said etc.*
>
> *I know the case is closed and all that jazz but just so you know, I watched Wrestling with Shadows for the first time last week, and there is a scene where Earl Hebner says to Bret "I swear on my kids I'm not going to screw you."*
>
> *It wasn't hearsay, the words came out of his mouth on camera.*
>
> *Just wanted to pass that on. Thanks for your time.*
>
> **- Jed Winter**

To which I replied:

> *Did Earl really say it or did Bret say Earl said it? I'll have to watch it again when I get home, I am having no recollection what-so-ever of this scene!*

Similarly:

> *I'm sure I'm not the only one that is going to e mail you but here goes: On Wrestling with Shadows Bret says himself that Earl swears on his kids that he [wouldn't] let anything happen. Dave Meltzer might have said that Bret said it because it is true. If I remember correctly it shows Earl in black in white while Bret says this. I think it's right after Bret talks to Vince.*
>
> *Thank you for your time,*
> **Devin Coleman**

And at the time I said:

> *I haven't seen it for a while, so I'm not sure about this scene. That said, if Bret is the one who said it, I'm still not convinced that those were Earl's exact words, or what Bret believes he heard.*

Due to the wonders of modern technology, I was able to re-watch the scene in question. At about the 1 hour | 14 minute mark, Bret Hart is talking to his wife and she is asking him what if something goes wrong. Suddenly, it cuts to a black and white image of Earl Hebner in the ring, ominous music starts, and Bret says:

> *Well I don't have to worry about the referee tomorrow because I talked to Earl. He swore on his kids that he's not going to let anything happen... and I can trust Earl.*

So here again we don't have Earl Hebner saying anything; we have Bret Hart's impression of what he allegedly said. But as noted above: I was able to view this with modern technology and was able to separate out the audio. These words are not from the conversation Bret was having with his wife; they are directly mic'd in a clear method without the background and quality of the recording in the seconds just beforehand. That means that this audio comes from some other conversation. Did it come before the screwjob, or afterwards? Editing put it in a place to make us think this is what he was saying this to his wife, but it seems more like he was telling a present-tense story or telling the thoughts in his head after-the-fact. Perhaps the experience of the event tainted his view of what happened? Or perhaps, more so, Bret was casting his own version of history for his own purposes—whether it was conscious or not?

Other than addressing this scene, there is one other thing I could have done better:

> *If we are asking if Earl was justified in the decision to "screw" Bret, then I'd happily change my vote to Not Guilty.*
>
> **Brian K. Eason**

I would like to have said that I lost only one vote due to semantics, but it was a lot more than that!

VINCE MCMAHON NOT BUYING OUT WCW'S CONTRACTS

INTRO

SOME DAME WALKED INTO MY OFFICE AND SAID...

Fixxer315 came in with a very convincing story about the InVasion and why Vince did not fail at it. Fixxer had a number of valid points, and I'd rather address them as we go than print them all here. The only problem was that there was too much to cover, and I wanted to focus on particular aspect in of the InVasion: the very beginnings.

But I don't even want to print what I wrote back to Fixxer because I think that will give too much away. So without further ado...

WHY THIS?

On March 23, 2001, I was in a club in Montreal when a more than inebriated man walked over to me and—in a thick French-Canadian accent—said, "WWF bought WCW! Can you believe it?"

Of course I couldn't, but was more surprised that someone would just think to walk over to me in a bar and start talking about wrestling. He then pulled out some sheets of paper from his pocket that he had printed out from a reputable website. It said right on top: WWF buys WCW. It was then I knew it was true.

I tried to get him to explain how this had come about, what had happened to Eric Bischoff and Fusient Media Ventures, how much the sale was, what was going to happen to WCW?

He could not tell me. It was loud, he was halfway gone, and there just was too much speculation and questions. Nobody knew what was going to happen.

It was probably one of the saddest days in wrestling I can remember. Here was the death of an organization I had spent a decade supporting. But at the same time it was exciting. There was a big question of "What's going to happen next?"

A few days later, Nitro would have its last hoorah and Shane McMahon would be revealed to be the man who bought WCW right from under Vince's nose. There was hope yet, even though it was kayfabe hope.

That hope would begin to arise on May 28, 2001 when Lance Storm ran into the ring during a WWF match, and the return of WCW seemed be floating to the surface. Things soon picked up with Hugh Morrus hitting the No Laughing Matter Moonsault on Edge the next week. And then it was quiet for a while, until June 25, 2001 when Mike Awesome jumped Rhyno in the back and won the Hardcore Title (24/7 Rules in effect). Thus, as PK said, the InVasion began!

But as time went on, something became obvious. Though important people like Booker T (the World and US Champion) and DDP (former World Champion) were on board with the InVasion, there were several people missing. Where were Hulk Hogan, Kevin Nash, Scott Hall, Scott Steiner, Ric Flair, Sting, Goldberg, and many others? Why had Vince not brought these men in?

And as the InVasion soured and slowly became WWF vs. WWF-turncoats, and finally ending in the Rock vs. Stone Cold, the question remained: why had Vince not brought in the big guns?

People say Vince intentionally wanted to destroy WCW, that he wanted to prove the superiority of the WWF, and that his ego would not let WCW shine. While this may or may not all be true, Vince had solid reasons for not brining in the big boys of WCW, and he was in the right to refuse them passage to the land then known as the World Wrestling Federation.

WHERE HAVE ALL THE GOOD PEOPLE GONE?

First off, you have to understand a little bit about the then AOL-Time Warner's corporate structure. Everyone who worked for any division of ATW had a contract with ATW, not with the division they worked for. Therefore, even if a division was sold off (like say when Time Warner sold off Warner Music), ATW could keep the key personnel they wanted and send the rest of the rabble with the sale. Much like in a bankruptcy sale, the person who buys these contracts also assumes all of the debt, that being the remainder of the employees' contacts.

Everyone is WCW was under contract to ATW (with the exception of Eric Bischoff who was being paid as an independent consultant). When ATW sold all of the assets of WCW, including the WCW brand name, they did not sell off their wrestling division. They simply renamed the division the Universal Wrestling Corporation, which was the actual name for the Wrestling division when Turner first bought JCP. Kind of poetic, isn't it?

UWC became a clearing house. Vince decided to take a lot of younger talent as prospects, and later Booker T and DDP negotiated for a settlement out of their WCW deals (which they did themselves) and then signed new WWF contracts. But what about the people left behind. What was wrong with them?

Scott Steiner – Scott wrestled on the final Nitro and lost the World Heavyweight Championship to Booker T in the first match of the night. But even if WCW was not going to fold, Scott Steiner would not have been champion for much longer. He was fighting dropped foot syndrome, a disease that makes it impossible to hold his foot in a single position and maintain balance. This was common knowledge, along with nagging knee, neck, shoulder, elbow, and back problems. Scott needed time away from the ring, and was making a good deal of money since he had been with WCW so long and had moved into the main event scene. Acquiring his contact would only get Vince a few months of service when Scott needed serious time off to treat his injuries. Allowing UWC to pay Scott to sit at home was the best decision and gave Steiner the monetary protection while he got to recuperate. WCW did not need a mouthpiece in the WWF like Steiner, as there were plenty of other logical choices.

Kevin Nash – Kevin Nash was another man facing serious injuries and was already 40 years old. His contact was thus that he could come and go as he pleased, so Vince would most likely have to pay him a bonus on top of his contract to keep him around. Nash was also extremely burnt out by this point and needed time away from the business to regain his earlier form. Also, before Vince Russo stepped in, Nash had been involved in the booking process, and would expect more creative control. Vince and the other personalities in the WWF at the time (see below) would not want that, and therefore Nash would have been a disruption at the least. Shortly after the sale of WCW, Nash was also suing the UWC for back royalties and compensations he said he was owed. The WWF would not want to get involved in that lawsuit, and Nash would lose all ground if he took a job with the WWF at that time.

Scott Hall – Although Kevin Nash would try to protect Scott Hall when Nash was head booker, he would not push him (as we covered in the earlier Kevin Nash case). This is because Scott Hall's personal problems far outweighed his professional ones. Despite dealing with some old injuries, Scott Hall had been away long enough to heal. But with so many other destructive personalities already around dealing with personal issues (Austin, Guerrero, Regal, Waltman), Vince could not afford to take on someone else who was going to need more help outside the ring than give back inside of it.

Sting – Sting was the franchise of WCW, and the only old-school main eventer who had never been in the WWF. Every dream match was possible with Sting, if it weren't for three things. First, Sting was burnt out on wrestling. The booking era of Vince Russo had taken the passion out of Sting, and he really did not have the drive to wrestle anymore (although he would later get it back to return to the WWA and NWA-TNA). Second, Sting's contract was set up so that he was only required to make a certain number of appearances per year (a la Goldberg), and he already surpassed that. He had 18 more months on his contact at the time, and therefore every appearance would be another pay special. Finally, well, I'll let Sting talk for himself:

> *I'm disappointed that we turned to shock and munch to hang with [the WWF]... All these years I had parents telling me, 'We're glad we can actually let our kids watch your show.' All those people that said that to me over the years can't say that anymore.*

Sting, as a born-again Christian and a believer in the family value of wrestling, could not stand the WWF's product. Although that has not stopped people like Chris Jericho or Ted DiBiase from being a part of the WWE, it is at least one of the factors (money and appearances being the others) that—at that time—had stopped Sting from making a WrestleMania moment.

Rey Mysterio – Although not a main eventer, Rey Mysterio was often lamented as a top choice to join the WWF, especially if they wanted to do anything with the Light-heavyweight and Cruiserweight divisions. People now-a-days point to Mysterio's excellent entrance and rise to the near top of SmackDown! as proof that Rey Mysterio would have been an excellent acquisition. Except people forget that Rey Mysterio was sans mask back then, and was running around as Konnan Jr. To keep up the storylines of WCW, Rey would come in as he was, which was not a very successful gimmick for him. Also, Rey was coming off of his about sixteenth knee surgery, an injury that has never healed (he had to take time off for it again not too long ago). On top of that, being in WCW so long, Rey was making substantially more than most WWF upper/mid-carders. Rey would most likely end up in a lower card position during the InVasion, but still be making more than guys that would now be pushed to the side. The investment was not worth it then, but giving him time to recuperate and come in at a lower cost with a new (old) storyline and mask became the best way for the WWF to capitalize on Rey.

Ric Flair – The other top name that personified WCW, Flair was well into his 50's at the time of WCW's purchase. Also, he was making top dollar beyond all over main eventers in the WWF. He was not in wrestling shape (why he wore a t-shirt on the final Nitro) and would definitely not work a full-time schedule. He had spent the past 10 years in frustration butting heads with Bischoff and Russo, and nobody thought then that he had any gas left in the tank. Although we were surprised later after the end of the InVasion to find out just how much Ric Flair could go, at this point in history it looked like Flair was ready to hang up the boots forever.

Goldberg – Arguably the man that could draw the most money for a WWF-led WCW, Goldberg was completely burnt out on the business. Vince Russo had treated him horribly, and Goldberg was not a fan of the direction he was going. Much like Sting, Goldberg had also used up all the days in his contact and was more than happy to sit at home and pursue his acting dreams. Unlike Sting, even if Goldberg were to have had his contact taken over by the WWF, he probably would not have shown up. Besides all of that, do not forget that Goldberg lost a "You're Fired" match to Buff Bagwell and Lex Luger in January.

But this was in fact so he could go and have shoulder surgery. So acquiring an injured, disgruntled, and WWF-hating Goldberg would not be the best move.

Hulk Hogan – Hulk Hogan is the biggest name in professional wrestling. No, he transcends the sport. You can be as much of a Hogan hater as you want, it does not matter. The man was more important to wrestling history and bringing it into the mainstream than anyone or anything else. Even someone who has never watched a single wrestling match in their life knows the name Hulk Hogan.

So why wasn't he brought in?

Hogan was last seen at Bash at the Beach in 2000, walking out with the Hulk Hogan Memorial Belt after pinning Jeff Jarrett. Because Vince Russo made so many disparaging remarks about Hogan, Hogan was busy suing WCW, a suit the WWF would not want to become involved with. On top of all that, Hogan had never fully recovered from his knee surgery, and obviously was well beyond his prime of adding to the product.

But Hogan's contact was the real kicker. Not only could he come and go as he pleased, he would have to be paid $250,000 per appearance. And if you wanted him on PPV, that would cost you a portion of the PPV revenue! Beyond all that is what led to the Bash at the Beach incident to begin with; Hogan had a creative control clause in his contact. Vince had already learned his lesson in creative control clauses from Bret Hart, and could not have another talent in his company who had the legal right to refuse to do anything they did not want to do.

As you can see, none of these men with their current contracts would have been a smart move for the WWF. But you still might think the WWF could have pulled it off with their deep pockets...

Economic vs. Normal Profit

Even though these superstars would have been expensive beyond belief, many people still say that Vince could afford it. After all, this was just after the peak of professional wrestling, and Vince had more money than anyone could imagine. The WWF/E was a publicly traded company with a very large profit margin.

Despite the fact that acquiring these talents would cost tens of millions, many people say Vince McMahon should have bitten the bullet for the short term. In the end, he could have negotiated out better contracts or they could have hit the road. By then, all of the WWF vs. WCW dream matches could have happened.

But there is one major flaw in this argument: profit.

And this requires a little more explanation than you think.

The average person thinks of profit this way: the selling price of the goods or services times the quantity minus the cost to produce those goods times the quantity (and once in a while they might remember to take out the taxes). Now, if you take this a step further and also subtract out the overhead, administrative, and general business costs, the money left over would be what we call normal profit. I sold this, and this is how much I made.

There is another type of profit, though, that comes into play, and that is Economic Profit. Economic profit begins with Normal profit; you take what you sold, subtract all your costs, and there you go. But then you also start to subtract what are known as "opportunity costs". Opportunity costs are what you gave up in order to make that money.

Take for instance your paycheck. Let's say you make $10 an hour at the stationary store and work 40 hours a week, so your paycheck is $400 a week. Take out taxes, insurance, and other benefits, and you are probably taking home $300 a week. That is your normal profit. Now, what if you had turned down a job at the card store for $12 an hour for 20 hours a week? That's another $240 lost opportunity, so you are down to $60 in economic profit. Or more so, what if instead of working for 5 hours, you could have gone to the beach with your girlfriend? What is the value of those 5 hours that you lost at the beach with your girl? Let's say it is $200. Now, suddenly, your economic profit (or rather loss) is negative $140. So if you had taken the higher paying job with fewer hours but spent more time with your girlfriend, your normal profit would be lower but your economic profit would be higher! Interesting, huh?

Let us now apply this to the WWF.

Overall, we'll say the superstars listed above would have cost the WWF $40 million. To make up those costs, there is a super PPV named InVasion that does a 2.0 buyrate, or about 800,000 buys. If this PPV cost $45, then that would be $36 million dollars. Add in the live gate attendance of 25,000 people with ticket, merchandise, and concession sales on average $100 a head, and that's another $2.5 million. On top of that, home video units sell another 100,000 copies at $30 a pop, for another $3 million. And finally, ratings go up so much that the WWF can charge advertisers an additional $10.5 million for the month to advertise on RAW and SmackDown!.

In summation, that brings us to a total revenue of $52 million for a total cost of $40 million, or $12 million in normal profit.

Sounds pretty good, right? A quick $12 million to line the pockets of the WWF, McMahon, and the stockholders, and everything would be great!

Except it is not really $12 million.

What were the opportunity costs to make that $12 million? Well, first off, you would put the pushes of Benoit and Jericho on hold, two superstars that could make you a lot of money down the line. And what about all of the guys in OVW and HWA who would now have to spend another year or two waiting to get up to big show because there wasn't a spot for them? There is a wasted cost of investment and future stars that could also be important to the company. More so than that, what about time? These guys were coming directly from the end of WCW, an extremely political environment. How much time would have to be spent to keep their egos in line and to stop problems from arising. How much time would be spent trying to convince them to go along with a storyline or a job? Even more than that, what could Vince, Stephanie, Shane, Slaughter, Brisco, Patterson, et al have been doing to earn the WWF more money if they were not so busy dealing with these personalities?

The time spent to create that $12 million "profit" could end up in the neighborhood of $100 million, and just like that the economic profit (loss) turns into a negative $88 million.

And of course, I was being extremely generous with the normal profit numbers to begin with. That is an absolute best-case scenario, and we all know that that never happens. In reality, bringing in the top dogs from WCW would have hurt the WWF short and long term financially, while also draining the other resources of the company. The true cost of business far outweighs the normal costs.

THE MILLIONAIRES YOU ALREADY KNOW

Let us not forget, though, that there were a number of big-name millionaires already in the WWF. The short list includes Stone Cold Steve Austin, the Rock, Kurt Angle, the Undertaker, Kane, and the Big Show (Triple H was out with injury). Do you think for a moment that any of these men, especially Austin and Taker, would step aside so that a WCW guy could take their place at the top of the card? Absolutely not! Look at how Austin reacted to being pushed down the card to fight Scott Hall at WrestleMania as proof. Not to mention that Rikishi, Benoit, Jericho, and Bradshaw were all getting sort-of pushed at this time, and none of them would want to lose that momentum.

Every political factor in the WWF would fight against any WCW guy getting a top spot above the people that had "paid their dues" in the WWF already. But there was another big outside factor with three initials that was holding WCW down, and it had nothing to do with wrestling!

THE "X" FOOTBALL LEAGUE

On February 3, 2000, Vince McMahon announced that the World Wrestling Federation would be branching out again. After having had so much success in professional wrestling, the WWF was sitting on a lot of cash. Investors did not want a dividend, because it would mean the company did not know what to do with money and had no growth prospects. To buck this idea, McMahon and other WWF officials came up with ideas to diversify the WWF's holdings and to branch out into new businesses. One of those ideas became the XFL.

Over the next several months, McMahon engaged in negotiations with NBC and his new partner for WWF programming Viacom and came up with the final concept. The XFL would be an off-season football league with less rules, more action, more cameras, more sex, and a compensation based on winning the game, not contacts. NBC bought into the idea so much that the two companies (WWF and NBC) formed the joint venture XFL, LLC. NBC would get the first choice prime-time games, and UPN and TNN would get to air other games. Thus, the XFL was born! And remember: the "X" did not stand for extreme. It actually didn't stand for anything. It was just to let you know that the XFL was different.

One year to the day of the initial announcement (February 3, 2001), the XFL kicked off with a game between the Las Vegas Outlaws and the New York/New Jersey Hitmen, which the former won 19-0. The game was seen by an estimated 54 million people, but that would not last. Ratings would continue to slide on NBC (despite doing well on UPN and TNN) until the Million Dollar Championship Game on April 21, 2001, which drew a paltry 2.1 network rating.

NBC shortly thereafter decided they wanted to pull out of the XFL and would not be renewing the league for television. UPN and TNN were actually ready to renew since the league did well for their networks. But when UPN said they would only do that if the WWF trimmed SmackDown! down to an hour and a half (probably so they could try to re-launch Gary and Mike or pick up the long-cancelled PJs from Fox), Vince would have none of it. Therefore on May 10, 2001 Vince announced the end of the XFL at a cost of $70 million.

A few weeks later, Lance Storm ran into the ring on RAW.

But there are a few things you have to take away from the history of the XFL:

(1) The XFL began before anyone knew that WCW was going to be on sale, and way before AOL-Time-Warner decided to cancel all WCW programming on TNT/TBS.

(2) Vince was extremely focused on making the XFL happen, and much of his development and marketing resources, as well as the resource of himself, were going towards that.

(3) With the falling ratings of the XFL, Vince was under pressure from stockholders and NBC to get the XFL to turn around, or at least to bottom out. He was not able to do either.

(4) At the end of the XFL, Vince lost at least $35 million (half the total shutdown costs of the league, of which he might have had to take on

more), and thus had taken a huge chunk out of the WWF's cash reserves.

You can see by all of this why bringing in a lot of those big-name wrestlers would not have even been possible with Vince. When WCW was bought out, Vince was in the middle of the XFL season trying to do anything and everything possible to make the league succeed. When was he going to negotiate through the incredible complex contacts of the big-name WCW stars and manage them and a new brand and his current roster? How would that even be possible?

By the time the XFL closed down, it had already been two months since the end of WCW. He knew he needed to start getting the guys back on TV and bring back the WCW brand. He could not wait any longer than he had to start the InVasion, so he started it. As the InVasion went on he was able to acquire some big names (notably Booker T and DDP), and that would have to suffice for the time being.

How much more money and time could Vince afford to lose? The answer was none. The XFL had drained so much from everyone. What resources were left for anything else?

YOU OWN WHAT?!

Believe it or not, there were quite a few "anything else"s.

The XFL was not the only asset that the WWF owned at the time. Looking over the 10Q (quarterly) report filed on January 26, 2001, it can be seen that the WWF had recently purchased the WWF Entertainment Complex for approximately $23.6 million and was amortizing the costs over ten years. OK, here is a little story about amortization: it's fake! Basically, you pay cash for something up front and on your balance sheet assets move from cash to fixed or other assets. That's fine. But you need to record the cost of the purchases as an operating cost somewhere, so you put it on an income statement. Now, instead of just saying "we spent $23.6 million this quarter and have negative results because of it" you spread the costs over years. That way, it does not look like you have had a really bad quarter or year on the bottom line, and you still get a tax benefit (less profit means less tax you have to pay. Don't worry, you still pay the tax in the end, it's just a matter of when). So when you look at the WWF/E's bottom line for the quarter and they look positive, they weren't. Follow the cash. Cash is king.

Anyway, the WWF sent this out in a press release:

> "We want WWF New York to be a showcase for all our brands, including the WWF, XFL and WWF Racing," said Linda McMahon, WWFE President and CEO. "By taking control at this time, we believe we can unlock the potential of this facility. We want to make WWF New York as synonymous with fun and entertainment as our other brands."
>
> The complex features a soundstage for TV production and live entertainment that was technically designed and equipped by WWFE independent of the licensee's investment. The complex also contains an active merchandise store and restaurant. In the first year of operations, the facility is expected to generate approximately $20 million to $25 million in revenue with $4 million to $6 million in EBITDA (earnings before interest, taxes, depreciation and amortization).

Although now we know that WWF New York (or the World, as it was later called) did not even come close to making these projections, it was still a substantial investment by the company at the time. So that is an additional $23.6 million that was being used for other resources and not for wrestling talent, not to mention the actual operating cost of the restaurant and store. Also take away from Linda's comments that there was a WWF racing team. Though the investment for that was not in the tens of millions, it was still another piece of the puzzle that held Vince's and the WWF's focus.

The World, actually, was not the WWF's first venture into real estate. Take a look at this press release from December 26, 2000:

> World Wrestling Federation Entertainment, Inc. (NYSE:WWF) today announced the sale of the WWF Hotel and Casino located in Las Vegas, Nevada. The net proceeds from the sale are approximately $11.2 million and are net of closing costs and other selling expenses.
>
> The property was purchased in the second quarter of fiscal year 1999 and classified as an asset held for sale on the balance sheet. The company expects to record a gain of approximately $1 million.

The WWF was trying to develop a casino in Vegas (can you guess why? ::cough cough:: Nitro Grill ::cough cough::). This was another unsuccessful operation that had the focus of the WWF prior to the WCW purchase. Although they made money on the sale of the land, that press release does not tell you about the amount of money and time they lost trying to create the casino. All of those costs were wrapped up into the SG&A expenses that hardly ever get broken out. But that still isn't all that was going on!

Remember how I said at the beginning of this piece that the WWF was trying to diversify their properties? Well, another one of those was SmackDown! Records. And look at this press release from March 1, 2001:

> *SmackDown! Records, a division of World Wrestling Federation Entertainment, Inc. (NYSE: WWF), and KOCH Records have launched WWF The Music: Volume 5 into the #2 spot on the Billboard Top 200*, making it the highest debut of the week. The CD is already Certified Gold in the United States, Canada, and the UK and is on its way to becoming Certified Gold in Australia and Chile.*
>
> *SmackDown! Records and KOCH Records shipped 1.5 million copies worldwide, including one million units in the US, 100,000 in the UK, and 70,000 in Canada. In addition to its strong showing on the US sales charts, WWF The Music: Volume 5 debuted at #2 and #5 in the UK and Canada, respectively. The CD is a top seller at retail chains such as Tower Records, Best Buy, Kmart and Target and continues to sell well at several other retail outlets.*

You see, SmackDown! Records was actually showing success, and so the WWE wanted to move forward with that. Maybe if they had someone like John Cena at the time it could have been more successful. They did sign a few bands to the label, but eventually dropped them when they dropped the whole division. But at the time, it was another part of the WWF becoming a multi-media powerhouse. And again, this is right before they purchased WCW, so yet another piece of what the WWF and Vince were investing in becomes common knowledge.

Stuart Snyder, then President and COO of WWF/E had this to say:

> We're extremely pleased with the successful launch of SmackDown! Records. As the company continues to grow and we diversify our entertainment product offerings, we expect the new label to be an integral part of our portfolio of brands.

But while branching out into a portfolio of brands, there was something else lurking behind.

LET'S TAKE IT TO A HIGHER POWER!

This came from the WWF/E's 10Q report mentioned above:

> On April 17, 2000, the WWF - World Wide Fund for Nature (the "Fund") instituted legal proceedings against the Company in the English High Court seeking injunctive relief and unspecified damages for alleged breaches of an agreement between the Fund and the Company. The Fund alleges that the Company's use of the initials "WWF" in various contexts, including (i) the wwf.com and wwfshopzone.com internet domain names and in the contents of various of the Company's web sites; (ii) the Company's "scratch" logo; and (iii) certain oral uses in the contexts of foreign broadcasts of its programming, violate the agreement between the Fund and the Company. On August 29, 2000, the Company filed its defense and counterclaim. On January 24, 2001, the Fund requested leave of court to amend its complaint to add a count of money damages. Leave has not yet been granted. The Company believes that it has meritorious defenses and intends to defend the action vigorously. The Company believes that an unfavorable outcome of this suit may have a material adverse effect on its financial condition, results of operations or prospects.

But as we know, leave was later granted. And not only that, the "Fund" won and became the WWF. By the way, be sure to check out wwf.com and wwfshopzone.com to see how much the "Fund" has done with the properties they fought so viciously over.

The point being, the WWF was getting sued... a lot. This was the biggest case going on, but not the only one. And all of those lawyer fees and court times had to be paid well before they would recover any damages (IF they ever recovered anything). This was yet another drain on cash, resources, and time that the WWF had to worry about before going into negotiations with some of the biggest names in the industry.

This might also be a good point to mention that the WWF was also fighting in bankruptcy court for the assets of ECW. Do not let anyone fool you, the WWF/E did not acquire the assets of ECW until June 17, 2003, well after the end of the InVasion. Again, this was yet another drain on the focus, time, money, and resources of the WWF.

But shouldn't they focus on their core business anyway: wrestling?

THE INTENTIONS OF THE MAN

And who is to say they weren't? The WWF was taking the WCW purchase very seriously. In a press release on March 23, 2001, these comments were made:

> *"This acquisition is the perfect creative and business catalyst for our company," said Linda McMahon, Chief Executive Officer of World Wrestling Federation Entertainment. "This is a dream combination for fans of sports entertainment. The incendiary mix of World Wrestling Federation and WCW personalities potentially creates intriguing storylines that will attract a larger fan base to the benefit of our advertisers and business partners, and propel sports entertainment to new heights."*
>
> *"The acquisition of the WCW brand is a strategic move for us," said Stuart Snyder, President and Chief Operating Officer for World Wrestling Federation Entertainment. "We are assuming a brand with global distribution and recognition. We are adding thousands of hours to our tape library that can be repurposed for home videos, television, Internet streaming, and broadband applications. The WCW opens new opportunities for growth in our Pay Per View, live events, and consumer products divisions, as well as the opportunity to develop new television programming using new stars. We also will create additional advertising and sponsorship opportunities. In short, it is a perfect fit."*

Linda was optimistic about being able to make WCW into a brand like the WWF, but Snyder was being a little more realistic. He saw the potential revenue in the extended tape library, something the WWE has really started to take advantage of in recent years. He, in this situation, was the forward thinker. Do not forget, this was the day of the WCW purchase, so the future was completely uncertain. All we could get then were intentions.

Still, some would have you believe that Vince would never want the WCW guys and he wanted them to fail from the get-go. Well, in a financial release on April 23, 2004 we saw this:

> *World Wrestling Entertainment, Inc. (NYSE:WWE) announced today that it has filed an amended Form 10-K for fiscal 2003 and amended Form 10-Qs for fiscal 2004 with the Securities and Exchange Commission to revise the accounting related to the March 2001 acquisition of certain assets of World Championship Wrestling, Inc. ("WCW"(TM)). These changes principally affect fiscal 2001 and 2002 as follows:*
>
> - *$6.6 million of costs, which were originally recorded and capitalized as intangible assets, are now recorded as $1.7 million and $4.9 million of selling, general and administrative expense in fiscal 2001 and 2002, respectively. These costs arose from the termination of certain WCW licenses and related agreement assumed in the transaction.*
>
> - *The remaining $2.5 million of purchase price, which was originally assigned an indefinite life for accounting purposes, is now being amortized over a six-year period. This increases annual amortization expense by approximately $0.4 million in fiscal 2002 through 2007.*
>
> - *There were no changes to revenue or costs of revenues in any of the periods.*
>
> *The company has also amended its fiscal 2004 quarterly financial statements to reflect the impact on the opening balance sheet, most significantly a $6.6 million decrease in its gross intangible assets, and additional amortization expense of approximately $0.3 million for the nine months ended January 23, 2004.*

I know, I know, that was a lot of jumbled mess in there. Let me put it to you this way: When the WWF purchased WCW, they listed everything as assets (IE, they just shifted the cash on their balance sheet into tangible and intangible assets, they did not record it as a normal operating expenditure). That means that the WWF had every intention to make WCW as much a part of the WWF/E umbrella as any of their other brands (XFL, SmackDown! Records, WWF Entertainment Complex, etc...), not the intention of just writing it off. It would not be until two years later, when it was apparent that there was no future for WCW as a separate brand in the WWE did the company write off the costs.

Despite this care for professional Wrestling, you have to realize that the WWF/E was not a wrestling company. It was a mass media company that had wrestling as one of its brands. Take a look at how the company viewed itself according to their own quarterly report:

> We are an integrated media and entertainment company principally engaged in the development, production and marketing of television programming, pay-per-view programming and live events; the licensing and sale of branded consumer products featuring our highly successful World Wrestling Federation brand; and the development and start-up of a professional football league, the XFL.
>
> Our operations have been organized around three principal activities:
>
> The creation, marketing and distribution of our live and televised entertainment and pay-per-view programming. Revenues are derived principally from ticket sales to our live events, purchases of our pay-per-view programs, the sale of television advertising time and the receipt of domestic and international television rights fees.
>
> The marketing and promotion of our branded merchandise. Revenues are generated from royalties from the sale by third-party licensees of merchandise, the direct sale by us, including from our internet operations, of merchandise, magazines and home videos, and from our operations at WWF New York entertainment complex.
>
> The Company's professional football league, the XFL, which consisted of costs related to its development and start-up through January 26, 2001.

That says it all. The WWF/E was a media company, and wrestling was not the only focus. While important (as it obviously should be for the first two points), the WWF/E was branching out in many different directions at once. The sale of WCW was just an additional windfall that they were able to take advantage of. But with so many other projects and concerns going it, the company simply did not have the resources to take advantage of the situation as many fans wished they could have. The cards were laid down, but there was nothing but mixed twos, fives, and sevens.

Sign on the Dotted Line

Wrestling was a different landscape in 2001, as different as Vince McMahon the person and the World Wrestling Federation Entertainment the company were. When Vince had finally vanquished his foes and gobbled them up, he was unable to execute on the dream WWF vs. WCW matches and events that people wanted to see. He was unable to capitalize on the hopes of WCW fans worldwide that their beloved promotion would live on. He was unable to save the InVasion.

The catalyst of that being he was not able or wanted to acquire the contacts of WCW's top performers. Much of that has to do with the performers themselves, whose contacts were enormous, filled with creative control clauses, performance bonuses based on just showing up for work, and date appearances that were already filled. Many of them were injured, too, or so burnt out at that point that they would not have been productive members of the organization anyway.

Still, there were many other considerations, from the existing top-tier performers' feelings, the costs of dealing with such large egos and obtuse contracts, and the costs of other existing enterprises—such as the XFL, SmackDown! Records, and WWF New York. All of these were a drain on the time, resources, and cash of the WWF/E and Vince McMahon; time, resources, and cash that could not be freed up for potentially dangerous contracts.

Vince McMahon had every reason in the world not to buy out WCW's contracts. And most of all, it was the right decision for the WWF/E as a whole.

The defense rests.

After the Trial

Hung Jury

IN THE CASE OF THE IWC VERSUS VINCE MCMAHON NOT BUYING OUT WCW'S CONTRACTS, VINCE HAS BEEN ACCUSED OF DOING THE WORST THING POSSIBLE FOR BUSINESS, DESTROYING ANY HOPE WCW HAD OF BEING A VITAL BRAND, NOT GIVING THE FANS WHAT THEY WANTED IN DREAM MATCHES, AND INTENTIONALLY TRYING TO HURT THE WRESTLERS AND THEIR FAMILIES.

With exactly 62 and 2/3 percent of the vote, Vince Not Buying Out WCW's Contracts was found:

NOT GUILTY!

And this verdict came despite a case of mistaken semantics and some people's interpretation of the law.

A number of readers who voted guilty did so because of the fantasy of everything that the InVasion could have been. I cannot stress this enough: Vince's trial was not about the InVasion, it was about not acquiring WCW's top tier contracts. And at that, to find Vince guilty based on what could have been (but still would probably have not been) is just against justice. Would you find someone guilty of murder because they chose to stay in bed instead of taking their normal root to school where they would have seen the murder happening? No! It's pure fantasy; and finding someone guilty of not living up to your hopes and dreams does not take away from the actual actions they have done.

Some people additionally came up with very rich and creative fantasy booking that I did enjoy, no doubt. I would have loved to have seen some of those matches, but people were trying to bend the laws of time and reality. Anything involving Triple H (torn quad), Chris Benoit (neck surgery), Scott Steiner (dropped foot syndrome), HBK (still retired), or Goldberg (shoulder surgery) just could not have happen. I mean that: physically could not happen. But yet Vince was voted guilty on those accounts. Since when is evidence of fantasy permitted in court?

Response

I'll skip over all the fantasy booking and InVasion criticism and go to a more interesting question:

> *I think you had a great [argument] about the contract dispute, but there is a question lingering in my mind about the entire situation. Why didn't Vince wait [until] the losses from the other ventures healed, sign the stars who were already free agents, wait [until] all the other WCW contracts had expired, and then bring in all WCWs name roster (only the ones who could draw money and were willing to work for Vince) in with deals on his own terms? There could have been a story about the [WCW] waiting to do a WWF invasion with "only their strongest" (an Eric Bischoff promo quote perhaps?) and Vince doing what he planned in real life and give them their own show.*
>
> *WCW vs WWF, with inter-brand PPVs, dream matches, and all profit going into his pocket because he runs [both] [companies]. Sure[,] it would have been about 2003 when it all could have happened, but it could have possibly... [been] HUGE business.*
>
> **N Rodriguez**

To which I replied:

> *Because the loses still have not healed.*
>
> *The WWF is still suffering from the loss of the XFL, they did not know the World and SmackDown! Records were going to fail (those were investments), and they had hired 20 WCW guys. What were they supposed to do with them? Send them all down to OVW?*
>
> *At that, there was no guarantee that any of these guys would have signed contracts, especially all together. I was still shocked years later that he got Hogan, Nash, and Hall to sign short term deals. But look, people came and left when they wanted to. How was Vince supposed to see the future and get them all to sign good contracts at the same time and manage all of their egos?*
>
> *And Bischoff was the biggest shock of all! We're so used to seeing him on RAW now, but it was the most shocking moment in wrestling history in my*

opinion when he showed up in the WWE. Nobody saw that coming (and anyone who says they did is a liar).

Waiting two years on a possibility while guys got older [and] the iron got colder did not make sense. Vince had to act if anything was going to happen. Also, do not forget that he was under pressure from the wrestlers he had hired, his own company, and the investors to do something with the WCW brand. Vince was forced to start to play that hand, and just because he only had a pair of 4's doesn't mean that he should have tried to hold out for a full house.

GOLDBERG

INTRO

SOME DAME WALKED INTO MY OFFICE AND SAID...

A while back, I received a note from **Damian Bartlett** who let me know...

> I have a REAL challenge for you!
>
> Bill Goldberg. I personally wasn't amazed with him in WWE at first, but over time I warmed to him. He wasn't boring in the ring, he was a fierce character who knew his role and didn't try to be anything but himself. Not to mention he sold really well, I was expecting far worse after hearing the IWC slam him on everything he did.
>
> He is constantly called a money grabber who doesn't care for the business, people say he has three moves, he's bland and a generic big man... I disagree on all accounts, but can you defend Goldberg?

Still, earlier I had heard from **Ben Jammin** out in Modesto, CA who wanted all the credit that credit deserves:

> How about one on Goldberg? That should give ya something hard to work on....

Even hardcore supporter and nWo 4-Life member **Andrew Strom** had this to say recently:

> If you ever defend Bill Goldberg and I vote NOT GUILTY then you truly are a master at this, because I am not really his biggest fan.

More so, a comment from **Justin Pelletier** (though not the only similar one) when I announced the case made it abundantly clear that I had to do this case:

> *Good luck trying to get a Not Guilty out of me considering GOLDBERG. I hate that douche bag.*

It's an uphill battle, but I love a good challenge!

WHY THIS?

Justin's and many other people's comments made it clear: the IWC hates Goldberg. But why? Why is he a douche bag? What did he ever do that made people hate him so? He went out there, wrestled, scored a bunch of victories, won some titles, lost some titles, did his job, and tried to watch out for himself in a dangerous business. What along the way made people turn their backs on him so much?

Part of me believes that when the WWF bought WCW, the wrestling world lost the vast majority of WCW fans and therefore there are only WWE, Japanese, and Independent fans left. But something goes deeper, even with the remaining WCW fans. What is it about Goldberg that ticks off so many fans? But more importantly, does he deserve their ire?

A while back, Matthew Sforcina did an Evolution Schematic on Goldberg that I thought was tremendous and really put his character in perspective. But it was not enough. Maybe those who read it understood the character better (especially those who did not see his initial assent), but there is a deeper problem underlying the surface—and it all comes from his detractors presenting false facts.

So often, I have read outright lie after lie about Goldberg repeated as if it were the only truth possible. Maybe you don't like Goldberg, maybe you don't like unstoppable babyfaces; that's fine. I generally prefer heels myself (Goldberg being one of the notable exceptions). But to take that hatred and spin lies around it to justify that hatred... that goes against everything this court stands for.

While Evolution Schematic may not have been a case of Goldberg the man—but the character—this case hopes to do a lot more. I want Goldberg the character to be a consideration, as well as the man, as well as the combination of the two. We will blur the lines back and forth without warning, but at the end of the day, I hope this case looks at what Goldberg has meant for wrestling overall.

But I suppose I cannot get there until I get the biggest lie out of the way...

STONE COLD RIP OFF

The absolute biggest and most outrageous lie I read every week is that Goldberg is a Stone Cold Steve Austin rip off designed to confuse the fans into watching WCW.

How this argument makes any sense is beyond me.

First off, yes, both men were bald, had a goatee, and wore black trunks. But this is going to come as a real shock: neither man was the first to go for this look! Hundreds of wrestlers over the years have had the same look, and hundreds more will in the future. Heck, I bet Gene Snitsky will lose a match at some point and have his head shaved bald and look the same. Well, OK, much more ugly, but the same. But Goldberg did not shave his head to look like anyone. He had played professional sports (notably football) for years and—as many athletes do—felt his hair got in the way and got rid of it. It's a quick and easy way to eliminate heat, sweat, and hygiene problems associated with constantly playing a demanding game.

Still, Austin really spent most of his time in denim shorts and a leather vest. Goldberg rarely appeared in anything but his black trunks while in WCW. Not until his trip to Japan and subsequent return to the WWE did he trade them in for black and white checker shorts. Back during the Monday Night Wars, though, you were more likely to see Goldberg in wrestling attire than Steve Austin.

But let's look beyond the surface. Steve Austin was an anti-hero who spent more time on the mic than in the ring. He was a loner who attacked everyone and talked trash non-stop. That was his character. But what about Goldberg? Goldberg was a quiet man who just came in, beat people up, and left. He rarely said anything, and most of the time it was "Who's next?!" Austin went around flipping people off and beating up the boss; Goldberg had a long entrance to the ring with security guards a la a boxer.

How are those two similar characters in the least? Just because both men were getting popular at the same time does not mean one was ripping off the other.

And I know I said "at the same time". The timing does not make any sense for Goldberg to be a rip off of Steve Austin.

When Goldberg signed with WCW in late 1996 and joined the Power Plant, Steve Austin was still nowhere near the top of the card. Heck, when Goldberg debuted on television on September 22, 1997 (he was tested at house shows starting in June 1997 as "Bill Gold"), Austin had just won the Intercontinental title for the first time a month earlier (and had to vacate in September due to the injury he suffered in that match). While his popularity was growing, his then current feud with Owen Hart gave no indication that he was going to be THE main event. Yes, Austin 3:16 was started in June 1996 after the King of the Ring, but that still did not mean he was going to reach the top of the card and become the phenomenon that he did become.

The same could be said for Hulk-a-mania. Just because Hogan defeated the Sheik for WWF Championship did not mean Hulk-a-mania was going to reach its great heights. It took years of cultivating, the growth of national cable TV companies, and the Rock & Wrestling connection to make Hogan into the true superstar he became. So just because Austin had a catchphrase and was popping the fans did not mean he was going to bring the WWF to heights they never imagined. It took years of cultivating him and the ultimate opponent in heel Vince McMahon to make him into Steve Austin.

And the same could be said for Goldberg. He was not just going to be pushed down our throats and become the merchandising masterpiece for WCW. It took years of cultivating and a compelling storyline to make that happen. More on that in a moment.

First, though, let's take a trip back to a Prodigy chat transcript with Eric Bischoff from October 1997:

> *maddog O (Prodigy Member):* It seems to me that Bill Goldberg is version of Stone Cold Steve Austin. Is that the idea?
>
> *Eric Bischoff (Speaker):* Not at all. Bill Goldberg is much bigger, and in much better shape, and is a far better athlete than Steve Austin has ever been. Bill Goldberg is going to be Bill Goldberg. He won't be a character per se. He's a very intense, very gifted athlete. Steve Austin isn't the only performer who happens to shave his head. That's the only thing they have in common.

You see, just one month after Goldberg's national debut and people were trying to compare him to Steve Austin. And he hadn't even said one word yet! Let us not forget that this was before anyone started counting wins and realized that Goldberg was undefeated. Bischoff wanted to demonstrate that Goldberg was an athlete, not a brawler—yet another character trait that Goldberg and Austin did not share.

A few months later in another Prodigy chat, Bischoff actually revealed that Goldberg was designed to mock Ken Shamrock. He was supposed to just be a "shoot" style wrestler. But the fans changed his and WCW's mind once they realized something special was happening.

Of course, there were still a few people who said Goldberg and Austin were the same based on looks. Well, Hulk Hogan looks a heck of a lot like Superstar Billy Graham (and he even notes him as being an influence on his career), but no one calls Hogan a rip-off or says that the WWF was trying to steal people away from the AWA by confusing them. Or the same with Triple H and Edge. Just because Edge has long blonde hair does not mean that he or the WWE is trying to get him confused with Triple H. They have two completely different gimmicks. Goldberg was a mixed shoot-fighter/strong man/silent killer. Austin was a loudmouthed/loner/underdog. Similarity of look does not make the characters even remotely similar and does not mean the fans are not intelligent enough to be confused by the two. As for "casual" or non-fans, the two attracted different audiences. While one attracted the person who wanted to beat up their boss and had to fight their way to the top, the other attracted people who liked an unstoppable machine. Anyone watching either program for three minutes would know which one they were getting.

As a matter of fact, **Josh** chimes in with his thoughts on this, Goldberg's wrestling style, and how it would match up in the real world:

> *I just sat there and watched him in the utmost awe. He was doing rolling queen arm scissors, standing to rolling leg bars, twisting arm-drag to arm bars (even off the top!), I mean this man was a VERY technical wrestler in the WCW days. To be fair, he wasn't a '[B]enoit' or even a grade A submission artist, but the man could deliver when he needed and wanted to. I am a [B]razilian jiu jitsu MMA fighter myself and I know for a fact that a lot of his [bleep] is not only HARD to do, but VERY effective in real life and he brought it to the ring. He could ground and pound, he could slam you down, and he could twist you around. He had it all and was a winning combination. This man was everything wrestling fans yearn for, a technical powerhouse that never spoke and just decimated his opponents.*

So you see, Goldberg had a wrestling prowess, natural strength, and an arsenal that reflected a true fighter. He was not the best ever, but why would he need to be. He did what the vast majority of fans wanted and did it effectively and convincingly.

THREE HUNDRED SIXTY-FOUR JOBBERS?

Goldberg was winning matches constantly, but it was more by happenstance than a full plan. However, the fans were noticing that he was slowly picking up win after win. The entrance got bigger, he became interactive with smoke and fireworks, got the fans on their feet, and got them chanting his name. Still, it was not an immediate push to the top, as some would have you believe. He continued to collect wins off of short matches but was left off of the

Uncensored PPV card. And even after that, he fought through the mid-card of Saturn and Raven (who had just defeated DDP for the US Title) and continued fighting in the mid-card for a long while after that until finally the fans got their wish and he plowed through the nWo to become WCW World Heavyweight Champion on July 6, 1998. A meteoric rise, yes, but not without precedent.

There are fans, and a number of WWE wrestlers, who will say that Goldberg's rise to the top by squashing his opponents was because WCW had an unlimited supply of people to feed him and that he would have never gotten to the top in the same manner in the WWF/E because of their smaller roster.

This, of course, is complete hogwash. Absolutely WCW did have a larger roster than the WWF at the time. Also at the time WCW was making about 10 times the WWF revenue and—more so—was profitable while the WWF was not. But their supplies were still limited and (despite what some will tell you) WCW did not hire everyone under the sun.

I catalogued all of Goldberg's 141 true wins during his streak (thanks again Matt!), excluding his 32 phantom wins. I then went ahead and broke the wins down by the wrestler's status. Here's how that came out:

Wrestler Status	Count	Percentage
Non-contracted Jobber	8	5.7%
Contracted Jobber	49	34.8%
Contracted Mid or Upper-Mid Carder	48	34.0%
Contracted Main Eventer	36	25.5%

You can quickly see that the majority of Goldberg's wins came from a combination of the main eventers he defeated and the mid and upper-mid card guys he beat up during his rise to the US Title and in its defense. But let's take a look deeper.

Breaking it down by wrestler, the top ten ones Goldberg defeated were:

Wrestler	Wrestler Status	Total Wins
Giant	Contracted Main Eventer	18
Saturn	Contracted Mid or Upper-Mid Carder	11
Jerry Flynn	Contracted Jobber	8
Curt Henning	Contracted Main Eventer	7
Brad Armstrong	Contracted Jobber	6
Fit Finlay	Contracted Mid or Upper-Mid Carder	4
Konnan	Contracted Mid or Upper-Mid Carder	4
Scott Hall	Contracted Main Eventer	4
Steve McMichael	Contracted Mid or Upper-Mid Carder	4
Yuji Nagata	Contracted Jobber	4

Thus of Goldberg's wins, the most came from the Giant, a no doubt main event player and former World Heavyweight Champion himself. That does not sound like someone plowing through jobbers. As a matter of fact, Goldberg only defeated 59 unique individuals, of which you have seen 8 did not even work for

WCW, 9 were developmental talents, and another 7 were over-the-hill veterans whose job it was was to make the new kids look better. That leaves just 35 unique individuals that Goldberg really went over in a significant matter.

Overall, though, of Goldberg's top ten wins, 41% were over main eventers, 33% were over mid or upper-mid carders, and only 26% were over jobbers. Sure seems like a credible build over worthy talent to me!

DEVELOPING INTO A WRESTLER

Many, though, complained during Goldberg's entire assent and career that he was too green, that he did not have enough moves, and that he had no longevity in the business. Once again, I remind you first off that the plan was not to make Goldberg a champion in just over a year, but that the fans demanded to make it happen. That said, let's look into Goldberg's past.

First off, Goldberg was an athlete before entering into WCW and already had an excellent physique and workout regimen. He had good stamina and a body willing to learn. He went to the Power Plant to train and while there he was put through the very best that Buddy Lee Parker had to offer. From there, he hit the house show circuit before making his television debut. He was learning on a high curve, yes, but he did not stop learning.

Across the country, Bill was staying with Fit Finlay and being paired up with him to learn more moves and in-ring psychology. And as we have seen Fit Finlay do with the Divas in the WWE, he is an excellent teacher. After his time with Finlay, Goldberg continued to try to learn more moves, including adding a number of leg and arm submission holds that are popular in Japan (these moves he learned for his tours over there).

Sure, he was no Chris Benoit, but Goldberg could still go when need be. More often than not, though, there was no need. Goldberg—much like his good friend Kevin Nash—knew that he did not have to do so many amazing technical things in the ring but could instead entertain the fans with his presence and charisma. Still, there were times he got to show off.

At Halloween Havoc in 1998, Goldberg defended his World Heavyweight Championship against DDP in a stellar ten-and-a-half-minute match-up. During that match, Goldberg performed the following moves: collar-and-elbow tie up, reverse arm-drag, overhead flip to reverse a legsweep (and landed on his feet! Take that Super Crazy!), fireman's carry, Jericho Armbar variation #547, shoulderblock, underhook suplex, side suplex, cross-armbreaker, attempted hiptoss (reversed), spear, jackhammer. That's more than a move a minute, not including all the moves Page was doing to Goldberg or the fact that the match was built around Goldberg hurting his shoulder on an attempted spear and being unable to lift Page for a jackhammer.

So wait: Goldberg has a full arsenal of moves, tries to learn new movies, and built a match around psychology? Guess that man did learn a few things about wrestling.

When discussing Goldberg's matches, though, one must address their length. **RC** says:

> *[Y]ou should have mentioned how many matches in which he used ONLY a few moves. Just highlighting one match of more than 150 matches is kinda wrong in my book...*

While it is true that the vast majority of Goldberg's matches were a few moves that lasted less than four minutes (with the intro being longer), that does not take away from his actual ability and willingness to learn. But Goldberg—much like Kevin Nash or Hulk Hogan—followed a less is more mentality. His job was to go out there and entertain the fans, and most were entertained by short squashes. He did not do a lot of moves per match because he did not have to. Sometimes, entertaining the fans means just doing the quick things they love best (i.e., playing the hits). His character was a demolisher; why should he perform a hundred moves he does not have to? Besides, when he did break out moves it make it that much more special. For instance, Booker T used to use the Harlem Hangover so much that it was not that interesting to see anymore. But now that he breaks it out only once a year (if that), it looks like a much more devastating maneuver. If Goldberg wrestled every match to the best of his ability, then what would be so special about those big PPV matches where he was taken to the limit?

Of course, there were others who recognized these facts long beforehand. Let us go back to March 1998 when Arn Anderson did a rare online chat on Prodigy:

> ***FlyerJon (Prodigy Member):*** *If the 4 Horsemen were re-formed today, who would you choose to become the newest members of wrestling's most elite and prestigious group?*
>
> ***ARN ANDERSON (Speaker):*** *Bill Goldberg*
>
> ***Bodinky (Prodigy Member):*** *Chris Benoit was an excellent choice as a Horseman. Is there anyone else in WCW who you think could join Benoit and Flair to reform the Horsemen?*
>
> ***ARN ANDERSON (Speaker):*** *Bill Goldberg and Dean Malenko*

> **bronco 94 (Prodigy Member):** Arn, what about BILL GOLDBERG, is he Horseman material???
>
> **ARN ANDERSON (Speaker):** Bill Goldberg is a special athlete/wrestler, that comes along only so often. Not only is he Horsemen material... but barring injury, he'll be as big a superstar as anyone in wrestling one year from this date.
>
> **Hoops01 (Prodigy Member):** Arn, who do you think the brightest star is among independent workers and you guys that haven't been given their chance yet?
>
> **ARN ANDERSON (Speaker):** I haven't had the chance to see any independent talent. I think the brightest star today is Bill Goldberg. It would be nice to see young talent being developed somewhere. New talent is always needed.
>
> **UPSETS (Prodigy Member):** How long do you see until Goldberg will get a TV, US, or even a World Title shot?
>
> **ARN ANDERSON (Speaker):** Less than a year.

How many times can you complement a man in one interview? Arn Anderson is a highly respected in-ring performer and considered one of the best mic men of all time. He said it in plain text: he thought Bill Goldberg was "it", that Goldberg was the total package and needed to rise to the top. Not only that, he did not seem upset at all by the idea of Goldberg growing to the top so quickly. Quite the contrary, he seemed to want it to happen as soon as possible. Guess who got their wish?

Unfortunately, **Erik Schwob** has found this whole interview suspect:

> That Arn Anderson interview was to shill WCW seeing that Arn did not mention other wrestlers. It would have cost him his job to compliment a non-WCW wrestler, especially since they were always under fire for not pushing fresh talent.

Well sir, here are some more excerpts from that interview:

GoUtes BA (Prodigy Member): *Compare working for Jim Crockett, Vince McMahon and Eric Bischoff.*

ARN ANDERSON (Speaker): *Crockett was a time when I was in my formative years. I learned wrestling etiquette in and out of the ring during that era. At that time, that I was with Titan, that was THE show, which made it an honor to work for McMahon during that period. It was the largest earning year I have had to date. As for Eric Bischoff. WCW is my home and is where I would like to retire. WCW has been very fair to me, and I'd like to return the favor with years of loyal service to them.*

nWoFan (Prodigy Member): *Will you watch WrestleMania XIV?*

ARN ANDERSON (Speaker): *Yes*

Techlight17 (Prodigy Member): *Who in your opinion is the best worker in wrestling today?*

ARN ANDERSON (Speaker): *You can't say any one. I think we have a lot of the best. I'd have to say Benoit, Malenko, Guerrero, Shawn Michaels, and never count Ric Flair out. Steve Austin is doing very well for himself. There's a lot of great young talent. Probably too many to cover in the time allotted.*

Techlight17 (Prodigy Member): *What is your opinion about shootfighters like Dan Severn, Ken Shamrock, and possibly Don Frye entering pro wrestling? Do you feel they will be good workers and would you be excited to see more ex UFC stars make the jump into wrestling?*

ARN ANDERSON (Speaker): *The only one that has even relatively proved himself so far is Shamrock, as far as making the transition. Time will tell. It's two different animals really.*

Wrestling GD (Prodigy Member): *Of all the wrestlers in the United States today, who do you think resembles you the most in terms of style?*

> **ARN ANDERSON (Speaker):** Probably Chris Benoit, but with a lot more talent. He has the same desire, the same business ethics, same work ethic. Chris has a lot more talent than I ever did.

OK, so he talked about several other WCW wrestlers, went out of his way to compliment a number of WWF wrestlers, and admitted that he was going to order a WWF PPV. Come on people, this conspiracy theory is too much! Bischoff was not controlling everyone and everything they said. I am sure Arn said a number of political things to protect himself and his job, but Bischoff was not over his shoulder and whispering in his ear. In order for any evidence to work, we have to take what people have said as their beliefs. Until the day that Arn Anderson comes out and says everything he said in that interview about Goldberg was a lie forced on him, then what he said was his testimony. Also, in the prior quote block he talked about Dean Malenko as the other potential horseman along with Goldberg.

QUID PRO QUO

Let's have a quick refresher on Goldberg's career. **Logan from Cincinnati** did not like how Goldberg wrestled at all, but for a different reason:

> OK going in I am already not liking Goldberg. The main reason I dislike him is his matches just were not that exciting. I cannot think of one good feud he had or series of matches from his WCW days that people are still talking about.

I never claimed at the beginning of this case that you had to like Goldberg. This is just to acknowledge that he was popular and had a lasting impact on the business. I, personally, do not like the Rock and find him boring in the ring and on the mic. But I would be insane to not admit that the vast majority of fans love the Rock, that he was popular, got over, made oodles of money, and has made a lasting impact on the business. Just because you, personally, may not find Goldberg exciting in the ring, it does not mean that there are plenty of others, like myself, who do. This is not a case of personal preference, though, and I do not expect people to come out of this case and buy the Best of Goldberg VHS (no DVD yet!). I do expect people to respect Goldberg's accomplishments at the end of the day.

As far as memorable feuds, Goldberg had several. First was against Steve "Mongo" McMichael when Goldberg was being managed by Debra (more on that later). Then he was fighting against the nWo as WCW's last hope, finally defeating Scott Hall and Hulk Hogan in one night. He followed that up with a series against Kurt Henning, and a drawn-out continuous feud with the Giant. And look no further than Goldberg's matches with the Giant to show that Goldberg was more than just hype. He picked up and jackhammered the Giant 18 times. No matter what anyone says, it takes significant upper body strength to hold someone up that is 500 pounds. The Giant did for Goldberg the same thing he would later do for Brock Lesner: he showed off that Goldberg could do the same to anyone, that Goldberg was a super-man to everyone—no matter the size.

Also, Goldberg had a series with Bret Hart where Bret defeated Goldberg three times (out of Goldberg's six WCW loses)!! We'll obviously talk more about Bret Hart a little later, but for now just remember that Bret Hart got Goldberg to run into a steel plate he wore around his chest (a la Back to the Future 3 where Goldberg was "Mad Dog" Tannen's bullet). How is that not memorable? And towards the end of WCW, he also had a great feud with Scott Steiner, a feud that turned Scott into a true main event player when he destroyed Goldberg at Fall Brawl 2000. And then there was Goldberg's final feud with Brock Lesner that is most definitely still talked about today, but mostly for the controversy of both men leaving the company at the same time. Still, it was a great and interesting buildup.

And all of that does not cover the one-shot feuds he had, like the match with DDP, the Rock, or the three matches with Sting. His feud with the Outsiders after the reformation of the nWo after the Fingerpoke of Doom was also of note. Sure, no one is walking around saying that any of those feuds were workrate matches of the year, but they were fun, enjoyable, and made money (more on that later, too), and that's what counts. Can you remember any Frank Gotch feuds that people still talk about today? How about Adrian Adonis? Memory is short, but the moment is what counts.

Peanuts for Sale!

Several readers wrote in that they were upset that Goldberg refused to sell any moves. To that I respond:

Who says Goldberg didn't sell moves? He sold a shoulder to the ring post against DDP, as we covered above. He sold an arm injury against Scott Steiner when Steiner defeated him at Fall Brawl 2000. That match was built up on the idea of Steiner working over Goldberg's previously injured arm (see window, limo) until Vince Russo saw fit to have three run-ins.

Earlier yet, at Slamboree 1999, Sting and Goldberg fought to a no contest where Sting had Goldberg locked in a Boston crab. When Goldberg escaped, he continued to sell the knee injury for the rest of the match. Then Bret Hart came down and waffled Goldberg in the knee, followed by the Steiner Brothers who came down to beat up both contestants. Rick went right after Goldberg's injured knee and kept up the momentum of the match and Bret Hart's run in.

Speaking of Bret Hart, Goldberg sold a steel plate from him. I enjoyed the way reader Josh put it:

> It really helped to sell Goldberg into an unstoppable, but not unbeatable, force to be reckoned with. Bret Hart broke him down mentally during [their later] match and we all got to see the smaller, but smarter, man dissect a beast.

Let us not forget as I said before: Bret holds three of the six WCW wins over Goldberg. Goldberg sold to Bret's moves and his intelligence multiple times.

The point is, Goldberg will sell when it is appropriate. He is Goldberg: his character is super-human. He knows and understands that and what it takes to keep that projection going. If he starts selling to Funaki then he's not a super-man anymore and you don't care.

Look at Kane. When he first debuted, it took multiple tombstones just to keep him down. Now a foot on the ropes can defeat him. They didn't raise anyone up to his level; they brought him down. Goldberg soared to a super-man level and by trying to "humanize" him it made the character less Goldberg and more generic nothing. Sometimes, a character is better for not selling 100% of the time, the same way the Harlem Hangover looks more devastating now that Booker T only breaks it out less than once a year. Sure, he COULD do it every match, but then what?

When Goldberg sold to someone, it made them look that much better. Anyone who could even hurt Goldberg had to be taken as a serious threat. And the people who defeated him were simply amazing. It all came down to protecting Goldberg the character.

PROTECTING THE CHARACTER OR WHEN TO FALL DOWN AND GO BOOM

People often complain that the WWE and WCW misused talent. When Chris Jericho, Christian, Chris Benoit, RVD, Booker T, Eddie Guerrero, or countless other are not getting the push or storylines that smarks say they deserve, then people get upset with the company and the writers.

But how often do these wrestlers do something about it themselves? Sure, we hear RVD complain, and recently have heard rumbles of Christian's unhappiness. But how many have actually tried to protect their character because they knew the storyline they were involved with were not helping them or the business?

When Goldberg first debuted in the WWE, he got off on the wrong foot. For whatever reason, Vince decided that it was necessary to "WWE-ize" Goldberg. The first thing to change was his music, which had been a signature of his character and entrance. The slightly off-beat tempo made it hard for fans to chant his name in time as the old music did. This, of course, would be changed back to his original music after much chagrin.

Then, Goldberg was put into a program with a recently heel-turned Rock. Rock was allowed to run rough shot over Goldberg and expose his weakness on the mic, as well as make him look bad going into the PPV by letting the Rock get the upper hand physically. Goldberg was also forced to resort to using a chair on the Rock. Goldberg is a weapon; he does not need one. That PPV (Backlash) was also held in a town not friendly to Goldberg. I know because I was there. The crowd, which was a solid base of WWE fans, turned on Goldberg as he defeated the Rock. They had seen a cowardly, weak Goldberg getting schooled by the Rock for weeks and did not want to see the homegrown People's Champ defeated by the outsider.

In order to make Goldberg more lovable, the WWE got him involved with comedy sketches involving Goldust. What had made Goldberg popular in the WCW was that he was so serious, completely intense in his matches. The funny Goldberg was not what old WCW fans wanted to see, and not something the WWE fans could get into.

As such, Goldberg took matters into his own hands.

In an interview with Filmmonthly.com, Goldberg was asked of his time in the WWE:

> **Gary:** Was it mostly an issue of them not utilizing your character?
>
> **Bill:** There's no question. Let's be honest, a moron can see that Vince holds a grudge, and when WCW was kicking their ass I don't think he'll even forget the people who were at the helm, that were managing the boat and beating him on Monday night. For some reason it always stuck. We were never really a member of the family. Maybe I'm the only one that thinks this, and if so that's still my thoughts. His pride gets in the way of his business sense, I think. And if you ask me that's pretty stupid. But it's a public company now.

And so Goldberg used his contract that he took years to negotiate with Vince and held it against him. He made changes in his direction, and got some help from his good friend Steve Austin. With Steve Austin's influence, the two worked together to get the WWE fans to accept Goldberg. Because of that,

Goldberg was able to work his way up and defeat Triple H for the World Heavyweight Championship. He returned to what made him great, while still being a little more "WWE" Goldberg.

Of course, this is not the first time Goldberg had used his creative influence.

In an interview with AskMen.com, Goldberg stated this when talking about his WCW contract:

> *I had creative control over my character, which means if they wanted me to do something that I didn't agree with, then I wouldn't do it. If it was good for the show, then I had no problem. If it was demeaning to the character and wasn't adding a positive light to the show, then I can guarantee that I wouldn't do it.*
>
> ***Q:*** *How did WCW and WWE differ?*
>
> *Vince McMahon, he was the determining factor. He was the main player at WWE. It was just a totally different atmosphere, it was more of a business-like atmosphere and, to me, it wasn't as fun. It was like we were infiltrating a tight-knit family and we weren't wanted. You don't need to demean and knock the character down because they were once part of the competition.*

You see, Goldberg tried to protect the character for the good of the business, not necessarily himself. And then when he went to the WWE, he wanted to do more of the same. That is, he wanted to use the Goldberg character for the betterment of all. Yet, in the WWE he felt shut out from Vince and company because he was an "outsider". And when they misused him and his character, he had to fight back. He could have just sat around and collected his money and did whatever Vince told him to do, but he wanted his run to be more than that:

> ***Q:*** *You have an amazing track record, do you ever get into a position where you really don't want to follow the script, or is it just a matter of getting a paycheck?*
>
> *There is no question in my mind that I am not doing it for the money. If I was doing it for the money then I would still be there. The fact is that I made a stand a number of times in my career, and I did it because I knew I was right.*

And it is not like Goldberg was not worried before he got to the WWE. Goldberg told The Palm Springs Desert Sun in February 2002:

> "I personally believe that everything I've stood for when I got into the ring would be compromised and succumbed to the circus-like atmosphere that's out [in the WWE], and that's putting it mildly... I would be an imbecile if I gave up half my money to work for a company that I didn't respect."

But was Goldberg a hypocrite for going to work for Vince? No, he would not let himself get involved with the circus atmosphere as he tried to protect his character. It is the same as Molly Holly or Ted DiBiase—two devout Christians—working for the WWE. They have personal convictions that stop them from getting involved with anything they deem inappropriate, despite the fact that inappropriate things (to them) do happen.

When Goldberg found he could not get to that point, that Vince was trying to force the circus on him despite everything he did, Goldberg stood up for his beliefs and left. Besides, he had more motivation than fans and money:

> Everyone in the business owes it to their career to be a performer under [Vince McMahon's] image. He pioneered the business.

Goldberg wanted to take the chance and do what so many had asked him to do. But he did not want them to be disappointed if Vince could not live up their hopes and dreams. Thus he protected himself and he protected the business. He did what so many smarks would love their heroes to do: he stood up to the man to get what he deserved.

Of course, there are those who think that Goldberg went too far with his creative control and did not want to make the jump to the dark side...

TURN THIS!

Many have said that Goldberg refused to turn heel, that he only wanted to be a babyface in the limelight. Well people, it's time to take a trip back in time. First stop: 1997!

This is going to come as a shock, but Goldberg was not a face upon his debut.

Well, at first he was nothing, but things began to change when Debra McMichael was putting together a stable to take out her ex-husband Steve "Mongo" McMichael. At Halloween Havoc, Goldberg ran in and speared Mongo in Mongo's match with Alex Wright, allowing Wright to get the win. Afterwards, Debra rewarded Goldberg with Mongo's Superbowl ring. The funny part was that the crowd loved how Goldberg beat up both Mongo and Wright.

But the feud would continue with WCW keeping Goldberg with Debra, thus keeping him "heel". Goldberg continued to pick up wins, and ducked out on fighting Mongo. Finally the two were set to meet at Starrcade 1997. On WCW Saturday Night two weeks prior, Mean Gene interviewed (I kid you not!) Goldberg about his thoughts on the match. Keeping his heel image, Goldberg first verbally assaulted Mean Gene ("No more first names! Do I look like a Billy to you?!"), and then ran down how Mongo "used" to be a legend and some other degrading comments. Then at Starrcade the two met, where Goldberg defeated Mongo in quick fashion. Even after that, he would not quit his "heel streak".

Still, WCW noticed that the fans were popping for him and starting to chant his name. It was unexpected, but they went with it. On the January 26, 1998 edition of Nitro, Goldberg dumped Debra and began his official run as a face, culminating with his 25th win over Brad Armstrong (not Glacier as WCW would have you believe).

See, Goldberg had nothing against being a heel from the start. He was supposed to be one, but the fans turned him, much the same way they turned the Rock or Austin. WCW saw the fans reactions and ran with it, and we all know where that ended up.

Goldberg continued unabated as a face until 2000 during the Russo/Bischoff era of WCW. The two were looking for a way to really shock the fans. Whether it was a good idea or not is debatable, but Goldberg agreed with their plans and turned heel at the Great American Bash 2000 by spearing Kevin Nash and allowing Jeff Jarrett to pin Nash and retain the WCW World Heavyweight Championship.

This heel turn would not go well, as the fans reacted badly. The angle did not catch on and Goldberg was turned face again. Many have said that it was Goldberg himself sabotaging the turn that did not make it happen. In an interview with Wrestling Digest in December 2000, Goldberg had this to say:

> **WD:** How did your heel turn develop, and what are your thoughts on it?
>
> **BG:** At first, I kinda liked the idea. I like the ability to go out there and beat the crap out of people without remorse, because that's how I am. It gives me an opportunity to develop my character more. The only thing that has been difficult is playing a

> heel in front of a Make-A-Wish kid who has cancer that I met before the match, and hearing her family say I made such a difference for her. After making a positive difference in a kid's life, it's difficult to go out there and do the heel stuff.
>
> **WD:** Let's hypothetically say that you see that kid in the front row, and you're in the ring swearing and playing a heel. What do you say to that kid after the show?
>
> **BG:** I'm an actor. Like Mel Gibson, I assume a character. It's hard for me to do something in the ring or in front of the camera if I am not totally behind what I'm doing. I have to do whatever I have to do in order to turn this company around.

You see, Goldberg was for the idea of being a heel so long as it made sense! He had been a face so long, though, that he did have doubts about it. From the Dallas News:

> It was hard for me because here I was making speeches to these kids and doing the things I do with charities during the day and then at night I was running those same kind of people down in the ring," he said. "Yeah, it was just a character, but for some of the kids, it's hard to understand.

Goldberg had doubts about being a heel. But so what? Having doubts does not make you a saboteur. He went out there, did what he was told, and tried to make the angle happen. He was not as into it as possible, that is for sure, but he did not fight it. It was Russo and Bischoff who saw that they had failed in the angle and hot shot their decision backwards. It was hard for Goldberg, but he was trying to make it happen. Just because the heel turn failed, it does not make it his fault.

There is one place it may have succeeded, though, and that was in the WWE. Goldberg was booed in his feuds with the Rock and Chris Jericho. He yelled at an audience member during his match with Chris Jericho, to boot. But the WWE chose to ignore their own fan base and continued to push Goldberg as a face. Yes, he did win over the fans with the time, but had the WWE asked him to turn heel, he may just have gone along with it.

In an interview with WWE.com, Goldberg had this to say:

> **WWE.com:** *Are you anticipating that some WWE fans might boo you because they perceive The Rock as "their guy"?*
>
> **Goldberg:** *If I worried about what the fans thought, then I wouldn't be here. I'm out here to do a job. If they like it, great. If they don't, get in line.*
>
> **WWE.com:** *Some of your critics have said you lack passion for this business. What do you have to say about that?*
>
> **Goldberg:** *The main reason why I'm here is to entertain little kids. Period. The main reason I came back to wrestling in the U.S. is to entertain little kids.*

Goldberg just wanted to entertain. If people booed him, he would have been fine with it, so long as it was good for business. As he has stated on many occasions throughout this piece, Goldberg never had a problem losing or doing something controversial so long as he felt it was right for the character and the business. He came into the WWE with high hopes and an open mind, willing to go along with the plan whatever that may be. It was only when it became obvious that there was no plan and that they were hurting Goldberg the character did he take a stand and try to change the tempo.

Of course, there have been other times in the past where people have questioned Goldberg's creative decisions...

WHY WON'T YOU FIGHT ME, GREENBERG?

Back in WCW, Chris Jericho began a feud with Goldberg as a joke. At Fall Brawl 1998, Jericho defeated a fake Goldberg via submission. Then, on Nitro on September 28, 1998, Goldberg (who was World Heavyweight Champion) and Jericho (who was World Television Champion) were set to do battle. Actually, Jericho had arranged for a little person Goldberg to be his opponent, but the real Goldberg came out with the little person on his shoulder. Jericho ran away while Goldberg beat up the Jericho-holic Ninja. But Goldberg was trying to prepare for his match with DDP at Halloween Havoc and didn't have time to deal with Jericho then. So Jericho said Goldberg ran away, and that was win number two!

The next win for Jericho came on the October 8, 1998 edition of Thunder. Knowing Goldberg was not there, Jericho challenged Goldberg to a match. Since Goldberg did not come out, Jericho won by countout. Two weeks later on the October 19, 1998 edition of Nitro, Jericho premiered his "Jericho 3, Goldberg 0" T-shirt. He would have to update this shortly as on Thunder on November 5, 1998, he told Schiavone he was now 4-0 against Goldberg (even I'm not sure where the 4th win came from!). Goldberg had heard enough, and speared Jericho on the rampway on Nitro on November 9, 1998.

And then... well, that was it. The feud was over.

It was not exactly the most paramount ending to a feud, but both went on with their lives. Jericho began a feud with Bobby Duncam Jr. while Goldberg beat up the Giant a few times before losing at Starrcade to Kevin Nash.

But critics will say that it was Goldberg's decision, that he asked not to be involved in a program with Jericho. Well, straight from Y2J's mouth:

> *I wanted to wrestle him. We started this angle (in WCW) on a whim, as kind of like a joke, and it became something that people wanted to see. I was calling him "Greenberg" at the time, because he was just starting out. And I always claimed victories over him whenever I escaped. It got to the point where I would always have a shirt that said, "Jericho 1, Greenberg 0." And then when I "beat" him again, it would be "Jericho 2, Greenberg 0" and then "Jericho 3, Greenberg 0." People had signs in the crowd counting along with me. People wanted to see him kick my ass, and that's what I wanted him to do. This was when he was in the middle of his winning streak, and the office wanted to end this in a two-minute squash match, as we call them, with him just spearing me and jackhammering me. I refused to do it because people wanted to see this match, and they were going to pay for it. I wanted to have a match on a pay-per-view, and he could kick the [bleep] out of me in a minute if that's what they wanted, but at least people would be paying to see it – not seeing it on free TV as just another guy that was part of his streak.*

Let me focus on one small part of that:

> [T]he office wanted to end this in a two-minute squash match, as we call them, with him just spearing me and jackhammering me. I refused to do it because people wanted to see this match, and they were going to pay for it.

To set the record straight: CHRIS JERICHO REFUSED TO LOSE TO GOLDBERG ON FREE TV.

The office wanted the match to happen, as did Goldberg, but it was Chris Jericho's refusal that made the match not happen. Look at the timing of this: Right during and after DDP and right before Kevin Nash. Jericho, as Television Champion, just did not fit in that spectrum in the eyes of the office. I am not saying they were correct in that belief, as I was excited to see the match, but that was the decision of the office.

So you see, it was not Goldberg who refused to work with Jericho, but it was Jericho's refusal to have the match on free TV and the office's decision not to make the match happen. Goldberg would have done this (and Jericho would have had no problem jobbing, don't think I am attacking him), but it was an office decision. The office was upset with Jericho's refusal to lose on Nitro, and thus pulled the feud entirely. I'm not trying to justify that decision, but it the words of Gene Snitsky, "It wasn't [Goldberg's] fault!"

DANGER WILL ROBINSON

What is Goldberg's fault is the injury to Bret Hart. Let's forget about the epic feud, the metal sheet, the three wins that Hart has over Goldberg. Let's forget about their professional relationship and just concentrate on what so many do: a kick to the side of the head.

Actually, no, let's not. According to Hart's RF Video "shoot" interview the whole storyline was Hart's idea. He pitched it all to Goldberg, who loved it and went along with everything Hart wanted. After getting approval from Bischoff (who wanted to make sure Goldberg was okay with it), the storyline began under Hart's direction. Hart actually listed this angle as one of his favorite two memories from WCW (the other being his tribute to Owen Hart match with Chris Benoit). So you see, Bret thought the situation was great, despite the outcome.

But Bret became bitter in the interview when asked about the career ending kick. He said:

> "I'd love to kick Bill in the head the way he kicked me."

Wow, that was bitter. He then went on to say how Goldberg never took responsibility for hurting him.

OK, pause right there.

First off, on the Wrestling Observer hotline Hart said:

> "I don't blame Bill. I don't have hard feelings toward Bill...."

And yet he wants to kick him in the head? And Goldberg never took responsibility?

Goldberg has apologized on numerous occasions both publicly and privately. As a matter of fact, Bret and Goldberg met at a Calgary Flames hockey game where both parties came out very amicably with each other. You can guarantee that Goldberg apologize then, as well.

Hart must have been having selective memory (or one of the other many brain traumas he seems to have suffered) the day of that shoot interview because on May 9, 2003 Hart wrote in his own article:

> *Making his way back into wrestling circles is Bill Goldberg, who is most famous for his incredible undefeated string of victories in WCW. Not to mention that he's the guy that accidentally kicked me in the head in December '99 causing my career ending concussion.*

There it is right there! It was an accident! Sadly, accidents do happen in wrestling, and this was one of them. Bret actually went to Goldberg after the match and said:

> "Accidents happen, don't worry about it."

But wait, this gets better. Back to the RF Shoot Interview:

> *After discussing the injury, Bret went on to describe how he DID NOT go to a doctor and just took some headache medicine and passed out in his hotel room. He then went back to work and took power moves from the likes of Kevin Nash and Sid Vicious. After a FEW WEEKS of seeing silver stars, he THEN decided to go to a real doctor and have his condition checked out.*

Now, I'm not doctor myself, but might I hypothesize that Bret's injuries were not as severe as they were just after the kick. That, if he had gotten proper treatment immediately and not been so stubborn, that the injury would have been much less severe. I am not suggesting that Goldberg did not ACCIDENTLY give Hart a concussion, but that Hart made the situation worse by his own actions. Goldberg did not end Bret Hart's career, Bret Hart ended Bret Hart's career.

BROCKBERG?

And when it comes to the end of careers, we should talk about Goldberg's last day. As we have discussed in depth, Goldberg was not happy in the WWE. He decided that no amount of money was worth it, and let the WWE know months ahead of time that he would not be renewing his contract. Shortly before his match with Brock Lesner at WrestleMania, Brock let the office know that, he too, was leaving the company. Since the wound was so fresh, the WWE decided to have Goldberg go over. It was not Goldberg pushing the decision on the WWE, for he would have lost on his way out, just like he lost to Luger and Bagwell to be retired in WCW. He did not care at that point. But the WWE and McMahon decided to have Goldberg go over in a last screw to Lesner.

The problem was that the fans were smart. They knew both were leaving, and the match was an abomination. The two did not know how to react to the crowd of smart fans attacking them both. But Goldberg explained in an interview with Filmmonthly.com:

> *My decision to become a member of the WWE was a very hard one to come by. And when I actually made the decision I knew what the road could be like and I knew what it was probably going to be like and unfortunately it was the latter of the two. Even though the only reason I went back was for the fans; still dealing with the B.S. at the WWE, it still wasn't worth it. It's hard for me to say that and I hope people understand what I'm talking*

> about. The fans are first and foremost the reason why I stuck with wrestling as long as I did. Fans are the reason why I kept coming back after injuries. It was very unfortunate that my first WrestleMania and my last match at the WWE had to be like that. As bad as the people felt, believe me Brock and I felt even worse. I would have loved nothing more for it to have been the hyped-up match it should have been. It should have been the main event. It should have been different than it was. It was a shame they didn't let it crescendo to what it could have been. And the people that got screwed the worst were the fans and the WWE screwed themselves.

Do you get what Goldberg is alluding to? He and Brock wanted to go out there and give the fans the power match they were looking for. They wanted to have a special match and leave on good terms. But Vince and company got nervous and had them only do a few moves and end the match. They did not want to go out that way, but it was the call from the back. Given any other circumstance, they could have made that match happen. Just like when Taz left ECW, he could put on a good match even when everyone knew he was leaving. Goldberg thought that he and Brock could do the same. But the decision was made to not let it happen, and what we got at WrestleMania was the result.

WE'VE GONE ALL THIS TIME AND WE HAVEN'T TALKED ABOUT THE NUMBERS?

We have gone on forever talking about Goldberg and we haven't talked numbers much at all? Well, let's do some quick ones:

One of the last times the WCW beat the WWF in ratings for a full night was when Goldberg defeated Hollywood Hogan for the World Heavyweight Championship on July 6, 1998 in front of over 45,000 fans jam packed into the Georgia Dome!

In June 1998, Nitro's average monthly head-to-head rating was a 3.98 (compared to the WWF's 4.54). In July it was a 4.68 (above the WWF's 4.65). In August it was a 4.73 (above the WWF's 4.58). And again in September is was a 4.33 (above the WWF's 4.00). Goldberg's win meant a lot for the momentum of Nitro and WCW for months to come.

Immediately after Goldberg's title victory, Bash at the Beach 1998 scored 1.50 PPV buyrate, the highest one of 1998 for WCW, and highest since Starrcade 1997 seven months earlier.

But here is the funny thing: Goldberg did not headline that PPV. He actually did not headline a PPV until Halloween Havoc, where he faced DDP for a 0.78 PPV buyrate, which was higher than the preceding month's Fall Brawl (0.70) and the following month's World War III (0.75). So Goldberg did not main event after Halloween Havoc until Starrcade against Kevin Nash, which drew a straight 1.15 buyrate. See the pattern: Goldberg in the spotlight, buyrates go up. Goldberg pushed to the side, buyrates go down. It is not Goldberg's fault (this is becoming a recurring theme) if management refused to keep him in the main event spotlight. But when he was there, he proved his worth.

But what about in the WWE? Well, Goldberg premiered against the Rock in the main event of Backlash 2003. That scored a high 1.10 buyrate. I say high because Backlash 2002 had a 0.80 and Backlash 2004 had a 0.54. OK, maybe that was just a fluke. So the following month's Judgment Day scored a 0.58 with no Goldberg on the card. But the next month's Bad Blood where Goldberg finally beat Jericho scored a 0.75 (oh, and Triple H/Kevin Nash Hell in the Cell was also on the card, in case anyone was questioning Nash's drawing power). Vengeance, the SmackDown! only PPV the following month, scored a 0.49. Summerslam's Elimination Chamber featuring Goldberg scored a 0.94. Unforgiven 2003 buyrates (where Goldberg won the title) seem hard to come by, but the story I hear is that they were higher than the following month's SmackDown! presents No Mercy, which had a 0.50. The point is, Goldberg drew buys for the WWE, despite everything they did to him!

Goldberg is money, but he also cares about how he is compensated:

> *When WCW was bought out by AOL Time Warner and they decided to not have wrestling on their programming anymore, Vince ended up buying WCW. Most of the contracts carried over, but if they wanted to work for him, they would get $0.50 on the dollar. I wasn't going to stand for that.*
>
> ***Q:*** *Did you suffer for that?*
>
> *I don't think so. I sat out and made my money. What kind of moron would go to work for half the amount of money, when they could sit at home and collect what's written in a contract?*

So what if Goldberg decided to sit around and get paid? Why should he accept half his money that he is guaranteed when from the evidence above he is the draw he thinks he is? Might as well stay home, make a lot of money healing up, and then come back and make a whole bunch more. He did just that, and who can blame him for it?

HUMANITARIAN AND HERITAGE

Of course, as I have said over and over, Goldberg is not just about the money. As you have seen in snippets, he spends a lot of time working with children and visiting kids in the hospital. He has used his fame to try to make people in terrible situations feel better about themselves. In his interview with WWE.com upon returning to the company, Goldberg stated that it was a boy whose brother had died in battle that made him want to come back. That boy looked to Goldberg for his hope, and Goldberg did not want to disappoint.

And it's not just people Goldberg is interested in helping. He spends a great deal of time working with animal shelters and humane societies, and owns quite a few pets himself. Surprisingly, Goldberg is a known vegetarian. I'm not saying he's a better person for it, but that his conviction to animals stems so deep that he refuses to eat them is a noble cause.

Goldberg also has a long storied history, from being a bouncer at a bar, getting a degree in psychology from the University of Georgia, playing college and pro-football, appearing in several movies, currently hosting AutoManiac on Discovery, and writing a biography with his brother. Through all of that, Goldberg has kept one thing about himself prominent:

Goldberg is Jewish.

Now, this is going to be hard to explain to a lot of you who come from areas where there are few or no Jews, but being Jewish in America is a hard thing. I know, because I am one. To explain to people how you are constantly outside regular society, how Christmas does not excite you, how you want to celebrate Rosh Hashanah, how Chanukah is the *least* important holiday in Judaism... it's difficult.

While doing my research, I came across an anti-Goldberg piece that said Goldberg refusing to work on Rosh Hashanah (the two day New Year holiday usually falling in late September or early October [Judaism follows a lunar calendar with an extra month needed to catch up from time-to-time]) was an example of the man just taking advantage of his born religion. After all, Goldberg said on numerous occasions that he is not a religious Jew.

Well, neither am I, but this is what is hard for many Christian Americans to understand. If you chose not to practice Christianity, the society is still built around Christian holidays and traditions. From having Christmas vacation from school to pee-wee soccer games being on Saturdays, there is very little difference in the life of a non-practicing Christian. Now I, and Goldberg, are ethnic Jews. We do not consider ourselves religious, but the traditions of the religion are important to us. Most non-practicing Christians like to celebrate Christmas and do. Goldberg and I like to celebrate Chanukah. They like to celebrate Easter, Goldberg and I like to have Passover dinner with our families (for at least the first two nights). But whereas non-practicing Christians already have their holidays and family time woven into society, Goldberg and I have to go out of our way to celebrate our traditions. Goldberg was not using his religion as a crux to get out work, but just trying to keep his tradition, the way he grew up, and his family time alive. I am taking three days off in October to see my family for Rosh Hashanah. I may not go to temple on any Saturday between now and then, but the symbolism of the holiday is not lost on me. I am not trying to skip out on work, I'm trying to keep my family and my traditions alive.

Kudos have to go to Goldberg for continuing to and insisting on using his real name. Face facts: the vast majority of wrestling fans, especially in America, are xenophobic. WCW's core audience was from south of the Mason-Dixon line. I'm not bashing the south here, but there are plenty of portions that are not accepting of others (not that the north and other countries don't have that problem, too, it's just not as pronounced). The fact that Goldberg was able to win over so many from a xenophobic base is astounding unto itself. And all the while he would never hide the fact that he was Jewish, and actually promoted it.

Goldberg has these things to say:

> "I was considering calling myself the Beast, or the Annihilator, and I even went so far as considering the name 'the Mossad,' after the Israeli secret service."

But Goldberg kept his real name, and was appreciated for it. The Jewish National Fund presented him with the prestigious Tree of Life award (go read the Giving Tree some time) in Israel. On top of that, Goldberg notes:

> "I've been asked to give out awards at the Maccabee [sports] games in Israel and to speak at the Young Jewish Men's conference. The Jewish National Fund wants me to dedicate a water project in Israel, and I was offered a ride on the Estee Lauder family plane..."

Of course, Jewish organizations were not the only ones to note Goldberg's accomplishments. He was the only wrestler in 1999 to be rated as one of Sporting News' "Most Powerful People". He also appeared on the cover of USA today as the representative for all professional wrestling.

More than all that, though, is this interesting fact:

> "[T]here is a marketing company in New York that conducts surveys to determine the popularity and marketability of celebrities and athletes. The result is called the Q rating. Michael Jordan [the basketball star] had the highest Q rating in the country for ten years. At one point in 1998, he dropped to number two behind... yes, as strange as it may seem, it was Goldberg the wrestler."

Some people claim that Goldberg was never really over. Goldberg was the most popular man in America for a short while in 1998!! How can you argue with that?

SPEAR, JACKHAMMER, PIN, GO HOME

Goldberg has been called a flash in the pan, a scam artist, a hater of wrestling, a rip off, and every other terrible name in the book. He was given a break in this business, no doubt, but his charisma and his abilities took him to the top of the game and kept him there. Yes, he wanted to protect himself, but for the good of the character and the business. When others backed down, he stood up to the bosses and tried to make a difference. Although money was important to him, it was not his only goal in business and in life. Goldberg has regrets in this industry, but he was looking out for the business. He is by no means perfect, and by no means the best ever seen in the ring. But he gave us everything and then some, and did a fine job of it. You may not have enjoyed him, but many people did. At the very least respect him; he has earned it.

Goldberg is a very private man, and that is why so much about him is misunderstood. It took a lot of research to learn this much about Goldberg, but he deserved it. He deserved a defense.

Now that Goldberg is off with his TV show and movies, will we get a chance to see him step into the ring on last time? Well, when it comes to future plans, I'll let the man speak for himself:

> "One thing's for sure, when I do decide to give up wrestling, I could have a long and profitable career on the Bar Mitzvah circuit."

The defense rests.

AFTER THE TRIAL

HUNG JURY

IN THE CASE OF THE IWC VERSUS GOLDBERG, GOLDBERG HAS BEEN ACCUSED OF JUST BEING A STONE COLD RIP OFF WHO WAS PUSHED DOWN OUR THROATS AND TREATS THE FANS, THE BUSINESS, THE WORLD, AND WRESTLING IN GENERAL WITH CONTEMPT.

With 81.1% of the vote, Goldberg was found:

NOT GUILTY!

Ha! That wasn't even close. I was so worried, as were many of the "not guilty" people. This shows me that people are capable of being incredibly positive and open, so I am proud of all that we have done.

RESPONSE

Before we get too far into this, it is important to note that **JorgeM** and **TASS** posted this case on the Goldberg fan message-board and basically rallied the troops to vote "Not Guilty". That said, the work was worth it due to responses like these:

> *I'm not a huge fan of Goldberg, but the fact is that he is a big draw.*
>
> **Jeff Devaney**

> *Dammit, man, this is the first time you've made me change my mind about one of these topics. Couldn't you have just let me go on hating Goldberg for no good reason?*
>
> **Brian Pelts**

Still, even the most ardent supporters had their doubts:

> *Nice case, thanks for defending him it was a great read. No doubt haters will still vote against him but that's their problem for being sheep and following the other haters.*
>
> *From **Damian**.*

To which I let Damian know:

> *Thanks Damian, glad to be of service. So far the "Not Guilties" are winning by a large margin, but the haters are still being haters. The number one reason for voting guilty? "Goldberg still sucks". God, sometimes, I just don't know.*

Even after the case, though, there were things to clear up:

> *Now, I'm not a Bill Goldberg fan. As a matter of fact, I have never liked him (as a wrestler anyway). I was with you when you proved that he was no Austin ripoff...*
>
> *But I do feel that Goldberg has always looked at wrestling (and the fans in general) with contempt. He wrestles for the "little kids". This points out to me that he feels wrestling is only for the kids. Not for those of us who are upper 20s and 30s or even older who love it. He blamed the fans for not following the Wrestlemania match and in turn, they didn't get the match Goldberg wanted to give them...*
>
> *So while I felt that you just might make me agree that he was not guilty, I feel that his words showed contempt for fans and the sport.*
>
> ***Gary***

And my response:

> *Thanks Gary, and I have to respect your vote even though I do not agree with it. I was talking to someone else about the "little kids" factor, and something to keep in mind is that Goldberg still talks to Steve Borden AKA Sting a lot. Sting is of the impression that he wants wrestling to be family entertainment, and Goldberg (tempered with is work with children) is in that same vein. The WWE, as we know, is not really family entertainment, and Goldberg was mistaken for believing he could be a family entertainer in that environment. But I look at it the same way I would look at the movie Shrek. Sure, it's a kids' movie, but it has adult themes and jokes that go over kids' heads. Kids and Adults will watch the same thing and tell you something completely different that happened. Goldberg being around kids so much wants to cater to their needs, which is fine so long as he can provide the subtext that adults want. I felt he did accomplish that, and that—although one of his goals was to entertain children—he did not believe everyone was a child.*

Then another one that came very late:

> *I'd like to introduce new evidence, proving Goldberg's guilt*
>
> *[Y]ou failed to mention the piped in chants during the latter years of his WCW stint. WCW comes down to the Southern VA, North and South Carolina area [a lot], and I've been to quite a few shows where he was on the card. Most of the time, my seats were near speakers, and you can clearly hear the piped in chants. I looked around, and nobody was on their feet chanting his name save for a few kids.*
>
> *Also[,] I'd like to mention that in ANY match Goldberg had to wrestle for more than 5 min in the WWE, the fans turned on him. They saw him for what he was. A fraud. No matter what Goldberg says in an interview, his actions didn't reflect someone who wanted to be there to entertain....*
>
> *Claims that the WWE didn't use Goldberg correctly, I partially agree with. But, in the WWE's defense,*

> they are structured differently. Squash matches really hurt how a wrestler is [perceived] in the fans eyes in the WWE. Prime example, they had to move away from Brock squashing people, and actually have him wrestle. That is the reason why Goldberg wasn't built up to be the "Unstoppable" Monster in the WWE. He couldn't go to Heat/Velocity and Squash the nobodies, because he would be [perceived] as a nobody, and you didn't want to bring the Heat/Velocity guys up for him....
>
> The reason why they had Goldberg get involved with characters like Goldust, is because [whether] you like to admit it or not, you can't survive in the WWE by just grunting and snorting, and saying "You're NEXT!" or "FEAR THE SPEAR!" [Y]ou gotta talk a little bit....
>
> **dman4life8017**

Luckily, I still felt like writing new material:

> Well, it's a little late now, but I'll respond:
>
> I went to a number of WCW shows myself, and I never heard the piped in chants. I have heard rumors that WCW did add them later to get the fans chanting earlier or to add to the smaller crowds, but that is not substantiated. Either way, it was WCW's call, not Goldberg's.
>
> I believe the fans in the WWE turned on Goldberg because he was a perennial WCW guy. Goldberg = WCW, WWE fans boo. The WWE lost 4 million WCW fans, so all that is left are WWE fans who are protective of their territory. They weren't booing him because he was a "fraud", they were booing him because he was an outsider. That's why I would have loved to have seen Goldberg as a heel in the WWE. But history happens the way it did, so what can you do?
>
> What are you talking about? The WWE does squash matches all the time. The LOD have been squashing jobbers on TV for a month. Whenever JBL needs a rub, he beats up Scotty 2 Hotty or Funaki or someone else. Big buys like the Big

> Show and the Undertaker beat up the Tag Team Champions (by themselves) on a regular basis! The WWE is full of squashing....
>
> I think you can survive fine anywhere if you have a connection with the fans. The Undertaker in the past and currently rarely says anything, and he's fine for it. The same with Kane. The same with Yokozuna, King Kong Bundy, Shelton Benjamin, Chris Benoit, and many others up and down the card over the years. Not that having the gift of the gab does not help, but not everyone needs it...
>
> My point is, politically you are right. In the WWE, you can't get and stay at the top unless you are everything management thinks is best for business. That does not mean that those who are different are not good, though, and have strengths that should be exploited.

And finally, we do have to delve deeper into societal norms:

> There is one thing I must comment. About Goldberg and his Jewish convictions. I understand that it is tough to be a non-Christian, or non-white person in this country. But Goldberg being over with the WCW crowd despite being Jewish, that is not an extraordinary feat. Hell, Booker T is black, and he was just as over as Goldberg in WCW. I know how tough this country can be against "different" people. I am an Arab-American, and it can be tough. And Batista is over with American white crowds, and he's half Filipino (half Greek, and I am quarter that). Trust me JP, times have changed, but we still have a way to go in this country. And it is easier for big white guys to get over with American crowds, but that doesn't matter too much anymore. In all honesty, I think Japanese crowds are more discriminate than American crowds. Whites are the minority over there, and it is tough for a non-Russian (or any other former Soviet ethnicity) white person to get over with a Japanese crowd. Hell, the term Gaijin (which just means foreigner in Japanese) is now more of a derogatory term towards whites in Japan. But times have changed over there now. I think Bob Sapp, who is African-American, proves that. .... And I said before, it is a small feat for a

> *Jewish person to get over with a southern crowd, but not an extraordinary feat.*
>
> **Chuck Betress**

So here in 2020, have things gotten better or worse since 2005? Or—does the fact that the fight continues—is the proof that it not a completely winnable war? While systems may be changing rapidly at the time of this writing, attitudes and perceptions take generations to evolve.

MORE GOOD THINGS

A few weeks after the original case I received a nice e-mail from a certain person who wanted to remain anonymous. These stories just go to show there's even more to the wrestlers we watch every week, great things they do that often go unnoticed...

> *Two quick stories about Bill that are not widely known.*
>
> *During Bill's run as a heel with WCW they were scheduled into Cleveland. A Make-A-Wish boy (age 8) wanted to meet Bill... [The boy] arrived about 2 hours before the show, and [he] had the run of the arena, getting in the ring, walking the entrance ramp, even playing with the sound system. Finally we were told that Bill was ready to meet us and we were brought backstage into a small room off the main corridor. We could see people hurrying back and forth as the show was about to start... [Goldberg] went directly the boy, who looked terrified - stood towering over him stuck out his hand and said "Hi. I'm Goldberg, you must be David" The boy couldn't even speak, just nodded. Bill went to one knee grabbed the boys hand and shook it. That broke the ice and the kid went for a hug. Five minutes later they're sitting cross legged on the ground together chatting like they're old friends. Bill spent about 20 minutes with David that day, and this is as Nitro is within minutes of starting. Finally someone sticks their head in the door and says "Bill, five minutes to gorilla" [m]eaning Bill had five minutes to get to the curtain as he was starting the show that night. Bill stood up, and reached down for David's hand. Pulling the boy up into his arms Bill said. "Dave,*

you understand this is all like a play right? That I'm really like this in here, and not the bad guy?" David nodded yes. "Good, because I'm going to go out now and do some bad things on TV, and later tonight with Booker T. That's OK, right?" David nodded again. Bill put the boy down, waved goodbye and was gone. That night was one of Bill's few 'almost clean' losses. He did take a chair shot before walking into a 'bookend' and being pinned in the middle of the ring - then the 'bad things' happened to Booker T.

The second story is virtually unknown because it's Bill's involvement with the WCW/WWF Invasion PPV. Yes, he played a hand there. The PPV you may recall was in Cleveland. When the location was announced, Make-A-Wish Ohio immediately got calls from kids wanting tickets. Many of them wanting to meet Goldberg, none of them believing that it was possible that their hero would not lead the charge as WCW invaded the WWF. Well, of course he didn't, and a quick call to Bill after Make-A-Wish called me confirmed his plans to be in San Diego that day. Still, I was left with the task of setting up a MAW event for Goldberg fans that would not involve Goldberg. Bill offered to help any way he could that would not involve a violation of his non-compete clause with AOL Time-Warner. No point in blowing several million dollars even for charity after all. It developed that I prevailed on the good hearts of the owners of Ohio Savings Bank to use their family luxury suite at the Gund to host [an] event party for the MAW kids. We had 15 kids and their families to the PPV. Ironically, the family that owns Ohio Savings is named Goldberg, and it turns out they're something like 3rd cousins to Bill's family - all from the same little village in Russia. We explained to the kids that Bill would not be there, and in the face of a catered party, great seats, and being able to meet several WWF/WCW stars they were happy. The highpoint though came about 1/2 through the PPV. We arranged as a surprise for Bill [to] call the suite. He spoke to each child in turn. He was on the phone for over an hour. Finally the last child was done and I got on the phone to thank Bill for his time... the connection was poor, and there was a lot of background noise. I asked him what the hissing sound was. 'Traffic' came the answer. Bill had been driving from LA to San Diego when it

> *came time to make the call, so he had pulled off to the side of the freeway and was standing outside the car in the desert talking to kids 2000 miles away. You have to love the guy.*
>
> *Sorry to go on so long, they were quick stories when I started typing. Thanks again for writing the defense.*

All I can say is... wow.

THE BRAND EXTENSION

INTRO

SOME DAME WALKED INTO MY OFFICE AND SAID...

Three and half months ago regular 411mania reader **Manu Bumb** (who appears in many reader write-in sections all over the net) came to me with a very compelling story:

> How about the Brand Extension? I hear people giving it crap all the time, but I still think [it's] awesome, even if it hasn't reached maturity yet. I think, 10 years down the road, with minimal interaction between the shows and minimal trading, the draft lottery will pay off... The brand extension was never meant to work overnight. They need to build superstars first, who will be the future of this business...

And there were quite a few good points before, the middle, and after those ellipses, but I think we will save them for the case!

WHY THIS?

Manu has a huge point; people have ripped on the Brand Extension since the beginning. It is the same thing I highlighted in The Elimination Chamber case. Before ever getting to see something, people have already judged its worth and decided whether or not they like it. From that point on, it does not matter what they see, they will let their initial prejudices blind them to all the good that is happening.

The Brand Extension is a long-term project meant to change the way the WWE does business. We are only a few years into it, but so much has happened. This case will explore the intentions of the Brand Extension, what it has accomplished, and where it is going. This will be an odd case because the evidence is not what has happened, but more about giving something the chance TO happen.

WHAT IS A BRAND?

When we talk about a brand, what do we really mean? In the normal business sense, a brand is an image, logo, or trademarked line that is immediately identifiable with a company or a product. For instance, when you see a swoosh you think Nike. Or when you see lightning bolts on a plastic bottle you think Gatorade. The most successful brands are the ones when you see it you know the product, the company, and the image it is supposed to represent.

A brand does not have to be limited to the visual sense. It could be oratory, also ("I'm loving it!" = McDonald's). In another sense, it can also be a feeling. When someone says, "Let's go to Burger King, Wendy's, or McDonald's" you have an immediate emotional reaction to each company's name, and a preference that comes to mind. That is your brand loyalty. Brand loyalty is the emotional connection you feel to a company name or image, and it is how companies consider you a customer.

For years, the brand of the WWF was the WWF, and you had a reaction to it. Whether that was positive or negative depends on the person. As time went on, the WWF established other brands, such as WrestleMania and Summerslam. These events became so big they were established names unto themselves beyond the WWF and existed whether someone were aware of the WWF as a company or not. Later yet, the WWF turned from a touring performance company to a television entertainment company. With that came the advent of "RAW" and "SmackDown!". During the late 1990's, people often knew of the shows RAW and SmackDown! whether or not they necessarily knew much about the WWF. The two shows had become brands unto themselves. More on this in a minute.

The WWF went through a major change when it was forced to drop the F and add an E. The WWF brand had become synonymous with wrestling in general. When people talked about wrestling, they often qualified it with "WWF wrestling". Or when someone mentioned a fight, they would say, "Like in the WWF?" You see, having a brand being recognized as the industry is not always a good thing, though.

Let's say you are the Band-aid company. Band-aid is a brand that has become synonymous with adhesive strips. Now everyone else who sells adhesive strips is living off of the Band-aid name and gets free advertising whenever someone says Band-aid. The same goes for Q-tips (cotton swab), Kleenex (tissue), Xerox (carbon copy), Post-It Notes (sticky pads), Tupperware (reusable plastic container), Rollerblades (in-line skates), AstroTurf (artificial grass), Jell-O (gelatin desert), and Ramen (instant noodles); and even FedEx (shipping) and Google (internet search) are recently falling prey to losing brand recognition. Some would have you believe that when your brand is synonymous with the product or the industry, you are the ultimate success, but that could not be further from the truth. When your brand is used to describe an entire industry or product, then it is worthless and you gain nothing from it. If all chocolates were called Godivas, then would you go to the Godiva store and spend four times the normal cost for chocolate? If all soaps were called Dove bars, would you buy Dove or the generic store brand?

The choice is clear. Losing your brand means losing all of the power and value that goes along with it.

Even during WCW's height, people still referred to this industry as WWF wrestling. Read the old interviews with Goldberg, Sting, or Hogan during WCW's top days, and the uniformed would still call them WWF wrestlers. WWF had become wrestling in general and was worth a lot less at that time.

When the WWF purchased WCW, then it did not matter anymore. They had a near monopoly on the industry and therefore did not need to reinforce to people that there was a difference between wrestling in general and the WWF.

But that was not so in the days of the Monday Night Wars. Since WWF already meant wrestling, they needed to find a way to attract and keep an audience on their programming and not on WCW's. Hence, a new focus came: RAW and SmackDown!.

The advertising for the late 1990's focused on getting people to tune into RAW or SmackDown!, not into the WWF. The same was true in WCW, people were asked to tune into Nitro and Thunder, not WCW. It was "Tonight on RAW: Stone Cold confronts the Rock". It was not "Tonight in the WWF: Stone Cold confronts the Rock". There is a subtle difference, but it was how the WWF attracted an audience. They made sure that people, especially the casual fans, knew the difference between RAW and Nitro since they could not teach them the difference between the WWF and WCW. This worked as people knew Stone Cold and the Rock were on RAW while Goldberg and Sting were on Nitro. They may have called it all wrestling or WWF, but they knew the difference in the shows.

This, obviously, became crucial in the deciding factors of the Monday Night Wars. By making their drawing factors in line with a television name brand it allowed the WWF to gain and maintain the casual fan audience and media attention that eventually led to them winning the war.

After the war was won and the dust cleared, the WWF faced a new problem. They lost the F and gained an E, but the mass media and the casual audience did not know. To them, the WWF equated to wrestling, and that was all there was to it. Those people (and most wrestling enthusiast) did not recognize the WWE as a brand name that they equated with wrestling. Even the few articles that did appear about wrestling at this point or with former wrestling stars usually said "WWF" (even if that person was never in the WWF). What was the WWE to do?

Well, because of the Monday Night Wars, they had developed RAW and SmackDown! into brands of their own, and they were the only brands (outside of the major PPVs) the company still owned that the casual audience would recognize.

When they decided to split the company into two traveling units, they decided that each company was going to go under the WWE (unrecognized brand) corporate umbrella. But they needed something the audience would recognize right away. They could not call one of them WWE and the other WCW or ECW or the Federation or any such thing (more on this later). They needed something the audience immediately recognized with the style of the WWE product, and those names were RAW and SmackDown!.

And as time has moved on, the WWE has discovered a new tidbit: 70% of the audience is Brand loyal. That means that only 30% of the audience watches both RAW and SmackDown! while the remainder only watch one or the other! Don't believe it? Just take a look though the message board at all the people that are "protesting" watching SmackDown! or don't get Spike TV (most people get USA, right?). The RAW and SmackDown! brands attracted and have retained different audiences based on their style, wrestlers, and availability.

So the WWE has been working for past year to create cross-over brand appeal to expand both audiences.

Now, a network rating point equals about 1,096,000 households and an episode of SmackDown! that took place a week before this was originally written did a 3.0 network rating. That means there are about 2.3 million people who are watching SmackDown who are not watching RAW. There is a potential audience to plow with a whole other product. The Brand Extension revealed that there is a WWE to be built with the existing audience, not just outside of it.

You might ask, though, why the WWE would go through the Brand Extension in the first place? After all, in 2002 they were the WWF, the InVasion was over, and there was a whole new world ahead.

BUT WHY OH WHY OH WHY WOULD THEY EVER DO THIS?

Who better to ask than the WWE itself. In December 2003, the WWE posted this in their FAQ section of their website in response to the question "What was the reason for the brand extension?":

> *The brand extension has enabled WWE to create two separate and distinct television shows that would provide the opportunity to develop and establish new WWE Superstars. The RAW and SmackDown! brands each have a touring company, thereby enabling us to increase the number of international live events yet lower the number of events at which each of our Superstars performs. Fewer events extend the careers of*

> *existing talent while provide more exposure to new talent. As well, there is the further opportunity to develop more pay-per-view events and distinctive consumer products. The company is considering increasing the number of pay-per-view events to 14 in fiscal 2005.*

Quite a bit covered there, and we will explore the success of each, but let us just now focus on the intentions of the WWE:

(1) They wanted to establish new stars. Being the only game in town, they had most of main event talent already under contract and would likely gain the rest over time. They wanted to split those talents up to have others enter the mix.

(2) They wanted to have more live events to create more gate revenue and give more talent a chance to get practice and develop. On the same token, they did not want a single wrestler to appear at 5 shows a week and instead be at 3-4, thus keeping their bodies and minds in better shape. This would also lower the probability of injuries for these wrestlers.

(3) They wanted to add more PPVs. Having one company meant they could only have 12 PPVs overall. But only a year before the brand extension there were 12 WWF, 12 WCW, and 6 ECW PPVs a year. The WWF felt that there was an untapped market who purchased those PPVs who now had extra income that could be used on WWF PPV products instead.

Of course, there was the unstated reason here: the WWF/E wanted to create its own internal competition. They ruled the wrestling world and needed to find a way to innovate and re-attract the casual and WCW audience. So the brands were set up and given distinctive flavors. You may notice that the color red now equates to RAW and blue equates to SmackDown!, or that big guest stars show up on RAW while the future champions first appear on SmackDown!. The shows have been developing more branding over time, quite different from where they started.

THE BEGINNINGS OF THE EXTENSION TO TODAY

On March 18, 2002, WWF CEO Linda McMahon announced that since co-owners Vince McMahon and Ric Flair could not work together, they would be separated permanently.

> *Aside: Just to clear this up so this storyline so it makes sense, McMahon and Flair each owned 50% of the Class B super voting stock, while the rest of us out in the stock market owned a percentage of Class A regular stock. Every share of Class B stock was worth 10 times the voting power of Class A— that is, one stock of Class A would get me one vote at a stock holders meeting while one stock of Class B would get me ten. Since each owned shares that far outweighed the voting power of Class A stock, they could do whatever they wanted in the company... to an extent. You see, the Board of Directors had become the official overseers and decision makers of the company in the best interest of all shareholders. Although they are voted on by the amount of stock you have, they are only voted on once a year. So even if Flair and McMahon did not like their decisions, they still had to adhere to them until they could use their voting power to remove a board member a year later. So the board of directors through Linda McMahon decided to split the company in two and give each of the two Class B controlling stock holders control over one half of the company. Since their personal rivalry was hurting the company and thus the stockholders, the only fair solution was to get them away from each other since they could not get the controlling stock away from either.*

The next week on RAW, each owner would get a chance to pick a superstar or tag team or stable (depending on the contracts of those teams) one at a time, alternating evenly. Each would have ten picks and then the rest would be randomly assigned. The Undisputed World Champion (Triple H) and Women's World Champion (Jazz) were off limits since they would float between brands to defend their titles, as was Stone Cold due to a contract clause. McMahon got to pick first since he won a coin toss.

There were a number of interesting choices, but at the end of the day SmackDown! had the Tag Team, Hardcore, and Cruiserweight championships while RAW had European and Intercontinental. Well actually, Raven defeated Maven for the Hardcore title on the last mixed brand SmackDown!, so that belt went back to RAW.

Problems arose early as Ric Flair tried to make the Undertaker the #1 contender, but McMahon said he had first pick by virtue of the coin toss. So Hollywood Hulk Hogan became the #1 contender for Backlash, and RAW and SmackDown! would trade PPV main events each month. At this point, there was very little difference in the brands, and they shared everything except a couple of titles and TV time slots.

Another problem arose after Hogan defeated Triple H for the title. Triple H then became a SmackDown! wrestler but still kept showing up on RAW. There was no way to control him and no penalty to do so. The Undertaker then started showing up on SmackDown!. What were the owners to do? This could not go on.

And then the WWF became the WWE! Too many things were happening.

Jazz also then lost the Women's Championship to Trish Stratus, thus making her part of the RAW roster as had happened to Triple H. Finally, all the superstars had a core brand (even Stone Cold had previously signed with RAW).

Later yet, we learned that when SmackDown! superstar Chris Benoit showed up on RAW he was allowed to do so because he was injured and not on the active roster. So apparently, only being an active wrestler kept you on a brand.

Things were going too crazy and the Brand Extension needed a new direction. Vince decided to do that by defeating Ric Flair in winner-takes-all-ownership match on RAW on June 10, 2002. It would seem that the Brand Extension would be over, then. But wait! Remember in the aside that I explained that the board of directors can control the final say in the WWE, and can only be voted out once a year? Well, despite Vince having so much clout, the board of directors, from a storyline point of view, were happy with the Brand Extension and wanted more of it. Vince, then, had to placate them.

After a month of planning, the WWE came up with a new direction: General Managers. Each would be in control of their brand and report to Vince as the ultimate overseer. On July 15, 2002, Eric Bischoff became the GM of RAW, followed a few days later by Stephanie McMahon becoming the GM of SmackDown! Thus, the Brand Extension Version 2.0 was born!

Vince also announced that superstars were now allowed to negotiate with either brand's GM to get the best deal they could. Immediately, an open back and forth trading war ensued. Not just people, though, but titles. The entire structure of the original draft was changing. Meanwhile, the European and Hardcore titles merged into the IC title, creating one major mid-card title.

Then the unthinkable happened. Brock Lesner, the Undisputed Champion, refused to appear on RAW or face any RAW challengers. The championship became in dispute. Refer to the earlier Elimination Chamber case to follow the storyline there.

At the same time, the women's championship also became exclusive to RAW for the same reasons, though Stephanie did not choose to dispute it. Now, each brand had a top World Champion of its own, with a Women's, Tag Team, and IC title on RAW and a Cruiserweight Title on SmackDown! On September 22, 2002, the open contract period came to an end, and each brand was forced to build from the inside. Version 2.5 had begun.

SmackDown! focused on wrestling and had two top athletes, Chris Benoit and Kurt Angle, win the newly created WWE Tag Team Championships. Over time, fighting between these two, Los Guerreros, Edge, and Rey Mysterio (affectionately dubbed the SmackDown! Six) would highlight SmackDown! for months to come. Meanwhile, RAW became more about storylines and flash, with things like Katie Vick, HLA, and returning stars like Scott Steiner and Kevin Nash. Also, the IC title merged into the World Heavyweight Championship, meaning each side now had an even (odd?) three titles.

WrestleMania approached and the Royal Rumble was given a new twist. Each brand would get 15 superstars, and the winner would get to face "the world champion" in the main event of WrestleMania. Brock Lesner won and went on to defeat Kurt Angle in the main event.

Things stayed quiet for a while with some minor trades and the return of the IC championship. That is until Version 3.0 of the Brand Extension began on June 15, 2005 with the first ever brand-only PPV (RAW), Bad Blood. In an interview, Jim Ross had this to say:

> **BS:** Wrestlers have the incentive for Sunday at the ppv, obviously putting on the best show they can besides the financial reasons, but this will be the first brand-only, RAW-only ppv. What's the mood around Connecticut? Are the WWE offices a little bit more tense than normal? Any sort of expectations or ramifications come out of this ppv?
>
> **JR:** No, I think it's business as normal. I think everybody's looking forward to it. The guys have a—there's a friendly, natural [rivalry] between the RAW and Smackdown rosters. We don't have that ECW 'Us Against the World' mentality. Which I think is counterproductive, as far as, the RAW guys hating the Smackdown guys. Or Michael Cole and Tazz knocking JR and King and vice versa. I don't think that, to me, is a positive. At least that's my view, I could be wrong on that. I think there is a very friendly, competitive nature with the rosters.
>
> You see that manifest itself when we have our co-jointly produced ppvs when all the guys are in the locker room at the same time. I think the guys on RAW are probably gonna be, will rise to the [occasion], because they know their peers are going to be watching. I think it's a pretty healthy environment right now. Really, Brian, I think

> *everybody is pumped up and it's gameday. Sunday, you go out and you get it done. And I think that's what we're intending to do.*

And life goes on. SmackDown! had its brand-only PPVs, the two shared major PPVs, King of the Ring went away, the United States Championship came back. Paul Heyman, Kurt Angle, and Theodore Long each became the GM of the SmackDown! while Mick Foley and Steve Austin both took temporary co-leadership roles on RAW. People came, and people went, trades happened, new people premiered, new gimmicks were formed. The mode changed, the day changed, there was a lot of change going on. New rules were formed (the winner of the Royal Rumble could pick their brand champion to face), new events were formed (draft lottery, RAW vs. SmackDown! color wars), and some wrestlers found they have never seen the other brand. This is Version 3.5 of the Brand Extension still going on at the time of this writing, but definitely not the end of it.

The point of all of that? The Brand Extension is a work in progress! The WWE has recognized that things need to change, and they are constantly trying to make it a better experience while also creating cross-brand appeal (have to attract the rest of that 70%). Is it perfect yet? No. Are they trying to get there? Yes!

And the WWE will not get there if all we say is "the Brand Extension sucks. It's a failure and they should reunite the brands." I'll get to that last point later, but you should know by now that being critical without a recommendation yields nothing. The only thing that is going to make the Brand Extension better is to let the WWE know what we like about it and where we can see improvement. They are in it for the long haul, and we as the audience have the responsibility to give suggestions that improve the product, not just be counter to it.

But I'm afraid there is one suggestion that just will not fly.

WHERE'S MY BRAND?

Over the life of the Brand Extension, one thing that keeps popping up to the surface is the names of the brands: RAW and SmackDown!. Many people have come on and asked why not name the brands WCW or ECW? Those are certainly recognized products that would draw well!

That may be so, but think about this. Let's say that SmackDown! became WCW. That means RAW would become the WWE, right? There would have to be a counter to the resurgence of WCW. But that brings us back to the original problem we stated at the beginning: the WWE is not a recognized brand name. While the WWF is a recognized brand that is synonymous with wrestling, WWE has not created that connection in the vast majority of people's heads. Meanwhile, RAW is an immediately identifiable brand that attracts an audience.

So while WCW might help one program, the other program suffers from being just WWE.

Then there is the other end. The WWF/E defeated and absorbed WCW and ECW. As much as we may not like it, that is the be all and end all of the Monday Night Wars and the wrestling revolution of the 1990's. You have to realize that Vince and many people in the WWE cannot and will not ever accept the resurgence of a brand that could overtake the WWE. Can you imagine if WCW SmackDown! got better ratings than WWE RAW? All those people who spent so many years working in the WWF while WCW demolished them would suddenly find themselves second banana to the brand they tried to destroy.

Yes, in reality it would not matter since WWE corporate would be reaping the profits. But there is psychological toll that is taken. Look at what happened at AOL Time-Warner. The Times and Warner people wanted nothing to do with the AOL people, and stopped all the synergies of the merger from forming. This, with the downturn in AOL subscribers, led to the company just becoming Time Warner again. Even though AOL was victorious in acquiring Time Warner, they lost internally and became what they had bought. Because of that, many AOL people left. Even though they were still in charge and were still making money, they could not deal with the psychological impact of working for a brand that had been under them.

Many of those people loyal to Vince and the WWE would not be able to handle it if the "enemy" brand became predominant. To them, it would be as if Vince had turned his back on his own creation just for the sake of money. It would be like if McDonald's bought Wendy's and then renamed all of its restaurants Wendy's. Where is the victory for all those who worked to make that acquisition possible?

Thus the Brand Extension in its current form becomes the compromise. Nobody in the WWE office will care whether RAW or SmackDown! is on top. Both of those exist UNDER the WWE umbrella, not beside it. It is completely psychological, but makes a big difference in the office and backstage employees who put everything on the line to bring the WWF to its superior heights of the late 1990's. Although it may seem neurotic to an outsider, it makes sense in the heads of those who have been there. And those are the people Vince needs to support to keep his empire going.

THE BIG GUNS

When the Brand Extension began, Triple H had just won the Undisputed World Heavyweight, and was not happy with the brands being split up. This was especially true after he lost the title to Hulk Hogan a month later and was relegated to SmackDown!. Hulk Hogan would in turn lose the title a month later to the Undertaker who would lose it two months later to the Rock. That was July 21, 2002.

Then, on August 25, 2002, a mere five months after the beginning of the Brand Extension, Brock Lesner defeated the Rock to become the first new champion of the Brand Extension era.

And what did the WWE say was one of their goals from earlier?

> *"...to develop and establish new WWE Superstars..."*

Well, that's one way to go about it. Brock Lesner also ushered in Phase 2.5 of the Brand Extension by only being on one brand, leading to the re-birth of the World Heavyweight Championship and his title becoming known simply at the WWE Championship. And since that time, the WWE Championship has been held by other first-time champions Eddie Guerrero, John Bradshaw Layfield, and John Cena. Meanwhile, the World Heavyweight Championship also met new holders in Chris Benoit, Randy Orton, and Dave Batista.

Of the ten World Heavyweight Champion reigns since the Brand Extension, 30% were held by new players, 10% were by young former champions in their first run in the WWE (Bill Goldberg), 10% by former stars coming back (Shawn Michaels), and 50% by Triple H. Ouch, that's a lot of Triple H. That would make you think that he totally dominated the title and that nobody was given a chance. Well, of the 1,107 days since the resurgence of the World Heavyweight Championship, 55% of the time it has been in Triple H's hands, 4% of the time vacant, 10% in older stars hands, and 31% in new stars hands. And every day that goes by, Triple H and the older stars numbers go down while the new stars' numbers rise.

Don't forget: at the beginning of the Brand Extension, the World Heavyweight Title needed some legitimacy. Although Eric Bischoff had genuine reasons to award Triple H the World Heavyweight Championship, he needed to win over the fans to the legitimacy and legacy of the belt. Having a credible champion like Triple H defending it against the best, and having big main even matches like the Elimination Chamber made the title seem incredibly important, despite the hurdle it had to get over in its path to re-existence.

Meanwhile, the WWE Championship had no such hurdles and could continue on unabated. Of the nine WWE Championship reigns, only 33 1/3% were by old stars and 66 2/3% were with new stars. Delving deeper, in the 1,115 days since Brock Lesner won the championship, 83% of the time the title was in new stars hands! That means old stars only touched the WWE Championship 17% of the time! How is that for developing new talent?

Combining the brands and the number of days of championship reigns, the titles have been vacant 2% of the time, in old stars hands 41% of the time, and in new stars hands 58% of the time. And like I said before, every day that goes by the old stars' percentage goes down while the new stars percentage goes up.

At the time of this writing, it has only been three years since the Brand Extension split the titles, and only three and half since the Brand Extension began. Yet still, the WWE has succeeded in their goal of creating new champions. As time goes on, only more new champions can rise to the top with the occasional run by an old champion to keep the scene fresh and bring legitimacy to the young contenders.

Of course, with so many young, new superstars, there's plenty we have not seen from them.

THE DREAM MATCH. OR IS THAT THE DREAM eHARMONY?

Who are the SmackDown! superstars at the time of this writing who have never been on RAW (TV)? Well, there's Doug Basham, Joey Mercury, Juventud, Ken Kennedy, Melina, Orlando Jordan, Paul London, Psicosis, Rey Mysterio, Sharmell, Steve Romero (I know, I'm sorry), Super Crazy, and Vito.

And what about RAW? What RAW guys have never seen SmackDown!? Looking down, there's Antonio, Ashley, Chris Masters, Gene Snitsky, Lance Cade, Maria, Rob Conway, Romeo, Trevor Murdoch, and Tyson Tomko.

What am I getting at? Well, most of these guys may not be huge now, but any one of them could be a future top tier champion. Stone Cold did not find his niche in the WWE right away, the Rock spent years developing, Triple H was not even Triple H for a long time. Stars take time to develop, and any one of these guys could be huge in the future.

One that is right near the top is Rey Mysterio. Sure, Rey-Rey has been beating up former WWE Champion Eddie Guerrero plenty, and holds wins over other former champions the Big Show, Kurt Angle, and Kevin Nash, but there are plenty of people he has not fought. What about Triple H? What about John Cena? What about Batista? What about older champions Stone Cold, the Rock, Mick Foley, or Hulk Hogan? There's just so many different opportunities for him out there.

But it is not just Rey Mysterio. What about the battle of the champions with John Cena and Batista? What about the Kurt Angle/Batista match? Where's John Cena/Triple H? John Cena/Shawn Michaels? Shawn Michaels/Batista? Hulk Hogan/John Cena? Ric Flair/John Cena? Chris Masters/Tyson Tomko?

OK, so maybe only I want to see that last match, but you never know! Maybe that will be the main event of WrestleMania 27? It's too early to tell!

The point is, the WWE is trying to recreate the idea of the dream match. By having PPVs on a bi-monthly basis for each brand and extending feuds, they are keeping guys further apart, extending title reigns, and making dream matches more possible. Let me put it to you this way: if cake is available for free all the time, then it loses its specialness. You get sick of eating cake and start craving some nice carrot sticks. The longer you can go without cake, the better it actually tastes.

Plus, just look at the Dream Matches the WWE has created with the Brand Extension. At WrestleMania XX we got the huge inter-promotional match between Goldberg and Brock Lesner, a match the fans had been chanting for since Brock started running rough shot over everyone (and well before Goldberg was in the WWE). At WrestleMania 21, we got two huge matches in Randy Orton vs. the Undertaker and Kurt Angle vs. Shawn Michaels. Both sets were forced to stay apart from each other for months leading up to the big main event.

Even recently at SummerSlam we got Hulk Hogan vs. Shawn Michaels, and we are likely to get a couple more Hogan, Michaels, Flair, Foley, and Rock matches.

Let us not forget that a few superstars are still out there, including Sting, Kevin Nash, Scott Hall, and Bret Hart. Though those men are not likely to appear in a WWE ring again (or ever, in the case of Sting, or wrestling for the rest), the possibility exists. They say "Never say never" in this business, and so that possibility exists. And because the possibility exists, the WWE through the Brand Extension has brought back the dream.

NEW RULES, NEW GAMES

But the Brand Extension is not just about the dream of the future; it's what it is adding to the here and now. What has the Brand Extension been up to? Well, let's look at all the new situations and events we have now because of its existence:

Draft Lottery
In what has become an anticipated event, the draft lottery shakes up the definitions of RAW and SmackDown! every year. And the draft lottery has not remained in one stagnant form, either. Oh no no no no no no! What started out first as an "Owner picks" moved the next year into a "Random Pick" where everyone was on the line. Fan interest was so high that the WWE opted to extend the event the following year into a month-long affair. Is this the final version of the draft lottery? Most likely not, but it remains an exciting and compelling bit of TV that we would not have without the Brand Extension.

Royal Rumble Stipulation
With the Brand Extension came some wishy-washy areas from the old WWE that did not fit in anymore. One of those was the fact that the winner of the Royal Rumble received a shot at the "Champion in the Main Event of WrestleMania". That little bit of ambiguity led to Chris Benoit being able to jump from SmackDown! to RAW in 2004, and was the crux of the storyline with Batista in 2005. The Royal Rumble stipulation is now an effective storyline

piece that helps keep the pace from the Rumble until WrestleMania and provides just a little bit more of drama and intrigue for the interim.

Elimination Chamber

In order to establish the brands (mostly RAW) and the rebirth of the World Heavyweight Championship, a monumental match needed to be created to capture the audience's attention. That match was the Elimination Chamber. And as we covered in the Elimination Chamber case, that match drew the big buy rates to prove it was worth the dollars and the interest it generated.

Super Shows

Since the brands have been separated for a while now, fans have come to expect just seeing RAW of SmackDown! superstars at the house shows and television tapings around the country. Now, the WWE has started to schedule super shows that contain RAW and SmackDown! matches on the card, or do back-to-back television tapings. This is reminiscent of the days when the NWA and the AWA used to put on shows together, or WCW and New Japan putting on international supercards. The WWE has used the brand extension to create a supercard with just the talent they have in house, without the mess of having to split the profits of the show and other paper work mess that would go along with working with another organization. And there is no worry of the two sides not getting along in the future and never working together again and disappointing the fans; they belong to the same company.

Contracts

Whether imaginary or real, the wrestlers' contracts come up during the year. In the old days, that meant that they might jump from the WWF to WCW of vice versa (and a few to ECW and from ECW, too). Nowadays, there is very little of this. TNA cannot afford the large guaranteed contracts, and the WWE has most of the talent locked up. But what the WWE can do is create the illusion of contracts being up. Last year, Matt Hardy switched from SmackDown! to RAW by saying his contact was up and he signed with over to the other side. This plot device can now be used for other wrestlers, especially those being harassed by their general managers.

Trades

Of course, the talent is not in complete control. The GMs can send their talent away in monumental trades. At any time (apparently) several talent can be traded for others in a chance to see talent move off cycle. At the same time, talent can be raised by what they are traded for. When the Big Show was traded from RAW to SmackDown!, five wrestlers came in his place. That just made the Big Show look like a huge value coming in to SmackDown!, and he used that momentum to propel his rebirth over there.

Suspension

For a while, Vince McMahon could threaten to fire anyone once he controlled the wrestling world. No one was safe, and it made it clear that he was in control and no one else. It was rather disheartening. With the GMs in control of each brand, firing someone can be a mistake. If they fire a wrestler (in a storyline), that wrestler can show up on the other show fresh as a daisy. To stop that, a GM can instead suspend a wrestler. This allows for slowing down a storyline, keeping characters fresh, and avoid the messy complication of "re-hires" at a later date. Besides, if someone were really fired, WWE.com would be sure to let us know. New honesty from WWE corporate: yet another repercussion of the Brand Extension.

But with all of these new inventions, some still criticized one brand or the other. As it is, I cannot go a week without reading that one brand is about to die.

THE DEATH OF SO-AND-SO

At the beginning of the brand extension, RAW was considered the "weaker" brand because it had less credible champions and challengers. After the draft lottery, RAW became the powerhouse while SmackDown! became the "second banana". As time has gone on, there have been scares that either show was about to be cancelled, and the rabble was more than willing to go along with the idea. But why?

Are those shows unprofitable? No, and as you will see later, quite the opposite. Are the ratings terrible? No, in comparison to the past they are not that high, but RAW is consistently rated in the top 5 shows on cable and SmackDown! is UPN's top-rated show. Are advertisers canceling left and right? Absolutely not; if anything the WWE has a large plethora of very supportive advertisers who know the market they cater to.

When Spike TV thought the WWE's asking price was too high and subsequently cancelled RAW at the end of the contract, everyone said RAW's days were over. Yet, just a few days later they were able to finalize their deal with USA. Do you think SmackDown! will not find a future home?

Just because SmackDown! is moving to Fridays, it does not mean the show is dead. First off, UPN's contract with the WWE runs until the end of 2006, so the WWE has quite a while to set up a new deal. At that, you have to realize why UPN is acting this way with the WWE. UPN is owned by Viacom, which also owns Spike (along with a lot of other networks). So you can imagine that the sister networks are working together against the WWE. UPN still wants to make money off of their contract, but not at the expense of the overall corporate parent.

SmackDown! is not going anywhere, and neither is RAW. Each is still a healthy brand with lots of life left separately and occasionally crossed together.

Still, there are those that say if competition arose the Brand Extension would have to come to an end…

BEWARE THE LOOMING SHARK

If you have watched Spike TV over the past few weeks, you have probably noticed something: commercials for TNA. That's right; TNA is coming to Slammin' Saturday Night and a late-night Monday replay. That being said, TNA is not competition yet. And even if they were getting a 4.0 rating every week, it would still not be full competition. That is for the following reasons:

#1: PROFIT – TNA is not profitable yet and requires the backing of Panda Energy in order to go about their daily operations. There is nothing wrong with that, and it makes perfect sense to do in the short term to grow at a rate faster than they would be capable of organically. That being said, both RAW and SmackDown! are profitable (see below) and are at a level that even in the best conditions TNA would take three to five years to get to. I hope TNA gets there, but they are not there yet.

#2: RATINGS – I said above IF they were getting a 4.0 every week. That is not going to happen, and when TNA premiers they will probably get about a 1.2. They might get higher in the first week and then drop immediately after that. It will take a good long time, but TNA can get there. RAW regularly gets a 3.8 cable rating and used to regularly get 5.0's. Even getting to RAW's current level, nonetheless their peak, is still a long way off. [*Editor's Note: TNA iMPACT premiered to a 0.8 rating in October 2005 and stayed in that range for quite a while. They did finally get that first 1.2 rating in May 2006*]

#3: TIMESLOT – As happy as I am that TNA has two cable timeslots now, they are not going head-to-head with the WWE. They are not there at primetime Monday's or Friday's, and they are only on for an hour a week. They can be as entertaining as they want (and I hope they will be), but that does not mean they are seen as much. Which leads to...

#4: BRAND RECOGNITION – As I covered previously, people equate wrestling with the WWE (well, WWF, but same difference). The other week while watching RAW, my co-worker (who hasn't watched the WWE since it was WWF and featured the 1-2-3 Kid) was over and the TNA commercial came on. I had to explain to her what the heck it was, and why I was looking forward to it. Do you know what she asked? "Why the heck would they call it TNA? That's a stupid name." You see, TNA has an uphill battle with the casual and fair-weather fans. Non-wrestling fans only think of the WWE/F, and there is nothing in their frame of reference to place TNA. TNA can become a recognized brand, but with a slow, thoughtful approach. And all those people who think they are going to die tomorrow because your mail man does not know what TNA is are wrong also. TNA is going through a long-term plan of their own and are aware of their battle, a battle they can win one day. I just need you to be aware of it as seen by the WWE, that they cannot win by tomorrow.

That being said, TNA could become true competition. Let us say that TNA lives up to all of their potential and they get as big as WCW in 1997. What should the WWE do then? Is the Brand Extension ruined?

Absolutely not! From 1996 to 2001, three major organizations were running full touring companies with weekly shows and PPVs. They were the WWF, WCW, and ECW. And during that time, the WWF was helping to fund ECW. So instead of helping to fund a different company, why can't the WWE run two companies and TNA be the other? Bobby Hennan once said that he thought there was room on Monday night TV for a hundred wrestling shows. While this may be an exaggeration of possibility, the point is there. The economy has already proven they can support three different organizations at the same time. So why could those organizations not be RAW, SmackDown!, and TNA? Wait, why am I using such a recent example?

Back in the 70's and 80's, three organizations in the WWWF/WWF, the NWA, and AWA were all running at the same time. Even further back the 30's the NB/WA, AWA, and NWA all were running (and a great number more, but those were the big players). The point is, three separate organizations can run at the same time.

Others will still say that the WWE would be a stronger force in that situation if they recombined. I will cover this point below. Just now, begin to think of all that will be lost should the brands recombine and the dream matches that will be lost.

The other thing to keep in mind is how the WWF survived their lean days in the mid-1990's. Remember at that point in time, RAW is WAR and WarZone were considered two different shows, even though they were part of the same two hour block. That is because they wanted to have two top rated shows on cable as opposed to WCW's one (well, two with WCW Saturday Night). That, and they could charge advertisers more for WarZone since it got higher ratings. Separation can actually lead to more money, and it's about time we proved how...

THE NUMBERS THAT DON'T AGREE

When the Brand Extension began, many people said it was a mistake because with fewer stars on each card ratings, buyrates, and attendance (and thus revenue and profit) would go down. Well guess what?

They were right.

Well, that was a fun case. Guess I lost. Time to go home.

Wait, what's that?

Oh yes, I have the counter-evidence! Silly me!

First of all, the drop in ratings and attendance at the beginning of the Brand Extension (and later PPV buys during the PPV split) was by design. On September 27, 2002, Vince McMahon went before the crowd at a stockholders meeting and began to address the issues of business being down. I turn to attendant Chris Perry:

> McMahon said part of the decline in attendance and television ratings was by design. In order to position WWE well for the future, the company has high hopes the "brand extension" of the separate Raw and Smackdown rosters. In implementing this "brand extension," WWE knew they would [lose] fans as the transition took place.
>
> The ultimate game plan is to build two distinct groups that can operate under the WWE banner.
>
> As discussed here before, separate storylines, TV shows, tour dates and Pay-Per-Views are the goals. All have been accomplished with additional PPVs scheduled for 2003.
>
> McMahon believes as future stars are cultivated and creative storylines improve, so [too] will the product improve.

So the WWE knew overall numbers were going to drop. Of course, you are supposed to ask if they knew the numbers were going to drop, why would they do it at all?

Think about it as a stock split. Let's say you are a public company with one million shares outstanding (able to be traded) on the New York Stock Exchange (NYSE). On June 30, 2002, your stock was selling for $100 per share, and therefore your company was "worth" $100 million. On July 1, 2002 you did a "stock split" where every single share of stock became two. So now you have two million shares outstanding. Each share is not worth $100 a piece; each is now worth $50, and essentially nothing has changed. The company is still worth $100 million. Why would you do it then? The company seems to have less value per share now that it is split.

Let's jump ahead to June 30, 2003. You still have two million shares of stock outstanding. But now they are worth $70 a piece, thus making your company worth $140 million dollars. If the company had not split, would the stock price have reached $140 a share to match that? Most likely not, there are few on the market that can afford that. But a much broader base of people can afford $70 a share, and now your company looks more attractive. It is owned by more stockholders, and may reach that $100 mark again to do another split!

Now think about this in terms of the WWE. When RAW and SmackDown! split, it was known that each was going to be "worth" less separately than if they had stayed together. $100 seems bigger than $50. But, as time moves on, each develops its own value and rises in price. Let's say the WWE completely spun off RAW and SmackDown as separate companies. At the day of this writing, WWE is trading at $13.18 a share. For simplicity sake we will jump back in time when it was trading to about $12 a share.

OK, let's pretend nothing else exists in the WWE (no WWE films, books, music, etc...) and it is just RAW and SmackDown! They split off tomorrow and each one is worth $6 a share. Because each is getting less revenue and profit separately, RAW drops to $5 and SmackDown! to $3.50. Now the company is worth even less than when this started!

That is where the WWE was in 2002/2003. The split lowered the overall value of the company. Jump ahead a few years. Now, RAW is trading at $9.00 and SmackDown! at $7.50. So the total WWE is worth $16.50, higher than when it started! Would the combined WWE reach that level? It possible, though not probable.

You are saying, 'sure, that sounds good in an imaginary situation, but that's not what is happening'. Oh contraire! That is exactly what is happening. How do I know? I read through five years of quarterly and annual reports and I ran the numbers!

First off, let me warn you that the WWE's fiscal year is very peculiar and does not being and end on normal months. They try to end their year the month after WrestleMania, which gives an odd pattern to follow. That's why sometimes a quarter will have an additional or one-less PPV. I did my best to normalize the WWE's numbers into "regular" years, but I will be the first to admit it may be off by about 5%-8%. Know that going in, I don't hide it.

In 2001, the WWE had revenues of about $431 million dollars and net profits of $8 million (net profits were so low due to the XFL). In 2002, with the beginning of the Brand Extension, that revenue number dropped to $411 million and net profits were at $26 million. Then in 2003, with the Brand Extension in full force, revenue dropped to $367 million while there was a net loss of $0.5 million (there was a correction on the balance sheet and some payments of discontinued operations. Profits from operations remained in the 15-20% of revenue range). This was not looking good, as many have said.

But something has begun to happen. In 2004, revenues popped just a little bit to $371 million with profits of $40 million. And with the additional quarter results release last week, the WWE is already up 3% to the previous year in revenue (and 9% on profit, though that is due to much cost cutting). By my calculations, the WWE does about 23% of their business in the next quarter, which means they are on track to make about $383 million in revenue for the year with $51 million in profit.

Do you see that? The Brand Extension is beginning to climb back up! All the loss that was expected at the beginning is giving way to the EVENTUAL growth. Given another few years, the WWE separated could be making much more than the WWE combined ever did from 1999-2001.

Looking for a few more signs? From Ashish and the newswire:

> WWE Summerslam drew roughly 530,000 buys this year, making it the most bought Summerslam PPV in years.

And it also crashed our server! But it's not the only PPV that has gone up:

PPV	2004 Buyrate	2005 Buyrate
WrestleMania	1.63	2.46
No Way Out	0.50	0.59
Backlash	0.54	0.74
Judgment Day	0.38	0.59
Vengeance	0.55	0.80
Great American Bash	0.57	0.58

Progress is starting to be made!

Is the WWE at the top of its financial game? No. Did they lose a lot of money in the short term that they could have had if they had not gone through the Brand Extension? You bet. Is that all changing? It looks like it! Is each brand beginning to grow at a faster rate separately than if the WWE were a combined company? The numbers don't lie. Can each brand be a success and take the WWE overall to new heights?

Only if we are patient to let the Brand Extension reach maturity and not pull the trigger at the inopportune moment.

REUNION SAYS WHAT?

Let's say, though, the WWE listens to the complainers and the brands recombine after the next PPV. These same complainers will say ratings will go up, PPV buyrates will go up, and attendance will go up!

And you know what? They are right again!

This does not bode well.

Sure, having all of your main event talent—your draws—all over your program will get people to watch both shows... for a while. This is just like the same type of crash booking that many complained about under Vince Russo. Just do something quickly and get the big pop! But then what happens?

Well, you'll have the Big Show, Edge, John Cena, Kane, Kurt Angle, Ric Flair, Shawn Michaels, Triple H, Batista, Booker T, Chris Benoit, Eddie Guerrero, JBL, Randy Orton, and the Undertaker as your main event talent all fighting for one title. What the heck can you do with the other 13 main eventers while two are fighting each other? Plus Hulk Hogan, Mick Foley, and Steve Austin can show up at any time. And there are still others out there like Chris Jericho, Sting, Nash, Hall, and Goldberg. How long until you are back to the original problem of feuds getting played out and talent getting burnt out and fans getting bored out with seeing the same people twice a week. Everything gets hyper accelerated again, but the WWE will not let these guys go.

Yes, there will be a big pop like at this year's Vengeance when RAW had both the WWE and World Champions in matches. What then? Then every problem still exists.

Does the WWE want to have two touring units? How can you tell the fans that only half of the main eventers can be there? People know who is on RAW and who is on SmackDown!, but if they are combined they will expect both and feel ripped off otherwise. Well, there went the second touring group. How many matches can you fit on a PPV? Somewhere in the neighborhood of eight seems probable. Are those main eventers going to give up those PPV spots to Carlito? Just look at all the stars that were not at a combined Summerslam, and all the titles that were not on the line. There just simply is not enough room.

And speaking of room, SmackDown! has 40 people listed on the roster and 47 over on RAW. Is there room in a combined WWE for 87 people? Most likely not, which means cutting at least 25% of the lower and mid-card. Where is the future of the WWE then? How can they develop new talent when they have to fire most of them and there are so many main eventers that there is no room to grow?

Besides, a recombined brand does not solve the WWE's deeper problems. Does a combined WWE have a more creative department? No, it will still be the same people writing the shows. Does it make WWE legal more forgiving of alleged trademark infringements? No, the legal department still will not allow Justin Credible and Billy Kidman to walk around with those names. Will cruiserweights be allowed to fly off the top rope? No, Paul London will still get that whiner gimmick. Will wrestlers be able to work to their top ability? No, Doug Basham and Rob Conway will still be told to kick and punch and not show what they can do.

The WWE has other problems that are not so quickly solved with a recombined organization. Nor are those problems any easier to solve with a combined roster. If anything, recombining now will create more problems that will take years to resolve, all the while causing several more years of loss after the initial pop.

Why go back now when the upside is just starting to become visible?

WHERE THE FUTURE LIES

The WWE is going through some major changes at the time of this writing. SmackDown! has just moved to Friday's (for now) and RAW is returning to USA. But what about the Brand Extension? What other changes are in store for each show?

Will RAW and SmackDown! get more PPVs? Will they only share two or even one a year? Will each brand introduce another title for lower-mid carders? Will RAW become more show and SmackDown! more athleticism? Will they reverse? Will bookers be given more control and Vince McMahon take a much more limited role? Will trades be allowed throughout the year? Will the draft lottery not cover champions? Will there be a RAW vs. SmackDown! tournament a la King of the Ring?

The answer is: I don't know.

The Brand Extension is a work in progress, forever changing. The WWE is not satisfied with where it is now and is changing it for the better. And that is the point, isn't it? We need to give it a chance to get there, wherever "there" may be.

TIME TO SPLIT

The Brand Extension has not been given a fair shake since the beginning. People have complained on everything from the brand names to the champions. Yet the Brand Extension has given so much, including 58% new champions, annual events, new storylines and plot twists, and new situations that can keep the WWE interesting for years.

There is a fear of competition, but the wrestling world has proven it can handle having three promotions running at once. Besides, recombining the brands only provides a momentary pop and does not solve the WWE's larger issues. Still, the numbers are beginning to turn around now, despite the initial drop that was expected and planned for. There is potential for growth.

And that is the point of this case. The Brand Extension needs to be given a chance to breath and mature. Calling it a failure and ending it does not prove anything, not when things are going just as the WWE said they would. The Brand Extension is plan in progress, and the WWE—and we the wrestling fans—deserve the chance to see where it can lead.

The defense rests.

AFTER THE TRIAL

HUNG JURY

IN THE CASE OF THE IWC VERSUS THE BRAND EXTENSION, THE BRAND EXTENSION HAS BEEN ACCUSED OF BEING AN ABYSMAL FAILURE THAT IS ONLY HURTING THE WWE, WRESTLING, WRESTLERS, AND THE FANS SINCE ITS INCEPTION.

With 90.5% of the vote, the Brand Extension was found:

NOT GUILTY!

RESPONSE

As you can imagine, with a score like that there was not a lot of controversy. Instead, people brought up more pertinent examples from their own experiences, such as this one:

> *I wanted to add something to your thoughts about more house shows on a regular basis. Back in 2000, there was a House show in Fresno, CA. Here is our card for the night:*
>
> *October 8, 2000 - WWF - Fresno, California:*
> *K.Krush defeated Joey Abs...*
> *Edge, Christian, and Jacquline defeated The Hardy Boyz and Lita...*
> *Crash defeated Just Joe...*
> *Light-Heavyweight Champion, Dean Malenko, defeated Essa Rios...*
> *Hardcore Champion, Steve Blackman defeated Sho Funaki...*
> *Chris Jericho defeated X-Pac*
>
> *... Chris Jericho vs X-Pac for a Main Event?????*
> *Yeah I was pissed off too, I mean we got to see 3 Champions (Blackman, Hardy Boyz, and Malenko)*

> but they weren't the top guys. While San Jose got the big boys
>
> October 8, 2000 - WWF - San Diego, California:
> The Goodfather and Bull Buchanan defeated Too Cool...
> Mideon defeated Brooklyn Brawler...
> Jerry Lawler defeated Raven...
> European Champion, Al Snow, defeated Saturn...
> Rikishi Phatu and Triple H defeated Kurt Angle and Kane...
> The Dupps defeated Rodney and Pete Gas...
> Chris Benoit defeated Billy Gunn...
> The Dudley Boyz defeated T&A in tables match
>
> There was also an [appearance] by Stone Cold Steve Austin too, this night in San Jose.
>
> ...
>
> With the brand [extension] most people who pay 40-50 bucks for house show tickets don't feel like they got ripped off, I know [I] sure did with a main event that [I] had just seen 2 days before as the opening match on Smackdown.
>
> **Eric Dodson**

A different Eric (Erik?) thought more about what would have happened to the up-and-coming wrestlers if there were less spots available for them:

> It's obvious it's not guilty, just look at the current two top stars, John Cena and Batista. If the roster split never happened, they would still be mid-carders, most likely still under the Prototype and Leviathan gimmicks. Without the roster split, Orton and Batista would never have joined HHH and Flair to form Evolution. Without the split Cena would never had been given the time to find his voice and polish his gimmick to the point that now he's the 2nd coming [of] Rock and Austin rolled into one. With one World Title, there is no chance that you would have seen Benoit or Guererro hold the belts, or see guys like Edge or Matt Hardy in TV Main Events. One Tag Team title would have stolen our chances of seeing MNM, The World's Greatest Tag Team, or La Resistance blossom like they did. Would Carlito, Eugene, Paul London, Ken

> *Kennedy..... Kennedy, Shelton Benjamin, Chris Masters, or Randy Orton have debuted without the roster split? Maybe a few, but they wouldn't be becoming anything worthwhile. I have to say the Brand Extension did far more good to the WWE than bad.*
>
> **Erik Vandermark**

To this I responded:

> *All I can think about is that Cena and Orton used to be "Team Vanilla New Kids With No Name". I think you are being generous with them being mid-carders, because I'm not sure they would have got on TV. I think we would have seen them make it to Heat and then subsequently get cut when they did not immediately win over the crowd. It took both nearly two years to find their voices and gimmicks, and that does not include the years spent training in OVW. Just remember all of the guys who were in OVW and HWA when the WWF bought WCW, and how many did not make it to the main roster for years or at all because of the sudden influx of talent. Most of that talent is still around, yet spots had to open up for them somehow!*

WCW Thunder

Intro

Some dame walked into my office and said...

This one comes from our resident **Stenographer**, believe it or not. Stenographer?

> *Thanks, JP. Well, since I figured I'd have the next couple of weeks off, I thought I'd get you to defend my favorite wrestling show: WCW Thunder. Whenever something bad happens on RAW or SmackDown!, writers and smarks go "that was as bad as an episode of Thunder!" But Thunder was enjoyable, and doesn't deserve to always be associated with bad wrestling.*

Thanks Stenographer, that does sound like a good case!

Why this?

Like Stenographer said, WCW Thunder gets a bad rap for being terrible Wrestling. But was it as bad as many would have you believe? Or was WCW Thunder truly an enjoyable program that more than pulled its weight in WCW. Only one way to find out, and that's to start the case!

Where the heck did this show come from?

That's the question that must have been running through Eric Bischoff's head. After a very successful 1997, Turner Sports and TBS wanted to capitalize on the success of WCW and Nitro and expand the brand outward. Without consulting Bischoff, Turner (the company, not the person) added WCW Thursday Thunder to TBS's lineup. Bischoff had just a few weeks (over the holidays) to pull together a set, an arena and taping schedule, and start writing the program. But feeling up to the challenge, Bischoff did not let the fact that he felt Thunder would cause an overexposure of WCW deter him.

Thus, Thunder premiered with a bang:

> *Thunders debut was on January 8, 1998. How do I know this for certain? January 8 is my birthday and I joked that WCW was giving me a new TV show for a present that year. I seem to also think that the main event on that show was DDP vs. Nash 1-on-1, but am not entirely sure. One thing I do remember for sure though was that it was on that Thunder that WCW made the announcement for the Hogan vs. Sting rematch at Superbrawl after the title had been held up due to the Starrcade silliness.*
>
> **Casey Trowbridge**
> **Huron, SD.**

The following week continued on top of that first week. The show featured seven matches, including Chris Jericho defeating Eddie Guerrero (a workrate dream match), Rey Mysterio winning the Cruiserweight Championship from Juventud Guerrera (pre-'Juice' days, a lot more real Lucha style), and Lex Luger and DDP teaming up to defeat Kevin Nash and Randy Savage.

With little promotion, no pre-planning, and no support from Turner corporate, the first episode of Thunder pulled in a solid 4.0 rating and the subsequent week held at a 3.6 rating (which was higher than a recent week's RAW rating at the time of this writing). But Thunder would soon start rolling in the numbers.

As the weeks went on, Thunder continued to pull in ratings in the high 3's and low 4's. Even on the weeks when Thunder was moved to Wednesdays because of a baseball game it would still get low 3's. This would all continue until July 1999, when ratings slipped into the high 2's as WCW's popularity waned. The ratings would continue to slide and hang in the upper 1's and lower 2's until the end of WCW. Even with Thunder being taped after Nitro, it was still pulling in ratings double to triple anything ECW on TNN got. Relative to the times, WCW Thunder was pulling in strong ratings.

But one would have to ask, what were they showing that would make people want to tune in?

WHERE ARE MY MAIN EVENTERS?

The biggest lie I read all the time about Thunder is that nothing important ever happened on the show, and the main eventers were never there. That could not be further from the truth. Look, we already saw that Lex Luger, DDP, Kevin Nash, and Randy Savage were on the premier episodes of Thunder, but that would not be the end. The Giant and Scott Hall main evented the following week, Bill Goldberg made regular appearances, Ric Flair most definitely fought on the show, Sting defended the championship, and even Hollywood Hogan lost a match to the Macho Man.

Not only that, but titles changed hands on Thunder. Above we mentioned the change in the Cruiserweight Championship. On the June 6, 1998 edition of Thunder the World Tag Team Championships changed hands. Even the World Heavyweight Championship changed hands, including one where Kevin Nash defeated Jeff Jarrett and Scott Steiner in a three-way dance on May 24, 2000. These are just a few of the examples, but most definitely not all.

Still, many complain that it was not always main eventers topping the program. One week, DDP would be defending the World Heavyweight Championship against Bam Bam Bigelow. Two weeks later, the show would be headlined with David Flair vs. Barry Horowitz. Seems rather inconsistent, doesn't it?

But consider this: WCW was using Thunder as a chance to give talent more exposure. Mid-carders getting into the main event gave them a chance to show that they were worth it, that they could go all the way. And it was not just mid-carders fighting other mid-carders. DDP defended his title against Stevie Ray, Hollywood Hogan defeated the Disciple, Evan Karagias defeated Randy Savage (you read that right) and Konnan and Rey Mysterio defeated the Outsiders. Where else but Thunder could the mid-carder work his way up and fight in the main event? There was no room for that on the superstar-filled Nitro, but Thunder gave them a chance to shine.

Not only that, but it was not just the people who were spotlighted. The US title was often in the main event, as were the Television and Tag Team Championships. These belts (which hardly get recognition now, if they even exist), were given top spots on Thunder. And who were often around those belts? Chris Benoit, Chris Jericho, Booker T, Eddie Guerrero, Raven, Perry Saturn, Scott Steiner, and basically everyone considered to be the top workers in WCW. Thunder was their chance to shine, and get their belts a nice shine, too.

Unique Situations

Since the real fight was on Monday Night, WCW got to have a little more fun with Thunder and try new things. For instance, on the June 18, 1998 episode of Thunder, Masa "My Hero" Chono and Hiroyoshi Tenzan defended the IWGP Tag Team Championships against Davey Boy Smith and Jim Neidhart. Where else in America could you see a major Japanese title defended? How often are other organizations even mentioned on national TV, nonetheless have their titles defended?

Or how about this one: On the July 16, 1998 Konnan and DDP teamed up to face Curt Henning and Scott Hall. Why was this a big deal? Because Konnan was a member of nWo Wolfpac and DDP a member of team WCW. This was the first time EVER that a WCW and nWo person teamed up. nWo had fought itself, but at no point had they ever joined forces with a WCW person. This was a first, and it happened on Thunder.

Also, Thunder was pretty much the unique home of Marty Jannetty. Without much fanfare, Jannetty would come out for weeks busting his butt in the ring and putting on a solid match with everyone. People talked about his matches in the WWE a few months before this writing as if they were his first wrestling appearances in a decade. But that is not true as WCW gave him a chance to show what he was made of on Thunder in 1998 and 1999.

Towards the end of WCW, Thunder became the home of new stars. A.J. Styles (you might have heard of him) and Air Paris were teaming regularly and beginning to show the new generation of the wrestling game. Thunder was all about the future of the business; it's a shame that that future was cut short.

(Fun Fact: Scott Steiner was in both the first and last Thunder matches. He was on the winning side both times.)

MORE BIG SURPRISES AND THAT OLD NITRO FEELING

Thunder was not just the home of future stars and unique events, but it also played an important role in the bigger scheme of WCW. On the January 26, 2000 episode of Thunder, Ric Flair returned to WCW television after a long absence. Hulk Hogan also made his return to WCW after a 4 ½ month absence on the February 2, 2000 episode of Thunder.

Of course, Thunder did not need big surprises to make it feel important. Despite being focused on younger talent and not trying to make every week a PPV, Thunder was still made to feel big. Notice something different about the lengths of RAW and SmackDown!? RAW always goes overtime (a leftover from the Monday Night Wars) while SmackDown! ends on time. It is a little distinction that makes RAW seem that much more important and give it that "anything can happen" feeling. Thunder actually shared this trait with Nitro, where both would go into overtime. Also, if Michael Buffer was the guest ring announcer for Nitro, you can guarantee that he would show up on Thunder. And who does not like to hear Michael Buffer announce La Parka?

FEEL THE THUNDER

WCW Thunder constantly gets ripped into as if it were the worst show in wrestling. But Thunder was given solid talent to work with, from main eventers and their World titles to the workhorses and their championships to the future superstars of tomorrow. The ratings would back up the fan interest in the show, even during WCW's waning years. The ratings were not the best ever at the end, but were much higher than ECW ever saw, and TNA has yet to see.

Big events happened on Thunder, from the return of stars to championship changes. And at the same time, unique events occurred from other organizations getting their titles on TV to the nWo and WCW teaming up for the first time. And Thunder was given the same rights as Nitro, with overrun main events and Michael Buffer doing the announcing.

Was every episode of Thunder the greatest night of wrestling? No. But on a weekly basis could it entertain the fans? You bet. How can anyone continually compare any bad event to Thunder when on any given week, Thunder could have been just as good as a PPV?

The defense rests.

AFTER THE TRIAL

HUNG JURY

IN THE CASE OF THE IWC VERSUS WCW THUNDER, WCW THUNDER HAS BEEN ACCUSED OF BEING A POINTLESS SHOW THAT HAD NO ENTERTAINMENT VALUE IN WRESTLING WHAT-SO-EVER.

With 89.4% of the vote, WCW Thunder was found:

NOT GUILTY!

Another lower voting (compared to the likes of Goldberg or the Fingerpoke of Doom), but high scoring case. I was happy to find many other people who enjoyed Thunder for what it was, and even more who were like me and preferred Thunder to Nitro. Who knew? Now it's IWC fact!

RESPONSE

A number of people shared their personal memories and experiences with Thunder. Here are a couple that were of particular interest:

> *Ahh, so many great memories of Thunder. Hell I can remember Thunder being my 2nd wrestling*

event that I ever attended, in the Roanoke Civic Center [Coliseum] in Roanoke VA. To me, Thunder was just as big as Nitro, and the best part at that time was they were taping two weeks' worth of shows in one night.

Ahh the memories of that night, Juventud Guerrera and Rey Mysterio Jr (Damn the WWE for dropping the Jr) went at it to a 15 minute time limit draw, and thankfully were allowed to finish the match. So many great high spots in that match, that you just can't catch in the WWE Smack Down! [Cruiserweight] [division].

And by the end of the night Goldberg had won yet another victory as the World Heavyweight Champion.

I thank you for letting me relive my [fondness] memories, and find WCW Thunder... NOT GUILTY!

Dave Jones

Some of my fonder wrestling memories actually come from what was consider WCW's "B" and "C" shows. While Nitro was hammering out 3 hour shows and (I believe), blurring the line between PPV spectacle and week-to-week build, Thunder was a two hour show with [its] own feel. I enjoyed having guys from the Flock or some of the better workers getting the nudge. Seeing a guy as entertaining as "The Mecca" Shawn Stasiak getting some quality TV time before he became a planet. Seeing an entire show dedicated to the cruiserweights. Seeing other belts get a little spotlight once and awhile.

Rick Steiner during his television title run had many prominent matches on the show with some of the younger guys, giving them a little rub. That's the sort of thing you weren't seeing on Nitro, that's for sure. I mean, why have them if they don't mean anything? WCW Thunder made them mean something, and I hold nothing against them.

Wolf Blitzer

Lex Luger

Intro

Some dame walked into my office and said...

Well, it all started on May 15, 2005 with resident Eric Bischoff hater (more than Joe Boo) **MATTHEW Roberts**:

> The Defense Of Lex Luger. Yes, he is a drug addict and scum bag now. However he was super over and a decent wrestler in the late 1980's. Yes, if Ric Flair had done business the right way and done 1 job for Luger from 1988 to 1991, Luger could have been a huge star. Yes, if Vince McMahon had given him the title following the Lex Express, he would have been a decent draw (definitely no worse than Chunkyzuna was).

Always interesting with the naming of things. Later on, **Ronevsorg** said:

> What about Lex Luger?...............

To which I wondered what all the periods were about, but then I said, "I'll take the case!" Well, actually I said I already took the case, but that he'd get credit, too.

After announcing the case, I did receive this from **Uncle Jason**:

> You see, no matter what you say about [Luger], I'm voting Guilty. I don't care if he was forced to have totally-suck-ass matches with his children at gunpoint. I don't care if his mother is needing medicine & he was working to help her. I don't care if he's been feeding starving people around the globe & healing the blind & teaching the lame to walk.
>
> I don't care. I hate Lex Luger.

That's a ringing endorsement right there!

WHY THIS?

Lex Luger is a man who has been mired in personal problems, especially since the demise of WCW. He came from an interesting time in wrestling, appearing just past the beginning of Hulk-a-mania, but before the complete demise of the territory system. He was a product of his generation, for better or for worse, and grew up to be a multi-time champion with a career spanning almost two decades long.

Yet, because of his recent personal problems, history has chosen to remember him unkindly. Suddenly, he was not the genetic marvel he was during the day, only a long line of people with a narcissist gimmick. He was not the PWI Rookie of the Year (1986), Comeback of Year (1993), Most Popular Wrestler of Year (1993), and Wrestler of Year (1997), but was a joke. He never belonged in this business; he was a loser who was pushed down our throats. Anyone with a modicum of muscle and gab could have been Lex Luger.

Of course, none of these lamentations on Luger are true. He has given so much to this business and we the fans, and his push to the top were the result of his hard work. Has he fallen mightily from grace (should he ever have been in grace)? There is no doubt. But should we kick him when he is down and bury his legacy as if he were a mere footnote at the bottom of a mud-caked shoe? I think not.

And to prove that, there is only one place to start: the beginning.

HE LOVES ME, HE LOVES ME NOT

We're diving right in, because the biggest lie I read about Lex Luger is that he has no love for the business and was only in it for the money. While money was definitely a motivating factor in Mr. Luger's life, that was hardly his sole reason for sacrificing himself to this business for so long.

Like many future wrestlers, especially from in and around his time, Luger (born Larry Pfohl, but that's the last time we'll be calling him THAT) found his athleticism expressed through football. He played college ball for the Penn State before transferring to the University of Miami in 1978. After college, he joined the USFL playing for the Memphis Showboats and then the Tampa Bay Bandits. This went on for a bit until he found himself in the CFL playing for the Montreal Alouettes before finally making it to the big leagues and playing for the Green Bay Packers in the NFL.

While out on a celebrity golf tournament, Luger met Florida wrestling legend Bob Roop. The two hit it off, and it was Roop who was convinced that Luger had what it took to be in the wrestling business. In case you were wondering about the credibility of Roop to make such a decision, here is Roop's description of himself:

> *I had an 18-year career as a professional wrestler. The first 15 of them I worked steadily, seldom having more than a day or two off at a time. Making a lot of money was not my goal, travel and adventure lit my fire. I made three trips to Japan and Australia, wrestled in Korea, New Zealand, Tasmania, England, Scotland, Germany, Iraq, the Bahamas, Puerto Rico, Grand Cayman, and from one side of the U.S. to the other. There were adventures along the way, some tragic in the form of a fatal plane crash, and others merely terrifying in the form of engine failures and near crashes or flying with maniacal wrestlers piloting their own planes...*

This was a former Olympian who had been on the professional scene for years before he met Luger. He understood the business and saw that Luger had the potential and the heart for it.

Just to make sure, Roop brought in Hiro Matsuda, who you might remember as the man that had previously trained Hulk Hogan and Paul Orndorff. So no, you were not going to get the technical expertise of someone trained by Stu Hart, nor the high flying prowess of someone trained by the Gory Guerrero, but he was going to learn how to excite a crowd and hold them in the palm of his hand.

After a relative short while, Luger made his professional debut in 1985 in Florida. He would have a monumental start, defeating Wahoo McDaniels for the Southern Heavyweight title on November 19th of that year. He would lose the title and win it back from Jesse Bar in February 1986, and do the same again in July 1986 with the Masked Superstar. He would later go on to also win the Bahamas title before being given a World Heavyweight Championship shot against Ric Flair at Battle of the Belts III. This match would go to a sixty-minute draw.

Sixty minutes? Lex Luger? Let's keep that in mind for later.

The point of all that success is that everyone from Roop to Matsuda to Kevin Sullivan (who ran the Florida territory) to Ric Flair saw the potential in Luger. He was not immediately given everything, though, despite what it may seem. Those were only Florida championships, and Crocket was the big game in the South at the point. Until he made it there, it was just like working in ROH today. Sure, he was succeeding at one of the biggest indies going, but it was still an indie.

But the opportunity came for Luger to join Ric Flair's Four Horsemen in 1987, and he jumped at the chance. The Big Show shares this memory:

> *I was bit by the wrestling bug as a kid. I remember when Lex Luger debuted. We were watching Georgia Championship Wrestling, and Ric Flair was talking about "The Phenom", and Lex came out, and I remember my dad and I were like, "Holy smoke! Look at that guy!" I had never seen anybody on TV with muscles like that at the time. At the time, he was so shredded. There are 30 guys in our locker room right now that look better, but back then it was unbelievable.*

And thus Lex Luger's real path to wrestling glory began. He went on have multiple US and Tag Title runs. He fought for the side of good, he fought for the side of evil. But it would not be until 1991 that he rose to the top when he pinned Barry Windham to become the WCW champion after Ric Flair left the organization. So for four years he worked in the mid card and fought his way up the ranks of the NWA/WCW. Nothing was handed to him overnight.

And why would he stick around? He could have gone into modeling with his body or tried for football once more. He obviously had a degree from the University of Miami or could have gone for more education.

But he kept on striving for more, and plenty of people all over the NWA put faith into him. Now why would they go ahead and do a thing like that? Because Lex Luger belonged in the wrestling business and loved it. He sacrificed on the smaller circuits, gave up big NFL money to take a chance to be trained, and ran with the ball when it was given to him. He could have packed up and gone home anytime, especially in the years of frustration that Ric Flair did not put him over. But he waited and waited, beating his body down, until his body could handle it no more.

Feeling frustrated by nagging injuries and the direction of WCW, Luger dropped the World Heavyweight Championship to Sting at SuperBrawl II in February 1992 and forthwith quit WCW. But his contract would not allow him to wrestle anywhere else until it ran out the following year (something Vince McMahon should have paid attention to later), so Luger joined Vince McMahon's World Bodybuilding Federation. Luger, unfortunately, was involved in a motorcycle accident that put him out of commission for the rest of the WBF's life. Without a wrestling contract and never getting to perform in the WBF, Luger signed on to the WWF at the Narcissist, but that is a story for another section.

But why did Luger come back at all? Was it for the money? No, he could have sat home and did nothing and made money. He wanted to wrestle, he wanted to be out there. On an interview on Live Audio Wrestling, Luger said he would rather perform and earn his money than sit home and just get paid like he did with his Time Warner contract. Just because he was smart enough to not to give up millions of dollars does not mean he loved wrestling any less. He is even at the time of this writing working with AWE in Winnipeg.

Lex Luger, if he wanted to, could leave wrestling forever. He still has his gyms, he still has real estate, he still has other investments. But he wants to go out there and wrestle.

The question is, do any of us want to see him?

WHO NEEDS MAT SKILLS WHEN YOU'VE GOT PECKS LIKE THESE?

The complaint has been that Luger is a punch-kick-clothesline-rack kind of wrestler, and that's all he does. First off, the vast majority of Lex Luger's matches are just that: he hits someone a few times, slams them around, and then puts them a torture rack to submit. But that is what he is paid to do! Look, his gimmick is a big strong guy with amazing muscles. As an entertainer, he is to go out there and perform what the crowd wants to see. Much like Goldberg and Kevin Nash, Luger was not destined to go out there and have half-hour classics every time up (although he has had several, back to that in a minute). The crowds, whether cheering him or booing him, wanted to see fast hard-hitting action with a few power moves whenever he appeared.

And that is what Lex Luger delivered. He was trained by some of the best and had years to learn in Florida and the NWA from Sullivan, Flair, Anderson, Sting, the Steiners, and others. During those years he not only learned how to push the boundaries of his abilities, but also learned how to reel them him. Luger learned a less-is-more mentality, and how to keep the fans interested in his matches. That's why when he defeated Hollywood Hogan for the title on the Nitro before Road Wild 1997 the fans were screaming and champaign was flying in the back. Luger did not need to perform a million moves a minute, he just needed a few.

Still, when he wanted to, Luger could pull out all the stops. That is why in 1987 he was nominated for the PWI Match of the Year award. Oh wait, that was a War Games match, can't attribute his contribution to that, no way. Well how about in 1991 when he WON the PWI Match of the Year Award? Wait, wait, that was because he was teaming with Sting and fighting the Steiner Brothers. Of course he had nothing to do with that match. Oh, what's this? That same year he was nominated for another match? Wait, am I saying that Luger was nominated for two matches of the year awards in one year? And the other one was a single's match? Against Ron Simmons?

That's history folks. Luger can pull out all the stops and impress when he needs to. Is he going to be in the match of the night most nights? Absolutely not! But that is not his job. He is a main event power wrestler who is supposed to go out there and perform big devastating moves. There is a balance to watching a wrestling show. So when Luger defeated Hollywood Hogan, the match before it was Villano IV y V vs. Hector Garza and Lizmark Jr. The fans got to see the high flying action to get them pumped up, and then a big powerhouse main event that sent them home happy and feeling like they got their money's worth.

But did the fans get what they paid for? Is Lex Luger really worth it? I mean, what has this man actually done?

I CAN'T REMEMBER ANYTHING IMPORTANT...

Many have claimed that Luger was never a part of anything big, that he was just bit player here and there that never had the spotlight. Well look into the last section: first off, he was a major player in WCW vs. nWo, a member of Team WCW in almost every super-tag match versus the fledgling nWo, and one of only three men to defeat Hollywood Hogan for the title while Hogan was with the nWo (the other two being Sting and Bill Goldberg). Also, Luger was in the nWo Wolfpac, both the face and heel versions.

Of course, this was not his first foray into group ventures. Luger was a prominent member of the Horsemen for a while, and fought against them for even longer.

Still, he had many memorable feuds besides these, especially those with Barry Windham (over the US and later World Title), Ron Simmons, and of course his on-again, off-again relationship with Sting.

More than these, though, is that Luger has been involved in some seriously shocking moments. On July 4, 1993 Luger landed a helicopter on board the USS Intrepid and body slammed Yokozuna to kick off the Lex Express (who saw that one coming?). He and Bret Hart were co-winners of the Royal Rumble when both of them touched the floor at the same time (an ending that would oft be repeated). But bigger than all of that was the day he returned to WCW in September 1995. It was the very first Nitro from the Mall of America, and out through the fans walked Lex Luger in an absolute shock to the world, especially since he had just wrestled for Vince the night before. But it turned out Luger was wrestling without a contact and as a favor to Sting, Eric Bischoff brought him on board. This ended up being a great benefit as it gave Nitro that "anything can happen" feeling that was so important at the beginning.

And despite the fact that Bischoff had no love for Luger, Luger would still go on to win both Tag Team and World gold. The man overcame the absolute disdain from his boss to prove he could be in the main event. What more could you want then that?

BOY THIS ARENA SURE IS EMPTY

Oh, that's right: sales. Well, how do the numbers stack with Mr. Luger?

Well, first we can look at SummerSlam 1993 when he fought Yokozuna for the title. As we know, Luger was given his position because Hogan had left the company. And of course, the Lex Express became a complete joke that no fan could get behind. Except for one problem: the fans did get behind it. SummerSlam scored a 1.2 that year. Let's fast forward to later that year when Luger and Hart were set to fight Yokozuna for the title at WrestleMania. That event drew an impressive 1.68.

Perhaps I am going about this all wrong. Let's jump to WCW in 1997 at Road Wild. Luger was defending his newly won championship against Hollywood Hogan. That only brought in a 0.65. But I will contend that that is because people already saw the main event on the Nitro beforehand and had no reason to tune in. They already saw what they were looking for. And taking a quick look, that night Nitro got a 4.4 rating to RAW's 2.7. I'd say Luger was holding interest there.

As for merchandise sales, well, it's hard to say. I do not have a copy of WCW's and WWE's books. But I do know that Luger was featured on credit cards, t-shirts, posters, toys, cards, magazines, and video games. And all of that is not sitting in a warehouse somewhere. People bought and owned Luger gear, and loved him as a wrestler.

Of course, when you get that high, you often come crashing down.

DAMN THAT BOY IS JACKED!

First, though, we really need to look at what got Lex Luger to the game. As noted by the Big Show earlier, there may have been a thousand guys with physiques as good (if not better) since Lex Luger, but Luger was the first. For his time he was unique, and don't forget it.

Of course, you are going to ask, "But JP, how did Luger get so jacked? Didn't he take supplements?"

And I'm going to tell you yes, yes he did.

What?

OK, let's take a trip way back in time. Do you know why marijuana is an illegal substance in the United States?

Is it because it is an intoxicating substance? Is it because it is dangerous to the health and wellbeing of the people who use it? Is it because of its debilitating long-term effects on regular users?

Absolutely not—it's because of outside interests.

Prior to 1937, marijuana was mostly legal across all of America. In the 19th century and early 20th century, marijuana could be purchased at shops or (according to wikipedia.com) *"it could be openly purchased in bulk from grocers or in cigarette form at newsstands"*. Then in 1937, a law was passed (against the advice of American Medical Association) to make it illegal to transport or possess cannabis. Now what would suddenly cause this change in attitude?

(1) Black culture – during the 1920's and 1930's, the Jazz scene exploded into the American underground and semi-mainstream society. The conservatives of this country feared the growth of Jazz and black culture in America and labeled it as the complete moral decay of society (hmmm... that story sounds familiar). Many jazz musicians were well known proponents and users of marijuana, especially the legendary Louis Armstrong. So, as an attempt to hold back black culture, white conservatives sought to make marijuana illegal.

(2) But they really wanted it illegal because these people were the same ones who got prohibition passed. You see, on January 16, 1920 the eighteenth amendment went into effect, thus making the transportation and possession of alcohol illegal in the United States. This, of course, paved the way for organized crime, importation from Canada, the growth of underground jazz bars, and the use of marijuana, but that is beside the point. The eighteenth amendment was repealed by the twenty-first amendment on February 17, 1933. Thus the Temperance movement needed to set their sights on a substance that they knew they could make illegal without an amendment, and one that most people would not miss. So they set their sights on marijuana and scared white America into buying the idea by saying blacks would be impregnating their daughters if they continued to let marijuana spread. Their plan worked.

(3) Still, there was one man who was most responsible for getting marijuana on the bad-guys book, and that was William Hearst, chief stockholder of DuPont. DuPont, as a chemical and materials processing company, had a heavy interest in a fabric called nylon. By eliminating hemp from the equation, nylon, cotton, wool, and linen sales went up, as did DuPont's profits. You see, it was Mr. Hearst's testimony to Congress that put the final nail in the head of marijuana in the United States, at least for a few decades.

In 1969, the Supreme Court overturned the laws against marijuana due to a loophole in it that violated the fifth amendment. In response, in 1970, Congress passed the Controlled Substance Act, and quickly added marijuana to the list of controlled substances. And that is where it has remained since, although some controls have been loosened for medical purposes in some states.

Now what the heck does this have to do with Lex Luger?

Well, those "supplements" that he was taking in the 1980's, they were just like marijuana. At the time, they were not illegal; they were just supplements! Weight trainers and other athletes are constantly taking supplements. The drug of choice today is guarana, which is really just a water retainer. It makes you look bulkier without adding real mass and also provides energy. But a few years ago ephedra was the drug of choice as a weight controller until it was banned by the Food and Drug Administration on December 30, 2003. How long until guarana or taurine meets a similar fate?

So Luger took those supplements for years. But wait, it was not until 1991 that anabolic steroids joined the list of drugs on the Controlled Substance Act, the same act that was created to control marijuana!

And why were anabolic steroids and other similar substances added to the list? Was it because of health concerns? Was it because of a fear for of long-term effects on the people using them and their families?

No! It was all about sports, a many-many-many billion-dollar business throughout the country and world-wide. Sports realized they had problem with their athletes using the substances to get better at their game while others chose not to. They then changed the public's perception AGAINST these supplements, saying they were illegal performance enhancing substances (long before they were illegal). Why do you think the US Congress was involved with the baseball steroids scandal? Was it because it was an important issue? No, it was because it would get them a lot of attention and they could talk about it with voters. Thus Congress became involved in 1991 with sports so that their constituents would re-elect them after the sports industry management turned against their athletes.

But by then, it was way too late for many workers. Luger was one of those men. He had been taking supplements for a decade and, at least in his own head, had seen no detrimental side effects. We know this is not true, but from his perspective he was fine. In reality, Luger was hooked. He continued to use substances as time went on, not aware of the effect on his body and mind.

Listen, up until the 1950's, doctors in China used to prescribe cigarettes for people who had bad coughs. How were they supposed to know it would make them worse over time? They didn't have the training or knowledge; no one around them did! The same with Luger—how was he supposed to know the long-term dangers of the supplements he took in the 1980s? Did you know the dangers of ephedra before it was made illegal?

A COUPLE OF MORE CRIMES

Still, it is obvious that either the long-term effects of drugs, two decades on the road, a career being started and halted a number of times, or a combination of all of that and more had a detrimental impact on Luger. He began to make life decisions that were not for the best. None of us can judge him because we do not know all the facts. But here is what we do know:

Ms. Elizabeth died in his house. From the Smokinggun.com:

> AUGUST 5--The wrestling personality known as Miss Elizabeth died from a lethal combination of booze and prescription drugs, according to this autopsy report from the Cobb County Medical Examiner. The coroner determined that the May 1 death of Elizabeth Hulette, 42, was an accident resulting from "acute toxicity-multiple drugs." Hulette was stricken at the Georgia home she shared with live-in boyfriend Lawrence Pfohl, who wrestles professionally as Lex Luger. She was later pronounced dead at a local hospital, where a police detective told the ME's investigator that Hulette "had been observed drinking Vodka and taking Soma and Loritabs several hours" prior to her demise. A toxicology screen found evidence of anxiety, muscle relaxation, nausea, and pain drugs in Hulette's system. Her blood alcohol level was measured at a whopping .299. As a result of the police investigation of Hulette's death, cops arrested Pfohl after discovering illegal bodybuilding drugs in his home.

Now, maybe Luger had the supply of those drugs on hand. And as we previously discussed, that is because of his earlier conditioning, not because he was a degenerate abuser. The man needed help and obviously was not getting it. His addiction was a disease, but that does not mean he is responsible for spreading the infection. Elizabeth had problems of her own, problems that far outweighed physical pain. Why in the world would anyone even have a blood-alcohol level of .299 to begin with? And then mix that with drugs? Something deeper was going on. From the LAW:

> *When asked about the last few years including the death of Elizabeth Huelette, [Luger] says is a very private person as was Elizabeth and that it's been very mentally tough. He says the real story has never been told and he wants to be private about that issue out of respect to Elizabeth's family. He says if he could change places with her he would have and misses her.*

Read between the lines. Luger was trying to protect Elizabeth. He may have been the one trying to wean her off of drugs for all we know. But we don't. Sting further alludes to Elizabeth's problems:

> *You know, it's all over out there. It's just ... there. You know actors and actresses in Hollywood and movies, sports, baseball, football, basketball it's everywhere, it's not just wrestling. Wrestling is set apart though because it's not seasonal. We don't go for 6 to 8 months to film a big blockbuster movie and go home. We don't play baseball for 6 to 8 months out of the year and come home. You know we're gone, traveling, and turning the light switch on every day of our lives. Every day. Actually, you're this super ball and bounce around and play and get trounced on and try to stay in shape and deal with the press and deal with the stress of traveling, and you know, it takes its toll. It takes its toll.*

Sting will not talk about it, but he put the idea out there. Luger will not talk about it either, and he will protect Elizabeth for the rest of his years. Say what you want to about Luger, but he cared for Elizabeth. And under no circumstances did he kill her.

In the months that followed, Luger's grief was strong and got him arrested again. On February 1, 2005, Luger was arrested for DUI. The problem was, he was not driving the car. He had passed out in the car drunk, and when the cops woke him up he tried to start the engine, so they booked him. He had expired tags and other illegal documents.

Almost two months later he was arrested again for failure to pay child support. Things were looking bleak.

But do you know what I say:

GIVE THE MAN A BREAK!

His live-in girlfriend DIED in his house! Stop all the jokes, that is seriously painful. Are you telling me that you would not be completely messed up if the person you loved, who you lived with, who was having problems, suddenly and violently died in front of you? How long would need before you could even BEGAN to function semi-normally again?

Luger obviously needed time. He was not in a good place, and with reason. Was being drunk behind the wheel right? No. Is not paying your child support legal? Absolutely not. But can we understand where Luger was coming from? Sure, he was in a hard place and needed time to recover. He needed to prove he was worth another shot.

GIVING THE BOY A SHOT

Just six months after the death of Ms. Elizabeth, TNA's Dixie Carter had this to say:

> *It is rare that TNA ever responds to media, no matter how off it may be from fact. But we strongly believe it is appropriate at this time to address what is being said about Lex Luger appearing on our November 12th pay-per-view telecast.*
>
> *TNA is about opportunity -- for wrestlers new and established. For the fans, TNA provides a weekly program that showcases today's hottest talent, introduces the stars of tomorrow, and provides the opportunity to re-experience wrestling icons. Since its inception, TNA has paid homage to NWA legends who have laid the foundation for our company.*
>
> *As far as TNA talent is considered, we could not be more proud of our entire roster who give their heart and soul week after week to build this special group. We believe in being compassionate and giving guys a chance. From new, incredibly talented young men to veterans who may need lifting up when trying to change their lives. Surrounding a man with the kind of environment we enjoy backstage at TNA can only be considered a very good thing. We are about accentuating the positive, not the negative.*

> *When our talent approaches management and recommends giving someone an opportunity, we listen, and that is the case with Lex Luger, as well as others. The success of bringing Lex to TNA won't be measured with pay-per-view buys. It will be measured by what a man does with an opportunity given.*

You see, despite everything, wrestling companies still see a reason to talk to and book Luger. He was on the WWA world tours. He has had informal talks with the WWE. His legacy in wrestling is not forgotten. And Lex has learned a lot, too. From the LAW again:

> *He says he blames no one but himself and wants to talk to youngsters about how he did things wrong.*

Luger has come to a point of understanding with his personal life. He is not all the way there yet, but he is getting there. But despite all of his personal problems, should we judge his final legacy on the mistakes of a few years that have nothing to do with the ring?

LISTEN TO THE FANS

If the e-mails I have already received are any indication, the answer is no. **Charlie S.** shares some memories:

> *I started watching WWF in 1991 and wasn't familiar with the man who said, "I'm the total package." I just wanted to say that to stress that I didn't know Lex Luger when he was arguably at his peak. Instead, I knew Luger as the guy who beat up Mr. Perfect a few times then "saw the light" and became the All-American. For those that don't remember, Yokozuna was astonishing when he started. He tore through the WWF. He put several people in the hospital (Jim Duggan for one), he dominated the Rumble, he beat Bret Hart, lost to Hogan (but who didn't), and then he KILLED Hulkamania (WWF Magazine, probably June or so 93). Alright, he's a HUGE heel, we get it. Then Lex comes around and slams him on a military ship after flying down in a helicopter, now that is*

> excellent booking. Then he starts Lex Express. He burns across America building HUGE momentum going into SummerSlam. He battles the unbeatable Yokozuna, knocks him out, and wins... by countout? No worries, he'll get another chance right? He battles through the Rumble, wins it (with Bret)! They both go to Mania for a showdown with the monster (who by the way, just beat Undertaker in a casket match with 11 guys, but still impressive to win a casket match against Taker). Now, if I remember correctly, Luger gets screwed over at Mania, Bret wins the title back, blah, blah. Luger's not done yet right? I mean he's still at the top with Bret and Yoko. Wait, who's this Diesel guy? Bob Backlund (well that chickenwing crossface is a cool move, I guess)? How can Shawn wrestle for a belt, he's too small? At WM 11, Luger will be back at the main event. He deserves it. What, he's teaming with British Bulldog as the "Allied Powers". He goes back to WCW and does a great job, winning the title in the feud with Hogan. Always a contender and a guy that kind of got left behind by Sting. You mentioned that he beat Hogan, but you need to point out that after Macho turned, it was basically Luger + WCW wrestler v. NWO. Luger was good, he knew how to work a crowd and he was not as shitty as people complain about in the ring. Vince McMahon and booking alone cannot sentence a man to death.

TTC also shares a more non-kayfabe look at Luger:

> I've met a handful of wrestlers in my day (at official signings), most just seemed forcibly polite (Kevin Nash and HHH for example), some were downright rude (Ric Flair), but one stood out... Lex Luger took time to have a short conversation with each of the fans in the long, long line. He was friendly and [full of compliments] and overall a really nice guy.

John Waraksa shares an interesting observation:

> *He was a very legitimate draw. EVERY female wrestling fan I ever met in the around 86 or so until about 94 liked him, and I know if they went to a show they were gonna get a t-shirt (and probably had their boyfriends buy it).*

And finally **Ron M.** sent in something that would have been the Hidden Highlight:

> *I saw Luger at a house show during the time he was doing the Total Package gimmick with the lights and all (like Masters now). It was at the Bryce Jordan Center in State College and he was complaining about not having the proper lighting. He went on to cut one of the most impressive heel promos I had heard that year. When let loose and comfortable, he is amongst the best. A funny part came when we all started chanting the "We are... Penn State" deal, alluding to his past which you mentioned. He just looked all around, paused for a long time and said "You know, you people are pathetic". Everybody loved it and laughed. Great stuff.*

That is great stuff. The point of all this is that Luger has entertained the fans both in and out the ring for years, and that deserves to be his legacy.

THE NARCISSISTIC FINAL COMMENT

Lex Luger is a man plagued by personal problems and an ambivalent internet crowd. But his true story is a man who worked his way up through the Florida system and was trained by the legends. He fought amazing contests with the likes of Ric Flair, Sting, Ron Simmons, and Barry Windham. He was involved in exciting stories and angles from the Four Horsemen to the Lex Express to the premier of Nitro to being the standard bearer for WCW against the nWo to being in both versions of the Wolfpac and countless other angles in between. He sold PPVs, he sold house shows, he sold merchandise. This is the man who Lex Luger truly is and was. A few mistakes should not define an entire career. A career should define a career. And more importantly: a legacy.

The defense rests.

After the Trial

Hung Jury

IN THE CASE OF THE IWC VERSUS LEX LUGER, LEX LUGER HAS BEEN ACCUSED OF BEING A TERRIBLE WRESTLER WHO NO FAN WANTED AT THE TOP BUT WAS PUSHED DOWN OUR THROATS ANYWAY. FURTHERMORE, HIS DESCENT FROM THE TOP WAS DESERVED, AND HIS PERSONAL PROBLEMS ARE JUST A MANIFESTATION OF EVERYTHING HE SHOULD GET FOR YEARS OF HORRIBLE WRESTLING ENTERTAINMENT.

With 88.1% of the vote, Lex Luger was found:

NOT GUILTY!

Response

When I got into cases about specific wrestlers like this, it usually evoked interesting tales of people's personal experiences:

> *A friend of mine is probably the world's biggest Lex Luger fan. He has sadly never seen him live, but has seen just [about] all there is on tape. In fact, he bought from Ebay a 14 tape set of the mostly complete works of Lex, from Florida to TNA. I watched these tapes with him slowly, over the course of a year or more. I saw every endless Nitro promo, and every WWE Superstars squash. I saw his elbow X-ray, him slamming Yoko, Him teaming with Buff, him beating Hogan and so much more. Let me tell you one thing about Lex Luger:*
>
> *[T]he man was OVER. He was Over for his entire freakin'*
> *career. [Y]ou know why people hate him on the IWC?*
> *Because he was such a good heel that he got them to hate him for real. Just like HHH.*
>
> *He learned how to work safe, and had a career largely injury-free. His workrate was fine, he just didn't have much flash. He knew, however, exactly when to do that powerslam, exactly when to apply*

> the rack, and exactly when to stand up and when to stay down. Lex Luger is an unsung great in the business that the critics just don't like because he was more successful [than] they'd like him to be. The hell with them. you've certainly done it again. NOT GUILTY.
>
> **-Cyrus Krapf-Altomare**

> The first PPV I ever saw was Summerslam 93, I was 12, Lex Lugar is wrestling. I saw a house show the following year with Bret and Lex teamed against Owen and Yoko and after Owen [clotheslined] [B]ret from behind when he had Yoko in the sharpshooter Lex came in and they cleaned house after the DQ victory. They spent the next 15 minutes shaking everyone's hand at ringside.
>
> Men rise and fall, [and] in the end their lives are made up of the moments that are remembered. I was too small and far away to get to the ringside area, but I know he would have shaken my hand, and I remember that.
>
> "A hero is no braver than an ordinary man, but he is braver five minutes longer."
> -Ralph Waldo Emerson
>
> **Maxtraster**

A lot of talk was around "workrate" and this response provided an interesting perspective on what that even means:

> This is just another case of the internet "smart" fans arbitrarily deciding what makes a wrestler good and what makes them bad. The fact of the matter is Chris Benoit's style of wrestling is no more real or legitimate than Lex Luger's. I watched wrestling before 1993, but I really got into it when Lex Luger was challenging Yokozuna. Summer Slam 93 was the first pay per view I had ever bought. I was pissed when Luger didn't win the title and was pissed when he lost at WrestleMania X. I was excited when he beat Hogan just before Road Wild a few years later.

> *Just because Luger wasn't a good "wrestler" doesn't mean he wasn't a good wrestler. There is more to wrestling than the matches, and the guy was a part of some really memorable storylines, and played an important part in the history of both WWE and WCW. With "smart" fan hindsight I can say I wouldn't go out of my way to see too many of his matches, but "smart" fans are just "mark" fans of different aspects of the same performance, and your column has helped me begin to realize that.*
>
> **John-Peter Trask**

Further, this response (among others) brought up memories of my own:

> *Yeah, he became a slug in the ring in his late years, but during WCW in 1997 (which I hated to death) there was one moment that made me mark out, and that was when Luger beat Hogan on Nitro. I jumped out of my seat and marked out like crazy. I didn't mark out like that for a wrestling show until Austin won the Rumble in 2001 (my favorite Rumble) and Benoit winning at WrestleMania XX. These are moments when I literally jump out of my seat and totally suspend my disbelief, and that was one of those moments. Luger was always a guy you could throw in there in a feud vs anyone and probably draw some money. He played the face role well, and the heel role well. And in the late 80's early 90's, he was a VERY GOOD wrestler.*
>
> **Brian Meyer**

To which I responded (an amalgamation of several different responses on the same theme):

> *I was actually at the Fleet Center in Boston the week before Lex won the title from Hollywood Hogan. We were supposed to get that title match, but Hogan chickened out. I was POed, to say the least, but Luger still got the rack on Hogan for the live crowd and made him submit. That sent us home happy. There was no doubt in my mind that Luger was legit over, and that the reaction out*

> back when he won the title was sincere. Hogan had a death grip on the WCW belt, and it was real emotion from the fans and the boys when he won. When he won the title the next week, I completely marked out. It was real emotion from the crowd, and I am convinced the boys in Luger's backstage celebration were giving their real emotions, too.

Something that is not always abundantly clear is what content has been cut from the case:

> I saw no mention of the infamous [Bruiser] Brody cage match.
>
> **Ronevsorg**

Luckily, I had just what Ronevsorg was looking for:

> I just ran out of space and it wasn't going with the tempo of the article. But I did have a blurb about it ready. From the LAW:
>
> "Dan Lovranski finishes off asking about the infamous Cage Match with Bruiser Brody in Florida where Brody started no selling for Luger. He said he was scared to death and walked to the back. After the match he asked if he did something wrong and Brody said "No" and that Brody was going to Dallas as a babyface and that since Luger was going to Crockett he wasn't going to work with him but that Luger never did anything wrong. Luger just felt it was a lesson to learn as a youngster in the industry."
>
> And there you have it. Luger tried to treat it like a professional, even after Brody no-sold and stiffed him in the cage. It was Brody who was being unprofessional, not anything Luger had ever done.

Since it was not a 100% win, there were detractors. However, this was the point where I really noticed the turn and got well-reasoned arguments back:

> *I would vote that Lex Luger is guilty. While I do agree with your comments regarding his recent legal troubles and the death of Miss Elizabeth, you made it seem as though he has only found trouble in his life recently and that it is all related to the death of Miss Elizabeth. You forget that Luger has, for lack of a better term, fucked up before.*
>
> *By far the best backstage story I have ever heard is how Luger screwed himself out of the world title at WMX. The original booking for the event was that Luger would win the title against Yoko and then go on to defend it successfully against Bret (possibly due to interference by Owen). Instead, Lex got drunk the night before, blabbed the booking to people at a bar where a reporter [overheard] him and the story was on the front page the morning of [W]restlemania. Vince changed the booking for 'mania and never let Lex get close to the title again as punishment for this.*
>
> *While you never came out and said it, there seemed to be a sense of "Vince dropped the ball with Luger" in your defense. No, to paraphrase Vince, "Lex screwed Lex" and also showed a great deal of disrespect for the business with his actions. For me, that is why Luger is guilty.*
>
> *...*
>
> *Regardless, I appreciate your work in opening up these dialogues, as it gives many immediately biased IWC'ers food for thought.*
>
> **Matt Jones**

And Lex Luger's personal demons would continue to be an issue, as the next section will show...

MINI-CASE: LEX LUGER (FOLLOW-UP)

A couple of months after defending Lex Luger, this came up on the newsboard:

> *Lex Luger was arrested on "outstanding drug charges" Tuesday upon arrival at the Minneapolis/St. Paul Airport. Luger was arrested on charges originating from the state of Georgia. He is currently in Minnesota's Hennepin County Jail and is scheduled for a 12/22 court date. He is being held without bail.*
>
> *Luger was refused entry into Canada earlier this week by the Canadian Border Services and was later sent back to Minneapolis where he was arrested.*

Now, you may think this takes away from my case, but I don't think so at all. For starters, my case was based off of you should not judge a man's wrestling legacy by his acts outside of the ring. This is just another moment outside the ring that cannot take away from everything that Lex Luger has accomplished and the major impact he has had on the industry as a whole.

Besides that, do a little reading between the lines (pun intended). He was arrested on OUTSTANDING drug charges... from Georgia! This is all dating back to stuff that happened two years ago. The justice system is slow, folks. Hell, when Luger was arrested in April 2003 for the 1000 pills found in his apartment following the death of Ms. Elizabeth, he was not sentenced until February 5, 2005.

So just because he got arrested again, don't think for a minute it is something that happened recently. By the way, it's really odd that he was allowed into Canada in October of this year but not two months later. What changed?

Mike Davidson of AWE (the promotion Luger was to make his second appearance for) had this to say:

> *"I'm very very frustrated. I guess they're protecting our country by stopping professional wrestlers from appearing at shows... The Government of Canada just cost a Canadian business a flight and a deposit."*

SLAM! Sports added this:

> *Loretta Nyhus, a spokeswoman for the Canada Border Services Agency, could not say why Luger was refused entry because of privacy laws, but said there are several reasons someone could be refused, including criminality, a danger to public safety or lack of funds.*
>
> *People with criminal records can apply either at the border or ahead of time for entry, and the circumstances surrounding each case can affect the decision, she said.*

In another article, SLAM! Sports said:

> *"It's very rare (wrestlers) can ever come in without a problem," said Andrew Shallcross, director of operations for Premier Championship Wrestling. "The worst feeling as a promoter is standing at the airport gate waiting to see if your guy comes through.*
>
> *"I've talked to guys who used to be in the WWE and they say Canada's terrible and Winnipeg is the worst."*
>
> *Shallcross said he even had trouble getting Steve Corino, a Winnipeg-born Canadian citizen, into Winnipeg recently. The border officer told Corino someone had phoned ahead and warned them he was coming, something Shallcross says happens suspiciously often in the wrestling world.*

It's all very odd, but in the end it doesn't change anything. Lex Luger is a former champion and impact player. He's had a terrible few years in his personal life, and it doesn't look like it's about to get any better.

THE UNDERTAKER

INTRO

SOME DAME WALKED INTO MY OFFICE AND SAID...

Way back on June 5, 2005, my main man **Brad McLeod** (now is that pronounced Mic-lee-odd, or Mic-cloud, because I've been doing the latter in my head) said:

> Now, for my case. The Undertaker.
>
> Yep, ol' Booger Red. No one wants to defend him, but I do at every step.

To which he listed out every step, but I'll get to those during the case.

A couple of months later on August 21, 2005, **Nick Gallagher** wrote in with similar thoughts:

> [A lot] of people {not myself} look at the [U]ndertaker as a meaningless player in the [WWE/F] circle and has been for years. [H]e has squashes and then when he [won't job] to someone he [doesn't] deem suitable and everyone gets pissed off[.] [N]ow myself[— personally[,] if [I] were in his position [I wouldn't] job to some nobody and hurt my character that helped build me up to the superstar [I] am if [I didn't] find my opponent worthy. [W]ho put over [M]ankind... it was long before the [R]ock and [S]ock [C]onnection[.] [I]t was the [U]ndertaker... defend the [Undertaker's] worth to the company[.]

And though Nick may be heavily edited, I only had one thing to say: "I'll take the case!" Well, actually I said I already took the case thanks to Brad, who wrote in to gently remind me that I had taken the case, but no worries! This was planned all along!

WHY THIS?

With over twenty years in the business and four WWF/E title reigns, how can one doubt the impact and ability of the man known as the Undertaker? People often complain about slow, plodding matches; about a lack of believability; about a lack of workrate; and about a lack of deserving his spot. Yet despite these claims, the Undertaker remains consistently over with the live crowd, a huge merchandise magnet, and a solid foundation at the WWE. Who else has been in the company for fifteen years straight whose last name isn't McMahon or Fink? How many of us have spent fifteen years at one job... or in our last five jobs combined?!

No, the Undertaker has been a consistent presence on our screen, yet many in the IWC bash everything he does. There does not seem to be a way for him to please the fickle community, yet the WWE does not listen to these critics. What is it the WWE sees in the Undertaker that the IWC seems to forget, and what has the Undertaker done over the years to earn the ire of the IWC? And more importantly, does he deserve it?

A LITTLE HISTORY, AND SOME EARLY COUNTER-ARGUMENTS

The first question that comes to mind when we talk about the Undertaker is this:

Who is the Undertaker and where did he come from?

For most of the IWC "elite", the answer if fairly simple: his name is Mark Calaway, he came into the WWF in 1991, promptly got pushed above everyone, won the title, and stole the main event from more deserving guys for fifteen years.

Pretty cut and dry, and not entirely based in fiction, which makes it believable. But as we have learned many times in these harrowed halls, believability does not make it true. Let's start from the real beginning.

Before 1984, the man born Mark Calaway was not sure wrestling was the path for him. Much like Kevin Nash and the Big Show, Calaway had aspirations of using his size and speed to become a basketball star. Unlike his brethren, though, it was not injury or rare opportunity that brought the Undertaker into wrestling, it was himself.

In 1984, Calaway had his first wrestling training session, and did not fare well. But that would not stop him at all. He began to train with Don Jardine, who some might know better as the Spoiler, the Super Destroyer, or (my favorite) Baby Face Jardine! What better way to tell your fans you are a baby face than putting it in your name? I digress. Jardine had a career spanning 25 years including headlining MSG against Pedro Morales for the WWWF championship.

Here was a man that obviously knew the business and was more than credible as a trainer.

Jardine helped the Undertaker get his body and mind in the proper shape, and then helped him find his way to Fritz Von Erich's World Class Championship Wrestling in Dallas, TX. Through the mid-80's, Calaway would wrestle under a number of pseudonyms (including according to Wikipedia the Commando, the Punisher, Texas Red [still trying to figure out if there is a connection from that to Booger Red], the Master of Pain, and Dice Morgan), but never found one that allowed him to fully connect with himself and the fans.

But his presence was undeniable, and he was able to work with what he had. Although not finding high success in WCCW, Calaway would move on to USWA. On April 1, 1989 as the Master of Pain, Calaway defeated Jerry "the King" Lawler for the USWA Unified Heavyweight Title. After losing the title, becoming the Punisher again, and winning the USWA Texas Heavyweight Title, Calaway had finally caught the attention of someone big. After sacrificing, scrimping, and working his way up for five years, the future Undertaker was discovered by Jim Crockett Promotions, a.k.a. NWA/WCW.

Upon arriving in JCP, Calaway became "Mean" Mark Callous and replaced Sid Vicious on the team of the Skyscrapers, teaming with none other than Dan Spivey to continue their feud with the Road Warriors. Interestingly enough, the team was once managed by future SmackDown! general manager Teddy Long. [Kafabe] Wonder why he keeps the Undertaker around? [/Kayfabe]

By the end of 1989, the Skyscrapers had run their course and "Mean" Mark Callous began his single's career in the almost-WCW. He would go on to defeat future head of WWE talent relations Johnny Ace at Capitol Combat and Brian Pillman at a Clash of the Champions, before finally losing to Lex Luger for the United States Title at the Great American Bash 1990.

But JCP was going through a transition into WCW, and much of the old guard and their opinions of wrestlers were going with them. A new breed of management took over and brought their ideologies with them. Towards the end of 1990, the now WCW opted to not renew Calaway's contract, and he was out of a job.

Calaway then began negotiations with Vince McMahon, who apparently had been waiting for just the right man to fill a new idea he had: THE UNDERTAKER!

At Survivor Series 1990 the Undertaker premiered on Ted DiBiase's team at the behest of Brother Love... and then got counted out less than ten minutes into the match. But his team won! The Undertaker was designed to be an impervious monster that had magic powers. You see, the WWE was moving to a more "cartoon" format, trying to capitalize on the ratings success of Saturday morning programming. Who in their right mind could pull off a gimmick with magic powers and being dead?

Apparently Calaway could. The crowd got into the Undertaker despite the fact that he was a heel and had switched to Paul Bearer as his manager. The crowd could not be ignored, and he went on to fight the Ultimate Warrior and Hulk Hogan before finally being one of the few people EVER to pin Hogan at Survivor Series 1991.

So yes, for someone who just saw the Calaway for the first time in 1990, it would seem he rocketed to the top! It was not an instant push, but still very rapid, especially for his time. But following his true career, the Undertaker already had seven years of sacrifice and paying his dues under his belt before he even made it to the WWF. Yes, that is a fairly fast rise to top the top, still, but not unheard of. This is a fact that should not be held against the Undertaker, but used as a testament to his skills. Why should he be punished for learning and growing so quickly? Here is a man who had accomplished a lot, but there was still so much more to do. Not only that, he had done it himself. He went through the system, he fought his way up the ranks, and he got a goofy gimmick over.

The Undertaker was not an overnight sensation, but the culmination of a long, hard haul. He had finally reached the top... if only for a week.

Ball... Errr... Belt Hog!

The Undertaker quickly lost the belt back to Hogan at the "This Tuesday in Texas" PPV. What the WWF/E has with alliterating PPVs on Tuesday I will never know. But it became more than apparent that this was a hot shot title switch to increase buyrates. That became even more apparent when the Undertaker would have to wait SIX MORE YEARS for his second title victory against Psycho Sid (yes, the man he replaced in the Skyscrapers. Don't you love the circles we weave with this guy?) at WrestleMania 13. This title reign would actually last five months before he lost the title to Bret Hart at SummerSlam.

So here it was, thirteen years in the business, seven in the WWE, and two title reigns. It looked like the Undertakers time had finally arrived.

Right?

Wrong.

The Undertaker would have to hold off another two years until Over the Edge 1999 when he defeated Steve Austin for the title with the help of Vince and Shane McMahon. Well, with two McMahons on his side, the Undertaker must have been able to hold on to the title? No, he lost it back to Austin a month later.

Three years later, the Undertaker would win the title again, this time from Hulk Hogan (again) at Judgment Day 2002. This title reign would be double the length of the last one—two whole months—before losing his last championship to the Rock at Vengeance.

Throughout this I hope I have made one point clear. The IWC accuses the Undertaker of being a belt hog, of having the championship too long.

In fifteen years in the WWF/E, he has had four title reigns. Lesner had three title reigns in his three short years, the Rock seven, Angle four, Triple H ten, and Austin six. All of those men have had less time in the WWE than the Undertaker yet all have had more reigns than him.

And it is not just number of reigns, it's length! Of the Undertaker's 5451 days in the WWE, he has only spent 254 as champion, or 4.7%. That does not sound like a man hogging the title.

Just to put that in context even more, JBL's run as champ was 280 days. Cena's and Batista's reigns are both at 205 days already at the time of this writing. In their first run, these three champions are already on track to completely outpace the Undertaker's total time as champion.

Yet he is still considered to be around the title too much. Some claim that he does not spend enough time putting over talent for the title. We will return to this topic later, but when it comes to losing chances at the title, no one does it like the Undertaker.

In the past fifteen years, the Undertaker has lost 54 title matches and number one contender shots. That's right, 54! How many people even get 54 shots at the title, nonetheless lose them all? And mind you, that is only on television! Quadruple that for his house show losses over the years.

You see, people think that the Undertaker is always around the title because he is a perpetual main eventer. And again, that is not something to be chastised for. The man has worked hard to create the aura that he is always at the top. Yet this has somehow become a negative?

No, facts are facts, and the numbers don't lie. The Undertaker has been nowhere near the title for most of his career, and has held it all together less than JBL. How can you hog something you never get to hold?

Want a little side story?

In 1998, Austin was the champion and put the title up in triple threat against Kane and the Undertaker. Kane and the Undertaker pinned Austin at the same time, and due to the controversy the title was held up. So at Judgment Day 1998 Kane and the Undertaker squared off with Austin as the special guest referee. Somewhere into the match, Austin decided to stun both men after mass interference, and then counted himself the winner. Backstage, McMahon fired Austin and put the belt in a thirteen-man tournament, which the Rock won over Mankind. That's right, the Undertaker pinned the champion in a title match and then the title ended up on the Rock. So not only has the Undertaker not been with the title, it has completely walked around him.

YET THEY STILL WANT HIM

I've researched a lot of less desirable people and events since I've started In Defense Of..., but with the Undertaker I have found something I have seen anywhere else:

An online petition.

That's right, someone actually created a petition in support of the Undertaker. Check it out:

> *To: World Wrestling Federation*
>
> *We, the fans, supporters and friends of World Wrestling Federation superstar the Undertaker ask the owners, leaders, and writers of the WWF to salute this great man for all he has given over the years by continuing to give him very high quality angles to work with, headliner competition, and main event status. We ask that you consider all that he has done, and not just think of the bottom line. We, the signers of this petition, believe he has the right to be a dominant force in the WWF for as long as he wishes to be. All we ask is that you allow him that.*
>
> *Sincerely,*
>
> *The Undersigned*

There were 489 signatures, many expressing their love of the Undertaker. This quite shocked me, as I would expect any petition to be AGAINST using someone in the WWF/E. Yet, here it was, fans so rabid that they wanted the Undertaker to not only be in the main event, but to be pushed to a level beyond where he was.

This is the type of loyalty and love this man inspires. The Undertaker may be a gimmick, but Mark Calaway the man makes it happen.

HOW COME HE ALWAYS GETS UP?

The first argument we have to tackle is that the Undertaker never jobs to anyone. Really? Well, looking at the Undertaker's television win/loss record as of August 21, 2005, he had 272 wins, 124 losses, and 33 no decisions/double count-outs, etcetera. So that means that overall he only has a 63% winning record. Want to get better? Of those 272 wins, 51 were against complete jobbers during the early years of RAW. Taking that out of the equation on both ends, that means the Undertaker only has a 58% winning record. Wow, that certainly sounds like someone who jobs a lot to me!

Shawn Michaels has an about 6% higher winning percentage, but he was gone for five years. As of the same date, Michaels had 312 wins, numerically far higher than the Undertaker despite the fact that the Undertaker has been around consistently over the past fifteen years.

But of course you'd want to say: what have you done for me lately? Well, over the past year at the time of this writing, the Undertaker has had 17 televised matches. Yes, very few for an active wrestler, but we'll return to this point later. Of those 17 matches, his record was 12-3-2, or a 71% winning record. Pretty high, much higher than his overall record, but apparently enough to make some people cringe.

Well, let's qualify this a bit more. Two of those wins were over jobbers/non-wresters, and five of those wins were over people no longer employed by the WWE. Doesn't seem like such a huge winning record. One of those wins he wasn't even supposed to have (over Hassan), so that brings it down even more.

In one-on-one matches with main eventers, the Undertaker has a 2-2 record. Also, just outside of our range the Undertaker had just lost to JBL for the first time. So in Main Event match-ups he is again on the losing side, as we noted in the title section before.

No, the Undertaker is not a winner, and has been putting people over for a while yet. Of course, this is not his only year of building up the main event.

WHO ARE THESE PEOPLE?

But you might be saying, "Sure, he loses some, but he never puts people over. Really, who has he made? He just buries people (pun intended)." And I'd say to you, "Boy, your puns are pretty weak."

First off, who has the Undertaker put over? Well let's see, in recent memory he has lost decisively to Randy Orton, JBL, and John Cena. As a matter of fact, both JBL and Cena have two consecutive wins over the Undertaker (i.e., they won the rubber matches), as have Brock Lesner and Maven. That's right, Maven got two wins over the 'Taker. But let's go back to Lesner for a minute. Lesner holds an incredible record with the Undertaker, going 5-3-1. So out of their nine matches, the Undertaker only won 33% of the time. And people say the Undertaker is not willing to make the new generation? Not only did he lose to Lesner, but he lost in both a Biker Chain Match and a Hell in the Cell.

Of course, these aren't the only men that the Undertaker has helped make over the years. His feud with Austin solidified Stone Cold in the main event. He helped bring the Rock into the upper tier circle, both by teaming with him on occasion and then against him when 'Taker was in the Corporate Ministry.

Still, there is one man that the Undertaker really made, and that man in Mick Foley. Mick Foley had an interesting career, traveling between Japan, WCW, and ECW, making waves wherever he went. But he had never truly broken through the top of the card, not until he ran afoul of the Undertaker.

The two had a series of matches, including the infamous Hell in the Cell where Foley was thrown from the top of the cage through the announce table and slammed through the roof onto a pile of thumbtacks. Despite losing this one encounter, Mankind/Mick Foley cemented his legacy that night. But just because he lost that night, does not mean he did not get the better of the Undertaker. As a matter of fact, his record against the Undertaker is 17-12-6 (including a KO, the only one in the history of the Undertaker). Therefore, the Undertaker only has a 34% win record against Mick Foley. Wait, that means Brock Lesner and Mankind have the same percentage record against the Undertaker. Well, certainly seems like the Undertaker was trying to bring more men into the main event by losing in these scenarios.

True, the Undertaker has not always been successful, and others have lost at his hands. DDP's loss along with Kronik are two big ones that come to mind. But those dominate wins had more to do with the WWE not wanting to look bad compared to WCW wrestlers. For every DDP, there is a Kane who the Undertaker helped create.

No one is arguing that he made these people, they obviously had a lot to do themselves and with others. But the Undertaker was a huge steppingstone in all of these men's careers.

Now, though, you are probably thinking of all the other people the Undertaker has beaten up who have not gone higher. You are thinking of Heidenreich, Luther Reigns, and Mark Jindrak. All I have to say to that is this: Chyna.

The Undertaker lost to Chyna in a triple threat match on August 9, 1999. The man let himself be pinned by a woman. Do you think, then, he understands storylines and the business? And if he ever has refused to job to someone (which has never been proven), that it was probably with good reason?

The Undertaker has been solid to the company that made him. The offers were available to jump back to WCW (although there is talk that Bischoff wasn't that interested without the gimmick), but he wanted to stay. The Undertaker became the personification of an era in the WWF, much like Sting was for WCW. While both men were never the gods of their organizations; they were always there to make everyone else shine brighter.

STEALING THE SPOTLIGHT

And since they were not gods, they did not get to have the big matches. If the Undertaker were such a hog of the spotlight, if he was really using his power to influence all booking decisions in his favor, wouldn't he have made better decisions? Would he have paired himself up with Nathan Jones to acquaint Jones to the WWE audience? Would he have let the sacrificing Stephanie angle go so far?

As it is, the Undertaker has stated in a number of interviews that he did not like the Satanic version of the "Lord of Darkness" because he "didn't enjoy it" and that he "did not want religious WWE fans to start thinking he is a satanic person." Yet he went along with it. It was his job, and he did it, for better or for worse.

Really, if the Undertaker was really flexing his connections, don't you think he would have ended up main eventing a few more WrestleManias? Despite his impressive record, the Undertaker has only headlined one WrestleMania: WrestleMania 13 when he defeated Psycho Sid for the WWE Championship in front of 18,852 fans.

Just as a little side-note: that WrestleMania took place at the Rosemont Arena in Rosemont, IL. The next time it would be that packed? At Judgment Day 1998, the Undertaker faced Kane in the main event in front of 18,153. The Undertaker is one of those rare men that brings people to an arena because people want to see him live. Sure, there are many superstars we want to watch, but it is the rare few who actually draw people in to pay money just to see them.

ENOUGH FOES, HOW ABOUT SOME FRIENDS?

The Undertaker has taken his gimmick and his presence, though, to bring others along with him. Previously, I mentioned Nathan Jones as one of the men who was paired with the Undertaker in order to get him over with the audience, but this isn't the first time this has happened.

Back in the Ministry (and later Corporate Ministry), the Undertaker brought the Acolytes into existence by teaming Farooq and Bradshaw. Of course, post-ministry these two would become the Acolyte Protection Agency, a.k.a. the APA. Also during this time, the Undertaker had Mideon and Viscera on his side, trying to give them something to do. These two would actually defeat Triple H in a casket match, if that can be believed!

Also, back in the Ministry were a couple of fairly new kids named Edge and Christian, getting their first rub from a main eventer. I wonder what ever happened to those two?

Whether friend of foe, the Undertaker has worked hard to bring people up the card, not hold them down. Some have been more successful than others, but the Undertaker is hardly to blame if some workers cannot get the traction they needed to take that next step.

BUT HE JUST WRESTLES WHEN HE WANTS!

Nowadays, the Undertaker is rarely seen. Like I said earlier, at the time of this writing, he worked 17 matches in the past year (on TV, he worked quite a few more house shows). To that, I have to say a hearty: SO WHAT?

First off, the man is almost 41 years old and has spent 15 years in the WWE. There is very little left for him to do on a weekly basis that he has not already done. In order to keep him fresh, he has become a special attraction. He shows up for a good feud here and there and gets the job done.

Also, because of his age and years in the ring, he has a lot of injuries. His knees are in terrible shape from doing so many tombstones (the real reason he did not want to continue to use the piledriver). On top of that, he has had several surgeries on his shoulders and elbows. With time, he is becoming more injury prone and does not want to be put on the shelf forever. He has two young children at home (one just born in May 2005) and does not want to take any more unnecessary risks.

After sacrificing his body for years, why should he do anything that is going to put him in major jeopardy? The bell tolls, the fans scream, and he sells a bunch of t-shirts. Everyone goes home happy. What is the problem with that?

FILLER FUN FACTS!

Because we have a little time left in this case, we should throw in a few fun facts that make the Undertaker that much more amazing. Here we go...

- Went to Angelina College in Lufkin, TX on a basketball scholarship (told you he was good at basketball)

- He was named one of the 100 greatest wrestlers of the 20th century by Inside Wrestling

- Won PWI Feud of the Year in 1991 with the Ultimate Warrior and Match of the Year in 1998 for his Hell in the Cell match with Mankind.

- According to PhenomForever.com: *From December 1991 to September 1993, Undertaker did not lose a single match. It was the longest undefeated streak of the 1990s.*

- According to Wikipedia: *The Undertaker is the only wrestler to have pinned Kevin Nash (6 ft 10 in), Kane (6 ft 11 in), The Big Show (7 ft 2 in) and Giant Gonzales (7 ft 6 in), four of the tallest men in wrestling history.*

- According to PhenomForever.com: *The Undertaker fought in the first-ever Casket Match, Boiler Room Brawl, Buried Alive Match, Hell in a Cell Match, Inferno Match, Biker Chain Match and Last Ride Match.*

- According to IMDB: *Is the first WWF wrestler to do a Bollywood movie. He played his famous WWF character The Undertaker in Khiladiyon Ka Khiladi (1996) and even spoke Hindi in the film.*

Anyone have a review of that movie?

And now from our very own news board on November 11, 2001:

> *The Undertaker has been in the main event of most WWF B House shows since the split of house show occurred early last month.*
>
> *Some of the B shows have developmental wrestlers appearing on the undercard, and the Undertaker has been spotted taking the up and coming wrestlers aside after their matches and giving them tips on their work.*

All I have to say to that is more proof of the Undertaker trying to help the next generation.

Also, there was a funny news-bite saying the Undertaker's wins over Kurt Angle and Chris Benoit in 2002 might hurt their careers. Guess not! You see, we extrapolated in the past saying what would become of people because of the Undertaker, but most of these horrible events have not come to pass. Yet, we have allowed the IDEA that fighting with and losing to the Undertaker can kill someone's career. Most of these events have not come to pass, yet the stigma remains. That is not fair to the facts.

But enough of that little stuff, because there are a few huge topics left.

BUT CAN THEY ~~DANCE~~ WRESTLE?

Did you know the Undertaker was a high-risk wrestler? Yes, nowadays the most dangerous move he performs is the top rope walk followed by a chop to the shoulder known as Old School, but do you know why it is called Old School?

Because it is part of the old repertoire. According to Thomas Chamberlin of the Wrestling Digest in April 2001:

> *The Undertaker was one of the first big men who could really move. At almost 6'10" and more than 310 pounds, [Calaway] had a unique mix of power and athleticism. When he first broke into the WWF in 1990, few had seen the top-rope moves [Calaway] performed.*

What Chamberlin was getting at was that the Undertaker has had a lot of injuries over the years and has changed his arsenal to reflect it. He stopped using the tombstone piledriver regularly not because of the WWE ban, but because his knees were in terrible condition from performing the move.

But in those days, the sky was the limit, and the Undertaker was still a young man. Unlike many men who find themselves thrust into the spotlight, the Undertaker continued to try to grow in all aspects in the ring. According to the Undertaker himself:

> *I think I learnt the most from Jake Roberts... He had, in my opinion, one of the best wrestling minds, as far as ring psychology and how to present his character to the audience went. I applied some of that to what the Undertaker was going to be about.*

Not only that, but the Undertaker is still an evolving wrestler. Let's just look at his finishing move. Before 1993, he was using the heart punch. Heart punch! He followed that up with the iron claw (comes from that Von Erich training), and THEN went to the Tombstone piledriver that became his signature. But he wouldn't stop there and added the chokeslam (because he's tall!) and the Last Ride. Then something interesting happened: The Undertaker started moving into submission moves! First he added a modified dragon sleeper known as the Taker Care of Business (not Takin') and followed that up with the triangle choke, reverse STO, and fujiwara armbar. These changes are due in part to his body wearing down with time, but also a desire to change and grow with the business and his current incarnation of character.

The Undertaker was not always in charge of his own wrestling evolution. He was often put in the most dangerous of matchups and made to live up to high expectations. This was the man involved in the first Casket Match, the first Buried Alive Match, the first Hell in a Cell, and—the most dangerous of all—the first Inferno match. The Undertaker had this to say on that match:

> *They told me the ropes would be set alight, and we'd wrestle until one of us caught fire. Real good idea... I can't even begin to describe how hot it was. There was no air. The flames were burning up all the oxygen.*

But the real story wasn't the match, but the Undertaker himself. Kane, who was actually set on fire, had this to say:

> *What was so impressive wasn't the heat or the flames. It was the sight of Taker, at six foot ten and three hundred pounds, flying over the top rope, through the flames, onto me.*

The Undertaker: a man who constantly laid it all out in the ring until he had no more to give, yet still tries to entertain to this day.

USUALLY WHEN I TALK ABOUT SELLING, WE'RE IN THE NUMBERS SECTION

Despite all of the dangerous risks he's taken, all of the evolution he's gone through, and his desire to continue to grow, the IWC elite has one big complaint about the Undertaker: He doesn't sell!

Guess what?

That's a good thing!

This has and always will be a major part of his gimmick. The Undertaker is a man who has developed an aura around himself that he is impervious to pain. And anyone who notices that he has a tattoo on his throat would believe it! Think about it from a real-world perspective: you have this huge, muscular guy covered in tattoos and has been wrestling for years. Do you think it is possible he has a higher threshold for pain than most? I like how **Brad McCleod** put it:

> *[H]ey, the man was a 6 foot, 10 inch, 325 pound BIKER!!!! You make him hurt. I dare ya. Go find a 7 foot, 325 pound Hell's Angel and kick him. See how bad ya hurt him. And, when you get out of the hospital, maybe you will see that Taker is just as real as real life.*

Being a short, skinny kid from the suburbs, I don't think that that is such good idea.

More than this, though, is that WHEN the Undertaker sells, it has much more meaning. Chris Benoit sells for everyone. So when [Miscellaneous Mid-carder Getting an Inexplicit Upper Card Push] beats down Benoit and makes him scream, it's not that big of a deal. Even when he beats him, that win can quickly be forgotten (see: Scott Norton). But not the Undertaker! Taking him off his feet is considered an accomplishment unto itself. When he grimaces and reaches for the rope yelling, when he falls down from a hit and stays down, and when he loses, it is a big deal. Despite the fact that he has a very low win percentage, the Undertaker continues to look strong because he has the mystique of an unbeatable monster. He lives a dual existence, balancing constantly losing with never looking bad.

And that's what people complain about more. "He never looks bad when he loses!" That's the point! It is not because the Undertaker is backstage pulling strings saying he will not lose cleanly; it is because he needs to look strong to make others look strong. When Brock Lesner beat the Undertaker in a Hell in the Cell, Brock became cemented as a dominant wrestler at the top of the card. Yet, despite being a pummeled bloody mess, the Undertaker was not the worse for wear.

In a feud with the Undertaker, both can come out looking strong. Just because the Undertaker can walk away from a match or loses from outside interference, it does not make the win over him any less pivotal. As time goes on, the details become less important. Remember, the Undertaker DEFEATED Mick Foley in their classic Hell in a Cell encounter, yet it is considered the match that was the springboard to Mick Foley's main event status. Losing to the Undertaker makes you famous? Maybe DDP was on to something...

So if this were an Evolution Schematic, would he be on Phase 943,304,424-C?

Of course, the evolution we've continually alluded to is not only in the ring, but in the character. It all began with a phone call. From Kristy Quested at Obsessed With Wrestling:

> "One day the phone rang," said [the Undertaker]. "It was Vince, and he says 'Is this the Undertaker?' I just thought - what the hell is this???" Vince went on to explain his idea. Having always been a fan of the old Western-style undertaker look, he wanted to create a character based on it. Mark, always fascinated with death and the dark side, felt it was

> fate, and clicked onto the idea immediately. "The idea was Vince's," said Mark, "but as far as styling the character went, he left that pretty much up to me."

I alluded to this in earlier, but this is where it comes to play. It's not just the lights, the smoke, the mirrors, or the music that make the Undertaker. Like most successful gimmicks, it really works if the gimmick is an extension of the person. The man behind the Undertaker was into death and the dark side. He believed in and developed the character, not the other way around. Despite the Undertaker being over the top at times, the gimmick was still an extension of the man behind it. Therefore, it was not really a gimmick in the way we think of it, but actually an honest look at a person.

As time moved on, so did the Undertaker. Realizing the need to change and grow, the Undertaker looked to make an impact after returning from injury. He had this to say:

> For years, people have wanted to know, what's the Undertaker really like? What's he like when he's at home or on the street, and not on television?... The old school Undertaker is very much a part of what brought me to where I am. And I don't want to insult the die-hard Taker fans by evolving my character, because the old Undertaker is still a part of me, still a part of who I am... I've always been fascinated with death and darkness, and I still am. I may not dress like Satan anymore, but I'm still down with the devil. It took me to where I am, and now it's time to move forward. But everything the old school Undertaker was, that's still very much a part of me.

Thus the Biker Taker was born! Of course, the Undertaker had been a motorcycle fan for years. When he defeated Hulk Hogan for the title years beforehand, he went out and bought a Harley Davidson motorcycle with his sudden cash windfall.

The Biker gimmick moved more into the American Bad Ass. Kurt Angle had this to say:

> Taker truly is an American Bad Ass. Not just in character, but in real life too.

Despite being radically different from the Undertaker, the American Bad

Ass/Biker Undertaker was not that different at all. All versions of the Undertaker were really just extensions of different parts of his personality. So when the Undertaker returned to a more morbid appearance, it was not a step backwards, but just bringing about another side of the man behind the gimmick. The Undertaker had this to say after returning to the dark side:

> *The key to longevity in this business is keeping what it is that you're doing fresh. Evolving as a wrestler, and evolving as a character. I think that's one of the keys to my success—the Undertaker has evolved from when he first came here. I continue to expand people's minds and expectations of what they're going to get from the Undertaker. I am the same person, I believe in the same things, I have a lot of the same characteristics, but what people have watched through this past decade is the evolution that has brought us to where we are today.*

And where he'll be one day. But then, there's the other side of a wrestler. How much did he make?

NOW, LET'S TALK BLING BLING

The Undertaker is a man who has made a lot of money for the WWF/E over the years. So much so that he is one of only 19 superstars (out of the about 80 currently employed) who has his own area on WWEShopZone.com. And actually, of those three are for part-timers (Mick Foley, Hulk Hogan, and Stone Cold), one is for a wrestler no longer around (Chris Jericho), and one is for non-existent character (the Hurricane). This week, the Undertaker's History of the Undertaker DVD is number 8 on the top selling chart. Fifteen years later, and the man is still selling in the Top Ten.

But looking over the years, the Undertaker has been a pivotal player in the main event scene. Although only getting one WrestleMania main event, the Undertaker has been in many more PPV main events. Below is a list of the PPVs that the Undertaker has main evented that he was at least 30% responsible for the overall buyrate:

PPV	Match Type	Opponent	Buyrate
1991 Survivor Series	WWF Title	Hulk Hogan	2.2
1991 Tuesday Texas	WWF Title	Hulk Hogan	1.0
1994 Summerslam	One Fall	"Undertaker" Brian Lee	1.3
1994 Survivor Series	Casket	Yokozuna	0.9
1996 In Your House: Buried Alive	Buried Alive	Mankind	0.44
1997 In Your House: Final Four	Final Four WWF Title	Hart, Austin & Vader	0.5
WrestleMania XIII	No DQ WWF Title	"Psycho" Sid	0.77
1997 In Your House: Taker's Revenge	WWF Title	Mankind	0.5
1997 In Your House: Cold Day in Hell	WWF Title	Steve Austin	0.57
1997 King of the Ring	WWF Title	Faarooq	0.5
1997 Summerslam	WWF Title	Bret "the Hitman" Hart	0.8
1997 In Your House: Ground Zero	One Fall	Shawn Michaels	0.45
1997 In Your House: Badd Blood	Hell in a Cell	Shawn Michaels	0.6
1998 Fully Loaded	Tag-Team Titles	Kane & Mankind	0.9
1998 Summerslam	WWF Title	Steve Austin	1.48
1998 In Your House: Rock Bottom	Buried Alive	Steve Austin	0.78
1999 Over the Edge	WWF Title	Steve Austin	1.24
1999 Fully Loaded	First Blood WWF Title	Steve Austin	1.07
2000 King of the Ring	6-Man Tag Team, WWF Title	Triple H, Shane & Vince	1.19
2000 Unforgiven	Fatal Four WWF Title	Rock, Benoit & Kane	1.5
2001 Backlash	WWF/Inter/Tag Team Titles	Steve Austin & Triple H	0.9
2001 Judgment Day	No Holds Bar WWF Title	Steve Austin	0.76

PPV	Match Type	Opponent	Buyrate
2002 Judgment Day	WWE Undisputed Title	"Hollywood" Hulk Hogan	0.94
2002 King of the Ring	WWE Undisputed Title	Triple H	0.82
2002 Vengeance	Triple Threat WWE Undisputed Title	The Rock & Kurt Angle	0.94
2002 Unforgiven	WWE Title	Brock Lesnar	0.75
2002 No Mercy	Hell in the Cell WWE Title	Brock Lesnar	0.77
2003 No Mercy	Biker Chain WWE Title	Brock Lesnar	0.5

There were some lean years, especially in the mid-90's when the WWE was suffering and a noticeable drop in the post-Brand Extension era. But overall, the Undertaker is still averaging a 0.9 PPV buyrate average, well above the "success" range we set WAAAAY back in our first case.

The bottom line: the Undertaker is directly and indirectly responsible for millions upon millions of dollars in revenue. But until the WWE opens their books up to me, we can only conjecture just how much this man has meant.

WHERE DO YOU GO FROM HERE?

But why should we talk past tense? Doesn't the Undertaker still have a future? What is the next step for the Undertaker?

Well, it seems we have already seen the next step. He is now a man working limited dates, but uses those dates to work with young talent. His next scheduled program appears to be to finish up with Randy Orton. No, the WWE does not seem interested in giving him the title any time soon, and the Undertaker is fine with that. He doesn't need the title, but he doesn't need to look foolish in his final years. He has given his body, mind, and life over to the business, and deserves a fair way to leave with his legacy intact.

Yet, there is still doubt. I am reminded of Snapple's review of WrestleMania 20:

> *Taker is finished. Vince will push Taker, and buyrates will plummet. I can see it all now. Everyone wins, except for the fans... and the wrestlers... and the sponsors... and the, well you get the idea.*

Really? Here we are a year and eight months later and the Undertaker continues to ride strong. Things are not as horrible as some would have you believe, and the Undertaker is not a man who is going to destroy the WWE.

Still, do not sell this man short; he'll come back, for one last ride.

Buried Alive!

The Undertaker has had a long, storied career. He worked his way through the independents and WCW until he found his way into the WWE. He was not pushed to the moon right away, but again had to work for his position. His time as champion was limited and his winning percentages were abysmal. Yet he remained one of the most consistently over, high drawing, and motivated wrestlers on the roster. He worked hard to evolve over the years, both as a wrestler and as a gimmick. The gimmick, though, really was an extension of himself and that helped him connect with the audience. He sold merchandise and PPVs and drew fans to live events and to their TVs. Meanwhile, he continues to journey to the future, putting over young talent and still looking strong, riding out his final years doing what he does best: resting... in... peace...

The defense rests.

After the Trial

Hung Jury

IN THE CASE OF THE IWC VERSUS THE UNDERTAKER, THE UNDERTAKER HAS BEEN ACCUSED OF BEING A WORTHLESS WRESTLER WITH NO TALENT WHO WAS PUSHED DOWN OUR THROATS AT THE EXPENSE OF EVERYONE ELSE AND CONTINUES TO UNFAIRLY PROTECT THAT SPOT BY HOLDING BACK THE SUPERSTARS OF TOMORROW.

With 89.1% of the vote, the Undertaker was found:

NOT GUILTY!

Oh, that was nice! I got a lot of good compliments from people telling me this was the best case they had ever read, that they really enjoyed it, etcetera. But you want to know the funny part? I don't even like the Undertaker! He's never interested me at all! But who am I to argue with my own rules? It probably helped that I knew all the arguments against the Taker because I believed so many of them myself. Good to prove myself wrong and see all the Undertaker has done for the sport. I still don't have to like him, but at least I got the lies out of my own head.

RESPONSE

While a solid victory, some people (rightly) questioned a particular bit of my methodology:

> Wasn't the UT a maineventer for ppv's when feuding with JBL`?
>
> You forgot to list those ppv's when showing the buyrates he's garnered as a ppv main eventer.
>
> **/RC**

And my response:

> Well, actually I said it was PPV's he was at least 30% responsible for the buyrate. There were a number of other PPVs that he was in the main event for that I dismissed as he was not at least 30% responsible for the final buyrate. His programs with JBL were actually not the focus of SmackDown! then, so I don't give him that full 30% for those PPVs. Maybe about 20%.

But similarly this question came in:

> Quick question? How did you determine the "at least 30%" equation for the buy rates of Taker headlined events? Not doubting you or anything, just curious.
>
> **Wendell**

To which I had to admit:

> *The "at least 30%" was a little more subjective then most things I do. I took into account the major programs going on, the amount of time the Undertaker took on TV, and the other specialty match-ups on the card. If it looked like the Undertaker was fairly important to the buyrate, then I included them. I admit, it's a bit flawed.*

However, there were some other bits left out of the case:

> *DDP and Booker T were the only two real stars brought over from WCW and UT and Austin made both look like fools. If Page and Booker were made to look strong by UT, Austin and Vince I believe the WCW invasion could have been a success.*
>
> **Justin Pelletier**

I let Justin know:

> *You'll find this interesting. During my research, I found some people who said that the Undertaker sent feelers to WCW after Hall and Nash jumped, and that Bischoff responded that he was worthless without the Undertaker gimmick. In response to this, the Undertaker was particular vicious during the InVasion in wanting to bury WCW. Now, there is absolutely no proof or corroborating evidence to use this, so I couldn't. It's just a rumor and seems like a convenient excuse to put heat on the Undertaker that belongs to the bookers.*

SID VICIOUS

INTRO

SOME DAME WALKED INTO MY OFFICE AND SAID...

First up is the king of the promo himself, **Tim Hamilton**, saying:

> The credibility of Pyscho Sid as a credible Big Man.
>
> The net basically ripped apart Big Sid, claiming his ring work was terrible, but he was real over with the fans wherever he went (ECW, WCW, WWF/E). He was just as solid as other big men (i.e. Nash, Hogan, etc.) if not better. [Th]e character of Psycho Sid was truly amazing and I loved seeing him snap. His facial expressions were priceless. Please come to the defense of Sid Eudy to ensure he is properly appreciated.

And then there was **Richard McClellan** who said:

> Could you please defend my main man Sid Vicious? From CWF with Shane Douglas up to his last appearance in Tennessee back in May 2005. Thank you and all the best.

Rick Cobos also threw in about 8,234,463,653,352,021 ideas, among them:

> [T]he WWF and WCW both putting their premier championships on Sid.

And since everyone called him by a different name, I thought I'd roll them up to one case!

WHY THIS?

I've wanted to do this case for a while. Sid is another Big Man™ whose value is often brought into question. This is especially true because his biggest years in the industry were during the "transition", when WWE was full of cartoon characters and WCW was changing head bookers every other day. It doesn't help that Sid has a tendency to rub people the wrong away, especially after his recent appearance on Voice of Wrestling. But does Sid have a ballooned view of himself, or is it all justified?

What was Sid's contribution to wrestling? Has he drawn as well as he thinks? Does he have a legacy worth maintaining? What about all the questionable actions he's been involved in? Stabbings, squeegees, and softball—what does it all mean?

All of those questions I want to answer. But I can't do that without a little background.

A LITTLE HISTORY, AND SOME EARLY COUNTER-ARGUMENTS... WAIT, DIDN'T I DO THIS BEFORE?

The man born Sid Eudy was brought into the world on December 16, 1960 (though some claim July 4th due to an old gimmick). He grew up in West Memphis, Arkansas, which is as redneck as it sounds. As a kid in the south, Sid found himself enamored with wrestling. According to Chuck Helstein in his interview with Sid in June 2003:

> *As a kid, Sid was a big fan of Jackie Fargo, Tojo Yamamoto, and others. "I always thought Memphis was the only territory when I was a kid," said Sid. Later, he discovered wrestling magazines and found out more.*

Growing up into a large, 303 lbs., 6' 9" man, Sid became an avid workout fan. One day while at the gym, he happened to meet the Macho Man Randy Savage, who was—to say the least—impressed with the big man's size and presence. Much like how Dusty Rhodes recommended that Kevin Nash give wrestling a try, so, too, did the Macho Man.

Sid began to train under Tojo Yamamoto. If you don't know, Yamamoto was a southern wrestling legend who began his career in 1953. By the time he started to train Sid, Yamamoto already had over three decades of experience that brought him seven NWA Six-Man Tag Team titles, twenty-two NWA Southeastern Tag Team titles, the NWA (Mid-America) Southern Tag Team titles, nine NWA (Tennessee/Alabama) Tag Team titles, the NWA (Florida) United States Tag Team titles, the NWA (Mid-America) United States Tag Team titles, the NWA Southern Junior Heavyweight title, the NWA Mid-America Heavyweight title, two NWA Mid-America Tag Team titles, the AWA Southern Tag Team titles, and the ICW United States Tag Team titles. To say this man had success in his years in the industry would be an understatement. Don't forget: this was before titles changed hands so often, and having a few reigns made you a legend.

Yamamoto taught Sid more than just wrestling moves, but how to have an entertaining match, how to engage the crowd, and how to make his presence project to the rest of the audience. Sid took these lessons in and made his debut in Memphis in 1987. His first match would be teaming with Austin Idol against Memphis kings Jerry Lawler and Nick Bockwinkel. When he first premiered, Sid was known as Lord Humongous and wrestled under a mask (which actually got cracked at the hands of Jake Roberts when he DDTed Sid straight on his head).

Sid continued to wrestler in Memphis and Arkansas over the next two years. Of course he was green and loose at the beginning; but the fans were getting behind him even though he was behind the mask. However, you can only wrestle so many of the Memphis greats before someone else takes notice. And that someone (or something) was WCW. Jumping at the opportunity, Sid moved up to the big time at WCW in 1989.

Was this an early jump to the big time? Yes and no. Sid was more than passable as a worker, though obviously not as technically sounds as someone trained in the Hart Dungeon. But did Sid have his own style to add? According to Calvin Martin, Sid had this to say on Xtreme Mayhem Radio in August 2003:

> [Sid] said a few years ago, everybody tried to take credit for the business doing so well. He brought up a segment with Edge on Tough Enough. Edge has said that he grew up admiring Hulk Hogan, but once he got into the WWE, he realized that he didn't have to be Hulk Hogan to get over and he got there because of his workrate. He said whoever came up with that phrase should be shot and killed. He said not everyone can jump through a table, but everyone can work hard in their own way. He said it doesn't matter who has good workrate, it matters who can sell tickets and draw money. They brought up Hogan, and Sid said that Hogan has always been credible and he felt that Hogan has been misused in recent years.

A little crass and scathing—and not how I would make an argument—but still to the point. Just because he could not pull off a top rope rana or trade move-counter-move for thirty minutes did not mean he was not working hard in his own way. We'll return to this point later, but let's just say for now that Sid had come a long way in a short time, and did not want to stop there.

And it was not like Sid was suddenly pushed into the NWA World Title picture. Far from it! Sid began tagging with Dan Spikey as the original Skyscrapers, managed by future GM of the blue team Teddy Long. The two would go on to some success and be involved with high profile feuds with the Steiners and, most notably, the Road Warriors. But luck would not be on their side as Sid went down with an injury in late 1989 before they could win any tag team gold. He was replaced on the team with Mean Mark Callous, who would later go on to be the Undertaker (but you know that from the last case).

WCW was not through with Sid, though, and were impressed during his short run. In mid-1990, Sid was able to return to the ring, but this time in a much more prominent role. Ric Flair chose Sid to join the Four Horsemen, seeing the potential and drawing power of the man. As it is, Sid is considered the first "non-technical" wrestler to join the Horseman, showing just how much WCW, Flair, and the rest of the Horsemen saw in the man. Under the wing of the Horsemen, Sid fought his way to the top, including losing a title match to Sting at Halloween Havoc 1990.

Though now near the top of the card, Sid returned to mid-card and tag team feuds for the most of 1990 and early 1991. He was even part of the winning team in the War Games match at WrestleWar 1991. All of these feuds, the reaction of the fans, and drawing power of Sid (we'll get back to this later, also) caught the attention of another man: one Vincent Kennedy McMahon.

Vince saw a plan for Sid and wanted to give him the push of a lifetime. The plan was this: push Sid Justice as a top baby face and then have him turn on Hulk Hogan to challenge him at WrestleMania. And that's exactly what was to happen, except there was a hitch: people booed Hogan! It really came to a head at the Royal Rumble in 1992 when Hogan pulled Sid out of the ring after he (Hogan) was eliminated. The crowd very loudly booed Hogan and those boos followed him for the rest of their feud, despite the fact that the WWF dubbed over the boos with cheers in every subsequent version of the match that has ever been reproduced since then.

It was tough. Sid was trying to be a heel, but the fan support was very real. People love who they want to love. It was an early version of Hart/Austin, but not the right time or the right people. Hogan went on to defeat Sid at WrestleMania VIII that year in the main event (sorry Ric Flair and Randy Savage, only the last match on the card is the main event) in front of a crowd that was definitely split.

By the way, this was not the only time Sid wrestled in the main event of WrestleMania. He would do it again at WrestleMania 13 against the Undertaker (which he also lost). And how many people have main evented at least two WrestleManias besides Sid? Well there's Hulk Hogan, Randy Savage, Yokozuna, Bret Hart, Shawn Michaels, Steve Austin, the Rock, and Triple H. That's a pretty short list of the elitist of the elite.

Want to go a step further? Let's do the list of men who have been in the main event of at least one WrestleMania and one Starrcade: Hulk Hogan, Ric Flair, Randy Savage, Roddy Piper, and Sid Vicious. That's it! Sid is on the short list of the most elite positions in the world of wrestling. Two organizations have trusted him as both champion and to help carry the biggest event of the year. That's some hefty responsibility, trust, and belief in someone. But I digress.

It was still 1992, and there was much to do. Though that did not seem on the agenda for Sid. Sid was feeling restricted in the WWF, and that Vince could not make him a big heel because he would limit what Sid could say. On a number of occasions, Sid has stated his disdain with tweener characters, and that he prefers heel/face lines. Again from Chuck Helstein's interview review:

> "Too many people are walking the middle of the road," said Sid. He thinks people who play half heel and half face characters are not taken seriously because the fans don't know how to react.

Sid realized the direction Vince wanted him and his character to go and did not think it was going to work. He wanted to return home to his southern roots. From the same aforementioned source:

> Sid left the WWF because it was not working out as well as he had hoped. He spoke to Vince about it who told Sid to stay and he'd "make him the biggest heel in the business." But, Sid felt it wasn't time for him to be there.

And so in mid-1993 Sid returned to the WCW for a short lived run. We'll get to the whys in the next section, but Sid was lined up to become the Unified NWA/WCW World Heavyweight Champion before he was fired from WCW and replaced with Ric Flair (who beat Vader in a match that is not replayed enough).

Sid would not sit idle, though, and went down to the USWA where he defeated Jerry Lawler for the title in July 1994. Less than a year later he returned to the WWF, re-fought his way up the card, and finally defeated Shawn Michaels at Survivor Series 1996 for the WWE Championship. He would lose the title back to Shawn and win it again from Bret Hart in 1997, before losing it to the Undertaker for good at WrestleMania 13. He would spend another few months in the WWF before leaving for other interests, working the independents in 1998, and spending half a year in ECW in 1999 before making his return home to WCW. In WCW he would feud with Hollywood Hogan, Goldberg, Chris Benoit (and even added the crossface to his repertoire), Kevin Nash, Jeff Jarrett, and Scott Steiner, again winning two World Heavyweight Championships along the way.

His in-ring career came to halt on January 14, 2001 at WCW Sin when Sid jumped off the second rope and basically split his leg in half. He would not wrestle a match again until June 12, 2004. Surely, times had changed for Sid.

Besides the points we made before, what was that history lesson for? To show that Sid was not just found, picked up, and pushed to the title. He worked hard in the independents and lower-card and got noticed. He moved his way up and around the major organizations, making money (we'll get to it) and drawing in people wherever he went. It may have been just five years after his debut when he was in the main event of WrestleMania, but it would still be another four years after that before he won a major world title. Nine years is not an instant push. Sid waited patiently and did what the bookers wanted, which is another point we'll get to shortly.

Sid's history is often misunderstood, especially some of his most controversial moments.

TOP THREE MOST INFAMOUS MOMENTS

Sid seems to be more famous (infamous?) for his out of ring antics then his in-ring accomplishments. There are three huge ones that come to mind that cannot be ignored.

NO RESPECT FOR THE HULKSTER, BROTHER

Back at WrestleMania VIII, something amazing happened. Sid Justice kicked out of the Atomic Leg Drop of Doom! This was an unfathomable moment in wrestling history. No one had kicked out of Hogan's finisher before, and few have done so since. The controversy stems from this:

> *Sid Justice double-crossed Vince McMahon by kicking out of Hulk Hogan's legdrop during their match.*

This is not what happened. Sid's manager Harvey Wippleman and the future Godfather Papa Shango were supposed to interfere in the match and get Sid out of the predicament. Shango or someone in the back missed the cue and he was running about two seconds behind. To keep the pace and plan of the original match, Sid had no choice but to kick out.

And it's not like Hogan or Sid have any ill will towards each other over the incident. As a matter of fact, Sid continually puts Hogan over as one of the best, and in ways that you would never expect. Sid had this to say:

> *Hulk is a real nice guy: Had his own style. Probably the easiest guy I've ever wrestled, he really was.*

Sid thinks Hogan is easy to work with. What bigger complement is there from your co-worker?

WHAT ARE YOU GONNA DO, CLEAN MY WINDOWS?

Another incident occurred in 1991 in an inter-promotional bar fight. Sid was working for the WWF by that point and ran into Brian Pillman who was still with WCW. As you can imagine, there would be tensions between two competing workers, and their exchange of words coupled with alcohol began to move to fisticuffs. Sid went to his car and then returned to the bar with his most dangerous weapon: a squeegee!!!

What was Sid thinking? I cannot say. Maybe he thought he was grabbing a tire iron or a shovel. Did he want to attack Pillman for real or just scare him a little? Who knows? The people at the bar had a good laugh and that was the end of it. Maybe he was really just trying to diffuse the whole situation?

But in the end, I really have to say: why does this matter at all? This incident was so far removed from the ring and has been blown out of proportion. What were the repercussions of this? A few guys got a good laugh and Sid hurt his pride a little? Big whoop! Sometimes when you are in fights you do silly things. I once threw a fishing pole at someone. Yeah, that'll hurt! It's really a very silly thing to hold against someone for their entire career.

TWENTY PUNCTURE WOUNDS?!?!?

But what isn't a small and funny thing is Sid's fight with Arn Anderson. In 1993, Sid and Anderson got into a verbal argument that escaladed as the night went on and ended up with Arn having twenty puncture wounds and heading to the hospital.

Now, there is no excuse for hurting someone like that. But when asked about it, Sid has this to say:

> *The thing about that, man, is it's over. Arn and I have sat down, talked about it, and hashed it out.*

So Arn and Sid have been able to put it behind them and worked together in WCW. Why should we judge if they don't? Well, there's a part of the story that is missed. According to Scott Bowden:

> *Even though Sid was stabbed with the scissors as well, he was singled out because it was felt he instigated the fight and because Anderson suffered considerably more wounds.*

Who grabbed the scissors? Was it Arn or Sid? We'll never know for sure. The bottom line is a fight got out of hand, but Arn is hardly without blame. Both went way too far over something very petty, no matter what their argument actually was about.

And even though both have moved on from the incident, Sid has grown a little more used to dealing with it in his everyday life. Scott Bowden tells this story:

> *Sid and I were standing behind the curtain at the Coliseum as we watched a six-man tag match involving Lawler and Doug Gilbert. During the bout Doug missed a spot, and Lawler got noticeably pissed in the ring.*
>
> *Handling the situation in a manner that his brother, Eddie, would have been proud of, Doug took an unscripted powder, leaving the rest of the boys to finish the match. Afterward, a steamed Lawler confronted Doug in the back, screaming at him for being unprofessional. Just when it looked like the two were nearly coming to blows, Sid said something like, "Man, sounds like it's getting out of hand back there." I laughed and said, "Yeah, I hope neither one of them have any scissors."*
>
> *I've never forgotten the look Sid gave me; it sent chills down my spine. Very quietly, but with a menacing tone, he looked down at me and asked, "What the hell does THAT mean?" With my heart racing, I said, "Uh, nothing. I just ... hope there aren't any, uh ... sharp objects around." He nodded his head and then screamed at me to "get the fuck away" from him. I quickly obliged.*

I ostensibly had heat with him for a long time; however, after a while, I got the feeling that he was ribbing me. All the heels were sitting in the small dressing-room area in Nashville one Saturday night when he abruptly shouted, "Goddamn it, I should have both them NWA belts right now. Instead I'm sitting here in this dump with Scott 'fucking' Bowden."

For weeks Sid would tell me that he was begging them to turn him babyface so he could finally get his hands on me and give me a powerbomb. He finally got his wish one night in the metropolis of Jonesboro, Arkansas. I was booked to manage Sid and Doug against Lawler and Brian Christopher (Lawler) in the main event. They were struggling to come up with a finish, one that would end inconclusively but leave the fans happy. Lawler finally suggested the following: After a ref bump (this is a Lawler finish after all), I'm supposed to nail Brian from behind with my Florida State football helmet (given to me by Uncle Bobby) but remain in the ring. Sid would then ready Brian for a powerbomb, but before the move could be completed, Lawler would gouge his eyes from behind. Sid, who wouldn't be able to see at that point, would then grab me by mistake and powerbomb me.

Upon hearing the finish, Sid looked at me, shot me a sadistic smile and said, "Bowden, it's time. You thought I'd forgotten about that scissors comment, didn't you? Never! Never!" Later that night, right on cue, Sid positioned me and whispered for me to jump. I closed my eyes as Sid lifted me over his head and sent me crashing into the canvas. Sid was a pro all the way and didn't hurt me in the least.

Still, the apparent heat lasted until a softball game at Chicks Stadium in Memphis. The heels, captained by Sid, were playing Lawler and the rest of the babyfaces in a charity game. Although Brian advised me to strike out on purpose to stay in character, I hit two triples, including one to drive in the winning run for the heels. This, of course, thrilled Sid to no end. From then on, he treated me like one of the boys.

> *Should have known that it would take softball to get back in Sid's good graces.*

Sid knows he did wrong, but won't deny or pretend it didn't happen. He has just integrated it into his life and moved on.

But, as Scott said, is what he moved on to... softball?!

THE SECRET OF LIFE: SOFTBALL STYLE

Let's get it out of the way real quick:

Sid has left wrestling to go play softball. FACT!

But as you must be aware by now, the facts do not end the case until we explore the meaning. Calling star witness Scott Bowden to the stand:

> *Sid had also taken a lot of flack over the years for playing softball when he took leaves from work to heal injuries.*

That's right, Sid has gone to play softball when he was INJURED. Look back at his career; Sid was a major workout buff and liked to stay in shape. He enjoys being physical. But when he could not get into the heavy pressing and bumps, he took up another activity. Are we to fault a man because he found enjoyment in another sport outside of wrestling? Also look how he ding donged around between companies over the years. Sid goes where he wants, when he wants. His goals were to enjoy life, make money, and try to stay as healthy as possible.

Many people, especially after the passing of Eddie Guerrero, have been critical that professional wrestling has no off season. While a football player may have time to heal some injuries (though many are permanent), a wrestler will continue to wear down his body until he can go no more. Well, Sid was not about to do this. He knew his limitations and knew that he wanted to be able to walk when he was fifty years old. So what did he do? He made his own off season! It was not every year. Hell, it was not even every other year. It was when he needed it.

Much like Chris Jericho, Sid had other opportunities and interests in life. He wanted to explore those opportunities and heal his body at the same time. How is that a bad thing?

And it is not like the companies held it against him! He was hired and rehired by the WWF, WCW, and ECW numerous times despite the fact that they knew he might take some time away.

On top of all that, it's not like Sid has not worked through pain when he could have just sat home. At the end of WCW, he was suffering from a major shoulder injury. Instead of sitting at home and playing softball, he came to work and did everything that was asked of him. He knew he was fighting a losing battle, but did it anyway, and it only cost him three years of walking ability.

No, Sid did not use softball as an excuse or a crutch. He did not get fired over going to softball games over wrestling shows. He left companies to heal and to enjoy himself. What's wrong with that?

WHAT IS THIS WORK ETHIC YOU SPEAK OF?

We just briefly touched on it about, but Sid is a hard, dedicated worker. He only left wrestling when he was really injured, not just to relax. And he did not always leave when he needed to, often sticking around well beyond his time. Hell, even when he could barely walk he still went on the WWA tour to contribute the only way he could: with his voice and crowd pleasing skills. Sure, he's no Rock on the mic, but he still works hard to entertain the fans.

And yes, he is not Chris Benoit or AJ Styles in the ring. But that has never stopped him from learning and getting better. He was quite green upon his first entrance in WCW, but got training from the best, including Ric Flair and Arn Anderson. He added their moves to his repertoire and sought out things that worked for him. Whether it was a powerbomb or cobra clutch slam, whether snake eyes or a popping vertical suplex, whether learning the crossface or a triangle choke, Sid never gave up on getting better. Hell, his final injury in wrestling was performing a move he never did before: a second rope sledgehammer. Sure, sounds simple enough... if you weigh 180 lbs. Sid, on the other hand, weighed 300 lbs. and was not good on the ropes. He did what he was told, though, if only to move on.

Beyond being a dedicated worker, he is also the kind the IWC loves: one not just looking to protect himself. Sid is the one that wants to do what is best for the product, not just for himself. From the Interactive Interview recap:

> *One thing that bothers Sid is the way guys worry about who you're working with and putting them over. Sid says he doesn't really care who he works or who wins as long as he gets out okay and can go home. He also does not play politics very well.*

And we know from history that Sid does not mind losing. He lost to Hogan,

Undertaker, Hart, Michaels, Benoit, Steiner, Goldberg, Nash, et al! The man is a human jobbing machine, but still comes out looking strong.

In the same interview, this was noted:

> Kevin Nash came up with the idea to hire a surgeon to cut Sid's forehead prior to a match with Goldberg. Sid said it ended up looking pretty gory. "I called home that night and my wife was just in tears, man."

If that doesn't say dedication, I don't know what does! He put his wife to tears for a match in a company he was not sure was going to live. That takes a drive like no other!

Despite his injuries and many people saying he could never come back from his terrible break, Sid has never given up. From the end of that same interview:

> Sid has been told "it's over" several times by doctors. About returning from this one, "I don't know man. I just don't know. I'm feeling a lot better but I just don't know. Once I'm able to run again, I'll make my decision."

You see, that interview was a couple of years ago, and Sid continued to work until he could run. Now, he's ready to go. From Voice of Wrestling interview recap:

> Although he could work often he took every book he was offered, he doesn't want to work for promotions that are "under the screen"...

Sid says he could work regularly now, but doesn't. He's ready to go.

Of course, that brings up our next point: Does Sid overvalue himself?

I'LL TRADE YOU THESE THREE BEANS FOR ONE SID VICIOUS

From the just mentioned Voice of Wrestling interview:

> *Chris finished the conversation by asking Sid a very direct question: "Where do you rank yourself of all-time in professional wrestling when it comes to drawing money"? Sid explained first how he wasn't in wrestling while Hogan was at his best. "As a matter of fact, when I came into the WWF, that's exactly what I came in there for," Sid said, "they thought I was the next person who was going to draw that kind of money... which I did draw that kind of money". Sid said that like Hogan, he also drew a lot of money with a lot of different people, which there's not many others that have done. Within his era, Sid said that he would put himself up there at One or Two, not counting Hogan. He even compares himself to Austin and the Rock claiming that they only drew major money one time, while he drew it a handful of times.*

And your first reaction would be: WHAT?!?!

Well, Sid thinks he's a draw, let's look into it, main event PPV buyrate style:

Event / Match	Buyrate
WrestleMania VIII vs. Hulk Hogan	1.68
In Your House I vs. Diesel (WWF Championship)	0.83
In Your House: Lumberjacks vs. Diesel (WWF Championship)	0.70
Survivor Series 1996 vs. Shawn Michaels (WWF Championship)	1.30
In Your House: It's Time vs. Bret Hart (WWF Championship)	0.35
Royal Rumble 1997 vs. Shawn Michaels (WWF Championship)	0.70
WrestleMania 13 vs. the Undertaker (No DQ, WWF Championship)	0.77

Not the most stellar I've ever seen, sure enough. All together it's a 0.90 PPV average, still above our "success" range (see the Eric Bischoff case). Of course, it needs to all be put into context. For instance, 1996 was a very bad year in the WWF. From WrestleMania 12, no PPV had broken the 1.0 barrier, and it was only at Survivor Series was that streak finally broken. And then it fell again and did not break the 1.0 barrier again until WrestleMania 14... in 1998!!

You see, Sid was a draw, but he was in a bad time in Wrestling. Sid vs. the

Undertaker is the lowest drawing WrestleMania of all time. Absolute fact. Want to know why? Because everyone had already seen the main event. They saw it just a few weeks beforehand! Why would you spend $45 on a PPV for a match you've already seen? Several times?! The championship had been going around between Sid, Michaels, and Hart (with others mixed in for fun), and the audience was turned off. Sid cannot be held responsible for impossible booking conditions, yet still managed to bring in quite the crowd.

So with no support of story in an old match, Sid was still able to pull in a respectable (though not successful) 0.77 buyrate. Just as a comparison, WCW (which in a few months would be at the peak of its power) presented Uncensored in the same month to a 0.89 buyrate. So the highly successful WCW was only pulling in a buyrate 16% larger than the dying WWF. Not too bad of a day.

Sid, too, was on everything. One thing we know for sure is that the WWF/E and Vince McMahon are marketing machines. There were t-shirts and video games and figures and cards and all of that, and Sid was selling. Think back to the mid-90's, did you see more people in HBK shirts, or Sid shirts? Hart or Psycho? The latter in both cases. Don't forget, Sid said "during that era" he was probably number one or two, not including Hogan. So that means he considers someone like the Undertaker above him. On more than one occasion he has stated that he is no Hogan and did not bring in that amount of money for that amount of time, but there were small blips when he was bringing it in big.

The other point Sid was trying to make is that he did not just do it in one run like Austin or the Rock. He is not devaluing their contributions, but they really did most of their drawing from 1997 until 2001/2, and that was it. Sid was drawing in 1991-1992, again in 1995-1997, and again in 1999-2000. He's had several runs. Yes, they were shorter than Austin's or the Rock's, but if you put them together, the man has had a long run being a top draw.

Does he overvalue himself? Maybe a little. It's hard to say without using the way-back machine and fixing a lot of booking mistakes. But there is no denying that companies keep hiring him back because they do think they can get something out of him. Would you hire a guy if he wasn't going to add revenue? Neither would Vince or Eric.

Sid, though, sometimes let's his thoughts on his value go a little too far.

WHY'D YOU SAY THAT? WHY'D YOU HAVE TO TELL ME?

Sid has a tendency to put his foot in his mouth. Back to that Voice of Wrestling interview recap:

> *[Sid] doesn't want to work for promotions that are "under the screen", that don't do much work to get his name out there, that don't have television, and are basically "devaluing" the importance of his return. "Over my history in wrestling," Sid explained, "I've just wrestled a handful of Independents. [I] just wasn't interested in it. I don't want to become someone who just does the Independents".*
>
> *Chris mentioned TNA and asked Sid what he thought about potentially working for them, but he's not very interested. "One, I really haven't had an offer from TNA," he began, "two, I probably wouldn't go into TNA because as it stands right now, they're way, way, way away from anything I would be interested in doing". Sid wants to have some sort of success before he retires and he doesn't think TNA could provide that. "That right there would a worse way of cheapening myself than if I did an Independent show". Sid doesn't want to burn a bridge with WWE by going to TNA and even says that if he can't work for Vince and them, he probably won't work at all.*

Does Sid have an ego? You sure as hell bet he does. Does he deserve it? You sure as hell bet he does. Why do I say that?

First off, the man has been wrestling for 18 years! Eighteen! This isn't some flash in the pan guy. He has main evented two WrestleMania's, a Starrcade, and has held the WWF Championship and World Heavyweight Championship both twice (equals four major world titles). Guess what? He's right. Working too many independent dates will devalue his legacy. If he keeps going out there just for the buck or the thrill, he's just another Jake Roberts or Terry Funk, a guy who can't stop and is hurting himself and his family. Instead, he chooses to do this as a business. He's staying smart. Not only does he have value, he wants to maintain it.

And by the way, Sid has been in independent shows, just select ones. He doesn't need the work, he's just trying to keep in shape. He's not against independents, he just does not have to be on one every week.

"Sure," you say, "that's fine. Do a few independents to look big. Right. Well, what's with the TNA bashing? I know you don't appreciate that!"

Well, in many ways I don't, but I understand what Sid is saying. First off, Vince now owns ALL of Sid's matches. Everything he did in the NWA/WCW, WWF/E, and ECW are under Vince's control. Like Bret Hart, Sid will have to play nice with Vince if he does not want to end up another Ultimate Warrior. I understand that. For the good of business and his legacy, he is willing to swallow his pride. The fact that he does happen to like Vince does help matters quite a bit. The fact that he thinks he has one major run left also goes a little way. How can he end his career in a company not affiliated in any way with his past? He's not ready for that yet.

Still, there's more to this story than meets the eye. Again from the same interview (hey, it's a good one, what can I say?):

> He described an incident with TNA when they first started that is part of the reason he has "a little beef" with them. They contacted Sid while he was still on crutches before they debuted over three years ago and they asked him to sign a Letter of Intent. He said that he was honest with them and told him he couldn't get around very well, but they told him not to worry about it. Jeff was just looking for big names to put on the list and told Sid that they would just show him around in the back a few times. "Of all the people they tried to get to sign, I was the only one that did it," he said, "then when it came time to get things going, they didn't really want to do those things they were talking about. From there, I really just didn't have much interest at all after that".

Sid's impressions with TNA are from his first dealings with the Jarretts. He does not realize that TNA is not under their control, that it is a totally different company. Remember how the Funks are having the same problem? Lex Luger in a recent interview said he was not aware of the changes there. Sometimes when you are so deep inside something you can't see everything that is around you. Many wrestlers on RAW don't even watch RAW. It seems strange, doesn't it, but that's their job, less their entertainment. Some are still fans and can watch, other can't. If you worked at Wendy's, could you eat bacon cheeseburgers every day? Would you notice if a new item was added to the menu? After a while, no and no.

So Sid really does not know what TNA is about nowadays, but that is forgivable. Normally I'd be the person to attack someone for not having their facts straight, but it is relevant to note where he is coming from. Sid, in his own way, isn't really being malicious. He's just trying to do right by himself for whatever the future may bring.

MARK OUT MOMENTS

But before the future, we have to think of the past. And just to help you remember a few favorite Sid moments, here is Richard McClellan with his top ten Sid moments:

> 1-ECW 99 when he showed up to a major pop and destroyed Kronus at GAC '99.
> 2-WCW 99 when he came back, attacked Nash, and then went on to feud with Goldberg
> 3-winning the WWF title
> 4-winning the WCW title
> 5-attacking HBK 4/3/95 after WrestleMania 11
> 6-WCW 93 joining Vader in summer 1993 as masters of the power bomb
> 7-his Memphis run 1994-95 (best year they'd done in a while, his 11/7/94 match in Memphis vs Undertaker was gold!)
> 8-turning on Hogan on NITRO 3/20/2000 which would've done a good gate for Spring Stampede until [Russo and Bischoff] scrapped those plans.
> 9-returning to WCW to punk out Steiner, [N]ov 27[,] 2000
> 10-Sid getting back into action 2004-05 after his injury by wrestling on various independents.

And then there are our favorite PWI Awards (via accelerator3359.com):

> - 1991 Most Inspirational Wrestler, 2nd Runner-Up
> - 1991 Most Popular Wrestler, 2nd Runner-Up
> - 1992 Match of the Year, 2nd Runner-Up (Royal Rumble)
> - 1996 Comeback of the Year
> - 1996 Most Popular Wrestler, 2nd Runner-Up

Whether a fan of the north, south, and everything in between, Sid had something for you. To deny his 18 years of entertaining you is to deny being a wrestling fan at all.

Powerbomb... SMASH!

Sid Vicious is a man truly misunderstood. People often think of him as a big, clumsy guy who just rocketed onto the scene and stole a couple of world championships. Nothing could be further from the truth. Sid had nearly a decade of experience before he got his hands on the big gold. For eighteen years he worked hard in the industry learning to entertain more than wrestle. Not that he could not wrestle. Sure, he may not be able to do a catch-as-catch can style match, but he never stopped learning. From power bombs to cobra clutches to learning the crippler crossface to the final move that he did not want to do that broke his leg, Sid was always trying to grow.

He made his own path in wrestling going from organization to organization, mostly by free will. He did the unthinkable by actually taking time off to heal his body and pursue his other interests in life. A strange combination for a wrestler, and one needlessly resented by IWC pundits.

Yet Sid is mostly remembered for his out of ring antics, which are either complete lies, overblown pointless stories, or one-sided arguments that have reasoning behind them. Sure, he does have a big ego, but it is well deserved. He was on the elitist of the elite lists when it comes to men who have held championships in two major organizations, been at the top of the card in three major organizations, being in the main event of multiple WrestleManias, and being one of the very, very few who has main evented both WrestleMania and Starrcade.

Wrestling companies believe in Sid Vicious for one reason: because the fans believe in Sid Vicious. He was cheered when he wasn't supposed to be, he sold when no others could, and created a following and legacy that is meant to be preserved. Why is he constantly attacked in our world when the simple matter is this: he has given us way more than we could ever ask for.

The defense rests.

After the Trial

Hung Jury

IN THE CASE OF THE IWC VERSUS SID VICIOUS AKA SID EUDY AKA SID JUSTICE AKA PSYCHO SID, SID HAS BEEN ACCUSED OF BEING A HORRIBLE WRESTLER WHO WAS PUSHED TO THE TOP WELL BEFORE HIS TIME TO THE CHAGRIN OF ALL. SID WAS NEVER LOVED BY THE CROWD AND HE DESERVES TO HAVE HIS OUT OF RING ANTICS RUIN HIS LEGACY AS ALL THE RUMORS ABOUT HIM ARE TRUE.

With 78.1% of the vote, Sid Vicious was found:

NOT GUILTY!

First off, Sid got a way higher voter turnout than I expected. I guess a lot of people are more interested in him (and despise him) than I thought. Which, in turn, only proves my point on how much he's meant to the industry.

RESPONSE

A lot of people shared their personal experiences of Sid, but this one just tickled me:

> *Sid is the man.*
>
> *Got my photo with him when [I] worked security, after his bodybag match with the [U]ndertaker in Cornwall[,] Ontario back in 1992 or so.*
>
> *Very, very cool guy, had just broken his hand, and said don't squeeze it.*
>
> *So we took the photo with a soft touch of the hands and off he went to do an interview...*
>
> *He is the man.*
>
> **Dean Ward**

MIKE AWESOME LEAVING ECW

INTRO

SOME DAME WALKED INTO MY OFFICE AND SAID...

First up is the man of 1004 Column Ideas, **Rick Cobos**, who said:

> Mike Awesome practically stabbing ECW in the back in 2000.

But before that was the man who hates my column more than anyone **MATTHEW Roberts**:

> Mike Awesome... he sucks for screwing over ECW while holding their strap.

I'm not sure if he feels that way or it is a suggestion. Either way, I'll take the case!

WHY THIS?

Mike Awesome is considered one of the better "big man" performers of our time. Unlike the Undertaker, Kevin Nash, Lex Luger, and Sid Vicious, Awesome hardly needs a defense of his wrestling style. He worked incredible hard to win over the FMW crowd in Japan, a fanbase known for being even more rabid than ECW in its lust for violence and action.

No, Awesome does not need a defense there. It's what he became most remembered for; not for his hardcore style, and not even for his endless string of bad gimmicks in WCW (fat chick thriller, anyone?). There is one defining moment in history for Mike Awesome: when he jumped to WCW while still ECW champion. And for that, he has been cast into IWC hell forever.

What's the Story Here?

It was April 10, 2000 and the event was WCW Monday Nitro. After a week off, Nitro was returning under the new direction that would be termed the Russo-Bischoff era. This was to be a new direction in WCW, with the New Blood taking on the old Millionaires Club, and all the belts were confiscated for good measure. Exciting and crazy to say the least, but would it pay off? Well, hindsight is 20/20, and we know that in the end Bischoff and Russo could not get along since neither of them was really in charge and the direction kept getting changed every week when ratings did not react quickly enough.

But on that night, Mike Awesome made his WCW debut by attacking Kevin Nash (on crutches) from behind, declaring his loyalty to Bischoff and Russo, and flipping off the camera. The one problem? Awesome was ECW Champion (as the announcers mentioned). That was a bit of a mess. How could the ECW Champion appear on WCW TV? What was ECW going to do? How much did this destroy their credibility? Why would Awesome do this?

To those watching at home it was either (a) a shock because they did not expect the ECW champion to show up on Nitro, (b) a bewildering moment because they had no idea what ECW or who Mike Awesome was, or (c) expected because this was known about for days.

Awesome had no-showed the April 8, 2000 ECW on TNN television tapings in Buffalo, NY and had sent word to Paul Hayman that he was going to WCW. This was after a long string of negotiations that we will get to below. Heyman reacted swiftly to keep up morale and to keep the show going. Mike Awesome, though, was already gone. What was going to happen?

Who Really Trashed the Title?

The rumors started flying right away. People said that Bischoff was planning to throw the ECW Heavyweight Championship in the trash, a la Madusa and the WWF Women's Championship years earlier. Actually, SLAM! Wrestling's John Powell on April 9, 2000 said it exactly like this:

> Sources say that WCW booker Vince Russo and WCW Vice-President Eric Bischoff want Awesome to throw the ECW World Title belt in the trash as part of their mega-hyped revamping of Monday Nitro which could also spotlight the WCW debuts of Tammy Lynn Sytch (formerly Sunny in the WWF) and Sabu, a tournament to decide a new WCW World Champion and the destruction of the old Nitro set.

Wow, that's a lot of rumors for one sentence, none of which came true (at least that night). Still, there is no actual proof to substantiate the rumor other than "sources". And who do you think those "sources" may be? Perhaps they were started by Paul Heyman and passed on by his cronies to try to discredit WCW and Awesome?

Actually, no. Troy Robinson had this to say:

> I attended the WCW show in Denver the night that Mike Awesome debuted. Anyone that knows anything about ECW knows the background of Awesome jumping ship while holding the ECW belt. After the show I ran into a large group of the wrestlers at the hotel bar, and began talking to Awesome. He had a few beers in him when I spoke to him, but he said something interesting...
>
> He said that during that day's legal negotiations, the talks were breaking down for Awesome to debut that night on Nitro. Awesome told me that at one point when Paul and the lawyers were trying to stop him from appearing on TV he got mad and told Paul that the only way to get the belt back would be to fish it out of the river. Apparently Awesome had planned to bring his own TV crew (not WCW or ECW) and throw the belt off of some bridge in Philly, and that Paul had begged him not to do it. Awesome had stated that he had the belt up in his room, and it was 50-50 even minutes after the show hit the air whether he would cave in and appear with the belt. He said Bischoff was pushing for another belt in the trash can angle that night on TV that would involve Madusa.

Did Awesome consider throwing the belt in the trash or the river? You sure bet he did. It would be shocking. But did he actually do it? NO! Honestly, what could stop him? If he did drop the belt and ECW sued him and/or WCW, what could possible happen? WCW had the power of TimeWarner behind it and dozens of lawyers. ECW had a couple of Jersey lawyers working part time. Any court case would take years and years, and it was obvious at that point that Awesome did not believe ECW had a future. And it's not like Heyman had not pulled a similar stunt himself. John Powell of SLAM! Wrestling had this to say:

> On August 27th, 1994, Shane Douglas beat 2 Cold Scorpio in the finals of a tournament to determine the undisputed NWA World Heavyweight Champion. In a move that shocked the wrestling community, Douglas vacated the title declaring himself ECW's first World Heavyweight Champion. Renaming itself Extreme Championship Wrestling, ECW followed WCW's lead and opted out of the NWA alliance to strike out on its own.
>
> The rest is history.
>
> Six years later, it may be payback time for Paul Heyman and the boys. What goes around, comes around. Universal karma, if you will. ECW embarrassed the NWA and now it looks like their competitor for the Number Two spot is about to shame them on national television. If Mike Awesome does appear on Monday Night Nitro tonight, whether he symbolically dumps the ECW World Heavyweight Title belt in the trash is insignificant. The damage is done. The fact that WCW has snatched away ECW's World Champion right from under their noses is a powerful statement in itself.

You see, Heyman was being a hypocrite about the situation. He had done the exact same thing before, and would have done it again given the opportunity. It's only bad when it happens to him, not anyone else. When he does it, it's controversy that is good for business. When someone else does it, it is a cowardly attack.

Even still, Paul Heyman felt he had recourse against both Awesome and WCW, and it was in the form of a contract.

WHAT ABOUT THE CONTRACT?

If you watched The Rise and Fall of ECW, you would have heard Tommy Dreamer say that Mike Awesome was under contract to ECW. No offense to Tommy Dreamer, but he did not run ECW's business end and was not privy to the negotiated agreements people signed. And when it comes to Paul Heyman, well, he had let others slip through the cracks. The Dudley Boyz said they only wanted one more dollar to stay with ECW but Paul would have none of it. Why wouldn't he work out that contract? What was Paul Heyman thinking?

And how often did we hear about one person or another jumping to WCW or the WWF from ECW at any time. Whether it was Dean Malenko, Chris Jericho,

Steve Austin, or the Sandman, these guys left when they wanted to leave. It does not seem like there were many iron clad contracts to me.

There were reports that Mike Awesome was being held up due to legal documents and that WCW bought out his contract in the end. Not true at all. From TheSmartMarks.com recap of Mike Awesome's 2003 Shoot Interview:

> Jumping to WCW with the title- He was not under contract with ECW. He was driving to the show one night and realized he wasn't getting paid, so he was wondering how much trouble the company was in and questioning why he'd left Japan. He wasn't even going to be able to pay his mortgage since Paul wasn't paying him. He ended up talking to Horace Hogan **[JP the EDITOR'S NOTE: Horace and Awesome are cousins. Horace is a blood relation to Hulk while Awesome is not]**, who put Hulk Hogan on the phone. Hulk then told him to take his ass home if he wasn't getting paid, so he went home and started to talk to Eric Bischoff and Vince Russo. They signed him, he showed up on WCW TV while still ECW champion, and then the lawsuits started flying. If he had signed the contract Paul wanted him to, he could never have done it.

Did you read that? Mike Awesome was not under contract. Paul gave him the contract and probably had a verbal commitment from Awesome, but Awesome was hesitant and did not sign. Why was he hesitant? Because he was not getting paid! And even if there was a contract, it was in complete violation on Paul Heyman's part. If Paul Heyman was not paying his champion the money he was owed for the dates he worked, then the contract was null and void. If this ever went to court, Awesome would win because he fulfilled his part of the contract (wrestling) while Heyman did not fulfill his part (paying).

But like I said, that's only an "if" since there was no contract to speak of. The legal holdups had more to do with ECW property (the title), signed dates, and trademarks, not individual contracts. Besides, there was only one thing on Mike Awesome's mind. From the same interview as above:

> What was the solution to the problem? He just wanted to give the belt back to them because making money to support his family meant more than the belt. He felt he'd made a bad career move by leaving Japan. He thinks that people saying he "sold out" don't realize that he couldn't afford to

> *support his family while working in ECW. All of Paul's promises went unfulfilled as well.*

Mike Awesome had a family to support. He needed to feed his family and live his life. Paul Heyman and ECW were making that impossible for him. As you'll see below, those sums were ridiculous and getting worse. So, it had nothing to do with him being champion, but everything to with his loved ones. And since he wanted to give the belt back, there was only one thing to do: the right thing.

DOING THE RIGHT THING

Like I said before, Awesome could have dropped the title in the trash and called it a day. The repercussions would have been so far off that they might as well have been non-existent. But he didn't do that. Not only did he not do that, but he went back to ECW and lost the title to a WWF wrestler in Tazz. That's right, in one of the most surreal moments in wrestling history, a WWF wrestler defeated a WCW wrestler for the ECW Championship.

Still, people lambasted Awesome for this. They said he just came in and escaped through the crowd, that he hid like a coward, that he would not face the locker room because he was so ashamed or afraid. Again, this was all conjecture, and here is what Awesome had to say (from the same TheSmartMarks.com recap of Mike Awesome's 2003 Shoot Interview):

> *Coming back to lose the belt to Tazz- The stories about him sitting out in front of the ECW locker room are true... "I wasn't ALLOWED in the locker room." He also had a piece of paper faxed to him from Paul's attorney spelling out where he was to stay, what would go on in the match, where he was supposed to be until they called for him, etc. They spelled out everything legally so that all would go right. Since Paul built the whole thing up on TV for a week, it was a packed house that night and they all chanted "You sold out!" at him. He loved every minute of it when they were chanting that because he knew what was really going on. The only thing that disappointed him was that he wasn't allowed to go out there with Rhyno and put together a match that would put him over the top. He didn't trust Tazz in the match and had his hand up while Tazz had the Tazzmission on him in order to keep him from hurting him. He says Rhyno was about the only guy he trusted enough to work comfortably against at that time.*

You see there. All of that, the security, the entrance, the exit, the match, the not going into the locker room—that was all Paul Heyman and ECW. And Awesome also noted that he wanted to put over a current ECW talent, and it was a deal between Paul Heyman and Vince McMahon that brought Tazz in. What ECW got for that, we'll never know (although it was discovered later that Paul Heyman was being paid as a consultant to the WWF while his own organization was falling apart). All we do know is that Tazz and Tommy Dreamer then proceeded to get embarrassed on SmackDown! when Triple H took them both out. And that was the moment that truly devalued the title, not Mike Awesome's jump.

BUT THE BOYS STILL HATE HIM

Yet, because Mike Awesome did not go to the locker room, and because Paul Heyman rallied the troops in Buffalo, people assume that the Mike Awesome was on everyone bad list for his actions. This, though, is completely untrue.

First up is Kid Kash from Mike Johnson's review of Kid Kash's Shoot Interview with BBrownVideo:

> [Kid] Kash defends Mike Awesome for jumping to WCW while he was ECW champion, saying that it's a business and the bottom line is making the money. He brings up his injuries, saying that he has to stretch and take a hot shower at the start of every day before he can even walk out to get his mail. Kash discusses breaking his tibia, a broken jaw, breaking his hand 15 times, a broken orbital socket, and breaking both ankles. Kash noted that he has a tube in his nose permanently since he has broken his sinus so many times, which makes it always look like he has a cold since he's always sniffing. Kash says that he doesn't understand why everyone realizes that this is a business, but the second one of the boys treat it like a business, the others get up in arms, and puts over Awesome for helping to make Kash a star in ECW.

What Kash was saying was that he, Awesome, and everyone else were breaking their bodies and minds for ECW and were getting nothing for it. At the end of the day, it's still a business, and a man needs to get paid. Even the man Mike Awesome was afraid of did not really hold it against him. Tazz said:

> "I have no problem with Mike Awesome. I had a problem with the way he did business. And Mike knew I felt that way, a lot of guys felt that way about Mike. I think if Mike had to do it all over again, he'd do it different. People make mistakes in life, make wrong moves, and it's fine. But I personally never had heat with Mike. If the fans want to think that, that's fine, that's good for business. But there was never heat."

Tazz probably wishes that Mike Awesome could have left like him, with three-months' notice. But that was not to be. Unlike Tazz—who was getting paid—Mike Awesome was in a bad situation that was getting worse. Awesome also wanted to make an immediate impact on Nitro to secure his spot in the bold new direction the company was taking. If he did not act then, he might miss that brief window. Though it did not turn out as planned, he still needed to take that risk.

And Mike Awesome met others in his situation when he got to WCW. From TheSmartMarks.com recap of Mike Awesome's 2003 Shoot Interview:

> Meeting up with people in WCW who used to work for ECW- They sympathized with him all right. "Almost everyone who worked for ECW ended up burned from what I hear."

And that is what happened. Awesome was burned, but was not about to get it as bad as some (RVD for instance, who was owed so much money that there was no way he was ever going to get it). They understood that Awesome had to make the move for his and his family's own good. Yet there is one man who especially cannot see that.

WHAT ABOUT PAUL E.?

The night that Mike Awesome no-showed the television tapings in Buffalo, NY, Paul Heyman gathered the troops in back. He told them to all sign exclusive contracts or they would not be on TV.

This tells me one thing: a lot of people were not under contract. Going back to our earlier discussion, it would seem that Heyman had a tendency to let people work without real contracts. Not only that, you have to remember the timing of all this. TNN was about to sign a deal with the WWF that would kick ECW off of national TV and leave them without a home. Paul knew he had to sew up all his talent or they, too, would start jumping ship.

Tommy Dreamer and this to say following his championship win:

> *"Paul [Heyman] put the belt on me because he knew I wasn't going anywhere. The only reason I won the title is because guys left."*

Of course, it would have helped if he were paying the existing talent; they may have wanted to stick around longer. It seems as if Paul were paying some people regularly and never missed a check (see: The Rise and Fall of ECW). Others, though, were not as lucky. Spike Dudley had this to say:

> *"And we had a choice. Look for work elsewhere or try and stick with this guy who's been bouncing checks to us for two years."*

Tommy Dreamer adds:

> *"It was a horrible time. We were... sometimes we weren't making payroll. Guys checks were bouncing. And, you know, that gets out there, too. And a company looks like it's starting to sink... I don't think a lot of TV companies are gonna pick us up. And they didn't."*

Want to go a step further? During ECW's bankruptcy hearing, several names came out with how much they were owed. This is a partial list:

Talent	Amount Owed
Bill Alphonso	$5,000
Justin Credible	$7,990
Lou E. Dangerously	$7,000
Simon Diamond	$9,000
Danny Doring	$2,100
Shane Douglas	$48,000
Francine	$47,275
Don Callis	$12,000
Little Guido	$25,000
Balls Mahoney	$4,000
Dawn Marie	$9,000
Nova	$4,000
Roadkill	$21,250
Rhyno	$50,000
Joey Styles	$50,480
Super Crazy	$5,000
Tajiri	$5,000
Rob Van Dam	$150,000
Jack Victory	$3,000
Mikey Whipwreck	$12,000

With money like that owed to them, can you believe any of those guys stuck around at all?

So anytime Paul Heyman tries to feed you a BS line about anyone leaving or betraying him or ECW, remember this: Paul Heyman betrayed them first by withholding large amounts of money that these people needed to feed their families. That, folks, is a true betrayal.

For Mike Awesome, that choice was still a hard one, but a necessary one. He was not being paid even though he was the champion. He was owed money from years ago that he still had not seen. Paul Heyman continually lied and manipulated him, and ECW was quickly sinking. Awesome knew the choices and risks he had, and he only saw one way out: go to WCW.

THAT'S AWESOME!

Mike Awesome has been called a betrayer and sell-out. Some claim he did business the wrong way and wanted to hurt ECW in many ways. This is not the true story of what happened to Mike Awesome. Here was a man who literally broke his body for Paul Heyman and ECW yet was continually being stiffed. He was carrying the company's championship on his shoulder yet was not even being paid the money for gas to drive to the arena. It was never about the championship when he left; it was about the once in a lifetime opportunity to be a part of WCW's reboot. It was about making a solid paycheck to support his family. It was about being given the proper compensation for his work and not being fed more lies to feed his empty stomach for another month.

The defense rests.

AFTER THE TRIAL

HUNG JURY

IN THE CASE OF THE IWC VERSUS MIKE AWESOME LEAVING ECW, MIKE AWESOME HAS BEEN ACCUSED OF BEING A SELLOUT TRAITOR WHO SET OUT TO DEVALUE ECW AND ITS CHAMPIONSHIP FOR HIS OWN SELFISH VENDETTA. MIKE AWESOME BETRAYED THE FANS, HIS CO-WORKERS, AND HIS EMPLOYER BY JUMPING TO WCW.

Maybe I should have called it THE WAY Mike Awesome left ECW. Either way, I still made my case. With 86.2% of the vote, Mike Awesome Leaving ECW was found:

NOT GUILTY!

First off, holy mackerel were there a lot of votes! Second off, holy mackerel, I can't believe I won that case with that high a percentage. Some people question whether people reading my cases are just marks of the people and would vote "Not Guilty" no matter what. Well, I would say that at least half of the people writing in said they wanted desperately to vote guilty, and that I had really changed their mind. Most common response: I had never looked at it that way before. Well, that's what I'm here for.

RESPONSE

Despite the large win margin, there was some criticism to address:

> *Sure, Mike Awesome wasn't under any contractual obligation to stay with ECW, sure he wasn't getting paid for all the bumps and bruises he was taking, sure he was struggling to make ends meet, but so was everyone else in the roster yet they still stayed or at least did business properly before leaving. Mike Awesome was the champion and holding that position means that Paul trusted him to help carry the company in especially trying*

> times in more ways than most of the roster. Sure, anyone such as Mickey Whipwreck or Don Callis could have no showed and leave for WCW or WWE in a heartbeat if they wanted to because they weren't champions. If he wanted to jump ship and move to WCW then no problem, he could have told Heyman, lose the belt and show up on WCW without being a complete ass about it. The fact that he left with the belt was really unprofessional on his part....
>
> ...
>
> There are things more important than fulfilling contracts such as maintaining a level of professionalism and ethics in your work and keeping the trust and respect of your peers. I'm sick of people using their family and hiding behind them as an excuse for unprofessional and unethical behavior. There's always the right way, which may not be the easiest path but at least whoever chooses that path can look at their family without a hint of shame.
>
> **w. lighter**

My issue with this response is the question of "When is enough, enough?" How long do you get to be screwed over before leaving would be considered "ethical"? Is there a point scale or a standard questionnaire that you can fill out to determine if you are making the most ethical decision? This is the point I tried to make in my response:

> Well, I will have to disagree with you there. Spike Dudley on The Rise and Fall of ECW said that most of the guys who weren't being paid continued on the road because they had nowhere else to go. A lot of them wanted to jump but the opportunity was not there. Mike Awesome was made the offer, and had to strike while the iron was hot, otherwise he might be trapped on the road destroying his body for no money (see: New Jack). The most unprofessional thing was that he was not being paid and they actually expected him to show up for work. If you had not been paid in a month, would you go to work, even if you were the safety engineer of a nuclear reactor? As important as he was to the company, they did not treat him in a professional manner and therefore did not deserve

> to be treated professionally back. Mike had done "the right thing" and played by their rules for a long time before he jumped. Who knows, maybe he told Paul E that he was thinking of leaving and Paul stopped paying him at all. Maybe it was just a game of chicken that Heyman lost.

Still, others tried to poke similar and different holes:

> If he was not getting paid, then give them the belt and leave. There was no reason for him to try to escalate the situation.
>
> Your article did not address whether ECW had to get an injunction from a judge to protect their belt, as Joey Styles claimed on ONS.
>
> Also other articles claim WCW had to have their head of security accompany him to Indy.
>
> ...
>
> **Thomas F. Glassman**

For this I noted:

> As far as dropping the belt, it was a timing issue more than anything else. The ECW show that was being taped in Buffalo would not play until after Nitro. He HAD to jump to WCW that week to kick off the "revolution", and WCW did not want one of their wrestlers losing to somebody later in the week on ECW TV. It's what happened anyway, but it would have been a deal breaker the week before. WCW did send security with him, but so what? It just added to the hype and Heyman loved it. They got an injunction that the belt was ECW property and that it could not be shown on WCW TV, which it never was. But the injunction had nothing to do with Awesome being champion or having to drop the belt. That was deal worked out between WCW and Heyman.

In an aside, in a response to a question about Joey Styles saying Mike Awesome was a "sellout" on One Night Stand, I sent this response:

> *I'm still not sure if Styles was schilling to the fans, he actually believes that, was brainwashed by Heyman, or just saying what Heyman wanted him to say. From what I understand they did not end on the best terms, but if the past few months have taught me anything is that Styles has no problem being a complete hypocrite. Listen, I have no problem with a guy selling out, just admit that you are selling out! The guy is re-writing his own origin! "I've always wanted to be a WWE announcer!" Since when?!*

While these particular criticisms were fairly easy to counter, this one has some legitimacy:

> *The fact that Mike Awesome said something in a shoot interview does not make it gospel. It makes it [testimony] at best, and even that's a stretch. History has repeatedly shown that when a public figure is under heavy scrutiny, they may wish to bend the truth a bit toward restoring their dwindling reputation. Does the phrase "I did not have sexual relations with that woman" ring a bell?*
>
> *While reading this column I noticed some internet rumors being presented as just that - rumors. Other rumors, however, were presented as [incontrovertible] fact. Inferences were made, which were then presented as fact. Speculation seems to be the theme here, rather than the dispassionate presentation of cold facts. Which, granted, does make for a very entertaining read. Just not a very convincing case.*
>
> **Jon Carruthers**

I was forced to concede here:

> *I will admit that this case was lighter on evidence than normal, but that is because much of it is just not available. Instead, I used the opportunity to present a different perspective of Mike Awesome's jump then is normally given and at the very least get people to think outside themselves.*

However, the justification for these tactics being reasonable is because of responses like this:

> *I never saw it that way. I really hated [M]ike [A]wesome. I was at [O]ne [N]ight [S]tand, I sat in the fourth row. When [M]ike [A]wesome came out to wrestle [T]anaka, I continuously shouted "FUCK YOU AWESOME" and I sat down and watched the floor throughout the match in protest. I've been told that I missed a hell of a match but from what I knew before, I thought it was a disgrace to have him there. Now, that I know this, I think it's a disgrace to not pay wrestlers. Like that wrestler [T]ony... said in [B]eyond the [M]at "[T]here's no reason why you should never pay a wrestler." [S]o thanks for the new insight, I forgive him.*
>
> **Andrew Lee**

There was no greater compliment than to know how I was able to break Paul Heyman's brainwashing and open someone up to a new and different perspective.

THE MCMAHON-HELMSLEY ERA

INTRO

SOME DAME WALKED INTO MY OFFICE AND SAID...

First off, the following people (in no particular order) have already asked me to defend Triple H in one form or another:

Rob Dow, Ben Albright, Max Smith, Tim Hamilton, MATTHEW Roberts, Ori Zeiger, John Dee, Rick Cobos, James "JT" Thomlison (I know, I couldn't believe it when I was checking through my archives), and about a million other people in passing.

The thing is, I find Triple H too broad of a topic, and asked these guys to pare it down. I got a lot of ideas, but there's one that I've liked since day one.

Thus **Ted Lach** peeked my interest when he said:

> *I'm pretty sure the McMahon-Helmsley era would be very interesting.*

That was followed up by **Mark Radulich** who added:

> *How about the McMahon-Helmsley era as being good for wrestling and not just an exercise in masturbation for both aforementioned people?*

And **Manu Bumb** also chimed in with:

> *Actually, I kinda liked the McMahon-Helmsley era.*

And that, my friends, is good enough for me!

WHY THIS?

As time had gone on, Triple H and Stephanie have become the iconoclastic figures of everything that has ever gone wrong in the modern era of professional wrestling. Whether this is true or not is actually irrelevant to this case. Due to limits of human memory and the compression of time, some would have you believe that Triple H and Stephanie McMahon were always evil control freaks who screwed each other, the WWF/E fans, and the on-the-rise stars. Nothing could be further from the truth!

The McMahon-Helmsley era truly marked the beginning of each of their collective rises. What we consider played out today was fresh and exciting then. What we see as yet another Triple H moment was something unique for the time. We overlook the accomplishments of the McMahon-Helmsley era because the accomplishments have been repeated with not as much success ad nauseam. Just because it has become played out today, does not mean it was not enjoyable at the time.

Not only that, but the McMahon-Helmsley era was about more than the two namesakes. There were a whole plethora of events and people that also existed and expanded, and these should not be forgotten.

So with that we begin a journey of rediscovery into the McMahon-Helmsley era.

How did this all begin?

On March 29, 1998 at WrestleMania 14, Triple H had defeated Owen Hart to retain the European Championship while fellow Degeneration X member Shawn Michaels lost the WWF Championship to Steve Austin. Michaels would not return to the ring for years, instead going into retirement to heal his back. Triple H then took control of Degeneration X the next night on RAW and recruited the New Age Outlaws and the returning X-Pac. Through the rest of 1998 and into 1999, Triple H continued his feuds with Owen Hart, D-Lo Brown (he lost the European Championship to him), the Rock (eventually winning the IC Championship from him), Jeff Jarrett, and Kane. On March 28, 1999 at WrestleMania 15, Triple H and Chyna turned on Degeneration X and joined the Corporation.

This began Triple H's rise to the top of the card. He became involved in three-way feuds involving Austin, the Undertaker, Mankind, and the Rock. Finally on RAW on August 23, 1999, Triple H defeated Mankind to win his first WWF Championship. This reign would be short lived as he lost the title to Vince McMahon on SmackDown! on September 16, 1999. Vince McMahon would forfeit the title and then try to screw Triple H over by making him win 3 out of 5 matches in one night. And not just any matches, but insane matches like an Inferno match with Kane. So Triple H did it, winning three out of five, wrestling FIVE TIMES in one night (that's just a lot of work!). This got him in the six-pack challenge where he won the championship on September 26, 1999. This reign would be short, too, as the Big Show (a last minute replacement to the run-over Steve Austin) defeated Triple H and the Rock in a three-way match for the title at Survivor Series on November 14, 1999.

Meanwhile, back in April 1999, the Undertaker had begun to stalk Stephanie McMahon. After much harassment and kidnapping, Vince McMahon actually turned to Steve Austin to save his daughter. This, though, turned out to be a giant swerve as Vince was revealed to be the "Higher Power" that the Undertaker was working for. In retaliation, Stephanie and Linda sold their stock to Steve Austin so that he could face-down Vince McMahon on a financial front as well.

As time went on, Stephanie and her father were able to patch things up (or so it would seem), and Stephanie started to date Test. Although this did not sit well with her brother Shane, the relationship would go on. In September 1999, the two were engaged to be married, but the October 11, 1999 wedding had to be postponed as Stephanie was suffering from post-concussion syndrome. She recovered and a new date was set: November 29, 1999. RAW.

Back to Triple H. Despite now being a two-time WWF Champion, he really was not established at the top of the card. Despite being the head of Degeneration X and a major player in the Corporation (before it became the Corporate Ministry), he had not found his spot. No doubt the WWF was behind him and thought he had what it took, but he had yet to find a groove all his own. He needed a moment to set him apart, he needed a moment to make the fans truly care... or truly hate him. They were becoming indifferent to his childish antics as much as they had become indifferent to his snob act. There had to be something he could do to set himself apart from the pack and solidify his place in the main event.

Back to Stephanie. The fans had really got into her budding relationship with Test. She was beloved by the audience and they were ready to see the little girl married. Stephanie was still so fresh to the scene, and every day was learning something new about her. She had already solidified herself with the audience by choosing Steve Austin over her father, and stayed that way by even getting in the ring (teaming with Test against Jeff Jarrett and Debra). This innocent girl could do no wrong.

And then the day came when their paths would intertwine forever. On the November 29, 1999 edition of RAW, Stephanie and Test were in the ring about to commit their vows when, suddenly, over the Titan-tron Triple H displayed a video that would change the direction of the then WWF. To get back at Vince for everything he had done, Triple H drugged Stephanie McMahon the night before RAW and had taken her to a drive-through chapel where the two were wed. Test was devastated, Vince was furious, and Stephanie was heartbroken.

Or so it would seem.

At Armageddon on December 12, 1999 Triple H defeated the enraged Vince McMahon in a Street Fight when Stephanie turned on him and sent him packing.

Thus, the McMahon-Helmsley Era was born!!!

Well, if you want to be technical, it did not begin until December 20, 1999 when Triple H and Stephanie actually announced it as the beginning of the McMahon-Helmsley era, but the idea was already there.

You see, Stephanie had never forgotten that her father had used her in his feud with Steve Austin, and that he had almost sacrificed her to the Deadman. That could not go without revenge. She had liked Test well enough, but it turns out that she was far less virginal than others surmised when they first started dating. But it was Triple H, daring to oppose her father, that gave her the idea for the ultimate revenge. And then she had found that she was in love with the man (in the storyline world) and everything seemed to come together perfectly.

Vince decided to take a leave of absence, and without Linda or Shane around, that left Stephanie in charge. Well, Stephanie and her new husband: Triple H.

WHY TRIPLE H?

The question is: why was Triple H given this opportunity?

A lot of pundits will say Triple H got to run wild because he was with Stephanie McMahon.

Time for a history check, kids! From Valleyboy's recap of Triple H on Off the Record in March 2002:

> *Michael jokes that he must be into extreme sports to start dating Vince [McMahon's] daughter. HHH laughs and agrees. Michael asks how it started and what Vince thought of it. Triple H says that it started right around the same time that they had started working together in the marriage program. He says that when you work with someone that you find you have a lot in common with and has as strong a passion for the business as they both do, you can't really control who you fall for. He and Michael then make a crack about how Steph has two huge passions for the business right [in front] of her.*

You see, it was the program between the two that created the relationship, not the other way around. Although Triple H was on a major push, that push was decided well before he became involved with Stephanie in real life in any way. The whole concept for the McMahon-Helmsley era and the first major programs (including Triple H winning the WWF Championship for the third time), were decided well before that relationship got under way.

But even if it did make a difference, it was not like Triple H was the booker for the WWE. Although on TV they were in control, it was just a storyline. There was only one man making the decisions there. From the same interview on Off the Record:

> *They then discuss what Vince thought of it and how he told Vince. Hunter says that it really wasn't something that surprised Vince because he would see the way they acted around [each other] at work and kind of looked like he was wondering what was going on. He says that they try to act as professional backstage as possible and try to just keep civil. Michael mentions the potential conflict of interest and asks if Hunter is worried about what the other wrestlers think about their relationship. Triple H answers that at first he was very nervous about it and it was actually Vince who was the one to convince him otherwise. He also talked to a lot of the guys about it and, in particular, the Undertaker because he is one of the real locker room leaders and Taker said that whatever happens, [no one] can question how hard you have worked to make it where you are...*

You see, Triple H was actually worried about the other guys and did not want to make it look like he was sleeping his way to the top. If he had had his way, the whole relationship would have remained as downplayed as possible. That, of course, was going to be impossible with Chyna lurking around. From the same interview:

> *Michael brings up his past relationship with Chyna and shows a clip of Joanie Laurer on OTR from a couple months ago in which she says that she doesn't blame Stephanie for stealing Hunter, but blames Hunter for leaving her. Hunter says that she's right and if she needs to blame him to move on then he is fine with that. He points out though that they were on a downswing in their relationship before the issue of Stephanie ever happened. He adds that when you are in this business and with someone 24 hours a day, that it can [wear] on your relationship, especially when you are looking for different things and [no one] ever forced any decisions on her that she made.*

Chyna and Triple H were over. He was not trading up; he was just moving on. It was just happenstance that it was Stephanie and he who fell in love with. They do have a great passion and history with the business, and care a great deal about the WWE.

But one thing has nothing to do with the other. Like we went through, Triple H and Stephanie became involved after the angle started. He and Chyna were on the outs and he and Stephanie were just heating up. Triple H wanted to keep it downplayed, but Chyna was making a fuss. Worried about what to do, it was actually Vince McMahon who said that they should be open about it. After all, he was the final decision maker and he would decide what was right for the show, program, and company. Triple H even went so far as to solicit advice from the Undertaker, and that made the decision easier.

So yes, Triple H and Stephanie had a real-life relationship, but that relationship did not dictate the direction of McMahon-Helmsley era, as we will discuss more in-depth later.

WHY STEPHANIE?

How was it, then, that Stephanie became involved in this whole storyline? Some would have you believe she just enjoys writing herself into storylines and TV. This, of course, is ridiculously impossible.

Why impossible? Because Stephanie was not on the creative team at that time! It would not be until a year later that she would join the creative team on the SmackDown! side. As a matter of fact, Stephanie had worked her way up in the WWE. From RAW Magazine in December 1999:

> [Stephanie McMahon said, "]I started off as a receptionist. At that time reception handled all fan calls, as well all company calls; there was no fan services department. I opened all the fan mail as well as controlled the stamps and everything else internal. Everything went through the receptionist. I was a receptionist for about two years."
>
> Stephanie then went on to intern in various departments- Human Resources, Marketing and Pay-Per-View, Media Relations, the television studio as a production assistant, New Media, and this year with the president and CEO- her mother, Linda McMahon.
>
> "That's when I became full-time," Stephanie continues. "I spent three months in my mother's

> office and it was the most incredible three months. It's a tremendous opportunity to be able to sit in every meeting and every phone call that the CEO has, for three months. Then I spent six months with my father, who is the chairman. I miss [working with] him very, very much."
>
> Today, Stephanie is an account executive in the New York sales office and still learning the business.

And that's where she was when she made her debut as either staying around Linda in the ring or becoming the eye of affection for the Undertaker. Even with her storyline with Test, she was not a part of the booking committee in any way. These decisions would still be a while off.

AND THEN WHAT HAPPENED?

Now that we understand the main players and their role in this, we can begin to follow their journey.

Like noted above, Triple H would quickly go on to win the WWF Championship against the Big Show on the January 3, 2000 edition of RAW. This time, though, the fans were firmly against him. He had cemented his place as a hated heel, but had yet to cement his spot on the top. That would come after a series of matches with Mick Foley, where he retired Foley in their Hell in a Cell match on February 27, 2000 at No Way Out.

The McMahons came back to get involved with WrestleMania 16, but their stay would be short lived after Triple H managed to retain his title in the four-corners main event. His reign over the title and the storyline company would continue, though he lost twice to the Rock along the way. While the Rock had the title, Triple H would then go on to feud with Chris Jericho. Strangely, this actually began to segue into the "rocky" period. From Slam! Sports:

> [P]roblems began between he and Stephanie, as Stephanie caught Hunter in a compromising position with Trish Stratus and Hunter becoming jealous of Kurt Angle's affection towards Stephanie. At SummerSlam 2000, Angle and Triple H battled the Rock for the WWE title but Angle cost Hunter the title, and the Rock again retained the belt. The love triangle between Stephanie, Hunter and Angle continued until, after a match against Chris Benoit, Helmsley blamed Stephanie for the loss and Stephanie announced that she would be

> *managing Kurt Angle. Helmsley would however rescue Stephanie from an attack from the Rock.*

Meanwhile, a few months earlier in March 2000, Stephanie had defeated Jacqueline for WWF Women's Championship and began a feud with Lita over said title. Stephanie somehow managed to hold on to the title until the RAW before SummerSlam 2000 when she lost the title to her erstwhile contender.

After SummerSlam, she and Triple H were still a bit contentious as Triple H and Kurt Angle continued to feud, with Stephanie in both men's corners. The two would get back on the same page as Triple H fought Chris Benoit in October.

On the other side of the fence, Steve Austin had returned from injury (or being run over) and was also feuding with Kurt Angle and Rikishi. On November 6, 2000 Austin was fighting those two when Triple H ran down... seemingly to save Austin. But no! He hit him with a sledgehammer instead and began their long feud while Kurt Angle continued on with the WWF Championship. This would go on until No Way Out on February 25, 2001 when Triple H defeated Austin in a best of three series matches.

After a quick loss to the Undertaker at WrestleMania X7 on April 1, 2001, Triple H changed his mind about Austin. The following night he attacked the Rock to save Austin, and the two joined with Vince McMahon as the Power Trip. Although Vince was back in the picture, he had not taken away the full power of the McMahon-Helmsley Era. Still, the era was waning as it seemed that Vince and Austin were becoming the team while Triple H and Stephanie were relegated in their duties and powers (on screen).

With Austin winning the WWF Championship, Triple H was forced to go for another prize. He defeated Chris Jericho for the Intercontinental Championship on the April 5, 2001 edition of SmackDown!. This was followed by a quick drop and regain to/from Jeff Hardy, a Tag Team title win with Austin over Kane and the Undertaker, a loss of the IC title to Kane, and a loss of the Tag Team titles to Chris Jericho and Chris Benoit.

And that last match would really be that: the last. It was on May 21, 2001, and Triple H suffered a major tear to his quadriceps that would put him out of action for eight months.

Thus, the McMahon-Helmsley Era ended in a silent scream. When he returned, the WWF had already gone through the InVasion and was in a new direction. It would be just a couple of months until they became the WWE, and a few months later the Brand Extension would begin. Although still married in the storylines, Triple H did not immediately appear with the disposed Stephanie. In February 2002, Stephanie faked a pregnancy to keep Triple H, but when the truth was uncovered, Triple H announced that he wanted a divorce.

Although this is the date for the end of the McMahon-Helmsley marriage, it is not the date for the end of the McMahon-Hemlsey Era. The Era ran from the week after Stephanie turned on her father until Triple H was forced out with his quad injury.

The McMahon-Helmsley Era: December 20, 1999 to May 21, 2001.

Remember those dates, because it will be important for everything that follows. We must remember what REALLY happened during the McMahon-Helmsley Era, and what has been erroneously attached to it.

THE SHORT-TERM GAINERS

There were quite a few people who had some short-term growth because of the McMahon-Helmsley Era that they would not have had otherwise. Though not always successful later, these people, events, and objects did have a moment of spotlight because of the Era.

Test — Test was fairly new to the scene and had not done much. He had been backup and he had squashed some jobbers, but he had not found a character or direction. When he started to date Stephanie, people began to take to him, and his short feud with Triple H following the wedding pushed him up the card. Yes, he did not become a main eventer and was slightly lost after the angle, but for a new guy he was involved in a very high profile moment that solidified his place for years. He would fumble around for a while, joining T&A and going on to some tag team success after a feud with the Dudleyz. And after the Era, he was heavily involved in the InVasion, joining his good friend Shane McMahon in the Alliance and winning Tag Team and Intercontinental gold (as well as winning the immunity battle royal). None of those would have been possible without his initial exposure during the beginning of the McMahon-Helmsley Era. If he had not been involved, then he would have just been your average big man searching for a gimmick.

Jeff Hardy — Edge/Christian and Matt/Jeff Hardy had done a lot to establish themselves just before the beginning of the Era. Fighting each other, the teams had gotten themselves over on pure athleticism and daredevil attitude. Going through the Era, the teams along with Dudleyz, Cheese Head, T&A, Hollys, and others danced with the tag team titles. But as with all teams, eventually there was a need to change direction and a heading of separate ways. And who would be the first to really benefit from that individual push? None other than Jeff Hardy. Jeff would have some success in the hardcore division (who didn't?), but really established himself as a single's competitor when he defeated Triple H for the Intercontinental Championship on April 12, 2001. Right near the end of the Era, but still in there to show what was beginning for Jeff. The Undertaker would later also provide this rub in a series of matches with Hardy (none that he won), but the foundation for that eventual push happened right in the Era we are discussing. Although Hardy would later leave the WWE and no-show TNA events, these cannot be attributed to what we first saw from him during the McMahon-Helmsley Era.

Mick Foley — You are probably saying to yourself, how can Mick Foley be considered a short-term gain of the McMahon-Helmsley Era? From James Walsh's recap of Mick Foley on the Wrestling Epicenter's Interactive Interview:

> Chuck asks why some veterans have such a problem putting young talent over. "Man, I don't know. I think some of it is insecurity. There's the old school feeling that you don't lose matches on TV. I knew I wasn't the greatest wrestler in the world but I strongly felt I had a good enough character to come back from losses," says Mick. Mick says for a lot of guys, it's not wanting to put people over. It's just not knowing how to do it without making themselves look bad due to the talent.

You see, when it comes to Foley, the greatest thing he can do is put over another talent. It was still the very beginning of the McMahon-Helmsley Era, and despite the fact that Triple H was on his third WWF Championship he was not solidified into the top of the card. No, it would be Mick Foley who would make that happen.

Also, Mick Foley got into the main event of WrestleMania shortly after his retirement match. It was always Foley's dream to be in the main event of WrestleMania, and he only got to accomplish that during the Era.

The Women's Championship — Of course, it was not just people who got a boost from the Era, but also certain inanimate objects. Although some detest the fact that Stephanie won the Women's Championship, and that she rarely defended it, it is hard to argue that the title was not brought into more prominence. The title had fallen into disarray and was won by "T&A" champions like the Kat and ring announcer Harvey Whippleman (a MAN!!) in a gravy bowl match. One could hardly understand the value of the title. But the feud Stephanie and Lita had over the title in the Spring and Summer of 2000 brought it into new light. So much so that the two main evented RAW for the Championship on August 21, 2000. From Ryan Watcher's report on 411mania (then 411wrestling):

> Stephanie McMahon vs. Lita, Women's Title - Special Ref: The Rock
>
> A woman's match is the main event. This is a first[.] Is a real wrestler going to hold the women's title for the first time since Wendi Richter? We'll see... Steph comes out with Angle and Triple, who are glaring at each other. BTW, Lita is alone. Triple H goes to yell at Lita, and The Rock's music hits.

> *Slow start, until Lita hits a hurricanrana for a 2 count. Rock's not looking, so H clocks Lita. The Hardys come out to stand in Lita's corner. Steph takes control and hits DDT after what Lawler calls "an [O]lympic monkey-flip". Steph slaps and kicks. Head scissor takedown by Lita. Modified second rope bulldog from Lita. Lita goes for the moonsault, but Angle pushes her off. [The] Hardys brawl outside with Angle and Triple H (and getting killed). Angle [attempts] to hand Steph her belt while Rock is distracted, but Rock sees him and pull[s] him in. Triple H comes in and attacks Rock, but Rock fights back. Angle goes to hit Rock with the women's title but Rock ducks and Angle hits Triple H. Rock Bottom on Angle. Spinebuster on Steph. Lita goes up and hits a moonsault on Steph, and the Rock counts three. They celebrate and the show goes off the air.*
>
> *Winner, and NEW WOMENS CHAMPION, Lita!*

The two also wrestled in several mixed tag matches in main events of RAW and SmackDown!. The Women's Championship, as Ryan said, had never been in a main event before. That was the direction the title took for a good long while.

Still, the championship's and these peoples' gains were nothing in comparison to some of the other people who grew out of the Era.

THE LONG-TERM GAINERS

Aside from those who gained in the short run, there were a slew of others whose true path to glory began and grew exponentially during their time in the McMahon-Helmsley Era.

Lita — Now that we've talked about the prominence of the Women's Championship, there is one woman who got an incredible push that put her into the spotlight, and that woman is Lita. After spending late 1999 and early 2000 with Essa Rios, Lita left her light-heavyweight friend to join up with the Hardy Boyz to form Team Extreme. The trio would go on to great success, but Lita really moved up the ranks. From follower of a jobber to be considered the establisher of the modern women's era in the WWE in less than a year is quite an accomplishment. And she has never left that high position, although only winning the Women's Championship one more time and having been seriously injured three times.

Chris Jericho — Chris Jericho had arrived in the WWF about four months before the beginning of the McMahon-Helmsley Era. After a confrontation with the Rock, Jericho floated around before feuding with Chyna over the Intercontinental Championship (winning it on the eve of the Era on December 12, 1999). Jericho's real rise, though, would begin in his feuds with Kurt Angle and Chris Benoit, establishing him as a star to be reckoned with. This came to a head when Jericho defeated Triple H for the WWF Championship on April 17, 2000 (only to have the decision reversed later in the night).

> *Just wanted to let you know that Vince is not the one that overturned that decision, it was Helmsley after bullying Hebner into admitting to a fast count.*
>
> **Todd Vote**

From going to fighting with Chyna to being a world title contender... all thanks to the McMahon-Helmsley Era.

Chris Benoit, Eddie Guerrero, and the Radicalz — On January 25, 2000 Perry Saturn, Dean Malenko, Chris Benoit, and Eddie Guerrero jumped from WCW to the WWF. While Saturn and Malenko went on to moderate success (including Malenko winning the Light Heavyweight Championship), it would be Benoit and Guerrero who would see the most prizes. Though the two would be future world champions, their stage was set during the McMahon-Helmsley Era. As a matter of fact, it was in the Spring of 2000 that Eddie Guerrero began to go with Chyna and developed his Latino Heat persona that would make him famous. On the same end, Chris Benoit fought the Rock for the WWF Championship, and then later got into a three-way feud that added Steve Austin to the mix. All of these developments and more happened during the McMahon-Helmsley Era.

Trish Status — Lita was not the only woman to rise to prominence during the Era. Trish's rise, though, was even quicker with a more lasting effect. On March 19, 2000, Trish premiered with the WWF. Shortly thereafter she was managing the team of Test and Albert (T&A) and being driven through tables. Though her promos were long and nonsensical at the beginning, Trish worked incredibly hard to better herself both on the mic and in the ring. But it would be later in the Era that Trish would find herself. Trish wound up teaming with Triple H and continually being caught in embarrassing positions, much to Stephanie's chagrin. This led to their early feud (and helped push the Triple H/Kurt Angle story) and put Trish on the map to stardom. She would remain a pivotal player in the entire McMahon family saga, the InVasion, and into the top-notch Women's Champion that she is today. And again, her roots began in the McMahon-Helmsley Era.

Kurt Angle — But there is no one, and I mean no one, who grew as much as Kurt Angle. Kurt premiered with the WWF on November 14, 1999, just one month before the beginning of the McMahon-Helmsley Era. Angle literally went from fighting Shawn Stasiak, to being choked out by Tazz, to winning his first title on February 10, 2000 (European Championship). Shortly thereafter he became the third "Eurocontinental" Champion. After losing the titles, Kurt went on to the aforementioned feud with Triple H due to his infatuation with Stephanie (she even went on to manage him for a while to make her husband jealous). The accolades would continue as Angle won the King of the Ring tournament in June 2000 and then defeated the Rock for the WWF Championship in October 2000. As a matter of fact, Kurt Angle had the longest single run as WWF Champion during the entire Era at 126 days, and had the third longest time with the title overall (at the time of this writing). Actually here are the standings:

Wrestler	Length with Title
The Rock	175 Days
Triple H	153 Days
Kurt Angle	126 Days
Steve Austin	50 Days (and last champion of the Era)
The Big Show	14 Days (and first champion of the Era)

That's right, the Rock was the longest reigning champion of the McMahon-Helmsley Era, not Triple H. Look at it this way: Triple H accounted for less than 30% of the total championship time during the entire Era. Hardly makes him seem like the belt hog and really makes it seem like the Era was more about creating Kurt Angle after it established Triple H.

Kurt became an early champion and rose quickly through the WWF to what we know him as today, and we have the McMahon-Helmsley Era to thank for that.

WHAT WE SAW FOR THE FIRST (THOUGH NOT LAST) TIME

Now that we know all of the people and some of the objects that grew out of the McMahon-Helmsley Era, we also need to look at what existed for the first time in the Era. Though some of these may be hackneyed today, let's reflect back and remember when it was new.

First off, I would like to go back to an earlier point about the Women's Championship. It was the first time we had ever seen the title in the main event, and that a women's feud could be the top of the card. Despite the players, it made women's wrestling into a serious event for the first time since Wendi Richter. I cannot stress what a breakthrough this was.

We also saw the first ever four corners match in the main event of WrestleMania. We had seen some tag team matches in the past, but never before such an all-out brawl for the championship. This multi-participant main event was a true rarity in the WWF at the time (though three-way dances became especially popular during the Era). Nowadays a typical RAW or SmackDown! could have this type of match, but it was something seldom used at the time which made it more special.

Also, we were able to get conversations like this from SmackDown! on January 6, 2000 (via the **lastrider2k1**):

> **Kurt Angle:** Hey guys, you know, it's so unfair that the Acolytes are getting a tag title shot at the Royal Rumble and not you, just like it's unfair that when I go to the ring I get interrupted by the lights going out and the number 13 flashing on the screen.
>
> **Christian:** Yeah, it's like the everyone is jealous of young, attractive, athletic, charming, dynamic dudes like ourselves.
>
> **Edge:** Yeah, but we are so totally used to it now, to be successful here, you've got to make a stand so people don't forget that we are the future of wrestling.
>
> **Kurt Angle:** You're right, I mean I was out in the ring, letting the fans in Fort Lauderdale see a real American hero, 'cos let's face it, I'm the only one they're ever going to see. Then all of a sudden the lights go out and the number 13 flashes on the screen. If it's someone trying to send me a message or scare me, well..... well.... it's not going to work because dynamic dudes like ourselves don't get scared, right guys!?
>
> **Edge:** Oh, it's too right Kurtster!

That was a classic moment every week, before it became taken over by writers in the back who determined every word.

During this period we had many re-introductions. One was the return of Mick Foley as a commissioner. Though he would have this and similar roles many times in the future (as would various other people), it was a fresher concept to try at the time. On the other end was Shawn Michaels making a special guest appearance as a referee. Nowadays, we are used to seeing Shawn every week. Back then, though, it was absolutely rare to see Shawn Michaels at all and only added to the hyped main events.

And back to the namesakes of this era; over time, the McMahon-Helmsley marriage morphed into the dysfunctional McMahon family. Today, many are tired of the McMahons fighting each other and loving each other, and a lot of the storylines have been redone. But at the time it was all new and unsullied, providing an interesting look at the first family of wrestling. Again, I cannot stress this enough: though played out nowadays, this was an innovative concept that drew in ratings and people to the arenas (more on this in a moment).

Yet these were things we saw for the first time. There were others less enjoyable and more played out moments to come in the future, but most did not actually happen during our time frame. Yet somehow, as we've stated, the McMahon-Helmsley Era has unreasonably taken the blame.

THE THINGS THAT DID NOT HAPPEN

Now, remember, the McMahon-Helmsley Era ended on May 21, 2001. Because of the condensing of perceived time, events post-Era have been erroneously attributed to it, and most unfairly I might add. For the record, these events DID NOT (I repeat **DID NOT**) happen during the McMahon-Helmsley Era:

Stephanie buys ECW – In the Summer of 2001, Stephanie McMahon revealed that she was the one who bought ECW and merged it with Shane McMahon's WCW to form the Alliance. This, coupled with the lack of talent and the fast-forward storytelling, led to a less than stellar InVasion. This, though, was the dawning of the new WWF/E, and not a part of the McMahon-Helmsley world.

Stephanie's Baby – Some will have you believe the McMahon-Helmsley Era ended with Stephanie's faked pregnancy and subsequent divorce. This, of course, would be impossible since it was post-InVasion (February 2002), and therefore could not have possibly been in the Era.

Chris Jericho vs. Triple H at WrestleMania – the buildup to this event took a turn for the worse when instead of focusing on the past history of the two, it became about Stephanie McMahon and her puppy that got run over. Jericho, the first and longest reigning Undisputed Champion, had a rather lackluster run topped by a loss to Triple H at WrestleMania for the title. These events happened in January through March 2002, after the end of the Era and InVasion.

Hulk Hogan winning the Undisputed Championship – Although I see nothing wrong with this, some pundits believed Hogan's time had passed and that he should be nowhere near the title. His win and reign happened in April and May 2002.

Being given the title – On September 2, 2002 Triple H was awarded the World Heavyweight Championship on RAW after the Undisputed Championship came under dispute (we'll get to this in a later chapter on the World Heavyweight Championship). Even though Triple H was just given a title, we cannot hold this against the Era since it happened so far after the fact!

Steph VS. Vince – Because the McMahon dysfunction really took shape during the Era, anything that has to do with it somehow gets tacked on. Vince and Stephanie McMahon fought at No Mercy on October 19, 2003 in a much-trampled angle. This was actually the culmination of the Zack Gowen story and

Stephanie's time as GM of SmackDown!. Not only was this after the Era, it was after the divorce! How this gets tacked on is a complete mystery.

All of these negatives (although that is a matter of opinion in some cases) have somehow gotten attached to the Era. Well they did not happen during that timeframe, and should not take away from all the true accomplishments.

NUMBERS GALORE!

And what are those accomplishments? Why money of course! Let's take a look at some of the big ones.

First off, the average RAW rating for the ENTIRE McMahon-Helmsley Era was a 5.6. What has RAW been averaging on USA recently in 2005? A 3.9?

Let's go a bit further. RAW broke the 7.0 ratings barrier on only five occasions. Three of those were during the Era: April 24, 2000; May 1, 2000; and May 22, 2000.

Let's look at it from a different perspective: the historical kind! In January of 1999, the average RAW rating was a 5.58. A couple of weeks after the beginning of McMahon-Helmsley Era in January 2000 the average RAW rating was a 6.50. And just to make sure this wasn't abnormal, the average rating for December 1999 was 5.93, November 1999 5.92, and October 1999 5.75. So in one month ratings jumped 10%! Not a bad day at the office at all.

But as we know, ratings only matter to advertisers and can fluctuate based on a number of small factors. When we want to see what people think directly, we head straight to the PPV buyrates!

For the entire McMahon-Helmsley Era, the average PPV buyrate was 1.37, well above our success range. Now, let's break it down by month comparing 1999 to 2000:

Month	1999	2000
January	1.88	1.60
February	1.21	1.20
March	2.32	2.35
April	1.06	1.65
May	1.24	1.05
June	1.13	1.19
July	1.07	1.04
August	1.47	1.40
September	0.85	1.50
October	0.88	1.35
November	1.14	1.00
December	0.97	1.15
Grand Total	1.27	1.37

As you can see, some months were up, some were down, but the ones that were up were up significantly, as was the entire year (it's just happenstance that 2000 is also a 1.37 average). This made the WWE less dependent on some months for a lot of their revenue and allowed them to spread costs and profits over the entire year. That means that they were able to change their business cycle and invest money differently, giving more flexibility overall to the company.

And of course, there's the biggest proof of all:

THE MCMAHON-HELMSLEY ERA KILLED WCW!!!

Well, that's an exaggeration, but we cannot deny that the success of the McMahon-Helmsley Era in part led to the continual downfall of WCW and its eventual cancellation on the Turner Networks. At the time, the shared audience of the two organizations was around 2.0, and many of those people were swayed to watch more WWF programming due to the storylines, excitement, and originality of the McMahon-Helmsley Era.

No, the Era was a huge money generator and everyone, from wrestlers to grips, were able to feel the financial windfall of the times.

AND WHAT BECAME OF OUR WARDS?

As the Era came to an end and the WWF/E had crushed its competition and the industry moved on. Creative began to lose the edge it had during the Era and started to rehash the same angles with the same people. Triple H dominated a lot of television time, as did Stephanie McMahon, in what many consider a waste. That is a fight for another day, though.

What we do know is that business dropped. Ratings, buyrates, revenue, profit, audience size, live event attendance—all dropped considerably from the height of the McMahon-Helmsley Era to today in 2005.

But all of that is not BECAUSE of the Era, it is because of the rehashing of the Era's successes. You favorite food tastes great on the first day. On the second day, it is all right. On the third day, it is kind of bland. On the fourth day, it makes you sick. Even if it was cooked the same way with the same ingredients to the same perfection, it will not matter. Too much of a good thing just isn't good at all.

This is what happened after the Era. A lot was repeated and rehashed, but to diminishing results. The important thing is to remember that first day, when the food melted in your mouth, and not the last day, when you couldn't eat one bite.

THE SLAP HEARD ROUND THE WORLD

Due to a lingering (and modern) hatred of Triple H and Stephanie McMahon, many people have let their opinion of the McMahon-Helmsley Era be colored by lies and misunderstandings. Looking back, we can see that the Era was really a birth of so many great moments and careers in wrestling. Even Triple H and Stephanie themselves were truly birthed out of this Era, and for a time were the most interesting parts of the show. Neither had political control at the beginning, and there was no relationship to speak of. The conspiracy theories just don't hold up.

Meanwhile, the Era may have gotten their names, but there were many more people, events, and objects that benefited. From the Women's Championship to Latino Heat to Kurt Angle's rise to the top—there was a growth all around the company. There were also some distinct moments of creativity and innovation, new for the time, though overused today.

And then there was everything that had nothing to do with the Era that gets attributed to it. From the Jericho-Stephanie-Dog fiasco to Stephanie and Triple H's divorce to Stephanie and Vince fighting in the ring—all of these did not happen in the Era and should not be counted against it.

All that should count is the large amounts of ratings, buyrates, and money the Era generated. It was the height of popularity in the WWF, and helped the WWF to finally defeat WCW once and for all.

The McMahon-Helmsley Era is the definition of success in the WWF. How can we forget that?

The defense rests.

AFTER THE TRIAL

HUNG JURY

IN THE CASE OF THE IWC VS. THE MCMAHON-HELMSLEY ERA, THE MCMAHON-HELMSLEY ERA HAS BEEN ACCUSED AS BEING A GIANT EGO STROKE FOR ITS NAMESAKES THAT ONLY SUCCEEDED IN PUSHING TRIPLE H AND STEPHANIE DOWN OUR THROATS AND DID NOT HELP ANYONE ELSE BUT THEM.

With 73.2% of the vote, the McMahon-Helmsley Era was found:

NOT GUILTY!

So Mike Awesome leaving ECW is less guilty then the McMahon-Helmsley Era? I don't know about that—and I wrote these cases!

RESPONSE

Most of the responses were fairly standard this time, but I enjoyed this response in particular:

> *You've really outdone yourself this time JP. I HATED the era in question. I got sick of HHH/Stephanie so much, that's it's still hard to watch either one of them on television, but in the case of not helping anyone else the era is not guilty. Really well written article...*
>
> **Jess Gaytes**

Aside from that, in the original version of the article I complained about the HTML coding I tried to do (poorly) in creating a table for first time. While I learned a lot more later, a regular reader certainly caught me:

> *So I decided to take a look at your HTML and see how you made it. Please [don't] take this the wrong way... How much do you know about HTML? I've always assumed that people who post on the net have at least a basic understanding of the simple tags, such as <table>, but looking at your source, I appear to be wrong. I know I'm sounding like an ass right now, so I'll stop.*
>
> **Manu Bumb**

I let Manu know:

> *Thank Manu, I really don't know much in HTML beside the basic tags like <b></b> <i></i> <u></u> <center></center> and <font></font>. I really don't need to know much because the site does most of it itself. I used to do a little work on webpages a few years ago, but I always used Frontpage so I really didn't know anything then. It's kind of like with databases. I know enough SQL to get by, but let Access do most of the work for me.*

Here in 2020, I needed to know almost no HTML to put together my own website. Still, knowing a bit helped when I wanted to do a few special things, but in those cases there were websites and other tools that helped me out. Even Microsoft Word can convert to HTML if you need it to!

NEW JACK

INTRO

SOME DAME WALKED INTO MY OFFICE AND SAID...

Matt C came around saying I should defend New Jack by coming right up with this:

> I've watched the guy for almost ten years now and he is an absolute maniac, in and out of the ring. He destroyed a seventeen-year old wannabe worker, confronted a crippled Brian Pillman, and worked ultra-stiff on an eighty-year-old man... and that's just for starters. It'd be a hell of a challenge at the very least.

To which I replied:

> Hmmmm... an interesting thought. What is the main charge against him? That he is too violent? That he is dangerous in the ring? That he isn't a "wrestler"? Actually, those do sound like charges. I'll take the case!

And so I shall.

WHY THIS?

Everything some people find funny or interesting about New Jack, someone uses as a reason to hate him. New Jack is an incredibly polarizing individual. Is he everything he says he is, or are the lines of character and person blurred with him? Do people hate New Jack because they don't like him or his style, or because he might be working them all the time? Does New Jack have any wrestling skill, or is he just protected by "garbage"? Should we even care that slicing people with a cheese grater is his most prominent move?

And this man has been involved in more incidents than most of the SmackDown! roster combined. He has spent time in jail, he has killed four men (in self-defense [while hunting them]), he has pissed off promoters by swearing his head off in front of six-year-olds. There is no sense in denying what has actually happened. The question is, how guilty is he really; and if he is, should it matter to us?

New Jack is a case I take on with some trepidation because even sometimes I am taken in by the myth and have worked hard to try to separate fact from fiction. But if New Jack has played me as well, would I still want to defend him?

You bet. If you can hide the truth from me, then you deserve an automatic buy!

For now, though, let's check in with where this man came from.

WARNING: THIS CASE CONTAINS A LOT OF GRAPHIC LANGUAGE. READER DISCRETION IS ADVISED!!!

How'd I come to be?

On the day of this original publishing in 2006, New Jack was 43 years and one day old. Born in Atlanta, GA as Jerome Young on January 3, 1963, New Jack did not have much in life. He grew up in a rough neighborhood but sought more for himself. He did not want to be taken in by the life around him, but at the same time did not want to forget where he came from. He worked odd jobs through the years, but one job in particular began to define the man: Bounty Hunter.

New Jack worked as a Bounty Hunter for years and all reports indicate that he had four justifiable homicides. Whether true or not, the man did risk his life for money, so it would seem that his next transition in life was not a hard one.

In the early 1990's, New Jack began training under Ray Candy in Georgia. Candy was a mid-south and Puerto Rican wrestling notoriety, having wrestled since 1973 and won the Mid-American Tag Titles and WWC Puerto Rican title. At the time of training New Jack, he had recently retired to Decatur, GA and was with a limited number of students.

This was not the only place that New Jack went for training. **Smitty** wrote in to tell me:

> *I knew Jack (Jerome) when he was training at the north Georgia wrestling academy here some years back. He was teamed with Bill "Festus" Harris who also ran the school with Uncle Sammy Kent and Danny Dees (I built crates for Harris and the academy was set up in the same building)[.*

> B]elieve it or not[,] Jack was a real easy going guy and just as funny as hell.

What does this all tell us? That New Jack is a trained wrestler! He went to the schools, he went through the ropes! He was not just some green guy that Paul E plucked off of streets and gave a shopping cart to and said, "Hit people with this." New Jack has all the training in the world to be a more than solid wrestler.

Why then, doesn't he?

Says New Jack:

> I will work rings around your ass, but I don't get paid for that kind of shit. I get paid to beat motherfuckers to death. But if you beat me up, I will SHOOT YOU! I'm licensed to carry a gun and I will shoot the shit out of you! All you motherfucking bitches! I ain't going to be no bitch!

Ahem... what Mr. Jack is trying to say here is that he has the ability, he just chooses not to use it. His gimmick over time has been to be the man that beats the crap out of you with everything in the building and then dive off a balcony. He does not need to, nor should he, go out there and wrestle Chris Benoit style. When describing one of his recent incidents (we'll get to that later) on New Jack: Undercover, New Jack added:

> If you book me, you don't expect armdrags and head tosses and lip locks...

Not since the days of Adrian Adonis had anyone been booked for "lip locks", but that's beside the point.

What is the point is that anyone booking New Jack today should know what they are getting: hardcore weapons and profane language. If you cannot deal with that, that is your own fault, not New Jack's.

THE ORIGIN, PART 2

But what became of New Jack after training? I already said that he was not just plucked off the street by Paul Heyman and teamed up with Mustafa. Well, half of this is correct—well, actually about a quarter. In 1993, at thirty years of age,

New Jack premiered in the USWA in Memphis, TN. This is actually where he acquired the name New Jack. From there he went on to SMW, where Jim Cornette paired him with Mustafa. According to Wikipedia:

> *The Gangstas took part in several controversial angles, on one occasion using affirmative action to enable them to win matches with a two count, not the conventional three count. They engaged in a long feud with the Rock 'N Roll Express (Ricky Morton and Robert Gibson).*

You see, it was not Paul Heyman that created or expanded New Jack or the Gangtas, but it was New Jack and Mustafa along with Jim Cornette that helped set the pace for what the team would become. When SMW folded in 1995, the duo made their way to ECW (still in its infancy).

Now, I've spent a couple of cases attacking Paul Heyman. The point I want to make with him is that he, and his devout followers, believe he has done no wrong and that everyone is out to get and steal from him. Well Heyman has done everything he has ever accused anyone of. Heyman would like you to believe he came up with the Extreme, that he invented the hardcore style. The hardcore style existed well before Heyman in the form of wrestlers like Terry Funk and Abdullah the Butcher, and the next evolution of hardcore existed in New Jack. New Jack is the one who came up with diving off the balcony as a regular event, or hitting people with everything and anything he could find, of scarring his head incessantly from blading, not Paul Heyman. As much as Heyman would like to take credit for the creation of New Jack, New Jack created himself.

As noted, New Jack was thirty-two years old when he came into ECW. He had already been around a long time, though not necessarily in the business. The man knew his tolerance for pain and violence, and was trying to turn that into a career. Paul Heyman gave him that platform, but did not create him.

New Jack would go on to win two ECW World Tag Team Championships with Mustafa and one more with former Eliminator rival Kronus. His brand of violence would be "borrowed" by the likes of Tommy Dreamer, the Dudley Boys, and countless others. But during his time in ECW and after, New Jack was involved in some of the most controversial moments in wrestling history.

YOU HAVE THE RIGHT TO REMAIN SILENT…

Above I noted that bookers should know what they are going to get when they put New Jack on the card: violence and swearing. Still, his in-ring antics and ability to blur the lines between reality and fiction have caused many wrestlers to fear working with him. Worse yet, some have landed him in jail.

THE MASS TRANSIT INCIDENT

On November 23, 1996, ECW was having a house show in Revere, MA and booked for the card was the Gangstas vs. D-von Dudley and Axl Rotten. For some reason or the other, Axl Rotten could not make the show, and instead of replacing him with any of the talent already there, Heyman turned around to some kid who SOMEHOW found his way backstage. From Steve Brinn over at Obsessed with Wrestling:

> Enter, Eric Kulas. He was a kid that wanted to make it big as a wrestler. He had no previous training, but he thought it would be his big break. He did have some in ring experience, wrestling midgets. He went by the name Mass Transit and he went to the ring wearing a bus driver's suit. Now not only did he have this against him, but he was terribly out of shape, weighing in over 350 pounds. Having talked to Paul Heyman, he was given a chance.

You see, Kulas was only 17, but his father vouched for the age on his fake ID and his claims that he had trained with Killer Kowalski (I met Kowalski around this time, and he was in no shape to train anyone). Somehow, this was proof enough for Heyman and he booked the match. Backstage, Kulas, New Jack, and the others went over the match and the high points they wanted involved. New Jack said that he wanted Kulas to bleed, and Kulas said that he did not know how and asked New Jack to do it. New Jack agreed.

During the match, New Jack went to cut Kulas with his exacto-knife, but the cut was deeper than normal. This is most likely because Kulas flinched significantly when New Jack went for the cut, and when New Jack hit him with a chair blood went everywhere.

The incident was incredibly violent, and fan recordings of the event got to PPV providers who cancelled ECW's first PPV. New Jack was falsely given the blame for what happened.

New Jack is not to blame here, though. He was put in a ring with someone who was screened through management, who he talked to in the back and said he could work. The kid's father vouched for him as well. Heyman and the father, these are your main culprits. And if anyone else thought something was wrong—the ref, Mustafa, or D-von Dudley (who were all there!)—why did they do nothing to intervene? No, New Jack was just doing the job he always did, and thought he was doing it with a professional.

Let us not forget what happened next. Kulas (two years later!) sued ECW and New Jack for physical and psychological damage. From our friends over at Obsessed with Wrestling again:

> In the trial, Kulas claimed that he did not know that New Jack would blade him. He denied that he knew he'd be treated the way he was in a match against The Gangstas. He also claimed that Paul Heyman told a reporter that it was an initiation for him into the ECW family. On the flipside, New Jack claimed that Kulas did know what was going to happen. He also said that Kulas said it was okay for him to get bladed and that Kulas' father knew of what was going to happen from talks backstage. New Jack claimed that you can see Kulas puffing his cheeks, a way to increase the bleeding. Jerome Young, aka New Jack, claimed that his first to attempts to blade did not work. This is due to the fact that Kulas had never bladed before. When he tried again, he accidentally pushed too deep and that caused the massive bleeding.
>
> Evidence used against New Jack was his mic claims and a shoot interview he later did. Young claimed that on the interview he was working in character. That his New Jack character loved to inflict pain and violence. Adding to ECW's case, although Kulas claimed to be scarred, no scars could be seen. Also, Kulas was reportedly walking around backstage and talking to wrestlers before being taken to the hospital. Supposedly he was only suing after he found out he would not be an ECW regular.
>
> In the end, ECW and New Jack were acquitted of the charges and Kulas would not get any money. Kulas could not keep his story straight, which severely hurt his case.

Kulas and his claims were complete baloney. The courts found ECW and New Jack had done no wrong. Oh, and by the way, when Kulas died in 2002, it was from a completely unrelated condition, and nothing to do with what happened that one night in ECW.

And again, as New Jack said, it was violence in character. This would not be the last time, though, that New Jack would get into trouble for something he did in character.

SCAFFOLD FALL

On March 12, 2000 at the Living Dangerously PPV, New Jack and Vic Grimes literally plummeted off the scaffolding and through some tables below. The match was abruptly ended and the show moved on. New Jack suffered a plethora of injuries, including blindness in one eye. Some people blame New Jack for the injuries because it looks like he pushed Grimes off of the scaffolding, almost killing the both of them. But in an interview with Jason Scales of Wrestling Digest in October 2001, New Jack had this to say:

> *Vic Grimes, the big stupid-ass, called a spot. He wanted us to go off this scaffolding that was very unstable. I asked him had he checked it out. He said yeah, but he hadn't. He didn't want to do it after he got up there; he said it was too high. I said, "Vic, pay-per-view. Let's go." He said, "Jack, it's too high. I can't do it." So I just snatched him, and we fell. The first table broke my fall, and he did a flip in the air and his back ran up against my head, and my head hit the floor. From that alone, I broke my leg, broke my right arm, cracked my sternum, cracked my skull, and lost my sight. I was laid up for a long time after that one, and I still came back.*

You see, New Jack knew it was PPV and knew he had to deliver. It was Vic Grimes trying to go back on a spot that he set up. New Jack just wanted to do the job they were paid to do, and give the fans in the arena and around the world their money's worth. How can he be faulted for just trying to deliver, and the other wrestler messing him up and hurting him so severely?

And New Jack was never paid for his injuries as promised. From Derek Burgan's recap of New Jack Shoot Interview Volume 3:

> *And since Heyman declared bankruptcy New Jack can't get any money that he is owned claiming that the WWE protects Heyman by only paying him $52,000 a year. Apparently you can put liens against people making even a penny above 52K.*

And more so, from Brian Lowman's recap of New Jack on Get in the Ring Radio in January 2004:

> Talk turns to Paul Heyman. New Jack says he has a $14,000 hospital bill that still hasn't been paid. He said he has a permanent limp and pins in his legs, ankle and hip because of the damage he did to his body in ECW. New Jack said Heyman told him they could no longer pay for his services. He said he told Heyman that if he doesn't, his ratings would go down. New Jack said he had no problem doing big spots in ECW because he is a pain freak and that it was good for the show. He said he would walk around for days with an injury until it [got] infected and when the time came to get it checked out, Heyman wouldn't pay. New Jack mentioned how when Paul Heyman went to California for a few weeks, he promised the talent in ECW that he was going to get a new TV deal signed for ECW. New Jack said he was actually filming for the movie "Rollerball" where he plays an announcer.

Interesting: another person like Mike Awesome who was giving everything to Heyman, but Heyman was giving nothing back (for example, the pay they were owed and just messing with them for his own agenda). New Jack elaborated a bit more in the aforementioned interview in Wrestling Digest:

> **WD:** In an interview posted on the Internet, you were quoted as saying that you "quit ECW before ECW quit on you." Elaborate on your fallout from ECW.
>
> **NJ:** At the end, I was really pissed. I saw it coming to an end. A lot of the boys in the locker room didn't want to believe it, just like a lot of the fans didn't want to believe it. It was time for me to start looking elsewhere, because I knew this [ride] wasn't going to be continuing much longer. A lot of the boys had false hopes saying, "Paul E. Heyman is going to bail us out." I was considered a vet in that locker room and I knew better. I was ready to leave and I did.

He left ECW when all he was doing was getting injured for no pay. Wouldn't you?

KILLING ECW ON TNN

Somehow over time, though, rumors became that it was New Jack who got ECW kicked off of TNN. I believe this is an amalgamated form of how ECW lost their first PPV because of the Mass Transit incident, but a little deeper. Back to Derek Burgan's recap:

> [New] Jack said that originally Heyman wouldn't put New Jack on the ECW show on TNN until he wanted to take the show off the network. Jack said that Heyman then aired New Jack matches and when they were kicked off of TNN he blamed New Jack.

Despite what Heyman said on the Rise and Fall of ECW DVD, he did tone down his product as Vince McMahon suggested. He did not just go out there and say, "This is what we are, deal with it!" No, no, he met their needs and wants, although many times going against them for reasons only he can fathom. Blaming anyone outside of Heyman or the TNN executives for ECW's cancellation is a bit asinine.

STABBY STABBY!

This one I'll leave to the source. From Derek Burgan's recap of New Jack: Undercover:

> For those unaware, during the fall of 2004 New Jack was arrested in Jacksonville, Florida for aggravated assault during a match.... After spending several weeks in jail, New Jack got out and [went] to RF Video and filmed a shoot about the whole situation.
>
> Only in wrestling.
>
> New Jack started off talking about the show which got him in so much trouble and explained he was booked against a "snot green" opponent (real name: William "Hunter" Lane) who didn't know kayfabe. Yep, the kid didn't know what terms like "get color" and "babyface" meant. To be fair, I didn't know what "gig" meant for the longest time either. Jack talked about the knife he pulled out

> during the match and the fact that he "kept stickin' him and stickin' him and stickin' him 'til my arm got tired. That act got Jack arrested and ended up putting him over $8,000 in the hole, although this figure would grow throughout the shoot.
>
> New Jack couldn't understand how what he did in the ring could possibly be considered assault because it happened in the ring. Tell that to Blue Meanie and JBL. New Jack compared it to a girl consenting to sex and then screaming rape afterwards. Jack called this incident "Mass Transit 2," but interesting said it was much worse than what went down with [Eric] Kulas. Jack said that [Kulas] just got sliced in the forehead while this suffering bastard got stabbed in the head, neck, stomach, leg and just about everywhere else. Was Jack apologetic about doing all of that to a guy who was clearly in over his head? Nope. "Welcome to the business."
>
> Indeed.
>
> RF Video steered the discussion towards New Jack's experience in jail. Jack said that he was in the maximum security area of the jail because of his past record and there were 50 other cellmates in his area, though he denied socializing with them. Jack detailed what an average day in jail was like:
>
> 3:30a.m. – woke up, given medication.
> 5:30a.m. – breakfast
> 11:00a.m. – let out of cell for recreational activity
> Noon – lunch, back to cell
> 4:30 – let out of cell for recreational activity
> 5:30 – dinner
> 8:30 – back to cell for night. No TV. No radio...
>
> Jack called the near three weeks spent on the above schedule, "the best vacation" he's ever had. Me thinks New Jack needs to find a new travel agent.

I just wanted to include that last part because it was funny. The more important thing is it was another situation that was taken out of context and out of control. What isn't mentioned here is that the kid who was stabbed never pressed charges, and later said that it was all part of the show. That is why New Jack got out of jail; he really did not do anything wrong. New Jack just likes the stories about him to grow because that's the type of person he is. Says the man to Wrestling Digest:

> *The way I carry myself in the ring and the way people see me, they think I'm really pissed off. When you see me jab a fork in somebody, you don't know if I've stabbed them or not. Mike Awesome almost pissed on himself when he found out that we had to work one night. Me and Raven kept picking at him about what I was going to do to him with a staple gun. He ran to Paul E. and said he didn't want to do the match. I had staples in it, and he didn't know if I was going to really shoot him or if it was going to be a work. There have been matches where Paul E. was standing by the curtain, because he thought I was in the ring mad at somebody. And it was a big work. When you can fool people in the locker room, I think it's funny.*

That is it in a nutshell. New Jack likes the legend of New Jack because he thinks it's damn funny.

MORE INCIDENTS

We could go on forever with more incidents over time that New Jack has been involved in, but they all lead back to the same story: There is a thin grey line between New Jack the person and New Jack the wrestler, and New Jack likes to play that game. This an interview on New Jack's website sums it up pretty well:

> **CM:** *New Jack! Holy Shit, aren't you in jail or something? Didn't you kill somebody in the ring?*
>
> **NJ:** *What the FUCK? You're really going to come at me with that bullshit? Aren't you in Jail? I'm about to be in thirty seconds!*
>
> **CM:** *No, No, No, No, I mean, No, I mean when I was reading up for this interview, everything I read online was like New Jack was arrested for killing somebody in the ring and things like that.*
>
> **NJ:** *Ain't that some shit? I see some of that stuff too and I'm like that New Jack is gangsta as fuck.*

> *The Internet shit can go both ways. In the day of ECW it was like underground smoke signals and shit. I'd be hittin the 1-8-7 in Philly and some guy on the Internet 5 states away knew about it before I put the bitch down. Those fuckers were high-tech and loyal to the bone. That network of crazy high-tech fuckers helped put a lot of us hardcore motherfuckers on the map and put ECW over the fucking top. A lot of those crazy fuckers are still out there looking for any [signs] of life on the web. So, you get some bitch that says he knows something and puts it out there, next thing you know I'm up the fucking river.*

And that's the point. All these rumors, all these unconnected events are brought together into New Jack because he is so controversial, because he is so hardcore. But he's just a wrestler, doing his best in the business, and giving back when he can.

A WRESTLER? DOING HIS BEST? GIVING BACK? WHAT?!

That was a pretty bold statement, wasn't it? Well, let's cover a couple of those points right here. In Josh Shibata's interview with indie sensation Trent Acid, New Jack made an appearance:

> **New Jack:** Who is this [interview] for?
>
> **Josh:** SoCal Uncensored?
>
> **New Jack:** Who?
>
> **Josh:** SoCal Uncensored.
>
> **Trent:** It's a shoot.
>
> **New Jack:** Who are you talking about?
>
> **Trent:** About myself. I'm talking about myself.
>
> **New Jack:** This is my buddy [Trent] right? And whatever he says is true. If he said I fucked a goat, I did. But I was drunk, and the goat had lipstick on so I thought the bitch was pretty.

> **Trent:** And the thing about training, this is the guy who taught me the most devastating punch in wrestling.
>
> **New Jack:** That's right because all I know is the punch. And those of you who believe that, you're out of your motherfucking mind. I will work rings around your ass, but I don't get paid for that kind of shit. I get paid to beat motherfuckers to death. But if you beat me up, I will SHOOT YOU! I'm licensed to carry a gun and I will shoot the shit out of you! All you motherfucking bitches! I ain't going to be no bitch!
>
> **Trent:** That man right there is New Jack. He is the man. He taught me the art of wrestling and how to make it look real. Actually, a true story real quick because this is a shoot, I broke my arm five years ago in a gym and everyone thought that I wasn't even hurt but [New Jack] knew it right away and he rode with me in my car with my mother to the hospital.

Two birds with one stone: New Jack is more than wrestling, he's about making it look real. Anyone can throw a punch, New Jack can make you believe he killed somebody. That's why people think he's just covering up with garbage, because he makes it look like he's hitting everything. The guy makes violence look violent, but he's still out there trying to protect everyone. Look what happened with Vic Grimes, look what happened with the Dudleys. Despite his hatred for both, he kept them safe and took the worse lumps for himself. But he was still out there diving off balconies night after night. Speaking of balconies, back to that interview with Wrestling Digest:

> **WD:** What goes through your mind before you jump off a balcony and how much longer can you keep doing it?
>
> **NJ:** Two words go through my mind when I get up there: "Oh, crap!" Everybody knows about the Vic Grimes thing, but that wasn't really my fault. He got up there and sissied out. I snatched his ass off the thing, and he just fell on top of me. I've cracked my ribs a couple times and landed wrong and broke my leg three times last year. I'll do it until I don't want to do it anymore. I've never been afraid of heights. Most of the time when I do it, the worst that happens to me is that I get the wind knocked out of me.

New Jack is trying to help the younger generation out. He tries to make them look good, but he still cares about himself and his paycheck. Why not if you go to jail for your fans?

And there have been times when it seemed that New Jack was supposed to show up in WWE as John Cena's stabber, but that never came to pass. Says New Jack on his website:

> *That fucking shit gets crazy. I'm not fucking sure that I know. There's very little direct communication. You get word floated to your fucking ass through backdoors and weird fucking channels. You get invitations to show up and hang out. Ideas are thrown around. People get called in and out of appearances as plotlines are developed and deleted on the spot. I've been there, I've been at the curtain and I've been patted on the back on the way out the fucking door. It's the way that fucking shit works. It's quick as a fucking chairshot. I'm always hearing shit. I've been a staple... ha ha... of a couple of major fucking promotions. I'll be there again, no fucking doubt. But, right now I got a good fucking thing going. I can be me and not worry about somebody losing 30 seconds of airtime or a sponsor because I screamed fucking die when I drop the 1-8-7. That's what's important to me right now is being true to me and true to my fans.*

Ismael Abdu Salaam's recap of New Jack's promo at Extremely Hardcore PPV taping says:

> - He stated the reports of him being unable to attend the ECW PPV due to an outstanding warrant were complete lies on the part of WWE. According to Jack, WWE wrestlers threatened to leave the ring if New Jack appeared for fear of being hurt.
>
> - He lambasted John Cena for being a caricature of Hip Hop. He briefly detailed the proposed storyline of him being Cena's attacker, but again WWE being too scared to bring in New Jack. According to New Jack he's the Original Gangsta and the only authentic Hip Hop influenced wrestler in the business.

On a side note, the recap also stated:

> Regarding Flair, he accused the Nature Boy of being a racist. Jack quoted Flair as saying "Wrestling is a white man's sport....and n****** have no place in it." As an African-American and [life-long] wrestling fan, I was shocked and saddened to hear those words attributed to Flair. Almost every fan went dead silent also. New Jack yelled he's a black man and has helped to revolutionize wrestling, and if anyone thinks he doesn't have a place in wrestling, they can "suck his d***." He continued blasting Flair as a rip off of Buddy Rogers, and stealing his chops from Wahoo McDaniel..

You may remember those exact last few words as the ones Edge said to Ric Flair on an episode of RAW in 2006. New Jack is right; they are afraid of New Jack the person, but are not too afraid to steal directly from him.

The bottom line is, New Jack wants to be New Jack, and is in a financially good enough position now that he can do that. He does not want to tone it down, he does not want to slow down, even at the age of 43. So why should anyone expect him to conform? He is New Jack, no matter what.

BALCONY PLUNGE

New Jack is a man completely misunderstood. He blurs the lines of reality and wrestling for his own amusement and financial gain. But the truth is, he worked hard to learn the business, to learn to wrestle, and fought his way up. He likes to wrestle his own way, and has become known for his hardcore style. When you book New Jack, you know what you are going to get. Sure, sometimes things seem out of control with him, but there is so much going on backstage that the truth is hazy at best. What we do know is that New Jack cares very deeply for the business and has put himself in the hospital and jail for it. Today, he gives back to the next generation and continues to make a name for himself. He is a trailblazer in hardcore and independent wrestling. He is a misunderstood masterpiece of the wrestling world.

The defense rests.

After the Trial

Hung Jury

IN THE CASE OF THE IWC VS. NEW JACK, NEW JACK HAS BEEN ACCUSED OF BEING A GARBAGE WRESTLER WHO HAS NEVER ACCOMPLISHED ANYTHING IN THE BUSINESS AND IS SOLELY RESPONSIBLE FOR SOME OF THE WORST ATROCITIES THIS BUSINESS HAS EVER SEEN. FURTHERMORE, HE ONLY LOOKS OUT FOR HIMSELF AND HIS OWN INTERESTS TO THE DETRIMENT OF ANYONE WHO WORKS WITH OR AGAINST HIM, ESPECIALLY NEW TALENT.

Oh man, what a character!

And with 66.7% of the vote, New Jack was found:

NOT GUILTY!

Did you read that, New Jack! I did it! I did it, brother! I got you a not guilty vote! Fire all your lawyers, because I'm the only man you need. And although I may not have a law degree, and you could not legally pay me to represent you in court, and I would never take on a record like yours without getting paid, umm... let me go take the LSATs and get back to you in a few years.

Response

We'll begin with a little additional background info:

> *When I trained with Chris Hamrick, he told us New Jack was one of the coolest guys he'd met in the business.*
>
> **-Eddie Lawson**

I asked for some more Chris Hamrick quotes but did not get any! However, this write-in reminded me of a silly point:

> SUBJECT: *New Jack: Can he plead insanity?*
>
> *The Man is clearly insane there have been other interviews he's done [regionally] that [he] says he holds no ill will toward [Heyman].*

> *He's starting to live his gimmick and you should see some of the e-mails he sends people.*
>
> *He's more [delusional] than Jack [Thompson].*
>
> **bemanisuperstar**

That point being:

> *I like the breakdown feature on his website where he shows all of his injuries. My favorite is the one pointing to his heart and says "Feelings hurt". That was too good!*

However, the real collateral damage from this case and some of the prior ones was Paul Heyman:

> *Every time I watch an episode of "Law & Order" (the original, natch), I'm struck by how a person can seem so totally guilty in a case, but then the case gets screwed up by a witness lying or breaking down.*
>
> *Much the same here... regardless of what I feel about New Jack, I have a problem finding anyone guilty when the main witness would be one Paul Heyman.*
>
> **Matt Simon**

> *In defense of Heyman .... (LOL) Someone else may need to do that based on your accusations.*
>
> **Chris Pineo**

> *I noticed in this story that you talked about Paul Heyman. Why not defend him?*
>
> **Ross Sims**

Among my responses to this topic included:

> *Yeah, I've kind of noticed that I've been attacking Heyman a lot lately, which I know will come back to haunt me. Either I'll be doing some In Defense Of... for Heyman or someone he is a key witness for, and I'll never be able to use his testimony. I've done a pretty good job destroying the guy's credibility!*

Scott Hall

Intro

Some dame walked into my office and said...

Oh, where to even begin? Well, how about **Christy** who said:

> I would like to see you defend Scott Hall against all these assholes that don't understand that alcoholism is a disease. They say "well why doesn't he just stop?" Well, [it's] not that simple. Furthermore, Scott Hall is a great and legendary wrestler and a good man.

And since I'm such a slowpoke, she also said:

> Hi, I spoke with you a while back about doing a defense of Scott Hall.... You said you'd take the case and I was just wondering if you had any idea when that might happen. I think considering he was just remarried to a good and decent woman this time and he is working really hard to get his life together, I think it would be a really great time to do this. Let me know. Thanks a lot.

That was four months ago! She must be so mad by now. I hope you are still reading Christy! Meanwhile, in between those four months, I heard from a few more people including **Bobbi** who said:

> Now..... since you did such a great job on Kevin.... how about helping us out and taking on Scott Hall? There are so many people out there that focus on Scott's personal life and the alcoholism that has a hold of him.... they forget what a great wrestler and influence he is to people. Everyone condemns him.... they don't understand that alcoholism is [an] illness..... one that thousands of people struggle with every day..... [it's] not like Scott can just wake up one day and say.... "OK.... I'm not

> drinking anymore". Several of us have tried to educate people, even referring them to gov links on alcoholism... but to no avail.
>
> Please take Scott's defense.... he needs SOMEONE to defend him.

And let us not forget **BDSTW FOM**:

> Defend Scott Hall
> Everyone knows his track record...

Plus everyone who has ever sent me something interesting (**Feroz**, I'm definitely using that tidbit you sent along), nice, or mean about Scott Hall over the past several months.

And I'll just throw **Andrew Strom** in here as well because he loves Hall and is nWo 4-Life!

WHY THIS?

Those folks have said it all. Scott Hall is a man mired in personal problems, ones that far overshadow the long and illustrious career he has had. He is one of the greatest wrestlers to have never been world champion with accolades dating back two decades. He's been involved in match of the year candidates (and winners), angles that revolutionized wrestling, and responsible for the catch phrases of our day. Yet this is all buried under unfair criticism and a lack of understanding about a disease (yes disease) that plagues this man forever.

Scott, though, has a long history to explore well before his problems surfaced.

THE HISTORY OF THE EDGE (NOT THAT KIND)

In a rare In Defense Of... moment, Scott Hall was born with that name on October 20, 1958 in Baltimore, MD, although many list him as born in Chuluota, FL (about 4 ½ hours north of Miami, so it's odd that he is sometimes listed as being born there). However, I was told by readers to check his marriage license to confirm the Baltimore, MD birth-town. However, being in a military family, Hall moved around a lot as a child, eventually finding his way to Munich, Germany and attending the All American High School. Returning to the states for higher education, Hall graduated from St. Mary's College in Maryland with a degree in Pre-med. According to IMDB Hall had "hopes to become a children's doctor", but had also begun training to be a wrestler.

Luckily for us, Hall continued to follow his ambitions in wrestling and trained under "Gentleman" Chris Adams. You might also remember that Adams trained Steve Austin (and Steve took his wife as thanks). Also according to Wikipedia:

> Adams is best known for being the trainer of Stone Cold Steve Austin in 1989, and bringing the Superkick to American wrestlers. Adams was also among the first wrestlers to use the Sharpshooter, which he called the Superlock (around 1985). He is also famous for using backflips and somersaults to catch his opponent off-guard.

And from our friends at Obsessed with Wrestling:

> Chris Adams was a National Judo Champion in England before getting into the world of professional wrestling... He was a three-time national champion in that sport and a member of the British Olympic Judo team... Chris Adams was trained by European legends Tony Sinclair and Shirly "Big Daddy" Crabtree....

So as you can see, we are talking about a man of considerable skill and ability who trained Hall, and would not let Hall get away with being anything less than spectacular in the ring.

After training, Scott Hall made his pro debut in October 1984 for Florida Championship Wrestling and began a program with Dusty Rhodes (Wow, Dusty sure seems involved in helping to bring along a lot of the best future talent, yet people still dump all over him for his choice of talent). In 1985, Hall moved over to the National Wrestling Alliance and became "Starship Coyote" in the Coyote tag team. This held on for a short time until Hall moved over to AWA, going from "Magnum" to just "Big" Scott Hall, and forming a team with Curt Henning.

On January 18, 1986 Hall (who looked a lot like Magnum TA with a fluffy mullet top and a big bushy mustache) and Henning defeated Steven Regal and Jimmy Garvin for the AWA World Tag Team Championships. Just two years into the industry, and Hall already had his first major championship (AWA was a major promotion at the time). As a matter of fact, according to Wikipedia:

> The "Perfect Combination," as they were dubbed by a Pro Wrestling Illustrated article, had many [hard-fought] matches against Buddy Rose & Doug Somers during this time. They eventually lost the belts to "Playboy" Rose and "Pretty Boy" Somers by count-out on May 17, 1986.

The "Perfect Combination", eh? I wonder where Vince came up with the idea to call Henning "Mr. Perfect" after luring Henning away from the AWA to the WWF (despite everything Vince has ever said about WCW and Eric Bischoff, he did the exact same things to the AWA and other regional promotions). But that was not the only thing Vince took credit for that was not his.

After leaving AWA, Hall spent some time moving about the independent circuits in Puerto Rico and Florida (becoming Latino along the way) and CWA until making his way to the early WCW in 1990. As "Scott Hall", he did not have a successful run, but in June 1991 the "Diamond Studd" was born (first as bodyguard to DDP, and later DDP became his manager). And during his reign what move did Scott Hall debut? Why it was the "Diamond Death Drop" aka the "Razor's Edge" aka the "Outsider's Edge".

So you see, Vince and the then WWF did not come up with most of what Razor Ramon was. Scott had already picked up the machisimo gimmick from his time in Puerto Rico and Florida and had already developed his famous finisher... **IN WCW!!!**.

When Scott Hall made his way to the WWF in 1992 as Razor Ramon, it was not the gimmick that Vince created that got the man over. It was the man Scott Hall had become from all of his training and experience. And when Scott Hall returned to WCW in 1996 to form the New World Order, he was not just playing Razor Ramon without the name. Razor Ramon the gimmick was nothing without Scott Hall. The fans got into Scott Hall, the man behind the character. Eight years of experience created Razor Ramon, not the other way around. To claim he was just using the fame that Vince and the WWF gave him to get over in WCW is asinine. Scott Hall blazed his own trail, and his own self got over.

In the WWF, Scott Hall became a four-time Intercontinental Champion, including his ladder match against Shawn Michaels at WrestleMania X. Although not the first ladder match in history, it was the one that put that type of match in the limelight. Voted match of the year by PWI in 1994, ladder matches became a staple of American wrestling because of the enormous effort of these two competitors.

Razor Ramon also had memorable feuds with Owen Hart, Psycho Sid, Goldust, and Jeff Jarrett, putting over all of them (among others, more on that later) along the way.

In 1996, after the infamous "Klique Farewell" at a house show at Madison Square Garden in New York City (where Triple H and Shawn Michaels broke their "face" characters to embrace their "heel" friends who were departing the company), Scott Hall made his reappearance in WCW as the start of the invasion that would become the Outsiders and the nWo. Let us never forget that it was Scott Hall who started off the invasion of WCW, that Eric Bischoff entrusted him to be the first man, and that he set the tone for everything the nWo would do for the next two years.

He and Nash as the Outsiders would dominate the tag team scene and with Hogan control WCW (in a storyline sense). He engaged in feuds with the Giant, Randy Savage, Lex Luger, and Goldberg, winning 7 Tag Team Championships, a Television title reign (the last true Television Champion, if you don't count Dugan's run when he picked the title out of the trash), and a 2 time US Champion.

But Hall would constantly be screwed out of the World Title. In the WWF he had fought Bret Hart for the title (once) and lost that match. In WCW, he actually won the World War 3 three-ring battle Royal which should have made him the number one contender for the World Heavyweight Championship at Starrcade 1997, but that was pushed off for the Hogan/Sting match (eventually getting his shot at SuperBrawl 1998). Hall would rarely ever get to fight for the championship, and often had his title-shots were forgotten.

After being let go by WCW in 2000, Hall made a short stint in ECW before heading to Japan and NJPW, putting over talent there. His personal problems (we'll get to it) mired that, and Hall was without direction before returning the WWF in 2002 for the rebirth of the nWo.

His stay in the WWF lasted a mere five months, and Scott made his way to the newly formed TNA for a couple of months. After some time off, he returned to TNA for the autumn before leaving wrestling for a couple of more years. At the end of 2004 through January 2005, Scott Hall made his last wrestling appearance in TNA (or anywhere for that matter) at the time of this writing in 2006.

What an amazing, storied history and impact Scott Hall has had on wrestling. We'll get into some particular detail momentarily, but for now we have a "big" thing to discuss.

CURSE OF THE BIG MAN

Because Scott Hall is such a large guy (6' 6", 260-280 lbs.), Hall often gets lumped into the "Big Man" category that we have talked a lot about. And much like counterparts in Kevin Nash, Undertaker, Goldberg, and Sid Vicious, Hall has a much larger repertoire than he uses on a day-to-day basis. First, let's have a look at JD Dunn's Countdown to WrestleMania - WrestleMania X:

> **Intercontinental Title, Ladder Match: Shawn Michaels (w/Diesel) vs. Razor Ramon.**
>
> *Probably don't have to go into much on this one. The thing that stands out for me is that Razor Ramon's music is just Stone Cold Steve Austin's music played really slow. Razor ducks under the ladder prompting shock and awe from the announcers. Diesel gets tossed early on by the referee. Or what, he gets disqualified? Shawn gets clotheslined over the top like a rag doll. He dropkicks the ladder into an unsuspecting Ramon. We get the first real uses of the ladder as a weapon as Shawn drives it down into him and finally just throws it down on Razor's back. Michaels [loses his pants] and Vince wusses out on saying Shawn has made an "ass of himself." Think about that one compared to today. Shawn splashes him off the ladder and goes up but Razor recovers just in time to push the ladder over. Shawn bounces off the ropes like a super ball. He sets up the ladder in the corner but gets whipped into it and falls all the way to the floor. Great googly moogly! This sets up the catapult into the ladder spot. UN-BE-LEIVABLE! UN-BE-LEIVABLE! Razor goes up but Shawn jumps off the top rope and pushes him off. UN-BE-LEIVABLE! (Those are Vince-isms if you're wondering). Razor slams him off the ladder but falls down himself. He sets it up again but Shawn dropkicks the ladder forcing Ramon off it again. Michaels hits Sweet Chin Music out of nowhere and nails a piledriver. He goes up but Ramon just does get up and pushes the ladder over. Shawn has no time to yell to Diesel, let alone make a wish. He falls crotch-first on the top rope and gets entangled allowing Razor to climb up and get the belts at 18:47. One of the greatest matches to ever come out of North America. It's lost a bit of its luster thanks to the Hardyz, Dudleyz, and Edge/Christian TLC matches, but it still ranks right up there with the best of them.*
> *****

I think JD hits it right on the head. If you watch this match today compared to TLC2, you would not think it was that innovative or amazing. But this was leaps and bounds above most of the wrestling quality that the WWF was showing at the time, and demonstrated what Scott Hall was really capable of.

So sure, in later WWF matches and WCW matches, he mostly did the paintbrush, abdominal stretch (with cheating), fall-away slam, sleeper, chokeslam, and the edge, but he had plenty of other moves and abilities in his arsenal. It's the same story we always tell: he did not need to do them. Scott Hall, as Razor Ramon, was a heel that the fans forced to turn face. In WCW, he was a heel that got bigger face pops then most of the face roster. The man was over, and did not need to lay everything on the line every night. He could do an easier (physically wear-and-tear) match any night of the week and still send the fans home happy. They came to take the survey and see the spray-paint; they did not care if he could pull off a top-rope plancha (which he could).

Of course, in the ring Hall was still trying to have some fun. But that did not mean he did not know how to do his J-O-B.

ONLY HIMSELF?

Being a Klique and nWo member, Scot Hall constantly gets berated for only looking out for himself and his own interests. Well if that's true, then why has he put over the following people:

Jeff Hardy

In his last wrestling appearance to date in 2005, Scott Hall put over Jeff Hardy at TNA's Final Resolution on January 16, 2005. Knowing he was on the way out, he still chose to show up at the PPV and give Hardy some additional credibility to fight in TNA's upper card.

Sean Waltman (The Kid)

In one of the most famous upsets in history, on May 17, 1993 the premiering Kid defeated Razor Ramon (who had already fought Bret Hart for the title) by roll-up. This, and ensuing feud where Ramon learned to respect Waltman and turned face, basically launched Waltman's career and gave him years of exposure.

Chris Jericho

On Monday Nitro on November 3, 1997, Chris Jericho defeated Scott Hall by a surprise roll-up (he's really susceptible to that move). At the time, Jericho was just a cruiserweight wrestler with some notoriety. This gave Jericho something he could brag about for years, and a huge win for his WCW career.

Hector Garza

In what I consider the biggest upset in Monday Nitro history, on September 9, 1997, Hector Garza defeated Scott Hall (with Syxx) with a roll-up (there it is again!). A cruiserweight with no fanfare whatsoever was put over by Hall of his own will and volition. If that does not prove how much this man tried to help other guys get over and be given a fair chance, then nothing does.

And making other people look good also made Hall look good in the long run. So good, that he got some recognition for it.

GOT AWARDS? WHY NOT!

There are lots of awards to look at, but the PWI awards are always of interest. According to accelerator3359.com (I love old website), Scott Hall has had:

> PWI Achievement Awards: (3 wins, 2 1st RUs, 2 2nd RUs, 2 3rd RUs)
>
> - 1986 Most Improved Wrestler, 1st Runner-Up
> - 1992 Most Improved Wrestler
> - 1994 Match of the Year (Razor Ramon vs. Shawn Michaels)
> - 1994 Wrestler of the Year, 2nd Runner-Up
> - 1995 Feud of the Year, 2nd Runner-Up (Razor Ramon vs. Jeff Jarrett)
> - 1996 Match of the Year, 3rd Runner-Up (War Games)
> - 1997 Tag-Team of the Year (The Outsiders)
> - 1998 Feud of the Year, 1st Runner-Up (nWo Hollywood vs. nWo Wolfpac)
> - 2001 Comeback of the Year, 3rd Runner-Up

That's a lot of high-up-there awards, yet this is not what Scott Hall is remembered for. His contributions to wrestling seem meaningless compared to his personal troubles.

WAIT, THAT WAS HIS IDEA?

Now, we've already covered how Scott Hall created his own gimmick and was not dependent on Vince or anyone else for his ideas. As it was, Scott had almost complete control during his interviews and came up with most of his gimmicks. And how many catchphrases did Scott get over in a short time? Well let's see, there was:

- "Hey yo!"
- "Chico"
- "Survey say..."
- "Don't sing it... bring it."
- "Down where you ask? You know where!"

And that's just the beginning. The crowds used to sing along with everything Scott would say, whether he was a good guy or a bad guy (usually calling himself by either he felt like).

But just as Scott Hall used to put others over, he also tried to help other guys and the promotion he was in. Regular reader/writer **Feroz Nazir** sent this along:

> I remember Scott Hall mentioning that one of the ideas behind the NWO was to create a situation for the fans: "Are you a fan of WCW or the NWO?" [opposed] to "Are you a fan of WCW or the WWF?". Meaning that they intended for the WWF to be completely out of the picture by offering them 2 wrestling factions(?) in 1 [organization].
>
> I think it was on the "documentary" NWO: Back in black.

This situation is exactly what happened. The WWF was mostly forgotten in WCW and it did become about the nWo and WCW. Perhaps it went too far in the end (oh, that's a case later in this series), but just as Scott set the tone for the nWo invasion with his initial appearance, he continued to set the stage for what the nWo vs. WCW was all about.

In the WWE, he was not given this free reign and they missed the point of the nWo. It was not a faction, it was a separate organization trying to take over and destroy tradition. DX and the nWo were very different, although DX was patterned after many of the mannerisms and attitudes made famous by Hall.

Back behind the curtain, though, Scott was still trying to help others. From Mike Johnson's recap of Sting during the Spike TV/TNA press conference:

> When asked about the Crow Sting look, he said it was a Scott Hall suggestion...

From Richard Trionfo's recap of Shane Douglas on Between the Ropes in January 2005:

> Shane was asked about some of the veteran talent that has come into TNA and how it has been received by the younger talent. Shane says that there was some concern from the locker room because of what they may have heard about

> *people not being 'team players'. Shane talks about Scott Hall, and says that Scott has worked hard in the ring and is teaching guys in the ring. Shane talked about a match between Scott and A.J. Styles that helped out A.J. because he was slowed down to tell a story in the first segment of the match.*

And in an interview with masked wrestler Bob Cook from DDT Digest:

> *Kevin Nash and Scott Hall showed me around. And as far as all the rumors are concerned, maybe he's changed in the last two years, but Shawn Michaels was a really nice guy when I was there. I also think he is the best worker in the business.*
> *The last time Scott Hall and I were together in the WWF, Scott got me so drunk I couldn't walk.*

So from guys you've heard all about and their major gimmicks to guys you have no idea who they are and made no television impact, Scott Hall was there, helping out in any way he could. He was a bright, energetic man. But this man was haunted by demons of his own, and an addiction that could not be stopped.

ALCOHOLISM

Scott Hall's problems with alcoholism and subsequent jail time, divorce, and other consequences are well documented. In many of our past cases, I have asked whether or not someone's addiction problems, jail sentences, or other out of ring shenanigans should have an impact of their legacy and what they meant to wrestling. Usually, the answer has been "No" because they have reached pinnacles in the industry, being world champions or being the definitive beginning of a genre.

This is not the case with Scott Hall. Because of Scott's addiction, he never was able to reach the true peak of his ability and wrest the top crowns of our beloved sport. As a matter of fact, Scott was let go by WCW and WWE for his behavior stemming from his addiction.

And this was true well after he got clean. No matter what, Scott Hall was under the constant scrutiny of his past actions. Although given multiple chances, his chances were met with a skeptic response rather than possibility. From Cool Dudes and Hot Babes (how's that for a source!):

> The source we spoke with would not comment on the specific grounds of Hall's possible wrongful termination suit. The source did tell sportstalkcleveland.com however that Hall believes his bad boy reputation led to a rush in judgment [by] the WWE and also states that because of his numerous second chances and previous arrests, they were less than fair in their decision to terminate him.
>
> "Because of everything that has happened with him out of the ring, they were quicker to be less lenient with him than anyone else," the source stated. "They are too quick to be afraid that Scott is going to slip back into getting into trouble every other day. They have no regard for the fact that he loves this business and he loves entertaining people. He doesn't do anything that anyone else doesn't do, they are just tougher on Scott."

Scott's legacy was forever tarnished because of his personal problems. The question is, to what extent do we hold Scott Hall accountable?

This is not the forum to debate how to treat people with alcohol abuse problems. I will not recommend the twelve-step program, checking into a detoxification clinic, or undergoing various forms of psychotherapy. The "cures" and treatments for alcoholism are a personal debate you will have to have for yourself.

What I want to stress here is that alcoholism is a disease, and that Scott Hall had limited control over his ability to stop himself.

"That's BS", you say, "If anyone wants to stop something they can just stop. Scott Hall just chose not to."

Really?

First off, I think we have to accept something about terminology. When I, and others, say alcoholism is a disease, the first reaction of many people is that it cannot be a disease because it is not caused by a virus or bacteria and is not transmittable to other people. But is cancer a disease? It is not caused by a virus or bacteria and cannot be transmitted, yet it is considered a disease. What about sickle cell anemia? There is another "disease" that does not meet that criteria. And on top of that, what about schizophrenia? This is a mental disease that is not caused by anything related to an outside force and cannot be caught by anyone else.

I submit that a disease is an ailment of the mind or body that needs an exterior force (whether a chemical change in the body a la white blood cells or some type of medicine or even therapy or medication) for proper treatment.

With that, we need to understand what type of disease alcoholism is. From Mental Health Matters:

> *Alcohol Addiction, or dependence, is defined as having at least 3 of the following signs: a tolerance for alcohol (needing increased amounts to achieve the same effect), withdrawal symptoms, taking alcohol in larger amounts [than] was intended or over a longer period of time than was intended, having a persistent desire to decrease or the inability to decrease the amount of alcohol consumed, spending a great deal of time attempting to acquire alcohol, and finally, continuing to use alcohol even though the person knows there are reoccurring physical or psychological problems being caused by the alcohol.*

Right, and we know that Scott Hall did meet those criteria:

(1) High tolerance for alcohol intake
(2) Took alcohol in larger amounts than intended
(3) Used alcohol for longer periods than intended
(4) Inability to decrease the amount of alcohol consumed (and even took pills that would make him sick if he tried to consume alcohol)
(5) Continued to use alcohol despite the problems it caused in his life

You see, alcoholism is sometimes a physical addiction and sometimes a psychological addiction and sometimes both. Think about the small things you do just by compulsion every day. I always tap a can of soda before I pull the tab or smack a capped bottle first on a table before opening it. Why? I don't see why not. And even though I am aware of the compulsion, that does not mean I can just stop, or see the need to.

This was the case with Scott Hall. His alcoholism was a compulsion that was beyond his control. Despite the negative effects on his life that he was aware of, his ability to control the compulsion was limited. It was more than a habit, but something he needed to do just as you and I need scratch an itch on our nose.

But Scott Hall was one form of alcoholism, and there are many others. From Wikipedia:

> *Alcoholics do not typically experience craving, unlike individuals afflicted with opioid dependence. Of importance is that frequency and quantity of alcohol use are not related to the presence of the disease; that is, individuals can drink a great deal without necessarily being alcoholic, and alcoholics may drink minimally and/or infrequently. As described in Psychiatric Annals by Pagano et al (June 2005), "alcoholism is a chronic, often progressive disease that can be fatal without intervention and treatment. Rationing or other attempts to control use fail as pathological attachment to the drug develops. Use continues despite serious adverse health, personal, work-related, and financial consequences. Comorbidity, genetic, and psychosocial factors contribute to the risk of developing this disease."*

So you see what I mean? Even if Scott Hall had the ability to stop drinking suddenly (which he did not), he would still be an alcoholic. Back to Wikipedia:

> *[A]n alcoholic in recovery is not drinking at all yet still has the disease just as a diabetic who keeps his blood glucose at precisely 100 (normal) all the time is still diabetic. Neither individual would be likely to suffer significant symptoms secondary to their ongoing illness, yet both are still afflicted.*

An excellent analogy if there ever was one. His disease may be in "remission", but Scott Hall will always be an alcoholic and always have to work to fight the disease.

WHAT ARE YOU ASKING OF ME?

Now that we understand that Scott Hall is an afflicted man, what do I intend to do with that information?

I am not asking you to forgive Scott Hall or excuse his actions. I'm not asking you to look past all of the destruction he has caused professionally, personally, and legally. What I am asking is that you understand where he is coming from, and that you do not let the rumors of Scott's behavior in the past few years blind you to the progress he has made.

When Hall was let go from the WWE in 2002 after the Insurrection PPV, several sites incorrectly reported that he was intoxicated and had fallen asleep backstage. The truth of the matter is that, yes, he did fall asleep backstage, but that was from being exhausted and staying up too long (he's in his 40's, you know). Hall had had a drink before the event, and not within hours of show time. Someone made the jump from falling asleep to blabbering drunk simply because of Hall's issues, not because there was any truth to the matter. From Cool Dudes and Hot Babes:

> "Following Monday Night Raw, they flat out told Scott he was fired," stated our source. "Scott told me that he wasn't drunk at the London pay-per-view or before that Raw. If you look at the tape of the pay-per-view, he doesn't walk funny or act like he has had a lot to drink. The fact that he fell asleep is inexcusable, however it isn't grounds to be fired. Besides, Scott wasn't even scheduled to wrestle that night, so why should they even care if he is sleeping backstage."

The type of paranoia that runs rampant in the WWE nowadays (don't play video games backstage, always wear your dress clothes!) made it a place ready to kick Scott Hall out fast. Although Vince and company wanted Scott Hall the character, they did not want Scott Hall the person. One does not go without the other, and there was a severe lack of understanding of both.

From an interview recap in March 2002:

> *Hall's problems went beyond attitude or management. He's battled alcohol addiction and marital issues, and spoke candidly about his ups and downs.*
>
> *Now he's divorced and raising his children as a single parent. He's been in and out of two rehab centers. He sees an addiction specialist and takes Anabuse, a drug which makes the taker violently ill at the mere taste of alcohol. He's thankful for another chance to earn a living in the business.*
>
> *"I've been searching to get in touch with Scott Hall, to find Scott Hall. He got lost in a blur of alcohol and immature decisions," he said. "I just want to be the best me I can be."*

Scott is well aware of everything he has done and tries to do better. Is he always successful? Not by a long shot. But since when is trying and failing a crime?

Where does it all come back to?

So is Scott Hall responsible for his own downfall? Well, yes and no. The beginning of Scott's disease begins with himself with questions and answers that only he can answer. But the snowball effect is not completely his fault. Neither is the fact that no matter what he does, he will always have this disease and he will never be able to break the stigma of what he has done. Even though Hall has had multiple "chances", each of those chances was laced with doubt. There was no fair, fresh start. He was already falling from day one, and the slightest mistake that he made would be blown significantly out of proportion. Where one person would get a slap on the wrist, Scott could be sent home.

Don't get me wrong. Hall has done some terrible things that he did deserve to get fired over and didn't. But you do not put the robber away for a murder he did not commit. He may rob people for a living, but that is not the crime he is being tried for.

And that is what has happened to Scott Hall. He has done bad things in the past, but he is constantly being tried and found guilty for things he did not do or were blown out of proportion. Given a second chance? Maybe. Given a fair chance? Never.

The Toothpick Flick

Scott Hall: a man whose personal demons have destroyed his legacy. We have forgotten how he came up the ranks in the independents, how he developed his own personality, his own finisher, and own style. He has impacted every organization he has even been in, setting off waves that forever changed wrestling. He gave back trying to teach the next generation how to be a performer, and put them over in the ring. Yet all we remember is that he had a problem, a problem beyond his own ability to control, and one that should never take the place of all that he has given for our sport.

The defense rests.

After the Trial

Hung Jury

IN THE CASE OF THE IWC VS. SCOTT HALL, SCOTT HALL HAS BEEN ACCUSED OF BEING A DRUNK WHO LET HIS OWN PERSONAL PROBLEMS PREVENT HIM FROM EVER ACHIEVING FULL SUCCESS. FURTHERMORE, HE IS ACCUSED OF BEING A LARGE, SLOW, UNINTERESTING CHARACTER THAT ONLY GOT TO WHERE HE IS WITH THE HELP OF OTHERS AND KEEPING EVERYONE BELOW HIM DOWN.

That case was different than any I had ever done before. But were the results?

With 76.5% of the vote, Scott Hall was found:

NOT GUILTY!

Another one... for the good guys. Yeah, like you didn't see that joke coming?

Response

Sometimes these cases go beyond the subjects and touch people personally. I was grateful that so many people shared with me their experiences with alcoholism, such as these:

> *I would just like to thank you for a superb defence of one of my all-time favourite performers. Scott's disease has overshadowed his accomplishments and I had always had a personal interest in defending the man no-one else would, as my own Grandfather was an alcoholic.*
>
> *My Grandfather's disease overtook his life so much, that he lost his marriage, his retirement fund and even alienated some of his closest friends and more [ignorant] family members. The disease [affected] him to the point that he developed a little known form of alcohol-induced Alzheimer's known as Korsikov's disease. Fortunately, after much work, he cleaned up but had to be taken into specialised residential care due to his constant fight of both alcoholism and the [literal] 5-minute memory that Korsikov's has left him with.*

I'm glad to hear that Scott has made every effort to clean-up and lead as normal a life as possible. I'm extremely thankful to you for your extensive research into the disease and have chosen to broadcast your findings on such a wide plateau. Hopefully, some people will be less eager to point the finger, and remember that alcoholism carries just as much pain as any other disease.

Regards,
Luke Howells.

I have seen up close what a chemical addiction can do to somebody and its effect on everyone that cares about them (it's not pretty). I have also seen first-hand how awesome it is when that person recovers. The key to it all is the person. They won't clean up until THEY want to. Nobody else can force them.

Rhett Walker

One thing that really pissed me off was his last stint in WWE with the nWo, WWE version. When he was being [interrogated] by Stone Cold, they had Stone Cold pouring beer all over the man... Now if that was real beer or not, I do not know... But to me [that's] like tempting a dog with meat above his head to see if he will jump at it or obey his master.

Dave Jones

I have known people in my life who are Alcoholics. One of my best friends is one, sober for over 30 years now.

But the stories he would tell me about his troubles with the bottle are ones I have taken to heart. I feel that Scott Hall has gotten a raw deal every time he's tried to come back. He was a single father for a while and he has always tried to correct the issues in his life. I feel that it is not fair

> to judge the man without walking a mile in his shoes, and I'd ever recommend someone become an alcoholic. He deserves our respect, not just from the fans, but from the industry he helped and gave so much of his blood, sweat and tears for.
>
> **~Michael Kenney**

> I know from being married to a Licensed Chemical Dependency Counselor the horrible trap that alcoholism creates: you want to stop, you can't, you drink, you hate yourself more, so you drink to quiet your self-loathing. An ugly circle that usually drags your loved ones down with you until they tire of you and disown you.
>
> **Matt Gonzales**

As I shared with these people and others, I, too, have dealt with people who have had alcohol and chemical dependencies in my life, and not usually to a happy ending. I share these stories not for the evidence for Scott Hall, but more for an understanding of where these people are coming from. Also as I told one particular critic: this is not enabling, just having compassion.

Larry Zbyszko

Intro

Some dame walked into my office and said...

Well, for the first time in a while, that dame is **me**. Being a huge NWA/WCW fan, I always enjoyed Larry's commentating skill. But because of when and where I was born, I never really got to see him wrestle. Were the stories he told true? Were the stories other people told true? Was Larry truly the living legend, or was he a joke as many others contend?

Why this?

As soon as I said this topic, I heard from a few people about it. First was **Rusty Nailz** who said:

> What the fuck is up with the next one being about Larry Z... No offense man, but I could give a fuck less about this guy... Please explain to me why you're wasting [your] time on this guy?

And there was also **Feroz Nazir** who said:

> What did Larry Z. ever do wrong?

And that about covers the why. Larry Zbyszko is truly an icon in this industry. He has had an incredible, lasting impact and deserves to be remembered as one of the best. For his time, too, he was a huge draw, making money for everyone involved.

Yet, as time has moved on, the WWE has re-written history. As a new generation of viewers has taken over, his place in history is threatened. If not stopped now, everything Larry Zbyszko has done will be forgotten.

This will be a case unlike any other. This will be more about learning history and understanding the industry in the past and less about disproving specific charges.

I did not and do not pick cases because they will be popular. If I always wrote about what people cared about, then there would be no challenge. No, this one is about getting you to see why you should care, and why talking about Larry Zbyszko is not a waste of time.

THIRTY YEARS IN THE INDUSTRY

On a cold windy night in Chicago on December 5, 1953, a man named Lawrence Whistler was born. Who knew that he would grow up to become a professional wrestler and call himself Zbyszko? Who would think to call themselves Zbyszko? Only one man, and that man was the living legend. But not quite yet.

In 1965, Larry and family moved to Pittsburgh, PA. Says Larry to George Wrestling History:

> [W]hen I went to Pittsburgh it was the first time I watched pro wrestling... And you know, Bruno Sammartino became my hero. And I loved it so much when I was a kid, I actually started wrestling in grade school back then. And then wrestling in high school, and did some wrestling for Penn State...

So even at a young age Larry was pursuing the sport. Kayfabe was much more alive then, and he believed more than enough to get the proper amateur training. That training was good enough to get him on the Penn State team, proving that he had all the basic skills prevalent in later wrestlers like the Steiner Brothers or Kurt Angle.

What happened next, though, was entirely Larry's doing. Says Larry in the aforementioned interview:

> I think my buddy was 16, and I was 15 or something, and we were driving around because I knew where Bruno lived. He lived a couple miles from my house. And we'd drive by his house every now and then to see if we could get a glimpse of him. And one day, there he was, I could see him through the hedges sitting in his backyard. My buddy stopped the car, so I jumped out of the car and busted through his hedges. (Laughs)

> *So he's sitting there in his yard playing with one of his kids, David -- who was little at the time -- and he looks at me, and there's this little kid, you know, coming through the hedges. And he gets up and kind of looks at me like, "What the hell?" And when he got up, my God, he looked like a gorilla. He was a big man. He was not that tall, maybe 5'11", but he was like 265 pounds. I mean, a gorilla. And I was a nervous wreck. I introduced myself, I was very respectful, you know. I told him that he was my hero, and my favorite wrestler, and blah, blah, blah, and I kind of started like that.*

And somehow out of that awkward introduction, Larry and Bruno became friends. They became more than friends, they became teacher and student, mentor and the mentee. When Larry was introduced later on as Bruno's protégé, that was not just some gimmick to get him over. That was the god's honest truth, but a lot more happened between them. Back to the interview:

> *As I got older, he met my folks, and he took me under his wing. I started training in his basement gym, that's why I sort of looked like him, I did the same workout for years. And he told me he'd start me in professional wrestling when I finished school because professional wrestling wasn't a guaranteed type of career, and it was smart to have a back-up plan. So I finished school and majored in basket-weaving and he got me in the professional wrestling game.*

Ever since he was a child, Larry wanted to be a professional wrestler. He had all the amateur credentials and he had the training of one of the best ever. Yet, instead of just using that to jump the gun and go right into the sport at 18 (or sooner), he respected his mentor's wishes. Larry did not want to go to college and had no huge need to go, but went anyway because it was what Bruno wanted. And as soon as that was done, he was right back in the sport. But it was not like he was just pushed straight to the top!

In 1973, Larry took the name Zbyszko. Since he was of Polish decent himself, he had a great respect for one of the most famous Polish wrestlers of just before his time: Stanislaus Zbyszko. You see, Larry was not just a fan of wrestling; he was the equivalent of today's smart mark, except with a work ethic. But Larry took his love and knowledge of the industry and premiered as a babyface under the tutelage of Bruno. Back to our interview:

> *I started wrestling around the Pittsburgh area doing some local TV and shows in the high school gyms. And then Bruno sent me to British Columbia. Vancouver --- there was a wrestling territory.*
>
> *[Interviewer:] Was that Al Tomko?*
>
> *No, it that was like Gene Kiniski and Sandor Szabo. And so I went there for about six months, because he (Bruno) wanted me to get experience. And then he brought me back and I started in the WWWF... as "Bruno's protégé."*

Tomko? Kinisk? What decade are we in?

Two points from this. One: Bruno wanted Larry to get some seasoning under his belt before he would help him get to the big time. He would not let Larry into the major circuits and wanted him to learn the industry and not be as green. Bruno knew how to open doors, but Larry would have to get better before he was allowed anywhere. Two: Although everyone in the industry knew Larry had trained under Bruno, he did not use that to get over with the crowd at that point. Again, Bruno wanted Larry to pave his own way before he would tie himself to him and the audience.

In 1974, PWI named Larry the rookie of the year. He was starting to make a name for himself, and that finally convinced Bruno to help him come to the WWWF (that's not an extra W folks) run by Vince McMahon Sr. And so finally Zbyszko was allowed to become Bruno's protégé on screen and in the papers. Back to the interview:

> *You know, to be Bruno's protégé was an honor. Everybody from the promoters, to the top guys around at the time, to the older guys that would really give you shit -- everybody was very nice to me. Everybody opened their arms to welcome me to the business, and would tell me things that they wouldn't tell everybody else. How to make money, the psychology. I had the best array of teachers in the business. I have an education that no one else in this business has from Bruno and these guys because they opened up to me, as 'Bruno's protégé.' It was all politics, and he was the man.*
>
> *[Interviewer:] When you say drawing money and little hints that you got from the jump, who were some of the guys and what was some of the advice*

> *that they gave you that they didn't give anybody else?*
>
> *Oh, God, you're talking about some dead brain cells. Everyone from Arnold Skaaland to Chief Jay Strongbow to Tony Altimore to Gorilla Monsoon, the Savoldi's. A bunch of people who have been in this business for years. Plus all of the wrestlers, the other guys. The George Steele's, the list goes on. It would take me hours and hours of sitting here thinking to remember what each quote from somebody was. But, it was just like a whole bunch of tutors.*

So yes, Bruno did open a lot of doors for Zbyszko, and lots of people told Larry stuff that they would tell no others. But this not a case of nepotism. Remember, it was Larry who made the jump to meet Bruno and befriend him. Larry trained, did the amateur ranks, did everything Bruno asked him to do. At the end of the day, it was still up to Larry to put on a compelling show in the ring and get himself over with the crowd.

If you think it was all Bruno's doing, then I have to ask you this: have you ever heard of David Sammartino? Exactly, you haven't. And if you have, you already know what's coming. Bruno's son David could not make it in the industry, even with his father. From our over-used interview:

> ***[Interviewer:]*** *What did you think of David as a wrestler? And what did you think of his future possibilities in the business?*
>
> *Well, he's a good wrestler. I mean, he was a good wrestler. A lot of fire. He just got frustrated easy, it just didn't work out like he thought it would being Bruno's son, and he couldn't fill the shoes. And the politics were bad, too, for him, because Bruno wouldn't take no shit, so there were a lot of promoters and people that didn't like Bruno, so it didn't help Bruno's kid, if Bruno wasn't involved.*

Once again, as you can see, it was not Bruno that had to work to get Larry over, Larry was responsible. But he also needed some more seasoning. Again with the interview:

> *[Interviewer:] Did you stay there long? Because I know you had gone out to California. Was that before or after you started with the WWWF?*
>
> Well I was with the WWWF for maybe a couple of years. Two or three years and then I hit the road a little bit to a couple of little places, and then I went out to California for maybe six or eight months in '75. And then maybe a wee bit in Georgia.
>
> What they wanted to do in those days was get you out of the area for a year or so, and then when you came back you were fresher... You know, six months here, three months here. And then I went back to the WWWF in probably '75-76. And then teamed up with Tony Garea and took it farther.

And over the next several years, he started to win championships, started fighting more challenging individuals, and working his way up the card. By 1980, though, it was apparent that he could not get out of Sammartino's shadow. And so Zbyszko began a campaign to face his trainer and prove himself once and for all. From Wikipedia:

> *Zbyszko became frustrated with his inability to shed his label as Bruno Sammartino's protégé. He challenged Sammartino to an exhibition match, claiming this was the only way he could step out of Sammartino's shadow. Sammartino eventually agreed to the match after Zbyszko threatened to retire if he was not granted the match. The trainer and pupil faced one another in Allentown on January 22, 1980, with Sammartino dominating the early stages of the match. After Sammartino threw him out of the ring, an irate Zbyszko seized a wooden chair and struck Sammartino, leaving him in a pool of blood in the middle of the ring and instantly turning Zbyszko into a reviled heel.*

And a little more detail from our beloved interview:

> *[Interviewer:] When did you find out you were making that turn? Whose idea was it to start the process along from making that turn from All-American babyface to...*

Well, it was my idea. It was at the time, Bruno was basically retired. He was doing the broadcasting, and the business was in the crapper. I mean, it was way down. Bob Backlund was the champion, and nobody cared. People wanted Bruno to come back, but he was all beat up and didn't want to come back. And there were a lot of guys in limbo. And I just put together all I learned from those guys, and said "damn, if..." -- because I wanted Bruno to make a come-back -- "if Bruno comes back whoever he wrestles is gonna be a big star." But, the whole thing would be great because the people want him back so bad that it can't miss.

So, then I went to Bruno and ran by the idea of what I wanted to do. And he sort of thought about it and said, "Okay, we'll do it." But, he was the one that programmed the whole thing, and along with some other circumstances, it became the biggest feud of the old school.

[Interviewer:] *Building to that, you asked him for a scientific match to try and escape from his shadow. What kind of led up to that match? Were you showing frustration in any of your other matches in trying to get ahead? How did that work?*

Well, it was just doing interviews basically about the story, which was kind of true, Saying, "Look if, Larry Zbyszko can't survive anymore here being Bruno's protégé. Surviving in Bruno's shadow, and Bruno's not even wrestling here anymore." And I said, "This is ridiculous." I said there's only one way for me to prove that I'm as great as my mentor, and that's to call Bruno out here and have the match of a lifetime. I said "He'll always be my hero, no disrespect." And then Bruno didn't want to wrestle me, because I was his protégé. And, of course, that made everybody want it more. And then I started getting more frustrated and said "Come on Bruno give me a shot," and blah, blah, blah. But, I did it so well, and it was laid out so well, that the people actually bought it. I mean, they actually wanted Bruno to give me a chance. And then when Bruno finally said "Okay, but it'll be a scientific match." And I said, "Oh, okay. That's great. I couldn't ask for more."

> *And then when I clobbered him with the chair, and he drowned in a pool of blood, my God, people hated me. Talk about wanting to kill me, I was stabbed in the ass in Albany, New York. God, I had cars smashed. I had cabs overturned. I had threats from Little Italy.*
>
> *Those were the days when people believed, and the hate was real—and the love was real too. The people loved Bruno so much in those days that when we were in the middle of a show where Bruno would get bloody and fall down, people had heart attacks. I swear to God. I think at the Civic Arena (Pittsburgh) one time the most I did was four heart attacks. I mean, people dropped dead because Bruno was bleeding! That's how serious it was taken, it's completely different today.*

From this, we can learn a lot. First, we learn that this great angle was really Zbyszko's idea, and not Vince Sr. or Bruno. Second, he legitimately had to convince Bruno to go through with it and put himself through another series of matches. And last, Larry put himself into legitimate danger. He was stabbed, shot at, hit with pipes, had his car overturned, his taxi attacked... he was no longer safe in his own home. But it was all worth it, according to Zbyszko.

And not just according to him. The records speak for themselves. He and Sammartino sold out arenas everywhere. But the biggest one of all was the Showdown at Shea on August 9, 1980. In the main event of the evening, Sammartino defeated Zbyszko in a steel cage in the largest wrestling audience of the time. From our favorite interview:

> **[Interviewer:]** *That match with Sammartino drew an insane amount. It was over 36,000 and, even more impressive, over a half million at the gate. (Dave Meltzer's Wrestling Observer Newsletter reports the numbers it drew as 36,295 – although it was announced as being 40,717, so it could be larger than the Chicago crowd that saw Buddy Rogers win the NWA World title over Pat O'Connor – and earned a then-record $541,730 in gate revenue.)*
>
> *Oh yeah. In those days, selling out a stadium for wrestling was unheard of. Unheard of.*
>
> **[Interviewer:]** *I think it was a quote from Bruno that said he was more impressed with the match with you than the match between Hulk Hogan and*

> *Andre the Giant at WrestleMania III drawing the crowd they did because, technically, it was a regional event.*
>
> *Oh yeah, I mean if we would have pulled it off down the road some years when national cable and they were on network? Shit, it would have been unbelievable. In fact, that Silverdome show that they claim was 90,000 people? They gave 30,000 tickets away.*
>
> *[Interviewer:] I remember Dave Meltzer reporting the actual paid was far, far less than that.*
>
> *Oh, yeah, so if you consider what we did at Shea Stadium to what they really did at the Silverdome, plus the TV in New York. The TV was on at like midnight to one in the morning, and that was it.*

The Showdown at Shea was the biggest North American wrestling event of its time, doing the largest numbers seen in an incredibly down time in the industry. And it was all thanks to the long feud between Zbyszko and Sammartino. Zbyzsko was actually named the PWI Most Hated Wrestler that year! Of course, this would not be the last time Zbyszko would set a huge attendance record, but we'll get back to that shortly.

After their feud, Sammartino went into retirement (well, about half a year later) and Zbyszko got to claim he sent him there. Zbyszko then left the WWWF and moved on to the NWA where he was involved in another controversial angle. From Wikipedia:

> *Zbyszko initially feuded with Tim Woods and Paul Orndorff, who he was unable [to defeat] for the NWA National Heavyweight Championship. After Killer Tim Brooks defeated Orndorff for the title on March 20, 1983, Zybszko immediately offered him $25,000 for the title, which Brooks accepted. His reign lasted until April 30 of that year, when NWA President Bob Geigel stripped Zbyszko of the title due to the manner in which he had acquired it. A tournament was held for the vacant title, which Zbyszko entered. He defeated Mr. Wrestling II in the tournament final on May 6, 1983 in Atlanta, Georgia to regain the title. His second reign lasted until September 25, 1983, when he lost to Brett Wayne in Atlanta.*

And where did I see that angle about five years later? Oh, that's right, when Ted Dibiase paid Andre the Giant for the WWF championship. How familiar!

You see, Zbyzsko was a pioneer in things that are now commonplace. Turning on a mentor and beating him with a chair? Trying to buy a title? Though they may be hackneyed today, they were original and shocking then. Back to our interview:

> **[Interviewer:]** How did the whole scenario with Paul Orndorff and buying the National title come about? Who's idea was that? And how did that kind of unfold?
>
> (Laughs) Argh, Jesus Christ! I don't really remember. All I remember is they had this thing with me and Orndorff, and they wanted to do something different. And I think I'm the one who came up with the idea, "But well then, why don't I buy it? And we'll have him (Brooks) do it." Because I always believed in swerving the people, and at that time, if I would have wrestled Orndorff and then somehow someone ran in and I won it, it would have been predictable. So I said let's make it unpredictable. We'll throw Killer Brooks in there, and it should look like Orndorff would kill Killer Brooks, and then we'll swerve it that way, and have Killer Brooks win the belt, which nobody would ever imagine.
>
> We swerved 'em, right? And as soon as you swerve 'em, Killer Brooks says "I'm the champion, I'm the greatest," and here I walk out and buy it from him, and he goes, "Oh, sure, here." Then I brag I'm the champion. I mean, it's just more heat for the complete unpredictability. That's what they don't have today. They don't have any unpredictability. This guy's in love with this broad, these guys are going to pop around, and on and on and on.

In 1984 he then moved on to the AWA and began a feud with Sgt. Slaughter. In this feud, Zbyzsko introduced another element he made famous: excessive stalling. The fans were more into booing his stalling during the match than any other match on the card. From Richard Trionfo's recap of Larry on Between the Ropes in April 2004:

> Larry talked about how Arn Anderson hated Larry's stalling during matches, and the longest he ever stalled was 16 minutes. Larry heard about it from the agent, Grizzly Smith. Larry said that the crowd was into his matches, while other matches were not getting the same fan reaction.

Zbyzsko's time in the AWA continued, leading to a feud with the champion Nick Bockwinkle. In yet another swerve, Zbyzsko helped Curt Hennig defeat Bockwinkel for the title instead of winning the title himself. From the original interview:

> **[Interviewer:]** They started pushing Hennig, and start grooming him to take the belt off Bockwinkel. Did you ever care about that mythical thing of having the World title, or were you just trying to get paid and do a good job?
>
> I'm in the business to make the most money. In fact, I'll tell you a secret, when I slipped Curt Hennig the roll of dimes supposedly, and Curt beat Bockwinkel to become the champion, that was my idea.
>
> There were thinking of the inevitable after the me and Bockwinkel program of having me win the belt. But I thought that would be anti-climactic, because it wouldn't have swerved the people. The people were thinking that's what was going to happen. Bockwinkel was getting older and blah, blah, blah, and the whole bit. So, I said, "Everybody is thinking I'm going to get the belt, let's swerve them," so we did this thing with Curt.
>
> Him and Bockwinkel had a 60-minute time limit, and I think it was going like 55 minutes, so everybody was convinced that it was going to be a draw and, all of a sudden, I gave him "the world's greatest advice," and he won the belt and everyone was completely swerved.

And that's another point. Larry was about business, not about himself. He could have taken the AWA title then, but didn't think it was best for business. He was never about just putting himself over; he was all about doing what was right for business.

After this matchup, Zbyzsko returned to the NWA (Jim Crockett Promotions, specifically) in 1987 and then won the Western Heritage Championship in 1988 (but not before claiming he also retired Bockwinkel, who did in reality retire shortly after Zbyzsko left). And when he left JCP in 1989 he took the belt with him and retired it to a storage bin somewhere.

Finally Larry ended up back in the AWA and won the World Championship. Late in 1989 he began a feud with Mr. Saito which led to a match at the Tokyo Dome. With wrestling in another downturn, this happened (according to Larry's website):

> [A]s the AWA Heavyweight Champion of the World, he wrestled a former Japanese Olympic wrestler, [Mr. Saito], at the first Tokyodome show in Japan. Over 70,000 fans were on hand to witness this scientific and brutal confrontation. This amazing attendance was more than twice the number of people to show up the following night at the Tokyodome where a championship boxing match was fought between Mike Tyson and Buster Douglas.

Once again Zbyzsko was able to prove that he was a huge draw all over the world, and he could excite with the best of them. Who else was drawing crowds that size in 1990? Want to know what else? Zbyzsko dropped the title to Mr. Saito. And unlike when Ric Flair used to drop the title, this one was fully acknowledged by Larry and the AWA. He regained the title in a rematch in the States two months later, and then left with the title in December 1990. The AWA was approaching its end. Despite being able to draw a crowd of that size, the AWA was a financial mess and soon collapsed as talent left, fans stopped showing up, and the show lost its creativity and finally its champion. Less than a year later the AWA would declare bankruptcy.

Thus in 1990 Zbyzsko was in the newly formed WCW, teaming with everyone and eventually joining the Dangerous Alliance a year later. Injuries would eventually catch up to him and he would become a color commentator. Leaving retirement a few times for some matches involving William Regal, Scott Hall, and Eric Bischoff, Larry was mostly done with active competition. He started off co-hosting Main Event in 1994, and found himself on Nitro by 1996. This put him right in the limelight again as the nWo war kicked off.

The crowds really got into him. "Larry" chants were heard all over the sold-out WCW arenas. The Living Legend was turned face by the crowd after fifteen years as a heel. Yet he never changed a thing! He said the same things, he kept the same attitude, and he talked smack on the same people. Yet, he was a new man for a new generation of wrestling fans. From our interview:

> *[Interviewer:] Yeah, doing the little salute, and just have people go nuts for announcing. Just for stepping up to the announcing stand!*
>
> *You know what? It felt great, it came full circle. I mean you know, you did a bunch of stuff and the people hated you, but after a while they loved you, because they hated you so much. And it was like they appreciated it. It feels great, even when I do these indy shows and appearances, people are chanting, and I do the little thing and they go nuts. They love me and I love them, and it was a great time.*

Larry stayed in the booth until the end of WCW. He spent some time out in the independents making appearances, and then found his way over to TNA for a short while until he had creative differences with Vince Russo. After Russo was gone, he found his way back and moved his way up from the Championship Committee and became the Director of Authority. And that is where we stand at the time of this writing in 2006.

So much had come before what we know about Larry Zbyzsko today, yet it is hardly talked about. And yet, there is so much more.

IS HE TRIPLE H?

Larry Zbyszko married the boss' daughter. In 1988, Zbyszko married Kathy Gagne, daughter of Verne Gagne. And Verne, of course, was the owner and booker for the AWA. To our favorite interview from Georgia Wrestling History:

> *[Interviewer:] When did you meet your wife?*
>
> *She was working there a little bit in the office when I was working for the AWA. And actually, it was funny, for like the first six to eight months it was a big secret, nobody knew that me and Kathy were dating...*
>
> *[Interviewer:] Even Verne or Greg [Verne's son, Kathy's sister]?*
>
> *Nobody. Then one day, Kathy and I went to like a Moody Blues concert, or something, downtown, and they had an intermission. And about two rows behind us, I hear this voice, and I turn around and*

it was Greg. Greg with somebody and they were at the concert too, and they saw me and Kathy sitting there. (Laughs)

[Interviewer:] How did that go over with Verne?

Verne hated my guts.

[Interviewer:] How long did it take for him to come around to the idea of his daughter dating a wrestler? And not just any wrestler, it was you.

After she got pregnant. (Laughs) As soon as she had the kid, I was okay.

[Interviewer:] Did that get you, like the Triple H-Stephanie (McMahon) thing, was it kind of the same thing at the time where guys look at you cross-eyed like, "Well, he's getting it with Verne's daughter, here we go"?

That's a natural, I guess. I guess because I was in the position I was, and I was who I was, I really didn't get a whole lot of it because I was a top guy. So it wasn't like it was something they couldn't handle. It wasn't like the daughter running off with a jabroni.

[Interviewer:] Like Jake Milliman, or something.

Yeah. It was interesting. I really don't know what the deal is with Triple H and Stephanie, but as far as I'm concerned, Kathy is just a great chick. Because she was Verne's daughter, she was raised in the wrestling business so that's in her blood[,] too. I mean, she understands the business. It's hard to have a wife in this business, but if you have a wife that was raised in it, and understands it, then you get along great because you kind of know where each others are coming from.

A lot of guys get divorced because they don't realize after you get married, you never see the husbands anyway. It's a weird life.

Then I was lucky because I got into the broadcasting, and I was home every day just about, so we could raise these kids. It was a good life.

Oh, where to start with this one? First off, Larry was already a main event wrestler and had been for eight years by the time he married Kathy. And marrying her did nothing for his career. Verne hated him, and you can bet that he still was not happy with Larry after he got his daughter pregnant.

Larry overcame the hatred of his father-in-law and boss and was able to win the championship. He won it because the crowds paid to see him (or rather to see him beaten). It was during this time frame that he sold out the Tokyodome with Mr. Saito in front of 70,000 people.

You see, Larry took this chance because he loved this woman and wanted to be with her. He could have been ostracized from this industry. There was no place for a non-muscle-head in the 1988 WWF, and WCW did not yet exist (and walking away with a title did not make him a friend of the NWA). No, Larry had found a woman who could be everything he was looking for in a wife. He saw how being married affected the other guys, and knew he needed someone who understood his life. Heck, he was 36 when he got married!

There was a man who lived the prime of his life unattached. He knew that getting married and having kids would be a major change from his bachelor days, bouncing territory to territory. But that was a risk he was willing to take because he loved Kathy and wanted a life with her; not to win championships or make more money off of the AWA.

THE LINE IN THE SAND

It just so happened, though, that Larry became injured and found himself as a broadcaster. This allowed him to be home with his kids and enjoy them growing up (as he grew older). Yet, this also put him in the position of constantly being on the mic. Because of this, everything he said was taken as his real opinions or his version of the truth. We forget, though, that despite everything he says on a microphone or in front of a camera, he's still in character (this goes for Jerry Lawler, too, but that's another day). Larry is the consummate professional, and his character is always in full gear.

But because he is playing the character so perfectly, the lines between his real personal beliefs and his character are continually blurred.

For instance, the character of Larry Zbyszko claims that he retired Bruno Sammartino and Nick Bockwinkle. Of course, in the real world we know both wrestled for months after Zbyszko left them behind! But back in the day, it was a way to maintain his heel heat. As I stated in the previous section, Larry also maintained his "heel" character when he joined commentary and continued to say such things, even after the crowd turned him face. This made some think that he truly believed that he had retired these men and was rewriting history. Of course this is not what he was thinking! Pretending to retire those two is just a part of his character as it has always been, and in the real world he is eternally grateful for all they gave him.

Another point is the title "Living Legend". From Richard Trionfo's recap of Zbyszko on Between the Ropes in April 2004:

> *Discussion moved on to the use of 'Living Legend'. Larry has been using it since suggested by Bruno Sammartino, since he was called the 'living legend' but it was not Bruno's style. However, it was perfect for Larry's character. The use of 'Living Legend' made him the biggest bad guy in the land, and got him a lot of heat.*

Some have claimed that Larry stole the title from Bruno, and that since he lost the cage match between the two he lost the right to call himself by that name (one of the stipulations?). But Larry said it right there. Bruno was called the "Living Legend", but that name was not for him. Zbyszko used it to gain heel heat, and it became synonymous with him. This is what Bruno wanted, and it is just Larry's character, not how he viewed himself (except maybe with his wife, but I won't go there).

That, sadly, has not stopped others from trying to claim the name.

It's suing time!

Even though Zbyszko is the "Living Legend", others like Chris Jericho and Randy Orton have tried to use it the past few years. From our famous Georgia Wrestling History Interview:

> *[Interviewer:] One of the smaller guys that Vince has is your buddy Chris Jericho...*
>
> Ah, yes.
>
> *[Interviewer:] The cynic of that whole situation (Larry and the WWE are tied up litigation over Jericho using the nickname "Living Legend" on television after he won the mini-tournament to unify the WWE and WCW World championships in 2001) would look and say, hey, Ric Flair took (the Nature Boy nickname/persona) from Buddy Rogers. Nicknames get passed around. What pisses you off so much about Jericho referring to himself as the "Living Legend."*

Well, it's not so much Jericho, because Chris, he's a good talent—he's one of Vince's puppets, you know, he does what he's told. And you can say, well, Flair took the "Nature Boy" from Buddy Rogers, but that's terrific, but Buddy Rogers is long dead. And, the fact of the matter is, after I'm dead, I don't care if he's the "Living Legend" or not. (Chuckles) But right now, I'm still using it to make my living. So it's like, you know, "Hey dudes!"

[Interviewer:] I guess Rogers let Flair have it too. They did that little thing in Crockett (Mid-Atlantic Championship) where Flair went over Rogers, and kind of like ascended to the throne.

Yeah, but Rogers was always Ric Flair's hero. And he wanted to pattern, well he did pattern, almost his whole bit after Rogers. But, you know, Buddy's dead, and great, but I'm still using it. And the thing that kind of got me was, after I called the WWF and said, "Hey guys, do you mind? I'm still alive here. I'm not dead." And working and making my living with what I've built up for 23 years. And the only reason it got to the lawsuit part was because their lawyers sent me a letter saying, "We are going to take it, and will continue to use it, and you will not interfere." So here we are.

[Interviewer:] Do you think it (the letter) was just a big "F.U." coming down from Vince, saying send him this, and "screw him"?

Well, it certainly sounded like it to me! I mean it was almost like, "Hey, look it. We're the WWF. We want to use what you made famous. And you're to go away now." Well, I'm sorry. I still got two kids to raise here, dude.

[Interviewer:] Do you have that trademarked, or how does that work?

Well, actually, it's in the trademark office, or whatever. But, even without that, as it is now, it's a common law trademark. Like common law marriage. If you use something in the public eye so long, it becomes your common law trademark.

> ***[Interviewer:]*** *Well, I think Randy Orton used it this past week. (On WWE Raw)*
>
> *Yeah, this ought to be interesting.*
>
> ***[Interviewer:]*** *Does this look to be one of those typical litigation things that never ends?*
>
> *It could be, you never know. It's been going a couple years. They did the discoveries, they deposed McMahon and Jericho, and they both admitted to everything. And, I did my depositions, and they sent everything to the judge, and now it's just a waiting game. And you could sit here for two months, you could sit here for a year, waiting for the judge's decision on the court date or whatever.*

All right, from the beginning; Yes, Zbyszko does not have a trademark on the term "Living Legend" like Christian has on "Captain Charisma". But he has been using it for so long it is synonymous with him. Actually, he has been using it since 1980, which would definitely put it in the "common law trademark" category. From Barbara Brabec's World:

> *Your constant use of an unregistered mark gains trademark status through the years. I had an interesting trademark case a few years back when someone stole my Homemade Money book title and applied it to a sleazy MLM magazine. The publisher hadn't yet applied for a trademark, so my attorney, Mary Helen Sears, was able to stop him from using this name. Because it has been so closely identified with my name since 1984, she was able to prove that my personal reputation would have been damaged if someone had seen this name on their magazine. Ms. Sears sent a powerfully-worded series of letters that convinced the publisher he had to stop using my book's title—or else.*
>
> *As Ms. Sears explained, "Because it is strongly associated with Barbara Brabec in the minds of persons engaged in, or interested in engaging in, home-based business enterprises, the term 'Homemade Money' has acquired a secondary meaning, not only as the identification of a book that has the reputation of being the handbook and primer in how to start, maintain and conduct a home-based business, but as the trademark and*

> service mark for educational materials relating to home-based business, and for educational and informational activity of all types in regard to such business." Thus, anyone using this phrase for their own profit would be in direct violation of trademark law 15 U.S.C. 1125(a), and I could take appropriate legal action against them.

Although now associated with something that would discredit him, Zbyszko could potentially lose money from the use of the term. Others might have believed he was associated with the WWE, or had given his rights over. But this could not be further from the truth. Larry was still using and making money off of the "Living Legend" trademark, and nothing but death is going to change that.

In an interview with Slam Sports in December 2003 Larry added:

> *Vince has a monopoly now, so he does whatever he feels like doing, even if that means taking something I've been using for more than 20 years. You don't see him being called 'Macho Man' Chris Jericho. It's just the arrogance.*

The WWE and McMahon truly were trying to take advantage of their monopoly position and force their will on the entire wrestling world, in direct opposition to the Sherman Anti-Trust Act (we've talked about this a lot, WWE).

Actually, Zbyszko did not just launch a lawsuit. He tried to play fair with the WWE. From an interview conducted with George Papoulias in January 2003:

> ***[George:]*** *What's the story behind your beef with Vince McMahon. We all know on the WWA tour last year, you shot a pretty riveting promo on him. What's the beef between you and him?*
>
> *Well, basically I have no beef on a personal level. I mean I've never worked for Vince or the WWF in 22 years. And I never badmouthed him, it was just business, I did mine and he did his. Then one day all of a sudden, Chris Jericho is using my trademark. And then I found out about it, called some acquaintances in Vince's upper echelon and said "hey man, you're taking my trademark here, my phone is ringing [off] the hook, people think I'm coming there to wrestle Jericho." Then I said "I'm not getting upset about it, but being the*

> business man I am, if you guys are going to take it, then maybe we can do some business." And to make a long story short, their attorneys contacted me and tried to con me into signing a release. They told me that they took it, they're going to use it and I'm not to interfere. So, they basically drew first blood by taking my trademark, which made no sense for Jericho anyway. WWE refused to stop using it; they ignored a cease and desist, and basically told me to go to hell. Well, I worked too hard for that, I can't go to hell and so here we are now with three federal lawsuits.
>
> **[George:]** What's the latest by the way, on the lawsuit that you filed against the WWE?
>
> Well, it was filed last April, so it's been close to about ten months. Some depositions have started. I did a deposition and I believe yesterday my attorneys were in Connecticut deposing Vince, so I'm sure he really likes me now (laughing). It's just too bad, they're kind of a monopoly and they think they can do what they want. There's nowhere else to go and they think the boys are just going to be run over. So you got to fight for what you work for, otherwise it's not going to work in your life.
>
> **[George:]** Before these lawsuits were filed, would you have ever considered working a program with Chris Jericho in the WWE?
>
> Well, it was one of the first things that entered my mind. I mean if they're using my name, then it would be a natural. But, it was half emotional, I'm trying to keep business as business, but at the same time when you work for something so long and after promoting myself as the living legend for 22 years, it's a stab in the back when they take it. I mean why couldn't they call him "Macho Man" Chris Jericho, "Hot Rod" Chris Jericho or "Undertaker 2" Chris Jericho? They just figured, "what's Zbyszko going to do to our corporation, screw him."

So you see, Larry tried to be the reasonable one and just do business as he's always done, but it was Vince and the WWE who wanted to just push the buttons because they can.

But you'll probably notice that nobody in the WWE is calling themselves the "Living Legend" today. Huh?

AND WHAT HAS HE DONE WITH THAT TRADEMARK?

Now, Larry is the Living Legend as the Director of Authority for TNA. But he is also making major strides in a new career—Professional Golf. From Wikipedia:

> Zbyszko is an excellent golfer (his handicap is zero), and has tried to build a second athletic career in the sport. As such he has competed in Hooters Senior Series events and has attempted to qualify for individual Champions Tour events. He also intends to enter the Champions Tour Q School to gain full membership in that Tour.

And from an interview with Scott Brown in Florida Today in June 2005:

> Zbyszko, who lives about 20 miles north of St. Augustine, is 6-feet, 240 pounds and said he regularly hits his tee shots between 270 and 280 yards. The biggest adjustment he has had to make as a touring pro involves the mental part of the game.
>
> It's a measure of the fame he earned as a professional wrestler that Zbyszko signed more than just scorecards while playing on the Hooters Senior Series.
>
> When some fellow competitors realized he was the Larry Zbyszko, word quickly spread that the guy who once wrestled in a sold-out Shea Stadium was playing on their rather anonymous golf tour.
>
> He was asked to sign his share of autographs, though requests were usually prefaced or followed with "for a buddy."

You see, Larry is not just bragging when he is talking about his golf game. He is a good golfer who is trying to improve his game on the professional circuit. On the same end, he is not forgetting what made him famous. There are some that would try to downplay their connection to professional wrestling (see:

Rock, The), but Larry just takes it in stride. It has been his life for over thirty years, so why would he not acknowledge his wrestling credentials while out on the greens?

And since when is pursuing a new career a crime? Larry has found something else he is good at and is working hard to better himself for it. If at 52 he wants to have a second career, how can we think to stop him?

It is not like wrestling is his whole life anyway. From Wikipedia:

> *In addition to being a proficient golfer, Zbyszko is a licensed pilot. He holds a black belt in Judo, and is trained in the usage of nunchaku.*

So you see, Larry has many interests outside of wrestling that he can follow, but none compare to everything he has given to the industry.

THE LEGENDARY WRAP-UP

Larry Zbyszko truly is the Living Legend. Aside from being in one of the 50 Greatest Tag Teams of All Time, he has had a long and illustrious career. His accomplishments in creative angles seen for the first time, selling out arenas around the world, winning championships, and always putting business first should forever legitimize him as one of the best. Yet, he is often overlooked because he is not the loudest, he is not the most revered, and often puts others above himself. His fame came at a time that most modern wrestling fans do not remember, and his misadventures have been blown out of proportion.

If we are to remember Larry Zbyszko, it should be for everything he has done, for the trails he has blazed, and for the money he has made. Let us not brush Larry Zbyszko aside, and instead prepare one day for his place in the Hall of Fame.

The defense rests.

AFTER THE TRIAL

HUNG JURY

IN THE CASE OF THE IWC VS. LARRY ZBYSZKO, ZBYSZKO HAS BEEN

ACCUSSED OF HAVING AN OVERINFLATED SENSE OF WORTH AND DID NOT MEAN MUCH IN THE HISTORY OF PROFESSIONAL WRESTLING.

And with 86.1% of the vote, Larry Zbyszko was found:

NOT GUILTY!

OK, so I definitely was expecting to win this one with little problem. And as expected, voter turnout was lower than normal. I know that Zbyszko isn't a topic that everyone is interested in, but he was definitely worth defending. If I just enlightened a few people to what Zbyszko has done for our industry, then it was completely worth it. And judging by the e-mails I did just that.

There was another reason I wanted to defend Zbyszko now. I have touched on this elsewhere, but what we are taking about is pacing. You bring the crowd down with a less heat-generating match right before the big matches so that the big matches have even more heat. Well, that's what I did here. As you can tell by the next chapter, we are stepping it up!

RESPONSE

This really being more of a history lesson, most people were just happy to learn something about a topic they were unfamiliar with. However, some people were around for the original run:

> *I am an old school guy. I grew up in the day of kayfab, and [I] must say that I have [gotten] real sick of all the bashing that [goes] on with the whole IWC. I came up in [an] odd way. My mom used to date one of the ring guys that worked for [C]rocket, so I grew up running around backstage (bugging the boys I am sure)[.] I went to the tv tapings in [downtown] [H]igh [P]oint. Hell I was there for [Flair's] first title win. Anyway I did not mean to get off track. I just wanted to say thank you for doing some positive [writing].*
>
> **Michael Roach**

Even people who voted "not guilty" were not entirely happy with our defendant, especially in light of what we just established with Scott Hall:

> *I feel that you do need to hold Larry accountable for one inexcusable breach of announcer etiquette. During the WCW v nWo feud, fringe member Louie Spicolli sadly passed away. When something like this happens, it's appropriate to take a moment to remember the man, not what side of the face/heel fence he's on. I distinctly recall the Nitro after the passing, when Tony made mention of it, and passed it over to Larry, who could have simply said that he'd be missed. But instead, he made some smart-ass comment about how "I really want to say what I think about him, but out of respect for the family, I won't"*
>
> *Come on man! The guy just died, maybe you could drop the storyline for just a second?*
>
> ***Matt Simon***

This I could not refute:

> *I vaguely recall the comment you are talking about. I think part of that, too, was Spicolli had some drug and behavioral problems and Larry really did not have anything nice to say about him. I agree, though, that in cases like that, you just have to keep your mouth shut or send your condolences to the family. Even if you don't like someone, you have to remember that someone out there does care about them.*

VINCE MCMAHON IN THE DEATH OF OWEN HART

INTRO

SOME DAME WALKED INTO MY OFFICE AND SAID...

That first dame was Patrick Kelly, who first walked in in May 2005. **Phatpat** said:

> I did not see the show personally, but it is an interesting situation from both an emotional and business point of view. Owen Hart's death. The case I want to see defended is Vince's initial decision to keep the show going and then the ongoing decision to keep the show going after JR made the announcement.

And then there was the man who I know no longer reads me, but will get a plug anyway, in one **MATTHEW Roberts**:

> Defending McMahon in the case of Owen Hart's death.

Well he had some other words, but I'm holding them for personal use, much like those of regular **Brad McLeod** who said:

> With all the discussions back and forth on the subject (I got into it today) how about a Defense of Continuing Over The Edge '99 after Owen died.

After announcing the case (the first time) **Charlie Sword** threw in:

> Kudos to you for taking on a crazy tough task in defending Vinnie in the death of Owen.

As did **Lost Soul** who said:

> [D]efending [V]ince in the death of [O]wen???
> [G]ood luck with that, you have convinced me
> before, but [I] dunno about this one.

Luck! Ha, I don't need luck! I just need... the truth.

WHY THIS?

Owen Hart is my favorite wrestler of all time. Period. I appreciated everything this man could do in the ring, and was always upset that he never got the chance to be a World Champion. I respect everything about him.

Vince McMahon I hold in a much lower regard. As an NWA/WCW mark, I automatically despise him. I really don't enjoy "sports entertainment" and think Vince more lucked into much of his success rather than created it (see: Hulk Hogan, Steve Austin, the Rock). Not saying he does not work hard (because he does), I just don't think he's as good as he thinks he is.

That said, there are times when Vince McMahon is right about what he does. Just because I do not like him, that does not mean I am going to let that blind me to the truth. Sometimes, Vince himself needs a defense (see: sexually harassing a tanning salon girl), and this is the place he gets it.

Vince McMahon, you and I might never get along in real life or philosophy, but when you need a defense, this is the place to come. And this time, you deserve it.

VINCE KILLED OWEN

Let's just get right to it. The accusation is that Vince killed Owen Hart through his actions by forcing Owen to do a stunt that (a) he did not want to do, (b) was not safe, and (c) was not part of his job. As a matter of fact, in Marc Ciampa's inflammatory article about the death of Owen Hart in June 1999 he wrote this:

> *Stu, along with the rest of the Hart family believed that Owen may have been a sacrifice for Vince McMahon and his constant need to better his competition, World Championship Wrestling. "Frankly, wrestling was getting so far out and my poor brother Owen was a sacrifice for the ratings," said Owen's sister Ellie.*

A sacrifice? That would mean that there was INTENT to kill or cause harm. There was no intent here; we are talking about a tragic ACCIDENT. Word choice during this emotional time led people to say incredibly incriminating remarks that were eventually picked up by the rest of the wrestling community and the general media. Listen, I cannot stress this enough: the death of Owen Hart was an accident. To suggest anything otherwise is a fallacy. But we'll get back to that in a second.

The question at the moment is: if it was an accident, who caused it?

For that, we first go back to Rajah's account of Owen Hart:

> In the early months of spring in 1999, Jeff Jarrett and Owen Hart had been building a reputation as a strong tag team, with Debra as their manager. Management had planned the team to eventually split up, and Owen [began] to lust after Debra, infuriating Jarrett, which would in turn plant the seeds for a bitter and very personal feud.
>
> Owen, happily married in real life, didn't want his young children to see him cheating on his wife every Monday night, so he outright refused the angle. It was an honorable, if stubborn decision.
>
> The result, was that Owen was saddled with the Blue Blazer gimmick. It was a persona he'd donned early in his career as a glorified jobber, and one he was forced to revisit. It was punishment for declining a well thought out angle, orchestrated to humiliate Owen, who has to don a superhero persona and spend much of his time mimicking the wrestlers in WCW.

I will highlight part of that for you:

> **[H]e outright refused the angle...**

He refused the angle? Everything I have read about Vince with Owen Hart was that Vince FORCED Owen into the stunt that took his life. Forced, huh? If Owen could refuse an entire storyline, then why could he not refuse a PPV stunt? It seems off that Owen would have the power to stop one thing yet not another.

Also, this article makes some rather large jumps in judgment, including that his decision was honorable and that the Blue Blazer was a glorified jobber. I'm not saying that I agree or disagree with these statements, but the truth is that these opinions of Owen Hart's actions and characters have been spread as the absolute truth and not the opinion it is. The same can be said that the Blue Blazer gimmick was designed to humiliate Owen. If that was the case, then why was he scheduled to win the Intercontinental title the night of his death? By Rajah's own volition:

> [A]t "Over the Edge" 1999, he was booked to win the WWF Intercontinental Title. After that, Owen was booked to break free of the Blue Blazer gimmick, and would go onto be called "The Game", and enter into a program with Edge.

Read between the lines. There was a plan to go with the Blue Blazer. Let us not forget that several other wrestlers were dressing up as the Blue Blazer as part of a running joke. Not everything in the WWE is designed to be a serious contest. Some things are meant to be comedies and create a break from the tension. Although this role was not normally associated with Owen, that does not mean it was not his responsibility when it was assigned to him.

So Owen accepted his role as the Blue Blazer and every angle and stunt that went along with it. Before the Kemper Arena, Owen had performed the stunt several times. On top of that, others had also done the same or similar stunts, from Shawn Michaels to Sting.

Speaking of Sting, who did the then WWF bring in to set the stunt up? Why none other than Bobby Talbert! Who's Bobby Talbert you ask? Why he's the man who helped rig Sting's rafter jumps for more than a year. Here was a man with a lot of experience who Vince brought in specifically to help Owen make sure nothing would go wrong.

The main reason for bringing in Talbert was because Vince did not like how Owen looked after he repelled from ceiling in St. Louis at Survivor Series 1998. After landing, Owen fumbled with all of the locks on his harness which took several moments and looked awkward. To alleviate this, Vince brought in an expert in Talbert and charged him with finding a better solution.

In turn, Talbert bought a quick release harness from Amspec, Inc. and attached it to his rigging. Keep that in mind. Back to our Rajah article:

> Bobby requested that Owen would rehearse the stunt, seeing as how the two had never worked together before. Owen declined. It was clear that he hated the stunt, and didn't want to do it for any more times than it was necessary. It is reported, that Owen tried to persuade management [that] being lowered from the rafters wasn't essential to

> his character in the days leading up to the pay-per-view, only for Vince McMahon to insist otherwise.
>
> As Owen was eating his lunch with friends, and Bobby Talbert was [taking] Hart through the protocol of the new quick-release system, Steve Taylor, the WWF's VP of Event Operations, interjected and told Owen he would have to do a dry run. Owen was reassured the equipment had been thoroughly tested earlier in the day, as Talbert had successfully lowered a 250-pound sand bag, and his assistant Matt Allmen, in two earlier attempts.
>
> Owen was [scheduled] to turn up to the middle of the arena to rehearse the stunt at 2pm. But, unbeknownst to anybody, he [snuck] out of the arena to catch some fresh air, and didn't return until 3.30pm. It was clear he left to avoid having to practice the stunt, and thought his absence would go unnoticed and management would quickly forget their orders.
>
> But they didn't. And they weren't happy with Owen either.
>
> The test run went perfectly, right up until Owen landed, when Owen inexcusably forget Talbert's earlier specific orders. He didn't pull the release cord, which caused a few WWF officials to get visibly annoyed at Owen. He was asked to do the whole thing again, but declined, and avoiding any potential argument, he walked forcefully back to his locker room.

Let's go through the facts. First, Talbert did the proper testing on the equipment with both a sandbag and a person. He then wanted Owen to do a test run, but Owen refused! Again, Owen refused! I find it odd that Owen is sometimes able to refuse and sometimes not. And here again, Owen went to management to try to persuade them out of doing the stunt. Why did he not use his power of refusal as before?

No, there is no doubt that management and Vince did persuade Owen to do the stunt. They wanted it done, and they wanted it to look good. But at the same time, they brought in an expert to help out. They wanted Owen to follow his lead and directions.

What did Owen do? First, he refused to show up to rehearsal. How could he not be afraid of the repercussions of leaving the arena for an hour and half and yet be afraid of the repercussions of not doing the stunt at all? These inconsistencies make me question the conclusions that Rajah, Ciampa, and others have come to.

Not only that, but read this line again:

> ***Owen [forgot] Talbert's earlier specific orders.***

Owen forgot specific orders? Might it be that Owen was not paying attention to his directions, directions designed to keep him safe? Might Owen Hart be in the wrong for not following directions on a stunt he agreed to do?

And what of the stunt? Why was a "wrestler" like Owen doing a stunt like that anyway? From MSNBC in May 1999:

> *McMahon said WWF wrestlers will stop performing the aerial move that killed Hart, but said other stunts will continue.*
>
> *"Stunts like this are performed at major sporting events on a routine basis in Hollywood," he said. "We compete with Hollywood for entertainment."*

McMahon is right. The WWE is not a wrestling organization. TNA is a wrestling organization. ROH is a wrestling organization. ECW and WCW were wrestling organizations. The WWE, as I stated above, is "Sports Entertainment."

Vince was not just in competition with WCW, he was also in competition with all of Hollywood and Television (and additionally today the Internet, Satellite entertainment, Podcasting, DVDs, etc...). Because of that, he did want to have wrestlers take on additional roles. Would the Undertaker exist if not for wanting someone to take on a role beyond a wrestler? Would the Rock & Wrestling Connection have ever happened?

Owen was just another person in a long line asked to go above and beyond the normal call of his vocation. And he chose to go along with it. There was no forcing. No one pushed Owen off the top of the Kemper Arena. As a matter of fact, he lowered himself. Back to Rajah:

> *Not wanting to be late, Owen briskly negotiated the catwalk, taking a right turn and walking along a narrow pathway for 30-feet. Now at the center, directly 100-feet or so below was the WWF ring. Surrounding that, were around 18,350 fans who were watching on as Al Snow fought Hardcore Holly for the WWF Hardcore Title. But Owen, could simply not let himself look down, because he had been afraid of heights his whole life.*
>
> *Owen began to get ready. He took his costume out of his bag and began to get dressed, but didn't put on everything until he hooked himself into the harness. Chief rigger Talbert made sure Owen was correctly fitted and helped him position his awkward cape[,] too, that had been [strangling] Hart in rehearsals.*
>
> *Once Talbert attached the rope to the lowering mechanism, the lights were dimmed, and Owen was seconds away from his descent. He had trouble properly positioning himself onto the scaffolding before getting a final helping hand from Talbert's assistant. For a couple of minutes, Owen hung there, in the air, floating. He was holding onto the railings as Talbert made sure not to release him until he got his cue.*
>
> *No matter how much you think you love somebody, your instinct is to step back when you see a pool of their blood edge up too close... Similarly, when a tragedy occurs, it's easier to move away and forget, than it is to stick around and help clean up the mess.*
>
> *As the backstage interview of the Blue Blazer was airing, Owen extended his elbows away from his body and tried to once again [maneuver] his cape.*
>
> *It was then that Owen accidentally triggered the quick-release. And it was then, that Owen fell 78 feet to his death, screaming all the way down, until he violently landed on his left side, shattering his left arm and causing fatal internal injuries, as the audience watched on in horror.*

First off, what is with the "inside Owen's head" stuff? I am not Owen, nobody is Owen, and nobody was with him to hear his thoughts. We do not know what

Owen was thinking up there. Even his supposed fear of heights comes into question. Who suggested this? Post hubris, several members of the Hart family said Owen had a fear of heights. Why did this not come out before?

Also, we look at the footage today and say the audience reacted in terror because we react in terror knowing what has happened. From our previously mentioned MSNBC article:

> "We thought it was a doll at first," said Robert McCome, 15. "We thought they were just playing with us. We were really shocked when we found out that it was no joke."

And from Wikipedia:

> The crowd, believing that this was "part of the act" (Ross stating repeatedly on TV that it was not), cheered with a standing ovation as Owen was carried out.

You can see from these examples that the audience thought it was the show, that there was shock but not terror. The terror comes from after the fact, ex post facto, not from what actually happened.

Hold on to that thought for a bit. For now, back to the events at hand.

Follow this pattern. One: Talbert and his assistant had the responsibility of making sure Owen was strapped in and properly secure. Amspec had the responsibility of selling quality equipment to the specific needs of this stunt. Owen had the responsibility of following Talbert's orders.

Yet, Amspec's equipment failed. Owen did not follow Talbert's orders. Talbert and his assistant did not keep Owen under control and safe.

And what of Vince McMahon?

He was trying to run a show, and had hired people to do work that he knew he could not do. He had entrusted others with his vision, and at that point it was well out his hands.

And the death of Owen was just the beginning.

THE SETTLEMENT

After Owen's tragic accident, the lawsuits began to fly. From the Stamford Advocate in October 2003:

> Three weeks after the fatal fall Hart's family sued the WWE, Lewmar, the city of Kansas City and 10 other defendants.

No waiting, no thinking, just suing, right away.

It took a while, but the WWE and the Harts settled out of court for $18 million in November 2000. Now, just because the WWE settled does not mean that Vince was admitting guilt. Sometimes, parties settle with people who make outrageous claims because it is cheaper to pay them off them to spend the days in court. Time in court for someone like Vince McMahon literally costs hundreds of thousands of dollars a day.

Also take into account where the money went to. From the Kansas City Star in November 2000:

> The terms of the settlement call for Martha Hart, Hart's widow, to get $10 million; the children, 8-year-old Oje Hart and 5-year-old Athena Hart, to get $3 million each; and Hart's parents, Stu and Helen Hart, to get $1 million each.

Basically, the money went to Owen's wife and his children. Do you think that Vince and company perhaps did want to make some type of payment to just help out the family for a long while? Is it beyond reason that Vince may have agreed to the settlement not only to end it quickly, but to try to end the suffering of the Hart family and support them for years to come?

Then again, the WWE was not even paying all of it. Back to the article:

> The settlement amount is being paid by the World Wrestling Federation and its insurer, TIG Insurance Co. The WWF, a publicly held company, said in regulatory filings last week that it would take a $7 million charge in the wake of the settlement amount from the companies that manufactured and sold the equipment involved in the accident.

So the WWF was insured for a good portion of the $18 million and only had to pay $7 million. But they were not stopping there. The article states:

> [Judge] Long approved the settlement over the objection of the manufacturer of Hart's trigger-latch shackle, Lewmar Inc., which argued that the settlement could impair its ability to defend itself against the WWF's claims for reimbursement.
>
> Both Lewmar and Amspec Inc., which sold the shackle to Hart's stunt rigger, were among the defendants originally sued by the Hart family. The family, however, dismissed both companies from the case in April.
>
> The dismissals came after Lewmar and Amspec reached settlements with the Hart family calling for a mutual release of claims. Notably, the settlement's did not call for Lewmar or Amspec to pay any damages.
>
> In court documents, the WWF has questioned whether those settlements were reached in good faith, and Long has yet to approve them. The WWF is concerned that the settlements will prevent it from recouping the settlement proceeds from Amspec and Lewmar.

And they had to question it with good reason. In the article it states:

> An additional impediment to the WWF's efforts to recover the $18 million arose Monday, when Amspec filed for Chapter 7 bankruptcy in Van Nuys, Calif. The bankruptcy petition lists the WWF and the McMahons as contingent creditors.

You see, Amspec knew the WWF and Vince was in the right and that they had lied and sold faulty equipment that could not do the job it was purportedly designed to do. In order to protect itself from litigation, it went into bankruptcy protection and listed the WWF and the McMahons as creditors, even though the lawsuit had not been launched yet. But it would not work out for them. From the Stamford Advocate article mentioned above:

> *Before settling with the WWE, the Harts dismissed the other defendants, including Lewmar, which had reached its own settlement with the family. The agreement did not call for Lewmar to pay any damages, although the WWE alleged that Lewmar had liability insurance of $50 million.*
>
> *WWE questioned whether the settlement with Lewmar had been reached in good faith. The WWE's protest stemmed from its concern that the settlement would bar it from seeking reimbursement from Lewmar. Under Missouri law, a defendant cannot seek reimbursement from a co-defendant who reaches a good-faith settlement with the plaintiff.*
>
> *After a hearing on that issue last year, Long, an out [of] state judge who presided over the original case, ruled that there was "overwhelming evidence" that the settlement was marked by fraud and said WWE's case against Lewmar could proceed.*

Additionally:

> *World Wrestling Entertainment Inc. has settled its lawsuit against the British maker of a harness whose premature release led to the 1999 death of wrestler Owen Hart in a fall at Kansas City's Kemper Arena.*
>
> *The case in which the Stamford, Conn.-based pro wrestling organization sought to recover $18 million from Lewmar Inc. went to trial three weeks ago in U.S. District Court at Kansas City and was expected to last at least two more weeks.*
>
> *The jurors applauded Tuesday after Craig O'Dear, an attorney for WWE, announced that the parties had agreed to the settlement on Monday. A gag order imposed by Judge Douglas Long Jr. prohibits attorneys for the parties from talking about the case, but jurors interviewed later by The Kansas City Star said the agreement called for Lewmar to pay WWE $9 million.*

The wrap-up? The courts found that the WWF and Vince McMahon were not in violation nor responsible for the death of Owen Hart. The manufacturer and sellers of the harness equipment were primarily responsible.

The Show Must Go On

Yet, despite not holding responsibility for the death of Owen Hart, Vince McMahon is responsible for having the show go on.

Now, we have already covered the fans in the arena. They were unaware that anything they were seeing was not in the script. Let's go back to another quote from the MSNBC article:

> "It was still tons of fun," said Barry Bickel, 21. "But that just dampened the whole thing."

The show was still a fun show. It did its job of entertaining the audience. But more than that, the severity of Owen's injuries were not known.

During the autopsy, it was revealed that brain functions had ceased six minutes after the fall. But at the same time Owen still had pulse and respiratory functions. For all those who could see, he seemed alive, though badly injured. It would not be until an hour later that he would be pronounced dead. The show had been going on for a while beforehand.

And it is not like this is without precedent. On a live episode of WCW Thunder Rick Steiner hit Buff Bagwell with a bulldog off the top rope, a move he had done a thousand times. This time, something went wrong, and Bagwell broke his neck. He was temporarily paralyzed and in the ring for twenty minutes, yet the show went on.

Years earlier, Owen Hart himself set up Steve Austin for a piledriver, a move he had done a thousand times before. This time, something went wrong, and Stone Cold broke his neck. He was temporarily paralyzed and Owen literally pulled him on top of himself for the win. Yet despite the scary injury, the show went on.

Injuries happen in and out of the ring, but the show has always gone on. There was no reason to believe Owen was dead or was going to be. No one even knew how far he had fallen from. Everyone in the arena was watching the screen, not watching the ceiling. For all they knew he had fallen from about twenty or thirty feet. And we already knew that it was possible to survive that. From Marc Chiampa's previously mentioned diatribe:

> People should have noticed that he was beginning to take things a little bit too far when wrestler Mick Foley (aka "Mankind") fought a cage match several months ago despite a separated shoulder. Another incident included Foley being body slammed from the top of a "cell" fifteen feet into the middle of the ring on a pile of thumbtacks.

Not to mention the matches that had happened between Edge and Christian and the Hardy Boyz. Hard hitting bumps were more common at that point in time. It was reasonable to believe that this was just another one, and that Owen was made of tough enough stuff to get up from it eventually.

The true extent of Owen's injuries and the actual cause of his death were not revealed until months after the incident. How was anyone to know he was dead in that ring when it took doctors months to figure out what really killed him?

And what would have happened had Vince suddenly stopped the show? He would have opened himself up to litigation from everyone who bought a ticket or ordered it on PPV. Though what happened to Owen was a tragedy, it does not stop Vince from having to deliver his final product. If he did not do that, the flood gates would be open. Even if all were dismissed, the time and money it would take fighting them would do the damage anyway.

No, the choice was simple but hard. The show had to go on. Not just for the money, not just for the fans, but because it made sense. Because it was what was always done. Because it was what was expected. Because the show does go on.

Martha Hart: Ultimate Martyr

Still, the animosity towards Vince and the WWF over the death of Owen Hart has only increased with time. Despite the fact that courts of law have found Vince and company without fault, there is one voice that has kept antagonizing them. And that voice is Martha Hart, widow of Owen Hart.

Mike D'Amour wrote in the Calgary Sun:

> Hart family members are expected to be at the Raw is War event and are expected to be discussing a new business deal.
>
> "There is that rumour and I believe it's true," Martha Hart told the Sun.

> "If anyone from (the Hart family) were to go to the show it would be disrespectful and disgusting."

The article continues:

> Smith Hart, who trains wrestlers, told the Sun he has no hard feelings about the WWF and will indeed be ringside tonight.
>
> The family patriarch Stu Hart told SLAM! Wrestling on the CANOE website that he would be open to meeting with the WWF.
>
> "I have no axe to grind with Vince," he said.
>
> "I haven't been officially invited yet, (but) if he wants me to be introduced ... I'd say, 'please, Vince, if you get a chance, just for old times' sake, give me a plug.' "
>
> That bothers Martha.
>
> "Whatever their motivation is, it's hurtful to me," she said.

So Martha continues to lament how horrible the WWF is, yet everyone else in the Hart family has forgiven them. Granted, she has a strong emotional attachment to the issue, but her judgment has to be called into question. Says the conclusion to the article:

> There were also rumours Owen's brother and wrestling legend Bret "The Hitman" Hart would be coaxed out of retirement by the WWF.
>
> But Martha said the idea was out of the question.
>
> "I talked to Bret a few days ago and I can tell you he would never have anything to do with the WWF."

We know that not to be true, either. Bret sure enough went back to Vince for his DVD. He may not be in the ring (yet) in 2006, but he has something to do with the WWF. Martha's ability to judge events and people is surely in question.

Beyond that, what is Martha's motivation? She had already won her court case, yet she continued (and continues) to attack the WWE and Vince.

The answer lies at Owen's funeral.

During her speech, Martha promised one thing: "a day of reckoning". She is still out for revenge against the WWE and Vince, no matter what the facts say.

And that is simply how many people react. In many ways I want to react that way, too. Owen Hart, as my favorite wrestler, makes me want to attack someone for his death. But the facts of this case compel me to realize he played a greater role in his own death than I ever wanted to admit before.

ONE LAST WALK DOWN THE TUNNEL

Owen Hart's death was a tragedy broadcast around the world. Because of this, and what Owen meant to so many people, we are ready to lash out at the first person we see, and that person is Vince McMahon. But Vince is not the one who holds the blame. He was just a man running a show, a man who entrusted others to carry out his vision. But a faulty piece of equipment, an overconfident stunt coordinator, and an over-antsy Owen Hart caused his death. There are so many inconsistencies and beliefs, but very few genuine facts. Those facts were fought in court and Vince and the WWF won on all fronts.

Vince did decide the show must go on, and looking back it seems questionable. But it was the correct decision for everyone involved. It's easy to look back with all the facts and say things should be different. It's a lot harder to be sitting in that big chair and making the decision without any facts and knowledge at all.

Owen Hart led a remarkable career, and it's sad that his legacy to the world is his death. But let us not drag an innocent man down with him. Vince has done enough horrible things in his life that he is guilty of. But in this case, he is an innocent man, and deserves to have that recognition.

The defense rests.

AFTER THE TRIAL

HUNG JURY

IN THE CASE OF THE IWC VS. VINCE MCMAHON IN THE DEATH OF OWEN HART, VINCE HAS BEEN ACCUSED OF BEING RESPONSIBLE FOR THE DEATH OF OWEN HART AND FOR BEING HEARTLESS AND UNPROFESSIONAL FOR HAVING THE OVER THE EDGE PPV CONTINUE.

If there was a chance I could lose a case, you would think it would start with this one. But with 84.9% of the vote, Vince McMahon in the Death of Owen Hart was found:

NOT GUILTY!

All I can say is... wow. I never, not for the life of me, thought I would get a Not Guilty with that high of a percentage. I honestly did not think I could have gotten above a 65%. I'm very happy that I did so well, and just hope the naysayers out there do not give up. I only get to become a better writer when I get challenged, so if you think something is off, I want to hear about it. Hell, even the people who vote not guilty sometimes tell me something is off.

Response

About two months after the original article was released, I got an e-mail with the subject line of **"I'm sure you were expecting this.."**. For the first time ever, someone directly involved in one of these cases reached out to me, but the person was not exactly a happy camper. Despite the subject line, I was not expecting to hear from **Bobby Talbert** himself, the man who did the rigging for the stunt:

> *Your article on Owen Hart was just brought to my attention... You should do more research[;] there are a few points at which you prove you are not and were not directly connected to this case... The calling me an "over confident stunt rigger" [is] not only untrue but lends another fact to show your ignorance in this case. I will give you credit for the amount of reading you did.. You seem to have [overlooked] a few points... you never mentioned that [L]ewmar had 2 prior accidents resulting from the faulty snap shackle which they not only knew about and didn't say anything, but also had an engineer who redesigned it so that the machining process could never produce this problem.. You also [mentioned] that Owen was still breathing and had a pulse, Did you not read any of the EMT's reports that stated the FIRST EMT to arrive immediately started CPR.. You don't start CPR on a person with an existing pulse that is still breathing....... [Although] your article made some valid points, you missed a few as well... It's seems like an [over-zealous] writer like yourself would be inclined to be truthful and accurate and not so quick to point fingers and name call.... good day to you sir[.]*

I was taken aback and had to think quite a bit on this response. And due to this, my own schedule, and the backlog of e-mails I had yet to respond to, it took me a good six months to reply:

> *Dear Mr. Talbert,*
>
> *Sorry for my delayed response. Your correspondence got buried in my files and I have not had the opportunity to revisit it until now.*
>
> *First to your point, you do need to understand my work. In Defense Of... is an anthology series and, as such, I do not have the time to research every single detail of a case. My points are more general in that I am trying to establish that those who have "over-reacted" to a subject at least see the other side of the equation. In this case, I was defending Vince McMahon against people who said he was responsible for Owen's untimely passing and his actions after the fact.*
>
> *Not once did I EVER proclaim that I am in way associated with you, Vince McMahon, the Hart family or anything to do with the case. It should be quite obvious that I am an outsider and have claimed so from the beginning. As an outsider, I was doing research on the material that was readily available, from [first-hand] accounts to reporters on the scene to my own experiences. For this case, I did about twenty hours of research, but to do more would go well beyond my capabilities.*
>
> *So yes, you are correct in that I did not read the EMT's reports, nor did I personally interview anyone else involved. These articles I write are not my [full-time] job and I cannot devote my entire life to a [single-issue case], no matter how personal it may be to certain parties. I am sorry if certain points were left out or other areas could have been more thoroughly explored, but that was not the intent of my article.*
>
> *I try to be as truthful and accurate as possible, but you need to read more carefully. I spent a good deal of the article talking about the prior accidents from the faulty snaps and the salesman who sold them not being totally honest. You were*

> overheated because of one off the cuff comment that may or may not have been out of line and read what you wanted to read, not what was actually there. For most of the article, I do defend you as a competent stunt rigger who did a lot right but whose directions were not followed. You skipped all the complimentary things said about you and focused on one negative comment.
>
> In response, I ask you take your own advice and do more research before you start name calling. I understand if you are upset with me and I hold no qualms about it. I wish you the best of luck and continued success in your career in life. Good luck out there.

Suffice to say, I never heard from Mr. Talbert again. Although perhaps I should be thankful as it would have probably led nowhere decent. However, upon re-reading my own article, I agree that I did not make my point about him well. What I was trying to say was that it was at least possible that he held some partial responsibility. Since this case was about Vince McMahon, all I wanted to do was deflect from my client and have the audience say, "Hey, aside from Vince McMahon, here are a bunch of other parties that may or may not have fault, but we should look more at them than at Vince."

I should have been more careful with my own words and not made suppositions about his character, the same way I correctly lambasted Rajah for going into Owen Hart's head. I am not Bobby Talbert and do not know what he was thinking as it happened, and therefore I cannot assign a mood and response to him. I still believe he overreacted in his message to me and did miss all of the defense I did of him (specifically putting blame on Owen Hart himself for not doing as Mr. Talbert instructed), but he felt the need to the defend himself against some internet reporter.

But then again, I was and am hardly the only one who questioned Mr. Talbert's abilities and his personal liability in what happened. In May 2019, Tom Buchanan—who was with the WWE for ten years at the time of the accident and headed up the internal investigation—made a since deleted Facebook post (that can be read in its entirety here, courtesy of Jeremy Lambert of fightful.com) that included the following:

> The photo accompanying this post is of sample hardware I purchased to show Vince McMahon what went wrong. This hardware is a different brand than what was used to suspend Owen, but it is functionally identical. The bottom silver piece is a "shackle" and the top silver piece is a spring-loaded "snap shackle." The shackle was attached

> to a harness Owen was wearing, and the snap shackle was attached to a rope that suspended him above ring. The red line represents the rope that ran from the snap shackle to the catwalk, and the green line represents a release cord running from the snap shackle along Owen's side to a small grip/hand release. Owen was to have been lowered to the wrestling ring and then pull the hand release which would open the snap shackle and allow him to step away from the rope. Somehow the snap shackle opened when Owen was being staged for the stunt, while he was suspended alongside the catwalk 80 feet in the air.
>
> Initial thinking on the night of the accident was that Owen may have accidentally grabbed the release line in fear as he hung above the ring (in spite of it reportedly being securely taped to his harness), but my experimentation with the sample hardware a few days later led me to believe the heavy cape/robe Owen was wearing pressed on an inappropriately [taut] section of the release line between the snap shackle and his shoulder, and when Owen felt his robe slipping or being lifted up by the line he grabbed at the robe, which further pressured the release line causing the snap shackle to open.
>
> It shocked me that a professional rigger would fly a wrestler with no stunt experience using just a single snap shackle without any back-up. When the rest of our crew learned how the stunt had been rigged they were equally aghast. By then our crew was mature enough that we wouldn't have hung a tiny light fixture with a single snap shackle, let alone a human being. This accident should never have happened, and probably wouldn't have happened if any of the WWF/WWE riggers had even a whiff of how Bobby Talbert, a newly hired independent contractor, was planning to rig the stunt. Mr. Talbert had apparently been involved in a similar stunt with WCW wrestler "Sting," and has since had a very successful career as a Hollywood stunt rigger and performer (see his profile on IMDb).

So perhaps Mr. Talbert was being defensive for one simple reason: he had a career and reputation to protect. Whatever the truth may actually be, he certainly had an interest in keeping his name clean of any potential fault. That said, reading this, my original comments do not seem so out of line. Further, a year prior, Mr. Buchanan has also posted this now deleted comment:

> *There were glaring technical mistakes made by the independent rigger who was hired to produce the stunt...*

So here we have one professional accusing another of incompetence, but both are highly emotional and have their own personal bias. Since the settlement with the Hart family included dropping Bobby Talbert from any future prosecution, there has never been an independent look by an unbiased court or other party.

Twenty years later and these snippets are as close to the full truth and understanding that we'll ever get.

The Ultimate Warrior

Intro

Some dame walked into my office and said...

First up I heard from **Casey Trowbridge** who said:

> *I'm sure you've gotten this one a lot, especially with the DVD hitting shelves yesterday but the Ultimate Warrior would be an interesting case to defend. Not that I have a great fondness for the guy necessarily but it would be a really compelling case I think.*

And then **Rick Cobos** joined the fun when he gave many ideas, including this one:

> *[T]he Ultimate Warrior's unprofessional conduct during his WWF tenures in 1991 and 1996[.]*

Of course, **Matthew Leisten** was not to be outdone. Here are his partial thoughts (the rest are for me and me alone!):

> *I [definitely] think that the Ultimate Warrior deserves a defense. I've never seen a wrestler as despised by his [colleagues] as he is. The guy is a little weird, and I cannot defend his remarks about Turban wearers, but otherwise he's just come across to me as a very intelligent person who just doesn't fit in.*

Strangely, **Migueal Sardalla** sent this in two months ago:

> *[C]an't wait to see you defend the Ultimate Warrior.*

Have you been peeking at my files?! Well one man who wasn't looking was **Cam**, who really laid it out best:

> *Defend the Ultimate One! Oh yes this would be the ultimate (sorry about the play on words) test. But there is hope in anyone who's ever had 4*+ main event matches[,] isn't there[?]*
>
> *Well I have laid the gauntlet sir, will you accept my ultimate challenge?*

Oh yes, I will take...

THE ULTIMATE CHALLENGE!!!

WHY THIS?

Have you ever heard a rumor about yourself? Have you ever happen to overhear someone talking bad about you?

How did that make you feel? How did you want to react?

We all have had experiences like this, where someone says something not true, or an exaggeration, or a misunderstanding about you.

And then they use it viciously against you.

Their motives may be numerous, but the point is made. You are the bad guy. You are wrong.

What if one day you discovered not only were people saying bad things about you, but your former colleagues decided to put together a documentary to reshape history and make you look like a complete chump?

After everything you did for them, after everything that you've accomplished, out of everything beyond your control, is seems that your legacy will be this:

You self-destructed.

This is what happened to our client Warrior. Eccentric? Yes. Misunderstood? No doubt. A destructive force in this industry?

I don't think so.

We will explore the Warrior in many ways, debunking the "Self Destruction" DVD along the way. We will delve deeper into his past, the motivations of others that are fighting against him, and just for a few moments at least try to understand where he is coming from.

The important question throughout this case will be simple: What is the legacy of the Warrior? Is he some flash in the pan nut job or he is a lasting testament to wrestling greatness, though eccentric and misunderstood?

I'll have to ask you to have patience as my points may not be clear right away. But the picture will form overall, and as always, I invite your feedback as we progress and delve deeper and deeper into......... Parts Unknown.......

HISTORY PART 1 – WHO IS JIM HELLWIG?

The year was 1959. The month was June. The day... it was the 16th.

And in the real world, the place was Williamsport, IN, and a man was born with the name Brian James Hellwig. OK, maybe he wasn't born with that name; it was the name given to him shortly after he was born, but that's beside the point.

The point is, he was born. And then he started to grow up—but not much. From Warrior Wilderness:

> Warrior was a [self-described] "skinny little 135lbs kid with no ass"...

He also had a fairly strained relationship with his father, to say the least. Due to being a lanky, skinny kid with parental issues (his dad split when he was twelve and provided no support; his mom was domineering, but he thinks that is a good thing), he became a recluse and outsider. His friends were limited and he was mostly by himself.

Then, one day, an odd thing occurred. During his High School days, he stumbled upon the weight room of his school (I assume Junior/Senior High School) and decided to give it a try. From Warrior Wilderness:

> [H]e became good friends with an old, rusty Universal weight machine, nothing fancy, it was oldschool. He started lifting and enjoyed seeing the benefits it had on his body, both in strength, looks and the discipline it gave him to push himself and his body to the limit, physically and mentally.

And thus Warrior pushed himself. Who else was there to push him? This was the type of support he got (from Warrior Wilderness):

> *Growing up, he wanted to become a Doctor of Chiropractics. This led to a meeting with the high school [councilor], he had a meeting because he wanted to discuss Further Education. Sadly, his reputation as a kid who was always in the wrong place at the wrong time reared its ugly head and the school [councilor] didn't want to know, let alone listen. Not giving him a chance, she immediately told him "This summer, you need to go down to the factory..." (In Indiana, where the a young Jim Hellwig grew up, many people worked in the factories there)... she continued "and put an application in, and you work there this summer. That way, when you get out of school next year, you will have a full time job."*
>
> *Young Mr. Hellwig left that office that day, continually questioning how that lady could make that life decision for him, without even giving the impressionable young man a chance to talk to her about his aspirations for HIS future. He questioned how not once in his 12 years of school, how nobody had ever stopped him and told him they didn't think what he had what it took to learn what they were teaching, how could she come to the conclusion he was a lost cause.*

Through his weight training, Warrior had grown an appreciation for physical and medical arts and wanted to pursue that further. But there was no help for him. His father was not his friend, his high school had turned against him, and he had no one else to turn to in all of Indiana.

But he would not let that stop him. He began his schooling, but life would give him a twist in the road. From the Warrior's own mouth in an interview with Dan Flynn:

> *Out of that [his work out discipline] I set an educational goal for myself to become a chiropractor. I turned my hobby of working out into a successful bodybuilding career. At the tail end of my schooling, the school being in Atlanta and it being a hotbed for pro-wrestling, my bodybuilding success created an opportunity to get into the business of wrestling.*

You see, Warrior was not a big guy when he left school. He still had not finished growing and at that point was about 5' 10" and 155 lbs. Compare that to his average size while wrestling: 6' 3" and 260 lbs. So while going to school, Warrior continued to grow, but there was much to learn. From Warrior Wilderness:

> During his third or fourth year of college, he went to California and saw all the bodybuilders like Robby Robinson pumping up. He was smart enough to realize that if these guys looked this way from repping out with weights and pumping up with strict form and not tossing heavy weights around, that was the way to do it. There was nothing to question. That was just the way they worked out and they all had the best physiques. Right then, Jim realized that working out with correct form and letting the muscle decide how heavy a weight to use was the way to go.

Seeing those guys gave the Warrior a goal. He was always a goal orientated person, thus so long as he had something to set his sights on he was willing to work for it. And so he built up his body, physique, and style and started to compete. Living between Florida and Georgia, he moved up in the ranks. He started off by placing 5th in a gym contest, but that was just the beginning. As time went on, he won the Junior Atlanta contest, he placed in the Collegiate Nationals, and moved on to the Junior USA. By 1984, his professional competing days were coming to their end. From Warrior Wilderness:

> In his final contest, he took fourth in the Heavyweights the year Ron Love won the Overall. He weighed 257 and was 253 the year he went to the Nationals. In his own words he says "I never seemed to get it together on the day of a contest."

You see, the Warrior's training regimen put him off-cycle with the major competitions, and he found that it was not the direction for him. Although he enjoyed working out and keeping in good shape, there was too much back and forth weight changes to feel good. And besides, another offer came along.

HISTORY PART 2 – AND THEN THERE WAS...

Our story begins in 1985. From Warrior Central:

> *Jim Hellwig began wrestling in November 1985. He started [training] with [Rick] Bassman for a spot as one of a quartet of bodybuilders known as Powerteam USA. The members of the team were Jim "Justice" Hellwig, Steve "Flash" Borden, Mark "Commando" Miller and Garland "Glory" Donnoho.*

Warrior went into greater detail in his interview with Dan Flynn:

> *I was going to chiropractic school and competing in bodybuilding. In 1984, I won the Mr. Georgia competition. From that, I went to the Mr. America competition that year in New Orleans. And there, there was a guy by the name of Ed Connors, who was one of three guys who bought the Gold's Gym that Joe Gold founded, and the three set out and turned into the worldwide franchise operation that it is today. Every year, back at that time, in the '80s, they would take two amateur bodybuilders they thought had potential to make it big, and bring the two out to California and put them up while they trained at "The Mecca" for a Junior National or National level contest. I was one of the guys in '84 or '85. I went out there and I trained for a Junior Mr. USA contest, took fifth in my class, if I remember right. Anyway, things didn't, in the contest, really go the way we expected them to go. The opportunity was still there. I was like one of the biggest, by bodyweight, bodybuilders at the time, got great reviews with [Joe] Weider and all the other top bodybuilders, just didn't hit my mark for that show. So, I decided to get back to Atlanta and finish the small amount of school I had left, mostly clinical requirements.*
>
> *Just as I got back to Atlanta, Ed called and told me there was a guy out there in California who's putting together a team of four guys to become pro-wrestlers, and he asked me if I'd be interested. I didn't follow the sport at all. Atlanta, of course, was a hotbed of wrestling at the time and I had crossed paths with a few of the guys—the Road Warriors, Paul Orndoff, Dusty Rhodes, Tony Atlas—but I didn't know them personally. But after some minor investigation, and the fact that I could use all the hard work I'd done in*

> *bodybuilding to capitalize off it—make some money, come back to the chiropractic later... I decided to go for it.*

But things were not so rosy. You see, Rick Bassman (who put the team together) knew nothing of the wrestling business and had no connections to anyone. After a very short time the team with no resources was quickly disbanded. But despite this, Warrior chose to continue his wrestling path. He wasn't indebted to the business, he wasn't without options, but he had found another goal to shoot for. Was he hoping for money? You bet! Why is that such a bad goal? Not everyone has to love the business to be a part of it. We'll get back to that shortly. For now, Warrior had this to say while speaking with Dan Flynn:

> *Turned out, within a couple weeks, that the guy who had the idea didn't have the money to float the beginning phases and the bottom fell out. We lost our place to live, had just enough to eat peanut butter, and do midnight snack runs at local grocery stores, eating in the aisles, funny stuff. To top it off, as Steve [Sting] and I later found out, this guy didn't know jack about how the business operated on the inside. Even if he'd had the money to feed us and get us fully trained, his big plan still would have failed.*
>
> *Steve [Sting] and I stayed positive about it all, and really our ignorance about things was a blessing. We sent pictures out to everybody on a list of wrestling organizations we had. We only had ten to fifteen hours of training. And that was basically just lifting each other over our heads and dropping one another on the floor—on the basic gymnastic mats.*

Oh, did I forget to mention that the other person to continue wrestling was fellow bodybuilder turned wrestler Steve "Sting" Borden? Well, it was. Sting, who is regarded quite differently from Warrior, yet had the same training. I'll get back to this in a minute, as well.

In the meanwhile, their story began. Warrior and Sting began to tag team together and send their pictures to promotions around the country. One finally bit. From Warrior Central:

> *But the wrestling seed was sown so Hellwig and Borden decided to tag together. They sent flyers out to every wrestling promotion in the country but only Jerry Jarrett was ballsy enough to take a chance on the two green but eager stars in the making. They wrestled in Memphis for Jerry Jarrett promotions as the Freedom Fighters. From there they moved on to Bill Watts' UWF (Universal Wrestling Federation). There they turned heel and renamed themselves The Bladerunners in which Hellwig changed his name to Rock and Borden changed his name to the more familiar Sting. They wrestled together in the Universal Wrestling Federation until after a contract [dispute] and his take no shit attitude not going down too well with Watts, Hellwig left the promotion.*

So it seemed like things were just turning out completely rosy for the Warrior. He was getting everything he wanted without the work. Or was he? From the Flynn interview:

> **FLYNN:** What kind of money did a wrestler make back then?
>
> **WARRIOR:** We were making $25 to $50 a night.
>
> **FLYNN:** Were you rooming with Sting?
>
> **WARRIOR:** We did everything together. Laundry, gym, groceries—always together. We had the one car. I'd sold mine so we could eat in California. We drove to the towns together. Sometimes 4-5 hours one way and with 4-5 guys in the car just to cover the cost of gas. Slept in a fleabag hotel until we got an apartment then we slept on the floor. Ate tuna fish out the can. Had to call Ed Connors to send us some money. It was really rough, but we stayed positive as we could. I thought a lot about going back to school, but didn't even have the money to get back to Georgia, let alone re-enroll. And we knew there was nothing we could do about it. It was about paying dues. One week we got a check for the whole seven days of working for like $150-$200. Beat all to hell, bummed out and all, we ask one of the boys, Rip Morgan, a guy from New Zealand, "How do you know when you are getting screwed (euphemism)?" He said, "Oh,

> *don't worry about that mate, you'll know when you are getting screwed. The question then becomes 'What can you do about it?'"* He was right. There was nothing we could do about it.

May I repeat one line for you?

IT WAS ABOUT PAYING DUES.

Did you read everything Warrior went through? Anyone who says the Warrior was just handed the world does not know what they are talking about. Warrior had to work for it, he did pay his dues. Sure, he did not do it for five years like some guys did. But that should be a testament of his dedication and unique connection to the audience, not used against him. It's a shame that some guys who were not good enough to hack it that quickly (or at all) feel the need to take it out on someone else who got a break.

Besides, it was not like Warrior did not have years of previous sacrifice. In the Warrior's words in his interview with Flynn:

> *I'd also busted my ass in painful ways they never had—years of training in the gym, self-discipline in working out and dieting. If they want to criticize anybody they should criticize the promoters who were, in effect, telling them, your little bag of fancy wrestling moves don't sell tickets t-shirts, posters, dolls, etc.—so leave them and your tears at home, instead show up with some muscle and some energy.*
>
> *What, am I supposed to apologize I did what it took, at that time, and they didn't?*

Just because Warrior had not spent half a dozen years on the circuit did not mean that he had not paid his dues in other ways. The training and work he did in the bodybuilding circuit was very similar. He was on the road, he had no money, he was stretched to his physical and mental limits, he was eating whatever he could find. How does any of this, coupled with his wrestling experience, not count as paying dues?

Back in Memphis, Jerry Lawler complained on the Self-Destruction of the Ultimate Warrior DVD that when Warrior came in he was green.

Really? What a shock! A man with a few weeks of training was green? Who'd a thunk it?

Lawler complained that he did not know what he was doing. Well how was he supposed to learn? You have to teach someone, you have to give them a chance to get better. That would be like Goldman-Sachs hiring a kid out of college and then handing him a billion-dollar account without training. Yes, you need young fresh blood, but you do have to train them and bring them up to your level, not fight against them.

And so Warrior and Sting (before either had those names) went on with their tag team, but the split had to come. From Wrestling Digest in December 2003:

> *While Sting stayed in the Mid-South, Warrior headed to the Texas-based World Class Championship Wrestling in 1986. Working as the Dingo Warrior, he entered the promotion as a heel but soon became a popular babyface. He went on to hold the WCWA Texas heavyweight title for four months.*

That was the quickie version because the most important part comes next.

HISTORY PART 3 – THE ULTIMATE JOURNEY BEGINS

In mid-1987 interest in the Warrior was high, and not just from the then WWF. Although Vince and company would like to have us believe that they brought Warrior in and made him, the Warrior was making his own name and had a buzz of his own. From Warrior Central:

> *Several promotions had taken notice of Dingo Warrior and approached Hellwig with offers. Antonio Inoki and New Japan Pro Wrestling outlined details of a new monster [character] they wanted Hellwig to portray in their promotion. Hellwig of course turned them down in favour of the World Wrestling Federation.*

Warrior could have gone to Japan and made good money with New Japan, but he knew that the bigger place was the WWF. If he could make it to the top there, then he would truly have made it and proved himself... to himself.

So the WWF career of the Warrior began. From Warrior Central:

> In 1987 The Dingo Warrior made his debut in The World Wrestling Federation. He impressed on his television debut in a 20 man Battle Royal which was eventually won by Bam Bam Bigalow. "Dingo" was soon dropped by Hellwig in favour of the more marketable "Ultimate" and he was given a guitar heavy [entrance] theme. His running entrance and the insane shaking of the ropes quickly made The Ultimate Warrior a crowd favourite and he took the WWF by storm. After taking care of jobbers in his early days he began feuding with another powerfully built wrestler, Hercules Hernandez. The feud began when[,] before a scheduled bout[,] Hercules challenged Warrior to a tug of war. Warrior accepted and ended up pulling on the steel chain so hard that it snapped! Their feud ended at WrestleMania IV with The Warrior emerging victorious in under 5 minutes. The Warrior was now an established WWF superstar but this was just the beginning.

And it continues:

> The Warrior became WWF Intercontinental Champion on 29/08/1988 when as a stand in for the injured Brutus "The Barber" Beefcake, he disposed of The Honky Tonk Man in just 31 seconds, the shortest Intercontinental Title match in history. Warrior defeated all challengers for his title and began a feud with "Ravishing" Rick Rude. He took part in a posedown with Rude at the 1989 Royal Rumble. Rude attacked Warrior setting the stage for a title match at WrestleMania V on 02/04/1989 in which Rude won the IC title with assistance from his manager Bobby "The Brain" Heenan. Rude's title reign was short lived though as The Warrior regained his title at that [year's] Summerslam on 28/08/1989. He entered a feud with Andre the Giant, most of which went on at house shows. Warrior [regularly] beat the Giant in under a minute and sometimes in only 10 seconds! A feature of this feud was Warrior's effortless bodyslamming of the 520 pound Giant!
>
> In the Royal Rumble of 1990 Warrior was eliminated by WWF World Champion Hulk Hogan. This set up their huge match at WrestleMania VI

> on 01/04/1990. It was the first time the top two babyfaces had squared off against one another. Title vs Title. WWF World Champion vs WWF Intercontinental Champion. Hulk Hogan vs The Ultimate Warrior. Before 65,000 ecstatic fans in Toronto Ontario, Canada The Ultimate Warrior defeated The Hulkster and became WWF World Champion. The rules in WWF at the time stated nobody could hold both titles at one time so Warrior had to give up his [I]ntercontinental title.

And in the Self-Destruction of the Ultimate Warrior DVD, the complaints rolled in. Again, the Warrior was too green for his spot. Again, he did not have the great wrestling skills. We'll cover the latter point in a bit, but let's return to the first point: GREEN!

If the Warrior was so green, then why would you put him in a main event spot? If his wrestling ability and interview skills were not to your wanted level, then why reward him?

This revisionist history is sickening. The Warrior worked hard, was on the road and doing what he did best: entertaining the fans. Whose fault is it if he wins the biggest title in the land with the only clean pinfall over the industry's biggest icon? Is that the Warrior's fault or the promoters behind him?

I'll answer that for you: it's the promoters. If Vince and the rest of his cronies really believed that Warrior was not capable of leading the company into the next generation, then they would not have given him this once in a lifetime opportunity. We'll spend a lot more time with this Hogan match later, but the important thing to take away is that Warrior was ready for the spot. If he wasn't, that fault belonged to the people who put him there, not anyone else.

And there is even more to this. From Wrestling Digest in December 2003:

> Three months after Warrior defeated Hogan, his former partner, Sting beat Ric Flair to win the NWA world title. The two wrestlers who five years earlier were passed on by every promotion except one regional group were now world champions of their respective companies after defeating two of the greatest legends of all time.

Sting won his first world title at the same time as the Warrior, yet we rarely hear complaints that he was too green or it was too soon. Why is that? What is the real difference between Sting and Warrior?

It's their relationship with the boys in back. We'll get a lot more into this as well, but nobody is going to attack Sting for the way and time he won his championship as they would Warrior. Yet, it was the exact same story.

Warrior would then have a turbulent relationship with the WWF, leaving the company in August 1991. He would return in 1992 for seven months before leaving again for four years. He would reappear in 1994 for another four months before leaving the WWF yet again for what seemed like it would be the last time. However:

> [H]e returned for WM 12 in 1996 and squashed HHH, he no showed a tag team match involving himself, Ahmed Johnson and Shawn Michaels. His stand in was Sid. 1996 was the last year that the Ultimate warrior was in the WWF(E)
>
> **Joseph Puopolo**

In 1998 he premiered in WCW for a short feud with Hogan before leaving wrestling for good. There's a great deal of detail to go over about each of these points in time, but that is for later.

After leaving wrestling, Warrior found he had a lot of excess energy. From his interview with Dan Flynn:

> *Being off the road and still having incredible energy and discipline and intensity, I began to want to do new things. I began a lot of self-study, including beginning a [self-learning] journey reading the Great Books of the Western world, and the study of American history and came to see and call the Founding people and times the absolute heroic models. This was special for me, having done what I did as heroic role model for young minds, and never before in my life able to point to any one identity as a role model.*

This is something that really bothers me. Here in the IWC elite we like to think we are so well versed, so self-discovered and aware that it makes us better than other people. Maybe it does, though I do not believe it. But here is something:

The Warrior began his journey of self-discovery in his later 30's, early 40's. Yes, most people who go through a process of self-discovery do it somewhere between 13 and 29. Yes, the Warrior began his discovery of history and knowledge and self-meaning at a later point in his life. So what? That is something we are to hold against him.

Or do we hold against him the answers he found for himself, and the answers he has taken on the road on his speaking tour?

What Really Happened?

As we went through the history of the Warrior, there were a lot of controversial points to go over. Now we will delve into the Warrior's wrestling history (we'll get to the speeches in a later section), and take a look at the other side of the coin that the "Self-Destruction of the Ultimate Warrior" refused to look at.

Unprofessional

There are several examples of Warrior being "unprofessional" in the Self-Destruction DVD, yet none are delved into or explained in any terms outside of those affected. Take for instance in 1996 when the Ultimate Warrior returned to the WWF and squashed Triple H at WrestleMania in just a few minutes. Triple H says that Warrior was the most unprofessional person he has ever worked with. One problem: he doesn't say what was so unprofessional about the Warrior. We are just supposed to believe at face value that Triple H, a man who was being punished and de-pushed, could criticize someone for being unprofessional? With no reasoning whatsoever?

Might it be that Triple H did not like having to job to a returning star? Might he be upset that he was embarrassed because he takes himself too seriously and never can get that win back? Might he be perturbed that a so-called non-wrestler was given another chance? Might he be upset that someone with much less in-ring talent than him drew a boatload more money? Just perhaps.

Another story I'd like to debunk is one where Bobby Heenan said Andre hated the Ultimate Warrior and had nothing to do with him. From the Warrior's interview with Dan Flynn:

> *Andre was at the end of his career. He was happy and wealthy... I had a great run with Andre and became good friends with him, really. I would even make the case Andre did more for the Ultimate Warrior than he ever did for Hogan. And that's saying a lot because Andre did not ever do what he did not want to. Ask Randy Savage.*

Randy Savage was not available for comment.

Although Andre and Warrior were never probably great friends, they were not the bitter enemies that Heenan (or the editing) made them out to be. Andre would not work with anyone he did not want to, and would not job for someone he did not think had a future. Yes, he probably did rough up the Warrior a few times for being green and not paying enough attention, but the Warrior learned from those mistakes and Andre was happier for it. It's much the same as Hardcore Holly or the Undertaker—an old school mentality to be rough to young guys to teach them the business, but it is not a sign of a lack of respect.

Contract Problems

These comments about Warrior's so-called unprofessional conduct led the DVD to use it as the reasoning around how the Warrior left the WWF under varying circumstances.

The first such instance came at SummerSlam 1991. Warrior was in a tag match with Hogan against Sgt. Slaughter, Gen. Adnan, and Col. Mustafa. Before the main event, Warrior went to Vince and said he would not go on unless Vince paid him some additional money. Vince, on the DVD, goes into a tirade against the Warrior saying you work out these things in the back before the event, you don't hold someone up. Hogan also went on the attack, saying that is just not how you do business. But why would Warrior do such a thing? From Warrior Wilderness:

> *Vince still owed Warrior his WrestleMania VII payoff, and after skirting around the issue time and time again, the Warrior gave Vince an ultimatum: He either paid Warrior what he owed him, or Warrior [wasn't] going to go to the ring that night. Vince paid up, and when Warrior returned to the locker room after the match, Vince suspended him, or fired him, or Warrior walked out, depending on who you ask.*

Do the math. We are talking five months after the fact that Vince was refusing the pay the Warrior. Warrior had done what Vince wanted, for months! He had tried to talk to him in the back, and Vince said he was going to pay him. But he completely lied to Warrior and did not give him his back pay. No offense to Hogan, but he was always paid for his events and had already been paid. This was not a negotiation for a raise, but for the money Warrior was owed for his performance and sales. Warrior only had one bit of leverage: himself. If he did not stand up to Vince, then Vince would continue to run over him for years to come.

As it was, Vince quickly realized he was better off with the Warrior and brought him back just seven months later. This quickly fell apart as well (for reasons we will get to in a minute), and Warrior was gone from the WWF until 1996.

By the way, the Warrior did not just sit around for four years. Aside from beginning his mental journey, he also worked a handful of independent dates and became the WWS Champion in Germany. He also spent some time in Hollywood and filmed the movie FirePower. It was during this time that he opened up his own gym and the short-lived Warrior University. The point being, he kept busy.

Vince needed a pick-me-up for the business. The WWF was down—way down—and the WCW was picking up steam quicker than ever. Vince McMahon, for all of his love of saying he creates stars, really does not. He chances upon stars who make themselves. Thinking that he could recapture the magic of the Warrior, he had Linda work out a contract with him. From the interview with Dan Flynn:

> *Vince called me at the end of 1995—I'd been out since 1992—and wanted me to come back to wrestling because the business needed a lift, and I guess, he had had the time to reconsider how he'd wronged me in 1992, using me and Davey Boy Smith as scapegoats to take the heat off his back when he was federally prosecuted over the steroid stuff.*
>
> *When he called I was already up to my neck in my own entrepreneurial projects using the Warrior intellectual property. Basically, I just told him no, especially if it was to be under a generic contract. There was no way I could do that after all the investments I'd made since leaving the ring. Linda called me, his wife. Of course, I knew Linda because I had met her before out at their house, at Titan. I don't know really how much she did business wise before, my business was handled with Vince really. But somewhere in the 1990s, she took a more active role, then eventually became CEO.*
>
> *She called me and said, "Can I meet with you?" So she came out to Phoenix and I just got the impression that it would really be different this time. So I said, "Look, I can't come back under a generic contract. I need a special contract. I got all these other projects going on. I got my gym, which is becoming a private facility—maybe to train guys who want to get in the business. I got*

> *my big comic book project I want to turn [into] an animated movie, got my mail order business, etc. I can't just up and leave these things." I said, "This is what I'll do. I'll come back. I'll be the wrestler. You can sell the t-shirts, the posters, you can make the money from the ticket sales. You give me a price for that. But I get to plug into your merchandising and networking with my other Warrior projects. And there's got to be a distinction between my new intellectual properties that I've developed, and those that represent who the wrestler is. So, we had our distinct agreement and four months after I came back they just started violating it. They didn't give a shit. And it turns out they never were going to live up to it. Screwing me again was premeditated.*

Lots of points to take away:

(1) In 1992, Warrior was used a scapegoat for the steroid trial (we'll get back to this momentarily [I know I keep saying this, but hang in there!])

(2) Warrior had been spending the past several years investing into the "Warrior" brand. You remember that the basis for the WWE's lawsuit against Brock Lesner is that they invested the money into creating Brock Lesner and therefore owned his wrestling rights. Well, Warrior had spent years investing his own money into "Warrior", a brand he felt was beyond wrestling. Therefore, the WWF had no claim to it, and the Warrior owned the outputs.

(3) Warrior would not accept the regular wrestling contract and Vince and the WWF, under good faith, agreed to the conditions that the Warrior outlined because they were desperate to have him back.

(4) As part of the agreement, the WWF was to use their vast marketing and distribution networks to promote and sell Warrior branded merchandise that did not directly benefit the WWF.

That said, the WWF refused to live up to their agreements. How do I know this? Because Warrior sued and won. Back to the interview:

> **FLYNN:** *So did you sue them, or did they sue you?*
>
> **WARRIOR:** *I sued them.*
>
> **FLYNN:** *So what happened in the suit?*

WARRIOR: The short answer is that I prevailed. Beyond that, I learned a lot about myself and life and my own integrity. I found out a lot I do not like about other people, especially the professional, expert suits in the world who get unchecked approval just because of who they are. I am more skeptical and cynical of others. I matured much, became a better man and came to know how I would define being one. I found out that it is never wrong to fight for what is right—never. In ways, having the experience has set me on the path I am now.

FLYNN: And when was the date of that?

WARRIOR: March, 2000, and then I fought my own lawyers for over a year, because they did an unbelievably corrupt turn and tried to screw me out of rightful settlement. I hung in there and beat them too. It was a rough five years.

FLYNN: So now, you have the right to "Warrior," "Ultimate Warrior"?

WARRIOR: Yeah, I have all the intellectual property rights and everything to it. I always did, the lawsuit was necessary to prove it, to put to rest Titan's fallacious claim that they did. Although just one aspect of the litigation, it was important from the stand point—a standpoint many don't want to understand—that I had worked hard to create it and make it what it was and wanted to be able to, should be able to, use it to do other business things outside of the ring—down the road at a different time in my life. Christ, what was I supposed to do: just lay down and give over all the work, sweat, toil, and value? Critics are so narrow-minded, like, "Yeah, he fought for it just so he could always have it as a [memento] of his wrestling days." The intellectual property is worth more than the memory of my career there. That chapter in my life signifies something about the whole of my life, what my life and the way I think about it and live it means to me. Of course, too, my full legal name is the one name of Warrior, and my family has it as their surname. It signifies the philosophy of life I live by.

Warrior proved that it was his investment into the Warrior name, and that the WWF had not lived up to its agreements at all. He was right all along, yet that is not what the WWE would admit in its Self-Destruction DVD. Instead they intended to make Warrior look insane and out of line for doing so. Yet the courts would say otherwise.

At the end of the day, Warrior made a stand few would make. From the interview:

> *In 2000, the day our trial was to begin and all was settled, he came up to me in the courtroom before the day got underway with his hand out and stared with his trademark, "Hey pal." I refused to shake his hand and told him, "I've been insulted enough and we have nothing to be pals about." Truly probably the only time Vince has had that done to him. Try it some time. Refuse to shake the hand of a person you don't respect when they have their hand extended. It's very hard to do. But man does it build your character and tell you something about yourself. Ever since that day, my handshake means something and I don't give it as if it does not.*

CRAZY ANGLES

And with all that, Warrior was involved in some crazy angles. But was he the one responsible? From his interview with Dan Flynn:

> *FLYNN: One thing that I remember, and I asked a guy today if I were dreaming or something like that—one of the gimmicks that Vince had you do which was probably the dumbest thing I've ever seen on professional wrestling...*
>
> *WARRIOR: With the Papa Shango thing?*
>
> *FLYNN: Yeah, you know exactly what I'm talking about. So, he had some guy put a voodoo curse on you and you [were] throwing up or something. Could you say to Vince, "Hey Vince, this is a bad idea?"*
>
> *WARRIOR: I did. But it did little good once he had his mind set on something. The big problem was*

> *that every three weeks you showed up at a television taping and they had it all laid out already. They got that one evening to tape three different television programs—whatever they were at the time. So, they can't modify things that much. You—the talent—have been on the road and you're worn down anyway, so it depends how much fight or how much creativity you have in you to make the case for doing something differently.*
>
> **FLYNN:** *If you tried to say to him, "Look, this isn't such a good idea." Is he the type a guy that takes criticism in stride?*
>
> **WARRIOR:** *Yeah, Vince was always good about hearing good ideas out. In fact, back then it was really up to the top talent to come up with their own creative ideas to make an angle work. But you had to come up with another idea really quick because they are going from one thing to the next. Papa Shango was a voodoo type of character anyway. So, in some way the office was already convinced that people were buying the voodoo thing. So taking it up a notch and having Warrior leak ooze or puke pea-soup wasn't, so they thought, wasn't going to make less believable the angle.*

Warrior was not really in charge of his angles unless he could come up with something better on the spot. And even then, his ideas could be rejected. But like a professional, he went through the angle and tried his best to make it entertaining. But in the end, Warrior cannot be held responsible for his crazy angles, that again belongs to someone else. Yet once more, his peers have held this against him.

Why would his peers, who were in the same situation, hold Warrior to a different standard? Well, there is the other side of the coin. Not just who Warrior was away from the ring, but who he was in the back.

F•R•I•E•N•D•S

I touched on this briefly earlier, but the question remains: what is the main difference between Sting and Warrior? The answer is friendship. Sting immersed himself in the locker room while Warrior distanced himself.

On the DVD, several people (including Heenan) said everyone hated Warrior. But on the same DVD, Hogan said everyone liked Warrior, just thought he was eccentric. To make it even more confusing, Vince said that most people were not friends with him, but nobody disliked him, and that if they got to know him better that that they would realize what a charming, funny man he was. How confusing!

So where is the truth in all this? Well, the first question to ask is if, and why, the Warrior distanced himself from the boys. From our overused interview:

> *Look, I'm cut from a different mold. Most of the guys have this loyalty to the business that I don't have. Even when it ruins their lives, breaks their character as a human being, or, worse, kills them. If things would not have gone sour with the McMahons, maybe I'd be more inclined. I mean, many of the old timers still work for Titan behind the scenes, as agents, gophers, real jobbers. It's their job. They've made the business their life.*
>
> *When I was having my success, you have to understand something: I'd been in the business a few years. Other guys had been in it 10 to 12 years and they never had the success I did. There was a ton of envy. I knew and was also smart enough to navigate the shark infested waters. I was despised in a lot of ways. I knew I had to be a loner to succeed—do my own thing. And I beat them at their own game—their own "work." I got out on my own terms. They didn't get to abuse the character or me.*
>
> *They want to think in some ways—the pundits at least—that they were instrumental in making you what you were. And they also want to write the obituary for you. They want to be the ones to ridicule you on your way out: "Don't let the door hit you in the ass." It pisses a lot of people off that I have gotten on responsibly with my life. Like I've said numerous times, if I had ended up a pitiful, drugged bum I'd be better appreciated for what I did in the business. If I OD'ed in a Budget hotel room doing dirty little street drugs, my wife and kids at home, I'd be a real superstar. It also bothers a lot of people in the industry that I don't have a problem defending the legitimacy of my career, using my mind to do so instead of muscle.*

Warrior laid it out pretty simply. Yes, he did intentionally distance himself from the boys, but that was only because wrestling was not his life; it was his job.

He felt he had enough interaction with them seeing them every day. Someone can work in an office with four other people they see each and every day but still not feel the need to hang out with them after work all the time or always talk to them. It's a job, not a life. Warrior thought the same way.

But because he was not their friend, and definitely not one of the good 'ol boys, they feel the need to badmouth him when he left. Hogan, being of a similar mode as Warrior, was more inclined to paint him in a better picture. But those who could not reach the success Warrior had, and had no strong connection to him, felt more of a need to speak harshly of him because they had nothing else to base it on.

Warrior has another point. Great wrestlers in the industry like Curt Henning who died dishonorable deaths due to drug overdoses will always be more revered than him, a man who has been able to hold his life together. And like I said, we'll get more into the drugs shortly, no need to worry.

Drugs are only one of the controversial issues we will touch. But this is the first taste of what the Warrior is reviled for. And then there is a bigger story.

TO HAVE WRESTLING ABILITY, OR NOT TO HAVE, THAT IS THE QUESTION

Throughout the "Self-Destruction of the Ultimate Warrior" DVD and around the internet for years, Warrior has been called green, sloppy, and just a poor wrestler. Unlike many of our past cases (Nash, Undertaker, Sid, New Jack), Warrior did not have previous extensive training that he chose to ignore. Instead, he chose not to continue to develop his training.

And I know many of you are screaming right there. How could someone choose to stop developing? Isn't that the point of being a professional wrestler?

Yes, if all you want is to wrestle. We keep forgetting that those were not Warrior's goals. His goals were to entertain, be the best he could be, and make some good money along the way. He did not need all of the Dynamite Kid's abilities to achieve what he did. As a matter of fact, they would have been a detriment. From the Warrior's interview with Dan Flynn:

> *Not being a technical wrestler is kind of a silly bad wrap I get all the time from guys like Bret Hart and industry pundits. My response is, look, you guys were in the business for a dozen years before I even got there. A dozen years and you never figured it out that wrestling skills per se were not where it was at. It was about being a gimmick. I got there and in two years I figured it out...*

> *It wasn't part of my gimmick—it wouldn't fit Ultimate Warrior—to keep doing the wrestling stuff. I was smart enough to know that. Making that decision is up to the talent. In other words, whatever a wrestler decides to portray himself as in the wrestling ring character-wise, he's the one who develops that.*

I have to agree with the Warrior. He did in a few short years what it took others decades to achieve, or never at all. Watching the DVD, guys like Ted DiBiase come off as bitter and angry. Now DiBiase is one of my all-time favorite wrestlers, but him never winning the championship while someone like Warrior did has dealt him a deep blow. And what about people like Steve Lombardi, aka the Brooklyn Brawler? How in the hell can Lombardi criticize anyone's wrestling ability when he spent twenty years doing kick, punch, lay on back? Not that Lombardi did not have any additional skills, but again he had no use for them as the "Brawler". I turn it over to 411mania's own Joe Boo:

> *Another time Jim Ross shows his hypocrisy colors is about why the title was put on the Warrior. Ross gets some help from the Million Dollar Man Teddy D. on this one. They both say that it was a bad idea because the Warrior had to be carried to a good match by his opponent and that the matches had to be short or it would stink up the joint. First off, I am not a huge fan of having a wrestler comment on another wrestler's in ring prowess especially when they wrestled in the same generation. It is in bad taste to do so and might just show envy, which is something that has been revealed about Teddy D. Somewhere it was said that Teddy D. was always bitter about not having a WWF Championship title run. He was a good solid wrestler but didn't realize that his potential was reached as a great heel and nothing more. Now back to Jim Ross is getting a superior roast by yours truly (thank you, thank you).*
>
> *Jim Ross praises champions like JBL and Batista and even Cena as the future. News flash Jimbo.... they have been keeping there matches short for a reason.... they all blow ass in the ring.*

Sorry to say, you don't need to be a five-star competitor to be a champion. If anything, it probably hurts you to the average wrestling fan. You need to be a character larger than life that people want to get behind (or run over), and that is what the Ultimate Warrior was. No doubt was he a sub-par in ring competitor. But wrestling, especially in the WWF/E, is not about in-ring prowess. It's about being able to drive emotion beyond where anyone will care what you do in the ring. One punch from the Warrior would send more ripples around the arena then an entire cruiserweight battle royal. People cared about the Warrior, people bought into the Warrior, and the Warrior became the epitome of wrestling—what everyone outside of the industry recognized as wrestling. The people who pay and the people who make the press don't recognize a reverse flying congitoro, they recognize a man who is beyond the ring.

LOVE OF THE BUSINESS

Throughout it all, there has been a question of whether Warrior really cared for the wrestling business at all. All those guys questioning his dedication seem to have retroactively forgotten what the Warrior was about.

First of all, yes, the Warrior was not a fan of professional wrestling growing up. His step-father used to sometimes watch it, and would embarrassingly change the channel when the Warrior came home with some friends. So what? Hulk Hogan rarely watched wrestling as a kid, and he's the biggest icon in wrestling.

Did the Warrior get into wrestling for money? Sure he did! But, as we noted earlier, that did not mean he did not pay his dues and scrapped by on nothing for years. Also, that does not mean he did not grow to love and respect the business. I turn it over to regular reader **Doug Bernard** who sent this in:

> *During Wresltemania All Day back in 2000 when they were going through the 15 WrestleManias up until that point they were discussing the Ultimate Challenge. Pat Paterson was being interviewed and began to tell [a] story of the Warrior after the match. He said he walked into the locker room to [congratulate] Warrior only to find the Warrior sitting down in tears saying he couldn't believe this had happened and how grateful he was for it all. Now-a-days you would never hear this mentioned but back then it was still OK to view the Warrior in a good light every once in a while.*

You see, even just a few years ago the WWF was willing to let the truth of the Warrior slip out, that he was grateful for everything he received in the wrestling business. The Warrior himself continues in his interview with Dan Flynn:

My match against Hogan, that was... I had a lot of great moments, but I would probably say that was the pinnacle of my wrestling career and one of the best matches of all time. I'm proud of it. It was significant for, as I've said throughout the years, many things.

One, I'd reached the goal I set for myself. Many people don't understand, many in the industry just don't want to hear it. But when I got in the business, I got in it to pursue success. If after a certain amount of time that would not have happened, I sure as hell wasn't going to stick with it just so I could be professional wrestler, like so many others in the business do. And when I got in it, Hogan was the guy. The facts are I set a goal and achieved it. Did the work, turned the eyes of those who mattered, and made it happen. And like I'd done my whole life up till then, once I had reached a goal, I began setting others. In some ways, having that match with Hogan was anti-climatic. And I would say, now, after greater life experience and looking back, that the way I was about setting new goals, having the confidence to and not having any doubts I could achieve them, likely, underneath everything else that went on between Vince and I, contributed somewhat to the fallouts we had.

That match was also very significant from this point: Hogan was the superstar and had been for a long time the only superstar. Doing the match the way it was done, having the big baby faces face-off was a huge statement about how popular The Ultimate Warrior character was. I mean, Hogan was popular, there was no doubt about that. In fact, buildups to previous WrestleManias were done by taking one of Hogan's buddies and having that buddy stab him in the back, turn the second hottest baby face heel. That's how they built WrestleManias. But Ultimate Warrior was selling merchandise at the same pace or better than Hogan. If they'd done that, turned The Ultimate Warrior heel, they'd have been cutting their own wrists. So they had to do the match the way they did. I know on a deeper level what that meant and I am proud of what I accomplished to make that happen. It meant something to beat Hogan then...

Warrior was very cognizant of the meaning of that match and his win, and he was thankful for it. At the same time, he had set a goal for himself and achieved it. Is that a bad thing? He achieved a goal and wanted to set a new one?

Also, who is to say that just because he did not love the industry as, oh, let's say Chris Benoit or Christopher Daniels does, means that he is not the best person for the industry? Some people become doctors because they want the money and prestige, not because they want to save lives. But that does not mean they are not damn good doctors.

If you needed brain surgery to remove a tumor, would you rather have the extremely skilled surgeon with an excellent track record who got into the medical business for money or the guy at the clinic who just wants to save lives but has no track record to speak of?

If you wanted someone to headline your WrestleMania, would you want the guy selling as much merchandise as your top face but is only in it for the money, or do you want the guy that can put on a wrestling clinic but couldn't draw a dime?

These super technical wrestlers may very well be the best in the world, but they are wrong about Warrior. He did not need to love the business as they did. He had the only tool he ever needed to succeed: the audience in the palm of his hand.

ONE LAST TIME OUT TO BAT

In the fall of 1998, WCW finally finished contract negotiations with Warrior and brought him in for a six-month deal with the intention of working out a longer deal if things were going well. Right from the beginning there was criticism, like why he was called "Warrior" and not "Ultimate". Said Warrior to Dan Flynn:

> *[Eric] Bischoff called me about coming to work there. I think Hogan called me too. I guess they were surprised the Renegade fiasco didn't drive me to make that mad dash to the ring they expected it to. Titan got wind of them contacting me about a return and rushed into the court and filed a brief making even wilder and broader claims about negotiations than even I knew myself, in an attempt to prevent it. In their brief they made the claim that I, Warrior, didn't own the Ultimate Warrior—that they did, that they owned the intellectual property.*

> So we had to file a response to it. What happened out of those two briefs being filed was that I came forward and proved through photos and footage—copyrighted footage I owned of the Dingo Warrior—that Dingo Warrior was really just a nascent version of the Ultimate Warrior; that I all along owned it, even before I went up to Titan. The judge said look, there's no question that Warrior owns the character "Warrior"—all the trademark indicia, all the mannerisms, and everything else—he had indisputably created it and was performing the Warrior persona before he even came up to Titan. Vince though had a couple of his cronies file affidavits telling a contrived story that they came up with and provided "Ultimate." So the judge decided that as the trial played itself out, what the truth about that specific matter would be determined then. So that's why when I went to WCW in 1998, it was only under "Warrior."

So you see, Vince and company were immediately threatened by the fact that Warrior was willing to go work for the competition and tried to sabotage him again, despite the fact that they had signed a contract giving Warrior complete intellectual control over his name and properties (a case that would take another two years from that date to finally be settled). But Warrior took it in stride and decided to make it happen anyway. He then appeared on an episode of Nitro to confront Hogan and Bischoff in the ring.

The initial response was huge. The crowd was so happy to see Warrior back, and had found yet another person to beat the evil Hogan. But his speech was long and convoluted, and Hogan and Bischoff just stood there listening.

All right, there are very few times I will attack Eric Bischoff, but this is one of them. Why was Warrior not given an outline and timeframe? Why didn't the director tell him to wrap it up? The Warrior's promo style was not unknown in the industry. It was a lot of energy with a lot of poetic metaphors, something that works in a taped promo leading to a match. An in-ring confrontation is a different animal, yet Bischoff decided to have Warrior go on. Yes, it was Warrior's words and his promo, so that gives him some fault, but it is Bischoff's job as the head of the organization to control the talent and the content. If an actor in a movie writes their own script and the director does not tell them where to stand and how to position the cameras, can the actor be given the blame for making a bad movie? This is what happened here.

But that is not even the crux of this discussion. On the "Self-Destruction of the Ultimate Warrior" DVD, Hogan claims that Warrior committed a cardinal sin and saying that he had defeated Hogan before, and now nobody would be interested in the match. Sorry to say, Hulkster, but that's not how it works. Everyone knew the history between Hulk and Warrior, and knew the outcome.

But it was eight years beforehand! One match... eight years ago! All he was saying was "I beat you before, and I can beat you again." The fans thought that would be great idea because Hogan was a heel and that is what they wanted. How else was Warrior supposed to put himself over? Hogan's argument makes no sense, and he and Bischoff blame Warrior's promo and that comment for killing the momentum of their feud.

What they fail to mention is some of the ridiculous things they did to "further" the storyline. For instance, Hogan saw Warrior's shadow reflection in a mirror while he wasn't there, and we at home saw it, too. That's like going into Randy Orton's head and seeing his father dripping in blood. Moments like that did more to kill the momentum of the Warrior/Hogan feud.

Still, Hogan and Warrior's match at Halloween Havoc 1998 would go on to draw a 0.78 PPV buyrate, higher than the previous month's Fall Brawl (0.70) and the proceeding month's World War III (0.75). Not exceptionally high, not WrestleMania levels, but still decent for a one-match show. The match itself was not up to most critic's standards, and it's hard to argue that point. But let's look at it this way:

This was Warrior's third match in three months, and those matches were his first in two years. To say he had ring rust would be an understatement. Also, on the DVD Hogan admits that his timing was off and he was missing all the spots, as well, so it was not just Warrior. Also, Hogan mentioned how he tried to set a fireball off in Warrior's face, and it ended up backfiring on him and burning his eyebrows off. Why was Hogan even trying to do that, I cannot even fathom. But what Hogan neglects to mention is that the fireball did end up scorching Warrior's arm, and he was working injured throughout the match.

What they also fail to mention is that Warrior lost, with little complaint. He had also lost one of his previous matches as well, and the only match he won was by DQ. And did Warrior complain about that? Did he say he would refuse to job and not do certain things? No, he went along with everything and let Hogan get his win back from eight years prior.

At the end of the program, Warrior tried to find out what the plans were for him. There were none, and WCW seemed to be disinterested in having a further relationship with the Warrior. They got what they wanted out of him, and then it was time to just let his contract run out. This would be Warrior's last time on the grand stage of wrestling.

WHAT'D HE SAY?

Of course, while on the grand stage of wrestling, Warrior often cut long, fairly incomprehensible promos. To that I say: so what?

First off, Warrior's character was to come out of left field and be from "Parts Unknown". Sure, nobody had ever incorporated "Parts Unknown" into their character quite like Warrior did, but that does not make it uninteresting or irrelevant. Macho Man Randy Savage is fairly incomprehensible. I find Ric Flair incomprehensible a lot of time (especially when he starts wooing, saying things quickly into a mic, and then dropping elbows on his jacket). The point is these guys get over with the emotion of their speech, not the words.

You could have Chris Jericho write a speech for Chris Benoit and have Benoit read it perfectly with Jericho as director, and it would still not have the same impact. Jericho has a skill Benoit does not: timing and charisma. Benoit, for all his skill, will fail to make the same type of impact in front of the camera that Jericho does. Likewise, Benoit will win over the crowd with his match alone (especially if it goes longer) while Warrior could lose a crowd just based on matches. Wrestling is not all about Wrestling, nor all about speaking lines. It's about the connection with the audience and getting them to care whether you are beating someone or they are beating you. A punch can be more devastating than any super flippy move if done by the right person. And super flippy move can look horrible and out of place if done by the wrong person.

But I digress, on the Self-Destruction DVD, they cut up a bunch of Warrior's promos and interlaced them with music and graphics. Of course he is going to look horrible if you do that! You have to look at each event in context. Perhaps one of those promos was two minutes, and got over a match with Rick Rude. Perhaps another one was long and just for character development. So long as they worked on that show, on that night, is all that mattered. I can string together a twenty minute highlight reel of Rey Mysterio and Kurt Angle blowing spots set to Charlie Chaplin music, and you would think they were the worst wrestlers in the world. But if you say that they hit 99% of everything else in a high impact fashion, then the context makes all the difference.

When it comes to Warrior, the important thing to remember is that in those moments, he captured the audience. They did not care what the words were (pick up a Kidz Bop CD to see what I mean about people not caring what the words are and just pay attention to the tune and emotion), they cared about their emotional involvement. And that kept them sitting in front of their TV and buying tickets to the arena.

Take for instance the aforementioned promo with Hogan in WCW. Now that was completely buried on the DVD, but Derek Burgan did a little research for me that proves my point (not that I wouldn't have made the same point, it just sounds better from a source):

> *Gene Okerlund said that "ratings sunk like a rock" during Warrior's promo, which most certainly [cannot] be true. After a little research, I found out Warrior's segment on Nitro did a 6.4 to Raw's 3.1. Now that I think about it, Okerlund might have been even harsher on this DVD to Warrior than Heenan. The difference being that Okerlund often comes across as totally clueless when he opens his mouth.*

Warrior has been right all along. His promos, although incomprehensible to most, are enthralling. People like to watch and listen to him. They are into Warrior, no matter what he's doing.

Shoot 'em if you got 'em

Despite being an enthralling character, Warrior also had a physique unique to the time. We have already gone into great detail about Warrior's gym prowess, but the accusations of steroid abuse run high. So, was Warrior gassed up?

From Mike Tenay's(!) interview with the Warrior on "The Wrestling Insider" radio show on March 20, 1994:

> **Caller:** In the WWF, was The Ultimate Warrior always you? There seemed to be a great weight loss. Did they bring somebody else in to be you?
>
> **JH:** There were a lot of rumors about that. I died quite a few times, too. From about every disease you could think of. Number one, there's always been steroid abuse and I've never denied taking steroids. The weight loss, yes, when I took time off in 1991 after the SummerSlam event after me and Hulk and the Iranian guys at Madison Square Garden. I went to Santa Fe, New Mexico, and lived in the woods for eight months. I had been [on] the road real hard, real strong, every day, cross country, international. So I decided to take a break, and when I came back, I hadn't been using the steroids. I was still training as hard as I could and doing all of the things I had to do, but yeah, steroids do work no matter what people lead you to believe. They are taken by people. They are taken by all kinds of people for different reasons, maybe not the right reasons. But when you're in a position and you're pilling down the money and making money and establishing security for yourself later in life, you do what you have to do. You do what you have to do to be number one to get there. Once you get there, sometimes the price is even more and you have to decide whether you want to pay that price.

Let's pause. Did you read that up above? Warrior said he never denied taking steroids! He did it. Well, think back to the Lex Luger case: steroids were not listed as a class three controlled substance until 1992, so Warrior was legally using them with a prescription. And again, all of the side effects were not known at the time; it was just what bodybuilders and wrestlers did. But why was he taking them? The interview continues:

> **MT:** *Vince McMahon, Jr., was recently indicted on anabolic steroid-related charges. Have you followed the news of the indictments? And what's your opinion overall of the situation?*
>
> **JH:** *I haven't really followed it that closely. I really haven't followed wrestling that closely. When I was doing it, I was so involved in thinking in The Ultimate Warrior character, that was the important thing. That the people get their money's worth from that character. Yeah, I've been following it. The New York Post and other people have called to ask me my opinion or what I thought. As Vince took the WWF banner and made that thing grow into the entity that it did, he made a lot of enemies. There used to be territories where people wouldn't bring your talent here or if we do we'll do a mutual thing. I think somebody wanted to see him fall. Based on the indictments and the time and the money that I know they spent bringing those charges against Vince, it's my opinion that it's a bum rap. Vince never told me to take steroids. There's not a wrestling fan out there who's gonna deny or say, if [we're] going to make a list of the wrestlers you think were taking steroids, The Ultimate Warrior was one of them. If I can say that, and I was part of the inner circle, so to speak, and made it to the WWF, who's a better testimonial of whether Vince did that or not.*
>
> **MT:** *Did you feel any pressure to maintain a certain look or find yourself out of the limelight?*
>
> **JH:** *I put that pressure on myself, and deservingly so. People bought the character for one reason. The guys used to tell me not to run to the ring, not to shake the ropes, don't do those things. I was at a point in the beginning where I was wondering if they were telling the truth or not. I finally said, "The people are going nuts over it, so let's do it." Those are things that made or established or created the mold of The Ultimate Warrior, if I was to back off on any one of them, he wouldn't be The*

> *Ultimate Warrior. The body and the physique was one part of it. I credit it to training. I went to the gym every day, no matter what time of day. I went to the gym after the matches at 2 or 3 in the morning. I went to the tanning beds every day. I worked deals with hotels and gyms. I had drivers who would find this and find that. I wanted to keep that up. It's much more than taking steroids. It has to do with discipline and making a decision that you're going to do it. If I neglected any one part of the mold that we had created, he wouldn't have been The Ultimate Warrior and I wouldn't have had the limelight.*

You see, there is no blame passing here, there is no crying about it. Warrior freely admits to what he was doing, and admits it was his decision overall. Sure, he felt the pressure to look a certain way, but that was still his decision. It would take years of reflection for him to realize what he was doing to himself. From our interview with Dan Flynn:

> **FLYNN:** *I've noticed that many wrestlers live a paradoxical lifestyle. So, on the surface they seem a paragon of health. But when you go beyond the surface, on the inside their bodies...*
>
> **WARRIOR:** *They're rotting.*
>
> **FLYNN:** *...are filled with drugs. They're rotting. They're battling inner demons...*
>
> **WARRIOR:** *Hey, when we are young it's built into us to think we'll never die. That you're invincible. And truth is you, your body, can get away with behavior when you are younger that later in your life you and, again, your body can't take. There are ways other than hard work, diet, and discipline to achieve a healthy look on the outside, yet be messed up and damaged on the inside. This is what definitely happened to some of the guys I worked with who have since died. They get some juice and keep taking it and continue, as they always have, to practice unhealthy dietary habits. None of them really exercised hard. When they were young they could [get away] with it. At 40-50 years of age, you throw in a bit of slimy street drugs and the fact you haven't consistently practiced healthy exercise and diet habits and BAM!—the body says, "No more."*

Also, in the business it's easy to get scripts for potent pain-pills and the like. In every arena that they go to there is a doctor there that's a big fan willing to write scripts for whatever the talent may ask for. Add to it street drugs and booze and fatigue and eventually there's a wall one is going to hit and hit hard. And, you are right, the inner demons. It takes quite bit of level headedness to put celebrity and life on the road into perspective. You have to be grounded in solid, genuine ways.

FLYNN: *You wrestled with several of these guys who are obviously no longer with us—Rick Rude, Curt Hennig, Kerry von Erich. Do you think there is something about the lifestyle that leads to self-destruction?*

WARRIOR: *Ultimately each individual is solely responsible for destroying their own life. I think there are always tell-tale signs one gets warning them that "Hey, you better take a hard look at what you are doing." Typically, self-destruction happens in stages and each person is given ample opportunity to get their act together. You can't keep tempting fate without there eventually being a serious, negative consequence.*

Shit, the autopsies came back and a lot of those guys died from street drugs. Hennig died from a coke overdose. Rick Rude died from [liquid] ecstasy. Davey Boy Smith was doing cocaine and ungodly amounts of growth hormone and all kinds of different steroids.

Look, these guys who have died over the last few years didn't just have that vision of death at that final moment of their life. The further and further out there they got with destructive behavior they knew inside themselves, many, many times along the line, that there was a price they were going to pay. They were doing the drugs to run from something. Something they didn't like about themselves, their lives, the way things had turned out. The more drugs they did the greater the escape from the reality they didn't like. Unfortunately, there are no success stories down that road. None. Not one. You don't drug yourself into a reality you would like better. You have to fix the one you are living. Too bad that fact isn't

> *enough to have people snap out of it and get their life act together before it is too late.*
>
> *People have criticized me about what I wrote in some posts when some of those guys died—like I didn't have any sympathy. Anybody who wants to can read them. Frankly, I'm sick of all the sympathetic praise we throw around adults who screw up their lives. Life is about finding the strength day in and day out to make it work. Most people do. I'd rather praise them than people who don't. We are a society, today, where we pathetically place praise of vice above praise of virtue and, as an adult, I'm not okay with it. My kids, if no one else, deserve better out of me, deserve better out of the world they will have to grow up in.*

Warrior understands now what he was doing to himself, but he did not understand as much back then. But on the same token, he does not have patience for the type of recreational drugs that other wrestlers have died from. He was never using steroids for recreation, he was using it for his career. And yet, that is what would do him in. Or so Vince would have us believe.

Flunking a steroids test was apparently the reason Warrior was fired from the WWF in 1992. Or was it? Back to the interview with Mike Tenay:

> **MT:** *Back in November 1992 when you left the World Wrestling Federation, I guess basically it was contractual differences with Vince McMahon, Jr. What exactly were those differences?*
>
> **JH:** *I wanted to go out and do other things. I knew things from the entertainment that came across Vince McMahon's offices were shoved aside because Vince McMahon wanted to have you on the road and drawing and producing out there so you could make money. That's totally understandable, but I wanted to reach a point where I could work with people out there as my representatives doing things like that. He agreed to it verbally, and when I presented him with papers, he terminated me.*

And there is more to this in the Dan Flynn interview:

> **WARRIOR:** The business has always had its highs and lows, but you are talking about the time when the crap hit the fan with the Dr. Zahorian steroid stuff, causing Vince and some of the talent, Hogan and Piper, to be implicated, eventually Vince being prosecuted.
>
> **FLYNN:** That's what I want to know. What was it like being in the WWF during that real dark time with the Steroid scandal, and the feds coming down on Vince?
>
> **WARRIOR:** Well, most of the guys took stuff. Even guys you'd never imagine, just to keep up with the pace of the road, the lifestyle, the hanging out with groupies, and drinking, and whatever else. Of course, steroids were legal. You could get them with a prescription from a doctor. It was just at the time that the government was initiating a [crackdown]. The war on street drugs was a bust, so they focused their attention on steroids. The word came down from the office to either to make sure you had a prescription or get off altogether. I can't remember exactly without a timeline in front of me. All the documents I have from my litigation with Titan lay it all out to the day, everything. I just know the office did things in stages. Just trying to go off the top of my head here, it [affected] a lot of guys negatively. I wasn't bothered by it. I never depended on just steroids to maintain my physique and knew I could keep right at what I was doing. In '92 when I came back you couldn't use them, and I reached a great physical peak by using the knowledge I had. Hogan, on the other hand, went on The Arsenio Hall Show and lied about having ever taken them, which just made matters worse and created, I recall, real friction between Vince and he. Both had different ideas about how to handle it all. Hogan would always say that Vince was going about dealing with all this the wrong way. But Vince got really scared about it all. I remember very vividly a conversation he had with me. He really thought he was going to do some time in prison.

Plus, remember what Warrior said about how he came back in 1996:

> *[Vince McMahon] had had the time to reconsider how he'd wronged me in 1992, using me and Davey Boy Smith as scapegoats to take the heat off his back when he was federally prosecuted over the steroid stuff.*

You see, Vince knew he was going to lose Warrior no matter what. Warrior had reached the pinnacle of the sport, and did not have the drive to stay in it just to stay in it (see: Funk, Terry). So instead he let Warrior go and then blamed him to get the heat off himself (admitting his own fears that he might go to jail, a humbling moment we rarely get from McMahon). In 1992, Warrior was clean when he was fired.

And do you think Vince might have held those comments Warrior made in 1994 to Mike Tenay against him? Remember Roddy Piper said basically the same thing on that HBO special a few years back, and Vince fired him immediately. Vince may give many chances, but he never forgets when someone screws him (or what he perceives as screwing), and so therefore has used his media power to re-write history instead of telling the humbling story that really happened.

THE FIRST RULE OF CONSERVATION

Warrior has parlayed his experiences in the ring, behind the scenes, on the road, and with his own endeavors into a new career: public speaking. Warrior has found after deep soul searching that he has conservative leanings. OK, leanings would be putting it mildly, but he has found a philosophy he believes in. And so he is trying to create a new career for himself. But he understands that he has to work for it. From the Flynn interview:

> *I haven't been doing what I am doing today for twenty years. But I know how far I've come in the last five years. I know how much further I'm going to go in ten years. I know how hard I work at it. Everything I'm doing now is a continual work in progress. I'd like to get some gigs writing columns but my pieces are longer and more personal, and it'd take someone spending the time to mentor me about how to tweak them to get that done.*

And elsewhere:

> *I'm pleased with what I've done thus far. Keep in mind, Ultimate Warrior started out as Dingo Warrior. It took some time to get to the full blown version. I plan to evolve in like fashion as a speaker.*

Warrior realizes that if he wants to be a better speaker and writer, he must work at it. He has to find others who are better than him to teach him, and he has to try new things to see what works and what does not.

Sometimes, though, his views can incite people. I believe the quote is, "Queering doesn't make the world work." From the Hartford Advocate:

> *On April 5 [, 2005], Warrior spoke to a capacity crowd at the Dodd Center on the UConn campus in Storrs. During that speech, many audience members, some intent on disrupting Warrior's speech, took offense at his comments, causing tempers on both sides to flare and voices to rise. The scene became so intense that a police officer, fearing things could get dangerous, called in reinforcements. A video of the speech and the mayhem that followed, filmed by UConn student Russ Passig (one of Warrior's most vocal opponents during and after the incident), was obtained by the Advocate.*
>
> *[Aside] from a kick-ass video introduction, consisting of kick-ass wrestling highlights, the first 44 minutes of Warrior's presentation were uneventful. He talked of rights and responsibilities, and his definition of conservatism: "preserving traditions that have worked throughout time, beginning with the simple idea that people need to think and provide for themselves."*
>
> *Yes, things were fairly calm until Warrior described how liberal thinking has created an "abyss of moral relativity where everything is as legitimate as everything else.*
>
> *"The broadest and most despicable illustration of this most destructive consequence of moral relativity," Warrior said, "is that barbarism, today, is as legitimate as civilization."*

I, too, have watched this video, and I have to say this is a pretty fair assessment of what happened. Warrior spoke his views for a good forty minutes with little incident, mostly on being a moral representative of the world, yadda-yadda.

Now, let me preface this by saying I am a liberal-leaning person in many respects. If Warrior and I were to meet in real life, he would call me an idiot who is destroying the very fabric of our society, except with a few more made up seventy-five cent words. And you know what? I'm fine with that. Everyone is entitled to their opinions and beliefs. Warrior happens to believe concrete, ego-centric Christian values are the true morality and everything else is bupkis. Well good, I don't believe that at all. But likely at least half the world does to some extent, especially if voting patterns can be believed in the United States.

That brings me to my next point. When Warrior made his inflaming comments, three quarters of the room was clapping and cheering. They either agreed with the man or the sentiment. Granted, it was in a room of young college Republicans (no offense, Mike LaFave), but even if they did not agree with the words, they enjoyed the intensity and meaning with which they were spoken.

Why did Warrior speak such words? Well, the Hartford Advocate alludes to it but does not outright say it: Warrior was being heckled. A group of extreme liberals went to the show with the express intention of heckling Warrior. Some were handing out fliers before the event with out-of-context quotes from Warrior to help prove their point that Warrior was no good. Basically, Warrior was antagonized and spoken over (during his own speech, no less!) until he was forced to respond.

Warrior has never hidden the fact that he does not believe in political correctness, and then decided to antagonize the liberals right back. He almost drove them to violence, proving his point, or at least in his own mind.

UConn, though, and the young Republican group chose not to back Warrior after the event and issued a retraction and apology. From Warrior's website:

> *Explain for me if you will, young College Republicans, how you square your applause and praise at the event, a 45 minute ride together back to the airport having a mature, engaging discussion, and further praise, handshakes, and appreciation for coming with an absolute denouncement of my appearance and the things I said?*

He's right. Whether they agreed with him or not (and his views were never hidden), the college Republicans betrayed Warrior and lied to his face. There was time before, during, and after the speech in which they completely supported Warrior, and yet turned against him when the PC police got on their case. If you have ever read Warrior's writings, this is one of the things he absolutely despises, and has criticized even Republican leaders for giving in to such tactics. Whether I agree or not is irrelevant, those are the Warrior's opinions and he is entitled to them.

As I noted above, other people do agree with Warrior and support him, he is not alone in his thoughts. From Melissa Beecher's report of Warrior at Bentley College in February 2003:

> ["]He exceeded all of my expectations," said Andy Prunier, co-vice chairman of the Bentley College Republicans, the group that sponsored the event. "He didn't sugarcoat anything and I appreciated that."
>
> "What you come to college for is to hear a variety of views, both liberal and conservative, and he really let his views be known," said junior Matt Revan. "He is direct and gave it to us straight."
>
> "I really didn't know what to expect, knowing that the Warrior is a rookie as a speaker. But this really was a great event. We couldn't be happier," said Chris DeRose, a freshman co-vice chairman of the Republican group. "He got up there and presented some important issues."

And from Nicholas Norcia's report of an appearance at Penn State University in October 2003:

> "That was the greatest speech I've seen at this school," said Mike Jozkowski (senior-mathematics). "He emphasized that what makes this country great is self-reliance -- the pull-yourself-up-by-your-bootstraps mentality."

I could go on forever with these, but the point it made. Warrior's views, taken in sound bites, can be made to look ridiculous. But his whole views, taken all together and in context, can make an argument that a large minority of people would agree with. He is not an insane lone wolf, but a man representing many people, though maybe not you nor me.

And then there is the big question:

Does what Warrior do at speeches take away from (or add to) his accomplishments in wrestling?

The answer is no! One has nothing to do with the other except they are by the same man. Do you judge how well you did on math test by how well you can swim? Do you judge how good your costing analysis was by that time you ate worms when you were three?

We are talking about separate worlds, and when I think of the Warrior in our world of professional wrestling, I want to remember the wrestler above all and his impact and meaning to the industry. What he does in his personal time and his new life are of little concern to me except if it means he will return to wrestling. More on that in a bit.

For now, what do other wrestlers think of the current Warrior? From the Flynn interview:

> **FLYNN:** Firsthand, or secondhand, have you gotten any sort of reaction from any of your old colleagues in wrestling about what you're doing these days?
>
> **WARRIOR:** No, well—yes, secondhand. Goes back to what I said earlier. I'm cut from a different mold. Most the guys I worked with are still trying to make a living off the business, in any way they can. They haven't grown in the ways I have. Of course, they think what I am doing is oddball. Truth is they don't really know and have never taken the time to find out. Everybody who finds out about what I am doing these days by reading some criticism of me elsewhere, when they take the time to come and find out truly where my head is, they are pleasantly surprised. Many are proud to have been fans of my wrestling career, but even more proud to say they are bigger fans of what I am doing now.

Like I said, Warrior is not Terry Funk, he's Warrior. He has to cut his own path.

THE ONCE AND FUTURE...

> **FLYNN:** Any chance you'll ever go back to wrestling?

> **WARRIOR:** *I don't foresee it. There's no place to go. I can't split my energies and always have in the back of my mind that I will return. I just keep on keeping on with what I am doing now. I have been able though to use quite advantageously the intellectual property. New dolls are out and they are selling better than all others. I just sold one of my collector's dolls for more than that has ever been paid for a wrestling figure. And I am in Akklaim's new "Legends of Wrestling" game. The response about that has been over the top—getting ready to do some promotional appearances for that soon. It's been, believe it or not, very humbling to see how Ultimate Warrior's popularity has sustained itself. Of course, I never expected anything less (laughs).*

As just seen in the Flynn interview, Warrior had no intention of going back to wrestling. He does not need wrestling like some, although he still has an interest. It was his life for fifteen years. Of course, since I've been laying out the case for Warrior, he had to flood the news board. From 411mania(!):

> *In an interesting commentary on his official website, the Ultimate Warrior (Warrior Warrior) says that if TNA is serious about competing, they need to bring him and Goldberg in and let them have a match together. Below is a portion of the commentary.*
>
> *"[Sting] also mentioned in the press conference that Ultimate Warrior coming to TNA would be interesting. Yes, I have to agree -- it would be very interesting. What would be more interesting is if the TNA execs had the creativity, integrity and balls to entertain it seriously. Frankly, what they should do, if they want to be competitive (there's that nasty blood, sweat and tears word again), is sell some of those construction materials Daddy Jarrett has laying around, and put up the financing to bring in Goldberg and Ultimate Warrior and let us try to beat the intensity out of one another.*
>
> *Now there's an idea -- an attention getting one, and a money making one. I mean, instead of always using "warrior" as the adjective to fallaciously describe all those who aren't -- bring a real, and Ultimate, one in. Let the hardcore, natural intensity rip. Let both of us take our*

> mischaracterized heads halfway out of our asses, just enough for us to be businessmen capable of discussing the serious potential success yet not enough to defuse a competitive grudge, and let the serious and creative thinkers at TNA, those without an agenda or envy problem, work out a program.
>
> Put your silly a** fear and prejudice for my strong, bold character away and think SUCCESS. Hell, I'm all for great ideas. But don't expect me to keep my mouth shut when you don't come up with any. Of course, as I hinted at, it won't be inexpensive. Goldberg has an agent and has to give him a cut. I'm my own and I charge even more. The bigger obstacle, and definitely the one that has us both the most hated in the industry, is that we are strong individualists who don't need, or even necessarily want, to be in the business and can get along having great lives without it. But, what a way it would be for the most envied and despised to shove the final word down the throats of those Nor'Easterners, while TNA capitalizes off the incredible heat of it all."

Warrior is not hiding anything. I like his last thought: "I'm my own [agent] and I charge even more." Warrior, as we have noted, is not into wrestling just to be in wrestling. He won't just accept whatever is being offered just to get back into ring. Wrestling is work to Warrior, not life. From the Flynn interview:

> **FLYNN:** You haven't wrestled since then. Has anyone approached you to come back since then, like the Jarrett outfit?
>
> **WARRIOR:** Yeah, when they first started up they did—others too, mostly dreamers. I spoke with both Jeff and his dad. They, the Jarretts and others, always present themselves like they think I'm sitting at home drooling for a chance to charge at the ring and that I should be grateful that they called, like, allowing me an opportunity to do so. Blows me away. Of course, that is how most other guys still working, outside WWE, are. They don't know anything else, are afraid to go out and attempt anything else and get all their [self-worth] from being in a ring, staying part of the circus of it all. They don't have any other means of making a living for themselves so when anybody calls and

> *says jump they say how high and when their feet hit they ask about how far to bend over.*
>
> *This type of attitude they have though, these promoters, like the Jarretts had when they called, creates a problem when it comes to negotiating with me. This has contributed to many mischaracterizations. They get offended when they realize I know how valuable the Ultimate Warrior is and if they want him he isn't going to come cheaply. They don't get away without discussing those details with me like they do with others, which is to say they don't really discuss them in detail at all with others. It's like, "Hey, we have a ring set up and are going to put your face on TV for a little while, come on down and we'll figure what we'll pay you afterwards." That's enough for most guys looking for work not doing anything else. That doesn't work for me.*

You see, Warrior is not a wrestler looking for one more day in the spotlight. He only wants to do something if it is going to make an impact and last in history. Is him fighting Goldberg in TNA one of those things? Perhaps it is. We'll never know until we see it. But Warrior is open to the idea, and honest about what he expects.

In the meantime, Warrior has a lawsuit with the WWE to go through (breach of contract and defamation of character) and many more paths to pursue. Will this be the last gorilla press slam by Warrior? I truly believe not.

> *While his lawsuit would be dismissed in 2009, Warrior and WWE eventually found a way to work together starting in 2013. On April 5, 2014 he was inducted into the WWE Hall of Fame. The next night at WrestleMania 30 he made an appearance, followed by a speech on RAW on April 7, 2014. It turned out that this would be his last appearance anywhere as he died of an apparent heart attack the very next day at the age of 54.*

AND SO ENDS THE ULTIMATE CHALLENGE

After reading such a long case, I don't think you need a summary. But instead, I'll leave you with a couple of quotes that sum up the basic ideas. First, from Warrior himself:

> *Gotta run...taking my daughter, Ms. Indiana Marin Warrior, to the Russian Ballet of Sleeping Beauty [tonight]... just another one of those 'self-destructive' things I do.*

And last, as Derek Burgan so aptly noted in his review of the Self-Destruction DVD:

> *Christian [closed] out the DVD with possibly the truest statement on it, "like it or not, everyone remembers the Ultimate Warrior.*

The defense rests.

AFTER THE TRIAL

HUNG JURY

IN THE CASE OF THE IWC VS. THE ULTIMATE WARRIOR, WARRIOR HAS BEEN ACCUSED OF BEING A MENTALLY UNSTABLE, FLASH-IN-THE-PAN WRESTLER WITH AN OVER-INFLATED SENSE OF WORTH AND DESERVED THE BURIAL JOB HE GOT IN THE "SELF-DESTRUCTION OF THE ULTIMATE WARRIOR" DVD.

With 66.3% of the vote, the Ultimate Warrior was found:

NOT GUILTY!

Oh.... Bwa hahahahhahahahahahhaha! Sorry, that was a major release. There were times when "Guilty" was winning by a big enough margin, but then people actually read the case and changed their minds. As further proof, the Ultimate Warrior and Goldberg were my two most voted on cases ever. Perhaps, then, Warrior has a point that a match between the two would be a huge draw?

More people than usual said it was my best case ever. I don't know, maybe. It was certainly the longest and probably the second-most researched (after Eric Bischoff). There was a lot of other projects going on at the same time, so I do have to appreciate that it came together so well.

Response

First up, I wanted to start with my own response to several people (both ones that voted Guilty and Not Guilty) about using Warrior as his own witness:

> *I liked using the Warrior as his own witness. Several people wrote in that I did a great job of making Warrior look sane. See, you can make Warrior look like a complete nut job if you take the right quotes out of context and plaster them together. But if you take the correct context and boil down what he is actually saying, he's actually rather eloquent. I don't agree with 90% of what he says, but he does make real arguments if you do not shut him out immediately.*

There were other questionable or unclear remarks I made that required some clarification as well:

> *Having been a Christian for nearly 20 years I would have to say that while some of Warrior's philosophical beliefs intersect with mine (and what I perceive to be Christianity) [his] belief system is not a Christian one. Warrior believes in an abstract creator, a Christian follows God's will (note capital G) who has definite preferences for our lives and models his/her life after Jesus Christ, my Savior and Lord.*
>
> *Example: I would not have blasted wrestlers right after they died. Jesus told us to love everyone. What about the families of those wrestlers. He showed zero compassion for them. He could have said the same things after the initial shock and while the families would have been upset it wouldn't have been rubbing salt in a fresh wound. He has the right to speak his piece (and I agree with some of what he said, death doesn't make you a saint) but it was too soon.*
>
> *Christian does not equal Republican or conservative. Too many Christians think so and thus it is understandable why you would describe Warrior's neoconservative philosophy as Christian (along with other adjectives). But God is neither conservative or liberal. He stands on His own.*
>
> **Christopher Pineo**

To which I responded:

> I'm sorry Chris, I didn't mean to equate Christianity as a whole to right wing politics. I meant that a number of right wing conservatives use Christianity as an excuse for some of their policies, even though (as you say) those values are not true Christian values but a bastardized version of them. That's all I meant, no disrespect was intended.

Of course, what was even more interesting was having liberal minded people defend Warrior after reading this piece:

> Thanks for writing such a fascinating article. I've been following your column since it started and I really do think this is your best work yet. Why do I think that? I do because I went into reading the article as a true Warrior-hater. Your article honestly changed my opinion of him and now I actually think the guy is pretty inspirational. Oh, and I am very liberal myself. So, your victory in winning me over is even more impressive.
>
> Good job, man.
>
> A fan,
> **-Matt Essary**

> I've been waiting a long time for some kind of intelligent, thought out defense of the Ultimate Warrior's wrestling career. Thank you for providing such. Regardless of my personal views on his current opinions, he made an undeniable impact on professional wrestling, and the Ultimate Challenge at Wrestlemania 6 will always be the match that makes my hair stand up on end through [its] sheer power and epic feeling. It was the closest I believe you can come to seeing two people who seemed more than mere mortals colliding.
>
> --
> **Derek Houck**

As an aside, sometimes it is just fun to hear little interactions:

> *I just wanted to add, [I] dealt with Warrior on EBAY, truly a class act to deal with.*
>
> **Justin Swift**

And finally was this little ditty:

> *Great article. The best complete [review] of [W]arrior I have read………*
>
> *[W]rite a book!*
>
> **s_brown**

> *I am writing a book! But it has nothing to do with wrestling. Would you like a wrestling book from me? You aren't the first one to suggest it. I've been thinking about doing a collection of the In Defense Of... series with some additional commentary from me (why I chose the topic, why I placed it where I did, why it was important). Would that actually sell? I'm not so sure.*
>
> **JP Prag**
> **April 16, 2006**

Hopefully I didn't miss the window…

Scott Steiner

Intro

Some dame walked into my office and said...

Several trials back I was thinking, "I really need a good medium-length case to help close out the first year of trials." Well, to my great surprise and happiness, **Lester Romero** came up with the answer:

> *How about something more difficult like Scott Steiner? It's a shame how many people forget how incredible he was and how he's mostly remembered for his later injury prone years.*

Thus, I made it so!

Of course, our main **fixer (#315)** said:

> *You must have read my mind when I thought of another guy that needed defending: Scott Steiner.*

Reading minds? Maybe...

But more than one person thought it would be a great defense. And more than one person thought I was out of my mind for agreeing to this case. Sounds like the perfect reason for me to take the case!

Why this?

For nearly twenty years, Scott Steiner has been a major figure in wrestling. But his career has been two-fold: one part helping to define the new tag team era, the other as the resurrection of the heel main eventer. Because Steiner has really been two, very distinct characters, his previous accomplishments are often forgotten. Not only that, but the more recent years have overshadowed even how much he accomplished in his second phase.

Instead of being recognized as a trendsetter and a major player, Steiner has become a joke. Instead of being recognized for his influence on the industry that is still prevalent to this day, Steiner has become just a bunch of quick one-liners.

Because some did not like his evolution, and others never knew him, and others yet only saw the worst he had to offer, Steiner has been buried. But here is a man whose career spans so much time and says so much; how can we sum it up with a laugh at his expense?

Before we get too far, though, we need to understand where we've been.

Scott Steiner Part 1 – Scott Steiner

On July 29, 1962, Rick Rechsteiner was surprised to find that he had a new baby brother. Of course, he didn't realize that he had a baby brother since he was just a year and half old, so the two grew up together. Their parents gave the new baby the name of Scott.

Scott and Rick spent their childhood in Bay City, MI. As brothers so close in age, they found themselves as their own best friends and worst enemies. Brothers fight, and brothers support each other no matter what. Neither growing up was a fan of professional wrestling, but both found a common interest in amateur wrestling. Their love of the mat-based sport led both Rick and Scott to the University of Michigan where they met with much success. According to Obsessed with Wrestling, Scott himself stated:

> [Received] 6th Place at the 1986 NCAA championships 190 lbs his senior year. He was also a 3x Big 10 Runner Up getting 2nd place his sophomore, Junior, and senior year.

Rick also met with similar success a little earlier, placing fourth in the NCAA Championship.

While in college, too, both got their full introduction to professional wrestling. Scott was not immediately drawn to the sport, but Rick was. After meeting with George "The Animal" Steele, Rick set himself to become a professional wrestler immediately after graduation. After training with Eddie Sharkey, Rick made his pro debut in 1983 and began a path that would eventually lead him to the NWA in 1988.

Meanwhile, Scott was still in school and was not sure of his direction. But, after watching his brother progress in wrestling up until that point (and listening to Rick go on about his new passion), and realizing that he could take his amateur career and turn it into a professional one, he felt it was a risk worth taking. Much like Kurt Angle, he realized that amateur and professional wrestling were two different worlds that required varied skills, but still had the same route. In order to bring about this route, he began to train in 1986 under one of the best ever: The Original Sheik.

Due to his amateur skills, Scott's training passed quickly and he made his debut in Indianapolis for the World Wrestling Association. His abilities and charisma, while severely subdued compared to later years, helped him win over the crowd and the WWA Championship. After winning the belt from Greg Wojokowski in August 1986, Steiner would go on to hold the belt for nearly nine months before losing it back to the former champ. From there, Steiner would move on to his tag team career. This began by teaming with Jerry Graham and winning the WWA Tag Team titles.

After a couple of runs, Steiner moved on to the AWA for a short bit before finding his way to CWA in Memphis. There, be won the tag team titles with both Billy Travis and Jeb Grundy between 1988 and 1989. All of his time spent in the tag team ranks had trained Scott to have a deep understanding and appreciation of tag team wrestling that is not truly prevalent in this day and age.

Finally the time had come to join his brother and shorten his name to just Steiner.

Rick had been in the NWA since 1988 and wanted to bring his brother in, but to no avail. From Brandon Truitt's recap of the Rick Steiner Shoot interview (July 2003):

> *Bringing Scott into the company- He tried to do it when Dusty was booking but couldn't even get a minute of his time. After his face turn, he pitched it to Flair and a few other guys who ended up bringing Scott in.*

There are people that said Rick just used his influence to get Scott a free ride right to the top of the NWA. This, as you have seen, cannot be further from the truth. Scott spent three years on his own in the independents and large minor organizations learning and honing his craft. At that, it took nearly a year and a change in booking power to even have his brother looked at. And so, Scott was brought in to see how the Steiners would do together.

The Steiner Brothers debuted in June 1989 and quickly lost to Mike Rotunda and Kevin Sullivan at Clash of the Champions VII. They impressed the office and the audience, though, and quickly got their win back at the Great American Bash a month later. Their feuds with Doom and the Freebirds led to the Steiner Brothers capturing the NWA Tag Team Championships on November 1, 1989, just five months after their debut. Part of that was Scott Steiner's unique finisher: the Frankensteiner. From IMDB:

> *Inventor of the "Frankensteiner", a wrestling maneuver that is more commonly used today by cruiserweight wrestlers. This move is now known as a "Hurricanrana".*

While it is debatable whether Steiner "invented" the Frankensteiner, the point is that he popularized the move in North America and Japan, and paved the way for future cruiserweight wrestlers. One problem: Steiner was no cruiserweight. At the time, Steiner was around 245-255 lbs. and was quite muscular (not as much as he was in later life), so the move was even more amazing when pulled off.

You see, Steiner realized that he could capture the audience through his look, his gimmicks, on the mic, and with his moves. He wanted to master of all of them, and this was just another step to prove how innovative he was. Steiner himself commented on keeping the move secret for a while. From Sean McCaffrey's review of the Scott Steiner Shoot Interview:

> *Scott talks about inventing the Frankensteiner. He talks about the origin of the move and how he waited to debut it in NWA because he didn't want people stealing it in Memphis.*

Steiner understood the difference between the big show and the little show, and he did not want to give it all away when it would not be seen. This was a lesson that wrestlers like Nova (Simon Dean) never took to heart. The often-lamented complaint in ECW was the moves that Nova did over the weekend were guaranteed to show up on Monday Night. And you know what? They were right. But that does not mean they were smart. Steiner was smart and understood the difference in his level, and understood he needed to save his best stuff for the biggest show in town.

Scott was extremely proud of the move and his tag team status. Said Steiner to the Wrestling Digest in June 2001 when asked about his biggest moments in wrestling:

> "The first time my brother and I won the NWA world tag-team title on November 1, 1989, and the first time I won the world heavyweight title this past November. Those are the two top trophies in the sport. You can't get any bigger than that."

Do you see what I mean? Steiner considered the tag team championships that he won with his brother in 1989 just as important as the World Heavyweight Championship he won in 2000. There is a man who truly respects tag team wrestling, which is most likely why he and his brother became such a dominating tag team. Unlike many wrestlers (or more likely writers) in this era, they wanted to be a tag team and saw prestige in it. Steiner said earlier in the same interview:

> The rest of my career, I have been focused on tag-team wrestling and winning tag-team championships. The world title really wasn't on my mind for the first part of my career.

The Steiner Brothers' tag team career continued, not only winning the NWA/WCW championships, but also holding the IWGP Tag Team titles as well. You see, Rick and Scott had also begun to make a name for themselves in Japan and became an international super team. For the first time ever, the WCW and IWGP tag team titles were unified (for four months) until Scott was injured.

After repeating this event in 1992, Rick left WCW to concentrate on Japan. Back in the States, Scott moved into singles competition for a while, even winning the Television Title. After the Steiner Bros. lost the IWGP tag team titles in November 1992, Scott vacated the WCW Television Title and the duo moved on to the WWF. From the previously mentioned interview in the Wrestling Digest:

> **WD:** You and Rick spent some time in the WWF and captured the tag-team rifle. What are your thoughts on your time spent there?
>
> **SS:** I have a lot of respect for Vince McMahon. He took a family business and made it bigger than it was. I am sure his son, Shane, will do the same thing. The time we were with them was a bad [time], because he was going through that steroid trial and wrestling was down. So, it was unfortunate for us that we picked that time to join the WWF. We still proved a point; we still won the tag [title]. At the end, we just got a better offer and went to Japan for a few years and made better money.

And also from Sean McCaffrey's review of Scott's Shoot Interview:

> Scott says he wanted a change of scenery and wanted some stability in his career, and that's why the Steiners jumped to the WWF. He also said he should've never jumped to the WWF at the time, and said everyone was miserable there.
>
> He says he left the WWF for Japan because the WWF was so depressing at the time.

You have to remember at that time in WCW, the boss was changing every few weeks. The organization was a mess and many people thought it was about to crumble. The Steiner Brothers hoped to find a more stable home in the WWF, but that was not to be. Due to the steroid trial, things were not going well. From the same review:

> Scott talks about Vince and the steroid trial and how Vince thought he was going to jail.

That seems familiar... where have I seen that before? Oh right! It was exactly what Warrior said was happening and what Vince said. I like when guys that have nothing to do with each other separated by years back each other up.

But the Steiners made their point and won the straps a couple of times in just a year and a few months. The Steiners then went on to Japan and made sparing appearances for ECW. Japan was all about the money, as Steiner noted in his interview with Wrestling Digest:

> I have always made it a point in my career to go where the money is.

ECW, though, was for different reasons. From the review of the Shoot Interview:

> Scott talks about working in ECW for a cup of coffee, and how his main concern at the time was Japan.

What ECW was for Steiner was just something to do while he was stateside. His real concern (and money) was Japan. Scott was never fired from WCW or WWF and forced to work in ECW; he had chosen everywhere he wanted to go.

In 1996, WCW came calling and the Steiner Brothers left Japan to return to WCW full time. It was a different organization then, much more stable and about to grow. They began feuds with the Road Warriors and Harlem Heat, but the birth of the nWo changed everything. The Steiner Brothers became the penultimate force against the Outsiders, even winning the Tag Titles at Souled Out 1997 before having the decision reversed on them the next night.

Their feuds would continue through 1997, winning the Tag Team titles a couple of times en route. After losing the titles back to the nWo in January 1998, everything changed...

SCOTT STEINER PART 2 – THE BIG BAD BOOTY DADDY

From Accelerator3359:

> *This was when Scott's attitude began to change. He became less of a team player, and engaged in a "body" feud with "Buff" Bagwell over who could flex better. This did not stop the two brothers from becoming 6-time WCW Tag-Team Champs, as they beat the Outsiders in February. Although the Steiners seemed united again, it was not to last. On February 22nd, at Superbrawl VIII, Scott betrayed his brother to the nWo, practically giving the titles to the Outsiders. Scott had jumped to nWo.*
>
> *Scott's next appearance showed him as a bleached blonde, with various nicknames (the White Thunder one was dropped due to possible racial suggestions). He offered an nWo membership to Rick as well, but Rick refused. Scott then had feuds with his brother Rick, Lex Luger, and others. Scottie joined "Buff" Bagwell as the two became a team, since Bagwell couldn't wrestle due to his injury. The Steiner vs. Steiner feud then continued for months, with Rick winning the tag belts from his brother and the Giant.*

It was a slow turn that people saw coming but could not wait for. Nobody knew just quite what was going to happen and who Scott Steiner would become. From Tim Baines in the Ottawa Sun:

> *After being a "face" much of his career, Steiner suddenly became a heel in WCW.*
>
> *"Eric (Bischoff) came up to me and asked if I wanted to be a heel," he [Scott Steiner] said. "I was ready for the change. I bleached my black hair blond.*
>
> *"Eric didn't have much faith in the booking committee so he let me do my own thing ... say whatever popped into my mind."*

In something you do not see today, Steiner was really in charge of creating his new character and his new story. And what he came up with was a true heel of the modern era, one who people loved to boo, but were captivated by. His catchphrases were numerous and interesting, but always pulled the audience in. From Wikipedia:

> - *"Say something nice and I'll make you scream twice!"*
>
> - *"This goes out to all my freaks out there. Big Poppa Pump is your hookup; holler if you hear me!"*
>
> - *"All my hoochies say: there's nothing finer than Scott Steiner!"*
>
> - *"You know where to find me: I'll be flexin' my PEAKS, pleasin' my FREAKS... and when they say 'BOOM-shakalaka!', that's when you KNOW that I'm the Big Booty Daddy! So Big Poppa Pump is your hook-up--HOLLA if ya hear me!!"*
>
> - *"Do you want to be [mesmerized] by the physical [phenomenon]?"*
>
> - *"All I care about is my peaks, and my freaks, nation-wide!"*

But it wasn't just the words and look, it was also the in-ring style. Steiner stopped using the ropes and became more mat and power based. Many complained that it was because he bulked up so much that he could not pull off the moves he once did. That was not the case, though. Steiner chose to change his style because he was a whole new character. After a decade as the same guy, he wanted to be completely different. That also included changing his finished to the Steiner Recliner (a submission move: a sitting camel clutch).

Steiner's new character would cause controversy in and out of the ring (we'll get to it), but eventually still led him from the Television to US and finally World Championship. In November 2000 at WCW Mayhem, Steiner defeated Booker T to win the WCW Championship for the first (and last) time. He would hold the title until the very last day of WCW, losing it back to Booker T in the opening contest of Night of Champions Nitro.

You have to realize that this was an extremely turbulent time in WCW and the fact that Steiner was able to stand out and find his way to the top is a testament to his professionalism and dedication. It was also during this time that he established himself as top wrestlers with impressive wins over not only Sid and Kevin Nash, but also Goldberg in a match that made him look even more powerful than the unstoppable machine.

During this phase, his rise to the title was really meteoric. If you consider Big Poppa Pump as a whole new man, then it was a relatively short time. From the Wrestling Digest interview:

> **WRESTLING DIGEST:** As of this interview [published three months later], you are WCW's world heavyweight champion. It was a long [time] coming. What took you so long to get there?
>
> **SCOTT STEINER:** I have heard that comment before, that it has taken me a long time to get there. Well, it hasn't taken me that long, maybe two-and-a-half years.

You see, Steiner was not looking to be the top singles competitor in the world when he was with his brother; he wanted to be the best tag team. But once he concentrated on his single's success, he quickly found his way to the top.

But with the death of WCW, it would seem like he would be forgotten.

WHEN AND WHEN NOT TO GO

Scott often gets criticized for not taking a buyout at the end of WCW and going directly to the (then) WWF. This, of course, led to him losing the title on the first match on Nitro. From the recap of Scott's Sheet Interview:

> *Scott talks about the final Nitro, and how he refused to take a buyout. He said he had an injury that he wanted to heal anyway.*

And further from IMDB:

> *Steiner decided to take things easy for a while to recover from some back problems that he had been having, along with a severe nerve problem in his left leg.*

So Scott stayed at home and got healed up (not heeled), what is wrong with that? The guy had been on the road for fifteen years at that point and had been in some brutal matches. He needed time to get healthy, and he was still a little sour from his last time in the WWF.

Even though he made a few independent appearances and did some shows for the WWA tour at the end of his Time-Warner contract, Steiner was not desperate for work. Wrestling was his career, but he was still well off. Back to the recap of Scott's Shoot interview:

> *Scott talks about joining the WWE, and how he was offered to join several times before he eventually accepted. Scott said he wanted the right amount of money to come back to wrestle, since he was financially set. He said the WWE product was some brutal shit at the time, so he wasn't in no hurry to join WWE.*
>
> *Scott talks about how he was basically brought in just to put over Hunter. Scott says that Vince didn't know how to use any of the WCW guys right. Scott says it was brutal to work for Vince.*
>
> *Scott talks about Hunter [trying] to make people look bad. Scott said he didn't care about being buried because he was getting paid no matter what.*

Scott did not need the money of the WWE, but that does not mean he would not accept it. From Scott's interview with UCW's Steven Goforth:

> **Steven:** I must say that I was very disappointed with the way WWE used you during your recent time there. How did you feel about your time spent in the WWE?
>
> **Steiner:** I wasn't very happy either. I had heard rumors that the only reason they brought me in was to work Triple H. But they signed me for 3 years so I got paid regardless, so who looks stupid[?] [N]ot me. It is [their] fault they didn't use me correctly. They never used or had good spots for any of the WCW guys. GOLDBERG didn't get used like he should have either. Vince never won over or got the WCW fan base.
>
> **Steven:** Why did WWE choose not to be more creative with your character and let you be involved in storylines with more wrestlers?
>
> **Steiner:** When you go up there, they make you into a robot, they even wrote my interviews, and that never happened in WCW. The same four people wrote everything for all the guys, so no one has very much personality that's different. But I don't think anyone on WWE now has much character.

And from Tim Baines' article in the Ottawa Sun:

> "I had a feeling they weren't going to do much with me," said Steiner (real name, Scott Rechsteiner) over the phone. "But it wasn't the first time they treated a guy from WCW like that. They seemed to s--t on the guys from WCW."

Steiner said it right. The WWE intentionally mismanaged his character because (1) they just wanted to use him to put over Triple H and (2) because there is no understanding of the WCW audience. At the time of this writing, RAW the prior week scored a 4.0 rating. Even during the low times of Nitro, the combined audience for RAW and Nitro was usually in the 7.0 range. Where are the other 3.0 ratings of people? Lost forever because Vince buried WCW.

Of course, there will be those who say that Steiner was ruined by his wrestling, especially Royal Rumble 2003. And let me tell you, that was an awful match to watch. How do I know? I was there live.

The match basically consisted of Steiner throwing the same two suplexes over and over for twenty minutes until Triple H hit him with a sledgehammer. To say the crowd turned against Steiner would be an understatement. Why, though, would the WWE put Steiner in such a position? He had a lot of ring rust and was told in the back how he should wrestle his match. And then to put him out there for twenty minutes?

Also, he had been a heel for five years, yet the WWE wanted him as a watered-down face (sound like a similar practice to, oh, John Cena? And to similar result, no doubt.).

No, that reeks of being set up for failure. That is like putting the female winner of Tough Enough in the ring a week after winning the competition and then blaming her because the match was bad. How can you do that? That is being intentionally set up to lose.

And if you watch Steiner's later matches, especially those with/against Test, he was able to shake off the ring rust and bring back his style. Those matches were often some of the most solid on the show, even though Test is not considered much of a worker either.

After December 2003, the WWE elected to just let Steiner's contract run out, again proving they had mismanaged him and could find nothing to do with him. The WWE somehow finds ways to use Mark Henry (nothing against Mark Henry, he's just been around for ten years), but could find no way to use Scott Steiner. Seems quite peculiar.

Of course, this would not be the end of Scott Steiner. He would be heard from just shortly after announcing this case...

HAVE YOU SEEN MY LOST PUPPY?

For a while now, Steiner has been making sporadic appearances on the indy circuit, usually in organizations that he was asked to come to by friends and family (notably Buff Bagwell and Rick Steiner). But as it would happen, immediately after announcing this case, rumors began that Steiner was in talks with TNA.

And as of Destination X, it looks like Steiner has joined the company. For how long? For how much? As of the time of this writing, nothing is for sure. What we do know is that despite everything that happened in the WWE, interest in Steiner has remained high, and he has one last chance to prove what he is made of.

Of course, many have had a hard time understanding what Steiner is about.

MISUNDERSTAND THIS!

Throughout his Big Poppa Pump years, Steiner has been characterized as a loose cannon, someone who could go off at any second. But, much like New Jack, is Steiner just working us? Kevin Eck of the Wrestling Digest seemed to think so in February 2003:

> Steiner then reminded fans why he is known for being as dangerous with his mouth on live television as he is with his fists in the ring. "Give me the [expletive deleted] [mic]," he screamed.
>
> Less than two minutes into his WWE comeback, he already had dropped his first "f-bomb."
>
> That intensity and "loose cannon" quality are two of the reasons why fans find Steiner so fascinating. You never know what he's going to say or do; whether he's playing a role or is truly out of control.

And...

> Steiner's publicized brushes with the law and backstage conflicts only served to give credibility to his volatile heel persona in WCW. With Steiner, the fans truly believed that he could snap and go off on someone for real at any moment.
>
> And unlike almost every other wrestling star on the current scene, Steiner refuses to ever break character in magazine or Web site interviews or acknowledge that the business is a work.
>
> "What happened outside the ring proved that what was going on in wrestling wasn't an act," Steiner told WCW Magazine in 2001. "It wasn't a character that was conjured up by someone in the back. I think the fans realize it is real with me."

Steiner is the ultimate "swork" character. We really do not know where the character ends and the man begins, and vice versa. Yet, he has let himself be pinned by everyone from Booker T at the last Nitro, Triple H, and even Test. So on one hand he seems to be all about himself, yet at other times he seems to be the ultimate professional.

Despite this, Steiner has been known to "go into business for himself". On two separate occasions on Nitro, Steiner actually went out with a live mic and ran down people he was not in a program with (Ric Flair and DDP, to be precise). Perhaps, though, he had good reason to act the way he did. Perhaps he was actually trying to vindicate someone. From Michael KopStick recap of Tammy Sytch's shoot interview:

> Her ECW stint didn't end with a happy goodbye, either. The internet rumor about this firing was drugs; she says that Paul just wanted to make an example of her and Chris since everyone else was doing worse drugs than they were. The Extreme locker room featured drinking, pills, pot, heroine, coke, you name it. Tammy and Chris drank and did pills, nothing more, but that didn't mater to Paul. "He can be a jerk that way," Tammy shrugs. But it wasn't that much of a big deal since they were already in talks with ECW-raider WCW.
>
> They were three for three, getting fired next from WCW. This one was reported to be drugs, too, but the story behind this, Tammy clarifies, is that Eric Bischoff called them aside and pulled out pills, saying that the other girls found them in a bathroom stall she was using. This was the worst [concocted] story ever on the part of the WCW females because these were bodybuilding pills. Tammy doesn't bodybuild! There were other girls on the roster that did like to bulk up, like Asia and Midaja, but not her. She [immediately] offered to take a urine test, which WCW officials [administered] the next day, eager to prove the former Boddydonna wrong. She took it and was then told that the results will be known in three weeks. In the meantime, she was given a paid suspension...
>
> When Scott Steiner heard what was going on, he got even angrier than Tammy was. He learned that Kimberly was behind the whole thing, ran into the female locker room, grabbed the Diamond Doll by her shirt, hoisted her down the hall with her bags, and threw her out the door, threatening that if she ever shows up again in WCW he'd kill her. That was the last WCW saw of Kimberly Falkenberg.

You see, Steiner was actually trying to help someone out, someone who got fired anyway. He has always had his reasons for acting the way he did, but being a private man who did not want to break kayfabe too much, he never let out why.

And yet after that he maintained his professionalism. Steiner and DDP worked together a number of times, including just two weeks before the end of WCW. No, despite personal feelings, Steiner was always one thing: a professional.

NOW THAT'S DEDICATION

How far, though, would Steiner take his professionalism. We already covered that Steiner was not a fan of wrestling growing up, so that would have you believe that he would not have a dedication to do anything necessary. Steiner, though, took his job very seriously. From Brandon Truitt's recap of Rick Steiner's shoot interview:

> *Is it true Scott asked him to punch him in the face as part of an angle? Yes. Scott was supposed to have a black eye for one angle but it didn't look good enough. He asked Rick to pop him one to make it look better but not to hit him too hard.*

Now if that doesn't show dedication to one's craft, I don't know what does!

THE AWARDS

That dedication paid off with a string of awards. From Accelerator3359:

> *PWI Achievement Awards: (4 wins, 3 1st RUs, 3 2nd RUs, 3 3rd RUs)*
> - *1988 Rookie of the Year, 3rd Runner-Up*
> - *1989 Most Improved Wrestler*
> - *1990 Tag-Team of the Year (Steiners)*
> - *1991 Most Popular Wrestler, 3rd Runner-Up (Steiners)*
> - *1991 Match of the Year (Steiners vs. Sting & Lex Luger)*
> - *1991 Tag-Team of the Year, 2nd Runner-Up (Steiners)*
> - *1992 Tag-Team of the Year, 2nd Runner-Up (Steiners)*

- *1993 Match of the Year, 1st Runner-Up (Steiners vs. Heavenly Bodies)*
- *1993 Tag-Team of the Year (Steiner Brothers)*
- *1995 Tag-Team of the Year, 3rd Runner-Up (Steiners)*
- *1996 Tag-Team of the Year, 2nd Runner-Up (Steiners)*
- *1997 Tag-Team of the Year, 1st Runner-Up (Steiners)*
- *1998 Feud of the Year, 1st Runner-Up (nWo Hollywood vs. nWo Wolfpac)*

And of course there were a string of titles en route. Same site:

- *WWA Heavyweight Champion (8/14/86 - 5/03/87)*
- *WWA Tag-Team Champion w/ Jerry Graham Jr (10/04/87 - 12/06/87)*
- *CWA Tag-Team Champion w/ Bill Travis (5/29/88 - 6/6/88)*
- *CWA Tag-Team Champion(2) w/ Bill Travis (6/27/88 - 8/15/88)*
- *CWA Tag-Team Champion(3) w/ Jed Grundy (2/18/89 - 2/25/89)*
- *WCW World Tag-Team Champion w/ Rick Steiner (11/1/89 - 5/19/90)*
- *NWA United States Tag-Team Champion w/ Rick Steiner (8/24/90 - 2/20/91)*
- *PWA Tag-Team Champion w/ Rick Steiner (9/17/90 - 10/1/90)*
- *WCW World Tag-Team Champion(2) w/ Rick Steiner (2/18/91 - 7/18/91)*
- *IWGP Tag-Team Champion w/ Rick Steiner (3/21/91 - 11/5/91)*
- *WCW World Tag-Team Champion(3) w/ Rick Steiner (5/3/92 - 7/5/92)*
- *IWGP Tag-Team Champion(2) w/ Rick Steiner (6/26/92 - 11/22/92)*
- *WCW World Television Champion (9/29/92 - 11/92)*
- *WWF World Tag-Team Champion w/ Rick Steiner (6/14/93 - 6/16/93)*
- *WWF World Tag-Team Champion(2) w/ Rick Steiner (6/19/93 - 9/13/93)*
- *WCW World Tag-Team Champion(4) w/ Rick Steiner (7/24/96 - 7/27/96)*
- *WCW World Tag-Team Champion(5) w/ Rick Steiner (10/13/97 - 1/12/98)*

> - WCW World Tag-Team Champion(6) w/ Rick Steiner (2/9/98 - 2/22/98)
> - WCW World Television Champion (2) (12/28/98 - 3/14/99)
> - WCW United States Champion (4/11/99 - 7/5/99)
> - WCW United States Champion (2) (4/16/00 - 7/9/00)
> - WCW World Heavyweight Champion (11/26/00 - 3/26/01)
> - WWA Heavyweight Champion (4/13/02 - 03)
> - SSCW Heavyweight Champion (10/29/02 - 11/18/02)

Yes, Steiner has done it all in this industry. But has he done it with a little... "help"?

MMMMM... DRUGS...

For years the speculation has been that Scott Steiner is not a genetic freak, but a totally drugged up pusher. This speculation has run rampant even before the Big Poppa Pump gimmick. Yet, I could not find one wrestler or associate who said they saw Steiner do steroids. I found several that said they had no problem with steroids, but none as witnesses. A few people even said that they never saw Steiner do steroids, but they just assumed.

Well great, Steiner's own peers are assuming that he did steroids and perpetuating the rumors about him. Yet, everything available tells us otherwise.

From the Wrestling Digest in October 2000:

> **BA:** Do you take steroids?
>
> **SS:** If I was on steroids, how could I pass the drug test? We're tested randomly once or twice a month. If I did steroids I would be out of WCW. They are pretty strict on enforcing the drug tests. People are jealous. They could never look like me because I am a genetic freak. It pisses them off so they try to cut me down by saying things like I take steroids.
>
> I weigh 265 now, and I used to weigh around 280. I changed my diet, cut down on the carbohydrates. I'm on a really strict diet, which makes you leaner

> and makes your muscles stick out more. I had to get my upper body lighter just to take the pressure off my back since I had some back problems. I'm a lot leaner, and I feel a lot better.

And from the same magazine in June 2001:

> PEOPLE WHO THINK I USE STEROIDS CAN:
>
> "Kiss my ass. I have never failed a drug test in WCW or the WWF."

Also, from Sean McCaffrey's review of Scott Steiner's shoot interview:

> Scott talks about his rumored steroid abuse. Scott says he never failed a drug test. Scott tells a story about how WWE wanted to test him and Scott says OK, he'll take the test with Hunter, and that was the last time the WWE ever asked him to take a drug test again.

Steiner seems pretty adamant that he's never taken steroids, and he seems to have proof, yet everyone still doubts him. Perhaps I should bring in an expert? From Bodybuilding.com:

> **Q:** Do you think Scott Steiner's arms are real or do you think they are synthol?
>
> **A:** Thing is that Scott's arms were huge long before synthol was ever around. So to answer your question Steiner's arms are as real as Monica Brandt's ass! Now Gregg Valentino is another story. Here is a man with so much oil in his arms he could run NASCAR pit crews for a year.

You see, Scott's physique is possible with a ton of hard work. Even if he was taking steroids, he would still have to work just as hard (if not harder) to sculpt his body in that way. I would try to explain Scott Steiner's work out program, but I don't have fifty pages, so feel free to check it out here.

And as for the supposed "'roid rage" incidents, Steiner has always been characterized as a malcontent. He truly does have a disdain for the human condition, and he has felt that way since he was young. Sure, Steiner is not your happy-go-lucky type of wrestler, but does that mean that he is a destructive force. TNA again seems to think he has something to add, and who's to say that he can't give back one more time?

TO ALL MY FREAKS OUT THERE...

Scott Steiner is a misunderstood man. He is a man who has had a bi-polar career, who has been viewed as the best and the worst. His last major appearance left a sour taste in many people's mouths and demolished a legacy spanning two decades. But Steiner is a man who was dedicated to the tag team ranks and did everything from invent a prominent move to win simultaneous international championships. He was able to completely change who he was and become one of the top people in the turbulent end of WCW. Yet, being very closed and a believer in kayfabe, many misunderstand where the character ends and the man begins. Controversy follows Scott Steiner like a dog follows a treat, yet he has been a sparing man who is still a millionaire today. He is not desperate for money, he is not in need. He can only be coming back to wrestling for one reason: he wants to make a difference.

I'll sum it all up with this quote:

> "For a number of years, over in Japan and in WCW, I've always admired his wrestling ability, his wrestling skill and his character... He's a true professional. When it comes to business, he's all about it. I'd love to be able to get back in the ring with him and have some more matches. We had some great matches over in Japan, and some great matches in WCW... I'm happy to have him on the crew."

That quote came from Chris Benoit.

The defense rests.

AFTER THE TRIAL

HUNG JURY

IN THE CASE OF THE IWC VS. SCOTT STEINER, STEINER HAS BEEN ACCUSED

OF BEING A JUICED UP, LOOSE CANNON WHO ACCOMPLISHED NOTHING IN WRESTLING BUT STINKING UP THE RING WITH OVERALL TERRIBLE SKILLS AND WREAKING HAVOK WHEREVER HE WENT.

With 87.9% of the vote, Scott Steiner was found:

NOT GUILTY!

Definitely not as close as that Ultimate Warrior case was! Some people criticized my defense of Steiner not being on steroids by saying just because nobody has ever seen him do steroids does not mean that he hasn't done them. What's that saying? "The absence of evidence is not the evidence of absence"? Well, check the rest of the proof: he's already passed all the drug tests and offered to take more. Yes, muscles like that are *nearly* impossible, but that does not mean they cannot occur naturally. Take the right person with the right genes and the right food and the right workout regimen, and you will be able to get Big Poppa Pump. And if I'm proven wrong, so what? He's still one of the best ever.

RESPONSE

First up, we'll go a bit deeper into a story briefly covered above:

> *I don't really get the point about the woman with the drugs and Steiner using this as a means of talking trash about DDP and Flair, but apart from that I found it enlightening.*
>
> **TG Corke**

To which I was happy to enlighten a bit more:

> *Well, a little more backstory. Scott Steiner and DDP did not get along at all. DDP's wife, Kimberly, was known as a little... demanding backstage. Steiner and her used to get into all kinds of arguments, which of course led to a lot of arguments between him and DDP. It got so bad that Steiner took a live mic and shoot called out DDP, who in turn punched him when he got backstage. Because Vince Russo was the booker, this led to a worked feud on TV.*
>
> *So anyway, among the women in WCW, Kimberly was not loved at all. There was another woman*

> there named Tammy Lynn Sytch, who used to go by Sunny in the WWF/E. Sunny had had drug problems in the past, but had cleaned up. Kimberly basically did not like Tammy and fingered her for drug use so that she would get fired (knowing that Tammy was on probation as it was). When Steiner got wind of this, he got so mad at Kimberly for trying to get another girl fired that he literally threw her out of the building, which didn't help matters between he and DDP.
>
> Kimberly was not with the company for long after that either, and she and DDP got a divorce several years later, although I did hear they were dating again.
>
> Hope that clears that one up!

With other people, it was not about educating, but discussing a shared experience:

> I love Big Poppa Pump and was at the Royal Rumble when he wrestled HHH.
>
> **Adam Fitzgerald**

To which I told Adam:

> I had really good seats that night, down in the first level about twenty rows back. Where were you sitting?

And he let me know:

> I was wicked high in the building. I could see the entrance way where they came out to the ring, but I was so high that the scoreboard at the Fleetcenter was straight ahead of me. All and all, it was still cool to be there.
>
> **Adam Fitzgerald**

To wrap it all up, here are a couple of hilarious anecdotes of Scott Steiner in people's lives:

> Before I saw Steiner in WCW, I had pretty much only enjoyed local indy wrestling. I hadn't watched wrestling in about 5 years because the PNW territory went out of business. So in a about 1998 I was at a bar when I saw this "genetic freak" get in the ring on WCW TV and cut a promo on the crowd for being fat and lazy and jealous of him. Maybe not the most original heel promo idea, but Scott made it seem so vivid. Just looking at him made me feel like a slug, and everything he said about my lazy ass was true. He forced me to admit that I'm a fat piece of crap, and I loved it. That's a great heel promo. I became a WCW fan because of Scott Steiner.
>
> **James Norbeck**

> [A]nd for the record dude, my mother was/is totally in love with the man and refuses to watch wrestling he isn't involved with.
>
> She used to openly admit to being one of his "[hoochies]".
>
> It got to the point when [I] went to see the E live a few years back and I told her he'd be on the card she told me to say hello to him for her.
>
> So there you have it, Scott Steiner, loved by middle aged women everywhere (at least in Australia).
>
> **John Dee**

THE WORLD HEAVYWEIGHT CHAMPIONSHIP

INTRO

SOME DAME WALKED INTO MY OFFICE AND SAID...

Well, a long time ago I started working on an article that was about how to really become the Undisputed Champion of the World. I have a really great Excel spreadsheet that proves my point, but just needed to write the words around it. But after all my research, Stuart Carapola beat me to the punch by writing **The History of the World Title** (Part 1 - Part 2). It was a great read that made about 80% of the points I wanted to make.

This was especially discerning because **"This Stillisntmyname"** asked me three months prior to that:

> *Someone really ought to do a "World Title" lineage article...*

Followed by nine questions about the true World Title.

This got me thinking about how I could still do this article without repeating Carapola. **Mike Mopett** also helped bring the idea into focus:

> *The World Title (Bischoff awards the title to HHH, thus people are pissed off and instead of a world title with a legacy in WCW and NWA, it is considered a new Raw title only. Why? The US title's legacy is recognized and the WWE Title is no longer the Undisputed Title, so what then happened to the WCW/NWA Title? Had Bischoff given Benoit the Title after disputing Brock, then the IWC would be hailing him as champ in the line of Thesz, Flair and the Funks) Sorry about the long rant on that one!*

Mike Ostcler added to that not too long ago:

> *Triple H's first world heavyweight title reign. His first three, technically. I'd like to see you defend the era spanning, I'd say, September 2002 'til WrestleMania XX. H-squared is reviled for many things by most of the IWC, but it seems the belt hogging and colleague squashing of this period is what cemented him as one of the most loathed superstars of our time.*

And that is when it all became clear (OK, so really I've been planning this for a while, but these guys added to it): I needed to defend the World Heavyweight Championship!

WHY THIS?

For a championship to be called a World Title, it is truly a distinct honor. But for a World Title to earn its name, that is a true rarity. And how does a title become a true World Championship? Well, it must be defended around the world for starters (or at least outside of Milwaukee). For another thing, it must be fought over by the top talent available. And last, it must have the ability to elevate its holder to another level.

The World Heavyweight Championship that as of this writing sits around Kurt Angle's waist on SmackDown! is such a championship. It recently took a trip to Europe, is being fought over by the likes of the Undertaker, Randy Orton, and Rey Mysterio, and it has brought men like Batista and Randy Orton (and perhaps Rey Mysterio) to a whole new level.

Yet despite its current spot, the World Heavyweight Championship got off to a rocky start. Some people were upset about how the championship came into existence, how it was defended in its first year of existence, and their general disagreement with splitting the championship.

But I am here to show why that split was necessary and logical. We will explore the history of the belt today and what it means to the sport. And we will prove once and for all that the World Heavyweight Championship is the prestigious belt that the announcers make it out to be.

Be fair warned: I will jump back and forth between kayfabe and reality without warning. It's your job to follow along. Good luck to you!

SUPPOSED HISTORY

If you were to ask someone who started watching wrestling in the early 2000's when did the World Heavyweight Championship come into existence, they would tell you September 2002. Well, that's not entirely true. But for now, let's center on that date. First, please review a bit of In Defense of... The Brand Extension to understand the beginning of how this title came into existence.

Are you back? Here, the point remains the same: Bischoff and the WWE always had the right to split championships on a dispute. It was not an uncommon occurrence at all. As a matter of fact, there would not be a WWE Championship if not for such a dispute.

TRUE ORIGINS

In 1957, the Undisputed World Championship (minus the European Heavyweight Title and parts of the AWA championship) had been back together for five years, but pressures were coming from different promotions. With the baby boom in full force, every region in America felt they could make more money if they could control the championship. And thus, the backstabbing began. In a world where 'shoot' meant someone might break your leg, wrestlers had to be legitimate tough guys to hold on to their titles; but there were also other methods.

Under Lou Thesz (the man who had brought the title back under control), the title began to fall apart. It all began with a DQ win over champion Edouard Carpentier (who won the title off of Thesz when Thesz could not continue due to back injury, another questionable move). From Wrestling-Titles.com:

> *[Lou Thesz] Loses to Edouard Carpentier by disqualification on 57/06/14 in Chicago, IL when Thesz cannot continue due to a back injury; Thesz defeats Carpentier in rematch by disqualification on 57/07/24 in Montreal, QC; however, NWA continues to recognize Carpentier as the champion; Carpentier withdraws his claim to the title when his manager and Montreal promoter Eddie Quinn leaves NWA; NWA voids all recognition of Carpentier as champion and returns the title to Thesz in 57; Carpentier continues to be recognized as World champion in Omaha and Boston and later by World Wrestling Association in Los Angeles to legitimate the lineages of their world titles.*

But it gets more confusing than that. Actually, there was the WWA World Title, and there was the Los Angeles Heavyweight Title, both of which claimed lineage. Boston was actually Big Time Wrestling, a huge organization that ruled the northeast. And there were plenty of small disputes along the way.

Eventually, some of those titles merged into each other (Los Angeles into the WWA, Omaha into the AWA) while others (like the BTW title) stayed regional and eventually lost their sheen. But it was the NWA who gathered up the most titles and had the most control across the country and the world.

With a loose organization of regional promotions, the NWA tried to maintained control over the title, and was successful in the South, Midwest, and Pacific Northwest. But the Northeast remained volatile at best. And it would all come to a head in 1963.

First, though, back in June 1961, Buddy Rogers won the NWA Championship in Chicago (again Chicago!). After a couple of confusing title fakes with Bobo Brazil and Killer Kowalski, Rogers was looking to be a lame duck champion. Already twice his title reign was in complete doubt, though he had held on to it for a year and half. This had put promoters in the Northeast ill at ease. Rogers was a draw for them, but he was being made to look bad in other regions and that was affecting their sales. And then the opportunity arose.

On January 24, 1963, Lou Thesz (again!) defeated Rogers in a one-fall match in Toronto, ON, Canada. You see, in those days 2-out-of-3 fall matches were much more common, and so a one-fall to the finish match would really be out of place, especially for a title. And so the World Wide Wrestling Federation was formed with Buddy Rogers as the champion.

Rogers, though, proved unreliable as he lost a 2-out-3 falls match to Thesz just a couple of weeks later, much to the ire of the WWWF. This made the decision easy to move the title over to uber-over Bruno Sammartino in May 1963, a title he held on to and brought to incredible prominence for eight years.

But as they say, time heals all wounds. The title transitioned (ha!) from Ivan Koloff to Pedro Morales in 1971, just in time for the WWWF to rejoin the NWA. The WWWF then willingly reduced their title to a regional title so that the NWA championship could shine. Unlike with the other titles, though, the WWWF title always remained separated from the NWA championship, something that would help the promotion later. Champion Bob Backlund would put the title up against the AWA Championship in March 1979 (double count-out) and against NWA Champion Ric Flair in July 1982 (double count-out again).

It was around this time that Vince McMahon Jr. bought the company from his father (in an installment plan) and dropped one of the W's. He also dropped the NWA and said his title was a World Championship again. And because his champion had just successfully retained against the NWA Champion, McMahon had every reason to believe his title was just as important.

The title found its way to the Iron Sheik in December 1983 shortly after the withdrawal from the NWA, and a month later was won by Hulk Hogan. And the WWF Championship would grow from there.

Meanwhile, the NWA was also growing, but very differently. Eventually, though, with the WWF becoming a national product, the NWA was suffering. In 1991, Jim Crocket Promotions—the major power of the NWA—was sold to TBS and renamed WCW. But much like TNA today, they continued to use the NWA Championships... at least for a little while. From Wrestling-Titles.com:

> *Stripped on 91/09/08 when Flair signs with WWF, where he claims the "Real World Heavyweight Title"; NWA World Heavyweight Title is vacant for the first time in its history; Flair wins WWF World Heavyweight Title on 92/01/19 in Albany, NY; some reports say Lex Luger, who has won the vacant WCW World Heavyweight Title by defeating Barry Windham on 91/07/14 in Baltimore, MD, is briefly given recognition as NWA World champion by the NWA board, controlled by WCW Vice President Jim Herd; Luger is not recognized by NWA as a former champion.*

So, to bring you up to date, the NWA World Champion was stripped of his title, but never lost, and then won the WWF title, making that title more prestigious. Meanwhile, WCW had Lex Luger win the championship while the NWA was not sure what to do. For a year and half, the NWA had no champion (Masa "My Hero" Chono won the title in August 1992), while the rest of the world thought of the WCW Championship as the real title (if not the WWF Championship).

Things became more confusing when WCW rejoined the NWA in 1993, as did Ric Flair. Big Van Vader was the WCW Champion and four months later Ric Flair won the NWA Championship. So there were two World Champions in WCW in 1993, but their relationship with the NWA would be strained. In September 1993, the NWA and WCW split again, and Flair became the "WCW International Champion". Meanwhile, there would be no NWA Champion again for a year, so the International title was the title as far as everyone else was concerned.

Flair quickly lost that title to Rick Rude and then went on to defeat Vader in December 1993 for the WCW Championship. The International Championship traded hands for a few more months before Flair unified the titles on June 23, 1994. So the WCW Championship had two direct links to the NWA Championship (which had a direct link to the Undisputed World Heavyweight Championship) and the WWF Championship had one direct and two indirect links to the NWA Championship.

And strangely, that's pretty much how it would remain for almost a decade. The NWA became incredibly regionalized and the title reduced to little value (especially after Shane Douglas threw it down in favor of the ECW Championship, and the NWA refused to let him throw it away), while the WCW and WWF Championships were raised to incredible heights and prominence during the Monday Night Wars.

In March 2001 that would all change when the WWF bought WCW, and a few months later brought their champions in. After a time and an InVasion, the two titles became combined on December 9, 2001 when Chris Jericho became the "Undisputed" (that's for another day) Champion.

Now the WWF Championship had three direct and two indirect links to the NWA (and thus real World) Heavyweight Championship and had the shared history of all of those belts. You see, when the belts were put together, they absorbed their history and champions. Although the exterior was different, the connections were quite real.

That also means that history can be split from the belt. So yes, the "World Heavyweight Championship" is a different belt physically, but it is the same belt emotionally. It does have a history that can be traced to 1880 with the American Greco-Roman World Heavyweight Title (and I did!), as can the WWE Championship. In reality, they were always the same belt, coming from the same origin, but just slightly different paths to get there. And when they came together all of that became intermingled, but that history is still there.

As we noted in the previous section, splitting championships is nothing new in the context of storylines and promotions. The only difference is in the past it was a legitimate heat between promotions that split the title, while in this case it was a calculated decision to establish separate brands. But both were decided for one reason: money.

Why did the WWWF split off in the first place? Why did the NWA have disputes? Why did the AWA and WWA spend years avoiding those organizations? Because they wanted to maximize their own profit in their own regions. It is not like the title split for any nobler reason than that, that there was some deeper meaning; it always came down to money.

So that same was true in the Brand Extension. The title was split for money, just an amicable split compared to the ones in the past.

Still, some people are upset about how the title was split and who was given the championship.

The Case for Triple H

When Eric Bischoff declared the Undisputed Championship in dispute, he named Triple H as champion because Triple H was the number one contender. We already covered the storyline reasons for this with past precedence, but people are still upset over this decision. Many wanted a tournament or some other way to come up with a new champion—at least one match.

But the Brand Extension was young and RAW had been suffering. Up until that point, SmackDown! had most of the talent and the storylines. RAW had in the main event scene:

- The Undertaker
- Kevin Nash
- Kane
- The Big Show
- Steve Austin

The Undertaker was really the prime player on RAW, but he was maligned at the beginning from getting his championship shot by Vince McMahon. Kevin Nash was not in good condition and was mostly injured, as was Austin. Kane and the Big Show had both been buried as transitional stepping-stones in the past, so RAW's main event scene was hurting. In the fringe there was:

- Scott Hall
- RVD
- Booker T
- Brock Lesner

Scott Hall was already having problems, so his time was limited. Booker T, RVD, and Lesner seemed like the best bets, though Booker and RVD had to "get over" being WCW/ECW wrestlers, and Lesner was extremely young. None, save perhaps Booker T, were ready to be taken as serious contenders to the Undisputed Championship.

It was not until the addition of GMs that this problem began to get fixed. The rosters were mixed up and cleaned up so that RAW became a whole new place. Again in The Elimination Chamber case, check out the summary of the contenders to the first Elimination Chamber itself.

You can see from the time Eric Bischoff took over until the Elimination Chamber, RAW had become a completely new world. But still, look at the roster: Shawn Michaels was a part-time wrestler, not ready to be a long-term champion. Jericho had some credibility, but only slightly more than Booker T and RVD. Kane still had the same problems listed as above. That left one person: Triple H.

Triple H was a truly established champion at that point in time, and was also the only one who could wrestle full time.

Yes, the ideal of the Brand Extension was to raise new talent to the title. But because we are talking about splitting a title, its worth had to be proven right away. Any time RAW spent without a champion would make them look even more inferior (see: SmackDown! during the 2005 draft lottery), and they needed a belt and a program fast.

Triple H was just the man for the job. He was a hated heel, so he could just accept a title without a fight. At the same time, he was considered a legitimate main eventer in the eyes of the fans, so the title would be given some prestige. Having Kane, RVD, Booker, or Jericho win the title would not elevate it to the level that RAW needed. They needed the title to look like a legitimate World Title, and it either had to be Triple H or Shawn Michaels. Since Michaels could not wrestle the full schedule at that time, he was not the person to carry the title.

Triple H lost to him in the Elimination Chamber for several reasons. First, it did put over the other wrestlers in there because all of them looked like they could take the title from Triple H. It actually created the programs for the next six months thereafter. But Shawn had to win to give RAW a happy ending to a huge event and also to have two huge names hold the belt.

Again, though, the WWE was faced with the same problem. Michaels was not a full-time wrestler, and there was no way they were going to sell MORE house show tickets without the champion at the show. Thus the title returned to Triple H as he was the biggest name on RAW to head into WrestleMania.

Triple H was not petitioning for the title and did not demand to keep it. He lost again and again, from Bill Goldberg to Chris Benoit. But that would all be later on when RAW had more people and began to become a powerhouse. Soon, it was because of his grip on the title that the World Heavyweight Championship became regarded as THE title while the WWF Title was used to create new champions in Brock Lesner, Eddie Guerrero, JBL, and John Cena.

It was not a point in the WWE where they could handle both championships being in new people's hands. They were also experimenting with what the Brand Extension meant. They were testing the waters to see what people wanted: their known stars or the new generation. Nothing was set in stone; it was all a trial. And in trials such as these, some things work and some things don't. As long as you learn from what you do then the effort is worth it.

And look, the WWE did change! They separated PPVs, moved more towards new champions (with Cena and Batista champions at the same time), and brought back different wrestlers. As we discussed in the Brand Extension case, the whole thing is a work in progress, as are the titles that are at the head of these organizations.

OVER YOUR SHOULDER OR AROUND YOUR WAIST

The World Heavyweight Championship is one of this most prestigious titles in the world. But it is not some magical belt created from nothing! No, it shares a long, storied history with the real World, NWA, and WWWF/WWF/WWE Championship. That history is real, and deserves to be recognized. At the same time, all these splits in the title's past have been about one thing: money. And the Brand Extension split was also about that. In the ideal world, the Brand

Extension would automatically mean new talent would get the title. But in a suffering brand, only the best of the best who could work full time could establish the title so that when other people won the belt it would mean something. The man at that time was Triple H, and his stranglehold of the title helped push it up to a value above and beyond the actual WWE Championship.

The World Heavyweight Championship is everything its name suggests. It deserves to be revered for what it really is. How many people can even say they have gotten a shot at a world title of that magnitude, nonetheless won it? No one who wins a title should ever be looked down upon, but only looked up to as the worthy champions they are.

The defense rests.

AFTER THE TRIAL

HUNG JURY

IN THE CASE OF THE IWC VS. THE WORLD HEAVYWEIGHT CHAMPIONSHIP, THE WORLD HEAVYWEIGHT CHAMPIONSHIP HAS BEEN ACCUSED OF BEING A PAPER BELT THAT WAS ONLY CREATED TO SOOTHE TRIPLE H'S EGO AND HAS NO REAL VALUE, PRESTIGE, OR HISTORY.

Well, with 71.1% of the vote, the World Heavyweight Championship was found:

NOT GUILTY!

That was way more contentious than even I thought it would be. I got a lot of heated responses from people who just blatantly did not accept points of my defense. The key areas being: (1) that the WWE does not acknowledge the history of the title (or they only do when it suits them) and (2) Triple H's stranglehold of the title. I think with the latter it has more to do with people looking back, not forward. Yes, today Triple H held the title too much beyond that first year, and looking back it is easy to critique. But I was talking about that decision at that point in time. As for the former, since when does the WWE have final say on history? We let them rewrite it too much, and it makes just as much sense by my history of the title. Besides, the WWWF title has just as much of a connection to the NWA championship as the WCW title, so why is the WCW title looked at as the only legitimate branch? The NWA championship is only a branch of a larger championship belt that preceded it, so how is this any different?

RESPONSE

This was the point that I fell hopelessly behind on my e-mail and never caught up. As such, any response from this point in is the first time I have actually been able to reply!

> There is no doubt in my mind that the Big Gold Belt is of monumental importance in the world of professional wrestling history and indeed carries the lineage of all the men that held it before Bischoff rebirthed it. However when you said "No one who wins a title should ever be looked down upon, but only looked up to as the worthy champions they are," you must have been lucky enough to forget the appalling act of crowning David Arquette World Heavyweight Champion simply to promote Ready To Rumble. But please don't consider this an insult to Ready To Rumble. To this day I boycott the Academy Awards for snubbing one of the top five films of the last decade.
>
> **Metalpunk140**

I wonder if this actually proved my point more? If David Arquette and Vince Russo could be WCW Champion, isn't a highly decorated wrestler even better?

> The real title is still the NWA title as it is still around. The others (WWE, Big Gold) are branches off of the original (NWA). So I say guilty of not being the real deal... the WWE versions, that is.
>
> **Mitchell Q**

That is assuming you would go with the NWA Championship as the full legitimate path, as well. So, I started working on a project in 2002 that I last updated in March of 2006 on how to become the Unified World Heavyweight Champion for real. This began with tracing every branch of the title visually. For this purpose, I have broken it up into several parts.

First, we look at the generation that gave rise to the real Unified World Heavyweight Championship:

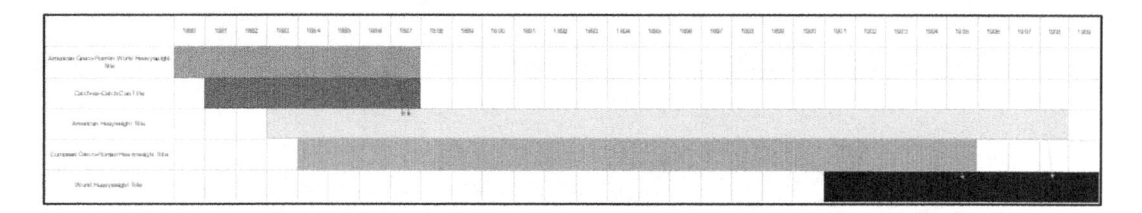

Then, we see the years of stability followed by the years of massive division:

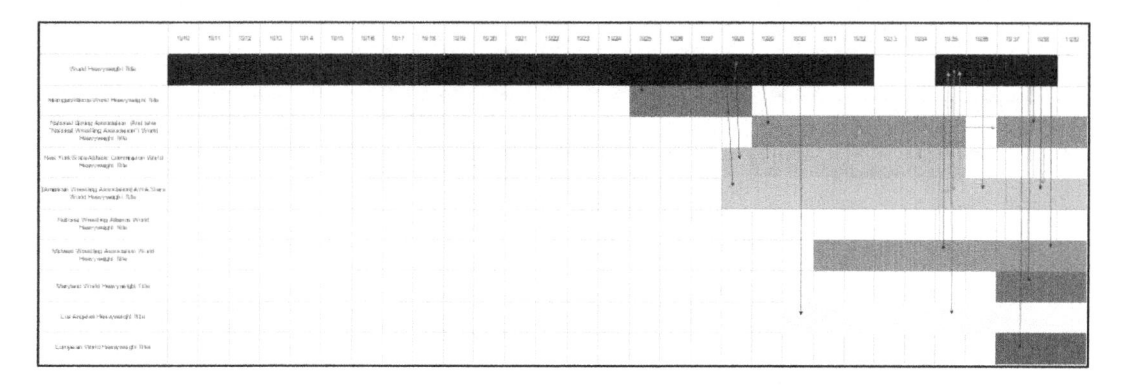

This is followed by the continued division leading back to the last unification, which in turn splits up the title for the remainder of eternity (to date):

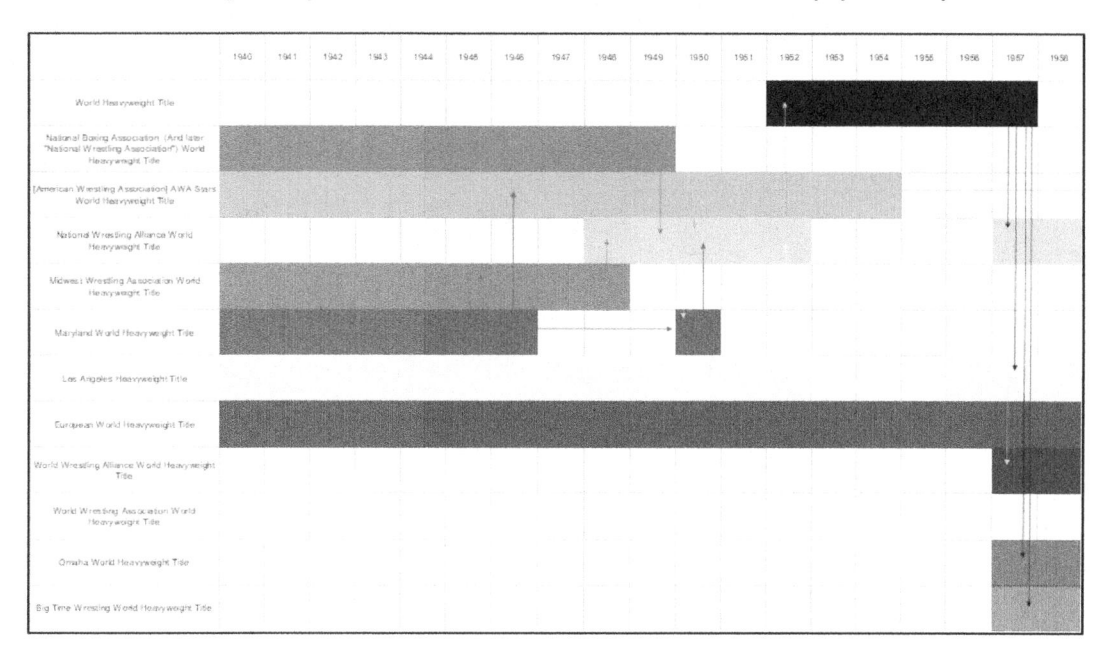

Then we see the age of territories, and most especially the dominance of the NWA system:

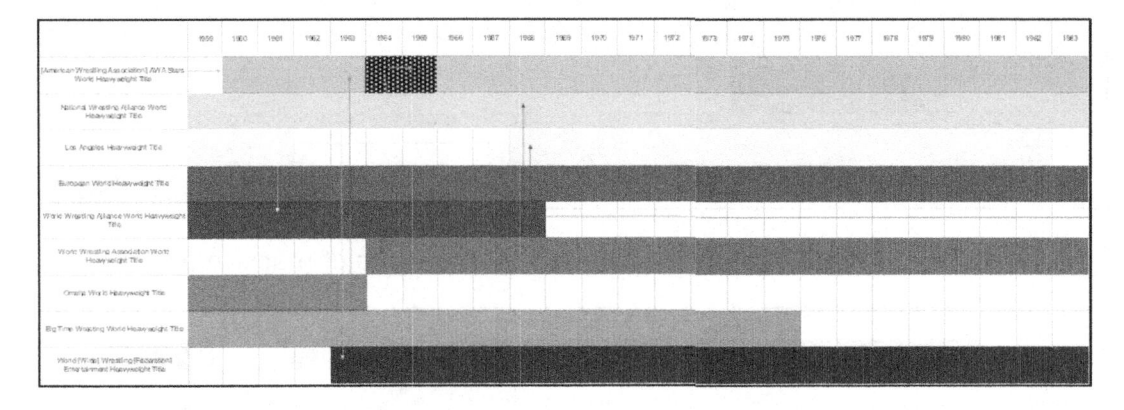

Things changed in the early 1980's with the rise of Hulk Hogan and Rock 'n Wrestling, culminating in the world as we knew it in 2006:

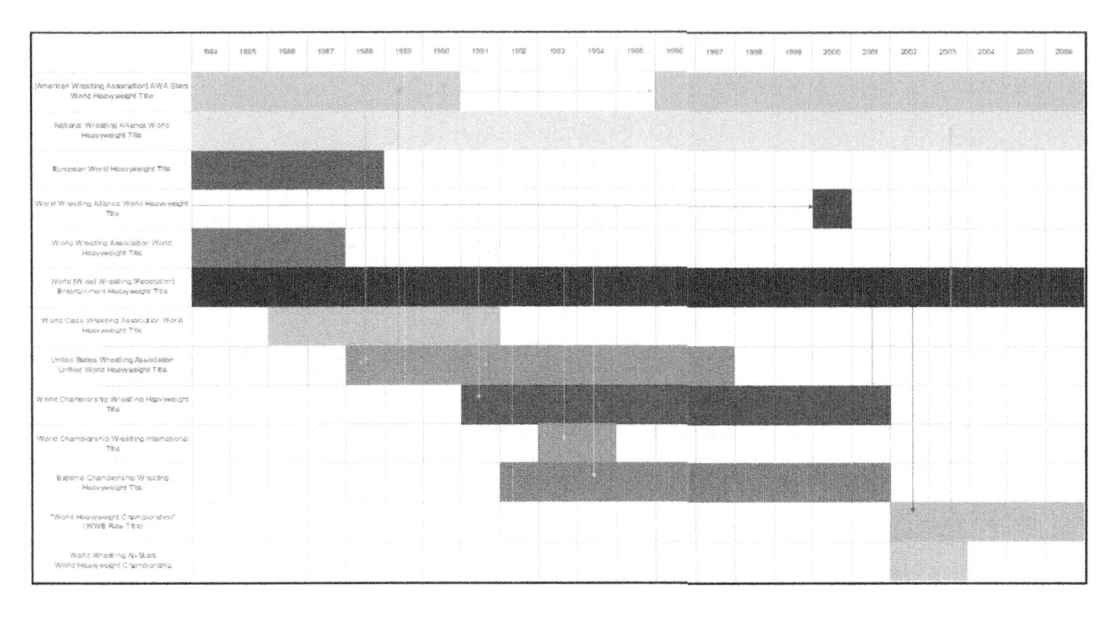

Among all those versions of the title, here was the final resting place of each:

Title	Analysis
American Greco-Roman World Heavyweight Title	Absorbed
Catch-as-Catch Can Title	Absorbed
American Heavyweight Title	Absorbed
European Greco-Roman Heavyweight Title	Absorbed
World Heavyweight Title	Exists in the lines of many active and inactive Titles
Michigan/Illinois World Heavyweight Title	Absorbed
National Boxing Association (And later "National Wrestling Association") World Heavyweight Title	Absorbed

Title	Analysis
New York State Athletic Commission World Heavyweight Title	Final Title split between many different promotions
[American Wrestling Association] AWA Stars World Heavyweight Title	Credibility of belt questionable at time of promotion's fall (did it join the NWA, unify champions, and then go back to its own lineage?), but still enough to say worth gathering for Undisputed Championship. The promotion restarted in 1996, but has yet to make a national presence.
National Wrestling Alliance World Heavyweight Title	Other remaining belts owe credibility to NWA, and NWA can be traced to the World Title with little dispute. Needed for Undisputed Championship.
Midwest Wrestling Association World Heavyweight Title	Absorbed
Maryland World Heavyweight Title	Absorbed
Los Angeles Heavyweight Title	Old claims to World Title do not really hold at the time the company folded. They left WWA because the WWA joined NWA and then LA recreated its own Heavyweight title. Though would be nice to have, not essential to Undisputed Championship
European World Heavyweight Title	This title has a lot of holes in its history, but its direct tie to the World Title make it essential to the Undisputed Championship. Unfortunately, since the title is inactive, this is impossible, unless some British Wrestling Authority names someone the World Champion.
World Wrestling Alliance World Heavyweight Title	Final Title split, but mainly absorbed by NWA since that is what the owners of WWA wanted
World Wrestling Association World Heavyweight Title	Similar to ECW, the first Heavyweight Champion abandoned the title when he won it and then went on to declare himself the first Heavyweight Champion of that promotion. Would be nice for the Undisputed Championship, but since the company folded that's not a consideration.
Omaha World Heavyweight Title	Absorbed
Big Time Wresting World Heavyweight Title	Although the title has direct lineage to the World Title, its value is questionable since it was only defended regionally. Still, the history makes it valuable, though not essential, to the Undisputed Championship
World [Wide] Wrestling [Federation] Entertainment Heavyweight Title	This title owes its lineage to the NWA. And since the fight over who was champion was a legitimate argument, the split still gives the WWE a fluid connection to the World Title, and thus makes its title essential to the Undisputed Championship
World Class Wrestling Association World Heavyweight Title	Absorbed

Title	Analysis
United States Wrestling Association Unified World Heavyweight Title	The title was abandoned in 1997 when USWA shut its doors. Given the history, if the belt and its connections to the NWA and AWA titled (both directly connected to the World Heavyweight Title), you would think it would be essential to the Undisputed Championship. But, because it became just a regional belt (re: Memphis), it cannot be considered essential. Still, it would be a good addition.
World Championship Wrestling Heavyweight Title	Absorbed
World Championship Wrestling International Title	Absorbed
Extreme Championship Wrestling Heavyweight Title	Even though ECW never claimed lineage to the World Title, deciding that their title should replace the NWA title (then won by Shane Douglas) shows that they are connected. The defunct promotion is still important to the Undisputed Championship, though not essential since they do not claim any lineage
"World Heavyweight Championship" (WWE Raw Title)	Since the WWE split their own World Title back into two titles to continue the Brand Extension, this title is as legitimate as the other WWE Title. It should not be confused with the WCW or NWA World Titles, as the WWE would have its viewers believe. Even still, it is essential to the Undisputed Championship.
World Wrestling All-Stars World Heavyweight Championship	Absorbed

Thus that leaves us with the final question: if you want to the Undisputed World Champion, which titles do you need?

Essential To Undisputed Championship	Highly Recommended to Undisputed Championship, but not required	Not need at all for Undisputed Championship, but would be good to have
National Wrestling Alliance World Heavyweight Title	[American Wrestling Association] AWA Stars World Heavyweight Title	Los Angeles Heavyweight Title
European World Heavyweight Title	Big Time Wrestling World Heavyweight Title	
World [Wide] Wrestling [Federation] Entertainment Heavyweight Title	Extreme Championship Wrestling Heavyweight Title	
"World Heavyweight Title" (WWE Raw Title)		

- This history does not reflect the addition of non-World and secondary titles that may have been absorbed into the many versions of World Heavyweight Championship over the years.

- Since the WWE and the NWA are the only two organizations still in existence with actual lineage to the World Title (and thus to several older titles), one needs only to win those three titles to be the Undisputed World Champion.

- At the time of this writing, the WWE title names are the "WWE Championship" and the "Universal Championship". The World Heavyweight and WWE titles discussed in this and other cases merged in 2013 (after the Brand Extension ended in 2011) and then split again in 2016 (when the Brand Extension started anew), although it was not necessarily presented as a split in the same way. As far as we are concerned, though, the "Universal Championship" is the equivalent of the "World Heavyweight Championship" for these purposes.

- Further, since 2006 there have been many changes to both the WWE versions of the championships, what happened between the NWA and TNA (iMPACT Wrestling), the start-up of AEW, and other such events. However, if you carry forward from here, this would mostly remain the same.

- To add more credibility to the champion, it would be good if he could somehow obtain the European version of the World Title and the AWA Title, since those date back around 80 years and make a drastic break in the World Title History. The BTW and LA Title are of questionable value, and the Undisputed Championship does not need them except to satisfy older fans who remember these champions.

- The same can be said for the ECW Championship (though that was retired in 2010 and is not readily available), which does not have a true lineage to the world title, but recent fans value the title, thus giving it credibility. One could argue that NXT is the defacto inheritor of ECW since it replaced ECW in the WWE's programming lineup, but that is a stretch at best (especially since the original NXT was nothing like it became later).

Hulk Hogan

Intro

Some dame walked into my office and said...

Oh my goodness, where to begin? Why not the beginning? It started with **Ernie** back in June 2005:

> I was wondering if you would be interested in doing a defense column on Hulk Hogan, who is [constantly] ridiculed and projected in a negative light. While I'm sure his detractors have a valid [argument], Hogan did [a lot] for the business. I'd just be interested in your perspective on this, and I'm sure others in my age group (mid 20's) would be as well.

About a day before or after, **Ken Batallones** brought up the same idea:

> And an even bigger challenge [than Triple H] would be to defend Hogan.

A short time later, **Ori Zeiger** also had a similar idea, except for different reasons:

> The person I would like you to protect is someone I'd think you'd have a real hard time doing so (at least as far as I am concerned but I'm sure also with [a lot] of other people)... and that is the piece of shit called Hulk Hogan. I've never liked him but even [more so] especially now after this [feud] with Michaels and him actually wanting to WIN BOTH matches.

That was a spectrum shift. **BDSTW FOM** had a more particular idea, but we'll get to it:

> *Defend the younger wrestlers from Hogan*
>
> *Defend the young guys from Hogan coming back on occasion and using his pull when they could be getting their own chance.*

Someone with lesser initials (**BGD**) brought it back to the big picture:

> Hulk Hogan
>
> Brother, if you manage to get a not guilty on him, [I'll] be mighty impressed and thankful. I personally [don't] think Hulk Hogan is the Anti-Christ, nor deserving of the bad raps he gets. Any chance of you doing a case on him?

Justin Swift had the same thought:

> I think you should defend Hulk Hogan, for as much as he has done for the business, he always seems to get a bum rap! I am personally hoping to see Austin Vs. Hogan at mania (and the mere rumor of it made me lay down 170.00 per ticket for nosebleed seats)

But where there is that much love, there is also hate, as **Andrew Lee** will tell you:

> I really hate [H]ogan, but maybe this because of the IWC. Will you ever write a piece on him?

Also, **Rick Cobos** gave me about a million different ideas for Hogan, but I just rolled them all up into one!

And throughout the past year, people have written in and said many nice and nasty things about Hogan that have all led to this case. As a matter of fact, Hogan tops the list of my most frequently e-mailed words. What were the other ones?

10. Chump
9. Chumpette
8. Yours
7. Up
6. Pimpmobile
5. Bite
4. My
3. Shiny
2. Daffodil
1. Hogan

There you have it!

WHY THIS?

Well, as the top ten list showed, Hogan is the most frequent topic of conversation in my In Defense Of... e-mails. More people have requested a case for him than anyone else. More people have referenced or written something directly about Hogan than most other wrestlers combined.

Hogan is the definition of wrestling. Without Hogan, everything that we take for granted in the world of professional wrestling would not exist. I honestly believe that Hogan is not just a pivotal player, but the key central figure of the wrestling revival. No one else could have been in his position.

There is some doubt there, but there is even more doubt about Hogan's worth today. Many feel that he should have been done in 1990, 1994, 1998, 2001, 2004, and 2005. Yet Hogan keeps returning, keeps coming back, keeps bringing them in. Why does Hogan return? Why is he allowed to return?

There are also questions about how Hogan attained his position in the sport, and more importantly how he maintained it. Going deeper, there are doubts about how over he was, and more importantly how entertaining he was.

Was Hogan a workhorse five-star grappler? No way in hell! Was Hogan much better than most people ever gave him credit for? You bet. Was Hogan long winded? Of course! Did what he have to say draw them in? You better believe it (and I'll prove it). Does his imagination get in the way of reality? Sometimes. Andre does get heavier and higher in the air every time I hear the story. But does that matter to the reality of our world?

Hogan has so much that we need to cover that he could not be contained to our normal format. Hulk Hogan is the biggest case to date, and as so, he deserves all the time he needs.

With so much material, it's hard to decide where to start. So why not start... in 1953.

CALIFORNIA... GEORGIA... WHAT'S THE DIFFERENCE?

Before Hulk Hogan legally changed his name to Hogan, he was Terry Bollea, the name his parents gave to him. His father, Pete, was a construction foreman and his mother, Ruth, was a homemaker and dance instructor. On August 11th, 1953, Ruth gave birth to the 10 lb. 7 ounces future Hogan (which is very large for a baby). He remained a big baby into his young life, much to the ridicule of his peers. From Obsessed with Wrestling:

> *Terry Bollea was an unathletic kid who weighed 195 lbs. at the age of 12.*

But despite this negative in his life, Terry found many interests, including the electric and bass guitar, as well as baseball.

After the family relocated to Tampa, FL, Hogan found his way to the gym in 1967. As he began to weight train, he found ways to sculpt and build his body. He put in hours of extreme dedication into creating a body that he could be proud of. At the same time, he continued to build is athletic prowess in baseball and other sports, and cultivated his mind in music. Beyond that, he also found a spiritual being by attending a Christian Youth Ranch in the area.

With such diverse interests, Terry was without focus. He was also without a lot of resources. His parents were not wealthy and were not in the best neighborhoods, so Hogan had to work for everything he wanted. And he wanted to go to college. He enrolled in Hillsborough Community College and began studying business. After a couple of years at the junior college, Hogan was admitted into the University of South Florida where he aimed to continue his studies.

But education was expensive, and he had other interests. From Warnet.net:

> *Terry Bollea was a part time body builder, bouncer, musician and [full-time] bank teller.*

With his physique and physical ability, body building seemed like a natural choice, but that didn't pay the bills. Being a bouncer helped pay the bills, but it didn't help Terry grow as a person. Being a musician was a love that tested his abilities, but did not have much of a future, and Terry was too smart to believe otherwise. Working at a bank was a way to apply some of his knowledge, but again it did not give him the chance to be more.

We can see from this that even at a young age, Hogan had an incredible work ethic. He was willing to do anything and everything to live out his dreams. He sacrificed so much of his time and life for his varied interests to make his dreams come true, though he was not too sure of what those dreams were. Hogan knew one thing, though: he wanted to be special.

Depending on who you ask, what happened next is up in the air. Hogan was playing with his band at a number of small venues that the Florida wrestlers frequented, and Hogan became friends with many of them. Now, either he began talking to Jack and Jerry Brisco at the clubs and became friendly with them or they spotted him sitting ringside at a wrestling event and recognized him or one night as a bouncer he met the two outside or he used to work out in their gym. Any which way, the Brisco brothers became the pivotal players that finally convinced Hogan to give wrestling a try.

Mike Rickard II sheds some additional light on Hogan's reasoning:

> Hulk Hogan's first dream was to be a rock star. He performed in a band called Infinity's End at a Florida nightclub frequented by wrestlers. Hogan also worked out at a gym frequented by wrestlers. At the time, Hogan worked at a bank and claims to have looked over wrestlers' bankbooks which gave him further inspiration to become a wrestler.

Whatever his inspiration, The Briscos (through Mike Graham) got Hogan in contact with Hiro Matsuda, a wrestling legend and very serious trainer. From Wikipedia:

> Yasuhiro Kojima (July 22, 1937 – November 27, 1999) was the trainer of Hulk Hogan, "Mr. Wonderful" Paul Orndorff, Lex Luger, Ron Simmons, Keiji Mutoh and many other professional wrestlers. He was better known as Hiro Matsuda, an identity he adopted while competing in the southern U.S., inspired by earlier wrestlers Sorakichi Matsuda and Matty Matsuda.
>
> He initially debuted under his real name at Rikidozan's Japanese Wrestling Association, but then left Japan to pursue wrestling in the Americas. Once in a while he would return to Japan, where he formed a tag team with Antonio Inoki that was only the outward reflection of the long-time friendship between the two men.

From that short list, it is obvious that Hiro trained some of the best and most well-known wrestlers in the world. But he was also a very unforgiving teacher.

On Terry's first day of training in 1976, Hiro intentionally broke Terry's leg (well, really his ankle, but that still sucks), putting him on the injured reserve list. It seemed like Hogan's wrestling career was off to a terrible start.

While healing, Hogan continued playing with his band the Gentrics. He was unsure of what he was going to do next, but after some time, he decided to give it another chance.

And so with his leg healed, Hogan returned to Hiro, much to Hiro's great shock and admiration. He did not go easy on Hogan and demanded he learn everything the same as everyone. Hogan was a quick learner, and showed he not only understood the moves, but understood the audience. He already had the telltale signs of being able to hold the audience in the palm of his hand, but there was only one way everyone was going to find out if that was true or not.

Rasslin' Down South

In August 1977, Terry made his debut as "The Super Destroyer" in Tallahassee, FL. He began to wrestle in the small circuits, changing his name several times between "Sterling Golden", "Terry Boulder", and "Terry 'The Hulk' Boulder", among others. But the money and prestige was not coming as quickly as Hogan hoped. From Mathew Sforcina's Evolution Schematic:

> *Terry continued to wrestle for CWF and other small Florida companies, but quickly grew tired. He just wasn't getting anywhere, and the small crowds' apathy and hatred got to him, and he quit.*
>
> *Phase 2- Well, that was short.*
>
> *Terry got a job as a longshoreman, and worked on the docks of Port Tampa. Within a few weeks, the Brisco Brothers and Terry Funk, who was also impressed with what he saw, and all of them tried to get Terry to reconsider. Eventually, Bollea did.*

Look, the man thought he might be done with wrestling, yet three wrestling legends already felt he needed to be a part of the game. Even back then, before the name, before the colors, before the hair, and before the maniacs, they saw in Terry the potential to be great. How often do you hear about any older star trying to convince someone to stay in wrestling? They went out of their way because they saw the potential in Hogan (though probably not to the degree that actually happened).

And so Terry returned, and a whole new career began. Others began to see in Terry what the three legends saw. From Cool Dudes and Hot Babes (edited for grammar):

> Terry was brought into Southeast Championship Wrestling in summer 1978 by Rip Tyler. On Terry's debut after defeating an unknown local mid-carder, Terry started to be called 'The Wrestling Hulk'. Terry helped heel manager Billy Spears and Ox Baker defeat local legend Masked Wrestling Pro (Leon "Tarzan" Baxter), putting him on the hated list. Then in September Terry had his most memorable angle during that time, against Andre the Giant, which was their first. That led to an Arm-Wrestling match, where Terry bloodied Andre with a loaded elbow and he and his manager Billy Spears destroy Andre with the table.
>
> Terry continued working for South East Championship Wrestling, including touring Alabama and Knoxville (and a couple times in [his] hometown [of] Tampa) during the rest of 78. In early 79 Terry [had] his first ever face turn. It was during an angle involving Ox Baker, Ron Fuller, and NWA champ Harley Race. Race had placed a bounty on Fuller so as to not to have to defend NWA World title against him. Baker & Terry Boulder had been having problems, shoving each other during tag matches after Boulder cost Baker a match, later during Baker's match Ron Fuller came to the ring only to receive the heart-punch (a move Baker billed as even killing somebody with it). While Ox [was] beating up Fuller, Boulder [came] out to help Fuller and even [carried] him on his shoulder back to the dressing room. That night Fuller was booked to face Race for the NWA title, [but] due to the heart punch was unable... Terry took his place, in what was Terry's first World title match. Due to Baker's interference Terry won via DQ, but didn't win the title.
>
> Then around February or March Terry defeated Ox Baker for his first wrestling title, to become the South Eastern Heavyweight champion recognized in Alabama. {Michael Calloway, who helped me with the Alabama-Knoxville [part], and was there in Dothan, Alabama to see these matches, can't explain why Terry Boulder/Ox Baker/Austin Idol were not recognized as South East Heavyweight champs in Knoxville. However in the unofficial list

> they're 100% recognized and there's no doubt they were champs!}
>
> Around June 1979 during an ongoing feud with Austin Idol, Idol beat Terry after cheating him out and got the South Eastern title. In July 1979 Terry received his 2nd World title match also against Harley Race, during the match Idol came down dressed up and flashed a camera in Terry's face, allowing Race to nail his top rope Head Butt for the 1-2-3. The Idol-Boulder feud continued in Alabama for the next couple months, which saw Idol 'break' Terry's leg. In mid-1979 Race and Idol brought Terry to NWA Georgia! He was given the Sterling Golden (bigger, better, stronger and improved gorgeous George gimmick) and he fought Handicap matches and used the Sterling Squeeze Bear Hug as his finisher. His major feud in NWA Georgia was against "Mr. USA" Tony Atlas. He was never pushed but his heel character was well protected. Terry offered $10,000 to [anyone] who [could] break out of his Squeeze. Terry then returned to Southeastern Championship Wrestling, under his new Sterling Golden gimmick and this time was given big push for the recognized Southeastern Heavyweight title, beating Bob Roop for the title[.]

Although the English may have been rough, the history was interesting. Terry was out there in the world paying his dues. He spent a couple of years in the independents, but still built up enough of a name for himself to find his way to NWA Georgia and get two shots at the NWA Championship.

What this piece fails to mention is that Terry spent some time in Memphis as well and feuded with Jerry Lawler. He also tagged with the future Brutus Beefcake, who at the time was wrestling as Dizzy Hogan.

Wait... so in SECW, Terry got the "Hulk" name and in Memphis he teamed with a "Hogan". Yet we hear all the time that it was McMahon (one of them) that came up with "Hulk Hogan" and gave him his name. Does not seem like that is the truth to me, but we'll get back to that in a minute. First, though, we have to get to the WWWF.

WRESTLING UP NORTH

In November 1979, Terry caught the eye of northeast promoter Vince McMahon Sr., head booker and majority owner of the WWWF. McMahon was looking for more "ethnic" characters, so he asked Terry to be Irish and dye his hair red. Terry agreed to the Irish part and became Hogan, but kept his blonde locks. With Classy Freddie Blassie in his corner, Hogan came in as a heel ready to take the WWWF by storm. From Warned.net:

> Hulk Hogan fought many handicap matches to prove his "giant" strength this [led] to a feud with Andre the Giant. On August 9th, 1980 - Showdown [at Shea] 1980 Saw Andre The Giant defeated Hulk Hogan. Andre again defeated Hulk Hogan. On September 22nd, 1980 at Madison Square Garden Andre defeated Hulk Hogan again. Hogan feuded with WWWF (World Wide Wrestling Federation) World Heavyweight Champion Bob Backlund, and Tony Atlas.

Although all of these similar feuds we would see later, Hogan was going through them at an early stage in his career. But let us not forget that he was four years into his journey at that point and was no longer a green kid. Even still, no one was going to just jump the gun with giving Hogan the title. He still had to earn his stripes.

Earning stripes was not Hogan's only goal. He wanted to be a star, a real star, perhaps even a "superstar". From Slam! Sports:

> For the first (but not the last) time in Hogan's career, Hollywood would come calling, and he found himself cast as "Thunderlips", a champion wrestler, in Rocky III. The move to Hollywood, however, cost him his job in the WWWF... at least for now, as Vince McMahon Sr. fired him.

And furthermore from Warned.net:

> In 1981, Sylvester Stallone personally offered him a part in the movie Rocky III. Hogan wanted to use this opportunity for a potential movie career. Bollea took film role. When Vince McMahon Senior found out, he fired Hulk Hogan from the WWE as a result.

But 411mania's own Mathew Sfornica brought it to a whole new level:

> *In the spring of 1981, the WWWF had agreed to lend Hogan's contract to the Crockett Jr. run companies in the Carolinas, and Hulk was supposed to go wrestle for them in order to help the two companies help each other and build bridges. Hulk refused, as he had been given a golden chance to go star in Rocky III by Sylvester Stallone, who wanted Hulk to play 'Thunderlips'. Vince McMahon Sr. was furious, and fired Hulk, since he wanted Wrestlers, not Actors.*
>
> *So Hulk went off and filmed his part, and then wrestled in Japan (who loved him, oddly enough) and back in some of the companies he came up in, this time as the main attraction.*

McMahon saw wrestlers as wrestlers and that was it. Hogan saw himself as a star, and he knew being in Rocky III would do more to increase his value in the industry and the world than being loaned out to another organization. Besides, what right did the WWWF have to loan his contract to another wrestling promotion? Did he not have the right to decide what territory he wanted to work for?

And so after filming, Hogan worked in Japan and made an international name for himself, something that would be quite useful later. Also, he and Stallone became good friend, another element that would raise his notoriety.

Hogan was correct, too. When Rocky III came out, Hogan's popularity skyrocketed. Of course, by then he had already returned to the States, but in a new home.

WRASSLIN' IN MIDWEST AND PURO IN THE LAND OF THE RISING SUN

After some time in Japan, Hogan joined Verne Gagne's American Wrestling Association out in Memphis, TN in 1981. From Mike Rickard II:

> *Although he debuted as a heel, Hogan won the fans over with his incredible charisma and larger than life look. Hogan's appearance in Rocky III served to increase his popularity even more. He turned babyface and began challenging AWA Champion Nick Bockwinkel for the world strap. At the time, Hogan was an incredible draw but AWA*

> owner Verne Gagne refused to put the title on Hogan because he did not think he was enough of a wrestler to hold the belt. Night after night, Hogan would seem to defeat Bockwinkel for the title only to have the decision reversed on a technicality. Fans grew frustrated with the screw-job finishes. They weren't the only ones.

Furthermore from Wikipedia:

> On two different occasions, Hogan had been scripted to win the AWA Championship from heel champion Nick Bockwinkel and have it revert back to Bockwinkel by contrived technicalities. This was a common plot device, used to milk audience anticipation that the face would topple the heel "next time." But this time, the crowd reaction was so furious that only Bollea's pleas (on the PA system, in character as Hogan) kept them from rioting. Hogan, for his part, grew frustrated with the AWA's backstage politics over the world title, and was upset with promoter Verne Gagne's demands for a percentage of his Japanese earnings in exchange for the AWA Championship.

The AWA of today (which holds almost NO relation to the AWA of that era) has since reversed those decisions and calls Hogan a two-time AWA champion. Little good that did at the time. Hogan knew he had done it. He was a superstar making big money and drawing in fans from everywhere. He had been wrestling for six years and had been fighting champions for years. Everyone was ready for the trigger to be pulled, but much like RVD and Booker T in the WWE today, the AWA refused to make it happen (that's right, I just compared Hulk Hogan to RVD). But unlike the aforementioned wrestlers, Hogan would not take it and left the AWA.

Finding his way back to Japan in 1982/1983, Hogan finally found a major championship. From Wikipedia:

> When competing in Japan, Hogan used a vastly different repertoire of wrestling moves, relying on more "scientific" (i.e., technical, more amateur style-seeming) looking traditional wrestling holds and maneuvers as opposed to the power-based (feats of strength), brawling style U.S. fans were accustomed to seeing from him. On June 2, 1983, Hogan became the first International Wrestling

> Grand Prix tournament winner, defeating Japanese wrestling icon Antonio Inoki by knockout in the finals of a 10-man tournament featuring top talent from throughout the world. Hogan and Inoki also worked as partners in Japan, winning the prestigious MSG Tag League tournament two years in a row, in 1982 and 1983. Also Hogan's popularity in Japan was so great, he even recorded an album there-a forerunner to the World Wrestling Federation's "Rock' n' Wrestlin' Connection" of the mid-'80's.

Hogan was still officially working for the AWA while in Japan, but things had changed at home. Vince McMahon Jr. had bought his father's company and dropped a W. He had a plan to take his organization national, and Hogan was to be a part of that plan. From Mike Rickard II:

> At the time, Vince McMahon was moving to make the WWF into a national promotion and he felt he needed a new type of champion to make his national expansion work. Hogan came in shortly after Bob Backlund had lost the WWF Championship to the Iron Sheik. Hogan debuted on WWF tv when he ran in to save Bob Backlund from a 3-on-1 beating from the Wild Samoans. Hogan told the crowd that he was back but that he had changed his ways and had a new attitude. Fans eagerly welcomed the babyface Hogan.
>
> In early 1984, Bob Backlund was scheduled to have his rematch with the Iron Sheik. However the combination of injuries from his title loss and his attack by the Samoans sidelined Backlund and Hogan replaced him as the challenger. While January 23, 1984 was not the birth of Hulkamania (Hulkamania had already been running wild in the AWA), it was the start of a new era in professional wrestling. That night in Madison Square Garden, Hogan defeated the Iron Sheik and helped launch Vince McMahon's national expansion of the WWF.

Exactly, so despite what Vince and the WWE may say today, Hulkamania existed in the AWA and Japan (and semi-nationally domestically) well before Hogan finally won the title. He had got into Rocky before all of that great fame, not the other way around. Yet, there was still much work to be done. It was not like Hogan was suddenly a legend: he needed to revitalize wrestling and change it in a way no one ever had.

AND SO THE TRUE AMERICAN ICON IS BORN

From Mathew Sforcina's Evolution Schematic of Hulk Hogan:

> *At first, Hogan was merely just very, very popular. He was not an icon, or a legend, or a part of Americana. He was merely WWF Champion. And for a few months, that was all he was, as he wrestled in both the USA for the WWE and in Japan for New Japan, as he still had commitments there, including defending his IWGP Title.*
>
> *See, after last year's tournament to crown a new champ, the 1984 tournament was held, and the winner would then get to fight Hogan for the title, it still being a yearly deal back then. Adrian Adonis, Andre The Giant, Dick Murdoch, John Quinn, John Studd, Ken Patera, Masa Saito, Masked Superstar, Otto Wanz, Riki Choshu and Tatsumi Fujinami all vied for the honor, but in the end, last year's runner up Antonio Inoki won the tournament, and got the right to fight Hogan. And he did so on the 14th of June, 1984. And Inoki, having learnt from last year, avoided getting knocked out and managed to beat Hulk Hogan to win the title, although the WWF title was not on the line.*

You see, it wasn't just like Hogan won the title and then the WWF became the center of pop culture, as many WWE documentaries would have you believe. There was a significant transition period. Hell, let us not forget how UNSUCCESSFUL WrestleMania was in comparison to future versions. Cable was in its infancy and PPV did not exist. WrestleMania was seen in select markets on Closet Circuit TV systems, i.e. you paid a ticket to go to an arena and watch the big monitors (which really weren't that big in that era). Some arenas did well, others did not. But it was not like getting 900,000 buys like 2005, not even close.

But I digress. The point was that wrestling was still wrestling. "Sports Entertainment" as we know it had not been born yet, and the WWF was just some northeast promotion that was paying well. The country and world was still divided into territories, and Hogan was an old school guy who was working his areas. And as an old school guy, he finished his commitments first, putting over a Japanese man before putting over the WWF. But with his head and responsibilities finally cleared, he could at last concentrate on the WWF and the vision Vince McMahon was talking about.

Sadly, though, McMahon did not have what it took to make his dream come true. You see, Vince McMahon was not the wrestling genius we know and love/despise today. First off, unlike Shane and Stephanie, Vince did not grow up entrenched in the business and did not actually meet his father until he was twelve years old. Although the two grew close after meeting, Vince Sr. discouraged his son from getting involved in wrestling, and at the very least convincing him not to become a wrestler (Wonder why in his mid-life crisis Vince started wrestling? Because his daddy denied him in his youth.). Vince Jr. was working as a traveling salesman in 1971 when his father gave him the opportunity to promote a card. Staying in his father's business, he even began doing play-by-play in 1972. He would stay involved in promoting cards through the 1970's, and then created his own business (Titan Sports) in 1980, which eventually bought out his father's company.

But in reality, Vince Jr.'s experience with all facets of wrestling was limited, and the idea of national promotion was beyond reproach (and against his father's wishes). With his father's death also in 1984, Vince was without any type of adviser who knew one of the most important things: how to manage and develop talent. Luckily, that is where Hulk Hogan came in. From HoganResoucez.com:

> *In the early stages, Vince Jr. did not have as much knowledge of the wrestling business as his dad. Hogan, by this time a veteran and the star, helped him out. He gave McMahon what he needed to keep the WWF company running, he gave him ideas and help, but most of all he gave McMahon himself. He did [whatever] he had to for McMahon; he even took risks for McMahon.*

Let us not forget, Hogan was a multi-media world star well before McMahon got his hands on him. Even more than that, though, was Hogan knew people. And on top of all that, he had a score to settle.

Through Hogan, Vince was able to make his contacts to wrestlers in the AWA and other promotions. From Wikipedia:

> *[M]uch of the AWA's other top talent, including announcer "Mean" Gene Okerlund, manager Bobby "The Brain" Heenan, and wrestlers Ken Patera, Jim Brunzell, and Jesse Ventura, among others, also left for the WWF.*

And from 411mania's own Ron Sarnecky's History of Vince McMahon's Wrestling Empire:

> *From Texas, [McMahon] grabbed the Fabulous Freebirds. He took the Junk Yard Dog from the Mid-South territory. Georgia Championship Wrestling said goodbye to men like King Kong Bundy, and Jake "The Snake" Roberts. Jim Crockett lost Ricky Steamboat, Roddy Piper, Bob Orton Jr., and Greg Valentine. Other stars from around the country that went to the WWF included Paul Orndorff, Sgt. Slaughter, Randy Savage, the British Bulldogs, Mike Rotundo, Barry Windham, and Brutus Beefcake.*

Quite the impressive roster, and just what Vince and Hogan needed moving forward.

So no matter what Vince may tell you retroactively, he created almost none of the stars of the early 1980's. These were men who had been around for a long time and had made themselves great by traveling the territories and the world.

Hulk Hogan was one of those men. But in order to become immortal, he needed to help the WWF reach a height that no one thought possible.

TIME TO REALLY START RUNNING WILD

Hogan was garnering a lot of attention as champion, and Vince was garnering a lot of hatred by continually invading other territories. Hogan was legitimately threatened on more than one occasion, but he knew he could handle it. He was willing to take that risk because he believed in Vince's dream and wanted to become the first true superstar. And was Hogan at home, sitting their collecting money? Of course not! He was on the road almost every day, defending that title at least once a day (sometimes more!). But something huge needed to happen to push the WWF and Hogan into the mainstream forever.

That something was Rock 'n' Wrestling.

In 1984, the WWF began a co-promotion program with MTV, the young and fresh cable network. MTV was about three years old (sort of, depending on how far you want to trace the history back, but we'll call it three years) and had recently reorganized and had its own IPO. As part of their bold new vision, they thought nothing would drive the youth market like teaming up with pro-wrestling. They were right.

At the spearhead of this effort was one Cindi Lauper. From Cool Dudes and Hot Babes:

> Cindi Lauper was a club singer from New York who had recently made it big with a hit record in the charts. It's not clear who came up with the idea (perhaps Lauper's manager Dave Wolf), but one evening out of the blue she turned-up on a WWF television show where an altercation broke out between her and long-time wrestler/personality, Lou Albano. After several weeks of this routine and a lot of hype on MTV, they decided to settle their differences in the ring. Of course Lauper had no intentions of wrestling Albano so she needed a stand-in. This angle gave birth to the so-called "Rock & Wrestling" connection. Richter would represent Cindi Lauper against Albano's stand-in, "The Fabulous Moolah", for the world title in Madison Square Garden.

And from an interview with Lauper with Michael Lano and Evan Ginzburg:

> **ML:** Do you feel your association with pro wrestling negatively affected your career at the time, or did you take some positives from it?
>
> **CL:** No, it was positive. Me with Hulk at the Grammies just got more attention from different areas than from people watching MTV. My ex, Dave Wolf, was always into the wrestling. He loved it. I remember watching Bruno and my Ma loved wrestling. Dave just thought we could reach out to a bigger and different audience by getting involved with the wrestling. He did everything, and set it all up. He still loves it, but I don't follow it as much. It's not like it used to be. Poor management and my p.r. guys not doing their job was what hurt me, I think. Not the wrestling. I enjoyed my time with it. If it was up to Dave, I'd still be involved with the wrestling. He and I are still friends, and talk. Who said it was a negative? P.R. is P.R. and I will always look at it as a positive. Dave just wanted more p.r., but we were doing pretty good airtime on MTV then. I learned a lot about hype and production from the wrestling, I have to say.

Lauper was particularly close with Hogan who, as we discussed earlier, had an affinity for music and therefore could connect with Lauper better than most.

With the attention of the world, Vince and Hogan came up with the plan of plans: to have a supershow! But not like any supershow. The NWA's Starrcade had already been around for years, so that was nothing new. No, WrestleMania would be broadcast around the country on closed circuit TV in arenas around the country.

Hogan, with Mr. T, guest hosted Saturday Night Live beforehand to help promote the show. Hogan was becoming a crossover star in every sense of the word.

And once the numbers came in and it looked like the WWF would live another day, Hogan boomed again.

You see, everyone wanted Hogan, and he was sure to oblige. The man got his own Saturday morning cartoon show in "Hulk Hogan's Rock 'n' Wrestling". He followed that up by being the first and last full-time active professional wrestler to be on the cover of Sports Illustrated. (Some would say that should belong to Dan Hodge, but he was on the cover during his collegiate wrestling days, not for his professional wrestling that would come later. Even much later when the Rock graced the cover in 2016 it was well after his days of regular in-ring competition.) The man became t-shirts, posters, toys, and light-switches. Yes, light-switches! I still have mine.

Austin and the Rock like to claim they are the highest dollar generating superstars ever in wrestling, and to an extent they are right. Depending on how you look at it, either Austin or Rock generated more money for the WWE than anyone. But here's the context: Hogan has one shirt for ten years. And that shirt certainly did not cost $25 (even adjusting for inflation). He did not come out with a new design every three months, he did not have DVDs, PPV barely existed and did not cost $40 an event when it did. There were no arm bands, glasses, jerseys, anything! If you look at it on an item per capita adjusted for inflation and availability—no one, and I mean no one, has ever come near the Hogan level of drawing people and money.

Hogan's legacy became finalized at WrestleMania III. Over the years he was defending his title successfully, packing the arenas and making everyone take their vitamins. But it is WrestleMania III that will go down as Hogan's defining moment. He slammed Andre the Giant in front of 93,000 (or 78,000 people depending on your perspective or which conspiracy theory you believe). Almost everyone wanted to see Hogan take on Andre, and when he defeated the Giant it set him in stone forever.

As Hogan himself said, Andre only let you beat him if Andre wanted you to. Andre believed in Hogan and was willing to lay down for him and pass the torch. The marks of the world got to see their hero do the impossible. The smarks (before the term existed) and boys in back who doubted Hogan finally realized that he was the real deal, and that he had earned their respect.

At last, Hogan was wrestling.

How to Build a WrestleMania

As the organization grew and wrestling became mainstream, everything began to revolve around Hogan. But that was all they needed. Hogan was all the draw the WWF required, and setting up confrontations was easy, but still loved. From the Ultimate Warrior's interview with Dan Flynn:

> *I mean, Hogan was popular, there was no doubt about that. In fact, buildups to previous WrestleManias were done by taking one of Hogan's buddies and having that buddy stab him in the back, turn the second hottest baby face heel. That's how they built WrestleManias.*

And what were the Main Events of WrestleMania? Well (all words below except roman numerals and colons from the Wrestling Information Archive):

> *I: Hulk Hogan and Mr. T defeated Paul Orndorff and Roddy Piper when Hogan pinned Orndorff. Muhammad Ali was the special outside referee.*
>
> *II: Hulk Hogan beat King Kong Bundy (11:00) in a "steel cage" match to retain the title. Robert Conrad was the special referee.*
>
> *III: Hulk Hogan pinned Andre the Giant to retain the title (12:01).*
>
> *IV: Randy Savage pinned Ted DiBiase (9:27) to win the vacant title. [JP Note: Hogan and Andre got double DQed during the World Title tournament earlier in the night. Which brings up another point: who said Hogan was not willing to give up the main event spot?]*
>
> *V: Hulk Hogan pinned Randy Savage (17:54) to win the title.*
>
> *VI: Ultimate Warrior pinned Hulk Hogan (22:51) to win the World title and retain the Intercontinental title. [JP Note: In a match considered by Warrior and his critics alike as his best match ever, of which most feel Hogan carried Warrior for 23 minutes]*

> *VII: Hulk Hogan pinned Sgt Slaughter (20:26) to win the title.*
>
> *VIII: Hulk Hogan defeated Sid Justice (12:44) by Disqualification.*
>
> *IX: Hulk Hogan pinned Yokozuna (0:21) to win the title. [JP Note: This was after Hart lost the title to Yokozuna]*

Two things to take away from this:

(1) Hulk Hogan did make other superstars. Guys like King Kong Bundy, Roddy Piper, and Ted DiBiase became regarded as some the biggest and best of all time DESPITE never winning the title from Hogan. And then guys like Randy Savage, Warrior, and Sid were completely legitimized by actually defeating Hogan. Hogan was willing to lose, so long as it made sense and helped everyone and the industry.

(2) These PPVs alone could not satisfy the audience's want of Hogan.

Survivor Series was created in 1987 specifically so Hogan and Andre could get in the ring together again but not give away another one-on-one match. It worked as the show drew 21,300 people to the Richfield Coliseum and a **7.0**(!!!!) PPV buyrate.

And of course, this is just talking a couple of major events. There's about a decade worth of filler in there as well. But towards the end of that time, things were changing.

HOLLYWOOD! LA LA LA LA LA LA... HOLLYWOOD!

As the years moved on in the WWF, Hogan started defending his title less and less. But that was because he had found another calling making movies. His role in Rocky III had helped propel his wrestling career to new heights, so why could his wrestling career not propel his movies to new heights? Don't forget what we learned about Hogan earlier: that he was motivated to continually be doing more. The man is a workaholic, always trying to bring it to the next level. He felt the real challenge for him was to try to be successful in Hollywood as much as he was in wrestling. Thus, the movies started. From IMDB:

> *No Holds Barred (1989) .... Rip*
> *Suburban Commando (1991) .... Shep Ramsey*
> *Thunder in Paradise (1993) (V) .... R.J. "Hurricane" Spencer*
> *Mr. Nanny (1993) (as Terry 'Hulk' Hogan) .... Sean Armstrong*

Let us not forget that when a movie comes out that it is not just made. It takes months of pre-production, months of filming, more months of editing and post-production, and finally plans for final release. When was Eye Scream Man filmed? Or the Marine? Two or three years prior to release?

Speaking of production, Hogan was also executive producer of the former three movies listed there. So when filming was done, he still had tons of work to do.

Were these movies great successes? Not hugely. None blew away the box office like Lord of Rings did, but few movies do. These were low budget family-style movies. They made profit when it came to video sales and syndication rights more than they ever made in theaters, but that's how movies worked at the time anyway.

People act like Hogan was trying to become Dustin Hoffman, Tom Hanks, Gene Hackman, or Max von Sydow or something. Hogan was not looking for any awards, just looking to entertain and make some money. He saw a challenge and was willing to take it. Did he fail? No, it wasn't as successful as being a pro-wrestler, but it was still interesting. And it's not like it led to the end of his tenure in the WWF.

Or did it?

THE SHOT (TO THE VEIN) HEARD ROUND THE WORLD

The year was 1993, and wrestling was at a turbulent point. Vince McMahon and the WWF were under scrutiny by the federal government during the steroid trial, business was way down, and the fans were booing or apathetic to Hulkamania. Hogan had tried to leave on many occasions, but Vince kept pulling him back. Finally, Hogan decided he no longer wanted to be in wrestling and wanted to set out in another direction.

Some people will tell you Hogan left because of his testimony against McMahon at the steroid trial. One problem with that: Hogan's testimony came almost a year and a half after he left the WWF. One had nothing to do with the other. Similarly, other people say that he left in 1993 because Vince McMahon was not happy with how he answered questions about steroid abuse in the WWF on the Arsenio Hall Show.

One problem with that one: That episode of the Arsenio Hall Show was in 1991, nearly two years before Hogan left the WWF. While it may have been a contributing factor, it was not the sole reason for Hogan's departure.

In a similar vein, others felt that since Vince was getting everyone off of steroids, Hogan was getting smaller and he did not want him around anymore. The problem with this one? Hogan had not had any steroids in four years. From Hogan's testimony to during the steroid trial (courtesy of Hollywood Built):

> **Defense:** You stopped steroids in 89?
>
> **Terry B:** Around then, maybe a little bit after.
>
> **Defense:** You and your wife have two children?
>
> **Terry B:** Yes.
>
> **Defense:** July 27, 1990 is the date of birth of your last child?
>
> **Terry B:** Yes
>
> **Defense:** Did you and your wife, in 1989, decide you would not be on any drugs?
>
> **Terry B:** I would wind down and come off.
>
> **Defense:** Did you use steroids after October 1989?
>
> **Terry B:** Yes. We had an argument about her getting pregnant while I'm on drugs.
>
> Defense reads GJ testimony of Hulk Hogan.
>
> **Q:** When was the last time you used steroids?
>
> **A:** About 4 to 4 and a half years ago. It was 9 months before our daughter was born.

Now, we'll get back to all this steroids stuff in a bit, don't you worry. But the bottom line is Hogan was not cycling off in Steroids and getting smaller. He still had the 22" pythons (oh, I have the best quote about that for later. This Steroid Trial is full of hilarious testimony), that had nothing to do with it at all.

Of course, we know at the time of this testimony Hogan had recently contracted with WCW. From Slam! Sports:

> *It seemed like a glorious day for Hulk Hogan. July 17, 1994. It was his first match with the Atlanta-based World Championship Wrestling, and that day he won the WCW World title from Ric Flair in Orlando, FL. He was taking a break from his new television series, "Thunder in Paradise." He had brought back the magic that was "Hulkamania." It seemed like the best day of his life.*
>
> *The week before [for] Hogan was not as glorious, though. He started the week off by promoting his new show, "Thunder in Paradise," and his match with Flair on "The Tonight Show" and "Live with Regis and Kathie Lee." But on July 14, Hogan had to testify in a Uniondale, NY, court against his former boss, Vince McMahon.*

The conspiracy theory is that Hogan was jumping to WCW and was going to turn against Vince and WWF. How ridiculous is this?

No, the truth of the matter is Hogan was tired of over fifteen years on the road, being the top of the business, literally carrying the company on his shoulders, and not spending any time with his family. So in relation to his Hollywood career, he began exclusively working on the television show Thunder in Paradise.

It was on the set of Thunder in Paradise that Hogan even met Bischoff for the first time. From Wrestling 101:

> *During Hogan's departure from the wrestling world, he embarked on a new project, Thunder in Paradise , Hogan portrayed an Ex-Navy SEAL turned mercenary with a boat which had all the gadgets of Michael Knight's K.I.T.T, but unfortunately the boat never spoke. Anyway, the series was fairly successful for Hogan, but it was while he was filming at Universal Studios Hogan met Eric Bischoff. Bischoff had started filming WCW events from the Disney MGM studios in Florida, and he decided to approach Hogan, the pair got talking and Hogan eventually signed a very lucrative deal with Ted Turner's World Championship Wrestling.*

It was just happenstance that Hogan and Bischoff were at the same place at the same time, and it turned out the two got along famously. WCW had been in turmoil for years, and Hogan realized that he may just be able to create another super organization again. WCW was in trouble after all, and he might be their savior. From Gery Roif:

> *After all the damage had been done [in the early 1990s], the financial losses due to poor buyrates, [non-existent] house show revenues, and generally insane spending habits from the controlling powers left WCW nearly 23 million dollars in the red at the end of the year.*

And immediately after signing, Hogan made an impact. The Bash at the Beach PPV did a 1.02 PPV buyrate. Compare that to the previous PPV that did a 0.48, or Starrcade seven months earlier that did a 0.55. The premier PPV of WCW did half the buys of the PPV with one Hulk Hogan match. He truly was the draw.

The PPV buys continued to stay mostly high... at least for a while...

THERE'S A NEW HOGAN IN TOWN

Hogan's return to wrestling in WCW helped lead the company out of the red and lend credibility to the organization. A year and a couple months later and WCW would be able to launch Nitro. With Hogan at the helm, Time Warner corporate felt more comfortable green lighting the program, much like Spike TV felt more comfortable with TNA when they got Sting and Steiner.

The problem was Hogan was facing the same problem. The fans had tired of the unstoppable babyface, and WCW fans were not fully accepting of Hogan. After all, these were the fans that were supposed to want to see more mat-based wrestling. Hogan tried to reinvent himself wearing black and giving himself an edge, but it wasn't enough. There needed to be something more. But he was frustrated and needed some time away.

While away, he worked on movies. His contract was coming to an end, and he thought that maybe it was all over. Strangely, an old friend made an offer. From Gery Roif:

> *Terry's contract was done, just when he finished Santa With Muscles and 3 Ninjas with Lonnie Anderson, he was offered 4.5 Million from Vinnie Mac, and would've signed, but when he heard that the new Bret Hart contract that he signed instead of being the 3rd nWo man... Terry did not [like] it, and somebody leaked it to him and re-signed for 3 years....*

You see, despite the accusations, Hogan never positioned himself to be the 3rd member of the nWo. He was actually away from wrestling, thinking about retiring or going back the WWF. Bret Hart and Eric Bischoff had already talked about him being the last man for the nWo (though it didn't have that name yet), and Eric Bischoff did not know what to do. He went to Hogan just to visit him and that is where they came up with the idea for him to be the third man. It would change wrestling forever.

This is the New World Order of Wrestling, brother!

At Bash at the Beach 1996, Hogan literally shocked the world. The "Outsiders" Hall and Nash were taking on a WCW dream team of Sting, Randy Savage, and Lex Luger. Rumors were running rampant. Who would the third man be? No one, and I mean NO ONE saw it coming.

Out of the back came a returning Hulk Hogan. The fans thought he was there to help out the WCW team after Luger was injured. But then, Hogan did the unthinkable! For the first time in fifteen years... Hogan turned heel! Hogan leg dropped Randy Savage, and the fans reacted bitterly. Mean Gene Okerlund on the Monday Night Wars DVD described it as one of the most incredible, emotional sights he had ever seen. The fans were so angry at Hogan and the nWo that they started to pelt the ring with garbage, a rarely seen event at that time.

You see, even after all that time Hogan still had the crowd in the palm of his hand. He still knew how to control them and get them to react. They had such a strong emotional investment that they felt betrayed in a way that no other heel turn before or after has topped.

Even when Austin turned heel, it felt contrived. Hogan's, though, became natural. He really did want the fans to stick it. He was upset that they had given up on Hulkamania. He was furious that they were turning on him.

So Hogan turned on the crowd first, and they loved to hate him for it.

Hogan and the nWo would turn the wrestling world on its head. From Wikipedia:

> *Hogan's turn to heel, after being one of the most popular and iconic figures in sports entertainment and sports in general, caused a great stir through the wrestling community. The next night on Nitro, Eric Bischoff announced that all night Sunday and all day Monday, WCW and Hogan received literally hundreds, if not thousands, of complaints from parents whose children had stayed up all night*

> crying and destroying Hulkster merchandise. Though intended as kayfabe, the statement was no doubt truthful. Hogan's move from face to heel signified a change in wrestling's character system, which in coming years would intentionally blur the lines between good and evil.

And the heel turn and the further pushing of the envelope with the nWo created a new boom in wrestling, one that has yet to be surpassed.

As the weeks went on, Nitro's ratings continued to rise. On August 26, 1996, just seven weeks after the heel turn and the formation of the nWo, Nitro broke the 4.0 ratings barrier that no one thought was possible (a 4.2 to be exact and put the icing on the cake). That same night, RAW scored a 2.0 rating, the lowest head-to-head rating it had received since September 25, 1995. EXACTLY a year later, on August 25, 1997, Nitro would be the first of the Monday night shows to break the 5.0 ratings barrier, although this was mostly due to there being no competition that night. But when RAW was unopposed just five weeks prior, they scored a 4.1 rating. The point was made. Hogan and WCW could convert people over while the WWF had yet to figure out a way to bring them back.

Now, I could keep going into all of Nitro's monumental ratings victories, even the 83 week winning streak, but that is for another day.

You may also remember from our Eric Bischoff case that it was under Hogan's reign as champion that WCW not only surpassed the WWF in monthly buyrates, but also in the twelve-month buyrate average. From March 1997 to September 1998, Hogan and the WCW/nWo literally topped the WWF in every category even looking over a year span.

But winning the money and the ratings was not the only thing Hogan did. He helped create the whole "spitting on tradition" counter-culture. He spray-painted the belt, he attacked people in group muggings that were not common, he told the world just how good he was and that they could stick it.

Hogan's presence drew into WCW some the most unconventional names. From Dennis Rodman to Jay Leno to Karl Malone, these men became a part of WCW history because of Hulk Hogan. Say what you will about what these people may have done or whose spot they may have stolen, they gave WCW and Hogan incredible mainstream attention that translated into ratings, merchandise sales, and buyrates. It made everyone's life better overall.

WCW was hurting before Hogan, and still shaky before the nWo. But under his guidance WCW became the predominant brand of wrestling in the world. Bischoff has thanked Hogan many times for helping to bring WCW to its only profitable time in history, and Hogan has thanked Bischoff for giving him the opportunity.

Not only, though, were there new events, but everything that was old was new again. Suddenly, Hogan was the heel and people were cheering Ric Flair, Roddy Piper, the Giant, Kevin Sullivan, and may more traditional heels. It was something completely different, to be on the other end of the screaming. To want Hogan to submit, to hope that someone kicked out of the leg drop. It brought new life to his career.

More than that, it brought new life to wrestling. Hogan had once again literally redefined the entire industry. He had helped create the national promotion and the superstar, now he had created the anti-hero and the attitude. He had created storylines with depth and shades of grey. He had given birth to yet another era of professional wrestling.

How many times must I explain how WCW died?

Yet despite all of this, despite bringing WCW to its only profitable time in history, and despite being the most influential person in a whole new era that paved the way for likes of Steve Austin, DX, and the Rock, Hogan has actually been blamed for the DEATH of WCW.

How is that possible?

People started to complain that Hogan's act was getting old. He came out and talked until the ratings sank. Except that is not what happened at all. Let me remind you what Derek Burgan said about the promo between Warrior and Hogan:

> *Gene Okerlund said that "ratings sunk like a rock" during Warrior's promo, which most certainly cannot be true. After a little research, I found out Warrior's segment on Nitro did a 6.4 to Raw's 3.1. Now that I think about it, Okerlund might have been even harsher on this DVD to Warrior than Heenan. The difference being that Okerlund often comes across as totally clueless when he opens his mouth.*

And this is true for many segments. Hogan was a personality who drew in more viewers, not turned them away. He remained one of the highest draws in WCW until he left the organization in disgrace.

I've already proven that the Fingerpoke of Doom (which many lament against Hogan) is Not Guilty, and that it did not cause the death of WCW.

Although many people attributed this to Hogan's booking power, over time Hogan's contract became structured so that he had creative control over his character. This made people feel that Hogan would refuse to job the belt to anyone, or that he would book himself at the top of the program no matter who was champ.

First off, who cares if Hogan got booking power in this contract? He had twenty years of experience and knew what it took to have the crowd in his control. Who is anyone to tell Hogan what programs he should be in and how to wrestle? Hogan literally re-created the industry twice. He knew what he was doing.

And Hogan was fine with any program, and losing, so long as there was a plan for him. During the New Blood time under Vince Russo, Hogan worked a program with Billy Kidman and lost to him twice. He was fine with that so long as he knew where his program was going.

Coming into Bash at the Beach 2000, Hogan was to defend his World Heavyweight Championship against Jeff Jarrett. Hogan came to the PPV prepared to drop the title, but under one condition: he wanted to know what the plan was for him afterwards. He was fine with dropping the title to Jarrett and understood that WCW was going in a new direction. Hogan understood that a new generation of wrestlers had to be created.

But when he went to Russo the day of the PPV and asked him what the plan for Hulk Hogan was after the PPV, Russo said, "Nothing."

Russo had absolutely no plans to use Hogan after the event! How can a booker have absolutely no plans for Hulk Hogan? The least he could have done was continue to use him in the New Blood storyline, putting over anyone from Scott Steiner to Booker T. But he had no plans for Hogan. He was essentially saying he was going to bury Hogan in favor of everyone else.

This was the final straw for Hogan. For the first time EVER he used his creative control clause to change the ending of the match. Russo was furious at Hogan, but Hogan was trying to protect his job. It wasn't him fighting the new wave of wrestlers or a change in direction; it was him fighting for his legacy.

With this decision, Russo told Jarrett to go out and just lay down, giving Hogan the "Hulk Hogan Memorial Belt" and then stripping Hogan of the World Title and putting it up in a match between Booker T and Jeff Jarrett later in the night. But that would not be before Hogan was verbally taken apart by Russo in the middle of the ring, breaking kayfabe in a way no one ever had before. Hogan left WCW and sued the company and Russo for defamation of character. Hogan's time in WCW was over in July 2000.

WCW would continue to spiral out of control for months while the bosses began to rotate. Things seemed like they were settling down in January 2001, and it looked as if Eric Bischoff and Fusient Media Ventures were going to acquire WCW. But in March 2001, AOL Time-Warner cancelled the highest rated show on their combined networks, thus ending any possible deal with Fusient. In some shady back door shenanigans, the WWF ended up being the highest bidder for WCW's library and copyrights, and that is what killed WCW.

Bottom line: WCW was killed when AOL Time-Warner cancelled programming. Hogan had been gone from the company for nearly a year, and had led it to its only profitable period in history. Neither Hogan nor his creative control led to the death of WCW. The complete opposite is the truth of the matter.

AND THEN THERE WAS QUIET

From Wikipedia:

> *From July 2000 to November 2001, Hogan was extremely quiet and out of the public eye. He had been dealing with self-doubt and depression following the Vince Russo incident, wondering if what Russo had said about him was true. Hogan was also dealing with the death of his father Peter Bollea in December 2001, which he took very hard. Fans at the time had largely agreed with Russo's sentiments, feeling that Hogan was "washed-up" and had been holding down younger talents for too long. Hogan wanted to prove his detractors wrong and show them that he still had another run or two left in him.*
>
> *In the months following the eventual demise of WCW in March 2001, Hogan underwent surgery on his knees in order for him to wrestle again. As a test, Hogan worked a match in Orlando, Florida for the XWF promotion run by his longtime handler Jimmy Hart. Hogan defeated Curt Hennig in this match and felt healthy enough to accept an offer to return to the WWF in February 2002.*

As the story above noted, Hogan overcame his depression and his worry. He trained and rebuilt his body. He did what no one thought would ever be possible: he came back to the WWF.

THE POISON IS INTRODUCED

Vince McMahon brought Hogan—along with Hall and Nash—back as the nWo in his storyline feud with co-owner Ric Flair. This time, the nWo was not fresh, and were not rebels. Vince never understood that the nWo was not a faction, that it was a different organization that was invading WCW. Also, Nash and Hall were having health and mental problems respectively and were not in the best condition of their life.

Something strange happened, though. Despite everything Hogan had done to the Rock leading up their WrestleMania match, the fans still cheered him. He may have tried to blow up the Rock's car, but it made no difference. He had passed to that status that was beyond anything, where he was just completely revered.

This newfound face status led to Hogan defeating Triple H for the WWF Undisputed Heavyweight Championship, which became the WWE Undisputed Championship under his reign, another first for Hogan.

After becoming a part of the SmackDown! roster, Hogan began to get involved in a program with young one-legged wrestler Zack Gowen that eventually led to him becoming Mr. America. The whole story ended abruptly when Hogan and Vince could not come to an agreement over money.

With Hogan gone from the WWE, he went to Japan to face Masa "My Hero" Chono before being attacked by Jarrett in what would become an aborted angle that was originally supposed to lead to the first ever Bound for Glory. But do not blame Hogan for this not coming to fruition. He never signed anything that said he would go to TNA. Besides, a very different offer came along.

Hogan was invited to join the WWE Hall of Fame, an event that he was truly humbled by as shown on Hogan Knows Best. Hogan continues to make sporadic appearances today, including a short program with Shawn Michaels. But Hogan knows how valuable his time and presence are. How do I know that? Glad you asked.

BUT CAN HE STILL DRAW?

Very few people doubt that Hogan was a major draw in the 1980's, there are doubts about how he drew in the 1990's (and I hope we've assuaged them above), but there are big lingering doubts if Hogan is a draw today. The most backwards comment is that he is good for short term draws, but does not draw for long. Is that so? From the 411mania newsboard on March 29, 2006:

> *The March 26th 12:30pm airing of Hogan Knows Best scored a 1.3 cable rating, with 3.1 share. The 9:30pm airing scored a 0.9 cable rating, with a 1.3 share while the 11pm airing scored a 0.9 cable rating as well, but had a 1.8 share.*

So already two weeks into its second season, Hogan is pretty much the top-rated show on VH1. This is the way I see it:

Hulk Hogan, by himself, has more drawing ability than the entire TNA roster. Sorry, but it's true! No matter how much I may heart their product and want them to succeed, the fact of the numbers show that Hogan in his lonesome outdraws the entire roster.

At this point in his life, Hogan cannot do a full schedule, nor could he even do just a TV schedule. His body and family will not let him, so he must sit back. But if he were around, those are the number he would draw in.

For through the years, Hogan truly has become immortal. His mere presence means more than some of the best laid storylines. One punch from him gets the crowd to cheer louder than any crazy spot off the X-ropes. Hogan himself said, "Why do just three elbow drops and put all that wear and tear on your body when you can do one and then look at the audience and get them to care."

Do you know when he said that?

On Hogan Knows Best.

Shoot 'em if you got 'em!

Still, people say Hogan would have been nothing without a little help. And that help came in the form of steroids. Let's get it straight out there: Hogan has done steroids. He used steroids for twelve years. From Hulk Hogan's testimony to the federal government in the steroid trial (courtesy of Hollywood Built):

> **Defense:** *Any orders placed to Zahorian by you were for your personal use?*
>
> **Terry B:** *Yes.*
>
> **Defense:** *Would you distribute steroids?*
>
> **Terry B:** *No.*
>
> **Defense:** *Which you [believed] steroids were legal?*
>
> **Terry B**: *Yes because I had a prescription.*
>
> **Defense:** *Do you remember Dr. War from Canada, Dr. Pannovich from Denver, Dr. Liebowitz from NY?*

Terry B: Yes, except for Dr. Pannovich.

Defense: Had other doctors dispensed steroids to you between 85 and 89?

Terry B: Yes.

Defense: War?

Terry B: Yes

Defense: Liebowitz?

Terry B: Yes.

Defense: Pannovich?

Terry B: Don't remember.

Defense reads Terry B's Grand Jury statements which said that all four doctors including Zahorian wrote him prescriptions.

Defense: Did you get deca from Ponnavich?

Terry B: Yes.

Defense: Did you try and use steroids legally?

Terry B: Yes.

Defense: Did you get a doctor to see you beforehand?

Terry B: Not so much that, just made sure that I had a prescription.

Defense: Did you get steroids in gyms in the 70s?

Terry B: Yes, 70s and 80s.

Defense: Once you started wrestling for large organizations like the AWA and Japan you starting seeing doctors for steroids?

Terry B: Yes.

Defense: It was better to get from a doctor because of the quality?

> **Terry B:** Yes a concern in the gyms would be that they might be fake.
>
> **Defense:** Today in 1994 you have more knowledge of steroids than in the 80s?
>
> **Terry B:** Yes.
>
> **Defense:** If you had this info back then would you not have used them?
>
> **Terry B:** That might have been the case.

And:

> **Defense:** Vince McMahon never directed you to take steroids?
>
> **Terry B:** Never.
>
> **Defense:** It was your choice and decision?
>
> **Terry B:** Definitely.
>
> **Defense:** Other wrestlers take steroids?
>
> **Terry B:** To my knowledge, yes.
>
> **Defense:** Ever hear Vince McMahon tell a wrestler he should take steroids?
>
> **Terry B:** No.
>
> **Defense:** Do you recall any conversations with Vince McMahon where he implied a [wrestler] should take steroids?
>
> **Terry B:** Never.

You see, Hogan did not view his steroid use as anything illegal or wrong. Elsewhere in the interview:

> **Government:** Did you carry steroids on the road?
>
> **Terry B:** Yes

> *Government:* Why did you use steroids?
>
> *Terry B:* To heal injuries, to keep on going, the schedule was tough. It gave an edge. For bodybuilding. When I first started it was to get big and gain weight.

And a little later:

> *Defense:* Did you believe steroids helped you to heal from injuries that you sustained?
>
> *Terry B:* Yes.
>
> *Defense:* Did you feel steroids speeded the recovery from injury?
>
> *Terry B:* Yes.

You see, we forget that there are legitimate uses to steroids, and Hogan knew what those were. He was already big, he did not need the 'roids to get there. He was using them to heal from injuries. And as covered in the Lex Luger case, the side effects were much less known. Back to the trial:

> *Defense:* Ever heard of a roid rage?
>
> *Terry B:* Yes.
>
> *Defense:* In your 12 or 13 years of use did you ever experience a roid rage?
>
> *Terry B:* No.
>
> *Defense:* Ever see Vince McMahon have a personality change known as roid rage?
>
> *Terry B:* No.
>
> *Defense:* Is it fair to say wrestlers are aggressive?
>
> *Terry B:* When performing.
>
> *Defense:* Being on the road, when the wrestlers were offstage were they boisterous?

> **Terry B:** Not all.
>
> **Defense:** Did some party?
>
> **Terry B:** Yes.
>
> **Defense:** Did they get into trouble?
>
> **Terry B:** Sometimes.
>
> **Defense:** Did you ever the make the connection of steroids usage and the wrestlers being boisterous at a hotel or bar?
>
> **Terry B:** Never.

Hogan never experienced some of the worst side effects of steroids. He also knew how to cycle the different drugs to stay healthy. He used them as they were originally intended—as a supplement, not the only way. Still, there were accusations that Hogan was illegally distributing. Back to the trial:

> **Defense:** Did you charge Dave Brower money?
>
> **Terry B:** No. He gave me 10 vials, so I gave him ten vials. We were friends. It is [similar] to how smokers share cigarettes.
>
> **Defense:** Between 85-91, you gave wrestlers steroids and the reverse was true. In your mind were you distributing steroids?
>
> **Terry B:** No, these were my friends.
>
> **Defense:** When they gave them to you, were they in your mind distributing steroids?
>
> **Terry B:** No. they were my friends.
>
> **Defense:** Did you believe as a lay person, that between 85 and 91, as long as a doctor prescribed them, they were legal?
>
> **Terry B:** Yes.
>
> **Defense:** Did you believe Zahorian was committing a crime?
>
> **Terry B:** No.

> **Defense:** You did not have knowledge that it was criminal?
>
> **Terry B:** No, I did not.

And it's not like Hogan was just seeing these doctors to get steroids:

> **Defense:** Did you talk to Zahorian about your physical condition?
>
> **Terry B:** Yes.
>
> **Defense:** Did you about problems apart from steroid usage?
>
> **Terry B:** Yes.
>
> **Defense:** Did you have personal and medical conversations with Zahorian?
>
> **Terry B:** Yes.
>
> **Defense:** Did you expect them to be confidential?
>
> **Terry B:** Yes.
>
> **Defense:** Did some concern your wife?
>
> **Terry B:** Yes.
>
> **Defense:** You used Zahorian for reasons unassociated with steroids?
>
> **Terry B:** Yes.
>
> **Defense:** Were you satisfied with the [advice] of Zahorian?
>
> **Terry B:** Yes.
>
> **Defense:** He helped you?
>
> **Terry B:** Yes.

So we can see from all of this that Hogan was not an abuser, he was just a supplementary person. He did what was normal, but only later came to understand the dangers he was putting his body through. When his wife became pregnant, they agreed that he would cycle off of all of the drugs, which he did and never turned back. It's been nearly fifteen years since then. The man learned his lesson and moved on.

"But JP," you'll say, "didn't he lie about steroid use or the Arsenio Hall Show?"

The answer is: no, not really.

First, let us remember that the appearance on Arsenio Hall was in 1991, three years before the trial. On there, he admitted to having used steroids "on a few occasions" but did not admit to any more. He explained about the healing factors and legitimate reasons for using steroids. Vince did not want to talk about it all, not even the legitimate reasons. That was the basis of their argument. And on top of that, that was just a show, not the grand jury.

No, Hogan didn't need the steroids, as we've said. He used them to help his life on the road, not realizing the full implications of what he was doing. But when he did he made the changes to his health in order to continue going without them. After all, he did not really need them. This wraps it all up nicely:

> *Defense:* You do not take steroids anymore?
>
> *Terry B:* No.
>
> *Defense:* Do you still refer to your arms as pythons when in character?
>
> *Terry B:* Yes.
>
> *Defense:* As 22 inches?
>
> *Terry B:* Yes.
>
> *Defense:* Are they still 22 inches?
>
> *Terry B:* Yes.
>
> *Defense:* Is one of your lines for the Ric Flair PPV (said in a Hulk Hogan voice) whats you gonna do Ric Flair when these pythons come after you?
>
> *Terry B:* Yes.
>
> *Defense:* And that's without steroids?
>
> *Terry B:* Yes.

And what is funnier than hear the defense do a Hulk Hogan voice?

HERE COMES THE PROSECUTION!

Now we can start new content, but I'm not even going to start! I asked you, the readers, what were some items that made you hate Hulk Hogan that I did not cover. Here they are (and whoever said them first gets the billing, sorry if you are not here). First up is someone many of you will recognize, **fixxer315** who said:

> *1. Curt Hennig is scheduled to win the Royal Rumble in 1990, but Hogan pushed to get it changed to him winning.*

That was never the plan at all. Curt Hennig had been in the WWF since 1988 and was still a very young man. He had a year-long undefeated streak that ended in an early shot at the WWF Championship against Hulk Hogan. Think of this as when John Cena faced Brock Lesner for the WWF Championship early in the former one's career. It was a huge push just to get a shot, nonetheless against the best. As the months were moving on, it became obvious that Warrior was becoming the huge face of the company. Hogan, wanting to take a smaller role and film more movies, agreed to move to the side. In order to build that match at WrestleMania VI, Hogan won the Royal Rumble to set up the initial confrontation, defeating the last man in the ring Mr. Perfect.

So just two years into his WWF career and Hennig had already gotten numerous title shots and proved he could hang with Hogan, a la Piper, DiBiase, Bundy, Hercules, et al.

And please take into consideration the WWF booking strategy of the time: the WWF title was to be held by a face for a long period of time who did more showmanship than wrestling. The Intercontinental Title was for those who were good enough to be champion but they just couldn't have them win the belt. And so when Warrior won the WWF Championship off of Hogan, Curt Hennig was the one to win the tournament for the vacant title.

It was never a depush or a plan by Hogan, it was a plan by Vince and the WWF to transfer the WWF Championship to Warrior, phase down Hogan, and give Hennig the reward he deserved without disrupting the top of the card.

Next!

> 2. Hogan pulls one of the most crass political moves ever as he walks out of WM9 with the world title, making Yokozuna and Fuji look foolish by challenging him after just winning the title. He then takes a vacation with the belt, rarely appearing on WWF TV until his KOTR defense. He is supposed to drop it to Bret at SummerSlam, but Hogan refuses, so McMahon pulls the plug on Hogan's run and has Yokozuna squash him at KOTR, and that's the last you see of Hogan on WWF TV for about 9 years. (That wouldn't be the last time Hogan screwed over Bret, but I'm not gonna get into Starrcade 97).

The WWF was in a bad position come WrestleMania IX. The steroid scandal was in full bloom, business was way down, and nothing seemed to help. Vince came to Hogan in desperation with a plea to help out his company. The problem was Hogan already had a crazy schedule with starring and being executive producer of two movies while also preparing for his new television show Thunder in Paradise. It was a mistake by Vince to put so much on Hogan when Hogan was not available. Anyway, Hogan's contract was coming to an end, and Vince decided it was worth pulling the plug on the reign early in order to get the title back into the main picture. He did not refuse to job to Bret Hart, it was just timing. Hogan's contract did not go until SummerSlam, and he was already scheduled to start filming Thunder in Paradise episodes. So he dropped the title back to Yokozuna, definitely not making him look foolish then, and then going on to film movies. As we covered earlier, Hogan did not leave the WWF to avoid putting over Bret or go to WCW; he went to film his new TV show. He thought he was done with wrestling until he met Eric Bischoff months later.

What else?

> 3. Hardly ever defending the title while in WCW, at least not in the pre-Nitro days.

This is the same story. Now we are just jumping ahead a few months. Hogan had signed a limited engagement contract because the intention was to use Hogan to bolster WCW but also allow him time to do his show and movies. And that is exactly what he did! WCW's ratings and buyrates hit new highs. Besides, Nitro was launched while Hogan was champion. His presence was one of the reasons WCW got a Monday night show. He even jobbed in a non-title match to Arn Anderson on Nitro. It was just a timing and booking decision by Bischoff to bring WCW to a new level, and that is exactly what happened.

Can we try a different story?

> 4. Using his backstage stroke to bring in all of the WWF castoffs whose gimmicks were getting old even in the early 90s. (Earthquake, Duggan, Ed Leslie, [Honkytonk]). Come on—Ed Leslie headlining Starrcade? The end result was to push many of the traditional WCW wrestlers to the side, as Sting didn't see the main event from mid-94 until late-95 unless he was tagging with Hogan. Flair couldn't be shunted aside as easily, but he was made into Savage's bitch. And all of the up and coming talent such as Pilman, Austin and Johnny B Badd were either removed outright or were put into supporting roles.

You have this backwards. Remember back where we talked about how Vince used Hogan to make contacts with all the stars of the AWA, WCCW, JCP/NWA, etc... and then lure them over? Pretty much the same thing. Bischoff was looking for more recognizable names to bolster WCW's roster. Do not forget how many people WCW lost from 1991-1993, a loss they were still recovering from. Bischoff wanted names that may or may not bring people in, but at least were recognizable. How they were used after that is not Hogan's fault. Sure, he probably wanted some of his friends to come over and have good jobs, but why is that a bad thing? You've never recommended a friend for a job before? These were all qualified people. The up and coming talent were not pushed down the card, and met mixed success later. We can look back now and say, "Oh my god, they were bad to Austin! He didn't get a push because Hogan was around!" But that wasn't the case at the time. Austin was some blond-haired guy who had not found his niche yet. He was a competent wrestler and was showing some signs that he could be good, but he was no higher on the card nor more important than, say, Ken Kennedy today.

You can't build the second floor of your house without the foundation first. Hogan and the older stars were the foundation that would make WCW strong. Only then could those younger stars grow. It just so happens that none of those three became main event stars in WCW (though only Austin did in the WWF/E), but there are others who were there then and later who did get to become stars because of the foundation that was built, including DDP, the Giant, and later Goldberg. And that's just the main event. Chris Jericho, Rey Mysterio, Steven/William Regal, Booker T... all were able to get the first major exposure in WCW in the years to come because of the foundation and risk Bischoff took through Hogan's contacts.

Next up in **Jim Moore** with a conspiracy theory:

> [T]ry to save face for Hogan for the Fast Count That Wasn't A Fast Count, when he colluded/paid off Nick Patrick to not do the fast count when he pinned Sting at Starrcade.

I believe you are referring to this version of history provided by Wikipedia:

> Rather than the triumphant victory that one would expect the most popular wrestler in the company to gain over the hated man he had been chasing for over a year, as Sting had Hogan, the finish was confused and chaotic, with the live audience visibly displeased at the entire spectacle. Hart "restarted" the match, and Sting quickly won the title, but given the circumstances, excitement was rather muted. It is rumored that Hogan paid Patrick a sum in cash backstage before the show in exchange for failing to execute the planned finish, with the intent of protecting Hogan's image. The entire debacle resulted in the title being held up for another Hogan-Sting pay-per-view match, which many WCW fans took as a slap in the face and a hapless attempt to draw additional money to see the result WCW had failed to deliver the first time around.

And that is why sometimes, Wikipedia is a VERY unreliable source. Commentary, psychological analysis, and ex-post facto examination of long-term impacts do make a good history book. Anyway, as is often the case, follow the dollar signs.

The first dollar sign was Bret Hart. The Montreal Screwjob was a shock to the wrestling world. Bischoff did not expect that he'd be able to get Bret Hart that way, and wanted to strike while the iron was hot. So he brought Hart in quickly without much direction because he just wanted him there. This created the need to get him involved in Starrcade and mess up the booking that had been in place for months. So Bret Hart was a combustible element that most were not used to working with.

Next was what happened after Starrcade. The "controversy" led to the title being held up and a rematch being set. Have you considered that this was just a swerve to get more buyrates? Do you know what the buyrates were for the next PPVs? 1.02, 1.10, and 1.10! Plan successful!

Now, if Hogan really did pay off Nick Patrick, how in the blue hell did he maintain a job in WCW for four more years and then be one of five refs to survive from WCW in the WWE. Even Earl Hebner got fired in the WWE, so how could Nick Patrick, if he were that corrupt, actually survive in these jobs? How could this be the only time he'd allow this to happen?

And why would Hogan pay him off? Why not just use his creative control clause and change the ending of the match? He already had it in his contract!

Now, I cannot speak for Nick Patrick, and he has never spoken aloud about it. Did me mess up and forget that this was the time to count fast? Or was this the story to set up more Hogan/Sting and eventual move a heel Hart (who, don't forget, was a heel coming from the WWF and didn't exactly make his intentions clear in WCW for almost his entire run) into the mix? I can only speculate on that. But Hogan paying him off? What would be the point and the actual possibility? Too crazy of a conspiracy for my tastes.

> *In 2017, Nick Patrick finally broke his silence on this issue on the Sitting Ringside podcast. During the interview, he had this to say (because he was retired and had nothing to lose anymore):*
>
> *"What happened was two people, Sting and Hulk, they were the two franchise guys and the two franchise guys were butting heads at that point in time... One guy came up to me and told me to fast count it to get some heat and give him an out and the other guy said 'Don't fast count it. Keep it nice and slow.'*
>
> *And so the person that was in charge evidently didn't want to make a call, didn't want to pick a side, and made themselves scarce all night long to where I couldn't find them to ask them 'Hey, what do you want me to do?'"*
>
> *Patrick further noted that he more often than not used a slow count, so just decided to go with that since he could not get better direction.*
>
> *Later on, Eric Bischoff addressed this in a response on his 83 Weeks Podcast. During that interview, Bischoff described the rest of the situation, explained how he had wanted the fast count but left the details up to the wrestlers, the ref, and the agents. He was not actively involving himself in the details, so it became a communication fiasco that resulted in what happened on screen. Nick Patrick made the final decision because Bischoff was not as involved as he could or should have been. Therefore, it was not politicking, not a payoff, but just a general disagreement of match specific layout details that led to a pure mess.*

Manu Bumb brings us back to reality:

> You kinda glossed over that whole part where Hogan lost to Lesnar on SD, then disappeared for a long while, at first to sell Lesnar's brutality, but eventually, didn't they have a problem causing Hogan to walk away sometime after that match, and before he returned to SD (prior to NWO and his WM match vs Vince)?

I did gloss over it for time purposes but we can return to it because you and a few others mentioned it. The bottom line is money and contracts. Vince and Hogan could not agree on how to use Hogan and what to pay him, but eventually came to an understanding. In the end, Hogan is still a businessman and knows his best product is himself. He does not need to work and will do it for the right fun and the right dollars. But not without a good combination of both. Since he came back after that, this point is rather moot.

After that I heard from **Steffan Jones** in the UK who just needs me to answer one thing before he votes Not Guilty:

> [O]ne issue [I] still have with Hogan which I'd like to you to answer is that I read in the UK's Powerslam magazine that HBK agreed to put over Hogan at SummerSlam as long as Hogan returned the favour at Unforgiven. After Summerslam Hogan basically blew them off, and refused to put HBK over and work Unforgiven for some reason or other. I'm a true HBK mark, so I gotta say, I view this as just plain bad sportsmanship, as HBK did a hell of a job putting Hogan over. Also, I heard it's written into Hogan's contract with WWE, that whenever he appears on a WWE ppv, he always has to be the highest paid wrestler on the card, even if it's just a quick mid-card run in, like WM 21. How can he justify this if he's only making a one off 10 min appearance in the mid-card?

Hogan's contract with the WWE was only through the match at SummerSlam, that is it. He never agreed to further matches and actually was quite busy trying to get his daughter's music career going. The whole point of Hogan Knows Best is to give his daughter publicity (and its working), and that is why she seems like the main centerpiece of the show—because she is! He may have verbally agreed to come back, but life and offers take you by surprise. Just a couple of months later and Hogan was on the set of Little Hercules (where he twisted his ankle and was on crutches).

Hogan does not have many matches left in him. His injuries, replaced body parts, and needs of his family means that he cannot just keep coming back to win and lose matches. He has no problem losing, as demonstrated by losses to Brock Lesnar and Kurt Angle (by tap out!), but he will not just come back for a match he's already had. He wants to wrestle Steve Austin, as he challenged him at Homecoming and teased it at the 2006 Hall of Fame Ceremony. That is his concentration now, not returning a "favor" to Shawn Michaels, a favor that Michaels does not need. Is Shawn going to be less over because of his loss to Hogan? Nope, it does not seem so. Hogan never got his win back over Goldberg, and never would have gotten it over the Warrior if Warrior had not come to WCW. He'll never get his back over Brock Lesnar! So Shawn has one person he's never defeated, it's no big deal. Magnum TA will never defeat Ric Flair, it does not take away from his career.

As for being the most paid person on the show, that is not what happened. It just so happens that on some shows he may be the most paid person on the show. But show pays are based on a number of things. First, there is the base pay. Most contracted WWE wrestlers have lower base pays than in the past, but Hogan only signs contracts with a high base. He will not be dependent on match residuals. And that's where the rest of the money comes from. First, there are the buyrates, of which wrestlers on the card get a cut. Then there is the actual gate and merchandise. This is where Hogan kills others. Despite the years, when Hogan's merchandise is available in the arena and he is there, it tends to be the top, if not near the top, of the sales list. And Hogan, due to his knowledge of contracts and his value, gets a higher cut of his revenues than other wrestlers like John Cena. While the WWE owns and copyrights everything John Cena related, Hogan owns almost everything related to his image and the WWE has to pay him to use his likeness in that way.

So yes, given the correct variables, Hogan could be the highest paid person at the show, it is very possible. But it is all dependent on Hogan being able to draw and sell himself, not just on the base pay of the contract.

All right, any other prosecutors?

Only repeaters of same or similar issues and **Andrew F.** accusing Hogan of vicariously creating Randy Savage's rap career, but that's for another day. There's also still the question of the relationship between Hogan and Hart, so I'll get to that first...

Do you have a Hart?

A lot of people claim that Hogan and Hart have a terrible relationship, and that Hogan has always held Hart back. They claim that throughout his career, Hogan has done everything possible to hold Hart back and Hart despises him for it.

The problem? Bret Hart totally disagrees. From Bret Hart's Calgary Sun article on June 8, 2002:

> *Hulk Hogan.*
>
> *He hasn't changed a whole heck of a lot from the way he was the first time I met him back in '79.*
>
> *The first time I met Terry Bollea we were both working for Georgia Championship Wrestling, which eventually evolved into the WCW.*
>
> *Back then he was known as Sterling Golden. He was very green. And very impressive. On the day I left Atlanta to come home I knocked on his door to say good bye and told him if he ever wanted to learn to wrestle he was welcome to come up and work for my dad any time. He thanked me, and meant it, saying he'd keep it in mind.*
>
> *The next time I saw him was in Japan. He'd just shot his cameo for the Rocky III movie and was on the verge of mega - stardom that nobody could have even begun to imagine.*
> *Still the same guy.*
>
> *When I started with the WWF, in August of '84, he was on his way to being, without question, the biggest name in the history of wrestling.*
>
> *I can remember, even during the glory days of Hulkamania, how Terry would come into the dressing room and say hi to every single wrestler. Every night he headlined there was a [sellout] and throughout the night all the wrestlers would come up to him and whoever his opponent was and thank them both for the house, for putting food on their tables and making wrestling something worth respecting.*
>
> *I can say that Hulk Hogan was not only a hero to millions of Hulkamaniacs, but to all the wrestlers too.*
>
> *If Vince McMahon was Julius Caesar, then Hulk Hogan was Alexander the Great.*

I remember one time at an airport, in about 1987, when Hulk signed one autograph after another to the point where it took him 45 minutes to get to the gate. They were closing the doors as he was boarding the plane and this one fan asked him for his autograph. He said apologetically, "I'm sorry, I can't, I'm gonna miss my flight ..." and he got on the plane. I was right behind him and I heard a bystander flippantly remark, "Just like I figured. I always thought he was a jerk." I thought to myself, that person has no idea how many autographs he just signed. Being a hero like Hulk Hogan it's hard to make everybody happy but for a guy that's been wrestling as long as he has he's certainly done a heck of a job.

Hulk was especially considerate of me when I joined him in the WCW.

I saw him a few days ago at Davey's funeral and despite the sad backdrop it was nice to catch up on things.

So then I opened up my paper and saw a picture of Hulk, taken in Calgary, with a fifteen year old girl named Amanda Marqniq who dreams of being a pro wrestler but needed a heart transplant.

It brought back what I remember most about Hulk Hogan, even more than his feats as a great wrestler. The countless times the office came to get him from the dressing room to make the wish of a sick or dying child come true. Despite the fact that he was pulled in too many different directions and had little time for himself or his family, Hulk always had all the time in the world for kids who needed him to be their hero. He somehow knew just the right things to say. It was never a burden to him. If anything, it gave him a sense of real purpose. I've always tried to follow his example.

In Friday's paper I read how Amanda has now gotten her new heart. I thought I might just give Hulk a call and let him know. He'd be happy to hear that.

Some things in wrestling have always been real and Hulk Hogan is one of them.

That sounds like a man who respects and admires Hulk Hogan, not only as a wrestler but as a human being. And notice about that remark about Hogan helping Hart in WCW? If Hart believed for a second that Hogan had paid off Nick Patrick or any other such thing, he would never say such a nice remark. Hart has never been one to pull punches, and if he had something to say against Hogan he would say it.

Sure, Hart would have liked to get that big one-on-one match with Hogan for the championship, but due to many reasons that we have covered it just did not happen. I understand that we are angry that we'll never get to see this dream match, but that is no reason to take it out on Hogan. The hands of fate and time do not make a man guilty of crime, and we cannot hold Hogan responsible because too many events did not align.

All right, with the big questions out of the way, one huge one remains...

CAN HOGAN WRESTLE?

The title says it all. Can Hulk Hogan actually wrestle? We've touched on his training and some specific matches, as well as how he thinks of showmanship over athletics. But what about his actual in-ring prowess?

For the first time in In Defense Of... history I submit video evidence for the jury. Below you can see video evidence of Hulk Hogan performing submission move after submission move rarely if ever seen in the US. Oh, and Muta kicks out of the Atomic Leg Drop! The video is made available courtesy of YouTube is available here and here, but screen captures for those of you just reading along:

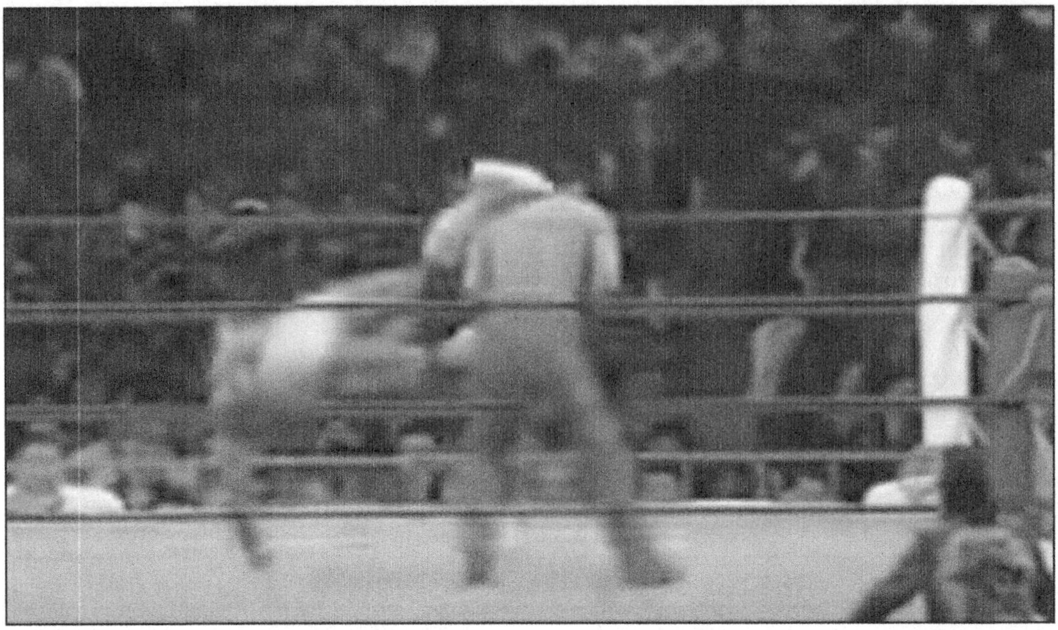

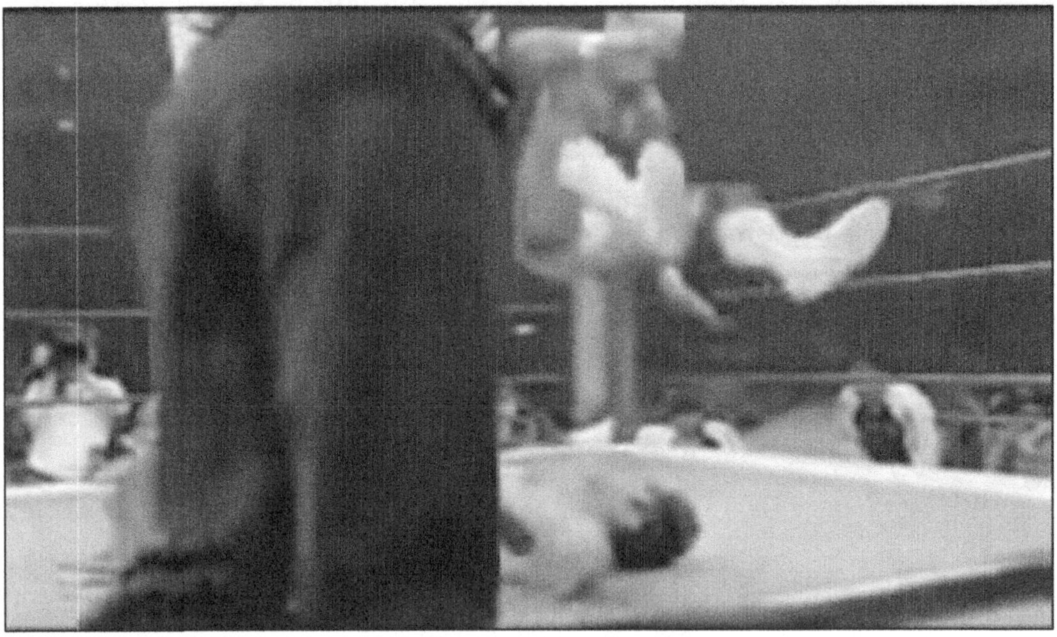

Just goes to show you: Hogan could wrestle and chose not to. Doing less moves elongates the career. Like I've said previously, why do a bunch of crazy moves when one punch can have the crowd eating out of the palm of your hand?

NOW WHAT?

So what is Hogan up to today in 2006? He spends most of his energy working on his daughter's music career, of which she recently signed a record deal. He is helping his son find direction and meaning in life. He is keeping his wife happy. He is starring in the highest rated show on VH1. He's in Arby's commercials. Hogan is still in demand, and will be for years to come.

HE IS THE IMMORTAL ONE...

Hulk Hogan is a man who at least twice revolutionized wrestling. He ushered in the ages of Rock 'n Wrestling and "cool to be bad". His presence has done more to define what it means to be a wrestler, and what the wrestling industry is. He has saved two companies from death. He has traveled the world defending his titles against the best the world has to offer.

Hulk Hogan has been the largest drawing wrestler of all time and created the true definition of the multimedia superstar. No one has been able to truly reach the cross-cultural iconic status that Hulk Hogan has set. Maybe no one ever will.

Yet despite all this there is hatred for the man. People question his place in wrestling history, they question if he is still valid today. They look at and older man today who does a few brief appearances and retroactively add it to the past. Forgotten are his great glories and in their place are events that never took place.

As a man who has been in this industry for so long, rumors run rampant. Most are untrue, and have long been proven untrue, yet they continue to this day.

Why? Why do these rumors persist?

Because when a man gets so big, so great, there are those that inevitably want to tear him down.

Some were peers who could never reach his level. Others were outsiders who felt that their heroes deserved placement above this showman.

But nothing they say can ever take away from the truth.

Hulk Hogan is beyond the sport of professional wrestling. He's beyond famous. He's beyond legend.

Hulk Hogan is one thing:

Immortal.

The defense rests.

After the Trial

Hung Jury

IN THE CASE OF THE IWC VS. HULK HOGAN, HULK HOGAN HAS BEEN ACCUSED OF BEING A DREG ON THE SPORT OF PROFESSIONAL WRESTLING WHOSE ACCOMPLISHMENTS HAVE BEEN GROSSLY EXAGGERATED, ESPECIALLY BY HIMSELF. HE HAS DONE MORE TO HURT WRESTLING THAN EVER TO HELP IT, AND HIS CONTINUED PRESENCE IN WRESTLING ONLY DISRUPTS THE INDUSTRY OVERALL.

With 76.3% of the vote, Hulk Hogan was found:

NOT GUILTY!

Although many naysayers still won't repent, I'd like to point out that almost immediately after the verdict Hogan Knows Best was renewed for a third season. Hmmmm... coincidence? My ego says not!

Response

In a case this long and detailed, so many points are covered it is difficult to satisfy everyone. Some people sent the usual "challenges" and "your facts are wrong, here's my unsubstantiated source that must be right", but I'll leave those to the side. An interesting one came from several people (including people who voted "Not Guilty"):

> *Bret did NOT talk to Hogan at HOF ceremony and made a point to mention he and Austin ignored him so the Bret Hart article makes little [sense] to me with all the ass kissing then to be so BITTER at HOF, something wrong in Denmark sunshine.*
>
> **Mike Sexton**

> *Before the Hall of Fame induction ceremony, I would have voted "NOT GUILTY." But after watching how The Hitman "snubbed" The Hulkster at the HoF, I decided to vote "GUILTY." This is despite you quoting Bret as saying Hogan is/was a good man.*
>
> **Leo**

> *Some points were simply proven inaccurate. Bret, for instance, ignored Hogan at the HoF ceremony as payback for what Hogan did to him. I don't agree with what Bret did there but OH YES, there is animosity.*
>
> **Ron M.**

What can I say? There is what the man said versus what these people perceived to be happening. I'll just let this response sum up my thoughts:

> *Hart's Calgary Sun article certainly gets rid of that conspiracy theory. A resounding NOT GUILTY.*
>
> **Kevin Mitchell**

There was a lot of new methods used in this case, including the prosecution (you can read about that in the Appendix) and the use of a video. Keep in mind that this was 2006 and how early it was to use embedded videos:

> *I loved the video man, but warn people that they are going to see Hogan do an Enziguri... I almost laughed out loud in the middle of my office.*
>
> *[A]nytime you can add video man please do, especially rare ones like that, [it's] fun to see matches you either never knew existed or would never have a chance to see...*
>
> **Doug Bernard**

Unfortunately, Doug got his wish as the Internet changed to shoving videos into everything because all things must be "multimedia" in the 2020's. You click on a news article because you want to **_read_** about it and BAM: it's an auto-playing loud video that provides no details beyond the headline or is completely unrelated. Thank goodness for auto-play blockers and the like.

That video did bring up something interesting that I was not aware of:

> *I was wondering how many readers will tell you that the reason that Muta kicked out of the legdrop was probably because Hogan uses the axe-bomber (clothesline) as his finisher in Japan.*
>
> **Feroz Nazir**

Feroz was actually the only person who brought this to my attention, but there you go!

Finally, to wrap it all up is a piece of evidence I did not get to use:

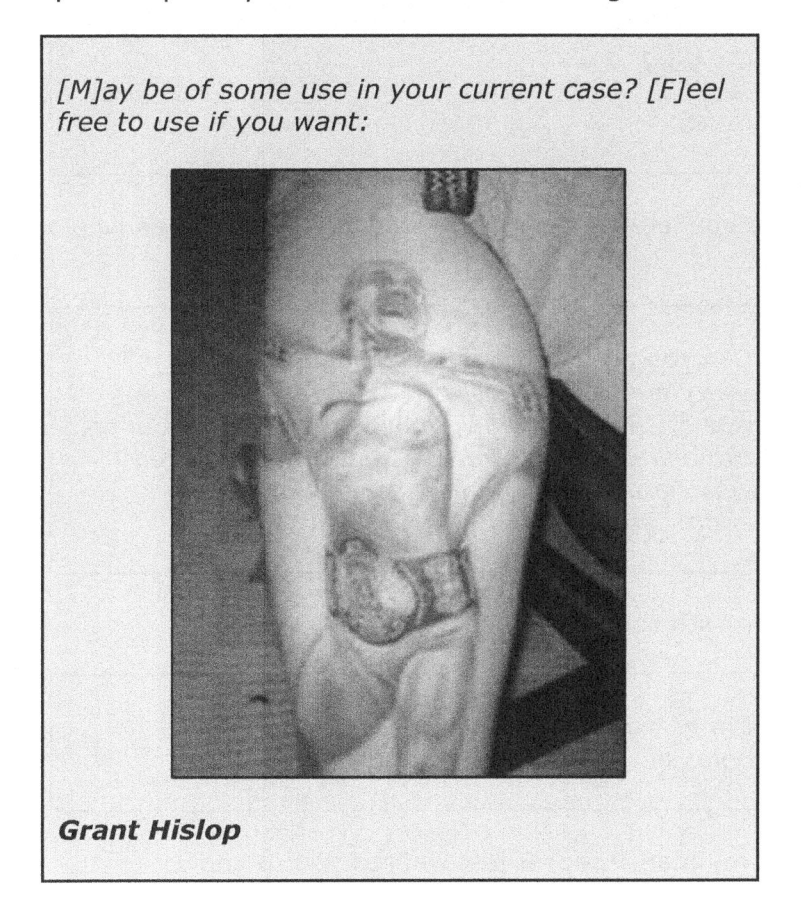

> *[M]ay be of some use in your current case? [F]eel free to use if you want:*
>
> **Grant Hislop**

DDP

Intro

Some dame walked into my office and said...

I can't believe I'm leading with this one, but the first person to e-mail me about DDP was **Jack Scum Bang** who... oh, you just have to read this one:

> [T]he real reason I have mailed you is about the man who knows all about that white stuff you get in the corner of your mouth when you...BANG...JACK SCUM BANG!
>
> What's your take on DDP? How does he fit in with the pedigree of world champions? Is Paige one of the great ones?
>
> BANG

Uhhhh... sometime later I heard from good 'ol **Bryan Jones** who asked... a little differently:

> Can you do a defense of Diamond Dallas Page? Everyone said he got where he was because he was Eric Bischoff's neighbor, but I was a fan of his. I think he was an average athlete who worked very hard and maximized his skills. I would appreciate it. Thanks!

Faye chimed in with some thoughts as well:

> I'm very much looking forward to the DDP defense.

But of course, my man **PeppeR** just wanted you to know:

> *I prefer DDP.*

And...

> *I can't wait to read DDP's.*

Well wait no longer!

WHY THIS?

DDP is an enigma in wrestling. He is one of few people who really came about in WCW during the hot nWo years. Goldberg and the Giant are really the only other people who can say they *became* legitimate main eventers in the golden years of WCW, though none of these men have found the same level of success elsewhere. Much like many people, DDP is not a person nor character that has staying power in today's WWE. There are many reasons for this that we will get to later on, but it does seem that—much like Sting, Ric Flair, and Dusty Rhodes before him—DDP was custom made for the NWA/JCP/WCW audience.

Unlike today's Chris Masters or Jay Lethal types, DDP did not go into wrestling in his teens. No, his career started later in life. The DDP story should be one of a man with a dream, a dream he came to at a much later point than most, yet was able to go beyond where anyone had dreamed. This fable of DDP should depict a man who overcame all odds to become a multi-time World Heavyweight Champion. All of these tales should speak of his in-ring skill, his ability on the mic, and his amazing charisma and connection with the audience. DDP should be one of the greatest hero stories in all wrestling, and we and our children and our children's children should know the legend of the man who went from nothing to everything, and that perhaps our dreams can come true, too.

This is not the DDP that is remembered, though.

DDP is seen as a man who never deserved his spot, a man who Eric Bischoff pushed down our throats because they were best friends, a man who perhaps engaged in wife swapping and other such events, and a man who was nothing in comparison to the deep pool of talent that was available in WCW during that day and age.

I am here to show how DDP really came about to be. I will dispel rumors, prove DDP's natural abilities, and let it be known that DDP has fans all over the world, myself included.

THE JERSEY TRILOGY PREQUEL

On April 5, 1956, Page Joseph Falkinburg was born to the community of Point Pleasant, NJ. Page was a child with excess energy, energy that would eventually get him in trouble. From DDP's official website:

> *From an early age, Page was an energetic kid, who would barrel through his grandma's kitchen on his tricycle, swing from chandeliers at the babysitter's house, and cannonball neighborhood pool parties.*
>
> *Page was big, lanky and athletic, and sports proved to be an outlet for his unbridled energy and saving grace for the grandmother who raised him. He played and excelled in both Pop Warner football, and youth hockey but he was captivated by the heroes of Saturday afternoon wrestling. He mimicked the moves and talked the talk of his favorite pro wrestlers on TV, and boasted to friends and relatives that someday, he would be the next Handsome Jimmy Valiant.*
>
> *At age 12, Page was hit by a car darting through traffic on his way to school, and the doctor's consensus assumption was that he'd never play contact sports again. Determined to compete in athletics, he picked up a new sport and became a star basketball player in high school and later went on to play collegiate ball.*

It seemed that even at the age of twelve, Page's career was destined for failure. Despite his love of sports and—especially—pro-wrestling, Page was supposed to be taken out of the game.

Let's look at another thing, too. Page was raised by his grandmother, meaning his parents could not be there for him. How can a boy with such energy possibly get along with an older grandmother? How can he find an outlet and direction in life?

Want to know more? Page is also dyslexic and has ADD; he couldn't even finish reading a book cover-to-cover until he was 35!

Despite the natural setbacks he was given, and the unfortunate events that took place in his life, Page showed an early determination that many others would not have. He was hit by a car, yet turned that into a positive to get involved with basketball! How many people do you know could take a life-threatening injury and turn it into a major triumph? A young Ric Flair quickly comes to mind, a man who survived a plane crash to become a sixteen to eighty-seven time World Champion. Page had that type of dedication; that when he believed in something, he felt the need to go for it. It was always his self-motivation that drove him, as we'll see again and again.

By the late 1970's, Page was already getting involved in the Night Club business. He was starting to find some success in the Jersey shore, and had earned the nickname "Dallas". From Derek Burgan's review of DDP's shoot interview:

> *Page had already given himself the nickname "Dallas" and explained that diamond's are his birthstone.*

Given that, and his fanaticism with Handsome Jimmy Valiant, Page thought he'd defy the odds and try to wrestle in 1979 as Handsome Dallas Page. He did not have any success and knew too little to get involved at that point. Also, the night club business was taking off, and his attention was needed elsewhere. From DDP's own site:

> *Page had established a successful and exciting career in the night club business, in several towns and states by the time he moved to Florida in the mid 80's. During that time as a master promoter and nightclub owner came the reawakening of his dream to become involved in the world of wrestling.*

And Derek Burgan's review of DDP's shoot interview continued:

> *[Scott] Hudson asked Page how he got started in the wrestling business, and Page went way back to his days of running a nightclub named Norma Jean's. Page's life at the time was one of complete hedonism and debauchery, which he makes no [apologies] for. One night while closing up the bar, Page saw the video for Cyndi Lauper's "Girls Just Want to have Fun." That gives you an idea of how long ago this took place as MTV was still actually airing... music videos back then. Anyway, Page saw Captain Lou Albano in the video and felt that it should have been Page himself as part of the Rock n' Wrestling Connection.*

You see, Page was the Rock n' Wrestling connection. He was a club promoter/owner who loved wrestling. As far as he was concerned, the connection would be perfect! But he did not have delusions of grandeur. The shoot continues:

> Page talked to the guys in his circle of friends at the club and thought that [he'd] try out to be a manager. Page felt that the girls in wrestling weren't that good looking and that he had access to a slew of "hot bitches," which would help his case as they would be his "Diamond Dolls." Page also noted that Jimmy Hart had the "Hart Foundation," so Page would have his own group called "the Diamond Exchange."

Remember, Page had already tried to be a wrestler and knew the physicality it would take. But also remember this: Page did not need wrestling. At this point in history he was already making excellent money in the club industry and would have been just fine for years to come. But he felt a calling and wanted to make an impact in the industry. And in order to break in, sometimes it takes the right connection. From the shoot:

> A local TV station did a small piece on Page because at the time he was semi-famous as the person who would host the club's wet t-shirt contests and other events of that nature. "[Someone] has to do it" said Page with a smirk. The TV spot was noticed by a local radio personality named "Smitty," who wanted Page on his show to [join], of all people, Captain Lou Albano. Smitty ended up knowing Rob Russen in Verne Gagne's AWA and told Page to send Russen a tape. Page ended up making a video with him and all his friends and sent it to Russen.

And the review continued:

> Page got a call back from Russen telling Page to bring his friends up for a try out, with the catch they had to pay their own way. Page admitted to Russen that many of the guys had no idea how to wrestle and Russen came back with the "don't call us, we'll call you" reply. That's never a good sign. A short while later, Paul Heyman (yes, that Paul Heyman) left the AWA and the company needed a new manager. Greg Gagne called up Page and told

> *him to fly himself up, bring his own clothes and they would give him a try out. Page flew up to Minnesota and brought a girl with him, who turned out to be nervous as hell. She'd be even more nervous if she had listened to the guys from Extreme Summit tell their 'rat stories. Page met Greg Gagne while wearing cowboy boots, which caused Gagne to remark that Page was the biggest manager he had ever seen. So of course Page was put with the much smaller Pat Tanaka and Paul Diamond as the tag team Bad Company. This mistake has been repeated throughout the last decade, including bringing up Matt Morgan and immediately putting him in a group with guys like Big Show and Nathan Jones to make sure not a single fan has any idea of how big Morgan really is. Page ended up working 15 months for the AWA, but since they only did one TV taping a month it ended up to only 14 days total.*

So you can see that Page's first break was no break at all. He had to use his own funds and bring his own "Diamond Dolls" to the ring with him, and 15 months of work equated to 14 television appearances. Obviously this did not translate into him getting much notoriety, fame, or money. As you might imagine, such decisions might actually burn through one's savings rather quickly. But Page felt that the sacrifices were worth it. He wanted to make it in the industry as a manager, and this was the way to go.

But while he was in AWA, Page met a man that would mean a lot to him in the future, but not as much as you think. Back to the shoot:

> *Page then went back to how he met Bischoff in the AWA. Page was talking to Pat Tanaka when he was rudely interrupted by Bischoff. Page said, "listen asshole, we're taking" and Bischoff's reply was "so?" The two men had a pull apart in the hotel bar. Later at the elevators, Page ran into Bischoff again except this time there was AWA management around. Bischoff buried Page to the office. At 8 a.m. the next morning, Page woke up with a [hangover] and was still pissed off. Bischoff showed up at his room and looked like shit as well. Bischoff said, "I understand I was a real asshole last night." Bischoff said there were two ways they could settle it. The first was to shake Bischoff's hand and accept his apology. The second was to let Page hit Bischoff in the face. Bischoff earned Page's respect and the two became friends.*

Let's put this straight right now: Page and Bischoff were not neighbors and friends before WCW. They weren't even really friends in AWA or WCW at the beginning either. At that, Page was just a manager when he was in AWA and at the beginning of WCW. It was in 1992 when the two bought houses from Dusty Rhode's wife (who I guess was a real estate agent) that they ended up being next door to each other. They did not know it until they both moved in, and it was after that point that they developed a friendship. Still, that friendship did not equate to a push to the top, as you'll see later.

STILL NOT QUITE FEELING THE BANG

Anyway, with his AWA career over, Page needed something to do and to continue to earn a living (or lose less money as quickly as he was). He ended up finding his way to Florida and wrestling for FCW/PWF. Again with the shoot:

> *When the NWA became WCW, they wanted Dusty Rhodes to turn heel and Big Dust packed his bags and went back to Florida. Mike Graham called up Page again and wanted Page to cut a promo on the phone to Rhodes. Page cut the promo and, at first, Dusty didn't reply. Rhodes finally asked "was that a recording kid?" Page went down to Pro Wrestling Florida and met Dusty, Gordon Solie and Steve Keirn among others. It's a sad state of affairs when I know Keirn solely from his absurd run in the WWE as "Skinner" than anything else. Rhodes' loved Page's energy and told Page he was "gonna make you the Jesse Venture of the '90s." Page had never done color commentary before, but The Dean of Announcing, Gordon Solie, walked him through it.*
>
> *Page worked for PWF for two and a half years and went from making 50 dollars a night to 150 dollars, while also being able to pick Dusty Rhodes' brain once a week while developing a friendship with Big Dust. Page learned that "the fake stuff hurts like hell" when he took his first bumps in the ring while training with Steve Keirn. While in Florida, Page met Scott Hall, who at the time had blonde hair and looked exactly like Magnum T.A. When PWF folded, Rhodes went to the WWE and Page a tryout as an announcer. Not surprisingly, the WWE wanted Page to change everything about himself. First Page tried out for a color commentary spot, then tried out for play-by-play.*

> *The late Alfred Hayes was impressed with Page's play-by-play and Page credited everything he knew to Gordon Solie. The WWE had zero interest in Page, and WCW ended up calling Page in just to "force" Paul Heyman to sign his contract by making Heyman think they had a replacement already lined up.*

So much to cover!

(1) Page tried a whole new direction with announcing and learned from some of the best there ever was.

(2) Page still was making next to nothing through the rest of the 80's to just try to live out his dream.

(3) Page began to take bumps in the ring and started to get a re-taste for wrestling that he had in his twenties.

(4) After the end of the PWF, Page tried out to be an announcer in then WWF. You might remember that this is THE SAME role that Eric Bischoff tried out for. So again, they were not friends at this point, but were in direct competition with each other.

(5) He had enough recognition to be used as a political tool, but not enough recognition that he could secure a job.

Things were tough, and Page took a one-time shot at driving his pink Cadillac out at WrestleMania XI, bringing the Honkey Tonk Man and Greg Valentine to the ring. Vince McMahon just wanted to rent the car, but Page demanded that he go with it, so he ended up driving it to the ring. And that would be his last appearance in the WWF/E for over a decade.

AND THEN THERE WAS ANOTHER "W"

But due to knowing Dusty and many of the NWA mainstays, Page was able to get a shot in WCW. Remember, this was 1991 and Eric Bischoff was a nobody in the wrestling industry and had nothing to do with anything Page got. As it was, they were fighting for a lot of the same resources (when Bischoff later joined the company). From the shoot:

> *Page went back to the clubs for several months until Dusty Rhodes left the WWE and returned to Atlanta. By this time Page was engage to Kimberly and she was going to school at Northwestern. Kimberly wanted Page to move to Chicago, but*

> Rhodes' implied that if Page moved to Atlanta he would have a job with WCW. Page convinced Kimberly to spend a weekend with him in Atlanta and in a funny story, Page's high end car that he wanted to impress Kimberly with, broke down, forcing Page to drive around in a U-Haul all weekend. Dusty's deal with Page was 350 dollars a shot, with no guaranteed dates. Page was put as a manager with the Fabulous Freebirds and immediately bonded with Michael P.S. Hayes. There were some great stories with Hayes, as Page said Hayes would, among other things, blow smoke right into Jerry Jarrett's face knowing that Jarrett hated second hand smoke.
>
> Scott Hall called up Page, as Hall was desperate for work, and reminded Page of the "Diamond Studd" gimmick that both men created while in Florida. Page called up Magnum T.A. to pitch the idea. Magnum said Dusty Rhodes wasn't interested. Page said they would change Hall's look (and added this story is fleshed out more in Page's Positively Page book.) Page told Hall to dye his hair "like Elvis blue-black." Hall agreed. Page saw a George Michael video and told Hall to copy the close-beard gimmick, although Page didn't know at the time it was a "gay thing." After a lot of coercion, Hall agreed. Magnum got Hall a tryout and when Page and Hall walked into WCW's Center Stage they quickly ran into Dusty Rhodes. Big Dust took one look at Hall and said, "he's in" while giving Hall a squash match on TV that very day. Hall was freaked out that nobody recognized him, but used that his advantage when pulling a great rib on Tommy "Wildfire" Rich.
>
> It wasn't long before Hall injured himself and was separated from Page. Magnum T.A. also broke the news to Page that his managing duties were no longer needed because the office felt Page was overshadowing the wrestlers. Magnum told Page he should have been a wrestler. That night Page convinced himself to give it a shot because at the time he was just a fourth string announcer with Eric Bischoff.

Actually, how they became announcers together is an interesting story. Page's shoot said:

> *Dusty Rhodes told the booking committee that Jim Herd was bringing in Eric Bischoff to replace Lance Russell. Rhodes told Page, who was Russell's partner, "If you like 'em (Bischoff), help him out. If he's an asshole, bury him. I don't care." When Bischoff heard he would be trying out with Page he figured he was screwed, and at the time Bischoff desperately needed a job as his wife had become pregnant. Bischoff showed up with a different look than his AWA days (the jet black hair, which is now gone) and he and Page quickly did a taping. Page realized that Bischoff didn't know many of the wrestling moves, so Page stopped the taping and explained all of the calls to Bischoff. This was quite a shock to Bischoff, who had to ask Page if he remembered Bischoff from the AWA. Bischoff eventually got the play-by-play job and Page said when Bischoff came back he "knew all the moves."*

So it was actually Page who helped Bischoff get his break in WCW and secure his position in the company, not the other way around. Bischoff might not have ever gotten a chance to develop in WCW if not for Page's help. Interesting how people want to only remember what happened in 1997-1999 and not what happened in 1991-1993. There is a whole other level of history that gets greatly ignored.

Anyway, Page started to mull over becoming a professional wrestler and headed to the Power Plant.

I'M A 'RASSLER!

In the Power Plant, Page started to transform into Diamond Dallas Page under the tutelage of Jody Hamilton. Although Jake "the Snake" Roberts is often credited as Page's trainer, it was really Jody Hamilton that taught him most of the wrestling that he knows. At the time, the Plant was a fairly empty place. Wrestlers did not come there to practice and it was not the breeding ground for future wrestlers that it would become later. So Page had some pretty exclusive training sessions and got to learn quickly. It was not like he had not previously been in the ring or taken bumps or learned the moves, but he had never put it together in a match.

The major hitch? Page was 35 years old! For context, Mick Foley retired from active wrestling when he was 35!!! To say Page was taking the road less traveled would be an understatement. Plenty of wrestlers had retired and become managers and/or announcers, but how many announcers or managers became wrestlers? Trish Stratus comes to mind, but that was ten years later.

Page gets a lot of criticism for being an old man in wrestling. Yet how many people can ever claim they reached the pinnacle of their sport in their later years in life? Perhaps if the Boogeyman goes on to be World Champion he'll be able to surpass the bar DDP has set, but that will be hard. After all, DDP did become a three time... three time... three time WCW Champion.

But as you can imagine, being 35 did not help Page's position in WCW. Most people saw him as a perennial jobber who had a year or two at most in the industry. He began teaming with Scott Hall (as the Diamond Stud). That lasted until Hall was injured and would be on the shelf for the rest of his WCW contract. That injury, though, became a blessing for Page as he was able to take over all of Hall's dates. Without that, Page would have had no bookings at all and absolutely no career.

As the months moved on through 1991 and into 1992, Page began to team with Kevin Nash (as Vinnie Vegas). Yes, the old Diamond Connection was paying off for DDP (he had managed both Hall and Nash in the past) and things seemed to be going pretty decent. PWI even named him Rookie of the Year in 1992.

Of course, he then tore his rotator cuff and Bill Watts fired him from WCW.

Well, that was working out for a while.

For many people, being 35, injured, and fired would be a major setback, but not DDP.

He would not give up, he would make his dream come true.

And that dream would be brought into focus as DDP and wife Kimberley brought a new roommate into their house:

Jake "The Snake" Roberts.

So that's why they consider him a trainer!

From Derek Burgan's review of DDP's shoot interview:

> Back in Florida, Page got a call from Jake "the Snake" Roberts, who had just separated from his wife Cheryl. Page let Jake stay in his house and learned from the Snake... Jake told Page that he already knew all the wrestling holds he would ever need to know and that Page needed to work on the psychology of a wrestling match if he was ever to become a star. Jake helped Page work on his

> *character and also got Page booked on all the indie shows that booked Jake. "If you're gonna be a top guy, you gotta learn how to handle the heat," said Roberts, explaining that when Page became a top guy his friends would become jealous.*

What? You were expecting something seedy? Sorry, it was all on the up-and-up!

And besides, whatever sexual activities DDP may or may not be in to is none of my business as it has no bearing on his wrestling career. Now, if DDP loaned Kimberly out to get a push, then we would cover it. And we'll get to that very comment later.

Anyway, the point is DDP was not just a nice guy to Roberts, but also used the opportunity to learn from him. Roberts taught DDP everything he would need to know about psychology and controlling the heat. DDP would put that to good use later on. And although Roberts told him he had all the hold he would ever need to know, DDP still strived to better himself in the ring.

So with a couple of years of seasoning (and even less money to show for it), DDP felt he was ready to return to the big league, but of course not before some trouble. From the shoot review:

> *Page had supplemented himself up to 280 pounds, but Kimberly was convinced being a wrestler was not in the cards for Page and told him to get a real job. Page told Kimberly to hit the bricks if she didn't believe in him.*

That's pretty amazing. From all accounts, Page would do anything for Kimberly, yet he still felt getting into wrestling was worth it. Even though at that point he was 37, had injuries, had no notoriety, and had hemorrhaged money for a decade, he still worked to make it in the industry. And that's when an opportunity came a'kockin'! From the shoot:

> *Fortunately for Page, Bill Watts was fired and Eric Bischoff was given Watts' job. Bischoff brought Page back in and Page asked for 150,000 a year contract. Bischoff said he couldn't do that and countered with 85,000, which was what Page was making when he got let go. Page said that after food and travel, 85,000 isn't much money at all and I can certainly believe that. Page claimed that Bischoff used "reverse nepotism" and made it tougher on Page than he would other wrestlers.*

> Bischoff wanted Page to sign a two year contract, but Page refused and instead went back the Power Plant to train. Page laid out three months of storylines to WCW booker Dusty Rhodes, and once Rhodes saw Page in the ring he said, "you got it."

All right, let's do this:

(1) Yes, Bischoff helped DDP, his friend and then neighbor, get back into WCW. BUT...
   I.   DDP had already worked for WCW
   II. DDP help Bischoff get into WCW originally
   III. Bischoff did not try to get DDP back earlier
   IV. DDP had seasoned up and paid even more dues

(2) Although Bischoff got him a job, he did not get preferential treatment. As a matter of fact, Bischoff treated him worse. And again, this goes back to our Eric Bischoff case, but anyone who said Bischoff just threw money at people has no idea what they are talking about. Bischoff was generous, and did eventually give contracts that worked against WCW, but he was ALWAYS looking out for the bottom line. That included a nothing wrestler like Page, friend or not.

(3) Bischoff's offer was so low that Page decided to just keep training and then lay out a long storyline so he could be a real part of the show and make some scratch.

(4) Even when Page was brought in, he was not going to the main event. And it was actually Dusty Rhodes who brought him up, not Bischoff.

And when Rhodes brought him in, it seemed good... for a couple of weeks. Back to our shoot:

> Page was back on TV with an angle where he would pick an opponent's name out of a fishbowl, and the person would always be a jobber. Four weeks into the angle, Dusty Rhodes was let go, Ric Flair was brought in as booker and the angle was dropped cold.

Can this guy not catch a break?!?! He finally had a storyline, TV time, and a job, yet it was all taken away in a month!

Still, DDP made the best of it, and he and bodyguard Madd Max went about losing to the mid-card through 1994 and into 1995. But then he won the Television Title from the Renegade! And then he lost it to Johnny B. Badd. He was named PWI "Most Improved Wrestler of the Year" in 1995! And then he "lost" all his money in storylines and became a pauper, lost Kimberly to Johnny B. Badd, and lost a Loser Leaves Town Match to the Booty Man in 1996.

Damn, storyline or not, things looked to be going nowhere for Page. Actually, someone else felt that as well.

WCW GROWS AND GROWS AND PAGE... GETS RELEASED?!?

From the shoot:

> *When WCW hit it big, Page was there to ride the wave. Page gave credit to his Power Plant training. Page wanted to be able to [wrestle] guys as diverse as Rey Mysterio and the Big Show. Hulk Hogan ended up putting Page over to Bischoff strong, but Bischoff didn't see it happening and offered Page his release. Page said he would talk about this in that damn audio book. Page does admit that Bischoff did help him in not getting screwed with by the wrestlers or outright fired by the company.*

Did you read that right? Bischoff actually told Page, his friend, neighbor, and whatever, that he should leave the company. Even Hulk Hogan, who Eric Bischoff holds in the highest regard, could not convince Bischoff of Page's worth. So once again, Bischoff did not push Page to the moon... he was ready to fire him!

DDP, 40 years old at this point, decided to stick around. And he was about to find some creativity:

> *The Monday Night War started and Page stayed in WCW. Ron Reis, who you may remember as the big goof from Raven's Flock in WCW, gave Page the idea for the Diamond Sign, which Page had trademarked. Page said he was growing on the WCW fans while adding they were chanting "D-D-P" in the same way they used to chant "D-D-T" for Jake Roberts. Page would tell the fans to "shut up" while playing the heel, but Scott Hall, who was now back in WCW as part of the New World Order, told Page to never do that again and just let the crowd react naturally.*

What's that? Just reacting naturally to the crowd and letting them boo and cheer what they want? What a novel concept!

So DDP had the diamond cutter that he could hit out of anywhere, a cool symbol, a chant-able name, and a NATURAL growing fanbase. I don't know how much I can hammer this home, so I'll do it some more. DDP was not getting the push of a lifetime! Before this, he had managed to win Battle Bowl in what was considered an incredible fluke at the time, and from there had gone on to feud with Eddie Guerrero, a feud Guerrero eventually won for the vacant US Title. It was during that time from Battle Bowl through Eddie Guerrero that he really developed the diamond cutter. From Obsessed with Wrestling:

> *Diamond Dallas Page credits Bobby Heenan for naming his finisher, "The Diamond Cutter" - which is a modified Ace Crusher.*

So yet another person DDP learned from and used to get better, not some grand push.

What finally solidified DDP as a face was when he was offered membership in the nWo, and became the first man to turn down the Outsiders. From Obsessed with Wrestling:

> *Early 1997: The Outsiders (Kevin Nash & Scott Hall) began approaching DDP and offering him a place in the nWo.*
>
> *January 25, 1997 - Souled Out: Scott Norton defeated Diamond Dallas Page by COUNT OUT.*
>
> *~~~The Outsiders once again tried to recruit DDP, but he gave them Diamond Cutters and escaped through the crowd!*
>
> *~~~This was the night DDP became a Megastar, surrounded by the fans and looked down at the nWo in the ring.*

Yes, this was the first time DDP exited through the crowd, which would become his trademark. This was yet another example of how DDP connected with the audience, how he became the "people's champion". But this was not what made him a megastar. Oh no, that would be what happened next...

SNAP INTO HIM! OOOOOOOOOH YEEEEAAAAAHHHH!!!

Wikipedia will tell you this:

> Page's career really took off in 1997. As part of the hot nWo storyline, Page began a feud with the nWo's "Macho Man" Randy Savage. On an episode of WCW Monday Nitro, Savage, aided by fellow nWo members Scott Hall and Kevin Nash, attacked DDP and sprayed "nWo" on his back. A few weeks later at the WCW pay-per-view Uncensored, Savage and Miss Elizabeth revealed to the world that Page and Nitro Girl Kimberly, were in fact married. Savage then proceeded to beat up Page, ensuring a future match between the two.
>
> At the 1997 Spring Stampede, Page and Savage battled in a memorable match where Page emerged victorious, but it was the not the end of conflict between the two. A few months later at The Great American Bash, they squared off again in an anything goes, lights out match what was dubbed "Savage-Page II." This match was far more brutal than their first encounter, and ended with Savage defeating Page with help from (then) Tag Team Champion Scott Hall. Savage and Page would continue their rivalry from there on. Page even dressed up as masked wrestler La Parka and beat Savage.

And while this is also statistically true, it does not capture the actual rise of DDP from mid-card to plausible main eventer. It also does not cover how this series came about.

Now I know what you are thinking. "Obviously, Bischoff wanted to push his best friend, even though you keep presenting evidence that that's not what happened. But this time it's different!"

Sorry my friends, this time it's not. From the shoot:

> Randy Savage said that he wanted to work with Page. Savage wanted to take the Diamond Cutter and Page said the fans blew the roof off when he nailed Randy with the move, first at a house show to test it out, than at the Spring Stampede PPV.

So once again, it was not Bischoff pushing Page, but other wrestlers wanting to work with him. Say what you want for Randy Savage's sanity, even then, the man was still a legend and a huge draw. If he wanted to work with someone, you knew that person had to be damn good. And page proved it, too. By the way, this won PWI's "Feud of the Year" for 1997.

As time went on, Page would continue feuding with the nWo, took a side-trip to win the US Title from Curt Hennig, defended the title against Chris Benoit and Raven, drop the title to Raven, and then got back to the nWo.

It was at this point that he got involved in the big storylines. It was here that he and Karl Malone fought Hogan and Rodman, and that he and Jay Leno fought Hulk Hogan and Eric Bischoff. And don't forget: it was not Bischoff pushing for DDP to have this spot, it was Hogan. Hogan trusted DDP enough to be involved in the biggest angles in WCW. No amount of nepotism is going to get a 40+ year old guy a spot like that without having the trust of the bookers, the brass, the wrestlers, and the guests. DDP had proven his worth.

After this and some War Games, DDP put over Goldberg in what is widely considered Goldberg's best match at Halloween Havoc 1998. From there he returned to the US Title feuding with the nebulous Bret Hart. It was 1999, five years since returning to WCW, five years of winning over the fans and being in huge main events. Yet despite all that, Bischoff did not want to pull the trigger on a title run.

As 1999 rolled on, Bischoff's responsibilities were slowly stripped from him and he was asked to stay home more often. It was only in this chaos that the trigger was finally pulled at Spring Stampede 1999. From Wikipedia:

> *Page finally became World Champion in April, 1999, at Spring Stampede when he defeated Sting, Hogan, and Ric Flair in a 4-way dance for the title. This match was ironic for Page, as it featured Randy Savage as the special-guest referee, and also saw Hogan eliminated early when Page seriously damaged Hogan's leg with a submission hold.*
>
> *Page was finally champion, and he had quite an unusual first month, as he lost the title to Sting on an episode of Nitro, only to gain it back in the show's main event.*

Bischoff was at home and was soon to be fired (September 1999, to be exact), so who put the title on Page? From the shoot:

> *Page said that many people credit Bischoff for putting the WCW world title on Page, but Scott Hall and Nash were the ones that pushed for that.*

Oh, and let's get this out of the way now. Page's last run with the title in April 2000 had nothing to do with Bischoff either. For the last time: Bischoff did not make Page a champion—Page made Page a champion.

THE END OF WCW

With Bischoff on his way out and gone from WCW, Page took a new direction, turned heel, and formed the Jersey Triad with Bam Bam Bigelow and Chris Kanyon, an experience used mostly to give Kanyon some exposure. But the Triad quickly disbanded in the rapidly shifting WCW as new directions became the norm. DDP would then spend the end of 1999 and the beginning of 2000 putting over Jeff Jarrett, Buff Bagwell, and Mike Awesome. DDP knew his days as an active wrestler were coming to an end (as late as they began), and he used the opportunity to give the rub to another generation.

As WCW started winding down, he and Nash teamed up as the "Insiders" to feud with the Natural Born Thrillers and what was left of the New Blood. He then main evented the last WCW PPV Greed, putting over new champion Scott Steiner to help solidify Steiner's top-tier status.

Two days later the WWF bought WCW.

The next week was the last Nitro.

From DDT Digest:

> *Earlier Today, DDP speaks positively about his WCW experience. DDP thanks all the fans for letting him make it. DDP says that it's not the promoters that decide who's over, it's the fans. DDP then brings up the forbidden name of Kimberly before closing.*

And that was the end of DDP in WCW. But it would not be the end of DDP in wrestling...

INVASION

A few months after the end of WCW, a few former wrestlers started showing up on WWF TV. These scant mid-carders were among the few that the WWF bought out the contracts of. But DDP, having a multi-million dollar guaranteed deal, was not one who was going to be brought over. Not only that, he was not in very good condition. From BJ Bethel's interview with DDP in 2001:

> **BJ:** How's the arm doing?
>
> **DDP:** Actually, [it's] my back. I ruptured my L4 and L5. It was actually an angular tear. [It's] because it goes around your spine and your disc. And I've been doing a lot of rehab...

Not only that, but DDP was 41. What type of shelf life could he possibly have? The WWF was not immediately interesting in the investment.

But as we have discovered, the money was not the most important thing to DDP, but living out his dream was. So he negotiated out of his deal with AOL-Time Warner and convinced the WWF to give him a shot. He was the first main event WCW star to appear in the InVasion. Things would not go so smoothly, though. From Derek Burgan's review of DDP's shoot interview:

> Page talked about his run in the WWE and that his angle with Sara Undertaker wasn't booked to go the way it did. I should hope not. Page takes responsibility for the angle flopping and said it would have worked with anyone else but Page was too much of a babyface to play the stalking heel gimmick. Page also didn't see the angle through all the way when it started or he would have realized it had to culminate with Undertaker squashing him.

Page takes responsibility for the Undertaker angle going sour, a responsibility he most likely did not need to take. The WWF bookers and writers were supposed to be the ones to think of these angles to the end and dropped the ball here. DDP, though, is not one to shift blame and tries to take responsibility even when it is not necessary.

DDP went out with injury at the conclusion of this feud in August 2001. He returned in January to a whole new gimmick. From Wikipedia:

> Page would eventually switch gimmicks and become a pseudo-motivational speaker, in what would come to be known as his "Positively Page" character. The name came from the title of his autobiography that was published during his WCW days. The character involved Page constantly smiling and acting optimistic, with his trademark phrase "That's not a bad thing... that's a good thing."
>
> In early 2002, Page became the oldest European Champion in WWE history. At WrestleMania X8, he defeated Christian, a former follower of his positive "philosophy" and retained the title.

Injuries, though, began to show their ugly head again and DDP knew he needed some time off. So, from the end of March to the end of April, DDP put over William Regal, Christian, and Hardcore Holly. During that match with Holly, though, things went really wrong. From Tim Baines article in the Ottawa Sun quoting DDP:

> I was fighting Bob Holly. He'd knocked me out with a kick to the face and clothesline. (Later in the match) I was trying to suplex him off the top rope. I was so worried about keeping him straight, I jackknifed myself.
>
> "It scared me and (WWE) didn't want to take a chance on me anymore. They wanted me to become a colour commentator. I was so beat up, I guess I just needed a break.

DDP was looking pretty rough. The almost WWE felt DDP was still worthwhile as a color commentator and wanted to move him into that role. DDP felt he still had more to offer as a wrestler. Because of this, he ELECTED to leave the almost WWE. That's right, DDP was not let go, he chose to leave.

With that, DDP went to check out his options. From Obsessed with Wrestling:

> April 17, 2002: DDP visited Dr. Jay Youngblood in San Antonio and was told that he qualifies for [surgery] on his neck.
>
> May 16, 2002: DDP again met with Dr. Jay Youngblood to get the painful diagnosis.

> ~~~Page has a lot of degeneration in his C5, C6 and C7 vertebrae.
>
> ~~~Page also has a spinal canal narrowing which is causing weakness in his biceps and numbness in his hands.
>
> ~~~Page's C3 and C4 vertebrae have almost completely fused together on their own.
>
> ~~~Youngblood said that DDP could continue wrestling as long as he can tolerate the pain.
>
> May 30, 2002: Page's third [doctor's] opinion was that he should retire from wrestling.
>
> ~~~Page later finds out that if he steps into the ring again, his insurance policy will be cancelled.
>
> June 2002: Page makes the most difficult decision of his life, and announces his retirement 'from the ring'.
>
> ~~~Page steps back from the wrestling business for a while, stating he needs the time because he "wasn't ready to leave"

Well, if that wasn't injured, I don't know what is!

TIME TO MAKE AN IMPACT!

Despite these devastating injuries, DDP found a way to recoup and work his way back into the squared circle. In order to get back into wrestling shape, DDP tread a path few western men had tried before (at the time)—Yoga. From DDP's own website:

> Now at the age of 42, it seemed that he should listen to all those who suggested that either surgery or retirement would ease the pain and be the best solution to the loss of mobility that his injuries had caused.
>
> But Page continued to search for a better answer, knowing that his positive attitude was equal to the challenge of rehabilitation. Along with the support

> of doctors and physical therapists, he decided to become an expert at healing his own body. He studied and experimented with chiropractic, applied kinesiology, nutrition, organic juicing and supplementation to create the perfect mix of wellness for a person who was trying to, as he put it, "put Humpty Dumpty back together again."
>
> His quest led him back to the mat, except this time it was a yoga mat. After studying the positive healing effects and increased flexibility that yoga positions provided, he became a devotee and adapted the discipline to meet his own needs. He developed YRG--Yoga For Regular Guys, which is a comprehensive, creative and motivational approach to longevity and better understanding of health and fitness that is presented in 20, 30 and 45 minute workouts.

Of course, this wasn't DDP first experiment with Yoga. From BJ Bethel's interview with DDP:

> **BJ:** I heard you were doing a lot of Yoga, is that helping out?
>
> **DDP:** I'm VERY into it. It's one of those things that once I get going I can't stop talking about it. My wife [Kimberly] actually got me into it, and I went and got a personal trainer. I won't be stretching here if I have to do anything, but I stretch [every day]. [It's] stretching from one move, into another move, into another. It's called Power Yoga and I have to make sure I'm doing it the right way. I also went to this spine specialist. [It's] the same one Perry Saturn and Raven went to and [it's] called Watkins-Glen Rehabilitation Method and what it is, is you know those five muscles around your spine, if you push your back flat on the ground, and you do stuff with weights and concentrate on your stomach, it strengthens your spine. I felt a difference the first week. I started doing it with dumbbells and the leg weights, cuz when I start doing something I do it right, I don't around.

DDP's quest to recover himself paid off. At 48 years of age after a mutual separation with Kimberly, Page started taking select independent dates. Then, in November 2004, DDP made his debut in the six-sided circle for TNA. From Wikipedia:

> [H]e debuted with Total Nonstop Action Wrestling on November 12, 2004, feuding with Raven and Erik Watts.
>
> Page received an NWA World Heavyweight Championship title shot on March 13, 2005 at TNA Destination X 2005 but was defeated by reigning champion Jeff Jarrett. He remained with the company until May, 2005, at which point he left to focus on his acting career and motivational speaking career.

There are a lot of rumors persisting that DDP walked out on TNA because he did not want to job out anymore. That's not what happened at all. From Tim Baines article in the Ottawa Sun two month before DDP left TNA:

> He's happy with his role in TNA.
>
> "That high impact stuff, drop me on my head ... that stuff ain't happenin' anymore," said Page. "I'd get to the arena and see guys like Cactus Jack and Terry Funk, and they could barely walk.
>
> "I'm having so much fun working with these guys. I probably have three or four more pay-per-views in me. I want to see how long I can do it, but I probably don't have too many more big singles matches in me."
>
> He's been to acting school, along with his wife Kim.
>
> "A lot of things that I did that got me over in WCW were things they teach in acting school," said Page. "Things like listen, feel and react."

DDP knew his time was limited. He was 49 years old! He also had other aspirations that he was looking to fulfill. He did three PPVs after this interview, living up to his word. He already knew his limitations, being old and injured, and went out putting over the Outlaw and Monty Brown while working with Ron Killings. What more could be asked for?

AND AFTER THAT?

For the remainder of 2005 through the time of this writing in 2006, DDP has made a few select independent dates, mostly to satiate his own wants and matches or to help out old friends. He does not need to wrestle, and by all accounts it is bad for him, yet he persists through love and desire alone. Also during this time he released his new book "Yoga for Regular Guys" and has been on a tour with it. He's also sued Jay-Z for use of the diamond sign, which he did have trademarked years beforehand. The case is not without merit, but that's for the courts to decide. What we need to know is this: what does this have to do with wrestling? Well, about as much as these things:

FUN FACTS

From Obsessed with Wrestling:

> *DDP is the only pro wrestler in history to ever be invited to the White House lawn and help with the President's Easter Egg hunt.*
>
> *Diamond Dallas Page went on a mission to help kids with reading disabilities.*
>
> *They donate money from DDP's autograph sessions at schools around the country to buy [books].*

So DDP has used his wrestling career to benefit others as well. He has lived by his motto of positivity, and has helped inspire many others, myself included!

THE CHING-CHING

Of course, the question remains is that even though DDP was over, was he a draw? Well, that's where my friends the numbers come in.

DDP's first (and second, since they were separated by an hour) reign as champion saw some impressive numbers. The four weeks that DDP was champion have an average Nitro rating of 4.0 (In comparison, RAW had a 6.2 average. How times have changed). Actually, DDP's first week as champ drew a 4.4 rating, the highest rating in nearly two months and the highest rating Nitro would have for the rest of its existence.

During DDP's last reign as champion, the second week saw Nitro ratings rebound to a 3.1. Three weeks before the rating was a 1.8. DDP help change the course of even a bitterly disturbed WCW. Even still, WCW was extremely turbulent at that point in time, and he had no chance to help turn the tide of the company as champion.

The one PPV defending his title during his second reign was Slamboree 1999, which drew a 0.48 buyrate. Now, we know that this is outside of the "success" rage we defined in the Eric Bischoff case, but the context is important. The previous year's Slamboree drew 0.44, and that was just off the peak of WCW (in a year where half of the PPVs drew over 1.0 buyrates). The Great American Bash 1999 the following month drew a 0.43 and Bash at the Beach after that drew a 0.39. So DDP was able to increase returns over the previous year, and buyrates went down without him in the title picture.

And what about his autobiography, Positively Page? How did that do? From BJ Bethel's interview:

> **DDP:** It was weird. It had so many similarities to me and Jake. Jake's one of my mentors. If you read Positively Page, you know which you can get off amazon.com. now ...*laughs*
>
> **BJ:** *laughs* When is it coming out on paperback?
>
> **DDP:** I'm not going to do that until I know where I am, or what I'm doing because I've been approached by people to do it. We published it ourselves, and that was our biggest mistake. *laughs* We sold 50,000 copies so far. I should've sold, in' 500 but we did it ourselves and when you do it like that you [don't] get the distribution.

So without any distribution DDP still sold 50,000 copies. Hey, at $28.95 a pop, that's about $1.5 million. Did you sell $1.5 million in merchandise in a year?

Of course, there is the merchandise. Unfortunately, WCW books are unavailable to this author, but DDP's extensive merchandise consisted of t-shirts, toys, magazines, posters, pennants and the VERY POPULAR foam hands in the diamond sign. DDP most likely made a very good chuck of change off his merchandise, especially by judging by his book sales numbers.

Is DDP the greatest drawing champion of all time? Most certainly not. He's probably not even in the top 20. But he was someone who put butts in seats and made dollars while doing so. That, especially at his age, is an accomplishment unto itself.

Diamond Cutter

DDP is a man you either love or hate, but you'll never forget him. His career is an odd one, one that began much later in life than most and went in the opposite path of others. He started off as a hanger-on, and through hard work and dedication made his dreams come true. DDP literally sacrificed all of his savings and life in order to have a wrestling career, one that he did not need, but one that he wanted. He grew in wrestling skill, in-ring charisma, psychology, mic skills, and storyline ideas; and got over with the crowd on his own accord. He won the admiration of his peers and they worked hard to put him over, despite the beliefs of his supposed best friend Eric Bischoff. Contrary to popular belief, Eric Bischoff was not DDP's ultimate supporter, but spent more time trying to get DDP out of wrestling for good.

Although his last few major exposures were tainted, they do not take away from the legacy of DDP. Spending time as a motivational speaker and Yoga guru, DDP has mixed interests that still involve his wrestling life. Looking back, his career actually did draw people and money, and DDP used that ability to parlay it into charities to help kids learn how to read.

Despite all of his disadvantages in life, DDP never let it get him down. He always stayed positive and always went the extra mile to make his dreams come true. Nothing was handed to him, he worked for every iota of his spot.

I think this line from DDP in his interview with BJ Bethel sums is all up:

> [Winning the World Heavyweight Championship for the first time] meant the most to me when I went into the locker room, and Hulk's sitting on the chair and as I walked in he's taking off his boots, and looks up to me, and says "that's the way [it's] supposed to be." And I didn't even say anything. And he goes, "A guy works as hard as you did, to accomplish what you accomplished when no one believed you could do it, that's the way things are supposed to be."

The defense rests.

After the Trial

Hung Jury

IN THE CASE OF THE IWC VS. DDP, DDP HAS BEEN ACCUSED OF BEING A NO-TALENT HACK WHO WAS PUSHED DOWN OUR THROATS BECAUSE HE WAS BEST FRIENDS WITH ERIC BISCHOFF AND NEVER WAS A WORTHY CHAMPION NOR DREW A DIME.

And with 95.0%(!!!!!!!!) of the vote, DDP was found:

NOT GUILTY!

Hot diggity landslide, Batman, that's an insane number!

Response

Being an overwhelming victory, most of the feedback was repeating back to me the facts of the case that really touched people. However, some people had other reasons for voting the way they did:

> *I have to vote not guilty, and it's not just [because] he went to college down the street from me, or that he's from the Jersey Shore in general.*
>
> *But, y'know, that helps him. :)*
>
> **Jim Moore**

Oh, New Jersey, always sticking together! Aside from this, I also got this little note that I thought was interesting:

> *I have another fun fact for you as far as DDP's Yoga for Regular Guys (he calls the program YRG).*
>
> *He did a book signing in Orlando which, while I heard it was a great turn out, I was unable to attend.*
>
> *No matter as he signed all copies of the book in store just in case anyone wanted to purchase it later.*
>
> **Andrew F.**

I am also a graduate of YRG and what he currently (in 2020) calls DDP Yoga. One time when I was with friends at WrestleMania—including fellow 411mania staff writer Jeff Small—I challenged them to do a 50-minute DDP Yoga session with me. Small was done and out at about 15 minutes!

Jeff Hardy

Intro

Some dame walked into my office and said...

It all started a year prior when **Ron Morris** said:

> You know what bugs me lately? The bad rap that Jeff Hardy gets. Especially right here on 411 where he is often referred to as "Hardly" or "Enema". I realize that his heart isn't totally in wrestling recently, but damn, the guy started his own [feud] with his brother when they were teenagers! The guy did [a lot] in a very short amount of time for the tag scene, often risking his body for the entertainment of others (ala Mick Foley). So I'm interested to hear you speak on that topic.

And then there was... wait, where are the rest of them? Well, **Jim Moore** said:

> GOOD LUCK with defending Jeff Hardy. You have your work cut out for you on that one.

Rob Hughes had some interesting feedback:

> Now Jeff Hardy I think You may have a more difficult time with.
>
> Love the wrestler!
>
> Can't stand the jackass!

And **Manor Admin** had a similar thought:

> *You'll struggle with Jeff Hardy though; when he went singles on Raw and had the same match for months; same moves, same order... He just didn't care about putting on a good match. But you may be able to change my mind.*

Of course, the man who challenges the challenges **Feroz Nazir** said:

> *Jeff Hardy might be an interesting case, you may have to convince me, depending what the charges are.*

No, seriously, I'm confused. I could have sworn I had heard this case from like five or ten other people. It's been on my docket for a year! Maybe I just talked about it a lot with other people. There was talk forever about defending Edge and Lita and firing Matt Hardy, and I was going to do a mixed case where it would be Edge/Lita, firing Matt Hardy, and then Jeff Hardy. But I nixed that idea once Hardy got a job and decided to wait to see his epic.

WHY THIS?

Jeff Hardy is a man who has fallen from grace in the eyes of the IWC. He is unrealized potential shaped in human form. Or so many would have us believe.

Here was a man who started his own wrestling promotion, was the independent star that did high flying tricks and made it to the grandest stage of them all. And unlike many indie stars, his timing allowed him to keep most of his style in the ring in the WWF/E.

Yet, because he did not reach World Heavyweight Championship level, because he let other interests take over his life, because he has tastes outside the mainstream, he has somehow become a failure. Everything he did was for nothing, and has all been swept away.

For whatever reason, Jeff is considered the "Marty Jannetty" of the Hardy Boyz (that's a case for another day), as if his path has led to some terrible self-destruction and his wrestling career was meaningless.

Well I am here to put all that to rest. We'll show just what type of career Jeff Hardy has had, who is really the most successful Hardy Boy, and what it all means in context.

Jeff Hardy is the charismatic enigma, but we are about to peel back some layers.

ON A LITTLE TOBACCO FARM...

On August 31, 1977, out in Cameron, NC, three-year-old Matt Hardy was given his future tag team partner in Jeffery Nero Hardy, better known to the world as Jeff Hardy. The two grew up together on their father's farm, but life was not easy. From Tim Baines' article in the Ottawa Sun in April 2003:

> Rising up through the ranks was a school of hard knocks for Jeff and his older brother Matt, whose mother died of cancer in 1986. Their father, Gilbert, was a tobacco farmer and part-time mailman, so the boys had to get domesticated in a hurry.
>
> "I was nine and Matt was 12 (when their mother died), so that became a very big influence for us," said Jeff. "It might have been meant to be. When we're in the ring, we know her spirit is with us."

And from the WWE's Cookbook (you have to appreciate the deep dive to get this source):

> North Carolina natives Matt and Jeff Hardy lost their mom when they were boys, so these two highflyers learned to cook and sew as youngsters.

Wrestling became an outlet for the boys, and they felt a real passion for it. In Brandon Truitt's review of the Jeff Hardy shoot interview he noted this exchange:

> Other gimmicks he used? They'd sit around the house thinking up gimmicks ever since they were about 10.

Though earlier in the interview Hardy gave this exchange:

> *How he got into the wrestling business- He and his brother, Matt Hardy Version One, watched Randy Savage win the WWF title at WrestleMania 4 then decided to start doing backyard wrestling.*

WrestleMania IV was in March of 1988, but it was probably the first big event the two saw. But let's not think that the WWE big man style of the 80's was the only influence on the Hardyz. Back to the shoot:

> *What promotions did they watch? They mainly watched WCW because they lived in the South and, as a result, saw a LOT of Ric Flair. One of the few times the WWF ran their area, they went and saw Andre the Giant, which was worth it because of how impressive it was to see Andre live.*

The bottom line is, Jeff and his brother Matt were really into wrestling, and because Matt was older, Jeff got introduced to it at a much younger age. They started working out together, fighting in the backyard (or tobacco field, it would seem) together, and then started to try to make a living out of it.

And so, the two followed their passion and tried to make it a career. From John Milner's Jeff Hardy compilation for Slam! Sports:

> *Jeff made his debut in 1994, in North Carolina independents. Wrestling as the Willow the Wisp, Hardy wrestled his brother Matt (as Voltage) in Robbins, NC, on March 25, 1995 and won the NFWA Championship, only to lose it back to Matt a month later.*

Pause. That means Jeff was just sixteen years old when he started wrestling professionally. Hulk Hogan didn't start until he was in his twenties. And it's not like they were making a ton of money at the beginning, or that it mattered to Jeff. From the shoot:

> *What was TWF? Originally, it was Trampoline Wrestling Federation. It was later Teen Wrestling Federation, but it was all a bunch of backyard wrestling. They used to do a lot of moves on the trampoline, which he feels is responsible for their high-flying moves today.*

Now, I was in a backyard wrestling federation in high school, as well. We used to wrestle in gym class (because we were told to just do SOMETHING). I was the high flying luchadore known as "Contablemente" (Accounting) and my finishing move was "El Queso Malo" (The Bad Cheese), a top rope guillotine leg drop. Though I was known on occasion to use the submission move "Paraguas de Tabla Hawaiana" (Surfboard Umbrella), a reverse sharpshooter/surfboard/crossface type maneuver. Anyway, despite eventually expanding into backyards, at no point did our little federation ever make money nor train any of us to do any actual wrestling. OK, one kid went on to have three matches in the same indie that started out Triple H in New Hampshire, but that doesn't count. The point is, while we were just goofing off, the Hardy brothers were serious. Back to John Milner's article:

> *Jeff and Matt started their own wrestling organization called OMEGA, a North Carolina promotion that [w]ould also boast future WWE stars such as Shane Helms (aka the Hurricane), Shannon Moore and Joey Matthews (now known as Mercury). As the Willow, Jeff defeated Jason Ahmdt (later Joey Abs) on August 2, 1997 to become the first OMEGA New Frontier Champion.*

That article fails to also mention former WWE Women's Champion Lita. Anyway, OMEGA became a breeding ground for a whole generation of performers, and many more who didn't make the big time. But a lot of those guys (and gals) are young, so there is still the possibility of adding more names to that list.

The problem is, people claim that Matt did everything and Jeff was just along for the ride. That is not true at all. From the shoot:

> *OMEGA- Matt came up with a lot of that stuff and, while it was strange, it really took off. "Matt did most of the work" and kept the promotion afloat through sponsorships while Jeff was still working as a landscaper part-time.*

And...

> *What did he learn when he was booking back then? That he didn't want to book, he just wanted to wrestle. His big part in OMEGA was playing two different characters and keeping them separate, such as selling differently depending on which one he was at the time.*

Jeff did not like booking, he just wanted to perform. What is wrong with that? So instead he pulled his weight in a different way and played two characters at once. Also, it wasn't a way they were making money back then, and Jeff had to work another job. In the ring as two different characters, Jeff taught himself a great deal of psychology and wrestling styles (I was also a different character in another back yard fed where I was "The Incredible Edible Egg" and had won the tag-team championships by myself when my partner turned on me and left me alone in the ring. I digress.). Still, because he wanted to be a performer, Jeff sought out ideas beyond Matt and OMEGA. From John Milner's article:

> *But Jeff wasn't content to stay within the safety of OMEGA, the Willow would win the NEW Junior title, the NDW Light Heavyweight title and even traveled to Iwate, Japan in June 1998, defeating Ikuto Hidaka for the UWA Middleweight Championship.*
>
> *However, Jeff and Matt didn't remain apart for too long. The Hardy Boyz defeated C.W. and Pat Anderson for the NWA 2000 Tag Team titles on March 7, 1998 in Hope Mills, N.C. and then, on July 24, 1998 returned to OMEGA to defeat Mike Maverick and Kid Vicious and capture the OMEGA Tag titles.*

It was Jeff Hardy who was pushing his limits and trying to learn the industry. He was the one trying to expand his horizons beyond just North Carolina and the local wrestling circuit. His efforts overseas and beyond probably did more to get the Hardy Boyz attention than anything Matt ever booked in OMEGA. And look, at seventeen and eighteen, Jeff Hardy was already traveling around the world for work.

Of course, the two did get noticed elsewhere, and actually had some experience with the WWF. From the shoot:

> *When did they finally get trained? They were trained by working shows for Stallion and George South, although they got ripped off on booking fees. As an example, they'd drive from North Carolina to New York to work tapings for three Monday Night RAWs and would get paid $150 each, but had to give up $100 each in booking fees. They didn't really care too much at the time, as Jeff was still a junior in high school and it was an experience to be on national TV while still in school.*

> Matches they had at WWF tapings- Jeff's first match was against Scott Hall while Matt's first match was against Nikita. "He beat the living shit out of me" and was about to cry afterwards. Apparently, Hall was having a bad day and decided to take it out on him. The next night, he faced 1-2-3 Kid (Sean Waltman, X-Pac) and had a good time.

A junior in high school and Jeff Hardy had already worked in the WWF, albeit as a jobber. Still, there are wrestlers who go their whole lives without ever getting to be a jobber for one night in the WWF/E. But here he was, just sixteen years old and already getting beaten up on a regular basis.

Eventually, all of this jobbing, traveling abroad, and OMEGA work got them the chance they were waiting for. From Milner's piece:

> That summer, Matt and Jeff were invited to participate in the WWE's "Funkin' Dojo" and trained under the tutelage of Dory Funk, Jr.

At the age of twenty, things were looking up for Jeff Hardy.

A CAREER BEGINS, LIKE A WILLOW IN THE WISP

In was the summer of 1998, and the Hardy Boyz had developmental contracts and were sent down to the Funkin' Dojo (no OVW or even HWA or UWF yet). From the shoot:

> Did the WWF send him anywhere after they got signed? They were sent to Dory Funk's Funkin' Dojo training camps along with Edge, Kurt Angle, and others. He remembers trying to do a reverse 450 one night and knocking himself out.
>
> Did anyone try to work very stiff with him because he was small? He feels that it was a common thing in his career but, since he could take it, he was able to get some respect.
>
> When were they actually signed to contracts? He thinks it was June of 1999 or 2000. The developmental deal was for only about two years but their contracts when they made the main roster about a year and a half after that were for five years.

The developmental program worked for Jeff, and he and his brother found themselves with five years contracts. Jeff, just twenty-one, was living out his dream in the top promotion in the world (well, just about to become top again. It was still another six months away, but still). After spending some time as jobbers on Shotgun Saturday Night, the duo started to find their way to TV. From the Jeff Nero Hardy fan-site:

> *Their first gimmick, or persona, didn't go over well with the fans. They wore brightly colored attire, and usually could not compete with the larger tag-teams. Soon, they joined Michael Hayes, who became their manager. He not only gave them different attitudes, he changed their look into a darker, edgier style. His alliance with the brothers [definitely] brought about a positive change when they won the WWF tag-team titles, but soon after they became annoyed of Haye's eagerness to control them... and joined Gangrel in the formation of the New Brood.*
>
> *With Gangrel by their side, Matt and Jeff entered into a feud with Edge and Christian. With their aerial-like moves and ability in the ring, the Hardyz became an instant hit with the fans, always breath-taking to watch. Come mid-1999, Terri Runnels offered both teams a chance at $100,000, as well as her management services. In what was def. one of the "match of the year" candidates in '99, the two teams clashed at the No Mercy PPV in a tag ladder match. The Hardyz won the 'bout, taking the money as well as Terri, and leaving Gangrel behind. However, her need for constant attention was too much for the Hardyz to suffice. As a result, she cost the Hardyz a shot at possibly becoming tag team champs after a number one contendership shot at No Way Out. After that incident, the Hardyz went without a manager for a while.*

There is an important piece missing in the middle of that. From Milner's compilation:

> *Jeff would take some time off from the WWE to compete in ECWAS's 3rd Annual Super Eight tournament in February 1999, losing in the first round to Devon Storm and, in May, lost to Super*

> Crazy in the first round of the IWA Junior Heavyweight title tournament.
>
> Jeff returned to WWE and teamed with his brother, Matt. After working their way through the tag team rankings, Hayes led the Hardys to a victory over the Acolytes (Bradshaw and Farooq) on June 29, 1999 to win the WWE Tag Team titles. The Acolytes regained the titles at Fully Loaded and soon after, the Hardys left Hayes behind, aligning themselves with Gangrel to form the New Brood.

Once again, it was Jeff who was out there trying to expand his horizons. Although Matt also competed in the same Super Eight (thanks to reader **Thomas Clinch** for pointing this out), he was more content to just be in the WWF and wrestle in tag team division. Jeff was the one who was always trying to expand beyond his basic setting. While Matt was happy to be a "sports entertainer", Jeff wanted to be a wrestler, and was more interested in expanding his abilities and reputation than in just making money.

Matt, too, it would seem recognized the money in his brother. From Wikipedia:

> Matt recently said that if they were compared to the Rockers, Jeff would be Shawn Michaels and Matt would be Marty Jannetty.

Being Shawn Michaels would be money enough. So Matt kept himself attached to Jeff for the longest time. From the shoot:

> Why did Matt ask for the original Hardyz split? He doesn't know, as Matt's the one that kept them together for so long. They never fully broke up until the WWF draft in mid-2002 which put himself, Matt, and Lita on RAW for the time being. The original split failed because they were fighting each other and no one wanted to see that instead of them teaming.

And elsewhere...

> Does he think anyone ever tried to hold him back? No, although tag wrestling held him back because he wanted to do more singles work.

Through his own experience, he wanted to get involved in more singles wrestling and push that career ahead. But he stayed behind in tag team wrestling FOR his brother. This helped give Matt more time to start to develop an individual persona that would eventually become Mattitude. But at the time, all he had was Jeff's daredevil notoriety.

Despite this, it was Jeff who was first given the ball to try to run with it.

I'M SINGLE, BABY!

From Milner's article:

> In addition to continuing to team with his brother, Matt, Jeff would begin competing in singles competition and wasted little time in adding many titles to his resume. On April 10th, Hardy defeated Triple H to win the Intercontinental Championship. He defeated Jerry Lynn to win the WWE Light Heavyweight Championship on June 5th, 2001. On July 10, 2001, he defeated Mike Awesome to win the Hardcore Championship. Rob Van Dam would defeat Hardy for the Hardcore title during the July Invasion pay-per-view, but Jeff interfered in a RVD/Kurt Angle match on August 13, 2001 to regain the title, only to lose it back to Van Dam at SummerSlam.
>
> But Jeff would return to the tag team ranks with brother Matt and in the course of just over a month would defeat Booker T and Test to win two different tag titles. On October 8th, the Hardys won the WCW Tag Team titles, and then on November 12, they won the WWE Tag titles.
>
> Near the end of 2001, dissention arose in the ranks of the Hardys and, at the Vengeance pay-per-view, Jeff defeated Matt in a bout in which Lita served as the special referee. However, the bitterness between brothers was soon forgotten.
>
> After teaming again with his brother Matt, Jeff began to strike out on his own (again), but made the mistake of angering the Undertaker who vowed revenge and, for the most part, had his way with Jeff. But Jeff earned a great deal of respect by

> nearly defeating 'Taker in a ladder match for the WWE Championship on the July 1st edition of Raw.
>
> Undaunted, a week later Jeff defeated William Regal and captured the European Championship. On July 22nd, Hardy lost a title unification match to Intercontinental Championship Rob Van Dam. A week later, a brief reign as Hardcore Champion began with a victory over Bradshaw and ended at the hands of Johnny the Bull.

So by the time he was twenty five, Jeff Hardy had won the Tag Team, IC, European, Hardcore, and Light Heavyweight championships. Not too bad of an accomplishment! As you can imagine, this type of toll can take a significant impact on your dreams and ambitions. Even a couple of years earlier before much single's success Jeff was talking about the trials and tribulations of the road. From Greg Oliver's article for Slam! Wrestling in November of 2000:

> He's only 23, but already the wear and tear on his body has forced Jeff Hardy to re-think his future in pro wrestling.
>
> Hardy knows that fans love his death-defying, high-flying moves but knows there's a change in his wrestling in the near future.
>
> "I just kind of take it day by day because I know that I'm not going to be able to do this until the day I retire," Hardy told SLAM! Wrestling before the WWF show at Toronto's Air Canada Centre on October 28. "I'll eventually [slow down]. My body's going to [slow down]. It's in the process of slowing down now. I'm 23 and I hurt sometimes when I get up in the morning."
>
> The pain becomes a regular part of life. "You adapt to this, but when you wake up you're going to hurt because we do this every night. It takes a toll on your body. I just hope that I can kind of ride it slow and not slow down as much."
>
> Retirement isn't thirty years away, like most 23 year olds. Instead, Hardy is thinking already of retiring at "somewhat of an early age", while hopefully still being able to get around without a crutch or a wheelchair.

Which of course brings us the end of his WWE career.

WHY DON'T YOU CARE ANYMORE?

Towards the end of Jeff's time in the WWE, the complaint was that he was not into his matches, that he was going through the motions. His style had become lethargic and sloppy, and he was not putting on the best matches in the world.

And you know what? That's absolutely true.

When he was twenty-three, he could more than deal with the pressures. From Greg Oliver's article:

> Besides the constant pain that results from his chosen profession, Hardy is not a big fan of the travelling.
>
> "It really gets to you sometimes. You get home, and sometimes you're home for an evening and have to leave the next day. It's pretty consistent though. We leave on Saturdays, and come home on Wednesdays, where we have Thursdays and Fridays off. But right now, being the champions, the appearances are crazy."
>
> Yet, it's all still worth it for Jeff Hardy. He's finally getting a real tag team title run, and the respect of the older, more established teams as well. What's the best thing in his life right now?
>
> "Just the vibe of everybody loving you for what you do and just knowing that so many people around the world can see you, look at you in a superhuman-like aspect," he said with a big grin on his face.

Jeff was in good spirits then, but time has a way of tearing someone down. From the shoot:

> Travel schedule- He was leaving on Friday and getting home on Tuesday. He'd either travel with Matt, Justin Credible, or just by himself. He and Credible used to sit around playing the guitar all the time.

> His burnout- It was a combination of the travel and the matches, as he would be leaving home as fast as he got back. He asked for time off at one point and Jim Ross gave him some weekends off here and there.

Plus...

> Did he start losing his passion from being on the road so much? No, it was from being beaten up so bad. When they first made it in the WWF, they would go all out every night but he almost screwed up his shoulder doing the Whispers in the Wind one night and had to change it up.

Also, his career was stagnant. As a person who wants to grow and change, this was beyond frustrating. Back to the shoot:

> Feuding with Steve Austin and Triple H- It was awesome but it sucked that it never went anywhere. He wonders what Austin and Trips were thinking since the crowds loved it. "Come on, Triple H."
>
> Was he ever able to talk to Vince or an agent why it never went anywhere? No, although he thinks Matt wanted to. If he ever goes back, that's one thing he's going to do because it pissed both him and Matt off intensely.

And...

> Were dropped programs like him and Matt vs. Steve Austin and Triple H a big part of why he lost his passion? Yes, he feels they played a big part in it.

That didn't mean he did not appreciate his feud with the Undertaker. From the shoot:

> *Memories of his ladder match with Undertaker- It built his confidence as a singles wrestler because of the comeback he made in that match before losing. For a long time afterwards, the road agents would tell him that he did a good job in a match but that he needed to have a comeback like in the match with Undertaker. He says that it's hard to do that when you're facing someone like Stevie Richards who isn't as legendary as Undertaker but that he still appreciates how highly they thought of that match.*
>
> *Working with Undertaker- Awesome. He isn't sure how he stayed on top for so long as Jeff attributes his own success to luck more than anything.*
>
> *Did he think he'd get a push after the Undertaker match? Yes, but he wasn't sure if he even still wanted to be wrestling at that point. He feels that match could have been even better if he'd been able to put his heart into it.*

But like he said, Hardy was aware that he was not at his best. But what was taking his attention? From John Powell's article for Slam! Wrestling just after Jeff was fired:

> *In a recent interview with Orlando radio host and SLAM! Wrestling writer Brian Fritz, Jeff explained where his focus is these days. "Music is a big thing. It's probably my #1 (hobby) now and that's what is drafting me away from wrestling," he told Fritz. "But my passion is still there. I still love it. I still get just as nervous as always before I go out for a match. I can't say that I love it more than I love life like Matt has said because he is 100% dedicated to pro wrestling. I give it my heart and soul but I give other things my heart and soul as well and I still try to follow my heart and go wherever it takes me. I can't give up things I really enjoy. I don't plan to stop wrestling at all. If anything, I'll just take a break within the next few years just to see what happens with the music but I don't plan to quit wrestling at all."*

So Hardy had other interests, much like Warrior, Hogan, and many others before him. Wrestling was dream, a passion, and something he was good at, but it was not his entire life. Although he had been wrestling professionally since he was sixteen, Hardy still wanted to see what else he could do. Put it this way, Jeff had been wrestling for nearly a decade and had already completed 95% of his dreams in professional wrestling. He wanted to do more! He wanted to follow and try something else! What is wrong with that?

Ten years is a long time to be at any job, especially one as mentally and physically draining as professional wrestling. And here was a man who had never gone to college, never got the chance to explore himself or his other interests, never got the chance to enjoy most of his childhood because he had been working since he was nine. All he wanted and needed was a chance to explore other interests.

So sure, he writes poetry, paints, and builds aluminum statues. We'll get more into Jeff's "art" shortly; the point is he is just now having the chance to actually find these things and is training himself. There is no guidance, no education, no help; just him trying to live out many dreams.

With so many different ideas pulling him away from wrestling, Hardy knew his time was up. He just was not committed in a way he needed to be. From the shoot:

> *How would he rate himself as a wrestler? On a scale of ten, he'd give himself a five right now but he feels he has potential to become a ten if he gets his passion back.*

And it must be commended that he was able to recognize his own lacking. And instead of just going through the motions, he decided to walk away from the WWE.

Yes, we'll get more into why and how Jeff and the WWE split ways momentarily.

With that split, Hardy was given time to follow other dreams.

BACK TO THE SMALL VENUE

While pursuing his other interests, Hardy stayed involved in pro-wrestling. Shortly after being release, Jeff found his way back to OMEGA. From Obsessed with Wrestling:

> May 24, 2003 - OMEGA WRESTLING: Jeff Hardy wrestled his first match since being released by WWE using old gimmick.
> ~~~Krazy K defeated Willow the Whisp (masked Jeff Hardy) to retain the OMEGA Cruiserweight title.

It was after this that Jeff decided to try Ring of Honor. Why Ring of Honor? From the shoot:

> How come he decided to work for Ring of Honor? He had decided after watching that tape that he wanted to go to ROH if he ever got fired.

So Hardy thought he could step up his game and show his wrestling ability again. Unfortunately, the ROH crowd had seen enough of the "five out of ten" Jeff Hardy and would not give him a chance. Back to the shoot:

> Did the fans have it in for him from the start? They weren't fair. He feels he deserved more respect for having wrestled some of those TLC matches he's done.

Jeff Hardy's wrestling ability has a rarely been questioned (his style, on the other hand, has—and we'll discuss it soon), but because he was not at his full passion level before the match, the fans dumped on him before he made it anywhere. This reaction most definitely affected the match (and people's perception of it) and did throw Hardy off his game. Even still, Jeff did not react to it as negatively as people claim. This part of the shoot interview was taped right after the match:

> He was interested to see the combination of ECW fans on one side and all the young girls cheering for him on the other. He jokes about how he was chanting "I fucked up" along with them at one point.
>
> Does he think he'd make a great heel in Ring Of Honor? Yes, and he loves how the business has changed to the point that you won't know how people will react to anything anymore.

> *Did he always want to have a run as a heel? Yes, but Vince McMahon shot it down because he didn't think they could pull it off.*

Hardy had an even, understanding response to the situation and thought he could have turned it into more money as a heel in ROH. This was not to be, as Hardy instead concentrated completely on his music and stayed away from wrestling for a year.

TOTAL NONSTOP JEFF

John Milner finishes off Jeff Hardy's career up to this point in 2006:

> *With a contract that included a promised World Title shot, Jeff Hardy didn't waste time earning the attention of Jeff Jarrett, who, along with Monty Brown, attacked Hardy on his first official night in TNA. Besides brawling with Jarrett and Brown, Hardy began teaming with A.J. Styles and Ron Killings before finally getting his title shot against Jarrett in September 2004.*
>
> *Jarrett retained the title but Hardy rebounded to win a #1 contender tournament and faced off with Jarrett, once again, at Victory Road, only to have his chances at victory spoiled by the interference of Kevin Nash and Scott Hall. Hardy would team with Styles and Randy Savage against Jarrett, Hall and Nash at Turning Point.*
>
> *After defeating Hall at Final Resolution, Hardy found himself under attack from Abyss. After further attacks from Abyss, Hardy took on (but lost to) Abyss in a #1 contender's match at Against All Odds but got the win at Destination X. The feud with Abyss widened to include Raven and the two men met in a Tables Cage Match at TNA Lockdown.*
>
> *Hardy was to have met Raven at Hard Justice but could not make the show due to transportation problems. Hardy was suspended from TNA over the incident but returned to attack Jeff Jarrett during the main event at Sacrifice and lost to Bobby Roode at Unbreakable.*

> Hardy found himself battling Rhino, Sabu and Abyss in a Monster's Ball match at Bound for Glory. Hardy lost that match but still impressed TNA officials enough to be pitted against Monty Brown in a contender's match at Genesis.
>
> Hardy lost to Brown, and his problems were just beginning. He no-showed the Turning Point pay-per-view, claiming to have overslept. Hardy remains on the active NWA-TNA roster, however.

At times, though, it seemed like Hardy was not fully with it for TNA, either. Especially with twice being suspended, Hardy does not seem to care either way. That might be because he does not. From the shoot:

> Is there any interest in him going to NWA TNA? He's kind of interested in it as he loved their Genesis show, but he would rather go back to the WWE.

And...

> If he was given a prime spot in a top [indie] and been guaranteed a huge push, would that get his passion back? It's a thought and he's impressed with the production values of NWA TNA but he doesn't think that he has the effort to put into trying to make a company compete with the WWE.

TNA, you were given fair warning right there. Hardy was not the person to try to build a major program around and help grow the company, and he told you so. He was only a part-time personality with interests elsewhere.

Yet despite this, and being suspended for months, Jeff still had three of the top eight (yeah, I don't know why the list ended at eight either) selling items on ShopTNA.com. They were:

#2 – Enigma: The Best of Jeff Hardy DVD
#3 – Jeff Hardy Glowing T-shirt
#4 – Victory Road 2004 PPV DVD (Jeff Hardy challenged Jeff Jarrett for the NWA Heavyweight Title in the main event)

Isn't it amazing that a PPV two years old is TNA's bestselling item? Oh, and what's this? The only other single PPV on the list is (#6) Final Resolution 2005 which has the Jeff Hardy vs. Scott Hall match with Roddy Piper as special guest referee. Coincidence? Not at all.

So you wonder why TNA will not fire him? Because Hardy sells. He makes TNA a lot of money. And recently, Hardy has been working for TNA, just not on TV. From Obsessed with Wrestling:

> *March 31, 2006--TNA House Show (UWF): Jeff Hardy & Kip James defeated Jeff Jarrett & Maven Huffman*
>
> *April 1, 2006--TNA House Show (UWF): Jeff Hardy & Amber O'Neal defeated Matt Bentley & Tracy Brooks*
>
> *April 14, 2006--TNA House Show (UWF): Maven & Jacqueline Moore defeated Jeff Hardy & Amber O'Neal in a Mixed Tag match*
>
> *April 15, 2006--TNA House Show (UWF): "Phenomenal" A.J. Styles defeated "Charismatic Enigma" Jeff Hardy*

Even now, Hardy is helping TNA sell tickets to their infant house show market, and also losing just as much as he's winning. Jeff proves his worth week in and week out, and here he is doing it again.

Yet despite this amazing career and strong drawing ability at just twenty-nine, Hardy faces sharper criticism every day. That, though, is coming up.

OH THESE LITTLE PILLS

Here it is from Brandon Truitt's review of the Jeff Hardy Shoot Interview:

> *Drugs in the business- You don't have to have them to make it in the business but the road schedule will raise the chances that you'll use them. He admits experimenting with drugs but denies being heavily addicted like many fans think he is. He talks about how addiction can completely change a person and brings up how Eddy Guerrero was sent to rehab in 2001. He talks about how he got surprised with a drug test, which he came up positive for and got released as a result. He says that it was a good thing for him because he*

> *needed to leave the WWE for a while. "They acted like I was going to die" and tried to send him to rehab, but he refused. He says he's changed his drug use and that he doesn't have a problem now. He refuses to name his drug of choice but says it was the one thing he kept testing positive for. Jeff also bitches about how everyone claims he was on drugs, plural, while he was only on one type of drug.*

You see, Jeff Hardy was taking some kind of recreational drug. I'm not going to say I agree with his choice, but the WWE made the wrong correlation. They thought that because he was late to shows and not putting on his best performances that he was completely out of control with drugs. The thing was, Jeff was just restless. He wanted to focus on his music but could not do that while under contract. The WWE wanted him to go to rehab, but he knew that was unnecessary. This interview was done just two months after his release. If Jeff Hardy had a major problem, he would not have been able to just stop using the drug. It was a choice then for him.

I hate to make excuses for anyone, especially when it comes to drug abuse, but the environment of the WWE locker room does have an effect on people. From earlier in the interview:

> *Was he ribbed a lot for being so young in the WWE? Yes, partially because they didn't drink. One of their assignments after their appearance in wrestler's court was to drink beers on the way home that night.*

So the Hardy Boyz came into the then WWF mostly innocent and picked up these habits from being on the road with the boys, some of it coerced onto them. We are still talking about a kid who grew up on a farm with very little parental supervision and never got to go to college. He never had time to experiment and discover who he was. There was no childhood and adolescence. Sure, he got to make a career out of play fighting, but it was still work from the time he was 16 onwards.

In the WWE he got introduced to something, and probably used the drug more because he felt stymied and locked out from being creative. Leaving the WWE gave him the opportunity to find creativity again and lessened his need to find other outlets. In this case, the WWE was the enabler for his drug use. This quote from the shoot helps sum up the environment at the time:

> Is he still a wrestling fan? Yes, but politics make him sick. "I wish I'd had a couple of terms in the White House" before working in the WWE.

And again, there was no "abuse", it was just the misconstruing of unrelated facts.

YOU ARE OUT OF HERE!

Of course, this was not the first time Jeff had been pushed aside by the WWE. Back in 2001/2002, the Hardyz and Lita got taken off TV for a while. From Obsessed with Wrestling:

> Matt & Jeff Hardy (and Lita) are written out of WWF storylines when the Undertaker injuries all of them.

But why? Team Extreme had just gotten back together, so it seemed like a rather inappropriate time. This question from the shoot may shed some light:

> Why were they taken off of TV in late 2001 and early 2002? That was when they were given the plan of him kissing Lita in a pre-taped segment. He went up to Stephanie McMahon and refused to do it and believes that it was a part of the office testing him because he'd never shot anything down before. Michael Hayes got the job of telling them that they were still expected to be at TV but that they were now off [TV and only performed on] the house show circuit.

Also from the other end and the Matt Hardy shoot interview review by Derek Burgan:

> Neither Hardy was a fan of their proposed "feud," but Matt said their one match at Vengeance wasn't that bad considering Matt was sick as a dog and Jeff clearly didn't give a damn. The "office" expected more from the Hardys though, and were still pissed that Jeff outright refused to an angle where he would kiss Lita and steal her away from

> Matt. Jeff told Vince McMahon himself, "I will not kiss her. I won't do it. I'll quit." Both the Hardys and Lita were then punished by being taken off TV till "creative" could figure out what to do with them. All three were still made to go to house shows though as the fans still couldn't get enough.

Well, you have to give Jeff props for standing by his convictions despite the consequences. Many others in his same situation have crumbled in order to keep their jobs, but Jeff has his own moral code that he kept. Because of that, he would not kiss Matt's girlfriend, even in a pretend world. It was not something he wanted to do (though judging by Matt's later reaction with Edge, he probably knew his brother's jealous streak).

Yet, much like what is happening in 2006 with TNA, Jeff and his brother were still a draw and were selling house show tickets. It was the story in 2001, and it was still the story in 2006.

Of course, this is probably what Vince McMahon saw in Jeff Hardy in 2002, just a year later. From Matt's shoot:

> By this time Jeff Hardy was starting to totally withdraw himself from the old cliques, to the point where even his relationship with Matt was strained as Jeff was "traveling with guys he shouldn't have been traveling with." I'm pretty sure that's kayfabe for "Justin Credible." Jeff had become disenfranchised with wrestling and started to look at it like just another job. Matt talked about the famous ladder match that Jeff had with Undertaker at Raw and how Vince McMahon, despite all the crap Jeff had pulled in the previous months, was all over Jeff after the match putting Jeff over. This was another example of Matt being frustrated as at the time he was training harder [than] ever, eating good, tanning and showing up for work on time while Jeff was blowing everything off. To be fair, I was at that Monday Night Raw (it took place in my hometown of Manchester, NH) and the fans there were ready to blow the roof off the building if Jeff would have won. It would have been just like when Foley won his first WWE title in Worcester, Mass.

And this goes back to our prior point. Jeff has a way of constantly finding a place for himself in wrestling, without even trying that hard. That is Jeff Hardy.

BUMPER

What Jeff Hardy is also known for is his daredevil style. The man did train on a trampoline, so that might have had some influence. But actually, Hardy had many diverse styles. From his shoot:

> What style did he think the promotion would be? They'd just started breaking tables and stuff like they'd seen on Sabu's tapes, so they started doing hardcore stuff. They began mixing it up with Lucha Libre after they saw tapes of Rey Misterio's matches in ECW.

And...

> Working in Japan- He'd seen tapes and was somewhat prepared although it was unusual to have quiet crowds during the match. That's changed, as the crowds were MUCH louder when he came back with the WWE during a recent tour. It wasn't hard working the Japanese style because he'd worked out with the two guys he wrestled over there and had laid out both matches beforehand.

As we've noted earlier, Hardy traveled the world, worked as two different wrestlers at once, and tried to expand his abilities. In the WWE, he became the daredevil. He still wanted to see how far he could take it. Because of the timing, the WWE was much more lenient on what they would let wrestlers do (the big push of the Attitude Era trying to dismantle WCW by any means necessary). From the shoot:

> Did the road agents tell them to tone their style down? A little bit, but that was mainly because they'd have to clear spots with them before matches. He says that the agents would usually come up to him and ask him if he wanted to do certain crazy spots.

Also...

> *Did the WWF ever encourage them to do crazier bumps? Only at PPVs, when they'd come up with crazy ideas for bumps that the agents thought no one else would do. The only thing he ever did shoot down was kissing Lita, as he and Matt had agreed that they wouldn't do an angle between them playing off the Matt-Lita relationship.*
>
> *Did he think he could do that style forever? He knew that he'd have to change it eventually and says that Matt has adjusted to the change in style much better than him, as proven by his recent match with Chris Benoit on Smackdown.*

Strangely, Jeff has taken on a much more brawling style and less off-the-ropes type maneuvers. Since he is wrestling less he can do more bumps compared to doing them every night. As we saw earlier, Jeff knew that his style in the WWE was taking its toll on him and he would have to slow down eventually. Actually, here is another good reminder from Jim Varsallone's article for the Wrestling Observer in December 2001:

> *"I'm 23 now, and some mornings when I wake up, I'm going, `Owww, man, my back, my shoulder, my knee. Oh my god,' ", Jeff says. "Then, I'll start the day, and I'll begin to feel normal again because I've pretty much adapted to it. We're used to being sore, but both of us have been really lucky as far as not suffering any really serious injuries. We've had all kinds of injuries, but nothing bad enough to really throw that huge stop sign in front of us. Then again, I don't think about the future much. That's what makes my crazy ass do what I do. I'm still growing up, and I'm still maturing as far as wrestling goes. I'm really starting to realize I am going to have to slow down. It all comes down to character and personality. In the WWF, you don't have to do the crazy moves every night in the ring where you're getting hurt. We hope [we'll] be able to slow down a little bit and still excite crowds, so we can save some years on our career."*

He now has a reputation that takes him further than his spots can, and his TNA T-shirt sales prove that. Only a man like Jeff Hardy could not wrestle at all and still be a top seller. His style has justified his life. He has found his success, as was his plan. Nothing else there truly matters.

YOU KNOW WHAT I'M THINKING?

Of course, the other side of wrestling style is psychology. Jeff has been accused of having none. But is that true? First, this from the shoot:

> *Who was his mentor early on, psychology-wise? Michael Hayes, because they met him around the time they began jobbing. "He was our wrestling daddy."*

So Hayes (and many others) trained Jeff in the idea of in-ring psychology. Your response would be, "Yeah, but he didn't listen." Or did he? Back to the shoot:

> *Michael Hayes- He and Matt are big Freebirds fans, although they mainly saw the Hayes and Jimmy Jam Garvin version of the team. Great guy and has a good mind for the business, as he taught them a lot about ring psychology. He then starts into a monologue about psychology and his views on it, which I'm not going to transcribe but can be boiled down to saying that he doesn't believe in traditional psychology and, as a result, people think that he doesn't know psychology at all.*

You see, typical in-ring psychology consists of working on a body part that leads to a conclusion of using that body part to win the match. Or, in similar situations, trading moves that are trying to lead to the end of the match. Hardy sees psychology as building up the audience for the big finish, not building up the wrestlers. That is the main difference. We have been conditioned to think that there is only one type of psychology, or only one type good "workrate". I'll get into this at a later date, but for now let's just note that there is more than one belief to how you can wrestle.

And how can you argue with Hardy's choices? His in-ring style and thoughts on psychology got him over in the ring and kept the money flowing in. So he does not have a "traditional" view of psychology. You know who else didn't have a "traditional" view? Freud. Just because it is "traditional" that does not mean it is best or the only. Slavery was traditional for thousands of years, that didn't make it right. Hardy is nothing if not an explorer, and he decided to explore another facet of being a wrestler. He re-wrote what it means to work in the ring to a design that made sense to him. If he was unsuccessful at it, I would still defend him. Instead, he found a way to make it a part of his whole performance and turn it into a profitable and entertaining franchise.

WIPE THAT BRUSH OFF

The other area that Hardy gets confused with is his "art". Now, I personally believe that art should have a message or a meaning. If I am looking at a painting, I (or someone with a better critical eye), should be able to know the purpose of the painting. For most of history, most art was created out of necessity. People were painters and sculptors for their jobs, writers and poets were trying to change the times (or maintain them), and glass blowers needed to make windows, albeit pretty ones.

But for the past half century, there has been so much additional leisure (especially in the United States) that many people have given up on "Art for purpose" or "Art for recreation" (i.e., a hobby) and have started to create "Art for the sake of art". Let me expand on this.

Back in college I knew a person that fancied herself as artist. I thought she was a hack. She used to do atrocious things like papier-mâché bottles. Yeah. So anyway, one day she painted something and asked me to look at it. The conversation went like this...

> *JP: So, what are you trying to say with this painting?*
>
> *Artist: I'm trying to convey... emotion.*
>
> *JP: Emotion?*
>
> *Artist: Yes... emotion.*
>
> *JP: Any particular emotion?*
>
> *Artist: No, just emotion.*
>
> *JP: Emotion?*
>
> *Artist: Yes, emotion.*

The point is, I—personally—do not believe that what she was doing was art. But there is a whole generation of people like her that do believe that is art. Jeff Hardy is one of those people. He feels that painting his body is like a form of expression. The conversation would go like this:

> **JP:** So what are you trying to express by painting your body?
>
> **Jeff Hardy:** I'm trying to express myself.
>
> **JP:** But what in particular are you trying to express?
>
> **Jeff Hardy:** I'm expressing the need for expression.

You can see the corollary.

Although most of the contemporary world would not consider Jeff's body painting, poetry, and music to be the greatest form of artistic creation, it is the wave of this generation. Jeff has the connection with the audience in a way than cannot be replicated for he truly believes what they believe. It's not like he's pretending to be an "Art for art's sake" type person; that is exactly who he is! Although you or I may not personally agree with that lifestyle, there is a large and vocal fanbase that stands behind Jeff Hardy, and all the expressions of expression he submits.

WHISPER THAT INTO THE WIND

Jeff Hardy is a man who, at 28 at the time of this writing, already has spent twelve years in the industry. In that time, he has captured almost every major tag team and singles title available, and made a ton of money along the way. Because he is so young, we see the potential for a long future unfulfilled. What we miss is the long past filled with glorious accomplishments. Jeff knew long ago that his time wrestling in the spotlight would be limited, and he was OK with that. It is only us who have failed to understand what Jeff has.

As time went on, the dream of working for the WWE became a job. As a man who always wants to expand his horizons, the WWE of the twenty-first century must be incredibly stifling. Because of this, Hardy let his skills and talent go. He wanted to explore other worlds, other ideas. He gave the world notice that he was no longer the man to build a promotion around, yet others refused to listen. They wanted Jeff to be something he could not be anymore.

Sure, the possibilities are endless. Hardy still selflessly wrestles today. Without being on TV, he is still the highest grossing merchandising person in TNA. His very presence brings in fans, money, and interest. Truly, he is the charismatic enigma.

The defense rests.

After the Trial

Hung Jury

IN THE CASE OF THE IWC VS. JEFF HARDY, JEFF HARDY HAS BEEN ACCUSED OF BEING A RECKLESS AND DANGEROUS WRESTLER WHO IS COMPLETELY UNRELIABLE AND SHOULD NEVER BE TRUSTED TO WORK IN A WRESTLING RING. HE WAS NEVER AS GOOD AS ANYONE BELIEVED, AND ONLY KNOWS HOW TO DO CRAZY SPOTS TO GET OVER.

And with a startlingly low 62.0% of the vote, Jeff Hardy was found:

NOT GUILTY!

I guess some people can never forgive someone for missing a show. My point was, TNA should not have put faith in him in the first place as he told them he wasn't into it, but they decided they were going to spotlight him anyway. I'm not saying Jeff should have missed the shows, or that he doesn't deserve his suspension, but that TNA should have known it was coming.

Response

With such a close result, it is important to see where the detractors were coming from. The most common reasoning can be summed up here:

> *Jeff was a spot monkey who spent a year stinking up my TV with [awful] matches because he couldn't be bothered. I can understand he had other interests, but if the question is whether he was as good as people said and/or reliable, then [I] have to say he is guilty.*
>
> **Manor Admin**

As noted, it was difficult to defend someone for poor performances and no showing, but his outside interests actually brought up a different train of thought:

> *I'm not quite sure if he's guilty on all counts but he is definitely been proven to be irresponsible in my book. And a waste of a great talent. He could have been one of the best pro wrestlers around and easily one of the biggest draws but instead he's barely employed and has ruined more than one chance. Then again I'd say the same thing about the Rock when it comes to being a waste of talent.*
>
> **BOB1318821342002**

That's the thing: everyone who is good at something but chooses not to do it can be seen as "wasting" that talent. But people have to at least attempt to do what they enjoy or find interesting, not just stay in a gilded cage forever. Also, people change with time, especially between their teenage years and their 30's. What you want to do then compared to how you view life can be drastically different. It certainly was for me; I would not even recognize nor like the person I was 20 years ago.

> *As far as [unfulfilled] potential, isn't that the reason everybody is down on Marcus Bagwell and Sean [Waltman]? Both when I saw Bagwell tagging with 2 Cold Scorpio and 1-2-3-kid debuting, I thought I was looking at the future. Certainly they deserve some level of criticism, but it is the 'hey, I expected so much of him'-thoughts, that drives the criticism into the Land of Unreason.*
>
> **Jansen Lisbeth**

It's actually a problem we see today in 2020 in so much media. A sequel to a movie or a second season of a show comes out and it does not meet expectations because the audience had not only built their own stories in their head, but they have listened to every YouTuber, theorist, and commentator coming up with how they think it can and should go. As such, the final product can never live up to the expectations that have been built up in our heads. And when we look at people like Jeff Hardy and we build their career in our minds, the letdown is even worse because they don't want to do it.

The European Championship

Intro

Some dame walked into my office and said...

I already had the World Heavyweight Championship on my docket, but the case hadn't happened yet. That would not stop **John-Peter Trask** from coming to task:

> I, for some reason or another, had quite the affinity for the WWF European Title. I think I may have liked it because I thought the WWF could use a [beginner's] title that could help keep the Intercontinental Title prestigious, while giving new guys a real chance to shine, sort of like the TV Title to the US Title in WCW. However, I know that when it came to liking the European Title, I was in the minority. For whatever reason people seemed to really hate that belt (which in my opinion looked awesome), and even the WWF didn't really seem to know what they were doing with it. Despite, the championships short comings it can be argued that it made the career of D'lo Brown, was the most prestigious singles belt held by X-pac, and provided one of the better matches at WrestleMania XV.
>
> Therefore, I request that you defend the European Championship. Convince people that it wasn't a bad title to have around.

Fixxer315 wasn't as forgiving:

> [T]he European title never really recovered from the HBK/HHH laydown of 97...

Sounds like a good couple of dames to me!

WHY THIS?

I always read today in 2006 about how the WWE mismanages their titles, that they cannot make a Cruiser, Tag, Women's, IC, US, World, or WWE division seem to work. Over time, titles have become devalued as props and whoever is champion does not really matter.

I don't agree. Whether shoot or work, we have heard numerous wresters on TV say the same thing: if you aren't in this business to become champion, then you should not be in the business at all. Sure, there are "less threatening" champions, and yes there are times when the focus is not on the champions (see: H, Triple). But that does not signify the title means any less.

If you figure that there are on average about 40 wrestlers on a roster, the chances of one of them holding a single championship belt is 3%. It's a goal to aspire to, it's a storyline to build around, and it is the meaning of wrestlers (except Tommy Dreamer, who did not want to hold a title during his entire run, because he was crazy).

Now, not everyone is World Champion material, at least not right away. If forty or fifty or a hundred guys were fighting for one title, no one would be happy and championships would have to change waists every other week. Also, there would be no way to judge growth and change over time. How would you know someone improved if you did not see them go up the rungs? Did DDP start out as World Champion? No, he worked his way up from Battle Bowl to TV Title to US Title and finally to World. Did Ultimate Warrior or Goldberg immediately get the World Titles? No, they both won the secondary titles first.

Sometimes, though, there is a large pool on top and a large pool near the top. Sometimes you need a rung below in order to have a title that the mid-card can fight for and aspire to.

Back on an edition of WCW Saturday Night, Lord Steven Regal (then Television Champion for nearly a year) had an interview in the back. Regal said that due to politics, he would never receive a shot at the World title, and being a proud Brit he did not want the US title ("Who would want to be champion of this despicable country?"), so he was happy to represent us all as TV Champion. It was the title custom made for a man like him, and he would defend it with honor.

The European Championship was the same way. It was a lower-tier championship meant to propel some to greater heights, but also to give those going nowhere something to fight for. Not everyone needs to be or can be World champion. For some, their home is that other championship—less prestigious, but still just as proud.

WHERE? WHEN? WHY?!?!

Most of 1996 had been terrible for the WWF, and 1997 was not looking much better. WCW and Nitro were killing their organization in every metric. Nitro beat RAW every week in the ratings, PPV buyrates were generally higher, and attendance was much higher for WCW television tapings. The WWF was in a rut, creatively and financially.

With the nWo red hot and the Sting year-long storyline in full-swing building up to Starrcade 1997, the WWF did not look like they had much to stand on. In desperation, Vince agreed to a number of radical changes in his organization, storytelling style, television production value, and the general direction of the company as a whole. But it would take time for him to come to accept many of the changes, and they slowly had to be brought in.

In the meanwhile, although the WWF was doing terrible at home, the international market was growing hot. While they could not sell out a 6,000 seat arena in Minnesota, the WWF found that they could sell out 15,000 seat arenas in Europe. In order to appease European fans and give them something special, a tournament was held to crown a brand-new title:

The European Championship.

Eight men participated, but it came down to Tag Team Champions Owen Hart and Davey-Boy Smith. From the History of the WWE website:

> *Berlin, Germany*
> *Deutschlandhalle*
> *Februrary 26, 1997*
> *Monday Night Raw - 3/3/97:*
> *- WWF European Title Tournament Finals: WWF Tag Team Champion Davey Boy Smith pinned WWF Tag Team Champion Owen Hart with a [rollover] out of a victory roll at 22:43*

As time went on, Davey-Boy Smith did not really defend his championship, although it did become a point of contention between the tag team partners. This did not materialize too much, but what did was the WWF's return to Europe in September.

By this point, McMahon had agreed with the likes of Vince Russo and was ready to change the WWF into a new "attitude". So, at the UK only PPV entitled "One Night Only" on September 20, 1997 things would change. In the main event, the European Championship was defended by the British Bulldog against Shawn Michaels. That's right, the European Championship not only main evented a PPV, but it was also above the WWF Championship match between Bret Hart (c) and the Undertaker.

And in quite the shock to EVERYONE, Shawn Michaels evilly cheated his way to the title and Degeneration X (a couple of weeks before it got that name) was formed! The arena erupted in disgust and hatred, it truly was a shocking moment. The European Championship had become the instrument used to set off the new direction in the WWF: The Attitude Era.

Just three months later, to show how rebellious they were, Shawn Michaels (then WWF/E and European Champion) laid down for his partner Triple H to lose the title. As mentioned above, this would seem to devalue the title.

But it was after this point that the title actually began to be defended. It was from this point on that it joined the regular rotation of defending and losing the title began. Before this point in time, the title was just a showpiece for the beginning of the Attitude Era and DX. This was the first opportunity for the title to exist on its own.

It was also after this point that the title got its most memorable storyline in the form of four-time champion D'lo Brown. Both he and Jeff Jarrett would also win the European and Intercontinental championships at the same time, creating the ground for the "Euro-continental" championship that Kurt Angle would make famous in his feuds with Chris Jericho and Chris Benoit.

You see, the laydown happened in December 1997, but there would be another four years of history for the title. There was nothing to devalue at that point, and the best and most important years of the title were still to come.

Sure, it was not like the European Championship reached the heights of meaning of the Intercontinental Championship, but who says it ever was supposed to? Maybe for some people, that's the best they would ever have to aspire to.

THE BEST WE COULD DO

With only so many hours of TV a week, and considerations of selling ability, pushes, and the financial situation of the WWF at the time, not everyone was going to become WWF Champion. And although a few more would become Intercontinental Champion, there were still many on the roster sacrificing their life and body to try to save the company. Was there any possible reward for them? Could they get spotlighted? Could they get a chance to prove they could carry the ball?

Enter the European Championship. As a testing and reward ground, many people who would never see other titles or never be able to move up found a goal and championship to fight over. It gave them an exposure that they would never get otherwise. In the list of people whose highest single's achievement (at the time of this writing) was the European Championship are:

- Al Snow
- Crash Holly
- Mark Henry
- Matt Hardy
- Mideon
- Perry Saturn
- Shane McMahon
- Spike Dudley
- Gregory "Hurricane" Helms

Perry Saturn may have been able to reach IC level, and Al Snow almost became ECW Champion. Gregory Helms is still early enough in his career that he may reach that IC/US Level. Matt Hardy seems like he could he a World Champion every other week, but that's a wait and see. The rest, though (with the exception of McMahon) were tailor made for a title like the European Championship. For everyone else—for people who work hard, who have storylines, who are able in different ways to get over, yet are not made to reach the pinnacle of the sport—do they not deserve a reward of some kind? Do they not need a title to call their own?

For these men, the European Championship was the perfect place for them. Actually, of the 27 European Champions, the 10 on that list account for 37% of all champions. That means that for over a third of all people who captured the title, that it would be the high point of their career.

Of course, that leaves another 2/3rd.

Is it a Steppingstone?

Even though we have discussed the European Championship as the highest level attended by some, it has been the steppingstone as promised for others. The following are people who won the European Championship who later went on to win a World Championship (or had already won a World Title):

- Shawn Michaels
- Triple H
- Jeff Jarrett
- Kurt Angle
- Chris Jericho
- Eddie Guerrero
- Bradshaw
- Christian
- RVD
- Diamond Dallas Page (had already been a three time... three time... three time World Champion)

In total, there were 27 individual European Champions, and of those 10 at one point or another have held a World Championship. That means the belt has a

37% success rate of helping to elevate people up the ladder (not even looking at others who also went on to hold IC/US Gold).

Let's put this in a little context. The WCW Television Championship (from when it became the WCW in 1991 until the title was lost in 2000) also had 27 champions (same amount of champions in double the amount of time, how odd), and of those 9 went on to be or had been World Champions, or 33%.

The numbers seem incredibly similar, don't they? That's because they are similar belts with similar missions. Also, the following people were both European and Television Champion:

- Chris Jericho
- DDP
- Perry Saturn
- William/Steven Regal

Two World Champions, a consummate professional, and man who has mostly disappeared. Three out of four is not bad.

But that is not the point. The point is that the titles were doing the same thing. They were giving some people a chance and elevating others. And 15% of the people were the same people! The WWE and WCW had the same idea and saw many of the same people with the same type of potential. The European Championship in the WWF/E was their chance to begin to shine or shine a little more.

The remaining 26% discussed in the previous section went on to also have Intercontinental/US Title success. Do any of them (D'lo Brown, Jeff Hardy, Owen Hart, Test, Davey Boy Smith, Val Venis, and William Regal) have a World Title in their future? Well, two have passed on, one is happy in Japan, one is happy with his music, one is likely to be fired, one is in a "veteran" role, and one was recently rehired yet hasn't been seen on TV. So perhaps not. But with an active Intercontinental/US title scene, could they still be involved in the European title hunt today, should the title exist? Absolutely; they have not left the title behind.

WHAT DID THE WRESTLERS THINK?

There are those, though, that claim even the wrestlers did not want to hold the European Championship. This quote from Chris Jericho would seem to be the proof (from a WWE.com article via Obsessed with Wrestling):

> "I kind of think it was a worthless title anyway," Jericho told WWE.com. "It was never promoted as (a prestigious championship). In boxing, there are too many titles. I think in WWE there might have been a few too many titles. So I think it's good that it's been unified, because it didn't really mean too much anyway."

Then again, even the article begins to disagree with Jericho almost immediately:

> But many superstars disagree with Jericho, and there's no denying that the European Title -- whether it was prestigious or not -- brought about some of the most memorable moments in WWE history.

I think that's an interesting way of looking at it. Was it prestigious? Maybe not as much as many hoped. But did it have a purpose and present memorable history? Most certainly. Besides, not everyone was as cynical as Jericho:

> D'Lo Brown upset Triple H on RAW to secure the title. D'Lo's reaction to winning and his subsequent reign as champion were priceless. Immediately after his victory, Brown's face lit up like the proverbial kid in a candy store. He jumped around exclaiming, "I'm the Champion of Europe!"
>
> "It was without a doubt one of the highlights of my career," D'Lo says. "I still have that picture framed and hanging up in my office."

And...

> [I]n February 2000, Kurt Angle won the title, his first in WWE.
>
> "I felt that the European Title was one of those titles that, not only does it bring another storyline and another dimension to the show, but it's kind of a catapulting belt," Angle said. "It's like, 'Hey, you're the next guy coming through. Keep your eyes on this guy because soon he's going to be

{ 573 }

> Intercontinental Champion. Or soon he'll be vying for the WWE Title.'"
>
> That was certainly the case with Angle. Less than three weeks after winning the European Title, the Olympic gold medalist won the Intercontinental Championship, and went on to that year's WrestleMania as the "Euro-Continental Champion." While he lost both titles at 'Mania, Angle defeated The Rock the following October at No Mercy in Albany, N.Y., to become the WWE Champion, and cap off arguably the best rookie campaign in history.
>
> "You hate to see a title like (the European Championship) get dropped," Angle said.

So while some forgot what that reign with the European Championship meant, there are many more who remember what it did for their career, storylines, and future. And there are just as many fans who remember the enjoyment they got out of the European Championship, not disappointment.

TODAY... WHAT ARE THEY DOING?

While looking through the WWE roster today in 2006 (just RAW and SmackDown!, not ECW), there are many at that European/Television level. What are they doing? Why are they fighting? What is their goal? Is Simon Dean, Tatanka, Vito, or Gunner Scott ready to be US Champion? What do they do every week that has meaning? What could they be fighting over?

Are Eugene, Johnny Nitro, Matt Striker, Rob Conway, and Rene Dupree ready to step up to the Intercontinental Championship? Or would they be better served putting each other over for a lower tier title?

Now I know there are fears, as stated above, that the WWE cannot manage the titles they have now. This may be true. But in the late 1990s, the WWE, Intercontinental, and Tag Team divisions were full and active, and the WWE was able to create another division that put over men like those listed in this section.

Is today the right time for the return of the European Championship? Probably not. The World/WWE title scene for three brands needs to be figured out first. But is it a possibility for the future? Why not?! The WWE has used the European Championship to propel a third of its holders to greater heights. It has proved its ability as a title, both as a place holder and as a steppingstone. It provides a central story for many wrestlers that would not have one otherwise. Perhaps it will have a home in the future.

STRAP IT ON

The short-lived European Championship is a title often maligned here in the IWC. Because it was not a cornerstone title and only had five years of history, people are ready to dismiss it as meaningless. But it had a very eventful life, from helping to kick off the Attitude Era to propelling ten people to World Championships to giving the mid-card something to fight over when nothing else was available. Its place in history should be recognized and revered, not forgotten and laughed at. For some, the European Championship was the greatest achievement of their careers. For others, it was the break they needed to become superstars. Either way, the European Championship always did what it was designed to do: be a true championship.

The defense rests.

AFTER THE TRIAL

HUNG JURY

IN THE CASE OF THE IWC VS. THE EUROPEAN CHAMPIONSHIP, THE EUROPEAN CHAMPIONSHIP HAS BEEN ACCUSED OF BEING A WORTHLESS HUNK OF METAL THAT DID NOTHING FOR ANYONE WHO HELD IT.

And with 84.4% of the vote, The European Championship was found:

NOT GUILTY!

A Television/European championship, I believe, is very necessary. It really does give people lower on the card something to fight for. And I'll be honest: my favorite championship of all time is the WCW Television Championship, especially when Steven Regal was the champ. That was the only title that was always defended, even when the World Heavyweight Championship (and champion) would disappear for a while. And what an upset when Prince Iakea won it!

RESPONSE

It was a lot of parroting back to me the same points, but I did enjoy particularly hearing from the Europeans and non-Americans in general on this one:

> *The fact that WWE was dipping into a ridiculously profitable market more than justifies the title itself. European fans are just as die hard as American fans, and there is no reason for them not to have a crowned champion they can be proud of as opposed to just rooting for the British Bulldog all the damn time. Christ, he's just one guy from one country! ...*
>
> *You were right to point out that the WWE was going through some serious changes during this period, but I think they were trying to emulate WCW flat out by adding more divisions and titles. That's perfectly fine except the WWE is notorious for dropping the ball on a great idea. The European championship was meant for a [separate] division. Whether that be a division that competed abroad or just a division of up and comers doesn't matter, all that matters is that the title be kept to a SINGLE DIVISION. WWE, as usual, tried to get the title to do everything at once, and thus it started to lose its flavor for many fans. But it isn't the belt's fault that the WWE doesn't know the meaning of continuity. The spirit of the belt, as carried on by the wrestlers who enjoyed it and the thousands of cheering European fans, even if only for one PPV, is still quality stuff.*
>
> **Damian S**

This actually gives me a reason to just drop in how amazing it was to hear from people all over the world. As noted, this was the wild west of the Internet, and finding like-minded people all over existence was just coming into being. The Internet helped make the world much smaller, but the amount of people online regularly back then was miniscule compared to what it would be just a couple of years later. It is part of the reason I wanted to release this collection; there were so many people who just were not there the first time around.

THE nWo SPLIT

INTRO

SOME DAME WALKED INTO MY OFFICE AND SAID...

Way back when, **Andrew Strom** said:

> I am a really big fan of the entire nWo era, including the Hollywood/Wolfpac split. I know you are a busy man, but maybe in your backlog you can throw in defending the nWo split for me. A lot of people in the IWC seem to dislike this time period, but I thought it was really cool and profitable for WCW. I remember going to Great America (a theme park in Illinois, which may give you a clue where "nWo 4-Life country" is...lol) and wearing a Wolfpac T Shirt and getting (I kid you not) over 50 reactions from people including "Too Sweet", "Wolfpac in the House", and even some heckling from an nWo Hollywood fan (even though I assured him I was a fan of all colors of nWo).

Well wait no longer! The backlog of nine months has brought you to the forefront today!

WHY THIS?

At the time of this writing, it is the ten-year (!!!!) anniversary of the founding of the nWo, and there has been little denying the impact of the nWo on the sport of professional wrestling. Before the nWo, WCW was losing tons of money, the WWE was full of clowns, and ECW was just starting to define the word "Extreme". Despite having two major powerhouse wrestling organizations, wrestling was in an incredible lull. Hulkamania had long since waned, the Horsemen had long since been a dominate force, the "New Generation" was met with yawns and empty seats, and the old guard were spinning in circles.

Enter the nWo. Eric Bischoff, inspired by an invasion angle he saw in Japan, originally conceived the concept when he was in the AWA. Since that company went out of business before he could do anything, the idea was tabled for another six years. When the time came, he launched the angle to great success, making WCW profitable, almost putting the WWE out of business, and creating a revolution in the sport that eventually morphed into Austin, DX, and the Attitude Era that catapulted the competition into heights thought impossible.

But before that could happen, the nWo had to go through many changes. At the end of a year and half storyline, WCW was without direction, without a central arc. In order to change this, the nWo split. But there were a plethora of other reasons why this happened. Though many lament this as the "end of WCW" (once again three years before WCW went out of business), we'll show why the nWo split was not only necessary, but profitable, and actually helped WCW for quite a while.

People forget: the nWo wasn't really a "storyline" in the sense of the word that we use it. Vince McMahon saw it as a storyline. But the nWo was a revolution, a separate organization, a change from the past. It's OK for it to grow and change and be different. It's not about a beginning, a middle, and an end. It is about the spirit of angle and the characters involved; it is about all the possible ways they could be used. This was another one of those ways.

What's the story here?

411mania's own Stuart Carapola in his That Was Then: The New World Order 1998 said:

> At the first PPV of the year, Souled Out, Hulk Hogan got some good news: due to the circumstances surrounding their two previous meetings, the WCW World Title had been held up and Hogan would meet Sting at Superbrawl to determine the true champion. Although Hogan was happy to get this news, there were other people who weren't quite as happy with the news. Among them was Sting, who had given up the title and now had to beat Hogan again to regain it. Also, Scott Hall was not thrilled to hear this because, by virtue of his win at World War III the previous November, he was scheduled to challenge for the WCW World Title at Superbrawl, although he was informed that his title match would be pushed back to Uncensored the following month rather than be cancelled outright.
>
> However, before Superbrawl came, dissension started brewing amongst the leaders of the NWO. The chief dissenter was Randy Savage, who had

again become tired of being a second banana to Hogan. Hogan tried putting Savage in his place by preventing the NWO from interfering in Savage's match against Lex Luger at Superbrawl. Without interference from the NWO, Luger put Savage in the rack and got the submission. Savage would get some revenge later that night, coming into the ring and knocking Hogan out with a foreign object, allowing Sting to get the pin and regain the WCW World Title. Hogan was livid that Savage, who was supposed to be on his side, cost him the title that meant more to him than anything. They ended up facing one another in a cage match at Uncensored, and were fighting tooth and nail when Sting (who had successfully defended the WCW Title against Scott Hall earlier in the evening) got in the cage and tried to help Savage against Hogan, but rather than allow Sting to get between them, the two NWO members instead put their differences aside and beat Sting down two-on-one to close the show.

They seemed to reconcile that night, but the tension between the members of the NWO would continue. Kevin Nash was granted a shot at Sting's title on [the] Nitro after Uncensored, but Hogan's interference (ostensibly on Nash's behalf) caused Nash to be disqualified and lose his shot at becoming WCW World Champion. Everything came to a head at Spring Stampede. Sting, angered at Savage's betrayal, agreed to put the WCW World Title on the line in order to get the Macho Man in the ring. In the meantime, Hulk Hogan would team with Kevin Nash to face longtime NWO nemesis Roddy Piper and the Giant (who had been chasing Nash since Nash skipped their Starrcade match, then almost crippled [the] Giant with a botched powerbomb at Souled Out) in a baseball bat match. The NWO side got the bat first and Hogan used it to put Piper down for the count, but then Hogan turned on his partner and laid Nash out as well. In addition to his already addressing his issues with Nash, Hogan still had a score to settle with Savage. Any reconciliation between the two men had disappeared the second Savage accepted a shot at the title Hogan perceived to be his. Hogan got involved and, ironically, attempted to help Sting beat Savage by attacking the Macho Man, but Nash got a little revenge on Hogan by

> powerbombing Sting and putting Savage on top for the pin and the WCW World Title.
>
> The official split came the night after Spring Stampede. Hogan came out and announced that the NWO had split in two, and that Nash and Savage had been booted out of Hogan's half (now called NWO Hollywood), and were no longer welcome in the group, then challenged Savage to defend the WCW World Title against him that night. Savage accepted, and they met again in the main event of the evening. After interference from Bret Hart, Hogan had ended his former friend's title reign after only one day, and was again the WCW World Champion. Nash and Savage responded by announcing that they were forming their own faction of the NWO, called NWO Wolfpac. The Wolfpac, which would use red and black colors instead of the traditional black and white that NWO Hollywood was using, already included Nash's partner Scott Hall, and in the weeks following, they recruited Konnan and Curt Hennig to their side, and even managed to draw WCW loyalist Lex Luger to their side as well.
>
> The battle lines were drawn.

That all makes sense to me, or does it?

FACE? nWo? WHAT?

The oft repeated complaint against this is that a face nWo made no sense. Why didn't the nWo members just leave the nWo and join WCW against the Hollywood members? Why would they stay in the nWo?

That's where I bring you back to this point: the nWo was not a "storyline". The nWo was a separate organization (in kayfabe), and they had one mission: to take over the world of professional wrestling. Kevin Nash did not want to just be a fan favorite and win praise; his character was always about winning the big money. As a member of the nWo, he had made the most money in his career. As one of the founding members with Hogan and Hall, he (in kayfabe) was a part owner of the organization. If he walked away from that, he would be giving up all the time and effort and money he had invested in the nWo.

Randy Savage was always a loose cannon, even when he joined the nWo. But he was no WCW loyalist. In his time in WCW, he was always pushed aside in favor of Hogan, and in return Hogan turned against WCW. He was the man who was first to get beaten down by the nWo, he was the one who always paid for the negligence of WCW management. When he joined the nWo, it was in an effort to take over, to take his place, and make WCW pay. Just because his hatred of Hogan was now being backed up by others, it did not change anything. He fought with Hogan while in the nWo because he was nWo. Again, the nWo was an organization, not a stable. They even said at the first Souled Out that they knew one day nWo members would have to wrestle each other, but not before they had taken care of WCW. Until then, they were a team. Unfortunately for the ideal, being a team was not working out. That did not mean, though, that he had given up on the dream of the nWo.

Konnan was a man who was always on the outskirts of the nWo, yet was a major superstar in Mexico. To him, being in Hogan's, or anyone's, shadow was intolerable. He was tired of being pushed to the side, but he knew going back to WCW was not the answer. In WCW he was hardly given much opportunity either, with a rare US title shot here and there. He saw how WCW just brought in his brethren from Mexico, used them to pop the crowd, and then forgot about them. His Latino passion, as is visible in his LAX story at the time of this writing, was on fire then. In order to make a stand, he needed the nWo. They were the best opportunity for him.

Speaking of opportunity, that brings up to Curt Hennig. Hennig was always an opportunist, and ready to switch sides when need be. At first, he thought that with the powerhouses in the Wolfpac, that they were sure to succeed. But it quickly became obvious to him that they were not strategists, and that the nWo Hollywood had the brains. Although he and Rick Rude could have served that function well in the Wolfpac, the Wolfpac had a more, "Let me show you what we can do" attitude than the sneakier Henning would have liked. So he and his friend Rude quickly changed sides back to Hollywood, where their skills were more appreciated. Beside, Hennig sure as hell could not go back to WCW. After turning on the Horsemen, he was completely hated by the remainder of the WCW locker room. There was no place safe for him than back in the hands of the nWo.

And of course, there was the last man to change sides: Scott Hall. It was just taken as automatic that wherever Nash went, Hall would follow. But people forgot that Hall was his own man, and was striving for independence. Hall was able to get his World Title shot because of the nWo, and all the money he ever needed. But it was the infighting of the nWo that caused Scott's title shot to get delayed. Specifically, Savage and Nash continually interfering in the affairs of Hogan and Sting made his shot get put off. And when he had his shot, his so-called brothers were not there to help him. Then the nWo infighting cost him from ever getting a rematch. No, he knew it was Hulk Hogan who gave him his greatest success, and he was prepared to follow him, until he went to rehab.

Henning, Hall, and Rude, though, failed to realize how disarming Kevin Nash was. Without changing a thing about himself, he was able to create an aura of "we're not the sneaky nWo, we're here to help." But Nash never stopped being Nash, as would be demonstrated by the Fingerpoke of Doom at the end of the split. But because he was so disarming, Nash was able to lure away WCW's prize: Lex Luger. For so long, Luger had fought against the nWo and was the face of WCW all summer. But that fight had taken a lot out of him. When he saw the nWo Wolfpac as a changed force, he thought that they could help rebuild WCW. How naïve he was. But Nash used that naiveté to his advantage by slowly manipulating Luger over time to the philosophy of the nWo. That's why, when the nWo merged, Luger was able to follow. He realized that he was fighting the wrong battle, and the nWo was the way to go.

And the last piece of the puzzle: Sting. I'll let 411mania's own Mathew Sforcina cover this one:

> But Sting then decided to focus on fighting the nWo. Thus, he challenged Hall and Nash, The Outsiders, to a match for the tag titles, choosing Giant as his partner, despite the fact that they were nWo Wolfpac, to Sting, the nWo was the nWo.
>
> Then Giant, a bit before the show, joined nWo Hollywood, Hogan's side, because he hated Nash so much. Thus Sting was left in a bit of a bind, but the match had been signed, so he went through with it.
>
> And was then shocked when Hall turned on Nash and he and Giant won the tag titles.
>
> Sting by this time had found a higher power, had become a born again Christian. And thus, when he looked at the three factions, he saw absolutes. He saw that nWo Hollywood was evil. And yet, he saw that WCW was chaos. And thus, that left the middle ground.
>
> And therefore, Sting took it, and joined the nWo Wolfpac, which at the time was the best option, and also had his pal Lex Luger in it.

You see, everyone turned against Sting, and he needed someone to trust. The only person he trusted was Luger. The war with the nWo had left WCW in ruins, and yet each faction of the nWo was strong. He had fought for so long for nothing, so now it was time for him. Enough with being WCW's savior, he just wanted to be with his friends again. And so, Sting became the final piece of the Wolfpac.

THE B-TEAM

Yes, I did just say that the nWo factions were both strong. Because of the compression of time, people often equate nWo Hollywood with the nWo B-team. They are not the same thing! The nWo B-team only came into existence AFTER the nWo Wolfpac and nWo Hollywood merged to become nWo Reunion (Black, White, and Red). Before that, nWo Hollywood was meant to be a devastating force. Let's look at who was in this crew (via Wikipedia):

- Hollywood Hogan – Undeniable World Champion Force
- Eric Bischoff – the brains and the money behind the nWo, still had power in WCW
- Brian Adams – Big huge guy good for backup
- Buff Bagwell – had found a personality and a winning streak in the nWo
- Miss Elizabeth – class defined and a great representative for "other" needs
- The Giant – he's a giant! And a former champ
- The Disciple – a mystery wrapped in an interfering enigma
- Scott Norton – helping to destroy Japan
- Dusty Rhodes – holds the history of the NWA and is connected to everyone
- Dennis Rodman – a cross media star and mainstream draw
- Scott Steiner – an explosion just waiting to happen, on many levels
- Vincent – OK, everyone needs someone to pick on

While not as many super champions as the Wolfpac, Hollywood still had its fair share of power and glory. Besides, Hollywood was designed to make Hogan look good, while the Wolfpac was trying to break out of Hogan's shadow in one way or another.

Of course, the nWo members were not the only ones who found opportunity in the split.

OPPORTUNITY

Because the nWo was feuding with itself, this actually left WCW to have storylines around the other wrestlers in the organization that were not nWo related. The most fruitful of these was the rise of Goldberg.

Over the year, Goldberg has been quietly gaining wins and momentum. People were chanting his name, his popularity was growing. But for the most part, he stayed clear of the nWo. The Wolfpac kept Hollywood in check, and Goldberg was more concerned with his growing streak than having an agenda with the nWo. Of course, this would greatly change by the time the nWo reunited at Starrcade, and even before that when Goldberg took the belt off of Hogan and beat Hall earlier in the evening. But these run ins with the nWo were not the norm for Goldberg, who was the first new wrestler not really involved with the nWo in any discernable way.

Also, Ric Flair returned from suspension and began to bring along Dean Malenko and Chris Benoit more. Though his main feud was with Eric Bischoff, the Horsemen still had separate programs, mostly involving the tag team championships. Eventually, this would morph into the feud of Benoit/Malenko vs. the Mysterio/Kidman, but that was still a bit off. The foundations, though, were built right here.

Booker T took most of 1998 to move away from the tag team ranks and begin his new singles career with the Television Championship. He and Chris Benoit had their memorable Best of Seven series (to get a shot at Finlay!), as well. Meanwhile, Malenko and Jericho continued their feud over the Cruiserweight Championship, which of course paved the way for Jericho to spend an entire commercial break listing out his 1004 moves.

Raven had made his WCW debut and quickly began assembling a flock. This, too, also led into the three-way feud of Raven, Saturn, and Kanyon, and its incredibly strong mix of hardcore and workrate.

Yes, plenty of other people used the nWo feuding with itself to build up what WCW was about. So many say WCW was without direction or characters, but there were a dozen stories and characters listed for you right there. There was a WCW beyond the nWo, though the nWo did have a central role to play.

TOPIC 1: THE END

The number one complaint about the nWo split was that it stopped the nWo from having what it needed: an end. There needed to be some huge blowoff match that would destroy the nWo once and for all.

Well sorry kids, but the nWo was not the Empire, and no one was going to be Luke Skywalker. Han Solo, maybe. But no Skywalker.

Let me ask you this: did the Horsemen ever get their comeuppance? Did someone thoroughly destroy them? What about DX? What about the Dungeon of Doom? What about the Un-Americans? What about the Dudley Family (in ECW)? What about S.E.X.?

None of these stables or organizations ever got the huge blowoff ending that everyone seems to think is possible. We have been conditioned by huge blockbuster movies that once there is a major battle, that's the end of it and everything is fine again. Happily ever after.

You see, in a movie or video game, you can have a huge blowoff and say that is the end. But in a weekly show (or in real life in general), there are consequences for all these actions. Even if there was some elimination style match that the nWo lost that caused them to be over, you would still have the problem of what to do with the guys next. How do you stop them from being the nWo?

Perhaps you recognize the problem. It is what happened during the InVasion. Vince had won the war, but there was a consequence to that: he had to do something with WCW. And once the InVasion was mucked up and he got that victory over the Alliance, there were still more consequences. He still had an additional 60 people sitting around. They could not just suddenly stop being who they were, and he could not suddenly forget what the stipulations of Survivor Series were. Sure, there was one last match, but it really was no ending. It couldn't. There are no endings in wrestling because the people always exist after the fact. Even when someone is retired in a match, at some point they will appear again, and everyone will automatically believe it is time to get revenge for that last match. The blowoff was meaningless because it ends up right where they last were.

I think the best way to look at this is this quote from a song:

"Every new beginning comes from some other beginning's end."

The end of the main WCW vs. nWo storyline was just the beginning of the nWo split. And the nWo split had one obvious end: the nWo reunion. The story did have an ending, it just was not necessarily the expectation that people had. The nWo split ended with the Fingerpoke of Doom. And it is not like that was the end either! That actually led to weeks of 5.0 ratings for WCW, not the destruction that many promised.

The nWo ended abruptly because of unforeseen injuries. Three-quarters of the main players in the nWo in 1999 were out with one injury or another. And then when the nWo reformed a few months later, almost everyone got injured again. THAT is an unforeseen circumstance that cannot be planned for. Who knows? Maybe there could have been something that really ended the nWo in a decisive way, or maybe the nWo was going to exist for another year with a huge storyline. We'll never know because life threw us a curveball.

Still, the nWo split was just phase 3 of the nWo. It prolonged the nWo for a reason: because it was successful and could continue to be so.

BILLIONAIRE TED SAYS...

Even though the nWo split had to eventually reach an end, in the meanwhile it had to be worthwhile. We have previously gone through the storyline and kayfabe reasoning behind the split, but does that make a lick of difference to the average fan?

If you read the IWC today, people will complain about how the nWo split was the downfall of WCW, how it signaled the end of all the hard work everyone had done, and that it was a complete mistake. My first problem with this train of thought is that WCW did not end until 2001, three whole years later. It would take a lot more to kill WCW than that. Back in the case for the Fingerpoke of Doom we saw the same argument, that the fingerpoke destroyed WCW. Yet as noted in that case and above, the Fingerpoke of Doom led to weeks of 5.0+ ratings, hardly the devastating end of WCW.

Well, that's true here as well. Except the nWo split was even more successful than the original nWo! How do I know this? I did the math.

From May through December 1997, during the biggest buildup to the highest payoff match in WCW history (Sting vs. Hollywood Hogan), the average Monday Nitro rating was a 3.8. From May through December 1998, during the turmoil of the nWo split and the rise of the Wolfpac, the average Monday Nitro rating was a 4.4! That's right, the nWo split and other storylines in WCW actually INCREASED interest in WCW, not the opposite. So no, the nWo split did not drive away viewers in droves, but actually brought them to new heights not before seen in WCW or wrestling anywhere.

As a matter of fact, Nitro was the first show to break the 6.0 rating barrier when on August 31, 1998 it scored just that rating. That's right, four months after the nWo split and WCW hit the highest rating mark in its history, a record that would not be broken until March 1, 1999 when RAW scored a 6.3 rating (and WCW still scored a 4.3 that night).

Nitro wasn't always winning ratings, but combined with RAW it was biggest audience ever seen in wrestling. Raw wasn't winning every week either, with wins going back and forth. Everyone likes to talk about the 83-week winning streak for Nitro, but it is not like WCW was dead the week they lost one to RAW. There was a long period of back and forth, and an even longer period when Nitro was getting big ratings, larger than those seen in the nWo vs. Sting storyline, but they just weren't as huge as RAW's numbers. We talked about it a number of times, but in those days when Nitro scored less than a 4.5 it was considered a terrible sign and that nobody watched WCW anymore. Here in 2006, when RAW scores a 4.0 rating it is seen as a huge triumph. Recently to this writing, SmackDown! scored a 2.2 rating. It does not seem so bad in retrospect.

Anyway, even though more people were watching WCW than ever because of the nWo split, did that necessarily translate into more dollars? Well, there's one sure fire quick look: let's browse the PPV buyrates for about the same period listed above.

WCW PPV Buyrates

WCW PPV	1997	1998
Spring Stampede	0.58	0.72
Slamboree	0.44	0.44
Great American Bash	0.60	0.75
Bash at the Beach	0.78	1.50
Road Wild	0.65	0.91
Fall Brawl	0.53	0.70
Halloween Havoc	1.10	0.78
World War III	0.56	0.75
Starrcade	1.90	1.15

In total the winners are...

- 1997 = 2
- 1998 = 6
- Tie = 1

That's right, PPV buyrates actually WENT UP for the most part in 1998 with the nWo split, much higher than during the Sting vs. nWo storyline. True, the summer of 1998 was bolstered by mainstream media attention, but why do you think people like Jay Leno and Dennis Rodman would even consider getting involved in WCW? Because WCW was huge, and the nWo split was a captivating and interesting focus for all of WCW.

I also personally know how much impact the Wolfpac made on my wallet. At that time, I was selling many wrestling shirts at the flea market. Some sold OK, some did not move, but there was one shirt I could never keep in: The Wolfpac. It wasn't even that greatly designed, and looking at it now, it is actually rather embarrassing. Yet that was the biggest seller by far. I still see nWo Wolfpac and Hollywood shirts, license plates, bumper stickers, flags, and everything else around today. The nWo cemented its legacy in its own personal war, and the monetary and cultural impacts are still prevalent today.

What did it all do in the end?

Besides the faded shirts that are around today, the nWo split began something that we see now. Even though the nWo had made it cool to cheer the "bad guy", the split made it possible for someone to be the true anti-hero. With a face Wolfpac, others could more readily be accepted as faces. Austin was already well on his way up in the WWE, but the Wolfpac turning face made his job much easier. DX was able to become an effective face unit because the Wolfpac had paved the way (poetic, considering the membership). Even in 2006, people like Eddie Guerrero could cheat to win, while someone who wanted to play by the rules was booed. Chavo Guerrero helped Rey Mysterio cheat on SmackDown!, yet people loved him for it.

True, the nWo was just a reflection of the changing times that Eric Bischoff was able to capture. But once people were able to accept the bad guys as good, it became easier to flip everything.

Also, the idea of a long-term storyline with a twist took center-hold. Look at a storyline like Test/Steiner, or Jericho/Christian/Trish/Lita, or even Edge/Hardy/Kane/Lita. A story can have many lives with the same characters, and it is a storytelling device still very much in use today. Is it always used correctly or effectively? Probably not, but the inspiration is the key in this case.

Additionally, the impact of the nWo and the split is still being seen today. In Japan, the invasion storyline continues with many of the same people, yet just a slightly different name. Here in 2006, ECW keeps invading RAW, and vice versa. ECW isn't really ECW of old, it's a new twist on the nWo. And with people jumping and moving apart, it's the same idea as the split. You have your mega-powers, just with a slightly different flavor.

No, the impact of the nWo split is quite obvious today, and will be for years to come.

TAKE OUT THE SPRAY PAINT ONE MORE TIME

Since the day the nWo formed, there was a thought that there had to be some huge ending, some insane blowup to finally put the idea to rest. Instead, the nWo used the ending of a year and half storyline to launch a new direction: a split. The ideas were sound in kayfabe, and that translated into a success in ratings and buyrates. Each nWo faction was strong and driving interest in WCW, while also allowing time for the rest of WCW to develop and catch up. In actuality, the nWo split did more to increase ratings, buyrates, and merchandise sales than even the original nWo did. After all, if you couldn't decide your loyalties, didn't you need two different color shirts?

Today, the effects of the nWo split are seen everywhere, from storylines to character development. Although the compression of time makes us forget just how long and interesting the nWo split was, and everything that came out of it (and what happened at later points in time), we cannot lose the knowledge of the true success the nWo split.

The defense rests.

AFTER THE TRIAL

HUNG JURY

IN THE CASE OF THE IWC VS. THE NWO SPLIT, THE NWO SPLIT HAS BEEN ACCUSED OF BEING A TERRIBLE MISTAKE IN WCW THAT LEAD TO THE END OF THE PROMOTION. IT WAS A WASTE OF TIME THAT HURT WCW AND THE REST OF THE WRESTLERS ON THE ROSTER, AND ONLY SERVED TO FURTHER BEAT A DEAD HORSE.

And with 76.2% of the vote, the nWo Split was found:

NOT GUILTY!

Another one... for the good guys. I love being able to use that phrase whenever we do an nWo related case. Anyway, that was all for the nWo 10-year anniversary!

RESPONSE

Whether people voted one way or another, there were a couple of comments that I felt deserved some additional exploration:

> [Here's] my problem with the NWO Split. The first is that you already had a WCW vs. NWO [feud]. Why not just put the Wolfpack guys back on team WCW? Why not let team WCW actually look credible for a change? Why do you need a third element to overshadow the main [feud] of WCW vs. NWO?
>
> **Rick Funcannon**

Don't forget that the nWo guys were "Outsiders" and had no loyalty or desire to be in WCW. They—especially in case of Nash—made more money being in the nWo and had more control over their matches and careers (at least from a kayfabe perspective). What benefit would they have to being in WCW with guys who hated them for everything they previously did? Also, how does WCW look good by absorbing the nWo guys and basically becoming the nWo? Isn't that exactly what happened in the InVasion when the Alliance took in WWE guys? Would not WCW actually just become nWo-lite and the storyline would end with the same anti-climactic fizzle?

> [Y]ou said episodic television couldn't have a final battle. Where the good guy wins at the end and the bad guy disappears. Not true bro. It's true for pro wrestling, but not true for episodic television in general.
>
> Look at most anime, or Japanimation if you will. God knows how many times Goku and his friends conquered evil in Dragon Ball, Dragon Ball Z, and Dragon Ball GT. I could also point out Full Metal Panic, any of the Gundam series, Yu Yu Hakusho, RuRouni Kenshin, etc. Take care man.
>
> **-Chuck B.**

Oh, you mean like how Goku defeated Piccolo Jr. and Tien Shinhan at the end of Dragon Ball, and how both became his allies in Dragon Ball Z? Or how the same happened with Vegeta in Dragon Ball Z to the point where Vegeta (who tried to murder everyone on Earth) married Goku's close friend and had two kids with her? Or how Majin Buu—who tried to eliminate all life in the universe—became a goofy companion to Mr. Satan and spent most of his time sleeping in Dragon Ball Super? Or like how Goku had a final climatic battle with Frieza on Planet Namek and then a short time later at the beginning of the Android Saga Frieza showed back up with a robotic body, and then after being killed and brought back multiple times has been both an enemy and an ally to Goku and team in several arcs?

I think I made my point: if you have something episodic—especially something that has a new episode/issue every single week—the stories can never have a true end. Sure, Goku and Frieza had a massive "5-minute" battle to end that particular storyline, but that just led into the next storyline arc. And worse, as time went on, the writers were obviously not as prepared as they were for the first big storyline, so there were diminishing returns in each successive pass. Gohan's arc was complete when he overcame his passivist ways to defeat Perfect Cell, but his character could not just be removed in the storylines to follow. As such, he became something less because the show must continue!

JEFF JARRETT

INTRO

SOME DAME WALKED INTO MY OFFICE AND SAID...

Our story begins a long, long time ago with a man named **JS**:

> *My case is Jeff Jarrett.*
>
> *I have been a huge fan of his ever since we started calling him J-E- Double F, J-A- Double R-E- --- Double T! Yet, it seems that every so-called smart fan on the net has it in for him. He seems to be the most hated guy this side of Triple H. And all I want to know is WHY? What has he ever done? He has always been the blueprint for a cocky heel, good on the mic, excellent in the ring, and could carry any feud.*
>
> *And I know a lot of the complaints are about how he is dominating TNA, but even when the WWF didn't pick up his contract during the [InVasion], no one shed a tear for him. So my question is, can you defend him? Or at least tell me why he's such a bad guy.*

Next up was 411mania's (sort of) own **John Dee** with:

> *I'm telling you now though dude, if you ever want to lose a case, take on the one I dared you to do - defending... Jarrett's never ending title runs. I don't think it could be done.*

After that is was **Mark Radulich** with:

> *In Defense of Jeff Jarrett - TNA Champion (I actually know what the complaints are and I think these people are full of crap, I'd love to see man defended).*

But that wasn't enough for **Rick Cobos**:

> Jeff Jarrett: TNA's constant "main attraction" regardless of who the TNA champ is.

Still with more was **Jon Foye** and this synopsis:

> I have a case I would love to see. Everyone in the IWC seems to knock Jeff Jarrett; saying he does not deserve the NWA title, that he uses his backstage stroke to regain the belt at the expense of others, and that he is not a great wrestler. This comes despite the fact that the man is a consummate professional, has been in the business ALL HIS LIFE, and is great at manipulating a crowd.

And then **Aaron Dorman** had to add this:

> Defend Jeff Jarrett. All folks ever do is crap on him, but ignore the fact that Austin held him down and how over he was in his last WWF run, not to mention that he was really the last great star of the territories.

But what about **Jason from Brooklyn, NY**? What did he say:

> I think you should do an in defense of Jeff Jarrett, he's probably the most hated man in wrestling today, due to supposedly keepin' himself on top, which is part of what I think makes him an effective heel.

Daniel Norman has less loving reasons for me to defend Jarrett:

> I'd love to see and try you defend Jeff Jarrett.
>
> The guy is only a multiple time world champion because during WCW's demise they threw the belt at anyone (see: Russo, Vince and Arquette, David)

> *and his daddy owns TNA. Even when he is not the NWA champion in TNA he is always trying to turn the focus to him. I might watch TNA more often if Jarrett wasn't pulling a HHH times 10. The stroke is a crappy finisher and he is not the wrestling god he seems to think he is, that's JBL's role!*

Plus there was... what? Oh, that's all Stenographer found on a quick search. But the Jarrett comments have been everywhere, which makes him a perfect candidate for In Defense Of...!

WHY THIS?

Jeff Jarrett. There are few people today more vilified by the IWC crowd than this man. TNA, whose audience his heavily hardcore internet wrestling fans, is faced with the dilemma of their hometown audience pelting the ring with garbage at the site of him. Despite being on a much smaller stage, the hatred for Jeff Jarrett in many ways surpasses those of Triple H, a man despised for marring the boss' daughter and always finding his way back to the championship when others seem more worthy.

Jeff Jarrett is the villain of the internet generation. He's part owner of the organization that he is champion of. He is the center of storylines and television above the homegrown talent. He is highly paid in a land where few are making money. He is screamed at constantly to not appear on TV, yet there he is every week.

But does Jarrett deserve all this hatred from the internet crowd? What has he really done to deserve the enmity of so many? And is this opinion shared by the rest of the kayfabe world, or is this just another instance of the IWC thinking it is better than anyone else who watches wrestling?

We will explore the life and times of Jeff Jarrett and find out what really makes this guy tick. We'll look at his record and accusations and find out if Jarrett is really a devastating force for professional wrestling, or a misunderstood hero who should be applauded for all he does and each and every day.

WHERE DID WE GET THIS COUNTRY BUMPKIN?

I liked the way Aaron Dorman described Jeff Jarrett above: "[H]e was really the last great star of the territories." This could not more accurately describe the early life of Jeff Jarrett. To understand the character and the person, to begin to relate to his actions, we must first explore his past and truly delve into what made Jeff Jarrett into the person he is today.

That means that our story will begin on April 14, 1967 in a well-known town called Nashville, TN. Actually, it starts a little before that.

You see, to understand Jeff Jarrett, you first need to understand his father: Jerry Jarrett. From Wikipedia:

> Born into poverty, Jerry Jarrett was exposed to the wrestling business at a very early age. His mother worked as a ticket vendor, and Jarrett began selling programs for a promotion owned by Roy Welch and Nick Gulas at the age of seven. After receiving his driving license at fourteen, he became a wrestling promoter, renting buildings, advertising shows, constructing the ring, selling tickets, and stocking refreshments. He worked as a promoter until he left Nashville to attend college. Upon graduating, Jarrett worked for Welch and Gulas as an office assistant, and became a referee by default after a referee no-showed. He soon returned to promoting, working his way up from local promotions to regional, then national promotions.
>
> While working as a referee, Jarrett decided to become a wrestler, and was trained by his friend and future tag team partner Tojo Yamamoto and veteran wrestler Sailor Moran, and wrestled his first match in Haiti in 1965.
>
> Jarrett became a successful wrestler in the South, particularly in his home state of [Tennessee], forming tag teams with Jackie Fargo and Tojo Yamamoto. At one point he participated in the extremely hazardous Scaffold Match.
>
> Jarrett operated multiple wrestling promotions throughout his career, including Mid-Southern Wrestling, the Continental Wrestling Association, the United States Wrestling Association, World Class Championship Wrestling and, most recently, Total Nonstop Action Wrestling. Jarrett was often the business partner of Jerry Lawler. In the 1970s, Jarrett began televising his shows.

And that is what Jeff Jarrett grew up in as well. Unlike many second and third generation stars (The Rock, Shawn Stasiak, Randy Orton, Bret Hart, Owen Hart, Rey Mysterio, Eddie Guerrero, Chavo Guerrero, Villano IV, Villano V,

Carlito, BG James, etc...), Jarrett was exposed to all facets of the business at an early age. He understood the needs of booking and storytelling, of selling tickets and captivating the crowd. While many of these others learned from their forbearers how to wrestle, they did not learn the secrets behind the business.

But Jarrett did. His education began behind the scenes. So when the question comes up (and it will later) what did Jeff ever know about running an organization, the answer is he was born into it. He was a part of his father's organizations and learned from him. Of course, it was an old-school territory-based system, and Jeff knew he had to be different to succeed. But we'll return to that later.

Anyway, much like his father, Jeff's first steps into the ring were in the referee's shoes. From Mathew Sforcina's Evolution Schematic of Jeff Jarrett (Part 1):

> *Jeff started his career following his father's footsteps directly, becoming a referee in the CWA, also known as the Mid-South Territory. But he quickly gave up being the law to become a wrestler.*

This could also be pretty close to the story of Shane McMahon, who learned the business and actually was a referee in the early 1990s. But unlike Shane, he was neither content to sit backstage nor just help the wrestlers out. He wanted to be a part of the spectacle. He wanted to learn to be the best.

So in CWA Jarrett began to hone his craft. Much like the Guerreros, Mysterios, Harts, and the like before him, Jarrett had really been training to be a wrestler since he was quite young. That is why it is no surprise that Jarrett was able to capture his first title when he was just 19 years old. From Accelerator3359:

> *Jarrett's first title reign came in August '86, when he teamed with Pat Tanaka to win the CWA International Tag-Team Titles from Akio Sato & Tarzan Goto. Sato & Goto won the belts back a week later. Jarrett, undeterred, found himself a new partner in Paul Diamond, and got the belts for the second time in November '86. Once again, Sato & Goto won them back.*

As a tag-team specialist, Jarrett then moved on to the AWA for a short while before making an appearance in the USWA Southern Title Tournament. Much like Larry Zbyszko before him, his mentors felt it best that he travel many territories to flesh out his ability. Although skilled in the ring and on the mic, and having a crucial understanding of the business behind the scenes, Jarrett was still young and in need of seasoning and experience. He accepted this advice and continued to try to build a path all his own. His work was recognized when in May 1987 he captured his first single's title by defeating Moondog Spot to win the NWA Mid-American Heavyweight Championship.

Jarrett's time soon was split between CWA, NWA, USWA, and WCWA (World Class in Texas with the Von Erichs). But times were changing. At this point, the WWF had become a huge national promotion and was destroying the territory system once and for all. JCP/WCW, the largest of the NWA territories, was losing money hand over fist despite being wildly more popular in the south than the cartoony WWF. That popularity made little difference in the effectiveness of running a promotion. The other territories knew they had to combine or die. So in 1989, the WCWA (where Jarrett was) was sold into USWA, and a new chapter was born.

WIN A TITLE, LOSE A TITLE, WIN A TITLE, LOSE A TITLE...

During all this time, Jarrett was winning and losing titles on a regular basis. As was the Southern booking style at the time, a title reign of two months was considered a grand success. Jarrett had most of his wins in tag action, but also spent a good deal of time around mid-card singles titles. Also, you must know that Jarrett was a beloved babyface during most of this period. Not because he was forcing it on the fans or that his father was booking for him, but because the fans were cheering him and wanted him to win. Jarrett had many years as a face and experience at being one that made him believe he could do it again. While the argument can be made that he is much more effective as a heel, Jarrett's own experience shows that he knows how to be a strong babyface and has the potential to be one again.

Anyway, with the 80's moving into the 90's, Jarrett found a new partner and mentor who also saw him as a future superstar: Jerry Lawler. From Accelerator3359:

> *In February '91, Jarrett found the ultimate partner in Jerry "The King" Lawler, who basically ruled over the USWA. They beat the Fabulous Ones for the USWA World Tag-Team Titles in February '91. But March turned out to be a bad month for Jarrett, as he would both lose the Southern Heavyweight Title to Tom Pritchard and fell to the Texas Hangmen (with Eddie Gilbert, recently returned, subbing for Lawler). As he always had done, Jarrett kept fighting, returning to beat Pritchard in a rematch for the Southern Heavyweight Title in April. The belt was held up a few days later, but Jarrett quickly won another*

> rematch, getting the belt for a fifth time. He would finally lose the belt for the last time to Eric Embry in May '91.
>
> Shortly thereafter, when Robert Fuller was turned on by his Studs, Jarrett remarkably came to his aid, forming a team with him. They quickly showed their skills by beating the Texas Hangmen for the USWA Tag-Team Titles. In June '91, the two also defeated Samu & Judge Dredd, which allowed them to unify the USWA Tag-Team and Western States Tag-Team Titles. They later lost the belts to the Barroom Brawlers, only to come back and get them a week later (a common thread, if you hadn't noticed). Two months later, the Brawlers, now known as the Texas Outlaws, retook the belts. Once again Jarrett & Fuller came back quickly and got the belts, for Jarrett's 9th reign with the USWA World Tag-Team Titles. In November '91, they lost the belts to Doug Masters & Bart Sawyer, and later broke up.
>
> Jarrett later teamed up with Jerry "The King" Lawler again, beating Moondogs Spot & Spike to get the Tag-Team Titles in June '92. After a week, Spot came back with Cujo as his partner, and stole the belts. It didn't take long for Jarrett & Lawler to get them back, but a month later, the Moondogs struck again, taking them in August. A week later, Jarrett & Lawler, for the fourth time as a team, became USWA Tag-Team Champion. In October '92, though, Lawler was forced to fight alone, when Jarrett reportedly had 'car trouble'. Lawler was beaten by Moondogs Spot & Spike, ending the title reigns. The feud between Jarrett/Lawler & the Moondogs was later named Feud of the Year by PWI Magazine.

How times have changed, eh? A tag team feud in an organization that was really no bigger than ECW at its prime (original ECW, not the WWE version) was honored in such a way. When was the last time any tag team feud came close to that? Edge/Christian vs. Dudleys vs. Hardy Boyz? Maybe. But we are talking about a feud that really put butts in seats, that sold tickets and kept the USWA afloat.

After this time, Jarrett also had a feud with Brian Christopher. Better known today as "Grand Master Sexy", Christopher was also son of the king of the USWA, Jerry Lawler. But during their feud, it was Jarrett who got the final dupe and most of the victories. That's right, Lawler let his own son be used to prop Jarrett up, that is how much potential and upside he saw in Jeff.

Also during this period (and a little earlier), Jarrett was a nine-time holder of the Southern Heavyweight Championship. In one match he had the title was held up, and later he won the rematch. Jarrett's opponent in this match would not forget this indignity, as he felt he was being held back in his young career. He would feel this way again in another organization that would lead to his firing, and he would have similar feelings later in the organization he had the most success in, and subsequently walked out on twice. That man's name was Steve Austin. And we'll get back to him later.

With time moving on, the power of the WWF began to wane as well. With Hulk Hogan leaving the WWF in 1993, the organization was in need of a new direction and fresh blood. They were aware of Jeff Jarrett because of an earlier inter-promotional feud that went nowhere. From Obsessed with Wrestling:

> *August 9, 1992: Jeff Jarrett participated in the first ever WWF/USWA [Inter-promotional] storyline.*
> *~~~USWA wrestlers Jerry Lawler & Jeff Jarrett were seated in the front row at ringside at a WWF card.*
> *~~~Jerry Lawler & Jeff Jarrett were upset that the WWF were running shows in their territory.*
> *~~~During the card, Jeff Jarrett challenged Intercontinental Champion Bret Hart to a title match.*
> *~~~Bret Hart replied that if he were to retain the IC title after Summerslam, then Jeff Jarrett would be next in line.*
> *~~~The angle was dropped when Davey Boy Smith defeated Bret Hart for the Intercontinental title at Summerslam*

Despite this story going nowhere, the WWF was incredibly impressed with Jarrett and decided they wanted him on the roster. They saw him as a possible future for the organization. From Accelerator3359:

> *Jarrett continued to climb up the ladder, managing to pin Jerry "The King" Lawler during a Battle Royal to become the USWA Unified World Heavyweight Champion. Lawler soon came back to regain the belt, something he did many, many times in the USWA. With 1993 running out, Jarrett was given the chance to head out of Memphis to try on the world, as a major trade took place between the USWA and the World Wrestling*

> Federation, who wanted to gain Jarrett's services. They gave up a lot of their lower-ranked talent, including "Hacksaw" Jim Duggan, Papa Shango, & the Orient Express, to acquire Jarrett's talent.

Did you read that? The WWF literally gave up four people just to get Jarrett. If that is not a vote of confidence, I don't know what is.

J-E-double F J-A-double R-E-double T. Double J, Jeff Jarrett

It was 1993. Jarrett had been wrestling for seven years and had found his way to the grandest stage of them all: the WWF. Although his father may have cursed Vince McMahon's name for destroying his territory, Jeff was a man of his own and knew that this was one opportunity he could not refuse.

Now, one would think that because Jarrett was such a hot prospect that he would be allowed to continue to do what made him so successful is the USWA. Everyone from Eddie Gilbert to Jerry Lawler saw that Jarrett had the potential to be a great true to life character, a man of southern pride and tradition.

That's not what Vince McMahon saw. Based on the evidence that Vince said he never saw in ECW show before One Night Stand, one can believe that he never saw Jeff Jarrett perform before he showed up in the WWF. Because of that, Vince heard "Southern" and thought "Country Singer"! Jeff Jarrett became "Double J" and was trying to use the WWF to launch his country music career. From the kayfabe friendly Evolution Schematic of Jeff Jarrett (Part 2):

> [H]e started to tell the world who he was ("J-E-Double-F, J-A-Double-R-E-Double-T, Double-J, Jeff Jarrett"), and what he wanted to do (Use the WWF as a platform to launch his music career in a specialized music genre... this is sounding more and more normal). But while many people felt a little confused by this, it did give Jeff one key that would stick with him for the rest of his career.
>
> No-one would blink twice when he walked down to ringside with a guitar.
>
> Jeff began his WWF career earning the crowd's ire, since he was such an asshole about his singing and wrestling talent. Plus his insistence on spelling out his name made people think he was insulting their intelligence.

Yet despite embracing the gimmick and being an important prospect, Jeff Jarrett seemed forgotten about. From Accelerator3359:

> [A]lthough his gimmick attracted attention, Jarrett did not move quickly into WWF stardom. He competed in the 1994 Royal Rumble, but was quickly tossed over the top rope by "Macho Man" Randy Savage. Jarrett continued to work on his image for the next few months, building up a small reputation. He entered the '94 King of the Ring Tournament, and made his first impact, surprisingly beating Lex Luger in the qualifying round. Unfortunately, he was defeated at the PPV in the first match by the 1-2-3 Kid (Sean Waltman).
>
> Jarrett's first major pay-per-view match occurred at Summerslam '94, when he faced up against the heavyweight, Mabel (later known as Viscera). After five minutes of battling back and forth, Mabel went for a sit-down splash on Jarrett, but Double J dodged, then made the quick pin, scoring his first WWF PPV victory. Jarrett then went on as a member of the Teamsters at the '94 Survivor Series. Teaming with Owen Hart, Diesel (Kevin Nash), "The Heartbreak Kid" Shawn Michaels, and Jim "The Anvil" Neidhart, the Teamsters faced off against the Bad Guys, which consisted of Razor Ramon (Scott Hall), "The British Bulldog" Davey Boy Smith, the 1-2-3 Kid (Waltman), and the Headshrinkers, Fatu (Rikishi) & Sionne (the Barbarian). Diesel proved to be a major force, eliminating Fatu, the 1-2-3 Kid, and Sionne. Later, Davey Boy Smith was counted out, making it 5-on-1. However, disputes among the ranks caused the Teamsters to all be counted out, giving the victory to Ramon.

This, though, would be very helpful as Jeff Jarrett would finally have a spotlight put on him... over a year after being recruited by the WWF...

Top of the Top... Nah, I've Had Enough

Finally the WWF was seeing Jarrett as Jarrett: a cocky southern wrestler with an attitude. Despite the long hair and funny singing, the fans were booing

Jarrett and McMahons saw that they could actually use him. From Accelerator3359:

> Jarrett continued his battles with Ramon, signing a match to face him for his Intercontinental Title at the '95 Royal Rumble. Ramon was injured, though, and during the match was tossed from the ring, where he was counted out. Jarrett got the win, but not the belt, and immediately began challenging Ramon's courage. Ramon opted to come back to the ring despite the pain, and the match started again. In the end, Ramon fell while trying to execute his Razor's Edge finisher, allowing Jarrett to get the pin and become the Intercontinental Champion. Ramon continued to challenge Jarrett in the next few months, but Jarrett enlisted the help of the Roadie (BG James) to help him stay the champion. At WrestleMania XI, Jarrett & Ramon faced in a rematch, which ended in a Disqualification loss for Jarrett due to the Roadie. However, this made sure that Jarrett retained the Intercontinental Title.
>
> In April '95, in a match against Bob "Sparkplug" Holly, Jarrett was surprisingly pinned, apparently losing the IC strap. However, video later showed that Jarrett's foot was on the ropes in time, which put the belt [up] in the air. Later on that night, Jarrett & Holly fought again, this time with Jarrett getting the victory, regaining the Intercontinental Championship. Jarrett continued to feud with Ramon, and in May '95, Ramon finally won the belt back over him. A few shows later, Jarrett won out again, getting the IC belt for the third time. Ramon finally challenged both Jarrett & the Roadie to a handicap match at In Your House I, where Ramon won out in the end despite the odds.

At first, things were going great for Jarrett. He was doing well, had an iron grip on the title (like many great IC champs before him), someone to follow him around, and wins over someone considered the top echelon of the business. He got to fight with a future legend in Shawn Michaels, and it seemed everyone was ready for him to continue working.

Yet despite doing everything he was told, despite strongly carrying a title, and despite getting the fans to hate him, someone in the WWF lost faith in him, and it all came crumbling down quickly. As if that handicap match loss wasn't bad enough of a burial, he was quickly knocked out of the King of the Ring in decisive fashion and had the Roadie turn on him and reveal Jarrett's singing ability was his. Jarrett realized that there may be nothing for him in the WWF and returned to the USWA for a period, defeating Ahmed Johnson for the USWA Unified Title in December 1995.

The WWF officials were impressed with the feud and copied it for WWF television with the two wrestlers. But after Royal Rumble 1996, Jarrett and the WWF got into a contract dispute (Jarrett obviously thinking he deserved more and should be pushed as a champion, the WWF thinking that they were losing so much money to WCW they didn't know what to do), Jarrett returned to the USWA. He thought that perhaps he and Vince could work out a deal, but in the meanwhile he feuded with Lawler for the title and then drove Jesse James (BG James/ Roadie/ Road Dog) out of the USWA. That was a good enough run for Jarrett, and negotiations with Vince failed. So with that, there was only one really good place to go.

WHERE THE BIG BOYS PLAY

Jarrett then signed a one-year deal with Eric Bischoff and WCW. This had to be a very surprising move, as everyone was signing multi-year deals for a lot of money. But Jarrett knew his greatest commodity was himself, and he wanted to make sure he was worth it. The WWF had robbed him of a lot of his shine towards the end of his run, and he knew that anything else like that could only diminish his value. His instincts from his territorial days took over, and he wanted to protect his image, trusting very few. But that distrust was unwarranted, as he was involved in a long storyline and very interesting program for the rest of 1996. From Accelerator3359:

> Jarrett appeared in WCW in October '96, demanding to be a part of the [Four] Horsemen, who were currently battling against the nWo. To prove his seriousness, Jarrett challenged one of the most dominating wrestlers, the Giant (the Big Show). At Halloween Havoc '96, the Giant dominated Jarrett, who still fought as hard as he could. In the end, though, the match was decided by Ric Flair, who attacked the Giant, causing the disqualification. Jarrett continued to challenge the Giant, while also insulting Sting, who he thought was cowardly for not fighting the nWo. At World War III '96, Jarrett took on the Giant again, and Sting appeared, attacking Jarrett for his comments. This helped the Giant get the easy victory. Later that night, Jarrett was tossed out in the World War III Battle Royal. He also competed in the WCW United States Title Tournament in

> November, but fell in the first round to Diamond Dallas Page.
>
> After various encounters with the [Four] Horsemen, Jarrett was finally given his chance. If he could defeat Chris Benoit at Starrcade '96, he would be allowed into the Horsemen. During the match-up, Kevin Sullivan, Benoit's major adversary, appeared, interfering in the match. Jarrett took advantage, getting the victory and finally getting what he wanted, a spot in the [Four] Horsemen. Jarrett then teamed up with Steve "Mongo" McMichael for a time, while he joined in the feud against the nWo, battling against Mr. Wallstreet.

Aside from the interesting storyline and wrestlers he was involved in, I want you to notice something else. Jarrett was a heel, trying to get into a face organization, to fight other heels. You see, Jarrett was in a true tweener storyline, where few had gone before. It wasn't about the face/heel lines, it was about being true to his character. Wrestlers were given a lot more leeway in WCW, and Jarrett used this time to flesh out who he wanted to be. Ric Flair was equally impressed and allowed him to become a member of the Horsemen, seeing in Jarrett what other legends saw as well: championship material.

As 1996 moved into 1997, Jarrett would live on fast forward feuding with the nWo, Public Enemy, Dean Malenko, and former partners Steve McMichael and Chris Benoit. From Obsessed with Wrestling:

> - *Uncensored 1997: Jarrett/Piper/Benoit/McMichael vs Hogan/Nash/Hall/Savage vs Luger/Giant/Steiner - 3-WAY Elimination match.*
>
> - *Spring Stampede 1997: Public Enemy defeated Jeff Jarrett & Steve McMichael.*
>
> - *Slamboree 1997: Dean Malenko defeated Jeff Jarrett by Submission to retain the United States title.*
>
> - *June 9, 1997 - Monday Nitro: Jeff Jarrett defeated Dean Malenko to win the United States title.*
>
> - *Jeff Jarrett was kicked out of the [Four] Horsemen and started a feud with former partner Steve "Mongo" McMichael.*

> - *Bash at the Beach 1997: Jeff Jarrett defeated Steve McMichael to retain the United States title when Debra turned on Mongo.*
>
> - *Road Wild 1997: Chris Benoit & Steve McMichael defeated Jeff Jarrett & Dean Malenko in an Elimination match.*
>
> - *August 21, 1997: Steve McMichael defeated Jeff Jarrett to win the United States title.*
>
> - *Fall Brawl 1997: Jeff Jarrett defeated Dean Malenko.*
>
> - *October 6, 1997 - Monday Nitro: Jeff Jarrett wrestled his last WCW match losing to Booker T.*

Quite an eventful few months. Also note that it was in WCW that Jarrett and Debra teamed up, not in the WWF. Another idea that was originated elsewhere that was not the WWF's or Vince's doing. And also note that Jarrett left WCW the right way, losing a match and putting someone else over. This will become a recurring story for Jarrett.

After not re-signing with WCW, Jarrett quickly returned to the WWF, using the momentum of his WCW run to propel him to greater heights. You see, sometimes in life you can only get promoted or move up the ladder by jumping around. Jarrett understood this and realized he was only as valuable as where he last was, and intended to make himself worth more.

The WWF, too, was going through a major change, and upheaval was happening over and over again.

WWF... ERRR... NWA... NO, I WAS RIGHT THE FIRST TIME

Jarrett began his new WWF career by continuing to show "attitude" before such a word existed. You see, the WCW/nWo feud had decimated the WWF and they were desperate to try anything. McMahon, though, was not yet ready to let the creative juices flow, but little cracks were forming. Jarrett actually had a sit-down shoot-style interview with JR where he bashed Eric Bischoff. And as was the (Vince Russo) style at the time, anything semi-shoot was made into a work. Jarrett also began to refuse his WWF matches as part of his gimmick.

After a battle with the Undertaker, though, Vince quickly gave up on this idea and Jarrett, too. Instead, Vince tried to copy WCW again and have an invasion by the NWA with Jarrett leading the fray. This, though, would never get much steam behind it because Vince refused to allow any other organization to look good inside his own, and he just could not get behind Jarrett. From the kayfabe friendly Evolution Schematic of Jeff Jarrett (Part 3) from 411mania's own Mathew Sforcina:

> Suffice to say, Cornette was trying to do an NWA invasion, or at least trying to bring the WWF back into the NWA fold. He first turned to Barry Windham, who had a great deal of affinity for NWA, as the guy to lead the charge. Cornette also brought in Tag Team Legends The Rock N Roll Express. But then when Jeff Jarrett pinned Windham to win the NWA North American Title on Dec 30th, 1997, Cornette dumped Windham and took on Jarrett as his main star and client.
>
> Jarrett and Cornette made a decent team (they had to when the Rock N Roll Express were quickly fired from the company). They removed Owen Hart from the 98 Royal Rumble before he got to the ring, right?
>
> Oh yeah, when Jarrett came in Owen ran back out and threw him out almost immediately.
>
> But he could put a good showing on at the special event of 'Raw Saturday Night' right? That would get respect for the NWA and thus Jarrett, right?
>
> Of course, few people would consider losing via pinfall to D'Lo Brown in under 2 minutes any sort of success.
>
> And in his first title defense on WWF PPV (the first time in WWF history that an NWA title was defended on WWF PPV) he got DQed for using Cornette's ever present tennis racket on Bradshaw, who at that point was just another Texas brawler and not a Wrestling God.
>
> This disillusioned Jarrett so much that he dumped the NWA title, ditched Cornette and reverted back to the last mindset that was successful.

As you can see, Jarrett made a mistake. Unlike his short-term contract in WCW to protect his reputation, Jeff Jarrett signed on for a two-year tour of duty with the WWF. Not long by the standard contracts at the time (Mark Henry signed for ten years), but still long enough to do damage. Despite the end of the NWA angle, Jarrett was then given his old country music singer gimmick and was managed by Tennessee Lee. This, too, lead him to tagging with "Southern Justice". It seemed like Jarrett was doomed to play one Southern stereotype after another if he stayed in the WWF. Yet, it seemed hope was around the corner. From Accelerator3359:

> *Jarrett next feuded with X-Pac and his allies in DeGeneration-X, leading up to a signed "Hair vs. Hair" match at Summerslam '98. Before the PPV, at Sunday Night Heat, Jarrett & Southern Justice attacked ring announcer Howard "The Fink" Finkle, shaving him bald, and promising to do the same to X-Pac. Due to this attack, however, Southern Justice was banned from ringside for the match-up. Both wrestlers fought hard for their long locks, but in the end, X-Pac was able to knock out Jarrett with his own guitar, scoring the victory. Afterwards, with Jarrett only semi-conscious, each member of Degeneration-X (including a one-night DX member, Finkle) took turns shaving off most of Jarrett's long blond locks. Jarrett would later reform the hair style into a crew-cut, a style which he kept, rather than growing it long again. Jarrett & Southern Justice later faced X-Pac & the New Age Outlaws at Breakdown '98, with the DeGeneration-X members again winning out.*
>
> *In October '98, Jarrett [began] a feud with Al Snow, which led to Snow costing Jarrett to lose in the first round of the WWF Intercontinental Title Tournament to X-Pac. Jarrett and Snow continued to feud for the next few weeks, leading up to the '98 Survivor Series, where they faced each other in the first round of the WWF World Title Tournament. Unfortunately for Jarrett, Al Snow's 'teammate' was also around: Head. Snow knocked out Jarrett with Head to get the pinfall victory, moving on in the tournament while Jarrett was forced to watch from the back, another title opportunity missed.*

Again, Jarrett did everything for the company, and they even promoted him as the "new attitude" Jarrett. Yet, the WWF machine failed to take up the point that Jarrett needed real feuds and wins. It seemed like they were off to good start with the Undertaker, but forgot all that and continually pushed his way down the card.

Many people would just let this happen and find no way to bounce back. Val Venis comes to mind. Jarrett, though, just tried to push his way back up. And he looked to find it in a couple of new partners. From John Milner's compilation of Jeff Jarrett for Slam! Sports:

> Jarrett was reunited with Debra and, as 1999 began, to team with Owen Hart. On January 25th, 1999, Jarrett and Hart defeated the Big Boss Man and Ken Shamrock to win the WWF Tag [T]eam titles. Jarrett and Owen made a successful title [defense] at WrestleMania XV, defeating D-Lo Brown and Test but lost the titles to Kane and X-Pac on March 30th.

Still, things were looking up for Jarrett and people were noticing him, especially with Debra back at his side. But one must wonder if Jarrett was burnt out by this point, if he thought he should give up? Absolutely not. From John Powell's interview with Jeff Jarrett in early 1999:

> **Q:** When you first returned to the WWF, you were trying to form yourself into a "man of his word", a "man of honor" and that kind of thing through the promos. What happened to that as direction goes. Was there a change of heart or something like that?
>
> - **John Powell** (SLAM! Wrestling).
>
> **Jarrett:** Well, it was the WWF's change. If you look back at my first night back in the WWF and you look at my persona now; it's exactly the same. I was pissed off at a lot of things and that's how I am today. What's happened between then and now is a lot of things the WWF regrets and I do too. But, it's not a strong regret. It's just we try things and you know, I don't think that myself and Tennessee Lee were given the proper opportunities. We didn't have title shots and I could go on and on about that but that's where we are at right now. I'm enjoying the direction that I am going now.

You see, Jarrett was still all business. He never took what happened to him personally, though I have presented it so here. He kept an optimism and a passive understanding that you do not find in many wrestlers, especially one we will get back to later. But in the meantime, let's look earlier in the interview to see what I mean:

> **Q:** Does he [Jerry Jarrett, Jeff's father] harbor any feelings towards Vince McMahon over what happened in the past?
>
> - **SLAM! Wrestling** (John Powell).
>
> **Jarrett:** Oh, absolutely not. Because when you get right down to it - and promoters know this better than anybody... even wrestlers - it's strictly business. It's not really on a personal basis. It is business and that's how he looks at the past. There was some decisions at the time that I am sure he didn't agree with or maybe still today he doesn't agree with, but that still goes under the classification of business.

You see, as trained by his father, Jarrett understood business first. And we know there is no ill will as Jerry turned his back on TNA to sell someone's contract to Vince, so their relationship remains the same as ever.

The point is, Jarrett always acted as a professional, and this is a point to keep later on. Others acted less professional to Jarrett than he to them.

With much momentum behind him, Debra, and Owen, the trio seemed destined for always something more. Unfortunately, tragedy struck at Over the Edge, 1999.

GOODBYE AGAIN, OWEN

This sums it up best. From Accelerator3359:

> When Val Venis began trying to flirt with Debra, Jarrett took offense, inspiring another feud, which featured Jarrett, Venis, Debra, and Venis' friend, Nicole Bass. They finally scheduled a mixed tag-team match at Over The Edge '99, for the two teams to settle their differences. This was the tragic night when Owen Hart fell to his death after trying to enter via a wire rig. After Hart was taken out of the arena, being rushed to the hospital with little hope of survival, Jarrett was forced to come out for the next match. He and Debra wrestled against Venis & Bass, in a match that could be loosely described as "disjointed". Eventually, Venis

> & Bass got the win, and Jarrett headed to the back to learn of his friend's fate. The next Raw, a special memorial show dedicated to Hart aired, with Jarrett faring prominently in telling stories of his former partner. Jarrett broke down, crying, during his segment, in one of the most moving moments in WWE history. Jarrett was then given the honor of taking on the Godfather [on the next week's RAW], who was supposed to be Hart's opponent at the pay-per-view. Jarrett defeated him, winning the Intercontinental Title that was supposed to be Owen's.

These were Jarrett's own words in that segment (via Wikiquote):

> In this business, I guess you got a lot of acquaintances but very few friends. And Owen, he was one of those friends. He did a lot of funny stories, his personality, the things he used to do.... and I told my wife a bunch of times about the last couple months I've been with Owen on the road.... I see Owen more than I see her and my little girl. And he said the same thing. And now that he's not here, it's.... you look at it almost selfishly. Owen, my buddy, my friend, not with me anymore. I know Owen's in a better place, life isn't cutting up. But when you really think about Owen's life, I think about integrity. Because in this business... it's cold, it's callous, it's selfish, it's self-serving, it's unrealistic, it's a fantasy world. But Owen was real. He was a man's man. His wife and kids..... are 3 of the luckiest people in the world, because he loved them more than anything in the world. And that's why he did what he did -- to provide for them. And he did it with integrity, and integrity in this business is few and far between. That's not a good thing to know, but it's the truth. And outside all of the laughs.... because on the road, without the laughs, you know..... the fans get to see Owen 10-15 minutes a week, but when you see him 24 hours a day for 10 or 12 days at a time, he's one of the guys that made it fun. Made coming to work entertaining off the camera, and that's just as important as on the camera. Owen........ I'll make the promise to you. 'Cause you've got 2 little kids and I've got a little one of my own, as they grow older, the only thing that they might have to find out what their dad was like is wrestling films. But

> *I'll make the promise to myself... as the years go by, I'll do my best to let Oje and Athena really know what a great man you were, Owen. That's it... I can't.... I don't know....*

Jarrett proved a lot to Vince and company over those two days and the following weeks. Despite his personal pain and devastation, he still went out there and did his job to the best of his ability. The WWF was impressed with Jarrett and finally understood him. No, he was not given a push because Owen died. He was finally seen for who he really was, the point he was trying to get across to the WWF since the beginning. He was a professional. He was a champion, and he wanted to do things the best way he could.

ONE LAST TIME

But the WWF quickly forgot this fact as well. From Slam! Sports:

> *A week later [after Owen's death], Jarrett defeated the Godfather for the Intercontinental Championship, a title he would hold until July 24th, when he lost the belt to Edge at a Toronto house show. Jarrett regained the championship the next night, but lost it to European Champion D-Lo Brown on July 27th.*
>
> *Jarrett and D-Lo Brown would meet again at SummerSlam 99 with both the Intercontinental and European Championship on the line. Mark Henry, Brown's partner, turned on D-Lo, costing him the titles. In gratitude, Jarrett gave Henry the European title.*

You would think that would be sign of things to come, that Jarrett had a future to move up the card. But the WWF had another fancy. From Accelerator3359:

> *He also brought out Miss Kitty to be Debra's official valet. Later that night, Jarrett issued an open challenge to any wrestler in the back. However, when Chyna came out to accept, Jarrett, enraged at the thought of a woman fighting him for the belt, knocked her out with his guitar. Over the next few weeks, Jarrett & Chyna feuded. Jarrett also attacked other ladies, striving to prove that*

> wrestling was a man's game. He tried to injure older female wrestlers the Fabulous Moolah & Mae Young, as well as turning on Debra when they lost a mixed tag-team match to Stephanie McMahon & Test. At Unforgiven '99, Jarrett was signed to face Chyna for the Intercontinental Title. During the match, both Moolah & Young tried to interfere, but Jarrett eventually fought his way back into it. Debra then came down to the ring, showing her knowledge of Jarrett's moves by knocking him out with his own guitar. Chyna then got the pin and apparently won the match, but Tom Pritchard came to ringside and informed the referee of the interference. The ref reversed the decision, giving Jarrett the win via DQ, and allowing him to retain the IC gold.
>
> Jarrett & Chyna continued to feud, with Jarrett's views on where a woman should actually be forming the basis for their next match, a "Good Housekeeping" bout at No Mercy '99. It was ruled that household items could be used as weapons in the fight. After much debating, Jarrett was able to convince the people in charge that his guitar actually was a household item, giving him a slight edge in the weapons department. During the match, Jarrett used his Intercontinental Title to knock Chyna out, apparently getting the win. But the ref then ruled that the IC belt wasn't a 'household item', and the match was restarted. Chyna then used Jarrett's own guitar on him, knocking him out and getting the pinfall victory. Jarrett lost the Intercontinental Title, and left the WWF after that night.

Surprisingly, it was not the woman-beater gimmick that made Jarrett not want to re-sign with the WWF: it was Stone Cold Steve Austin.

In interviews around the country, Jarrett had stated many times he would like to work with Austin, but the feeling was not mutual. You see, Austin was still upset from back in the USWA days when Jarrett defeated him in a rematch for the Southern Heavyweight Title, feeling Jarrett was holding him down and that Jerry Jarrett (who had influence in the USWA) would only favor his son. But that wasn't the only reason he didn't like the Jarretts. From Wikipedia:

> *According to industry insiders, Austin never forgot an incident that happened when he broke into the business and worked shows for Jeff's father, Jerry Jarrett. The story goes that Austin was sitting in the locker room after a show looking at his paycheck, which he felt was very small, and Jeff made a sarcastic comment along the lines of "it's not going to get any bigger by staring at it".*

Of course, Jarrett was not the only person Austin refused to work with. Billy Gunn was another man that Austin did not want to work with at all. Although Austin may have had a point in saying that his match with Brock Lesner should not be given away on free TV, he had no point for not wanting to feud with Jeff Jarrett except a personal vendetta.

Jeff Jarrett was all business and never took anything personal, as he stated above. Yet Austin took everything personally and actually refused to help elevate Jarrett.

Yes, Jarrett only reached an IC level in the WWF, but that was for a reason. The WWF was finally, finally willing to get behind him, but a top of the card person refused to work with him. Jarrett knew that there was no hope for him in the WWF if Austin was not willing to work with him, and he could not deal with that. He decided that he was not going to re-sign with the WWF and would instead go to the WCW. After all, his good friend Vince Russo had just taken creative control of the company, and he felt it was the best opportunity to prove himself once and for all. There was only one problem:

Jeff Jarrett was still Intercontinental Champion when his contract expired.

In one of the greatest blunders in WWF/Vince McMahon history, Jarrett was no longer a WWF contracted wrester yet held one of the biggest belts in the promotion.

So Vince and Jarrett worked out a deal for him to appear at the No Mercy PPV and drop the title to Chyna. And what is more professional than agreeing to work a show and losing to a woman, despite planning to be a champion at another promotion starting the next night? Jarrett could have seriously hurt his reputation with that loss, but he decided to do it anyway.

"But JP," you'll say, "didn't Jarrett hold Vince up for a whole bunch of money?"

The answer is yes... and no. Vince would have you believe Jarrett made Vince pay him a bunch of unearned money or he would show up in WCW with the IC title and throw it in the trash. That is not what happened at all. Jarrett wanted all of the money that was owed to him for past PPVs (PPV bonuses are paid out months later), merchandise, and the current show. He asked for the few hundred thousand dollars of money he was owed and that was it.

Listen, when you leave a job, you get all the money you are owed. You cannot have a company owe you anything in the long term because there are too many legal ramifications. Worse yet, Jarrett was going to work for Vince's competitor, and because of that Jarrett could never, ever guarantee that Vince would pay him. Jarrett may have been a professional, but he no longer saw Vince as one. Since Vince let Austin tell him how to run his company, Jarrett had lost faith in Vince's power as head of the company. With that, he wanted to make sure he was given everything that was owed him and leave no loose ends.

That is just business, people. It doesn't matter what company you work for, you do not walk out the last day with money owed to you. That's not the way business is done, and that is not what Jarrett was about to do. It was quite a chunk of change, and Jarrett was not prepared to work for free.

It was simply a smart and safe move. Yes, Vince made a big mistake by letting Jarrett hold on to the IC title past the end of his contract, but Jarrett would have made the same request anyway.

With the loss behind him and the money in his pocket, Jarrett was set for his last run in the big leagues (for now).

Now It's Time to Be Chosen

All right, in Mathew Sforcina's Evolution Schematic for Jeff Jarrett (Part 3):

> *Jarrett ran out and [in] his first act back in WCW broke a trademarked guitar over Buff Bagwell's head, seconds after Bagwell had lost to La Parka. Jarrett's second act was to talk about how much he hated the WWF and certain people there. His third act, perhaps, was to lay out Elizabeth with a guitar. It's hard to say if he did that or not, he left his Women Hating days behind him at the WWF. But his first major act was to confirm that he was The Chosen One of the Powers That Be, and that he would be the PTB (Vince Russo)'s main man. He would continue to get up in Bagwell's grill (i.e. hit him over the head with his guitar as often as possible) leading into the World Title Tournament to crown a new champ after Hogan, Goldberg and Sting had controversy and stuff. Really, any excuse to hold a tourney. Everyone loves a tourney.*

> Jarrett had a tough, but successful run to the semis of the tourney, getting past Booker T (impressive), Curt Hennig (expected) and Bagwell (thankfully). But then at Mayhem in the [semi-final] against Chris Benoit, Creative Control (Russo's hired goons, [aka] The Harris Twins) came out and screwed up, allowing Benoit to grab Jarrett's guitar and use it on Jeff to advance to the finals. Jarrett took his anger out on Disco Inferno as he headed to the back.
>
> Jarrett then was convinced by Russo to leave the World title for now. Jarrett was OK with this, since Russo promised him success without the belt, and that's all he wanted. At Starrcade, Jarrett won the Bunkhouse match against PTB enemy Dustin Rhodes with help from Hennig. He then helped Nash beat Sid with (what else?) a guitar shot. However, third time was not a charm, as when Jarrett replaced an injured Scott Hall in the US title ladder match against Benoit, Benoit had little trouble beating the tired Jarrett to win the title.

Jarrett's new WCW career was off to a start, but not as much of a start as the re-writers of history would like us to believe. You see, despite being friends with Russo and being the Chosen One, Jarrett was not immediately just thrust into the top of the card. Although heavily profiled, this was mostly because WCW was going in a new direction under Russo, a creative direction WCW had never been in before. Russo, like many of the promoters and wrestlers in the past that we've covered, saw Jarrett as someone who could be built as a huge star.

Jarrett was 32 at this time, still young enough to build the future around (as Russo had a penchant for younger wrestlers [see: Billy Kidman vs. Hulk Hogan]), but had 13 years of in-ring experience that made him a veteran. Of course, that did not even come close to including his true experience from growing up the son of a regional wrestling promoter.

But WCW was in an incredibly turbulent phase. Vince Russo was pushing the buttons of everyone, money was beginning to be lost, and the departure of Bischoff left the company without a true head. Although Russo was in charge of storylines, he was not in charge of the business. In reality, nobody truly was, as temporary heads from Turner Sports and TBS would make their presence known.

Meanwhile, Jarrett managed to capture the US title from Chris Benoit with much shenanigans. But what happened later that night was more important as Jarrett joined with Bret Hart, Scott Hall, and Kevin Nash to form nWo 2000 (Black & Silver). This, though, again did not lead to success. From

Accelerator3359:

> Jarrett feuded with Benoit for the next few weeks, as well as joining Nash in his fight against the Commissioner, Terry Funk. Because of this, Funk put Jarrett into three matches during a Monday Nitro, against Funk's old friends. Jarrett lost all three, falling to George "The Animal" Steele, Tito Santana, & "Superfly" Jimmy Snuka. During the final match, which was fought in a steel cage, Snuka jumped off the top and tried a splash, but accidentally hit Jarrett in the head with his knee, giving him a concussion. Due to the injury, Jarrett was forced to vacate the US belt, and did not have his scheduled "Triple Theatre" match with Benoit at Souled Out '00.

Despite being plugged into the most important group in WCW and being best friends with the booker, Jarrett was still going out and doing his job. He did not make demands or have his friend give him huge wins. He went out there and lost to three non-regulars (and particular ones that were way past the use by date). The injury was a setback, but he was able to come back and regain the US title when then Commissioner Kevin Nash (having won the right from Terry Funk) gave the belt back to Jarrett.

But then more interesting things happened. Vince Russo was ousted from WCW and WCW was without a creative head, nonetheless a business head. This, as you can imagine, led to some levels of insanity in WCW storylines, and Jarrett was no exception. From the Accelerator:

> Jarrett then added the Harris Brothers to the nWo, making them his personal allies in his battles to retain the belt. When Nash was injured, he handed over the responsibilities of the Commissionership to Jarrett, who used the power to battle against the current World Champion, Sid Vicious. But Jarrett & the Harris Brothers had trouble combating Sid, and when Nash returned a few weeks later, he stripped Jarrett of the power, taking it back for himself.
>
> This caused friction between Jarrett & Nash, especially after Nash made a #1 Contenders match for the World Title shot between his 'friends' Jarrett and Hall, which ended in a Double Disqualification. Nash then opted to make the match at Superbrawl X a Triangle match between

> Jarrett, Hall, and the World Champion, Sid Vicious. He also announced that the Harris Brothers were barred from ringside, which was too much for Jarrett, who bashed Nash with his guitar, putting Big Sexy out of action and causing even more heat between Jarrett and Hall.
>
> At Superbrawl X, Jarrett made things better for himself, as he took over the Commissioner spot once again. He changed the ruling, allowing the Harris Brothers at ringside, giving him an edge against the other two opponents. During the fight, many referees were taken out, usually by Jarrett. It soon became [apparent] that Jarrett had been doing it on purpose, as Jarrett's personal referee, Mark Johnson, came out and took over, making Jarrett a serious favorite to win the belt. However, "Rowdy" Roddy Piper then reappeared, wearing a referee's shirt, and took out Johnson, taking over the match. Jarrett was then taken out by Vicious' Powerbomb, ending the match and causing a loss for Jarrett.
>
> In the next month, a furious Jarrett, still carrying the powers of the Commissionership, continued to go after Vicious at every opportunity, bringing the Harris Brothers with him. He assigned himself a rematch at Uncensored '00, where he again faced off against Vicious for the World Title. During the match, the referee was once again taken out, bringing Johnson to the ring, who began to make fast counts for Jarrett. Hulk Hogan then came out, however, stopping the counts and tossing Johnson to the wind. He then attacked Jarrett, beating on him, which allowed Vicious to come back and get the Powerbomb. Once again, due to outside interference, Jarrett had missed his chance to be the World Champion.

But then something amazing happened! Russo was back, and he was with Bischoff. After a week off, WCW "reset" and all the champions were stripped of their titles. It was an incredibly refreshing time in WCW, one filled with great excitement. Unfortunately, Bischoff was mostly just a consultant and on-air character, nobody was really in charge of WCW, and Russo was making rash decisions because his choices were being changed on him. From John Milner at Slam! Sports:

> At Spring Stampede 2000, Jarrett defeated Diamond Dallas Page in the finals of a tournament to win the vacant World Heavyweight title. Page would, in turn, defeat Jarrett on April 24, 2000 to end Jarrett's title reign but a second title reign would begin when Jarrett defeated Page and David Arquette in a "Ready to Rumble" match.
>
> On May 15th, 2000, Ric Flair would defeat Jarrett for the belt, but the title would be stripped from Flair and Jarrett would defeat Kevin Nash for the vacant belt a week later. This latest title reign would last only two days, as Nash would win a Three-Way Dance involving Jarrett and Scott Steiner but Jarrett would, of course, regain the title.

Four title reigns in two months? Something else! But if you were Jarrett, what could you do? Jarrett was doing everything possible to get over the New Blood and make WCW a fighting organization again. Was he to refuse the world title? No! He knew that he was the future of wrestling and wanted the chance to prove it. Unfortunately, no time with the title and quick decisions by Time Warner Corporate led to excessive demands being put on Russo for changes. And then came the Bash... at the Beach...

CHOP IT DOWN WITH THE SIDE OF MY HAND

In what can only be described as one of the most controversial moments in wrestling history, Jeff Jarrett laid down for Hulk Hogan in the middle of the ring, as covered in detail in the Hulk Hogan case.

You see, there was no controversy between Hogan and Jarrett. Hogan felt Jarrett was worthy of defeating him. If there were any hard feelings, then why would Hogan have agreed to let Jarrett hit him over the head with a guitar in Japan? Jarrett and Hogan were of the same mindset: it's a business and they are the product. It was Russo's relationship with Hogan that was strained, and Jarrett was just doing the company's bidding. If Jarrett refused to go out there and lay down for Hogan, what would happen to him? He may have been friends with Russo, but he had already lost the title enough times to know that his reign was tenuous as best, as was all of WCW. Besides, he still lost the title to Booker T later in the night, as Russo and others wanted to work with the future King Booker and move him up the card as well.

This incident also led to Bischoff completely leaving WCW until the week before the Night of Champions (aka, the season finale of WCW). WCW spiraled out of control for the following months and into 2001, and Russo was ousted once and for all. Jeff Jarrett never regained the World Title, but he did put over the champion Booker T again as well as Scott Steiner when he had the title. WCW had a brief glimmer of hope when Eric Bischoff and Fusient Media Ventures looked to purchase WCW. But as soon as AOL-Time Warner corporate mysteriously cancelled their top-rated show, the deal was off and Vince McMahon and the WWF bought WCW.

On the final Nitro and during the RAW simulcast, Vince McMahon polled the audience on many members of the WCW roster and what the crowd through of them. But in a final humiliation, Vince let his feelings about Jarrett be known as he "fired" him over the air (in reality, just not picking up his contract).

Sure, Vince had the right to not want to do business with Jarrett nor absorb his contract. That is fine. But he purposely went out of his way to try to ruin a man's career. And why? Because he was still vindictive over the thought that Jarrett had screwed him out of money when he left for WCW. As we covered earlier, Jarrett was just trying to recover what was owed him from his time in the WWF and did not want to leave the company without the money he had previously earned. He was just doing smart business. This is just another example of Vince's hypocrisy with his policies and beliefs. I'm sure in a DVD review, Vince would say something (like he did in the Rise and Fall of ECW) that he is not sure why he (Vince) would do such actions, and that he should regret them. But Vince knows why, and the reasons are listed quite clearly here.

Jarrett, unlike many wrestlers, could actually get out of his contract in a rather short fashion, and did not turn to Vince McMahon for work. Instead, he helped the World Wrestling All-Stars get off the ground by joining the tour. From Slam!:

> [Jarrett] joined the World Wrestling All-Stars on a tour of Australia, joining such stars as Buff Bagwell and Bret Hart. Jarrett's tenure with the WWA was highlighted by being crowned the first WWA Champion, defeating his former roadie, the Road Dogg, in the finals of a tournament on October 26th, 2001.
>
> Jarrett would retain the WWA Championship at several house shows before losing it to Nathan Jones during a four corners bout (that also featured Scott Steiner and "Grandmaster Sexay" Brian Christopher) on April 7th 2002.

It was a short time, but Jarrett enjoyed touring the world and working with many of his friends. But it also whet his appetite for something more.

IT'S A BIG WORLD

Over the spring and summer of 2002, Jarrett and his father, along with some other financial backers, got together to form Total Non-Stop Action Entertainment, an affiliate of the NWA. In a matter of months, they were able to secure a weekly two-hour PPV block, exclusive rights to the NWA World Heavyweight and World Tag Team Championships, and a roster mixing old, new, and misused stars. In June 2002, NWA: TNA launched on PPV, changing wrestling in the twenty-first century forever.

And I cannot leave this part without stressing this huge point: Jarrett put up HIS OWN MONEY in order to help create TNA. Jarrett took a vast financial and personal gambit in order to get TNA off the ground and running. He didn't have to do that. Jarrett had enough money to retire comfortably, and Jerry Jarrett had plenty of other side businesses that he did not need wrestling. Instead he risked it all for the possibility of creating a new business, for taking it to Vince McMahon, and to make sure there was another place for all his fellow wrestlers to work.

By this time, the InVasion had been a complete disaster and it was apparent that the WWF had no idea how to use former WCW stars (or did not want to use them). At that, without WCW a whole chunk of the wrestling audience had completely disappeared.

On the final Nitro, WCW scored a 3.0 rating and RAW a 4.6, thus a total audience of 7.6. This was far from the peak of a combined 11.0 seen just a year and half earlier, but there was still a much larger audience. But what did RAW Score in the following weeks?

DATE	RAW RATING
2-Apr-01	5.7
9-Apr-01	5.4
16-Apr-01	5.1
23-Apr-01	5.1
30-Apr-01	5.0
7-May-01	4.6
14-May-01	4.5
21-May-01	4.2
28-May-01	4.2
4-Jun-01	4.3
11-Jun-01	4.1

Immediately, ratings dropped almost 2.0 points. That means that millions of people just stopped watching wrestling that night! And as the weeks went on, the audience continued to decline. Not everyone liked the WWF-style. There is a whole echelon of southern-style, catch-as-catch-can style, and free-base style wrestling fans out there that were not being serviced.

In this, Jarrett saw the opportunity. Once again, let us not forget that he had grown up in the territory days and understood what the business was like before a national company. Because of that, and his travels, he knew that there was a difference in the audiences, and an audience was not getting what they wanted. Jarrett was not looking to necessarily steal the WWE's audience, but was looking to recapture all those wrestling fans that had been lost, seemingly forever.

Things got off to a rocky start as within a couple of months the other financial investors in TNA backed out. Since PPV revenues take upwards of 6 months to clear, TNA was about to go under. But did Jarrett give up? Absolutely not! Instead he found a new partner in Panda Energy, who became majority shareholder, corporate parent, and good friend. Because of that profound sacrifice by Jarrett—giving up control of his company—TNA was able to celebrate its fourth anniversary just a few months ago here in 2006.

Also during this time, Jarrett did not put himself at the top of the card, nor with the championship. The title went from Ken Shamrock to Ron Killings while Jarrett feuded with the likes of Bill Behrns, Bob Armstrong, and Apollo. This would all finally change in six months at a PPV in November. From Accelerator3359:

> *Having finally earned his World Title shot, Jarrett got his chance on the November 20th, 2002 PPV, to wrestle Ron Killings. In a bloody match that featured chairs, guitars, & tables, the two men fought it out for the belt. In the end, Mr. Wrestling III suddenly appeared and hit Killings with a guitar shot, allowing Jarrett to get the victory and become the NWA World Heavyweight Champion! The mystery man then unmasked to reveal former WCW booker Vince Russo. Jarrett defeated Killings in a rematch for the belt the next week, this time ignoring Russo's attempt to help and instead beating Killings with 3 straight Strokes. For the rest of the year, the puzzle was whether Jarrett was joining Russo's Sports Entertainment eXtreme, or S.E.X. On one December card, Jarrett [retained] the NWA World Champion over Curt Hennig, thanks to Russo's interference. But on the final December '02 PPV, Jarrett decided that he wouldn't be joining Russo. This led to S.E.X. beating down Jarrett. Jarrett came back later in the night to attack S.E.X., but was surprised and beaten down by AJ Styles, who joined Russo's team.*

TNA was again going in a new direction, or just starting to find a direction. TNA did not know what it stood for yet, and so a lot of new things were being tried.

One of those things was AJ Styles, who would go on to dethrone Jarrett not once, not twice, but three times, more than anyone else in TNA.

The times that Jarrett did have the belt, he was always out touring. He went to the small independent shows, the WWAS tours, the international dates, always representing TNA and the NWA. Christian Cage made a few sporadic appearances outside of TNA TV and PPV with the title, but Jarrett had taken it around the world. Say what you will about his death grip on the title, but Jarrett had always gone the extra step to defend the title and represent TNA everywhere he went.

Meanwhile, TNA moved from having a weekly PPV to an odd spot on FSN (not available in all markets) along with some syndicated television. Jarrett then convinced the rest of the owners of TNA to let the deal expire and work to get a deal that was good for TNA over the summer. That eventually led the organization to Spike, but that was hardly the definitive outcome. WGN was a possibility for a while, and while they may have gotten a better timeslot than Saturday at 11pm, they would have been in far fewer homes. No, Jarrett helped take another risk because he wanted to make TNA succeed.

Does he have selfish reasons? Of course. He wanted to get his investment back. He wanted to make boatload of money. He wanted his legacy etched into stone forever. He wanted to stick it to Vince McMahon. He wanted everyone to see him as a genius on many levels.

But he also had many selfless motives, too.

HAVE YOU EVER TRIED TO PROTECT A MOUNTAIN?

Despite wanting to keep himself over, Jarrett did think highly of others on the TNA roster. From the TNA chat with Jeff Jarrett in 2003:

> *Submitted Question:* Who is the best wrestler in TNA after you of course[?]
>
> *Jeff Jarrett:* Well, you'll have to get more specific if you want an exact answer.
>
> Best Technical? In my opinion, Chris Daniels is very technically sound. A couple guys in X Division that are very technically sound but [if] you're looking at a style and "the best wrestler" at displaying a persona? Monty Brown has unlimited potential. Abyss has the ability to work many different styles. Some would consider him to be the best in TNA.

Interesting choice of people, especially his comments on Abyss. And we know that these were people that had been featured on TNA television and surrounded around Jarrett for some time. He was trying to help bring them up, and he wanted their talent to make himself look better. And what is wrong with that? Remember: Jarrett has JUST turned 39 here in 2006. Despite being around for a very long time, he is still very young and has many more fruitful years to add to the product. He does not need to completely step away, just slightly change his role.

And who knows where this current title reign is going? It seems that this time it may be his last as a transition role. He was the champion for a while because he was the most recognizable name in TNA, and Spike TV wanted someone who they thought the audience would know. Once TNA earned a lot of trust with Spike, they were allowed to make more changes that they wanted.

When it comes to the audience at the iMPACT Zone, I do not find them a fair gauge. Yes, they chant derogatory remarks at Jarrett demanding his dropping of the title, but that audience is the second most smarky in the business (next to ROH, of course). There are over a million regular viewers of TNA every week at this time, and we cannot believe that 200 people represent the entire audience. As entertaining as that audience is, they also do things just to be a part of the antidisestablishmentarianism movement. There was a "heel section" that had to be broken up, if you want proof.

No, out of a million people, more see Jarrett as he is portrayed on TV than the dictator of TNA. Granted the audience of TNA is among the smart mark crowd, there is also a much wider base now. That base will continue to grow, and so too will the reactions of crowds change. Anyone who has seen Jarrett live knows how different the crowds in other parts of the country react to him.

But as conveyers of wrestling news and programming, we are apt to take the iMPACT zone reaction as dogma. This is not what is true reality, though it is hard to accept given what is seen on TNA iMPACT every week.

And what does Jarrett think about his time in TNA. From the chat:

> **Submitted Question:** What's it like wrestling for TNA? Do you have fun?
>
> **Jeff Jarrett:** I absolutely have fun! It's a 24/7 situation. I don't like to call it a job because wrestling has always been my passion. My family's been in the business for 3 generations. It's in my blood. In early 2002 me and my family "hatched this idea" and it has been a dog fight every step of the way but makes the good times all the more rewarding

More importantly, what does Jarrett think of the belt he holds in his hands now?

> **Submitted Question:** Hey Jeff what do you feel when you wrestle and held the NWA World Title belt here in TNA!
>
> **Jeff Jarrett:** The World Title is something I always dreamed of attaining. Everyone knows this is a business first and foremost, but that being said, gaining the title you grew up watching is a great feeling.

Yes, Jarrett wanted to be a champion, but he was about the business first. He had and has a long-term interest in making sure TNA succeeds, and wants to see it go long beyond him. But he still has many years left in that ring, and is going to use them to cement his legacy and put over the next generation ready to take his place.

SWING THAT GUITAR

Jeff Jarrett is the last of the old school. His history is long and storied in this sport, and he was met with much resistance as he went. Nothing was easy for Jarrett, and he could have given up at any time. Instead, he worked hard to create a business of himself, setting up deals that no one thought were possible, moving on when he decided it was right. He never just let himself sell out for money or pushes, but always went where the opportunities would be the best. And when the opportunities were not in the existing companies, he dared to put everything on the line to start another organization. In that short time, he has dominated a promotion he is part owner of, but for good reason. He is still young and has much to offer. It is now the time that he can begin to move aside for the next generation, but not before establishing a platform for them to take.

Misunderstood? Yes. Needlessly berated? Yes. Turbulent history forgotten? Yes. True Champion? Most definitely.

The defense rests.

After the Trial

Hung Jury

IN THE CASE OF THE IWC VS. JEFF JARRETT, JEFF JARRETT HAS BEEN ACCUSED OF BEING A NO-TALENT WRESTLER WHO SELFISHLY USES EVERYONE ELSE TO JUST PUT HIMSELF OVER AND NEVER DID ANYTHING TO GIVE BACK TO THE BUSINESS OR MAKE ANYTHING BEYOND HIS OWN EGO.

With a mere 57.1% of the vote, Jeff Jarrett was found:

NOT GUILTY!

Skin of my teeth people, skin of my teeth. There were times when the numbers were not in my favor, but never by much. It hung out in the 50% range the first few hours, then moved up to about 55-57% where is stayed around until the end of the voting. That was a tough one, because there were points even I was doubting what I was saying was making sense. But it did! Jarrett lives another day to rule TNA!

Response

We'll begin this one with the best way to sum up how those who voted "Guilty" came to their conclusion:

> *My Vote: "Guilty"*
>
> *Okay... if you look at this from perspective you have presented... I would have to agree... "Not guilty." Good amount of what you say I have to agree with... and on that note... I would have to agree that Jeff Jarrett is probably misunderstood on more than several things (I am not going to debate you there).*
>
> *...*
>
> **Robert Kilgore**

There was a lot more to this response, but I think the opening lines cover it quite well, in addition to what other guilty voters said. They agreed with the arguments but they just never liked Jarrett as a performer or were upset with how much control he had of TNA TV time and/or his grip on the title. So what can you do with that? "You are mostly right, but it does not matter because I cannot stand the guy anyway." With a case like Goldberg we had the opposite problem where literally his fan club was flooding me with "Not Guilty" votes. Here, the anti-fan club of Jarrett's flooded me with "Guilty" votes. Both cases are skewed in their results because of it.

> *He's the heel every promoter could ever want. Hell, I'll be going to Bound for Glory to see Double J get his ass beat and then somehow steal the win. Everyone on the internet who hates Jeff Jarrett is just a mark, because JJ is making them do exactly what he wants. And he's laughing all the way to the bank.*
>
> **-Zack Macomber**

That's an interesting perspective. Since TNA fans were more of the "smark" variety who at the very least were internet knowledgeable, how does one get the audience to hate them? Was Jarrett actually working the IWC crowd and getting them react in the way he wanted by using classic tactics in a modern technology?

Since the nWo, heels have had a problem that if they are too hated then they will not sell merchandise. The late 2010's made it even worse with the explosion of social media. Heels should probably not even have social media accounts, but instead they have ones with a "wink", ruining the character. Having met many wrestlers in person during my career, I can tell you how much having a personal relationship with them ruins the character. There are performers I enjoy just because I like them personally and cannot get behind whatever evil machinations their characters are up to. Similarly, there are ones that I dislike and had poor interactions with that made me never be able to accept them as faces.

As such, perhaps Jarrett recognized that this condition was coming early on and was working us all with just how he ran the company and took up time on TV and with the belt? Could his actions be not self-serving in that he just wanted to dominate those things, but because he knew those things would get him heat?

All right, let's wrap this up with what I love to see and hear most of all:

> *You reminded me how good JJ is and how much I used to like him before the internet changed me. Thanks for helping me find out what I really think about JJ and not what I think I should think of JJ.*
>
> **Patrick Sullivan**

CHYNA WINNING THE INTERCONTINENTAL CHAMPIONSHIP

INTRO

SOME DAME WALKED INTO MY OFFICE AND SAID...

Our first dame happens to be **Rick Wiltsie** who was inspired by the 411mania forums:

> There was some discussion about titles being devalued, more particularly the IC title during the Jericho/Chyna dual title reign. One person argued that it was in fact a good thing for the IC title based on the fact that Chyna was a mainstream entity. I however disagreed for various reasons.
>
> Perhaps I'm just stubborn in my thoughts, but I would like to try to be swayed the other way. That and I don't see how anyone can defend it appropriately.

And then there was... well, that was it. But a case is taken by quality, not quantity!

WHY THIS?

After having defended the World Heavyweight Championship and the European Championship, it should be obvious that I have great reverence for titles. Their prestige and lineage is something I take seriously in the world of professional wrestling. I do not appreciate anything that scars the legitimacy of the title or hurts its overall placement in history. That is why I do not condone David Arquette or Vince McMahon winning their respective championships, even for storyline purposes. Luckily, both the WCW World Heavyweight Championship and the WWF/E Championship have enough history and greats that have held them that one or two blemishes would not tarnish them forever.

That brings us to the WWE Intercontinental Championship. From that previous statement, you might believe that this case is about the IC title being able to overcome the scar of Chyna. This could not be further from the truth. This case is about proving Chyna was a worthy IC contender and champion, and her reign was actually a benefit to the title, both in the short-term and the long-term. Because of Chyna's personal problems, she has been degraded in our eyes. Losing a bout to a nobody on Celebrity Boxing did not help matters. But we must wrap our mindset around the timeframe and the kayfabe, and what Chyna winning the Intercontinental Championship really meant.

DYNASTIES IN CHYNA

The woman who would later be called Chyna was born Joanie Laurer on December 27, 1969. She showed much promise in early life and actually went to Spain to finish High School on a UN Scholarship. This parlayed into studying at the University of Tampa and graduating with a double major. From there she joined the Peace Corps and taught literacy in Costa Rica.

Meanwhile during all of this, Joanie got involved in fitness competitions. It was through these connections that she ended up in Killer Kowalski's wrestling school, a school that has produced other wresters such as Perry Saturn, John Kronus, Big John Studd, Chris Nowinski, Frankie Kazarian, and (of course) Triple H. She trained under Kowalski and began to wrestle for the independents in 1995. Her skills were recognized then, as she had two major achievement. From Obsessed with Wrestling:

> - *September 28, 1996: Joanie Lee defeated Violet Flame for the IWF (International Wrestling Federation) Women's title.*
>
> - *1996: Joanie Laurer was named the PGWA (Pro Girls Wrestling Association) rookie of the year.*

This was a great steppingstone, and people were starting to notice Joanie. From Wikipedia:

> *Her career reached new heights when she met World Wrestling Federation employees Hunter Hearst Helmsley (Triple H) and Shawn Michaels in a bar in 1997. Struck by her appearance, they helped her get into the WWF. Her original role was as Chyna, the laconic bodyguard of D-Generation X, often getting physically involved in Triple H's matches.*

As we also know, this striking appearance also led Triple H and Chyna to becoming an off-air couple, a relationship that came to an end when Triple H had an affair with Stephanie McMahon, who is now his wife and mother of his children. But that is neither here nor there, for it has nothing to do with anything related to Chyna winning the IC title.

You see, this is a part of the problem when it comes to Chyna. Any one event in history is overwritten with the trouble she had later in life. We'll get back to this forthwith, but for now we must remember where Chyna was.

Chyna continued to be involved in Triple H's stories, but also began to get more involved in the ring. She got stunned by Steve Austin in 1998, and later had her own love triangle story with Mark Henry. After turning on Triple H for the Corporation, she and Kane defeated Triple H and X-pac in a tag match, her first official match in the WWF/E. Although the two would later rejoin, the stage had been set. From the Official Women of Wrestling website:

> *Taking time off towards the end of 1998 Chyna returned to the WWF after having gone to a plastic surgeon and having her jawline reconfigured. A few weeks later a much "bustier" Chyna appeared with Triple H who was returning from an injury. Chyna and the WWF were obviously on the right track for propelling her towards Diva status. Male hormones began to stir when the new and improved "Ninth Wonder" entered the ring to kick some guys ass.*
>
> *After publicly stating that she had no desire to go after the WWF Women's Championship Title since she didn't feel that there was much of a challenge facing other women, Chyna began blossoming into a well-liked (by fans anyway) and respected woman in a man's world. Obviously reveling in the excitement of testing herself in the ring against the men while enjoying her new found status as an up and coming Diva, she did quite well for herself while seizing several firsts in the wrestling world. In January 1999 Chyna became the first woman to compete in a Royal Rumble PPV as she continued her assault on the WWF men's division. Not content in just confronting her one time mentor Triple H (who was now in real life her significant other) she decided to battle the two Superstars of the WWF - Stone Cold Steve Austin and The Rock - and held her own against either in several matches.*

Chyna had done everything right. She was taken as a threat and contender, especially after her Royal Rumble appearance (not to mention the battle royal that she won to get into the match). She was over with the fans because of her look, style, and her stand; and the audience believed she could hang with the top dogs. There were questions of whether she could beat the top men in the company, but there was no question that she could beat some of the upper-mid-card.

She was poised to take the next step up the ladder.

WHERE IS INTERCONTINENTAL?

As the WWF was growing in 1998 and early 1999, the smashmouth style took over. Everything was quick, swerving, and shocking. And with each new surprise, the next one had to be bigger in order to have the same impact. But because of this, title reigns were often short or happened to further a storyline, not reward a wrestler. This was the case for the Intercontinental Championship especially. From Colm Kearns' History of the Intercontinental Championship (Part 3):

> *1999 would not be a good year for the Intercontinental title; frequent title changes and [substandard] champions would diminish the belt's prestige over the next 12 months. Venis looked to be a competent champ but he lost the title a mere month after winning it to Road Dogg[,] a popular and fairly talented wrestler but primarily a tag team star. Road Dogg managed to retain his title in a 4 way at WrestleMania XV but he didn't go much further than that as he lost it to Goldust on the following night's episode of RAW.*
>
> *Goldust wasn't champion any longer than Road Dogg, he was defeated by The Godfather on April 12th and again in a rematch at Backlash (he left the WWF shortly [thereafter]). The Godfather was popular but he wasn't popular enough to excuse the fact that he was [substandard] in the ring. Despite [this] he held the belt longer than most had in 1999, his eventual loss came at the hands of Jeff Jarrett on May 25th in under 4 minutes.*

What Colm misses here is what happened before Jarrett won the title. As covered in previous cases, at Over the Edge 1999 Owen Hart (as the Blue Blazer) was to face the Godfather for the title before falling to his untimely death in the ring. Although Jarrett was more than a competent and capable wrestler to take the title in his stead, that does not mean that people were not aware that his win came at the expense of Owen's life. What did not help is that the then WWF did not get behind Jarrett and instead continued to be wishy washy with the title. Back to the history:

> Fans who despaired at the IC title's recent loss of value saw a glimmer of hope in Jarrett's victory. He was a more than competent in ring performer and an established WWF [mid-carder]. But Jarrett's title reigns in 1999 would be marred by pointless losses. The first of these occurred at a Toronto house show on July 24th 1999. Jarrett was to face Ken Shamrock but instead WWF decided to have Jarrett drop the belt to Edge to capitalize on the shock factor. The next night at the Fully Loaded PPV Jarrett recaptured the title. This may have served a purpose if it helped elevate Edge to singles stardom but it didn't [as] after his title loss Edge went back to teaming with Christian and would not become a successful singles wrestler for another two years.
>
> One week after regaining the title Jarrett lost it once again, this time to European champion D'lo Brown. Over the next few weeks the two men had an interesting feud that teased that Jarrett's [long-time] manager Debra would leave him. This continued until Summerslam in Minneapolis where Jarrett with the help of Debra and D'lo's former partner Mark Henry defeated [D'lo and] won both titles. The next night on RAW Jarrett presented Henry with the European belt and thus began the D'lo/Henry feud. D'lo was popular and quite good in the ring so you couldn't be blamed for thinking that WWF had big plans for him if they made him the first man to simultaneously hold the European and IC championships[;] sadly this was not the case [as] after a final European title reign following a win over Henry[,] D'lo did little of note for the rest of his WWF tenure. By the time Kurt Angle was billing himself as 'Euro-continental' champion six months later D'lo's double belt winning feat was largely ignored. These pointless changes made the IC title look like a useless piece of metal that was traded between wrestlers with no meaning or value[,] not something that had once been a prestigious prize used to help create future main eventers.

Again, what Colm is missing is what else was happening by the sudden changes and new storylines. By doing this, the WWF was trying to move the

Intercontinental title as far away from the Owen Hart disaster as possible. The wresters involved were weeded away from the title, but it was at such a pace that it was hurting the title in the short term.

Now it was time for a radical change of pace, something that would get people to notice the IC title and reward one of the growing stars in the company.

THE EMPEROR'S NEW GROOVE

Jeff Jarrett had recaptured the Intercontinental Championship and had decided that he hated women. This led to him hitting several over the head with a guitar. The perfect foil for him in this story was Chyna, a woman strong enough to fight back. The two began a feud that started with a different victory. From Obsessed with Wrestling:

> *# September 2, 1999 - Smackdown!: Chyna defeated Billy Gunn to secure an Intercontinental Title shot.*
>
> *# September 26, 1999 - Unforgiven: Jeff Jarrett w/Miss Kitty defeated Chyna by DQ to retain the IC title.*
>
> *# October 11, 1999 - RAW: Steve Austin & Jim Ross vs Triple H & Chyna ended in a No Contest after a brawl!*
> *# ~~~Jeff Jarrett & Miss Kitty attacked Chyna and put her in a laundry bin and pushed it off of a ledge with her inside!*

You see, when Chyna defeated Jarrett for the title it was not just out of the blue. Not only had the two been fighting for nearly two months, but Chyna had won a shot at the title over Billy Gunn. She was not thrown in there to embarrass Jeff Jarrett on the way out, but part of the long-term plan. Perhaps the feud would have gone another month longer if Jarrett had not left the WWF then, but we will never know that. What we do know is that Jarrett did not refuse to drop the title unless he was paid $225,000, he refused to show up unless he was given the money he was owed. The payout had nothing to do with Chyna and everything to do with Jarrett wanting money he had already earned. Jarrett had no problem losing to Chyna, as evidenced by him still pulling out a full match and making Chyna look good on the way out, despite working without a contract.

From there, Chyna moved on to a feud with Chris Jericho. She lost the title to him in December 1999, but two weeks later they pinned each other in the same match. Because of that, they became co-champions, and Chyna found herself interfering in Jericho's matches to make sure he retained the title. This came to an end a few weeks later when Jericho defeated Chyna and Bob Holly in a triple threat match, ending Chyna's second reign as champion.

What people forget is that Chyna won the title one more time in August 2000 in a mixed tag match against Val Venis and Trish Stratus. Official Women of Wrestling fills in the details and tells the other story going on at the time:

> *In April 2000 during a European Title match between titleholder Y2J and Eddie Guerrero, Chyna turned on Chris. The referee had been inadvertently knocked out and Chyna entered the ring and administered an unofficial three count, and then raised Jericho's hand as if he had won the match. Then she surprised everyone - including Guerrero himself - when she kicked Y2J in the midsection and delivered a DDT. She dragged Guerrero [on] top and threw the referee back in the ring, who made the three count and awarded the European Championship to Guerrero. From then on she partnered with Eddie who became "Latino Heat", while she became known as "Mamacita".*
>
> *In August 2000 Chyna regained the Intercontinental Title after Commissioner Mick Foley set up an Intergender Tag Team Match for the Summer Slam PPV. The match pitted Val & Trish Stratus against Eddie & Chyna, but with the stipulation that whomever got the pin would be declared the Intercontinental Champion. After a lengthy and hard fought battle Chyna was able to pin Trish and become the Intercontinental Champion...*

She would lose this championship to Eddie Guerrero in a three-way match that included Kurt Angle when Eddie was "crying" over a fallen Chyna and pinned her while hugging her.

Now here is the simple question for you:

Would the WWF have ever put the title around Chyna's waist **_three times_** over two years if they did not believe in her and the fans had not accepted her as a credible contender? The answer is "no", Chyna had proved herself a worthy contender and defender of the title, and had storylines outside of the title that led to her eventual reign.

Besides, do you know who else falls into the exclusive three-time IC champ club? From Wikipedia:

> *The most times the title has been won by one man is seven, by Chris Jericho. The next-highest number of reigns is six, held by Jeff Jarrett & Rob Van Dam, then Triple H & Edge with five, Chris Benoit & Razor Ramon with four, and Shawn Michaels, Chyna, Christian, Shelton Benjamin & Goldust with three.*

Not a bad club to be in at all!

FUTURE IMPERFECT

Of course the question is: what were the short-term and long-term effects on the title because of Chyna's reigns. Well, let's look at the championship for the year before Chyna. From Wrestling-Titles.com:

WRESTLER	DATE WON
Ken Shamrock	1998/10/12
Val Venis	1999/02/14
Jesse James	1999/03/15
Goldust	1999/03/29
The Godfather	1999/04/12
Jeff Jarrett	1999/05/25
Edge	1999/07/24
Jeff Jarrett	1999/07/25
D-Lo Brown	1999/07/27
Jeff Jarrett	1999/08/22

And then what happened in the year after?

WRESTLER	DATE WON
Chris Jericho	1999/12/12
Chris Jericho & Chyna	2000/01/03
Chris Jericho	2000/01/23
Kurt Angle	2000/02/27
Chris Benoit	2000/04/02
Chris Jericho	2000/05/02
Chris Benoit	2000/05/08
Rikishi Phatu	2000/06/20
Val Venis	2000/07/04
Chyna	2000/08/27
Eddie Guerrero	2000/09/04

Let's compare. In the year before there were eight different holders while in the year after there were seven. Not much of a difference there. But of those eight, only one (Edge, thanks to readers **Bryan Hayes** and **Dave Rozewski** for pointing out that Edge was WWE Champion at the time of this writing) went on to be WWE/World Champions, while two went on to be NWA Champions (and one a WCW Champion). Of the seven in the later year four went on to be WWE/World Champions. Not judging too much on the skills of these wrestlers, but they do seem a higher caliber.

Chyna was the beginning of the upswing that began with her and continued to the unification of the title with the World Heavyweight Championship. She was instrumental in segueing the title away from the looseness of the past and the storylines it was involved in to bringing it back to a title for contenders and having the best wresters around fight over it.

And what of Chyna herself? Well, she was not so lucky. She did feud with Eddie Guerrero and Right to Censor, and eventually found her way pushed down the card and into the Women's Division. She let her contract expire because she felt, as a former Intercontinental champion, she deserved a contract at least as good as Val Venis. But that is not how WWE brass saw it and wanted to keep her pay low and put her in her place. Thus she left the WWE with the Women's Championship, never to be seen on WWE TV again (except in archive footage).

The rest of her life was not so great. Her music and acting careers went nowhere, she had an embarrassing loss on Celebrity Boxing, had emotional breakdowns on the Howard Stern Show, and released several sex tapes (starting with one with Sean Waltman). Although that particular video won a major porn industry award, one cannot consider that a highlight for a former champion. While she had brief runs in other organizations, in the end she died of what was ruled most likely an accidental overdose in April 2016.

The reasons, causes, and blames for all of these things is not what we are here to debate today. We must remember that THIS is not how Chyna was in the days as champion. At the time, she was completely credible. Her ex-post-facto actions have been retrofitted to make her appear as an unfit champion, but that is unfair. That is like saying Mohammad Ali should not be considered one of the greatest boxers of all time because he could barely speak in later life due to the debilitating effects of Parkinson's Disease. One has nothing to do with the other. Chyna was no embarrassment to the title, and if anything helped bring it back to the level of interest and prestige it should have enjoyed in the first place.

THAT WONDERFUL LISP

Chyna was a woman whose life after wrestling was not great, resulting in her eventual early death. She has had her troubles in life, so much so that we forget all she accomplished. Chyna winning the Intercontinental Championship was not an embarrassment at the time, but a logical evolution that needed to happen. She went on to become a three-time champion not because she failed, but because she succeeded in a man's world, a feat that has never been repeated at such a grand stage. She should be lauded for accomplishment and forever remembered as a worthy champion, not torn down because the sands of time have not been kind. Chyna had the faith of the WWE management and the fans, and it would take a long time to erode that. But when she was champion it was good for all, and helped bring the Intercontinental Championship back to a former level of glory.

The defense rests.

AFTER THE TRIAL

HUNG JURY

IN THE CASE OF THE IWC VS. CHYNA WINNING THE INTERCONTINENTAL CHAMPIONSHIP, THE WIN HAS BEEN ACCUSED OF BEING COMPLETELY UNREALISTIC AND ONLY FURTHER DEGRADED THE INTERCONTINENTAL CHAMPIONSHIP, A STAIN THAT IT CAN NEVER ERASE.

But, with 74.6% of the vote, Chyna Winning the Intercontinental Championship was found:

NOT GUILTY!

Bwa hahaha! I got you! You know you thought you were getting a guilty this time, but no way! You are looking at the man who got the Fingerpoke of Doom to be less guilty than Jeff Jarrett. Even I think that's crazy. A lot of people did pick up on the point that they were judging Chyna's win harshly based on the mess her life turned out to be. Once again, her life later on and our perception of her as a contender eight years ago at the time of this writing are totally different. You have to think within the time period.

RESPONSE

Let's start off by again trying to reset our post-conceived notions:

> *Vince knew Jarrett was going to become a major player in the new WCW under Russo[,] so maybe the theory could be that he made Jarrett job to a woman of little ability to make [WCW] fans realise that one of their main stars was no better that the [WWE]'s top woman!!*
>
> *I realise that sounds sexist but it just wasn't believable at the time that a woman [would] beat the top [mid-card] guy in the industry and looking back on it, it still isn't.*
>
> **David Garnett**

There's a bit of an assumption that Jarrett was going to end up as a major player or not. We look back in hindsight, especially at WCW in 2000, and realize that is what happened. However, Jarrett could have flopped upon his re-introduction to WCW and been pushed down the card. Sure, Vince could have been trying to make him look bad in general, but this match was booked well before his contract expired. And I would disagree that it wasn't believable that this particular woman could beat a top mid-card guy. Chyna's character was never built as a "woman who was as strong as men", but as "a very strong and dangerous person who happens to be a woman". There's a fine difference there, as shown here:

> *People seem to forget that When [C]hyna won the [I]ntercontinental [C]hampionship she had already gone toe to toe with "The Rock"[,] "Stone Cold Steve Austin"[,] "HHH"[,] and "[M]ankind"[.] [N]ot only that[,] but she had won a number one contender shot for the WWF title. So she proved she [c]ould hang with the big boys.*
>
> **Alex Windos**

Of course, we cannot get through this case without talking about Jeff Jarrett even more!

> *Well argued, but did not Jeff Jarrett hold the "E" hostage for $250,000 on the eve of the event where he was to drop the title to Chyna? His contract had expired like a day or two before the event and he wanted a quarter million bucks to cleanly drop the title to Chyna.*
>
> **Will Johnson**

We covered this in the Jeff Jarrett case itself, but I wanted to revisit it here for a few reasons. First, the figure for this money varies from $225,000 to $300,000, depending upon who is talking. Further, these rumors about Jarrett were exacerbated by Chyna herself in her 2001 autobiography (that was mostly written in 2000) "If They Only Knew". At the time, she was thoroughly employed by the WWE and still giving their version of events, including where she accused Jeff Jarrett and Vince Russo of engaging in a conspiracy to make the match happen after Jarrett's contract expired so that he could hold Vince McMahon up for money. This is the true origin of these accusations. In 2008, Jeff Jarrett addressed these accusations again in his TNA "King of the Mountain" DVD set where he not only covered the points we went over before, but that he also got WWE stock options right before they went public (which happened just two days later). Jarrett actually had nice things to say about the WWE and the negotiations for the match and money owed.

So no, he was not holding the WWE hostage so much as trying to make sure he had the money he was owed and made sure he was set up for the future. Now what became of the stock Jeff Jarrett received is a story for another day!

MINI-CASES

OVERVIEW

When beginning another anthology series entitled "Hidden Highlights", I was not completely sold that the concept could live on its own. While I was proven dreadfully wrong and went on to write or co-write 201 issues, I felt it was important to give Hidden Highlights the benefit of a proven commodity to prop it up. Thus, I added some mini-In Defense Of... cases to try to attract readers in. Again, this proved unnecessary, but it did give me an opportunity to discuss some smaller issues that could never fill up a full case but deserved to be heard anyway. You have seen a few of these sprinkled throughout this book when they directly related to larger cases, but here we have the remainder for your enjoyment!

As an aside, there was no "voting", per se. Instead, my co-writer James "JT" Thomlison would chime in with his singular judgment. I have not included those results here as they were not a true poll of the audience, so I leave you to your own conclusions.

TONY SCHIAVONE "THAT'LL PUT BUTTS IN SEATS

On January 4, 1999 on a live episode of Nitro, Tony Schiavone let the audience know that Raw was taped, and that former WCW wrestler Mick Foley—now known as Mankind—won the WWF Championship. In response to that win, Tony sarcastically said, "And on the other channel you will find that Mick Foley has won their world title. Yeah, that will really put butts in seats." Consequently, 600,000 people switched the channel to see Mick Foley win the title instead of watching the Finger Poke of Doom. Boy, was that a controversial night!

Many people have said that it was the most horrible thing Tony has ever done, and he is a terrible person for ever saying it. Except the problem is that Tony was told to say this from the back. As an announcer, he was often told to say things he did not agree with. And it is not like this is without precedent as Eric Bischoff used to go on the air and give away the RAW results and make fun of their matches.

Some have said that Tony should have stood up and refused to say the comment. To what end? So that he could be fired from the largest wrestling organization in the world (at the time)? What would that accomplish? It is not like he and Mick Foley were best friends, or that saying the comment would physically hurt Mick. Schiavone was just a pawn in the big game, and could be replaced at any moment with Scott Hudson, Mike Tenay, or Dusty Rhodes. He had no job security, but did have one of the greatest opportunities in the world for a company that always treated him right. Whether he agreed with the line or not does not matter: his job was to put over the talent and product, sell the merchandise and PPVs, and say whatever else the boss wanted.

Besides, on July 27, 2005 on the Wrestling Epicenter's Interactive Interview, Foley said that he knew right away that it was a comment that Tony did not want to say, and that he was just told to say it. He understood that Tony had a job to do, and despite everything holds no ill will towards him because of it.

If Mick Foley—the man most affected by Tony Schiavone's comment—does not have a problem with Tony because of the comment and understands Schiavone's position, then why have so many of us held a grudge against Schiavone for it till this day?

The mini-defense rests.

Brock Lesner leaving the WWE for Football

Two weeks before WrestleMania XX, Brock Lesner let Vince McMahon know that he would no longer be working for World Wrestling Entertainment and would instead be seeking a career in football. Though Brock had not played football in some years, he believed his natural athletic ability and strength, along with his determined training regimen would make him a viable candidate. So, with no one's blessing, Brock left the WWE and started down that path.

Many have said that Brock was an absolute idiot for doing this, giving up a multi-million-dollar dream job. They say he was ungrateful and should have just shut up and done whatever he was told.

But why? Brock Lesner was not happy at his job and decided to leave. What is wrong with wanting to be happy? Was it the smartest decision in the world? Probably not; he did give up a boat load of money and a giant push to the top. Brock had to ask himself, though, what was the price of his happiness? He did not like his work environment, his co-workers, or what he was doing. In a couple of years, he had already made it to the top, so he did not have any prospects of going anywhere. Where was the challenge, where was the fun?

A lot of people will tell you that work is not supposed to be fun, that sometimes you just work and that is it—and you should be grateful for anything. That is a defeatist attitude that will get you nowhere in life. Brock wanted to grow and expand, and felt the WWE was stifling him. He wanted the opportunity to do something new, something he loved, and did not want to be less than he could be.

And we should be grateful for that. Let us pretend that he did stay in the WWE. What would he do if he was not happy? Every week he would just be phoning it in, and we would complain that he does not care and was going through the motions, which would be true. Brock decided he did not want to do anything at half speed, and if he was going to commit it was going to be with his whole self. By leaving the WWE, he actually spared the WWE and its fans a disgruntled man who would not be adding to the product.

So he went off and tried football. Was he successful? Depends on your definition. From many people's ends, they will say no since he did not actually make it onto the Minnesota Vikings football team. From my perspective it is yes, because he made it through their training camp. Would you or I even get close enough to the field for ten minutes, nonetheless to the training camp? Brock was right in his belief that he stood a chance at making it in the NFL, and he had a right to pursue that dream, that happiness.

Others higher up in the NFL were sure of Brock's ability, too. They made a number 69 Vikings jersey which became one of the top selling items in the entire NFL. Football fans were excited to give Brock a chance, but he was not ready that year. The Vikings asked him to go to NFL Europe, but he had no interest. There was only one dream he wanted to pursue then, and that was to be with the Vikings.

Has Brock changed his mind since then? Perhaps. Did he sign a bad release deal with an insane no-compete clause? Most definitely (though no no-compete clause for ten years will not hold up in court. There is precedent that a no-compete clause cannot hold you from making a living for an 'unreasonable length of time', even if the contract is signed in good faith. So Brock does have a case when he says the no-compete clause is invalid, as he has a limited amount of time he can compete athletically. But that is a different story). But did he have the right to pursue a dream outside of wrestling without persecution? Absolutely!

The mini-defense rests.

THE WWE BANNING HIGH-RISK NECK MOVES

During an issue of In Defense Of..., I asked the audience to read Michael Weissman's The Paradox of Excellence. The reason for this is so that you can understand that hard work does not necessarily equate to large success. And why is that? Why is it that you can do the best job in the world, get everything perfect, and those benefiting from your work are still not happy?

It comes from the idea of managing expectations. Now imagine a line graph that looks like this:

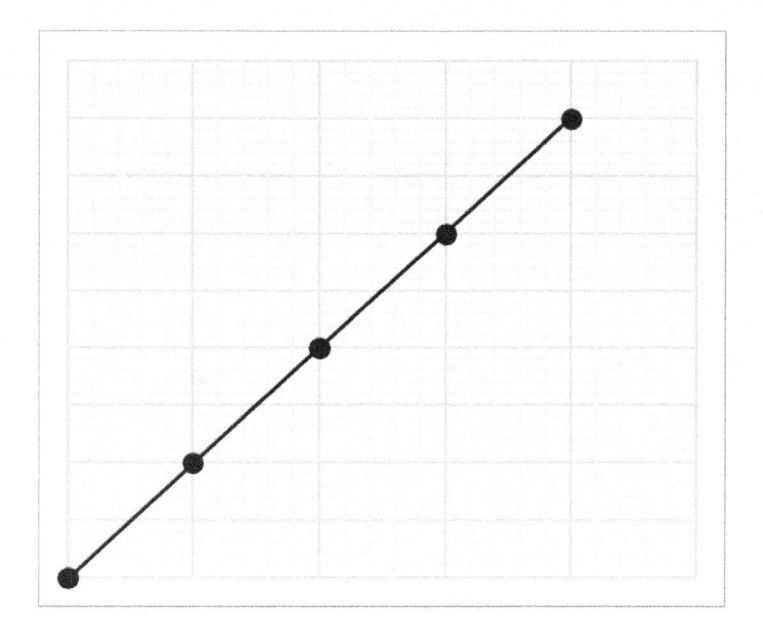

Connecting those circles, you will see that they form a straight line. Let's call this line your productivity. Now as your line goes up, you are getting more accomplished, and you'd think people would be happier with what you are doing, right? Well, look at this one:

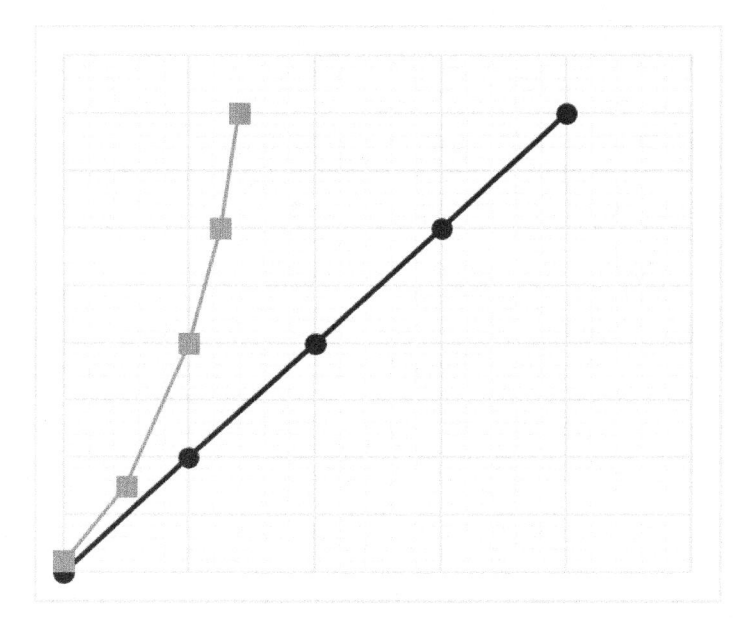

OK, you see those dark grey squares? That line is curving exponentially upwards away from your productivity line. And what is that line? That line is expectations. The more work you do, the more people expect. The better job you do, the more you have to do to meet others' satisfaction. And as time goes on, the gap between their expectations and your productivity grows so much that one of you will break. Either the recipient of your work will not appreciate or see the need for you anymore, or you will get sick of doing all that work for nothing. This is the Paradox of Excellence.

Right, now what does this have to do with banning high risk neck moves?

Well, letting the recipient of your work set the expectations is a sucker's game because, as you have seen, you can never truly reach their level of expectations no matter how much work you do. That is why you should propose this scenario:

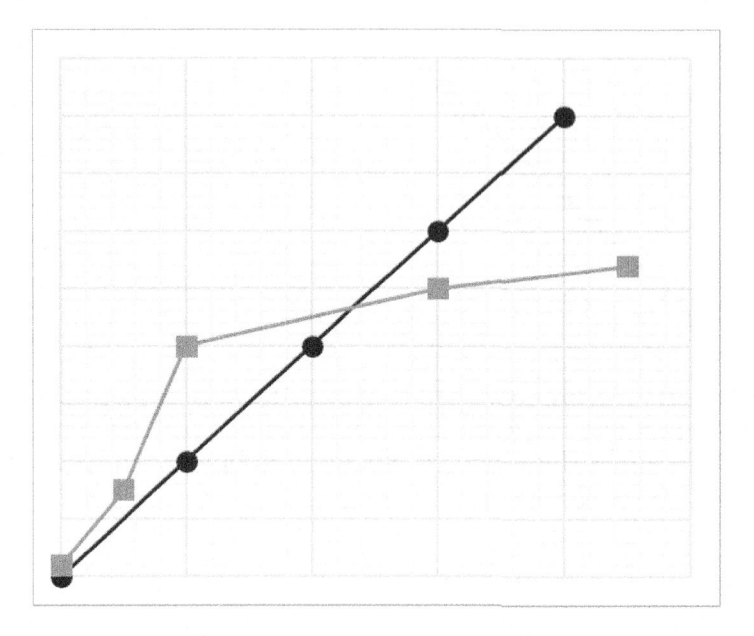

In this chart, expectations go through the productivity line so that doing exceptional performance stands out. And how do you get to this point? You manage their expectations of you!

Ready? By banning high risk neck moves, the WWE has said that the audience can no longer control the expectations. For years, the audience had complete control because the three top competitors (WWF, WCW, and ECW) were always trying to outdo one another, especially ECW. As first, just putting someone though a table was a big deal. Then it had to be stacked tables. Then it had to be stacked tables after jumping off a balcony. Then the wrestlers had to cut someone with a cheese grater first. Then the tables had to be set on fire.

Do you see where this is going? The audience could never be fully satiated because they came to EXPECT the total full-on violence and mayhem as the regular occurrence. And when the organizations did not deliver or tried to play safe, they were lambasted for it. Or worse yet, after setting a table on fire, the next time a table got set on fire it would not have the same impact or importance. Was the table any less on fire? Was there any less danger? Was the spot any less incredible? The answer to all of these questions is no, yet the spot had less of an effect on the audience. Expectations had run out of control.

When the WWE found they were the only game in town, they noticed that a fair number of their superstars were struggling through neck injuries (Steve Austin, Chris Benoit, Edge, Kurt Angle, and many others). They realized that the problem lay in the fact that the wrestlers had to go out every night and not just wrestle like it was a PPV, not even like it was WrestleMania, but that it was WrestleMania/Starrcade 100! The powers that be realized that they had let expectations get out of control, and that there was nothing special wrestlers could do anymore without getting into potentially lethal areas.

So over time they created a calculated plan to lower expectations. Slowly, large dangerous neck moves like the Piledriver, the Vertibreaker, head-first bombs, and others were weaned out of the weekly diet. And over time, the wrestling style we see today became the norm. So when Kurt Angle and Shawn Michaels have a four snowflake match, it isn't "Eh, it was just four snowflakes", the reaction is "Wow, what a great match, four snowflakes!" You see, the quality of the in-ring work has not changed, it is just the WWE has conditioned us for lower expectations.

In an interview with Michael Strider, Jake Roberts had this to say:

> **M. S.** – *You basically invented the D.D.T., right?*
>
> **J. R.** – *Yep! Every time somebody wins with it, they tell people, "Jake did it! He kicked your ass, so Jake must be better than you are!" See how stupid this is? These guys are going out there and doing it and I'm thinking, "Go ahead and show them I'm better than you are!" That's psychology right there! When you can take people and make them think they're doing something smart when they're doing something stupid! When you hit a guy with 9 clotheslines, you're not smart! You're telling the people that you're a phony and he is too! If I can't knock a guy on his ass with two lefts and one right, I'm not gonna hit that son of a bitch anymore because I'm not gonna be the guy that can't knock you on your ass with one punch! I'm damn near 50 years old! I don't need that bullshit!*

Do you see what Roberts is saying? By using a move like the DDT as a transitional move, wrestlers are setting themselves up for failure. Jake used it as a finishing move and made it look devastating. But now, people do not expect someone to get pinned off of a DDT; it is not believable. And it is not because Roberts overused it, it is because others saw fit to ignore the psychology of a match and just use it to get from one move to another. That was what was happening with these dangerous neck moves. People were getting injured off of what were essentially becoming transition moves, and in order to finish a match wrestlers would have to go to extreme lengths to please a finicky audience. The results may be predetermined, but the dangers are real. And these men and women were putting their bodies over the line for our entertainment.

Because of this, the WWE pulled in the reigns. So now when the Undertaker hits a rare tombstone, it is a big deal. When the Hurricane gets to use the Vertibreaker, it's simply amazing. When someone is allowed to fly through the air and into the crowd to take out their opponent, it is an intensely great PPV moment. RVD does not need to use the Van Daminator—nonetheless the Van Terminator—as a transition move! Those moves are special and deserve to be held in reverence.

We, the audience, should not be comparing every week whether one table spot was weaker than the other. That is expecting too much, and puts the wrestlers at too much physical risk. Look at all the wrestlers that have died from pain killers or have been seriously injured in the ring to never return. Is this what we should expect? Should we expect these people to hurt themselves viciously just because our appetite is insatiable?

No, the WWE decided that to protect their wrestlers—their investments into the future of the business—to limit the moves that we see on free TV. This makes the moves that much better, that much more special, when we do get to see them; gives a reason to order the PPV; and makes it so that each time we see these now rare moves, they always exceed our expectations.

The mini-defense rests.

APPENDIX: SUSPENDED SENTENCE

NEWS FROM PRAG'S PLACE

For my last official full article for 411mania in November 2010 (News from Prag's Place: Second and Final Edition), I took a look back at my career there and filled in some additional details on this series. This is a bit of a view of what could have been (and what may be should I ever decide to write a sequel to this book).

SOME DAME WALKED INTO MY OFFICE AND SAID...

Now, perhaps you didn't read all 64 issues of In Defense Of...? Maybe you didn't read about Chyna Winning the Intercontinental Championship, Jeff Jarrett, the nWo Split, the European Championship, Jeff Hardy, DDP, Hulk Hogan, the World Heavyweight Championship, Scott Steiner, the Ultimate Warrior, Vince McMahon in the Death of Owen Hart, Larry Zbyszko, Scott Hall, New Jack, the McMahon-Helmsley Era, Mike Awesome Leaving ECW, Sid Vicious, the Undertaker, the Sport of Professional Wrestling, Lex Luger, WCW Thunder, the Brand Extension, Goldberg, Vince not buying out WCW's contracts, Earl Hebner Screwing Bret Hart, Dusty Rhodes: Head Booker, The Finger Poke of Doom, Kevin Nash, the Elimination Chamber, or even Eric Bischoff. Well, for those new to the concept, this article came with a pretty simple premise:

Certain people, events, organizations, and storylines in wrestling history have gotten a bum rap. Some writers have presented overtly critical comments and outright lies as fact, and others have followed suit. Well no more! "In Defense of..." has one reason: to bring the truth to the wrestling fan!

And that's what I did.

Officially, In Defense Of... has been on hiatus since August 3, 2006 so I never got to finish off the articles I wanted to do. Below was the plan:

- Issue 65-66: The Ministry of Darkness
- Issue 67-68: The Bushwackers
- Issue 69-70: Marty Jannetty
- Issue 71: Steve "Mongo" McMichael
- Issue 72-74: Sean Waltman
- Issue 75: SPECIAL - Different Styles of Professional Wrestling
- Issue 76-77: Shane Douglas
- Issue 78-79: Kane
- Issue 80: Coliseum Home Video
- Issue 81-83: Vince Russo

- Issue 84: Women's Wrestling
- Issue 85-86: Brian Pillman
- Issue 87-88: Tito Santana
- Issue 89: The Diva Search
- Issue 90-91: Billy Gunn / Kip James
- Issue 92: The Hardcore Title
- Issue 93-94: Bob Holly
- Issue 95-99: WCW
- Issue 100: SPECIAL – TBD

And there were another fourteen cases that were accepted and not booked, including (in no particular order):

- Billy Kidman
- Booker T's WWF/E Run
- David Flair
- Demolition
- Doink the Clown
- Double Shot: Matt Hardy, Edge, and Lita
- Giant Goncalves
- Muhammed Hassan
- Randy Savage
- Ron Garvin... World Champion
- Tammy Lynn Sytch
- The Black Scorpion
- TNA Cutting Off ROH
- Verne Gange

Not to mention there were dozens of other cases that were under consideration or not accepted. I hope this is a lesson for theme writers today and the future of how far in advance I was planning things out and how it translated into the work.

The only one I regret not being able to do is the five-part WCW one. Growing up a NWA/WCW fan, it saddens me to see how people talk about the promotion today. Of course, 95% of all NWA/WCW fans stopped watching wrestling all together upon its demise (WWE's rating did not go up when they bought WCW), so I'm the last of a dying breed there as well. Heck, I wrote the first In Defense Of... for Eric Bischoff because there was pretty much nothing but pure WWE smarks left by the time 2005 rolled around and they had no sense of what really transpired in that company. Even today I read people who say how Eric Bischoff put WCW out of business. No, Eric Bischoff led the company to their only profitable time in its history. When things started to sour, he was sent home and others took over the reins leading to major losses and the eventual backroom deal to sell the company by a former WWE employee who was part of the AOL-Time Warner merger. But you can read all of that in the archives, therefore there is no need to rehash that here.

In any case, what are we going to defend now? Well nothing as these articles take way too long to put together. Instead it's time to move on...

IN DEFENSE OF... IN DEFENSE OF...

In Defense of... was normally about spreading truth to the wrestling fans. It was also about enjoying everything in wrestling, or at least understanding why other people do. Things don't just suck because you say so, and people's lives are not screwed up because you think so. There is too much out there that is pure speculation yet has become the diehard fact.

Over the course of the series, I took on a number of controversial subjects. As you can imagine, that sparked some rather... heated responses. People questioned my conclusions, my facts, my methodologies, the voting results, pretty much everything. As such, I originally wrote this piece to meet the critics, explain why I did and did not do certain things, and let the audience delve a little deeper into what this article meant to me.

WHERE'S THE PROSECUTION?

This article is called "In Defense of...", and it is that: a defense. That's the gimmick. That's my whole synopsis of what this article is. I designed it to be a counter-measure to the net-gativity (© Meehan) out there and to try to stop the incorrect rumors from being spread. I wanted to get people to at least think about the other side of the equation instead of just accepting what the likes of any IWC journalist said as fact. You would hear things like "Everybody hates Hogan" and "Why can't he retire, nobody wants to see him" or "I hope he gets hurt and is gone from my TV forever." Ouch!

These types of words made people who are fans of the IWC's most hated targets to think they were alone in the world. They would think that they were crazy for wanting to see Hogan hulk up, see Randy Orton deliver the RKO, see Lex Luger put someone in the rack, or actually enjoy the McMahon-Helmsley Era. What I have found is that these small-pockets put together actually overwhelm the louder IWC voice. Just because someone can yell the loudest does not mean he is saying the truth.

Because I was so frustrated with the IWC's portrayal of certain wrestlers and events in history (and the compression of time, which gets to me to no end), I felt the need to be the defender against all of those people spreading the falsities. It was me against the entire IWC, and I was ready to do it.

Yet because I want to be a defender of wrestling's "most hated", I get labeled as one sided. People say I need the prosecution to be the balance. ***I*** need a balance. Little me against the hundreds—thousands!—of other negative liars out there—I'm the one who needs to have a counter!

Take this letter from **Brendan** for example:

> I do find your arguments have a certain bizarre logic to them. First and foremost, though is that you're defending things against well... what, I'm not sure. It's a prosecution without a voice, it instead incorporates ideas, hearsay, and generalities from so very many different sources. This prosecution ghost has no voice in your column, except from you. The person who wants to prove the defendant [innocent]. It's like some reverse 1930s soviet show-trial.

Or this one from **Frank Adetoye**:

> I wanted to suggest that how about having a prosecution side of stories, [i.e.,] have a guest writer in the prosecution of....... and then putting it to the public vote maybe it will be a fair reflection of things. It will be really interesting to see how it works.

Or this one from **Lev.**:

> You only present the defense.
>
> What about the prosecution?
>
> Now I know you explain what the accusations against the wrestler are, and then you dissect and counter them, but the problem is there is no one to counter your counter-points. You're swaying the readers by trying to disprove the accusations, as the defense does, yet there is no prosecution trying to prove the accusations. Does that make sense?

And let me tell you, there are a lot more similar. Unfortunately, not many of them are as clear and reasonable as these three, so I included them.

All right, let me answer the accusations.

I don't need a prosecution for two major reasons:

(1) The prosecution already exists. As I state in the rules every week, each one of my clients has already been found guilty in the court of IWC opinions without ever hearing the other side. My job is to be the countermeasure to that and show what the IWC haters do not want you to know or, more likely, what they never knew. Most of these negative opinions are based on a lack of facts, not a vendetta. Brendan is right in his accusation that he is not sure who I am defending against because the prosecution seems to be a mix of different voices. That's because it is. For every source I quote in my article, you can guarantee that are at least ten more that I have read, listened to, or watched in my quest for answers.

Sometimes, I don't find the answers I'm looking for and my argument changes. I do not pick an objective and stick with it. The final accusations come out of what I find as I research. Sometimes I find hatreds I never knew existed. I've also taken on clients that I do not like and felt were terrible before I started. Yet through my own research I convinced myself of my client's innocence. After all, I am my harshest critic.

The point is, the prosecution, if you will, has hundreds of different forums (pun intended) to get their message of hatred out. I have one article a week to make a counter measure. And once the case is done, it is done forever. My single article, with a splattering of others who care deeply for my client, are the only small voices against the overwhelming, pre-existing prosecution.

And (2) the other thing is this article is called In DEFENSE of…! Now, I wouldn't be much of a writer if I did not show what people opposite me felt and then write a refutation. That's all this article is: a refutation. Now why should I use my limited amount of space to provide those who already have unlimited space more time to show their arguments? I don't care about their arguments beyond my refutation. This is not a debate; this is just trying to see the other side.

Which of course brings us to our next point: Why isn't this a debate?

THIS SHOULD BE A DEBATE

You want the honest answer?

I can't.

There is no way I can make this article into a debate.

First off, who would I debate against? Look at it like this:

It takes JT and me on average about 36 hours to write an issue of Hidden Highlights. The only thing Hidden Highlights requires is that we watch the shows and take notes. Yet because of the logistics involved in just trying to get the two of us to get our parts done and send the draft back and forth, Hidden Highlights takes some considerable time. And we have a template we use!

Now look at In Defense of.... A one-issue case usually takes me about eight to ten hours of research and another four to seven hours of writing. Now double that for a second person. Plus add in the logistics of getting it back and forth. Now add in the fact that In Defense Of... does not have a template and will require a fresh copy every week. I'd say a single issue of this article would take three weeks, minimum.

As another example, the Great Positivity Debate took three weeks to complete. That involved four people, so the logistics were insane, but that is nuts. A single issue of Fact or Fiction takes about three days, but that's only because Ashish controls the topics, participants, and lengths. The level of detail in Fact or Fiction or the Great Positivity Debate is nothing in comparison to the level of detail I put into a single issue of In Defense Of....

And who would I ask? Another writer on the site? No offense, but other writers have different styles that do not mesh well with mine, and others just plain don't have time. Do you think my schedule could work with someone like Sforcina? The guy lives in Australia!

That's the other thing. My schedule is horrible. Anyone who reads me regularly knows that I can be on the road for any length of time. I might be working on this article a week or two ahead of time, or I might be going until the midnight deadline. No one can depend on me to get them a draft or schedule a time for an AIM chat. You will never know where I am, what time zone I'm in, and when I'm free. Plus it will change every week.

No, the logistics of a debate are virtually impossible from my end.

Now might I suggest that if you still have issue with, or want to spread the message in my article more, go on to a message board on any site (preferably a competitor's), put a link to my article, and debate it. Sadly, beyond the initial article and my e-mail responses (and sometimes additions in Hidden Highlights), I don't have the time nor ability to do it myself.

Besides, I put myself over enough. That'd be really weak linking to myself on other sites.

MORE COUNTER-EVIDENCE

All right, now that we understand that this is just a defense and why this is a defense, you do have to realize I get challenged after the fact. I do try to respond to everyone, and I appreciate people with logical arguments. I don't appreciate, "He just sucks" without any reasons. You will often get a response from me just saying, "Why? Could you clarify your reasoning for me?" IF (and that's a big IF) I get a response, it will most likely be, "I don't have any reasons, I just don't like him."

Sigh.

That's not what I'm about and those aren't the people I'm writing to. This article does ask you to at least come in open minded, and if you have something to use against me after the fact, then sure, I'll hear it and respond.

That said, I do not accept challenges. You can rant and rave all you want, even if you are the most logical person in the world with an argument that trounces mine, I will never return to a subject within the confines of my column.

And no, it's not because I'm scared or that I don't want the "truth" to be known. It is, once again, that I just don't have the time. I have my entire caseload planned out months in advance. So when I finish a case, I'm done with it.

Listen, right now I'm averaging seven weeks to respond to an e-mail. Seven weeks! So by the time I re-read (I always read the majority of them when they first come in, except the really long ones) and respond to your e-mail, we've already moved two or three topics ahead.

It would be counter-productive for me to go back to a subject I've already completed, as well as extremely redundant. Due to time and space constraints, I cannot hit on every single subject. I always try to hit the biggest issues with a few key small ones that make the impact I am looking to have. So yes, I will "forget" or "skip" or "gloss over" something that was extremely important to you. It happens, and I'm sorry! But I'm human and there is a limit to my time, space, and ability to research and write.

If there is something that particularly bothers you, please tell me when I first announce the case. Nine times out of ten I'm already planning on covering it, but it might make my case better if I hear from you before I start. Telling me everything you hate after the case does not help me at all.

"But JP," you'll say, "You just did this in the Hulk Hogan case. You met the prosecution, so how come you can't always do that?!"

Because that was a special case. I made it four parts and designed it so that it would end at a certain point that would allow feedback. And it's not like I haven't changed my cases due to feedback before. Goldberg gained a whole other part (and Lex Luger became one less) due to reader feedback. It just needs to be appropriately timed to be included.

So yes, I can include the counter-points, but not after the fact. There is nothing I can do then but respond to you directly.

MANIPULATING THE LAST WORD

But the biggest complaint I get after the fact is how I word the final accusation. Take for instance **Feroz Nazir** who says:

> You really have to watch your semantics.

AK lays it out in plain English:

> You win all your cases by a land slide. The reason being is how you word your accusations. It's easy to defend one angle of an argument, especially when every article the accusation is worded in ways that don't reflect what the [internet] is really accusing people of.

That is where I have to disagree.

As some of my examples from above show, most people in the IWC **DO NOT** know why they truly dislike something. They just have a disdain for certain people, events, storylines, etc... without knowing why. A lot of it has to do with the flippant remarks by other columnists that get written over and over. If I read a thousand times that Triple H is evil, I'm very likely to believe it. I can also read a thousand times that CM Punk is a wrestling god, and I'd be likely to believe it. Now people in the IWC swoon over almost every single Chris Benoit match out there, but let me clue you in: every single Chris Benoit match is not a classic.

As a matter of fact, many of them are slow and repetitive.

Remember when Peter Kent was doing the number of moves that Triple H was doing per minute and it came out to something like one move every two minutes? Chris Benoit is not that far off. A chop is not a move. Throwing people in the ropes, not a move. Stalling, not a move. Staring people down, not a move. Laying on the mat for a minute, not a move. In the restraint of the WWE style, Chris Benoit does almost as few moves as Triple H. It's true.

Yet people in the IWC will watch his matches and say it was great! If he and Triple H both wrestled Viscera on the same night and did the exact same sequence of moves, Triple H will have had a boring match where he dominated while Chris Benoit would have carried a broomstick to a passable match and sold like a champ. Think about it.

I honestly believe there is a large amount of passive aggressiveness (and passive passion) that people in the IWC have because of what they read, not what they believe.

The accusations at the end of my article put EXACTLY what I have read through my research into concise words. Do you want to know why you get upset? Because you have to face your beliefs in real words. People get angry when they are faced with the complete truth. That's what makes this article effective. It's also what makes an effective heel. When Ric Flair calls someone in the front row fat and lazy, and they are fat and lazy, what does that person do? Boo and yell and flip Ric Flair off. When Daivari tells the audience that they are racist and they boo his client because he is of Arab decent, and the audience starts booing and chanting "U-S-A!", is he not telling the truth?

The truth hurts. It really does. To face your own prejudices in clear, defined packages makes it hard to admit your true intentions. When you are allowed to hate without qualification, it is very easy. I can say any day of the week, "I hate Steve Austin." Yet someone would come up to me and say, "How can you hate him? He kicks ass, has cool catch phrases, beats up the boss, and drinks beer!"

Now, I could just slink away and say I hate him and let the hate just seethe in me under the surface without any reason. Or I could face myself and define my hatred. I can say, "I don't like wrestlers who brawl, I happened to agree with Vince McMahon during their feud, I agree with Eric Bischoff's reasoning for firing him from WCW, and being a huge WCW mark I don't like how he contributed to the WWE's rise to dominance." Now I have reasons. Are they good reasons? They are to me. But at the end of the day, I can still say, "I hate Steve Austin, but I get why you like him."

And that's what I'm talking about.

I want you to face the REAL accusations that are out there and not just have some undefined hate. If you hate someone/thing, that's fine! You can tell me you still hate it. But you better have reasons. Still, you should be able to look beyond yourself and see why other people would find a defendant "not guilty". If, even with all my evidence, you believe I am completely wrong and that the "guilty" people are right, and you have the true proof and reasoning to go with it, then vote guilty. If you are basing it off a "feeling" that I just cannot respond to, what can I possibly do to convince you?

I was at a client a few weeks back and we had a chart on the screen generated from a database of data. One of the people in the room said, "That doesn't look right." I asked him what didn't look right, if he could clarify for me. He couldn't. He had no answer. Yet he questioned my data on the screen for no reason other than the visual was not meeting his expectations. Well, going back the data was 100% right and he was 100% wrong, but the damage was done by his "feeling". Other people in the room took his doubts as their own, even though those doubts were based on nothing.

To say I was frustrated would be an understatement. I thought about this article at that moment, and how people vote guilty based on a feeling. I wonder if they even read the cases, or if they just wait until the last part and vote? I put in a lot of work, and nothing makes me feel worse than someone voting guilty based on nothing at all.

THE "RULES" ARE UNFAIR

When it come to the vote, people sometimes say the rules I put at the end of my case for voting are unfair. Unfair?

Well, I practically copied them from a combination of American and British laws, amendments, and declarations. So I guess the judicial branches of most of the western world are designed wrong!

(By the way, I am in no way saying the judicial systems in the western world are without flaws; and are in need of an overhaul. But the base laws that exist were not designed for the level of corruption that we see. They can be added to, though, to make up for it. But I digress.)

The other thing is that they are not "rules", they are "guidelines". Hell, they aren't even really "guidelines", they are just reminders. The "rules" are just a way for me to remind the readers to stick to the topic at hand, to read everything I've written, and to take the accusations seriously. They came about because in the case of Vince McMahon Not Buying Out WCW's Contracts, people found Vince guilty based on the cRaZiEsT fantasy booking you could have ever seen. People like Triple H weren't injured, Norman Smiley became World Champion, and SpikeTV was willing to give the WWE fifteen hours of TV a week. It was ridiculous. Because of this, I felt the need to focus people and remember what we were talking about and what they had just read.

And besides, the rules actually came about as a suggestion from a reader. Much like the voting, the major changes to the style of the column have come about from reader feedback. The rules were just in response to a need.

YOU DON'T FOLLOW THE "RULES"

But because I wrote the rules, I often get accused of not following them. For instance, **John Carruthers** said:

> *You may wish to remove the list of rules at the end, however, if you're unwilling to adhere to all of these same rules.*

To which I asked how I broke them and never got a response. But why not delve into this anyway? Let's take the rules one at a time and see how I follow them and how other may think I break them.

> *(1) All parties, events, circumstances, etc... are innocent until proven guilty. In this court, the defendants have already been found guilty without trial, and so therefore this is an appeals court. Finding a defendant guilty means you disagree with the evidence presented.*

Ummm... I'm not even sure how I could break this rule. I assume my clients are innocent and face the charges. OK...

> *(2) The jury must find the defendant guilty beyond reasonable doubt. That means that if there is doubt in your mind that the defendant is guilty, then you cannot find the appellant guilty. Reasonable doubt means that the average person, looking at the facts presented, could not find the defendant guilty on all counts despite personal feelings.*

Yeah, I'm not really sure how I could break this rule either. I'm not the jury, I'm the defender, and I try to make sure you have at least a little doubt.

> *(3) This is a court of fact, not fiction. Fantasies of what could have been or should have been do not fly here; especially fantasies of the impossible (such as a wrestler not getting injured at an untimely moment). All we have is what did actually occur and the intentions of those being accused.*

I guess this is one people may try to find me guilty of, but I have not fantasy booked. I have never said, "Imagine if this happened..." or "If so-and-so hadn't done that, then things would be different." That's not how I work. I may pose the question from time-to-time about a definite plan that was out there that did not come to fruition, or I might present the actual plan that would happen. For instance, in the Brand Extension case I posed the question of what would happen if the brands came back together. Using historical data, I showed that there would be an initial jump in ratings, but then brought it back to the bigger question of what is wrong with the WWE's booking. Being separate brands is not what is causing poor writing and feud development, they are totally separate issues. So the WWE would have problems beyond that point and the Brand Extension coming to an end would not fix those bigger issues.

Sometimes, I do ask to allow things to develop. For instance, when I was defending Scott Steiner, I said give it time to see what he can do in TNA. I didn't fantasy book and say he was going to bring TNA to the mainstream and beat the WWE. I said just keep an open mind and wait and see what happens. That is not making something up, that is just asking a request and not judging his run in TNA to be crap before he even made his premier. That seems reasonable to me.

> *(4) A defendant cannot be judged by events outside the case at hand. For example, if we were trying a particular contract signing by a wrestling promoter, you cannot use that ten years later that wrestler died from a heart attack relating to the drug use that the wrestler started when he signed with the promoter. One has nothing to do with the other in terms of the case at hand.*

This is the one I probably get the most crap on. Take for instance in the Owen Hart case. Some people felt like I was being vindictive against Martha Hart and it was irrelevant to the case at hand. While I may not have been clear in why I included Martha Hart, it was not irrelevant. I was trying to make the point that she is one of the people pushing the idea that Vince is guilty because she has a direct benefit from it. Remember, the case was about Vince McMahon, not Owen Hart, and anyone who was dragging Vince down had to be spoken against.

Another example would be where I talked about Eric Bischoff having a pilot's license or Larry Zbyszko being good at golf. People say these are irrelevant to the case at hand. I disagree. When we are talking about a whole person and their career, I like to remind everyone that these people are PEOPLE! It's very easy, especially behind this keyboard, to just think of these people as objects that are there to be critiqued. I want everyone to remember that when talking about a person that they have a life and interests outside of wrestling. It's also about setting the character. In real court cases (or maybe just TV and movies ones), lawyers often call character witnesses in order to prove their client's being. I am doing the same. I want you to understand the whole person, although it may be irrelevant to their wrestling career.

Look at Warrior Warrior. Nothing did it more for me when he said he had to take his daughter to the ballet, being one of the self-destructive things he does. Many people just want to call him insane, and then use that insanity as a reason to hate his wrestling career. Yet lines like that go a long way to prove he has a normal life and didn't blow up the way the WWE and IWC would like to have us believe. The character witness was important to disproving the wrestling connection.

> *(5) You do not have to like the accused before or after the case at hand, and a vote of not guilty does not change your personal preferences. You can make it clear that you feel the accused is the worst thing you have ever seen, but if the facts compel you to see that the accused cannot be found guilty beyond reasonable doubt, then voting guilty would be unconscionable.*

This is where people get the most confused. They say that I write subjectively and that I break the rule by putting my feelings into my arguments.

Do you know what that is called?

Passion.

I argue with passion, and it has feeling behind it, but the words are still the facts. The only time I ask for feelings is when I ask if the facts even matter. Like does it matter if Hogan had bad movies? Does that have anything to do with wrestling? But I'm not asking a feeling, I'm asking for relevance.

Also, I guarantee you will never figure out which clients I believe or do/did not believe in. I argue with the same passion for any one of my clients. Yes, I use passion as a tool in my arguments, but the arguments could stand on their own if they were just a list.

Of course, this would be a really bad article if it were just a list. How enjoyable would that be to read? You need to feel something to get from point to point. Sometimes I joke, sometimes I'm serious, sometimes I say something ridiculous. I'm still trying to make this an entertaining read, so of course I want you to have an emotional response. But the emotions are just a backdrop to the facts, nothing more.

THE VOTE IS SKEWED

Of course, when it comes to voting, there are two much larger complaints. The first one is that it's not easy enough to vote through e-mail. **Bill** says:

> *You should get one of those polls that Larry's got.*

I thought long and hard about this one, but decided the risk was not worth it. With that external poll, people can vote multiple times, set up bugs, and hack them. It actually happened to Larry, and that's why he no longer uses the polls. The polls on the outside are not safe when it comes to voting.

So yes, the number of people voting would probably be ten times higher than what they are now. I do understand that. But I also believe I get a fair representation from e-mail. I also have complete control over voting.

If someone votes twice, I see that very quickly. And believe me, people try to vote multiple times. But even if someone has multiple e-mail addresses, how many could they possibly have? Five? After a while it's just not worth it.

Also, I find that doing an e-mail poll invites more reader feedback. If people just voted, then they may not want to take the effort to write in. But since they are already writing, many feel the need to write more. So in the end, it's a win-win for me.

The other problem is people do not like answering all the charges at once. **cubfan75** over in the 411mania Forums said:

> *I wish you had split the charges.*

Here's the thing with splitting the charges: it's probably a good idea. It'd be great to split everything up, but it's just not feasible. Some cases have two charges, some have twenty. That means that each charge needs to have a separate e-mail (I use e-mail subject lines to count the votes, so please make sure you use the correct subjects otherwise your vote will not be counted), and it would go on forever.

If we were using the system described above, it could work out better. But the drawbacks of using that system make this not a viable option as well.

Also, how would we judge my success rate? Really, either I win the case or I don't. I can't sort of win and sort of lose. Either I got my message across or I didn't. It's really an overall question about the wrestler/event. At the end of the day the question is really this: "Is this person/event as bad as the IWC has made them out to be?" That's all I really want to know.

PREACHING TO THE CHOIR

Through my accusations and arguments, I have been able to have a long-running winning streak. But the complaint is that I'm just preaching to the choir, and that the lovers of such a person/event are flooding my inbox.

I will admit, I do get a fair share of people that say they would have voted not guilty no matter what I said. But I also get a lot of these:

> *When I saw the header I thought, this is going to be an easy one, he's guilty.*
>
> *You have changed my mind.*
>
> *- **Noah Madison** on Mike Awesome Leaving ECW*

> *[O]nce again you changed my mind. I have always looked back and felt that that era was the one that started the downfall that we are in today. But with your hard work and research I realize that it was fresh and new, but like all good things they get old with time. NOT GUILTY*
>
> *- **Nick from the Package Center** on the McMahon-Helmsley Era*

> *Thanks for writing such a fascinating article. I've been following your column since it started and I really do think this is your best work yet. Why do I think that? I do because I went into reading the article as a true Warrior-hater. Your article honestly changed my opinion of him and now I actually think the guy is pretty inspirational. Oh, and I am very liberal myself. So, your victory in winning me over is even more impressive.*
>
> *- **Matt Essary** on the Ultimate Warrior*

> *That very article changed my opinion about Triple H more than about the World Title. He was indeed at that time the only guy worthy of that title, and for that matter, as #1 contender and potentially or realistically (cough) next in line for a shot. Great article, and in my opinion, the best you've written as well as the most convincing. Nice Work.*
>
> *- **Matt Adamson** on the World Heavyweight Championship*

> *[A]lright... [I] cannot believe it, but you convinced me...*
>
> - **Weyoun** on the Finger Poke of Doom

> *I don't know how you do it, but you convince me every time!*
>
> - **ShiHigh2005** on Lex Luger

And **Andrew Lee** sums it up best:

> *I just wanted to tell you how much I enjoy your column and have just spent 3 hours reading your columns on Dusty, Bischoff, Hebner, Nash, Goldberg and Awesome. All these men I have hated in the past, yet I couldn't help but keep coming up with my own verdict of not guilty. You have really helped me see a new side to each controversial wrestler and allowed me to step away from the bias views of the IWC that were becoming my own...*
>
> *Thanks for really helping me see new sides to things and keep up the good work.*

And this was just a small sampling of everything I have received. I think the evidence speaks for itself.

WHY DO I PUT UP WITH IT?

Throughout this article, I may have come across a little more angry than usual. Being the King of Positivity, you rarely do get to see me flip out a little bit. You must be saying, "If this is the stuff he gets every week, why does he put up with this crap?"

The answer: I really enjoy this.

For everyone who doesn't read the case and votes guilty are people like those listed in the above section who come in with an open mind. For every person who never reads my work and continues to spread the lies are the plethora of people sending my article to their friends and continuing to spread the good word of In Defense Of....

Also, I'm a wrestling fan, and I'm a history buff, and I'm a truth fanatic, so I found a way to combing all three. I do think that I am making a small impact out there, and that it is spreading every day. I also think its spreading in more subtle ways than many people realize.

Between Hidden Highlights and In Defense Of..., many other writers' styles have changed to a positive message about pro-wrestling. Some posters on the board use similar argument styles to mine. There is change out there.

Plus I am touching people around the world. I have gotten messages from Austria, Bangladesh, Guiana, and some countries even I have never heard of.

I've also discovered a new feeling that is hard to describe. I find it very odd when people are talking or writing about me in the third person. I don't consider myself famous or even well known, but now I realize that complete strangers are reading and talking about my work. As a matter of fact, more than your average IWC kid is reading me...

REAL WORLD IMPACT

I don't talk about this much (or at all), but I have heard from people involved in the cases. Not to name any names, but during the Goldberg case I did hear from a close acquaintance of his who thanked me for defending his friend. I've also heard from people who have met Scott Hall and Kevin Nash and said I captured their real-life spirits. But that is just the tip of the iceberg.

Recently, I heard from someone HEAVILY involved in the Vince McMahon in the Death of Owen Hart case. I'm not going to mention who because I have not had a chance to respond to this person yet, but I guarantee you would be shocked. I was shocked! Oh, and it wasn't as nice a letter as the ones mentioned above. This person was not happy with how I argued my case. Quite interesting.

We always like to pretend that the bookers and personalities in the world are reading our stuff and stealing our ideas. I used to laugh at these very notions. But after seeing things I've said show up on TV and having heard from people involved in the industry, I'm not laughing as much anymore. We really do have an impact in the world, and it makes this job very intriguing.

MY SECRET REASON FOR DOING THIS

There is a reason beyond all that, though, about why I write this article. And it involves a lie.

In Hidden Highlights before the Reader Write-in section, we say something like "We aren't just doing this for our health...". Well, that's not entirely true.

I do this article for my health.

In case you haven't been able to tell, I live a very turbulent life. In the past year, the only stability I have had is this article. I've lived in two different homes (and look to be going to my third, as I just found out on Sunday), I've traveled back and forth across the country, I've eaten at more nameless restaurants than I care to count.

Sometimes, this article was my only sanity, my only stability.

I've also had a lot of personal trials, and writing this article has been the thing to cheer me up, or at least keep me focused on something else for another day.

This has not been the easiest year of my life. It hasn't been horrible, I haven't faced things that made me question life or anything like that. But then again, I'm a pretty optimistic guy.

But writing this article has been a joy. Even when I was dreading the deadline or writing until 4am (four hours past my deadline), it still felt worth it.

I've seen myself grow as a writer, grow as a person, and expand my own horizons based on just what I have done here.

This article has been an important and pivotal part of my life, and I'm glad that Larry, Randle, and Ashish gave me this opportunity.

I want to thank them, and all of you, for giving me a chance this year. I also want to thank you for reading this issue, even though it had next to nothing to do with wrestling.

It's been a great ride so far, and I promise good stuff coming up right down the road!

The defense continues!

AFTERWARDS

ABOUT THE AUTHOR

J.P. Prag is a Pisces, even though that does not mean anything. However, ten of the stars in Pisces are known to host planets, though these stars are nowhere near each other. One of the planets (GU Pisces b) takes around 80,000 Earth years to circle its sun. Of note, some of the stars are not stars at all, but are entire galaxies! Further scientific examination has discovered many other faint galaxies, nebulae, stars, and other stellar objects within the Pisces general area. A couple of those galaxies are on a collision course, so look out for that over the next several hundred million years or so.

When not observing the stars at the Ladd Observatory, J.P. Prag can be found several blocks away at his home and office in Providence, RI, U.S.A. with his partner Caroline and their many tall ferns and philodendrons, lazy lying down cacti, outside pet squirrels (including Squirrel the Raccoon), and a stuffed pet sloth named Peeve.

For more irreverent details (and perhaps some pertinent ones, too?) and contact information, please visit www.jpprag.com.

OTHER WORKS

Please visit www.jpprag.com to see all upcoming works, prior works, general articles, and current status.

Upcoming works include:

- **NEW & IMPROVED: THE UNITED STATE OF AMERICA:** The United States government is broken to the point where we can no longer have a single discussion without claiming partisan favoritism. Perspective does not matter because the entire political process has become a quagmire where nothing happens. Why is it so out of control? Every side will blame each other, but where are the solutions? *NEW & IMPROVED: THE UNITED STATES OF AMERICA* goes beyond the 230 years of how we got here. Instead, a myriad of amendments, laws, and policies are explored to show how we can do better. With these fundamental and forward-looking Constitutional updates, hope will be restored to disenfranchised voices and there can finally be a real conversation in the United States government!

- **COMPENDIUM OF HUMANITY'S END:** Humanity's scientific and societal achievements have reached unprecedented heights and now people are populated on distant planets throughout the galaxy. Despite the vast distances and technology required, no life has been found at all—not even a microbe or a fossil of one. Colonists have never discovered an Earth-like planet no matter how exactly close it is to the real thing, but have to work tirelessly to keep a fragile balance in the ones they have created through terraforming. If thousands of years have been spent looking for life to no avail, what would that do the psyche of those who have been tasked to find it? If we are truly alone in the cold emptiness of the universe, then is life a mistake?

- **HERRENVOLK:** During World War II, Hitler managed to set up an underground lair that the Nazis populated with "perfect" people. As the war turned, the secret society was forgotten about and everyone who knew about them was killed. Nearly a century later, they are discovered by accident. As archaeologist, psychologists, historians, and others are exposed to the lost nation, they are impressed with how peaceful the Nazi descendants are and how well their society runs. The Nazis do not know much about the war and do not carry a hatred of other people. They just know they are the chosen ones destined to be the best.

- **LOST RUMORS:** What would happen to you if you woke up to find several days of your life are completely missing? As you go out in the world and speak with others, you slowly realize this, but something more: everyone has distinct memories of you and they do not align to who you think you are. Told entirely from your perspective, you have many questions: What is real? What is just a rumor or perception? How do you separate facts from fiction, and how do you even know which one is which? What does is mean about you personally? And, most of all, what are you going to do now?

Prior works include:

- **HIDDEN HIGHLIGHTS:** Hidden Highlights was about the small, hardly noticeable acts in entertainment that made large, positive differences. This could be camera people catching things perfectly, announcers making deep references, or even just interesting people in the audience. There were just so many unsung heroes that deserved to be highlighted for making what we watch that much better!

- **THE HAMILTON AVE JOURNAL:** The Hamilton Ave Journal was the _only_ professional wrestling news report focused solely on the business side of the industry. Looking not only at the stories that were important to investors and business-minded people, the Journal also delved into reports that most fans of wrestling would overlook. That was because the Journal was about getting the heart of the matters that affected the companies and outlooks of the wrestling world.

DEDICATIONS AND NOTES

First and foremost, all my gratitude goes to my bestedest partner Caroline. During date night, I know that listening to me drone on about wrestling articles I wrote nearly 15 years ago was the highlight of your evening. I love you^3!

Next up, my deep appreciation goes to my editor Mary Rockwell. I already had Mary working on something else when I dropped this on her, so she got the joy of spending so much time with me!

Of course, this work would not exist without the fine folks from 411mania.com, including the people who hired me and helped me develop as a writer: the late, great, and irreplaceable Larry Csonka (not that one) and Ashish Pabari. Over the years at 411mania, I also had the great pleasure of working with many other writers who inspired and pushed me including my writing partner James "JT" Thomlison (yes, we got together just so we could be "JP and JT"). Other great members of staff included and were certainly not limited to Jeff Small (who became a real-life friend I went to many WrestleMania's with), Steve Cook, Mathew Sforcina, Stephen Randle, John Meehan, Andy Clark, Jordan Williams, and many more you can still find there today. We had some crazy and memorable times together, both in the super-secret staff forums and out in the real world!

Even more than my fellow authors were the readers of 411mania who were actively engaged in the wild west of the early internet. Their direct feedback and interactions helped shape both the original article and me as an author, especially as my work morphed into the ultimate interactive article Hidden Highlights. And yes, I still have all of your e-mails and will definitely be getting around to responding to each and every one of you as soon as I have a chance. Do @aol.com and @msn.com e-mail addresses still work?

Hopefully, my lack of ability to respond to everyone directly will not dissuade you from leaving a review on Amazon or wherever you happen to buy or rent books. As an independent author, reviews have a direct correlation to my visibility, which turns into more sales, which turns into the ability to eat, which turns in the ability to produce more works like and unlike this one. Be sure to visit jpprag.com to find out about those works and sign up for the mailing list to stay up to date!

VERSION HISTORY

Version Number	Version Date	Version Notes
0.00	2019-10-29	Draft Started
0.10	2019-10-30	Shell Outline Transfer Complete
1.00	2020-01-28	Alpha Draft
1.50	2020-07-06	Alpha Draft – Edited
2.00	2020-07-21	Beta Draft
2.50	2020-07-22	Beta Draft – Edited
3.00	2020-07-22	Final Release Form

COPYRIGHTS AND DISCLAIMERS

Copyright © 2019-2020 JP Prag

All rights reserved. No part of this publication may be reproduced, distributed, or transmitted in any form or by any means, including photocopying, recording, or other electronic or mechanical methods, without the prior written permission of the copyright holder, except in the case of brief quotations embodied in critical reviews and certain other noncommercial uses permitted by copyright law.

This is a work of nonfiction. No names have been changed, no characters invented, no events fabricated except for hypothetical situations.

The advice and strategies found within may not be suitable for every situation. This work is sold with the understanding that neither the author nor the publisher are held responsible for the results accrued from the advice in this book.

Printed in the United States of America

First Edition August 2020

Edited by Mary Rockwell

Cover design by SelfPubBookCovers.com/ Fantasyart

ISBN 978-1-7353287-3-7 // ebook
ISBN 978-1-7353287-4-4 // hardcover
ISBN 978-1-7353287-5-1 // paperback

Basil Junction Publishing
11 S. Angell St. #366
Providence, RI 02906

www.jpprag.com

Made in the USA
Monee, IL
15 November 2022